The Globalization of Business Firms from Emerging Economies
Volume II

The Globalization of theWorld Economy

Series Editor: Mark Casson
Professor of Economics
University of Reading, UK

1. Transforming International Organizations
   William G. Egelhoff
2. Strategic Alliances
   Paul W. Beamish
3. Structural Change, Industrial Location and Competitiveness
   Joanne E. Oxley and Bernard Yeung
4. Developing and Newly Industrializing Countries (Volumes I and II)
   Chris Milner
5. Historical Foundations of Globalization
   James Foreman-Peck
6. Trade and Investment Policy (Volumes I and II)
   Thomas L. Brewer
7. The Globalization of Financial Services
   Mervyn K. Lewis
8. Foreign Direct Investment and Technological Change (Volumes I and II)
   John Cantwell
9. The Globalization of Business Firms from Emerging Economies (Volumes I and II)
   Henry Wai-chung Yeung

Future titles will include:

Privatization, Deregulation and the Transfer to Markets
David Teece, Leonard Waverman and Pablo T. Spiller

Financial Market Integration and International Capital Flows
David Vines

Globalization and Labour Markets
David Greenaway and Robert C. Hine

Wherever possible, the articles in these volumes have been reproduced as originally published using facsimile reproduction, inclusive of footnotes and pagination to facilitate ease of reference.

The Globalization of Business Firms from Emerging Economies Volume II

Edited by

Henry Wai-chung Yeung

Assistant Professor of Economic Geography
National University of Singapore, Singapore

THE GLOBALIZATION OF THE WORLD ECONOMY 9

An Elgar Reference Collection
Cheltenham, UK • Northampton, MA, USA

Published by
Edward Elgar Publishing Limited
Glensanda House
Montpellier Parade
Cheltenham
Glos GL50 1UA
UK

Edward Elgar Publishing, Inc.
136 West Street, Suite 202
Northampton
Massachusetts 01060
USA

A catalogue record for this book is available from the British Library.

Library of Congress Cataloguing in Publication Data

The globlization of business firms from emerging economies / edited by Henry Wai-chung Yeung.
(The globalization of the world economy)
Includes bibliographical references and index.
1. International business enterprises—Developing countries.
2. Corporations—Developing countries. 3. Investments, Foreign—Developing Countries. 4. Developing countries—Foreign economic relations. I. Series. II. Series. III. Yeung, Henry Wai-chung
HD2932.G58 2000
338.8'89172421—dc21 99–026744

ISBN 1 84064 053 7 (2 volume set)

Printed and bound in Great Britain by MPG Books Ltd, Bodmin, Cornwall

Contents

Acknowledgements

The editor and publishers wish to thank the authors and the following publishers who have kindly given permission for the use of copyright material.

Blackwell Publishers for article: Krishna Kumar (1982), 'Third World Multinationals: A Growing Force in International Relations', *International Studies Quarterly*, **26** (3), September, 397–424.

Blackwell Publishers Ltd for articles: Rachelle L. Cherol and José Nuñez del Arco (1983), 'Andean Multinational Enterprises: A New Approach to Multinational Investment in the Andean Group', *Journal of Common Market Studies*, **XXI** (4), June, 409–28; Premachandra Athukorala and S.K. Jayasuriya (1988), 'Parentage and Factor Proportions: A Comparative Study of Third-World Multinationals in Sri Lankan Manufacturing', *Oxford Bulletin of Economics and Statistics*, **50** (4), November, 409–23.

Economic Geography for article: Henry Wai-chung Yeung (1997), 'Business Networks and Transnational Corporations: A Study of Hong Kong Firms in the ASEAN Region', *Economic Geography*, **73** (1), January, 1–25.

Elsevier Science Ltd for articles: Sanjaya Lall (1982), 'The Emergence of Third World Multinationals: Indian Joint Ventures Overseas', *World Development*, **10** (2), February, 127–46; Rajiv Lall (1986), 'Third World Multinationals: The Characteristics of Indian Firms Investing Abroad', *Journal of Development Economics*, **20**, 381–97; Michael McDermott (1991), 'Taiwan's Electronic Companies are Targeting Europe', *European Management Journal*, **9** (4), December, 466–74; Tain-Jy Chen (1992), 'Determinants of Taiwan's Direct Foreign Investment: The Case of a Newly Industrializing Country', *Journal of Development Economics*, **39**, 397–407.

International Economic Journal for article: Yongwook Jun (1987), 'The Reverse Direct Investment: The Case of the Korean Consumer Electronics Industry', *International Economic Journal*, **1** (3), Autumn, 91–104.

JAI Press, Inc. for articles: Louis T. Wells, Jr. (1978), 'Foreign Investment from the Third World: The Experience of Chinese Firms from Hong Kong', *Columbia Journal of World Business*, **XIII** (1), Spring, 39–49; Seamus G. Connolly (1984), 'Joint Ventures with Third World Multinationals: A New Form of Entry to International Markets', *Columbia Journal of World Business*, **XIX** (2), Summer, 18–22; Pang Eng Fong and Rajah V. Komaran (1985), 'Singapore Multinationals', *Columbia Journal of World Business*, **XX** (2), Summer, 35–43; Christopher Wells (1988), 'Brazilian Multinationals', *Columbia Journal of World Business*,

23 (4), Winter, 13–23; Erderner Kayank and Tevfik Dalgic (1992), 'Internationalization of Turkish Construction Companies: A Lesson for Third World Countries?', *Columbia Journal of World Business*, **26** (4), 61–75.

Journal of International Business Studies for articles: Krishna Kumar and Kee Young Kim (1984), 'The Korean Manufacturing Multinationals', *Journal of International Business Studies*, **15** (1), Spring/Summer, 45–61; Donald J. Lecraw (1993), 'Outward Direct Investment by Indonesian Firms: Motivation and Effects', *Journal of International Business Studies*, **24** (3), 589–600; Chol Lee and Paul W. Beamish (1995), 'The Characteristics and Performance of Korean Joint Ventures in LDCs', *Journal of International Business Studies*, **26** (3), 637–54.

Journal of Southeast Asian Studies for article: Lim Mah Hui and Teoh Kit Fong (1986), 'Singapore Corporations Go Transnational', *Journal of Southeast Asian Studies*, **XVII** (2), September, 336–65.

Kluwer Academic Publishers BV for article: C.M. Rogerson (1990), 'Sun International: The Making of a South African Tourism Multinational', *GeoJournal*, **22** (3), 345–54.

Kiel Institute of World Economics for article: Yoong-Deok Jeon (1992), 'The Determinants of Korean Foreign Direct Investment in Manufacturing Industries', *Weltwirtschaftliches Archiv*, **128** (3), 527–41.

Management International Review for article: Stephen B. Tallman and Oded Shenkar (1990), 'International Cooperative Venture Strategies: Outward Investment and Small Firms from NICs', *Management International Review*, **30** (4), 299–315.

Jeffrey B. Nugent for his own article: (1982), 'Multinational Joint Venture Companies of Developing Countries as Instruments of Economic Integration for Development', *Development and Peace*, **3**, Spring, 52–60.

Oxford University Press for article: Qi Luo and Christopher Howe (1993), 'Direct Investment and Economic Integration in the Asia Pacific: The Case of Taiwanese Investment in Xiamen', *China Quarterly*, **136**, December, 746–69.

Routledge for articles: Chyau Tuan and Linda F.-Y. Ng (1995), 'The Turning Point of the Hong Kong Manufacturing Sector: Impact of Outward Investment to the Pearl River Delta', *Journal of International Trade and Economic Development*, **4** (2), July, 153–70; Christopher M. Dent and Claire Randerson (1996), 'Korean Foreign Direct Investment in Europe: The Determining Forces', *Pacific Review*, **9** (4), 531–52.

Sage Publications Ltd for article: Nicholas A. Phelps, John Lovering and Kevin Morgan (1998), 'Tying the Firm to the Region or Tying the Region to the Firm? Early Observations on the Case of LG in South Wales', *European Urban and Regional Studies*, **5** (2), April, 119–37.

South African Geographical Journal for article: C.M. Rogerson (1986), 'Third World Multinationals and South Africa's Decentralization Programme', *South African Geographical Journal*, **68** (2), September, 132–43.

United Nations Conference on Trade and Development (UNCTAD) for article: Ye Gang (1992), 'Chinese Transnational Corporations', *Transnational Corporations*, **1** (2), August, 125–33.

University of California Press and the Regents of the University of California for article: Xiangming Chen (1996), 'Taiwan Investments in China and Southeast Asia: "Go West, but Also Go South"', *Asian Survey*, **XXXVI** (5), May, 447–67.

University of Michigan Business School for article: K.C. Fung (1996), 'Mainland Chinese Investment in Hong Kong: How Much, Why, and So What?', *Journal of Asian Business*, **12** (2), 21–39.

John Wiley & Sons, Inc. for article: Raul de Gouvea Neto (1995), 'Brazilian Emerging Multinationals: A Conduit for Export of Technology', *International Executive*, **37** (6), November/December, 583–97.

V.H. Winston & Son, Inc. for article: Kris Olds (1998), 'Globalization and Urban Change: Tales from Vancouver via Hong Kong', *Urban Geography*, **19** (4), 360–85.

Woodcock Publications Ltd for article: Rik Donckels and Johan Lambrecht (1995), 'Joint Ventures: No Longer a Mysterious World for SMEs from Developed and Developing Countries', *International Small Business Journal*, **13** (2), January–March, 11–26.

Every effort has been made to trace all the copyright holders but if any have been inadvertently overlooked the publishers will be pleased to make the necessary arrangement at the first opportunity.

In addition the publishers wish to thank the Library of the London School of Economics and Political Science and the Marshall Library of Economics, Cambridge University for their assistance in obtaining these articles.

Part I
The Organization of Transnational Corporations from Emerging Economies

[1]

World Development, Vol. 10, No. 2, pp. 127–146, 1982.
Printed in Great Britain.

0305-750X/82/020127-20$03.00/0
Pergamon Press Ltd.

The Emergence of Third World Multinationals: Indian Joint Ventures Overseas

SANJAYA LALL*
Institute of Economics and Statistics, Oxford University

Summary. – The more industrialized LDCs are emerging increasingly as exporters of capital (or of technology in several forms). This paper draws on the recent experience of Indian MNCs to re-examine the factors which give rise to Third World multinationals. The author summarizes the current state of research in the analysis of LDCs MNCs, drawing upon specific MNC literature and other related literature on trade and technology. He deals with the evidence on Indian capital exports, placing it in the broader context of technology exports, discussing some examples of interest and drawing comparisons with foreign investment by some other LDCs. He assesses the Indian experience, using the distinctions drawn by Dunning's 'eclectic' theory but concentrating on the processes of technical change that underline the growth of its MNCs. The final section draws some tentative conclusions.

1. INTRODUCTION

The emergence of developing countries (DCs) as exporters of capital (we refer only to direct investment here) has attracted some interest in recent years. In particular, academic discussion has been stimulated by the publication of seminal papers on the subject by Carlos Diaz-Alejandro (on Latin America) and Louis Wells (on LDCs generally), both in Agmon and Kindleberger (1977),[1] and by Lecraw (1977) on Thailand as a host to LDC MNCs. The phenomenon itself is not new. Indeed, the 'internationalization' of LDC firms seems to have started around the turn of the century with overseas activity by Argentinian firms. Data on Hong Kong firms are scanty, but it would not be surprising if some of its giants like Jardine Matheson (really still a British firm in terms of its management but based in Hong Kong) also went international over half a century ago. However, the real upsurge of LDC internationalization came in the late 1960s for open economies like Hong Kong and Singapore, and in the 1970s for other industrializing countries like Brazil, Mexico, Argentina, Korea and India. These were trailed by small bursts of overseas activity by firms from a variety of smaller LDCs in Latin America and Asia.

The amounts involved are still miniscule by the standard of the 'real' MNCs from the advanced OECD countries. It is, however, the longer-term trends which are interesting. The internationalization of LDC firms is growing relatively rapidly. It is linked intimately with the growth of their manufacturing capabilities and sophisticated industrial exports, since the same set of forces determine the development of technology, skills and international competitiveness in all forms. Thus, as the LDC share of world industrial production and exports grows, so will their share of international investment. The link between the growth of technological and other skills, exports and direct investment is not a straightforward one, of course; nevertheless, we think that one is reasonably safe in assuming that industrial development is positively correlated with its internationalization.

Placed in this rather broad historical perspective, it may not appear surprising that the more industrialized LDCs have emerged as exporters of capital (or of technology in several forms). On the contrary, it may even seem inevitable.

* An earlier version of this paper was presented to the International Economics Study Group Annual Conference, Sussex, September 1980, and will be published (editors J. Black and J. H. Dunning) by Macmillans. The evidence reported here was collected during a research project for the World Bank on exports of technology by India. The Bank's sponsorship is gratefully acknowledged, but it bears no responsibility for the views expressed here. Rajiv Kumar provided valuable assistance with the empirical work.

The standard tools of economics have not, however, been forged to deal with dynamic historical processes, and to use them to analyse the growth of LDC MNCs should require some effort and readjustment. The recent literature on this theme has attempted such readjustment, but has, in the process, obscured some interesting new tendencies and some important differences between MNCs from different LDCs.

This paper draws upon the recent experience of Indian MNCs to re-examine the factors which give rise to Third World multinationals. The evidence on India is, in the nature of things, still rather anecdotal, and, for other LDCs, rather patchy: the hypotheses derived from it must, in consequence, be treated as very tentative. Nevertheless, it appears that many of the conclusions which have been reached about LDC MNCs, in terms of their comparative advantage *vis-à-vis* DC MNCs, need to be qualified. LDC firms appear to be entering much 'higher' levels of skill, size, capital intensity and technological capability than current thinking allows for, and the line between them and the 'real' MNCs should be drawn more carefully. The factors which give rise to their 'ownership advantages', to use the current terminology, need to be explored more deeply, particularly in terms of technological learning, so that different types of MNCs, from different environments, can be identified.

Section 2 describes the 'state of the art' in the analysis of LDC MNCs, drawing upon specific MNC literature and some more obliquely related literature on trade and technology. Section 3 deals with the evidence on Indian capital exports, placing it in the broader context of technology exports, discussing some examples of interest and drawing comparisons with foreign investment by some other LDCs. Section 4 assesses the Indian experience, using the distinctions drawn by Dunning's[2] 'eclectic' theory but concentrating on the processes of technical change that underline the growth of its MNCs. Section 5 draws the main conclusions.

2. CURRENT ANALYSIS OF LDC MNCs

There are several branches of economic analysis that touch on the explanation of international involvement by LDC firms. Since such involvement necessarily requires the enterprise concerned to put together and transfer a 'package' of finance, technological knowledge, marketing expertise and managerial skills, each of these elements of the package may be examined separately to see what conventional theory leads us to expect about the role of LDCs in international investment. As Dunning (1980) explains, the package must be such as to yield the investor a *competitive advantage* over all potential competitors abroad, the elements on which it is based must be *transferable* overseas, there must be certain *location-specific factors* which make the choice of the host country profitable, and direct investment must be the *form* of operation that is preferred to other ways of exploiting the package.

Conventional theories of direct investment, drawing upon Hymer's pathbreaking thesis, have argued that the same forces that make for larger firm size and greater market concentration within the developed countries (i.e. barriers to entry of new competition) provide the advantages that are exploited overseas. Thus, technological leads, product differentiation, managerial skills, scale economies and capital market imperfections enable certain firms to grow at the expense of others. Not all the advantages are equally transferable, of course; some are necessarily exploited at home, at least to start with, while others have to be exploited overseas from the start (Lall, 1980). It is generally assumed that an advantage developed in the home country yields a *net* advantage over similar firms abroad: this assumption may be justified if firms are highly specialized in their activities, if the home environment is different from others and so breeds a different set of advantages, or if the home market is so large that the sheer size of its dominant firms yields an edge over leading firms abroad.

This explanation of the origin of monopolistic advantages works fairly well to explain the internationalization of developed country firms, but even there it does not work perfectly. In particular, doubts have been expressed about the relevance of the standard monopolistic advantages theory to the growth of small firms, from relatively competitive industries, operating in low-technology activities.[3] The answer that seems to be emerging is not that monopolistic advantages do not exist – by now it has become almost tautological to say that a foreign investor has some 'advantage' – but that all advantages are not necessarily 'monopolistic' in the original sense (i.e. of the sort that lead to entry barriers in developed countries). Firm-specific advantages may derive from mastery over particular adaptations to well-diffused technology, from access to cheaper or more appropriate management, from ethnic factors, from better knowledge of particular markets or simply from 'being first' in a newly industrializing economy. Since these are the sorts of factors which have been generally used to explain the emergence of LDC MNCs, let us consider them at some length, harking back to the main elements of the 'package' mentioned at the start of this section.

(a) *Finance*

While the 'real' MNCs undoubtedly enjoy considerable financial clout in the imperfect markets for international capital, it is unlikely that firms from LDCs can have an edge here. Not only are their home countries likely to be capital and foreign-exchange scarce, they are themselves of a size unlikely to command a premium in conditions where sheer size is the preponderant factor.[4] Thus, we expect LDC firms to suffer a net disadvantage in providing this element of the package.

(b) *Technology*

It is generally argued that LDC firms cannot have an advantage in what are normally regarded as high-technology industries, or, within industries, in activities which are at the complex, capital-intensive, innovative end of the scale. Current trade theory assigns LDCs a role at the bottom of the ladder of skills and technology, the two factors which dominate the new theories of comparative advantage. Furthermore, the accumulation of local skills and technology (the two are often merged with each other) is taken to be a direct function of *per capita* income (Hirsch, 1977), so that the poorest countries have a natural comparative advantage in the production and export of the lowest-skill and simplest-technology products,[5] while those higher up the income ladder have a corresponding advantage in the production of somewhat more complex goods.

This need not preclude LDCs from building up monopolistic advantages in their respective spheres of production and so becoming direct investors. The necessary conditions for this are:

(a) Production know-how is adapted in such a way that it becomes a unique asset. Thus, the product is changed to suit LDC conditions; the process is adapted to smaller scales, to particular raw materials or to particular skills (or lack thereof); older techniques or machines are used which other firms cannot operate efficiently. This assumes that there are dualistic product markets in LDCs, with distinct markets for older, more 'appropriate' products which are not served by DC MNCs; or that technical progress is evolutionary (in the Nelson sense, see his excellent 1980 summary) so that a DC firm cannot 'go backwards' and efficiently handle technologies which exist but which are of a smaller scale or older vintage than those it is currently using. These are realistic assumptions, but not in accordance with the standard theoretical analyses of technology, which take for granted production sets of existing techniques which are fully known to all firms and over which they can range costlessly in response to changed factor prices.

(b) Even if technology does not become a unique asset in this sense, LDC firms can go abroad with a well-diffused technology if their technology-transfer and/or managerial costs are lower.

In general the few studies which have been done of LDC MNCs have concluded that they specialize in labour-intensive, standardized technologies, usually adapted to local conditions. Wells, Lecraw and White [all in Kumar (forthcoming)] all concur that LDC firms have developed some special advantages in the operation and transfer of relatively simple, old technologies and that these advantages are strengthened by cheaper manpower. White, in describing Latin American MNCs, allows for greater innovativeness than do Lecraw and Wells (who base their observations mainly on Asian firms), in terms both of independent contributions to technology based on their own research work and of rapidly internalizing and diffusing very new technologies introduced in the developed world. Wells and Lecraw stress the down-scaling of standardized technology and its lesser automation. Wells points to the innovativeness of LDC firms in making technologies (equipment) more flexible and more amenable to using local materials; Lecraw, on the other hand, emphasizes their 'experience in using and adapting labour-intensive, small-scale production techniques to produce undifferentiated products of low to medium quality at low cost'.

These studies conform to the expectations raised by the trade literature, except perhaps in the importance they attach to the local technology. It is expected, therefore, that LDC firms will have advantages which are: (a) exploited in other LDCs, generally lower down the income (or industrialization) scale; (b) confined to mature technologies, not competing directly with DC firms, or else to technologies where their specific adaptations have given them a unique asset; (c) confined to small-scale operations, using more labour-intensive technologies than obtainable from DCs; and (d) subjected to a rather rapid erosion of their advantages, so prone to retract from foreign operations. This literature offers neither specific hypotheses about which developing countries are most likely to be the home of MNCs, nor about different sets of technological advantages that are likely to be generated by different LDCs. In his more general analysis of the dynamics of net international investment, however, Dunning (1980) mentions two ownership-specific determinants of outward investment: the stock of human capital and expenditures on R & D (appropriately deflated). According to these, a country like India should have the smallest (and, by implication, least sophisticated or diversified) foreign involvement.

(c) *Marketing skills*

There are two, closely related aspects of marketing skills: product differentiation (the ability to distinguish one's own branded product on the basis of real or imagined advantages), and the ability to understand and meet customer requirements (quality control, product adaptation, after-sales service). Product differentiation generally requires large and rich markets, and is generally an acknowledged area of strength of DC MNCs. Thus, firms from LDCs are thought to be unable to compete in products where advertising, product variety, rapid model changes etc. are important in corporate strategy. A few exceptions are, again, noted among Latin American firms by White (in pharmaceuticals and soft drinks), but in general LDC MNCs are said to specialize in undifferentiated products where price is the main element in competitiveness.

Other marketing skills are not so dominated by large MNCs from developed countries. LDCs like Hong Kong and Singapore, with long experience of selling to sophisticated markets, have learnt to keep abreast of fast-moving fashions, to 'package' their wares nicely and to maintain quality (within the range of products they can handle technologically). Countries with fairly rich markets and 'Western tastes', e.g. the big Latin American countries, may also set high standards with poor, highly protected markets, strict and pervasive official controls on all aspects of industrial activity and low exposures to international consumers, but are expected to be much worse at marketing. Analysts of Indian industrialization [led by Bhagwati and Srinivasan (1975)] have roundly attacked the evils of its import-substituting strategy, and cited instances of poor quality, neglect of consumers' needs, and short-sighted attitudes to product development. It is probably the case of such firms which leads Lecraw to talk of 'low quality products' made by LDC MNCs in Asia.

The expectation with respect to LDC MNCs, then, is that they will not possess product differentiation advantages, and that they may or may not possess other marketing skills, depending on their domestic markets and the industrial strategy pursued. Any advantage they possess here is likely to give them an edge over other LDC firms, not over the 'real' MNCs.

(d) *Managerial skills*

The early MNC literature had tended to accord to DC firms a significant edge in all types of managerial and organizational skills. The emergence of LDC MNCs has led to some implicit revisions of these views, since the latter have clearly shown themselves to be aggressive and able in their own sphere of technical capabilities. In so far as managerial skills other than those related to technology and marketing are concerned, the main advantage perceived for DC firms arises from their size and greater international spread and experience. Thus, they are much better geared to large-scale operations, global communication, rational allocation of resources internationally, and highly developed forms of transfer pricing, financial planning and avoidance of exchange rate losses.

As far as standardized technologies and small-scale operations are concerned, however, earlier doubts about the entrepreneurial vision, adaptability and speed of LDC firms have been cast aside. This particular factor now rarely appears as a significant discriminator between developed and less developed country investors. What does appear important is the much greater willingness of LDC firms, especially in manufacturing, to accept minority equity positions (in this they are similar to Japanese, and very different from US MNCs); and a marked propensity on the part of medium-size firms to go abroad (especially from Hong Kong).

* * *

Let us conclude this section. The literature on MNCs has always been more a *post hoc* rationalization of changes that have already taken place than a coherent theory derived from a clear set of assumptions: rigorous neo-classical trade theory fails to explain the growth of MNCs in any form. The earlier theories of monopolistic advantage would probably also have failed to predict the growth of Third World MNCs, since the perceived competitive edge of these firms has little to do with high levels of innovative and product differentiation expenditure that sustained the spread of developed country MNCs. The realization that MNCs are emerging from LDCs has led to further refinements to the understanding of monopolistic advantage and traced its sources to such phenomena as evolutionary (non-reversible) technological growth, technical and product adaptation, learning by doing and the accumulation of unique skills in LDCs: all aspects of 'minor' technical change and human capital formation rather than the standard determinants of oligopoly in advanced countries.

What does all this lead us to expect of Indian MNCs? India is the poorest (and so the least capable of generating ownership advantages), the least export-orientated (and so the most burdened by the inefficiencies of import-substitution policy) and slowest-growing (and so, if growth is linked to increases in productivity, the least capable of absorbing and creating technical progress) of the LDCs with significant industrial structures. These conventional views of its economy, thus, lead us to predict it will be a minor exporter of capital and that its MNCs will be at the lower end of the technology/skill scale, using more labour-intensive technologies, operating at smaller scales, concentrating in poorer (or as poor) countries, and specializing in low-quality products not in direct competition with DC firms. Its poverty and lack of dynamism suggests that its MNCs will enjoy fewer 'ownership advantages' based on technology. Its relatively poor export performance suggests that they will be deficient in marketing skills. The revealed comparative advantage of LDC MNCs in small-scale labour-intensive technologies should be accentuated for India by two factors: lower wage rates, and the strong monopolistic positions established by the leading business houses (which should make them more prone to stay at home in sheltered markets rather than go abroad with their inappropriate, capital-intensive technologies). Thus, we should observe a negative correlation between foreign investment propensity and domestic size, capital-intensity and product sophistication.

Let us now turn to the evidence and see how far these hypotheses are vindicated. Our discussion will focus on the manufacturing sector, with only passing reference to other types of activity.

3. INDIAN MNCs: EVIDENCE AND COMPARISONS

(a) *Overall stocks of direct foreign investment*

A few Indian firms had launched foreign production during the 1960s in Sri Lanka, Iran, Kenya and Nigeria. They were concentrated in light engineering products and textiles, the traditional 'low-technology' products where production know-how is widely diffused, small-scale operation is profitable and a great deal of 'learning by doing' is possible on the shop floor. These projects did not exceed 10 in number; the total equity participation of Indian firms came to Rs.14 million (under $2 million) and total dividends earned abroad until 1970 came to Rs.1 million.

Between 1970 and 1978 there was a rapid increase in equity exports by Indian firms (nearly all of it was in kind, i.e. equipment and capitalized know-how, rather than cash). The 8 years saw Rs.192 million ($24 million) invested abroad, with total dividends repatriated of Rs.19 million ($2.4 million) and technical fees and royalties of Rs.42 million ($5.2 million). During this period the government acquiesced in, rather than encouraged, foreign investment, and few efforts were made to liberalize foreign exchange availability for investment, travel or promotion. However, with a realization of the export-generating capacity of overseas affiliates (exports of intermediate goods to affiliates came to Rs.425 million or $53 million up to 1978, or 2.2 times the value of equity investment), with growing foreign exchange reserves which the sluggish domestic economy could not absorb, with the pressure of growing oil imports and with growing demands by Indian MNCs, policies became much more positive in 1979. It was decided to speed up approval procedures, to allow the taking of majority equity participation (again in exceptional cases), to allow wholly-owned subsidiaries in trading and other service activities, and to generally use foreign investment as an important tool of export promotion. However, further liberalization of foreign-investments is restrained because of the obvious anomaly of India seeking massive amounts of foreign aid while simultaneously exporting capital in the form of direct investment.

The year 1979 thus witnessed a virtual explosion of foreign investment activity. By early 1980 total equity overseas came to Rs.800 million ($100 million), in 192 projects in production as well as under construction; about 95% of the investments were in manufacturing in-

Table 1. *Indian joint ventures abroad: cumulative data as at end of January* 1980 *(Rs. million)*

Projects under production	109
Projects under implementation	83
Total No. of effective projects	192
Total investment in effective projects	Rs.79.45 crores*
Investment in projects under production	Rs.30.45 crores
Investment in projects under implementation	Rs.48.91 crores
Total earnings repatriated	Rs.9.70 crores
Dividends	Rs.2.60 crores
Other remittances including managerial fees and technical know-how fees	Rs.7.10 crores
Exports	
Additional exports generated	Rs.62.00 crores

Source: Federation of Indian Chambers of Commerce and Industry, *Report of Workshop on Indian Joint Ventures, Turnkey and Third Country Projects* (New Delhi: 1980), p. 36.
* 1 crore = 10 million.

dustry. The value of projects under construction far exceeded the total value of past investments, and the value per project of the former (Rs.6 million or $740,000) was also far larger than the value per investment in projects in production (Rs.3 million or $350,000). However, it is not clear whether the data on the value of existing investments include reinvested profits in the affiliates; if they do not, as I suspect, then the Indian stake abroad in functioning enterprises is understated to an unknown degree. The available data on the values of investment, earnings and additional exports generated are shown in Table 1.

Since Indian investments are almost entirely in minority-owned ventures, the value of total investments with Indian participation should come to between two and four times the size of its stake, i.e. to $200 million–400 million. More recent indications are that the boom in overseas activity is continuing, with several hundred proposals now under active consideration by the government, and an increasingly aggressive search for new opportunities by existing and prospective investors.[6]

In view of the scantiness of the data on other LDCs, it is difficult to make comparisons of the relative position of India as a capital exporter. The process of internationalization is just beginning in India and in countries like Brazil and Korea, while it is much better established in open economies like Hong Kong or those with longer histories of industry like Argentina. Moreover, its progress will be erratic, depending on foreign exchange availability, political changes, and relationships etc., all unrelated to the competitive advantages of LDC enterprises. Bearing these problems in mind, let us piece together some scattered bits of information.

According to White, the existing investments of the Latin American countries in that region (which probably accounts for the great bulk of their activity) by 1978 came to $60 million for Brazil, $62 million for Mexico, $37 million for Argentina, $55 million for Colombia and $54 million for Venezuela. By some aberration, Uruguay, which does not seem to have any MNCs, recorded $144 million in overseas investments. This is not the only peculiarity of White's data: the Argentinian figure seems much too low given the anecdotal evidence on its firms abroad,[7] as does the Brazilian figure (IMF statistics give its total accumulated direct investments by 1978 at $580 million, of which equity capital comes to $163 million). Roughly half of Latin American overseas investments are in manufacturing; no country-wise breakdown of this is available.

South Korean foreign investments [according to Jo's paper in Kumar (forthcoming)] came to $90 million by the end of 1978, of which $15 million (17%) was invested in 19 manufacturing affiliates. Hong Kong keeps no records of its foreign investments, though some data are available from host countries. The value of its investments in other countries includes funds channelled by DC firms via Hong Kong subsidiaries; furthermore, the presence of such giant international firms as Jardine Matheson, which is, while nominally a Hong Kong firm, to all intents and purposes a British expatriate firm, distorts the contribution of indigenous enterprises. Despite these problems, local Chinese enterprises from Hong Kong do seem to have gone multinational in a significant way since the early 1960s.[8] Hong Kong investments in Indonesia (till 1976) came to $219 million, in Malaysia (till 1977) to $251 million, in Taiwan (till 1978) to $223 million and in Singapore (till 1973) to $155 million – a total of $848 million in these main areas of its operation. Recently Hong Kong firms have invested in Sri Lanka and are on the brink of entering the EEC. At a very rough guess, Hong Kong has a total foreign investment stake of around $2 billion today.

Singapore has important investments in Malaysia ($80 million of total fixed assets in 1973, value of equity not known) and Indonesia ($116 million in 1976). Presumably it also invests in other ASEAN countries, though far less vigorously than Hong Kong: its total foreign equity may be about $500 million. Malaysia itself has some overseas investments [over $50 million in 1976 according to the limited data provided by the UN Centre on Transnational Corporations (UNCTC)]; here, as with Hong Kong, the operation of a large 'expatriate' UK firm, Sime Derby, may distort the picture. Taiwan is a relatively minor foreign investor, according to the impressions conveyed by the few studies that have been done of Asia; IMF figures show a total outflow of $12 million up to 1978.[9] The Philippines had, according to the IMF, direct investments of $59 million abroad by 1978 (though none of this is recorded as 'equity capital' in the 1979 *Balance of Payments Yearbook*): the UNCTC shows its equity stock to be $273 million by 1976, almost certainly an overestimate.

As far as the stock of direct foreign investments by LDCs is concerned, therefore, Hong Kong appears to be far and away the leader, followed at some distance by Singapore. Other LDCs are difficult to rank because the data are poor and often apparently misleading. A weaving together of impressions, anecdotes and conflicting bits of data leads us to place Argentina, Mexico, Brazil, Taiwan and India at about the same level as the second group of overseas investors. The third group comprises Colombia, Peru, Venezuela and Korea. The other LDCs seem to have only occasional ventures abroad (despite the figures) and can be placed in the fourth group.

If *per capita* income in countries with significant manufacturing sectors are used as a composite index of factors leading to ownership advantages (industrialization, literacy, R & D etc.), the general picture is more or less as one would expect. Hong Kong and Singapore are the richest countries of the LDCs, with *per capita* incomes of over $3000 in 1978.[10] Taiwan, Brazil, Argentina and Mexico have incomes in the range $1300–1900. The third group of countries is more variable. However, if we take Venezuela out (oil accounts for its high income of $2910), they range between $740 for Peru and $1160 for Korea. The last group of countries, the recent industrializers, are in a rather lower range (Thailand, the Philippines around $500), though some natural resource-rich countries (Malaysia, Chile) are relatively rich.

The odd-man-out is clearly India according to this simple predictor. With a *per capita* income of $180, its actual participation in international production far exceeds its predicted share. Not that this is very surprising, of course: India is an odd case more generally in having the 13th largest contribution to value added in manufacturing in the world in 1976, and the third largest in the developing world (after Brazil and Mexico). Any sort of deflation of Indian figures, by population or total GNP, obviously tends to understate the size of its manufacturing sector.

Value added in manufacturing is not, however, the only determinant of the internationalization of a country's manufacturing industry.[11] While the size of the manufacturing sector may be a good proxy for skill accumulation and technical knowledge in a country, sheer size does not capture such important elements as international competitiveness, export experience, technological progressiveness etc., all of which affect the building-up of ownership advantages by the firms involved. Furthermore, outward investment also depends on 'location' and 'internalization' factors in Dunning's technology, which depend in turn on relative costs of production, the possession of unique rent-yielding assets, company strategy and government policies at home and abroad. We will touch on some of these later. What may be noted here is that at first sight the inclusion of these variables would also not prepare us to expect India to be an important capital exporter: its obsessively inward-looking strategy has been accused of fostering widespread inefficiency and a reluctance to enter foreign markets, its tight control on MNC entry and on the purchase of foreign technology of perpetuating obsolete technologies, and its restrictions on private domestic companies of stifling entrepreneurship and breeding complacence.

There may be a puzzle here, and it grows

Table 2. *Indian joint ventures abroad – industry-wise as on 31st January 1980*

Industry	Projects under production	Projects under implementation	Total effective projects
Textiles	17	7	24
Chemical products and pharmaceuticals	6	9	15
Pulp, paper and paper products	3	2	5
Cement, cement products, sugar and sugar products	1	3	4
Engineering products	30	17	47
Restaurants and food products	14	9	23
Construction, trade and consultancy	16	18	34
Oilseeds, crushing and refining	7	8	15
Miscellaneous	15	10	25
Total	109	83	192

Source: As Table 1, p. 37.

Table 3. 101 *Indian joint ventures in production abroad: industrial distribution by value of Indian equity holding (September 1979)*

	Equity			
Industry	Value of equity (Rs. million)	% total	% manufacturing	No. of ventures
Textile, garments	88.5	28.2	29.8	17
Sugar	11.4	3.6	3.8	1
Other food processing*	32.1	10.2	10.8	11
Steel, rolling mills	3.8	1.2	1.3	3
Chemicals and pharmaceuticals	20.2	6.4	6.8	9
Paper and pulp	92.4	29.4	31.1	4
Metal products	19.0	6.0	6.4	13
Machinery	12.0	3.8	4.0	6
Electrical products	0.5	0.2	0.2	1
Transport equipment and parts	10.3	3.3	3.5	10
Glass	6.1	1.9	2.1	2
Other†	0.6	0.2	0.2	2
Subtotal manufacturing	296.9	94.5	100.0	79
Electricity distribution‡	1.8	0.6	–	1
Civil construction	5.5	1.8	–	3
Trade, management and engineering consultancy	0.7	0.2	–	9
Hotels, restaurants etc.	9.2	2.9	–	9
Total	314.1	100.0	–	101

Source: Data provided by Ministry of Commerce.
* Includes palm oil processing, beverages and other foods.
† One rubber and one construction materials.
‡ Venture set up to undertake transmission line projects.

more interesting when we consider the nature of India's activities abroad.

(b) *Industrial composition of foreign investments and some interesting cases*

Tables 2 and 3 set out the industrial distribution of Indian foreign ventures. Table 2 provides the most recent data on the *number* of investments, both in production and under implementation, by broad industrial categories. Table 3 provides rather older information on the *values* of Indian equity participation and ventures in production by a more detailed classification.[12]

As far as the number of ventures is concerned, engineering products broadly defined dominate Indian foreign investments (the Indian classification of 'engineering' products includes simple metal goods as well as machinery and transport equipment); in terms of value of investments in operational ventures, however, they accounted for only 15% of the total. Textiles and garments, the traditional areas of strength of LDCs, are strongly in evidence both in terms of number and values, though their importance is declining over time. Paper and pulp projects are few in number but very large in size, and so constitute the largest sector in terms of value (most of the equity is accounted for by two ventures in Nigeria and Kenya). Food processing, dominated by some large palm oil processing investments in Southeast Asia, constitutes the third largest industry by value, followed by chemicals and petrochemicals; both seem to be gaining in importance in recent years.

Non-manufacturing investments do not contribute much to the value of equity, but their numbers have been rising dramatically with the shift in policy to establish sales agencies, consultancies, civil construction offices and the like abroad (banks seem to be left out of the available data). The Middle East has attracted a number of such investments, since the promotion of various forms of technology (turnkey projcects, consultancies) and commodity exports requires an active continuous presence there. Indian hoteliers have been notably successful overseas: the Oberoi group, operating mainly under management contracts, has set up a chain of 20 or so luxury hotels from Australia, via Southeast Asia, Sri Lanka, Egypt and Spain to the US. The Taj group, part of the Tata conglomerate, is now venturing abroad with a Ceylon Rs.500 million hotel in Sri Lanka and other luxury hotels.

Our main interest, however, lies in manufacturing. Here the aggregate figure shows that, despite their late entry, Indian firms have spread abroad (geographical distributions are discussed later) in a very diverse range of activities. While a number of simple, relatively low technology and labour-intensive ventures are, as received theory predicts, present (textiles, sugar, simple metal products), roughly half of foreign equity is accounted for by ventures in more complex, capital-intensive (steel mills, paper and pulp, chemicals) or skill and technology-intensive (machinery, pharmaceuticals, transports equipment) activities. The grouping of industrial activities into broad 'high'- and 'low'-technology groups is, of course, a risky procedure. Even 'low'-technology industries like textiles have very modern, innovative branches, while such 'high'-technology activities as machinery or electronics have pockets of stable and/or well-diffused technology like simple machine-tools, radios or consumer electronics.

It may be useful, therefore, to mention some of the more interesting cases of Indian foreign investments, both existing and in the pipeline, to get a 'feel' for their nature and capabilities. The description is necessarily anecdotal, and is patchy in that we describe only a few cases on which information happens to be available. Moreover, it is focused on instances of 'unconventional' behaviour, to highlight points where we propose to challenge the accepted wisdom on LDC MNCs.

Let us start by briefly reviewing the identity of the main MNCs from India. Table 4 sets out the values of foreign equity held by the top seven enterprises in the 101 operational ventures in September 1979. The figures may not be completely accurate in that it has not been possible for me to identify the conglomerate

Table 4. *Main Indian foreign direct investors, as of September* 1979

Firm	Main activities abroad	No. of ventures	Value of investments (Rs. million)	Investment per venture (Rs. million)	Share of total (%)
Birla Group	Paper, rayon, textiles, palm oil	12	122.6	10.2	39.0
Tata Group	Oil mills, trucks, tools, metal products	5	27.6	5.5	8.8
J.K. Group	Textiles, metal products	4	27.1	6.8	8.6
Shahibag Enterprises	Textiles	2	21.1	10.6	6.7
Thapar Group	Paper, trading	3	14.8	4.9	4.7
Sarabhai Group	Chemicals	2	11.4	5.7	3.6
Kirloskar Group	Engines, machinery	4	8.8	2.2	2.8
Total		32	233.4	7.3	74.3

Source: Compiled from Ministry of Commerce data and FICCI (1980).

origin of some enterprises; however, the broad magnitudes of concentration accord with figures given by other observers..

There are over 100 Indian enterprises active in various types of joint ventures abroad. Some of these are relatively small enterprises by Indian standards. Some very large Indian enterprises (especially those in the public sector or those which are themselves affiliates of MNCs) are not foreign investors, and some of them are just dipping their toes into the cold but exciting waters of international production.

At present, however, there is a very high level of concentration of overseas activity in the two largest industrial groups in the country: Birla and Tata.[13] Birla by itself accounts for nearly 40% of total Indian foreign equity and Tata for another 9%. (This excludes ventures under implementation or under active consideration – their inclusion would probably raise their share even further.) The top seven investors together account for nearly three-quarters of total foreign equity (at the very least). All of them are large, diversified and long-established business houses, with considerable industrial experience. Nearly all are in a much broader range of activity at home than overseas, and all are major exporters of products.

Size, experience and exposure to foreign markets are clearly of great importance in determining exports of capital from India. This is hardly surprising, since it reproduces (in a more extreme form) the pattern of concentration observed for foreign investments by the developed countries, and is in accordance with what we would expect given the costs, risks and requirements of going abroad. White finds a similar pattern for Latin America (where the role of giant state corporations, especially from Brazil, is noteworthy), though he does not provide enterprise-level data. Analysts of Hong Kong and other Southeast Asian investments have, on the other hand, stressed the large role played by medium/small enterprises: whether this is a peculiar feature of Hong Kong and Singapore enterprises, or is simply a mistaken interpretation based on the size of *foreign* ventures (especially in comparison with investments by DC MNCs), we cannot say.

Let us now consider some examples. Birla had 12 overseas ventures in operation last year. Our most recent compilation of data shows that it now has 16 in operation and a further nine in the process of implementation (plus an unspecified number under active scrutiny).[14] There are several companies of this group which are independently investing overseas, with no apparent attempt to co-ordinate their activities. Recently, however, a 'Birla (International) Private Ltd' has been set up to control some of its foreign affiliates, though even this, with its nine ventures, does not cover more than a part of the field. The 25 ventures exclude a textile firm nationalized in Ethiopia, an oil processing plant sold to local interests in the Philippines, several management contracts, and, most interestingly, a large ($125 million) turnkey contract won in China (the first of its kind by India) to build a rayon plant with Indian technology and equipment.[15]

Birla first went abroad in 1966, with a light engineering goods plants in Nigeria. This was followed by textile plants in Thailand (1970) and Malaysia (1972), a jute plant in Uganda (1971), a paper plant in Kenya (1974) and subsequently Nigeria (1979), two palm oil refining plants in Malaysia (1974, 1979) and a coconut oil plant in the Philippines (1979); rayon plants in Thailand (1976) and two in Indonesia (under implementation); a cement products plant in the UK (*ca.* 1976); and other textile plants, including one in the Dominican Republic. It is currently setting up, jointly with a US and a local firm, an export-orientated canvas shoe plant in Sri Lanka, a dyestuff plant in Indonesia and a chemical plant in Thailand.

There are innumerable 'stories' of interest in the Birla experience abroad. Of interest here are:

(a) In 1976 Birla was invited by the International Finance Corporation to take over the management of a loss-making textile affiliate of a US firm (Spring Mills) in Indonesia, Daralon Mfg. Co. This firm had been poorly managed and saddled with a limited product range and outdated equipment. Birla ordered new looms (from Switzerland) and other equipment (from India), rearranged the organization, and are about to declare profits. It undertook a similar operation in the Philippines with Evertex Industries, and turned the loss into a profit in 3 months.

(b) The Orient Paper Mills' paper plant in Kenya is the largest on the African continent, financed by the World Bank, with extremely modern equipment and technology, and highly profitable. In 5 years it has earned dividends of Rs.11 million (on an equity of Rs.41 million) and created additional exports from India of Rs.57 million.

(c) Birla's Gwalior Rayon developed its own rayon technology from scratch, set up the Thai Rayon Company in 1976 (equity Rs.10 million, dividends Rs.1.1 million and additional exports Rs.25 million) and is constructing the Indorayon plant in Indonesia. Its Indian technology and equipment (selected by the Chinese) will, curiously enough, have to compete with Swiss technology and equipment in a rayon plant built by Tungabhadra Ind., another Birla company, in Indonesia – evidence of the relative 'freedom' within the Indian conglomerates. Gwalior Rayon has just brought into production, jointly with Phillips of the US, the Thai Carbon Black Co., the largest plant for carbon-black (a sophisticated chemical used in tyres) in Asia outside of Japan.

(d) Birla's Edible Oil Products in Malaysia was, in 1973, the first company in the host country 'to develop the concept of refining palm oil for export' (rather than exporting the kernels).

(e) The canvas footwear plant in Sri Lanka was set up, jointly with CITC of the US (in turn a subsidiary of Mitsubishi), to export to the US. It was located in Sri Lanka rather than India because of the former's cheaper rubber and better fiscal incentives. Careful evaluation of location was made between the two, as well as Malaysia, Indonesia and the Philippines: an example of the true global planning that marks the MNC. The plant is to be imported second-hand from a failed facility in the US – it was too labour-intensive for US standards – rather than from India (not efficient enough) or from Uniroyal (new US machinery was too capital-intensive): another interesting example, this time of considerable entrepreneurial initiative in selecting technology.

In sum, Birla's expansion overseas is a mixture of aggressive and imaginative entrepreneurship and technological capability, with the former element predominant. The group has areas of technological excellence (Orient Paper and Gwalior Rayon) solidly rooted in Indian knowhow and equipment (both firms have large R & D facilities), though it is quite open to Western technology and sometimes uses its affiliates to gain access that is denied to it in India. However, many of its affiliates (especially in textiles) operate with fairly low technologies, where its competitive edge lies in good management, marketing and productivity (including the ability to select appropriate technology). It is *quality* of entrepreneurship which seems more important than its low cost, in contrast to the impression conveyed by Chen, Lecraw and Wells [in Kumar (forthcoming)].

(i) *Tata*[16]

The Tata group is far less involved in direct investment than Birla, but is a much larger exporter of technology in the form of turnkey contracts (Rs.1042 million executed and in hand, mostly in power generation and sugar and cement plant), consultancy earnings (of Rs.152 million in 1978–1979), licensing and sale of training services. In contrast to Birla's tradition of aggressive entrepreneurship, Tata has a reputation of cautious but excellent management, technological dynamism and far-sighted strategy.

The Tata Engineering and Locomotive Company (TELCO) is the largest truck manufacturer in India, holding about two-thirds of the total domestic market. It is also a major exporter: 15% of its output is sold overseas, making it the largest private-sector exporter of engineering products in India. With a production capacity of 37,000 vehicles (all 7½ tons), it is one of the largest truck producers in the world of a *single* model. It thus reaps most economies of scale; its products have a reputation for rugged reliability; and the design (originally imported from Daimler Benz, but subsequently greatly modified by TELCO's own R & D) is well adapted to LDC conditions. It has set up an assembly plant in Malaysia, TATAB, with a capacity of 1000 vehicles per annum, for which it designed and manufactured all the equipment and fixtures. It will provide know-how and training to local technicians for free for 15 years: it claims that its products are already outselling those of Daimler Benz (which also has an assembly operation) in Malaysia. TELCO has also licensed and equipped five licensees (Indonesia, UAE, Guyana etc.) to assemble its products; presumably most of its exports are channelled through these assembly facilities. To our knowledge, TELCO is the first automotive transnational to emerge from the Third World which is exporting its own equipment, components and know-how.

TELCO built up so much expertise in the building of special tools for its own second plant that it set up, jointly with the host government, a plant for making precision tools in Singapore. In 1977 Tata Precision Industries was producing $4 million worth of tools, 80% of which were exported to the OECD countries. It is widely regarded as the most advanced facility of its kind in the Southeast Asian region, and it runs the Technical Training Institute of Singapore, one of two such institutes helping Singapore to move up to high-skill activities.

The UNITATA palm oil complex in Malaysia, is the 'largest, most integrated and diversified facility in the world based on palm oil'. Tata Oil Mills have been involved in oil refining and soap manufacture for decades in India and their first overseas venture proved an enormous success, with sales exceeding Rs.360 million in the first year.

Tata is also setting up a truck plant in Saudi Arabia jointly with Mack Trucks of the US to assemble their respective products (management will rest with Tata). Unlike Birla, this joint venture with a DC firm involves a full use of Indian technology for the Indian product. The same is true of pre-stressed beam plant being set up with Polliet of France, again in Saudi Arabia. The group is considering another six foreign investments at this time, including one for making shoes in Europe (with Bally designs). We have already remarked on the internationalization of Tata's hotel group.

(ii) *Kirloskar*

Three companies of this group are operating overseas to manufacture power pumps, diesel engines and milling machinery. Kirloskar is now one of the world's largest manufacturers of small diesel engines, carving a significant export market as the developed countries have been forced into larger engines. It is operating a diesel engine assembly and milling machinery plant in *West Germany*, and has earned dividends of Rs.2 million and sent Indian equipment of Rs.10 million for this venture; its other plants are in Malaysia and the Philippines. This case is particularly noteworthy because Kirloskar's early experience of making diesel engines, with a Cummins licence, was the subject of a very critical and pessimistic book by Barason (1967) some time ago.

(iii) *Mahindra & Mahindra*

Another large engineering company, Mahindras are renowned for their export success with jeeps and tractors. They started an auto component plant in Iran in 1976, and are setting up a jeep and truck assembly plant in *Greece* with 40% equity. The original licence from Willys (American Motor Corporation) expired some time ago, and the firm has apparently successfully internalized and adapted the basic technology.

(iv) *Hindustan Machine Tools (HMT)*

A very successful 'high-technology' public-sector firm, HMT is a major exporter of turnkey plant for machine tools to LDCs,[17] an exporter of numerically-controlled (NC) tools to the DCs, a provider of consultancy and technical services, a licensor of designs (e.g. a chucking lathe to the UK), and a direct investor. It was persuaded to take equity participation in two turnkey ventures for the local governments in Nigeria and Kenya. It has set up a small operation in the US to attach General Electric computers to its own-designed NC tools (apparently Indian computers, though equally efficient, would not be acceptable to the US market); it is setting up a similar operation, to attach Japanese electronics, in Singapore.

Much of HMT's technology sales to LDCs has been at the well-diffused end of the scale, for simpler varieties of tools where it has complete mastery of the product and process technology, and where it is more active than firms from DCs. Some of its technology exports have, in fact, occurred to 'simplify' overspecified, expensive and unworkable technology supplied by European companies. This does not, however, mean that its technological competence ends with such 'low' technologies: its own R & D is concentrated on frontier technologies, to develop export markets in the advanced countries and to give it the capability to absorb the latest developments in its field. Its US operations, small as they are, are a proof of its competence, as are the very advanced facilities under negotiation with Iraq and Algeria.

(vi) *Hindustan Computers Ltd (HCL)*

HCL is a medium-sized manufacturer of minicomputers which has unusually high R & D activity (10–15% of sales) for an Indian company, and which has been selected by the Singapore government to set up a computer manufacturing plant there.[18] It was chosen over some 40 other international firms which sell minicomputers in Singapore. It is planning to set up three other offices in the Middle East and Southeast Asia to sell its Singapore products in 13 countries.

HCL is an obviously interesting case because it is in a truly 'high'-technology activity. While India has no production base in micro-chips or sophisticated peripherals, HCL has devoted considerable effort in product design and software. It claims to have developed a much better system of computerization for LDCs than the larger manufacturers, and can back it up with cheap programming manpower based in India. The components for its computers in Singapore will not be exported from India (and in this it differs from the usual Indian MNC), but will be sourced internationally. This will eliminate the 6-month technology lag which it claims it suffers in India.

(vii) *Fertilizer Corporation*

The state-owned Fertilizer Corporation is currently negotiating a giant $500 million fertilizer complex in Saudi Arabia, in which it will take 45% equity. A feature of the deal which is new for India, though common elsewhere, is that India will buy back 75% of the output at exceptionally favourable prices: this is the first time that India has gone for a natural-resource based venture abroad.[19] The project is very capital- and technology-intensive (competitors include French and Spanish firms). With a projected output of 500,000 tons of urea per annum, clearly no down-scaling or simplification of the technology has been attempted.

(viii) *MECON*

Metallurgical and Engineering Consultants are a large public-sector consultancy firm specialized in iron and steel. While it is only one of several major exporters of advanced consultancy services from India, it has the unique distinction of having been approached by a large European counterpart, Alusuisse, to set up a joint firm. Thus, Indo-Swiss Engineering, with 50–50 participation, which came into being in 1980, was termed a 'breakthrough' in the field of Indian joint ventures by the *Financial Times* of London.

(ix) *Other investors*

We have given enough examples to establish the variety and sophistication of Indian investors. There are numerous others in fields requiring very high levels of mechanical engineering skills (automotive pistons, tractors, scooters), chemical skills (pharmaceuticals), marketing skills (soft drinks, pharmaceuticals) and so on, but a longer discussion would add little.

The main points we should note about Indian MNCs are as follows:

First, while a number of small–medium enterprises occasionally venture abroad, the field is heavily dominated by large conglomerate enterprises with considerable managerial, technical and financial resources and a detailed knowledge of foreign markets. The process of internationalization seems a cumulative one, with experience creating a stronger base and providing greater incentives to those who have gone abroad. While no direct evidence can be cited on this, it seems that spare managerial and financial resources are an important factor pushing the larger enterprises abroad.

Second, a strong motivating factor on the part of the large enterprises has been the slow growth of the domestic economy compounded by tight anti-monopoly restrictions which has held back diversification. Thus the desire to grow and spread risks initially pushed the big houses abroad: once established, they have become relatively 'multinational' in their outlook, finding many advantages in spreading overseas.

Third, many investments have been made to counter import-substitution threats to established markets. However, most of them have served as an export promotion measure, to enter markets which could not be served by product or other forms of technology exports.

Fourth, company strategies differ. Birlas seek, for instance, to exploit their expertise by direct investments, though occasionally they sell turnkey projects and technical services. Tatas are much more diversified over the whole range of export transactions. Public-sector firms prefer to sell turnkey projects, but are sometimes obliged to take equity participation.[20] A number of large Indian enterprises remain inward-looking, and the structure of incentives remains such that they can afford to do so (Bhagwati and Srinivasan, 1975).

Fifth, Indian enterprises are not major innovators in the sense of creating new technological breakthroughs: clearly, they do not undertake that sort of massive R & D activity. It would, nevertheless, be wrong to describe them as producers of 'unbranded, low R & D, low quality products that competed on the basis of price'. Nor is it correct that they invariably were 'smaller, used more labour-intensive technologies', as Lecraw and others have done. Certainly, there are areas in which this sort of characterization is apt. There are others, increasingly important, in which it would be wrong: many investments are large and technologically advanced, often very capital-intensive, the products are sophisticated and backed by extensive advertising and after-sales service. In some cases they compete directly with established MNCs, especially in the production of intermediate products (chemicals, rayon) where continuous processes render down-scaling and adaptation nearly impossible, where (as with mini-computers or jeeps) considerable production know-how has been accumulated, or where (trucks or machine tools) they offer a slightly older but more appropriate product. In others, they operate at a 'lower' level, as received theory leads us to expect.

Sixth, the technology which is transmitted by Indian enterprises has a very high 'embodied' content in terms of Indian plant, equipment and components. While a few investments 'source' their equipment and components elsewhere, in general Indian investors go abroad to exploit their country's comparative advantage in the manufacture of a wide range of capital and intermediate goods, and their own know-how in setting up projects and operating the relevant technologies.

Seventh, a number of foreign ventures are highly export-orientated (and very few are aimed at providing low-cost goods to the Indian market). This is particulary true of investments in Southeast Asia. However, there are no MNCs with vertically integrated production structures spanning countries, and no MNCs have a truly global system of corporate planning.

Finally, a number of firms going abroad have felt a deficiency in their product differentiation capabilities. The protected domestic market has not engendered the right selling skills, especially for mass-produced consumer goods (and here they certainly do differ from export-orientated LDCs). A few firms have nevertheless learnt these skills quickly, by entering into partnerships with DC multinationals or by benefiting from their own mistakes. Some joint ventures have gone out of business, especially those involving smaller firms unable to finance these learning costs. By and large, however, the relatively low consumption standards of the Indian market are reflected in the weakness of Indian investors on highly differentiated consumer goods.

So much for the Indian MNCs: how about other developing countries?

Hong Kong firms seem to be much more specialized in their areas of export strength: textiles, plastics, footwear and toys in the early days; garments and consumer electronics more recently. A few firms have taken equity participation in chemical ventures launched by other MNCs; this may allow them to learn the technology and import it into Hong Kong at a later stage. They export little from their home country except their managerial expertise: lacking a basic capital/intermediate goods production capability, Hong Kong firms source their equipment and components world-wide [though they may, according to Wells (1978), have an advantage in knowing where to get second-hand equipment]. Their technological capabilities reside in the organization and implementation of production of light consumer goods: this is backed by formidable marketing expertise (and presumably considerable financial access) and excellent export contacts.

Chen points out that the main motivation of Hong Kong investors has been to find low-cost bases for exporting to the developed countries, not to substitute for imports in the host countries. He also cites the desire to acquire new technologies and to exploit profitable investment opportunities as the motivation for investing in industries like chemicals, machinery and opticals, where Hong Kong has no experience. The majority of Hong Kong investors seem to be medium-sized firms (though the absence of comprehensive data makes this conclusion very suspect).

Latin American manufacturing investors follow patterns more similar to those of India, though non-manufacturing activity is much more important in overall flows of Latin American capital. Of a rather small sample (77 cases) collected by White, roughly a quarter (by number, apparently) were in 'engineering' defined broadly, 16% in food products, 15% in chemicals, 5% in metals, 5% in textiles and the rest in miscellaneous activities.[21] The much greater importance of food as compared to India is explained by the importance of food production and exports by the major Latin American countries; the lesser importance of textiles is explained presumably by the already semi-industrialized nature of most of the smaller economies. Private-sector enterprises are concentrated in simple engineering products (like bicycles, agricultural implements, and simple machine tools), pharmaceuticals, and consumer electronics. A few large public-sector firms dominate the sophisticated, capital-intensive metallurgical and petrochemical sectors.

The three big Latin American countries differ among themselves, of course. Argentina has a strong and experienced local private sector, which is active abroad in pharmaceuticals, food processing and light engineering goods; there is no state participation in foreign activity, and there is a relatively weak showing in high-technology, capital-intensive activities. Argentina has a fairly well-developed capital goods sector with some local design capability, and has undertaken some low to medium technology turnkey activity abroad (Katz and Albin, 1978). Brazil, on the other hand, has a large capital goods production base but a weaker national private sector. Its high-technology industries are heavily dominated by DC MNCs, and only the giant state corporations provide a counterbalance in sectors like mining, petroleum, petrochemicals and steel. Its foreign investments reflect this dichotomy; private firms invest abroad mainly in light consumer and engineering goods, while the state enterprises sell much 'heavier' technology overseas. A few MNCs also use their Brazilian experience and production base to serve investments elsewhere (e.g. VW will assemble its Brazilian model in Egypt).

Mexico is also heavily dominated by MNCs, but still lacks a substantial capital goods sector. Its areas of local strength are petroleum and petrochemicals (following the setting up of the powerful PEMEX after an early nationalization of foreign oil companies), paper, cement, iron and steel. It invests abroad or sells technology in other forms in many of these sectors, but relies heavily on capital goods and engineering expertise from the developed countries. In general its basic technological capabilities are narrowly developed and suffer from the lack of basic design work in equipment manufacturing.

These countries are similar to India in that their foreign investments are diversified into complex, capital-intensive and high-technology activities, especially in the process industries.[22] They differ from it by their lower capabilities in areas of advanced mechanical engineering, where their domestic industries are predominantly foreign owned and indigenous design capabilities are less developed.

Some of the enormous Korean integrated trading–manufacturing companies have entered fairly advanced areas of foreign investment (tyres), but in general they are concentrated in traditional products like textiles, plastics, cement and simple metal goods. A few have invested in natural resource extraction activities, while one or two have taken equity participation in high-technology US firms to gain direct access to new (electronic) technologies. Jo describes its manufacturing investments as 'horizontal investments in the production of labour-intensive standardized products' in which there had been some 'firm-specific adaptation of foreign technology and/or standardized process to a relatively small scale of operations and some adaptation of product designs to LDC conditions' (p. 40). Since the country still lacks a capital goods base (its plans to shift quickly into heavy industry have been drastically cut back as a result of last year's recession), its overseas investments embody relatively low levels of local technological capability, and depend heavily on foreign licences and components.

In sum, therefore, India emerges as the most diversified and technologically advanced foreign investor in the Third World, with the highest embodiment of local goods in its overseas activities. A consideration of technology exports more generally [see Lall (forthcoming)] strengthens this impression. The puzzle becomes more intriguing: how, despite its poor growth and export performance, its stifling policies, its low income levels and (in relation to Brazil and Mexico) smaller industrial sector, can this be explained?

We shall turn to this question after briefly describing the geographical distribution of Indian investments abroad.

(c) *Geographical distribution*

The distribution of investments by the value of foreign equity of 101 operational ventures last year was: South and Southeast Asia 66%; Africa 30%; Middle East 1.5% and DCs 2.5%. By number of projects, the 192 'effective' investments in early 1980 were distributed as follows: South and Southeast Asia 92 (48.5%); Africa 39 (20%); Middle East 38 (20%); and DCs 23 (12%). The divergence between the two sets of figures is explained by the low equity value of the several service ventures in the Middle East and DCs, and by the relatively high level of new activity (ventures under implementation) in the Middle East.

Malaysia has been the single largest recipient of Indian capital, but data on approved future investments show that Indonesia and Thailand have overtaken it, and Indonesia will soon account for the largest stock of Indian equity. Nepal is rapidly becoming a favoured area, as may be expected. With the growth of domestic manufacturing, some OPEC countries are also drawing much more investment than before (they were the largest market for Indian 'project exports' in industrial and civil construction fields). In Africa, Nigeria is increasing its share but East Africa is attracting much less than before. In the developed world, the US and Yugoslavia are drawing the most Indian capital.

A number of analysts have remarked on the propensity of LDC investors to enter culturally, linguistically and ethnically similar countries. Hong Kong investments, in particular, have clustered in countries with large Chinese communities. Latin American countries have tended to stay in the LAFTA region. Indian investors have concentrated on Malaysia. With all these countries, however, there is now a marked shift to more diversified patterns. Having found their feet in 'psychically close' areas, LDC MNCs are becoming more confident and aggressive. Tata and Birla certainly gave the impression (in interviews) that the ethnic factor mattered little to them; in fact, as resentments built up to the new 'imperialists', they tried to play down the Indian connection and to blend as much as possible with the local colouring. What was more of a problem was language: Latin America was a very tempting market, but linguistic distance (and physical distance too: there are no direct shipping routes between India and South America) held them back.

4. AN ASSESSMENT OF INDIAN FOREIGN INVESTMENTS

Let us now quickly examine the determinants of Indian foreign investment using the extremely helpful scheme developed by Dunning (1980) for expounding his 'eclectic' theory. In the absence of detailed data on several aspects of direct investment behaviour, some of the factors mentioned cannot be given due consideration. We will concentrate particularly on the 'ownership' factors which affect an investor's monopolistic advantage in international markets.

(a) *Ownership advantages*

Dunning (1980) distinguishes three types of factors for each set of determinants of foreign investment: economy level, industry level and firm level. Let us take them in reverse order.

Firm level factors that, according to Dunning (1980), give rise to monopolistic advantages are size of enterprise, diversification, market-orientation, attitudes to risk and economies of joint production. The Indian evidence suggests strongly that such advantages are significant for its MNCs: large size, conglomerate identity, access to domestic capital markets, political muscle, efficient and aggressive management, all characterize the dominant foreign investors. Furthermore, the act of going abroad reinforces these advantages: the experience and confidence gained, the contacts established and the new sources of management tapped abroad all enable the investor to tackle the next project with greater ease. Some other factors which may be stressed for firms from a country like India are: large firms are particularly adept at dealing with cumbersome bureaucracy; and they have built up considerable managerial and technological manpower which provides them with a cushion of 'excess capacity' when their growth is restricted domestically by deliberate policy or sluggish economic conditions.

Industry level factors are those which enable Indian enterprises to 'learn' technologies efficiently to the extent that they gain an edge over international competitors. The literature reviewed at the beginning of this paper had suggested several such factors: the technologies should be simple and well-diffused; they should be amenable to scaling down and being made more labour-intensive; they should be for products where price rather than quality or differentiation are important; they should not be in high-skill or technology sectors populated by DC MNCs. Our review of the evidence suggests that such factors do apply to some LDC MNCs, but there is a substantial and growing part of their activity where they do not. Thus, MNCs from developing countries are showing the capability to set up large-scale, complex, 'leading edge' technology, marketing-intensive projects where they compete head on with established MNCs. They compete, moreover, not in a well-defined set of low-technology industries, but over a broad range of MNC activity.

This is not to say that there is no distinction between DC and LDC multinationals. Far from it: the dividing line is sharp, though it shifts over time. It is drawn, not by requirements of high skills, advanced technologies or capital-intensive processes *in general*, but by the specific conditions under which they are acquired. In other words, LDC enterprises can acquire high skills and advanced technologies given the market and technological learning conditions of their home economies. Since their home economies will support technological activity which takes them to international frontiers in some cases and not in others, the final determinant of their competitiveness will be the *scale of R & D required to assimilate internationally saleable technologies*.

It may be noted that internationally saleable technologies may be the most advanced in some cases (where there is little scope for intermediate technologies, e.g. chemicals or electronics) and rather out-of-date in others (e.g. some consumer or engineering products). Since LDC enterprises are, for the foreseeable future, going to be imitators and diffusers of technology rather than major innovators, they clearly cannot establish an advantage in activities requiring enormous R & D: in all other activities, however, they can become competitive, regardless of skill requirements. The only limitations are those imposed by scale and income levels: if the minimum efficient scale is larger or the level of income required higher than their 'learning base', even if the technology is not highly R & D intensive, they will not assimilate it.

What we arrive at is essentially the 'product cycle' theory, but the 'cycle' is very short, and the poor countries are not confined to the bottom of the skill scale. We have, therefore, to distinguish clearly between skill- and R & D-intensive industries: the latter are the real problems for LDCs, not the former.

It is the *country* level factors which can explain the different patterns of 'revealed comparative advantage' in capital exports by LDCs, and so help resolve the puzzle of India's performance. To reiterate: small, open economies without indigenous capital goods industries set up MNCs in light consumer goods industries with little 'embodied' (equipment and component) technological content from their home countries; they exploit managerial and marketing expertise and a mastery of production know-how. The larger Latin American countries set up a more varied range of ventures abroad, with some very advanced ones in metallurgy and chemicals where state enterprises are powerful; they have greater technological embodiment; it is relatively weak in sophisticated consumer goods, but relatively strong in the complex mechanical engineering sector.

The difference between the first group and the others is obvious: the size of the economy, its openness and the nature of viable domestic manufacturing in the former explain why they export their form of multinationals. That between, say, Brazil/Mexico and India is not so obvious: all have large economies, long histories of import-substitution and fairly 'heavy' industry (though Mexico lacks a capital goods base). The difference lies in their *technological strategy*. The Latin American countries have, in the past, adopted a policy of passive reliance on foreign technology, mainly in the form of direct MNC presence and in the licensing of local producers. Where MNCs predominate, of course, the multinationalization of such local competitors as are present is difficult; they tend to be too small and technologically dependent to venture abroad. MNCs themselves may generate some local technology, but this would tend to be in terms of minor process and product adaptation rather than in basic design technology: it would simply be uneconomical for them to relocate major R & D activities to affiliates in LDCs [on the relocation of R & D by MNCs see Lall (1979b)]. Furthermore, any technical progress experienced by MNC affiliates would get transmitted abroad through the firm's own international network rather than through investment by that affiliate or by other means of selling technology. This is why there are few instances of technology exports by MNC affiliates based in the LDCs. Where local producers are strong in Latin America, as in light consumer and engineering products, foreign investment by them does occur, but often with a lower degree of embodiment because of the relative lack of basic design skills and R & D in the enterprises and their local suppliers. The main exceptions are state enterprises where their size and status enables them to finance the heavy 'learning' costs of acquiring and assimilating very complex technology, and to set up a strong local supplier industry.

India has followed a strategy of greater technological self-reliance. It has applied to licensing and foreign investment the same sort of obsessive controls that it has applied to import substitution [described in Desai (1980)]. While this has resulted in various inefficiencies and technological lags, it has also enabled its national enterprises to build up a very broad base of technological competence. They have acquired the 'know-why' (i.e. basic design capabilities) of many industries rather than simply the 'know-how' (production technology): a strong foreign presence inhibits the movement of LDCs from one to the other, even with high growth rates and large manufacturing sectors. The success of many Indian enterprises which only a decade or so ago were regarded as hopelessly inefficient leads us to believe that there is a strong case to be made for the protection of 'infant technological learning' rather than only the classic protection of 'infant industry' (where production know-how is mastered). Such protection of learning requires the protection of domestic output against imports, but this is not enough; it requires that local enterprises be made to invest in the risky and costly process of learning the basic technology, by restricting the entry of foreign technology and raising the returns to indigenous R & D.[23] The assimilation of production know-how is inherent to the production process – it occurs in every enterprise, local and foreign, regardless of where the basic technology is obtained. The assimilation of *know-why* requires a local capital goods industry and often a substantial components supplying industry with which close linkages are established. It requires R & D activity and independent engineering consultancy activity. To some extent, it also requires the periodic injection of foreign technology to supplement local efforts.

The interaction between imported and local technology is a highly complex one, varying across industries and products: in cases where local efforts can, within a reasonable period, completely substitute for foreign technology, their relationship is competitive; in cases where local efforts cannot begin to master the technology, it is complementary; and, in cases where periodic injections of foreign technology followed by periods of assimilation are needed, it is both. India has gone so far in the search for self-sufficiency that it has pushed many technologies to their limits in terms of local development: to render these technologies internationally competitive, it will have to import new technologies.

5. CONCLUSIONS

The two main conclusions that may be drawn from this paper about LDC MNCs are:

First, the multinationalization of LDC enterprises is a dynamic and complex phenomenon. The existing literature has tended to underplay its sophistication and dynamism, and relegated it to too low a place on the technological scale. LDC firms will increasingly enter the haunts of DC MNCs with large, high-skill and capital-intensive foreign ventures: the ultimate dividing line between them will be scale of R & D required to generate or assimilate particular technologies[24] rather than some general notion of technological complexity or skills. The historical evolution of Japanese enterprises may well serve as a model which industrializing LDCs may follow. Thus, it would be wrong to portray LDC MNCs generally as small, low-technology, labour-intensive and low-quality manufacturers. There are numerous cases of this sort but the number of exceptions is large enough to lead us to reject it as a generalization.

Second, there are important differences between the 'revealed comparative advantage' of MNCs from different LDCs. India emerges as having a much 'higher' RCA than its income and admittedly inefficient import-substituting policies would lead us to predict. According to the (admittedly patchy) evidence at hand, it seems to have the most diverse, complex and technologically advanced set of foreign ventures of the industrializing LDCs, with the highest local 'embodiment' of skills, capital goods and components. My evaluation of technology exports more generally (Lall, forthcoming) suggests that this is true of its exports of turn-key industrial projects and consultancy services also.

This pattern is explained, in my view, by the technological strategies followed by the different countries. Countries which have pursued an 'open-door' policy to foreign technology, especially in the form of direct investment by DC firms, have built up a smaller base of indigenous capability in the design, improvement and adaptation of technologies, even if they have enjoyed high rates of growth and industrial production. This is not to argue that foreign technology is a substitute for local technology: their relationship is a complex and continuously changing one, and needs further research. Countries which have deliberately restricted access to foreign technology (but not cut it off altogether) have been able, after considerable 'learning' costs, to assimilate an unexpectedly high level of technological 'know-why', and this is reflected in their foreign activity.

The lessons of this are, however, not as obvious as may appear at first sight. Is it necessarily a 'good thing' to have a high level of multinational activity by one's firms? Or even to have achieved a stronger indigenous technological base? If rates of growth are the sole or prime objective of economic policy, the answer is far from clear: Japan succeeded brilliantly with a highly protectionist policy towards local technology, but, then, some LDCs have also done well with a highly open 'dependent' strategy. The longer-run implications of different technological strategies are hardly understood; even the most advanced countries today worry a great deal about the mainspring of technological progress. Thus, economics by itself does not enable us to find an answer to questions about the value of technological strategy. If other national objectives besides growth of GNP are introduced, answers become even more complex and remote. The aim of this paper has been to raise these interesting questions, not answer them.

NOTES

1. Since this, a conference has been held at the East–West Centre, Hawaii, exclusively on Third World multinationals [Kumar (forthcoming)], and several articles have appeared on various capital exporting and importing LDCs. Our own interest arose from MNCs as one form of technology export by LDCs – an early paper presented at a conference in 1978 (subsequently published in 1979) was followed in 1979 by a book (forthcoming), and now by field work in India and perhaps other developing countries.

2. Dunning (1980).

3. These doubts have surfaced most strongly in the case of Japanese overseas investment. See Kojima (1977), Ozawa (1977) and Mason (1980).

4. Neoclassical trade theory would, of course, take a more extreme stand: capital scarce countries cannot, under market forces, export capital. If at all, they may invest in countries which are even more short of capi-

tal, but by this reasoning a poorer country (India) cannot invest in a much richer one (Malaysia).

5. These products may or may not be capital-intensive, as Hirsch (1977) points out. However, there is a general tendency for capital intensity to be associated with skill, if not with technology intensity. Thus, countries with no skill endowments will tend to specialize in products which are also labour-intensive, while those with greater human resources may move up to more capital-intensive products even if they have no innovative capabilities. Offshore processing of high-technology components by MNCs can, of course, cut across these patterns.

6. Interestingly enough, figures published by the US government for foreign investments in the first 6 months of 1979 reported in the *Financial Times*, 6 May 1980, show that India accounted for 10 projects out of a total of 15 investments by non-OPEC, non-tax haven developing countries.

7. According to UNCTC (1978) figures, Argentina had 69 foreign operations in 1976, Colombia 21, Mexico 19, Peru 16 and Brazil 15. This seems to greatly understate the contribution of Mexico and Brazil. The latter, in particular, has recently entered Nigeria to assemble consumer products in a big way, and has also bought shares in some US companies.

8. See Chen's paper in Kumar (forthcoming). Most Hong Kong investments seem to be in manufacturing, though financial institutions based in Hong Kong are also extremely active abroad. Hong Kong is undertaking several export-orientated operations in China, but no data on values are available yet.

9. More recently, however, several large Taiwanese companies are investing abroad in plants to supply resource-based products (petrochemical and coal) to its industries. Thus, the Formosa Plastics Corp. is launching a $100 million petrochemical complex in Texas jointly with a local US firm; Taiwan Fertilizer Co. is negotiating a $300 million urea plant on a 50–50 basis with Saudi Arabia. See *Business Week*, 9 June 1980, p. 44.

10. These income figures are taken from the World Bank's *World Development Report* 1980, pp. 110–111. Note that we are leaving out South European countries from our group of 'less developed' countries.

11. According to data provided by the World Bank (*ibid.*), manufacturing value added (1976) was: Brazil $19.1 billion, Mexico $12.2 billion, India $9.0 billion, Hong Kong $1.3 billion, Singapore $0.7 billion, Korea $3.9 billion, Taiwan $4.3 billion, and Argentina $8.3 billion.

12. Note that the classifications in Tables 2 and 3 may not be identical: the former was carried out by the source mentioned, the latter by the present author.

13. The 20 largest business houses in India control 50–60% of the entire corporate sector in the economy. Birla and Tata account for about 40% of the stock controlled by the largest 20 houses, and so far about 20% of the entire corporate sector. I am grateful to M. S. Siddharthan for this information.

14. Much of this information was kindly provided by Mr Ashok Vardham Birla earlier this year.

15. Reported in the *Financial Times* (London: 7 July 1970), p. 2.

16. I am grateful to Mr B. Nehru, Managing Director of Tata Exports, for much of the information given here.

17. Its major turnkey projects include a Rs.120 million meter plant in Algeria, a Rs.94 million training centre in Nepal besides the ones in Nigeria and Kenya (Rs.151 million together). It is negotiating a Rs.2.5 billion plant in Iraq and a Rs.2.6 billion cutting tool complex in Algeria. This information was kindly provided by K. Kutty, Managing Director of HMT International.

18. Information provided by Mr A. Malhotra, Director of HCL.

19. Although the Oil and Natural Gas Commission is involved in oil exploration in Tanzania and the Gulf states.

20. The largest turnkey exporter from India, Bharat Heavy Electricals Ltd, is setting up power stations worth $270 million overseas. Partly because of the nature of the customer, and partly because few other LDCs can enter this highly complex and capital-intensive activity, it has not entered into production activity overseas. It has, nevertheless, set up an electrical turnkey construction company jointly with the Libyan government.

21. Paper and cement are significant areas of activity for Mexican firms. A Mexican firm HYLSA has also pioneered a direct-reduction steel-making process which has been licensed to several countries; as far as I know, however, HYLSA has not exploited its invention by direct investment.

22. India does not exploit its metallurgical skills by direct investment in a major way since the industry is dominated by public-sector firms which are, unlike Brazil, reluctant to go multinational, and which are fully stretched to meet local needs. However, Indian firms have built some steel mills overseas by turnkey contracts, and consultants like M. N. Dastur and MECON (mentioned earlier) are very active internationally.

23. Local R & D may be undertaken by foreign affiliates as well as local firms, given appropriate policy measures. In India MNCs are heavily involved in R & D activity and so support the growth of multinationalization in vertically related local firms, though they themselves 'stay' in India.

24. In very advanced technologies, especially in the engineering industries the difference between creating and assimilating new products/processes is not very great. Thus, I have mentioned both together, realizing that LDCs will be assimilators rather than innovators of technology.

REFERENCES

Agmon, T. and C. P. Kindleberger (eds), *Multinationals From Small Countries* (Cambridge, Mass: MIT Press, 1977).

Baranson, J., *Manufacturing Problems in India: The Cummins Diesel Experience* (Syracuse: Syracuse University Press, 1967).

Bhagwati, J. N. and T. N. Srinivasan, *Foreign Trade Regimes and Economic Development: India* (New York: NBER, 1975).

Chen, E. K. Y., 'Hong Kong multinationals in Asia: trends, patterns and objectives', in Kumar (forthcoming), *op. cit.*

Desai, A., 'The origin and direction of industrial research and development in India', *Research Policy*, Vol. 9 (1980).

Dunning, J. H., 'Explaining the international direct investment position of countries', Reading University, paper presented to the International Economics Study Group Conference, September 1980.

Hirsch, S., *Rich Man's, Poor Man's and Every Man's Goods: Aspects of Industrialisation* (Tübingen: JCB Mohr, 1977).

Jo, Sung-Hwan, 'Overseas direct investment by South Korean firms', in Kumar (forthcoming), *op. cit.*

Kojima, K., 'Transfer of technology to developing countries – Japanese style versus American style', *Hitosubashi Journal of Economics*, Vol. 4, No. 1 (1977).

Kumar, K. (ed.), *Multinationals from Third World Countries* (Lexington: DC Heath, forthcoming).

Lall, S., 'Developing countries as exporters of technology: a preliminary analysis', in H. Giersch (ed.), *International Economic Development and Resource Transfer* (Tübingen: JCB Mohr, 1979a).

Lall, S., 'The international allocation of research activity by US multinationals', *Oxford Bulletin of Economics and Statistics*, Vol. 41, No. 4 (1979b).

Lall, S., 'Monopolistic advantages and foreign investment by US manufacturing industries', *Oxford Economic Papers*, Vol. 32, No. 1 (1980).

Lall, S., *Developing Countries as Exporters of Technology* (London: Macmillan, forthcoming).

Lecraw, D. J., 'Direct investment by firms from less developed countries', *Oxford Economic Papers*, Vol. 29, No. 3 (1977).

Lecraw, D. J., 'The internationalization of firms from LDCs: evidence from the ASEAN region', in Kumar (forthcoming), *op. cit.*

Mason, R. H., 'A comment on Professor Kojima's "Japanese type versus American type of technology transfer"', *Hitosubashi Journal of Economics*, Vol. 20, No. 2 (1980).

Nelson, R. R., 'Production sets, technological knowledge, and R & D: fragile and overworked constructs for analysis of productivity growth', *American Economic Review, Papers and Proceedings*, Vol. 70, No. 2 (1980).

Ozawa, T., 'International investment and industrial structure: new theoretical implications from the Japanese experience', *Oxford Economic Papers*, Vol. 31, No. 1 (1979).

UNCTC, *Transnational Corporations in World Development: A Re-examination* (New York: UN, 1978).

Wells, L. T., 'Foreign investment from the Third World: the experience of Chinese firms from Hong Kong', *Columbia Journal of World Business* (Spring 1978).

Wells, L. T., 'Foreign investors from the Third World', in Kumar (forthcoming), *op. cit.*

White, E., 'The international projection of firms from Latin American countries', in Kumar (forthcoming), *op. cit.*

[2]

FOCUS

Joint Ventures with Third World Multinationals: A New Form of Entry to International Markets

Dr. Seamus G. Connolly

Besides domestic competition in steel, textiles and electronics, US firms face competition from Third World Multinationals in Third World markets in industries such as construction, service contracts as well as manufacturing. Third World firms have advantages such as lower labor and management costs, lower input costs, a more appropriate technology supplied without strings, and a greater familiarity with the business and working environment that is characteristic of Third World nations. However, these companies lack capital, are often subject to exchange controls in their own country, and lack a flow of up-to-date and improved technologies in manufacturing. These are the complementary assets that firms from the US and other industrialized countries can provide in a joint venture partnership as well as providing management and marketing skills and head office services that often are scarce resources for many Third World firms. There are certain situations in Third World countries where the combined advantages of the US and Third World firms make market entry or survival possible where otherwise neither could go it alone.

DURING THE PAST ten years much attention has been focused on a group of developing countries that have achieved high economic growth rates and have penetrated Western markets by following a strategy of exporting manufactured goods. Known as Newly Industrializing Countries or NICs, they have drawn attention in the US because of their impact on American unemployment. They have become attractive locations for overseas manufacturing and are now the source of a large volume of imports ranging from textiles and garments to steel. What is not so well publicized is the competition US companies face in the international market not only from NICs' exports but also from Third World Multinationals.[1] Obviously, these Third World companies are no immediate threat to the dominance of the US multinationals on a global scale; but as many US companies have discovered, the Third World companies have a distinct competitive advantage in such areas as, for example, construction in the Middle East, financial services in some of the Pacific rim countries and in certain areas of manufacturing in the Third World.[2]

This article examines some market situations where Third World Multinationals and US companies (especially smaller companies) can form joint ventures where the distinctive advantages of each can be combined for mutual benefits. Not that such joint ventures can compete on an equal basis with US, European or Japanese multinationals or even domestic firms in all markets, but rather that in certain areas and for certain products or services it is this combination that makes entry possible and enables the US firm to be competitive. The Third World Multinational may be particularly useful to the smaller US firm that wishes to export to several countries or wishes to establish an assembly, processing or manufacturing plant overseas and does not have the resources, experience or personnel to go it alone. Larger companies that already are international in scope also find rewarding opportunities in joint ventures. These exist, for example, in the service sector or where a skilled or semiskilled but cheap labor force is required, or where governments or mul-

Dr. Seamus G. Connolly is coordinator of international business studies at the Rutherford Campus of Fairleigh Dickinson University. He is also Vice President of IRI Research Institute, Inc.; a New York-based international management, technical assistance and research firm.

tilateral lending agencies require regional experience or language ability in awarding contracts under international competitive bidding.

Competitive Advantages of Third World Multinationals

The potential for rewarding joint ventures lies in the ability of the US and the Third World firms to complement one another's specific advantages and develop an enterprise that either would not be possible or equally rewarding if both acted independently. It is in this context that some of the advantages of the Third World firms are examined.

The most distinctive advantage of the Third World firm in the international market is the same as that which has enabled them to penetrate the US markets (i.e. lower labor costs and cheaper materials). Labor costs include the cost of management, technical skills as well as unskilled labor. A Korean company bidding on a construction contract in the Middle East, or an Indian company involved in manufacturing in Malaysia has a distinct advantage. Not only will management and skilled workers be paid significantly less than their US counterparts, but these firms also often use their own unskilled labor force paid at home country salary levels. For Third World managers, an overseas assignment may not involve much of a salary increase. For a US manager, working in a Third World country usually means a significantly higher salary and extra fringe benefits. One study estimates that it costs a US firm about $100,000 to keep a middle level executive in Malaysia for a year, while the corresponding cost for an Indian firm is about $20,000.[3] But salaries and fringe benefits are only part of the price difference; costs for housing, office space and equipment, administrative overhead and transport are also lower.

The lower cost of supplies and materials from the Third World countries is also significant. This applies to both the machinery and technology used in manufacturing as well as other inputs that may be required such as, steel or cement. In some cases the production costs of the inputs may be subsidized directly or indirectly by the home government.

A second distinctive advantage of the Third World Multinational is the appropriateness of its technology. It is labor intensive in a context of high unemployment and underemployment; it requires less maintenance, fewer spare parts and is cheaper. In many cases basic technologies have been purchased in the developed economies and adapted to local conditions where lower output is required for smaller markets, or the same machine performs several different functions. Because of severe competition, the emphasis is on low cost production rather than economies of scale with cheap labor performing many peripheral functions.[4]

The technologies of these firms, however, are not all imitations or adaptations. Several countries have developed new technologies suitable to small scale agriculture and rural construction (e.g. multipurpose two-wheeled tractors and smaller scale processing equipment), while countries like India, Brazil and South Korea have made significant progress in the development of heavy machinery and machine tools which they use in their investments overseas.

A third advantage of the Third World Multinational is its first hand familiarity with working conditions in many developing countries. These conditions include inadequate infrastructure, a large public sector, cumbersome bureaucracies, cultural similarities and work attitudes and the general manner of doing business in such an environment. Two aspects of this advantage are important.

- First, many Third World multinationals operate in countries that are ex-colonies of the same mother country. As such, they have many legal, accounting, tax, labor and government regulations in common. This applies to companies from Hong Kong in Sri Lanka, Indian companies in Malaysia and Latin American multinationals.
- Second, there is often an established network of family and ethnic connections that give many investors points of access in the host countries. This is true for Chinese investors in Asia and for Indians in East Africa. However, while these connections may be helpful in gaining access to a market they also may be a liability in the way the host country government views a joint venture because of the dominance that group may have in a particular sector (e.g. the Chinese in the retail trade in the Philippines).

A final distinctive asset of Third World Multinationals is that precisely because they do not have a global reach and are from weaker home countries, they are perceived by the host country to pose little threat to political or economic independence.

In many cases, lack of capital has forced these companies into local joint ventures where their contribution is scarce technology or skills. This enhances local control and even where the foreign firm is state-owned, there is little basis for the charge that it dominates any particular sector of the economy. A joint venture with such a firm will make entry for the US firm more acceptable because it is not seen just as a part of a global plan, or a link in an international production chain. The Third World government will find it easier to control such a joint venture, and if it needs what the joint venture has to offer, it will prefer it to a wholly owned subsidiary of a large multinational corporation.

Complementary Assets of Firms from the US and Other Industrialized Countries

Third World Multinationals have significant advantages when investing in other Third World countries, but very often they lack several factors in the investment mix that are necessary for a successful long term investment. Small firms from any country may have the missing factors the Third World Multinationals need. In such a case a joint venture could give access where otherwise it might be difficult either because of the size of the company, its resources, its operational experience or the attitude of the host government. This form of entry may be particularly attractive to firms from the smaller countries of Europe as well as US firms. The concentration here is on US firms, but the complementary assets would generally be the same for firms from all industrialized countries.

Probably the single greatest constraint of Third World multinationals is their lack of capital resources. For countries like Brazil, India, South Korea or the Philippines, foreign exchange is scarce and often rationed. This creates severe operational problems and limits investment possibilities for many Third World firms. It is particularly true for state-owned multinationals at a time when internal spending is being severely curtailed and outflows of capital kept to a minimum. In these circumstances it is difficult for many companies to survive or to withstand the costs of normal competition. A US firm that has investment capital or the capability of raising it in the financial markets, has a scarce resource of great interest to a joint venture partner. Moreover, this supply of capital may be the price a Third World government is willing to pay to allow a US firm access to its market.

Another asset the US firm can contribute to the joint venture is a flow of more advanced technology. Mature, standardized or adapted technology is a definite advantage in increasing employment and production for smaller markets, but since it is not exclusive and is not new it can be easily replicated by local entrepreneurs who could replace the foreign investor in local and export markets. There is already evidence that some of the early NICs are now being replaced by other developing economies in the production of textiles, shoes and cement and that because of higher costs, the early NICs are being pushed into higher levels of production. If the Third World firm is to stay competitive or move into new areas of production, it may be essential to have the new updated technology which the US firm can supply.

Moreover there is a certain ambivalence in many developing countries' attitudes towards technology. Because of the level of unemployment and underemployment, policy statements and development plans emphasize labor intensive technology. At the same time many nations do not want what they consider to be second class technology and if there is a foreign exchange cost, they may insist on state of the art production. The US firm can supply a flow of updated technology, and this may be an important factor in the host country's decision to allow the joint venture to enter. While some host governments may have reservations about wholly owned subsidiaries of large US firms, they still respect the technology and quality control that goes with it particularly at higher levels of production for export. In a joint venture arrangement they may be getting the best of both worlds.

Another complementary asset of the US firm is the highly developed management, marketing or technical skills available to them. While the Third World firm has a distinct advantage from an operational point of view within another Third World country, management, marketing and technical skills may be scarce and/or underdeveloped. In their home environment managers may have had a protected or semi-captive market and may be ill-prepared for the competition of the international market place. Moreover, there may be a significant difference in scale of production especially if the foreign investment is used as a step into a larger regional market. A US partner can supply scarce skills and back up services either on-site or through technical assistance or management contracts. Moreover, some such arrangement can give the joint venture access to international financing sources, communication networks, information systems and marketing channels that either would not be available or would be too costly for the Third World firm on its own.

Joint Venture Opportunities

Joint venture opportunities exist where both sides need the complementary assets of the other. In the case of the Third World Multinational, it is where present competition or the desire to expand heightens the need for capital, newer technologies or scarce skills. In the case of the US firm, it may be difficulty of access, lack of welcome by the host country, lack of operational experience, or limited resources. In such cases where a US firm has a product or a technology or a service that is marketable, a joint venture with a Third World Multinational may be the only way to go and could open up not only one market but several, and give access to regional markets (e.g. in the ASEAN region). The US firms likely to be in such a situation are smaller companies that have reached the limits of expansion in the domestic market and who see the potential of international markets. Large multinational corporations that can penetrate and successfully operate in Third World markets without entering a joint venture, are likely to do so. If they enter a joint venture, it is likely to be with a host country partner precisely because they do not need the assets the Third World Multinational possesses. They may also prefer a weaker partner that can give them access at the local level while not exercising much control in the operation of the joint venture. But again, there are the areas and enterprises where even for the large US multinational a joint venture with a Third World multinational may be the only or best way to go. It is estimated that the Third World share of foreign demand for US goods and services grew some 33 per cent faster than the developed country share in the seventies.[6] As some of the NICs raise their levels of production from consumer products, and industrial supplies into capital goods and higher technologies, US firms will face increasing competition for these markets. In some cases it may be only by joint ventures they can remain in the market at all.

The service sector is one area where joint ventures may be mutually advantageous to US and Third World Multinational firms. For example, US service companies seeking technical assistance or financial and management contracts in Indonesia or Malaysia now face direct competition from Filipino companies with a staff trained in the US tradition at a high level and that can be supplied at a fraction of the US cost. For example, the Filipino firm of Sycip, Gorres, Velayo and Company (SGV) has a significant position already in the Pacific Basin and can compete and hold its own against the "Big Eight" from a professional point of view at a much lower cost.[7]

The same is true for Indian firms in Hotel Management in the Middle East. Not only does the Indian firm get the contract, but then of course India becomes a source of supply. US firms cannot compete on a cost basis, but they have ownership-specific advantages that when combined with the cheaper Third World factors can give a service that is competitive in price and also provides a level of service that otherwise may not be available. Such advantages include worldwide information systems and communication links, more advanced skills and technologies at headquarters and international mechanisms for reservations and sourcing of supplies. A recently announced joint venture between a Cleveland construction company and the People's Republic of China combined the expertise of the former with the cheaper factors of the latter to get an international construction contract in Kuwait, a contract that neither could have gotten on its own.

Another area of mutual interest to US and Third World Multinationals is the development of supplies of raw materials. Most of the large Third World Multinationals are natural resource development companies. This interest in raw materials indicates the dependence of both the developed and Third World countries on imported strategic minerals for their dustrial growth. Investment in raw material development has proved to be a risky business for US firms, but two factors may be changing the situation. Firstly, the period of resource nationalism may have peaked as the growth of manufactured exports has slowed and the demand for raw materials has declined as a result of the world recession. Many countries are again looking to extractive industries to help them resolve external imbalances and bring in more foreign exchange. Even Brazil, itself a multinational natural resource developer, has welcomed a resurgence of foreign investment in extractive industries.[8]

Secondly, for many Third World countries that took control of their natural resources and now lack the capital or technology to operate or expand, it is much easier to allow a Third World multinational to return in a joint venture with a US firm that has the capital and technology for the project. For the US firm it lowers visibility and political risk, while at the same time allowing for a profitable investment and a source of supply of raw materials. As more and more Third World governments move into overseas natural resource development either through state enterprises or incentives to local firms, this could be an increasingly important area for joint ventures. Petrobras and other Brazilian multinationals are exploring for oil and helping other Latin American countries in their mining industries. Scarce capital may make this an attractive area for US partners. Interestingly, the fact that many of these natural resource multinationals are state-owned appears to be of little concern to host governments possibly because neither the company nor the home government have the power of the large multinationals, and at the same time the state owned firm is less likely to be allowed to fail. Malaysia, for example, has advertised as a plus the backing it can give its state owned multinationals.[9]

Looking at joint venture opportunities from a geographical point of view, an area of great interest is the ASEAN region. As indicated earlier some of these countries have their own multinationals expanding in the area. Economically, the region is one of the fastest growing in the world and the business climate is one of the most hospitable in the developing world. A major thrust in the region is rapid diversification into both light and heavy industry and high technology. There are extensive links between those nations through Chambers of Commerce and Industry, Regional Industry and Commodity Clubs and there are also extensive contacts with US business organizations.

A distinct advantage of entering a multinational joint venture in the region is that it gives access to a regional market with some preferential trading arrangements for member countries. Possibilities for joint ventures with multinational companies in this region exist in such areas as food processing in Thailand, construction, engineering and irrigation projects in the transmigration programs in Indonesia and technical assistance, management and service contracts associated with the large programs of public investment. Attractive opportunities exist in a whole range of projects involved in extracting, refining and adding value to the abundant resources of the region such as timber, metals, rubber and petroleum.

In less friendly environments it may not be politically advisable for the host country to allow US companies to enter with wholly owned subsidiaries. At the same time they may need the resources, markets, technology, or quality that a US firm can supply. In such an environment the US firm will have large reservations about entering anyway. However, the market may be important because of the actions of competitors, the volume of business associated with a large public sector or large multilateral lending, or the presence of rewarding opportunities in raw materials development. For example, Brazilian companies have access to the resource-rich former Portuguese colonies of Angola and Mozambique. These economies lack capital, technology and skills that US companies could provide and would probably be welcome in joint ventures with Brazilian companies and subsidiaries of US companies in Brazil.

Conclusion

Third World Multinationals have become increasingly important actors on the international business scene, whether it is in construction in the Middle East, financial or management services in the Pacific Rim or natural resource development in Latin America. These firms have distinctive advantages which could be complementary to US firms trying to enter or expand in overseas markets. In some products and services and in certain countries this may be the only way they can be competitive. Some of the broad areas of possible joint ventures were outlined in the previous section. No mention has been made of the operational difficulties of the joint venture itself involving as it does three national systems with different legal, tax and business practices and two headquarters management whose interests may conflict. Questions of decision-making, control, allocation of costs and other factors will be complicated. However, there are markets where neither company can penetrate alone or remain competitive. If both firms possess significant complementary assets that are mutually advantageous, the rewards of the joint venture will make the operational problems manageable.

NOTES

1. See Wells, Louis T., "The Internationalization of Firms from Developing Countries," *Multinationals from Small Countries*, eds. Agmon T. and C. P. Kindleberger (Cambridge, Mass.: MIT Press, 1977), pages 133-156. And eds. Kumar K. and McLeon, M.M. "Foreign Investors from the Third World," *Multinationals from Developing Countries* (Lexington, Mass.: D.C. Heath, World Markets," *Asian Development Review*, 1983, *Review*, 1979, Jan-Feb. pages 101-109.
2. See Heenan, Davis A. and Warren J. Keegan, "The Rise of Third World Multinationals," *Harvard Business*
3. Kumar, Krishna, "Third World Multinationals: A Growing Force in International Relations," *International Studies Quarterly*, 1982, (26), September, page 406.
4. Wells, "The Internationalization of Firms from Developing Countries," page 138.
5. Sicat, Gerardo P. "Newly Industrializing Countries and World Markets, "*Asian Development Review*, 1983, page 60.
6. Wallace, James R. and Lynn Quincy, "Annex A, Table A-5, Indicators of US Third World Interdependence," *US Foreign Policy and the Third World Agenda, 1983*, eds. Lewis, John P. and Valeriana Kallab (New York: Praeger, 1983), page 178.
7. Heenan, Keegan.
8. Quintella, Sergio F., Seminar held at Plaza Hotel by Grande Carajas Development Project on "Investment Opportunities in the Carajas Project, a Model for a Joint Venture of Foreign and National Capital" (New York: September 10), 1982.
9. Heenan, Keegan, page 107.

[3]

mir vol. 30, 1990/4, pp. 299–315

mir
Management
International Review

Stephen B. Tallman/Oded Shenkar

International Cooperative Venture Strategies: Outward Investment and Small Firms from NICs[1]

Abstract

- This study analyzes the preferred models of overseas outward investment in cooperative ventures for 340 small and medium sized Korean firms in 1987.
- The analysis suggests that firms in the sample have strategic concerns that are different from those of the large MNCs typically studied in such research. Current models of the international firm and of cooperative ventures are shown to have a strong situational component and limited application to a sample of firms which are not large multinationals

Key Words

- Current models of the international firm and of cooperative ventures are shown to have limited application to a sample of firms which are not large multinationals.

Authors

Stephen B. Tallman, Assistant Professor, Graduate School of Business Administration, University of Utah, Salt Lake, Utah, U.S.A.
Oded Shenkar, Senior Lecturer, Graduate School of Business, Tel-Aviv University, Ramat-Aviv, Tel-Aviv, Israel.

Manuscript received March 1990.

Stephen Tallman/Oded Shenkar

Introduction

The study of international cooperative ventures (ICVs) is gaining increasing popularity among researchers. Much of the literature in the field addresses cooperative ventures in less developed countries (LDCs), but does so from the point of view of large multinational companies (MNCs) from industrialized countries (ICs) (Beamish 1985; Hladik 1985; Hennart 1988). The local partners are treated as passive partners of the foreign multinationals, which use them to provide relief from local customs, biases, or regulation. The objectives of the local partner are addressed only in terms of their potential to disrupt the multinational's strategic investment (Stopford and Wells 1972; Franko 1971; Kobrin 1988).

This emphasis on outward investment from the ICs fails to recognize the increasing role of the LDCs and the newly industrialized countries (NICs) in the world economy. Investment abroad from the Republic of Korea alone surged to almost $400 million (US) in 91 projects in 1987 for an aggregate total of $966.1 M (US) in 546 projects, and has taken place in both LDCs and in ICs. While a few studies have examined the role of LDC firms as outward investors, they have retained the typical large firm focus (Wells 1977; Ghoshal 1988; Kumar and Kim 1984). However, smaller firms are also becoming more important in international business. The Business Korea Yearbook indicates that small and medium sized firms accounted for 101 aggregate overseas investments with a total value of $23.1 M (US) by the end of 1987. The totals from smaller firms include 31 new projects in 1987 alone.

This paper investigates the strategic plans of smaller Korean firms seeking ICVs in other countries. It examines firms from a NIC as sources of investment capital, knowledge, or technology, and addresses locational differences in the methods by which these firms exploit their competitive strengths. The paper also provides insights into the role of smaller firms in international business in general and a detailed look at an emergent part of the Korean economy. This study offers a combination of features which, to the best of our knowledge, is unique in the literature on ICVs. It examines *outward,* rather than inward, investment flows from a NIC; it focuses on small and medium sized firms in the international economy rather than large firms; it investigates strategic venture plans, rather than completed investments.

Theoretical Framework

Study of the strategies of MNCs, to include cooperative ventures, has generated a number of models of international activity. Kogut (1988) finds that the most relevant perspectives on international equity joint ventures (JVs) are the strategic behavior model (Hymer 1960; Caves 1971; Graham 1974) and transaction cost models (Teece 1981; Hennart 1982, 1988), to include internalization theory (Buckley and Casson 1976, 1988). Kogut suggests the need for a third approach, based on organization theory concepts, which he calls the organizational learning model (Kogut 1988). The strategic behavior model is primarily focused on oligopoly competition among large firms, not a relevant concept for small forms from a small country. Therefore, this paper examines the relevance of the transaction cost perspective and the organization learning perspective to a sample of small NIC-based firms, and suggests a model of their ICV planning which is somewhat different from either perspective.

In discussing the transaction cost perspective, Kogut suggests that in a situation where whole ownership is economically infeasible, equity JVs offer "mutal hostage" positions to guarantee performance on the part of both the foreign firm and the local firm. Such as guarantee is needed when opportunistic behavior by either side in a contractual venture would seriously harm the other. Buckley and Casson (1988) address this same topic within their internalization model. They find that equity forms are needed when other means of guaranteeing forebearance from cheating (legal protection, reputation, or threat of retaliation) on contracts are weak. Cooperative forms are found to be related to minimum efficient scales beyond that of a single firm, to product indivisibilities, and to complementarity of skills.

Hennart (1988) suggests that pooled knowledge, market access, and reduced political risk are key incentives for ICVs. He finds that the risk of losing intellectual property rights is critical to the choice of equity JV over contractual forms. Hennart proposes that tacit, or implicit, organizational knowledge is particularly susceptible to compromise in a market transaction. Transaction cost based models in general predict a preference for internal forms of transaction among firms in knowledge intensive industries, due to the high cost of compromising firm know-how in a contractual situation.

Kogut's (1988) organizational learning model for international equity JVs focuses on the same condition of tacit knowledge described by Hennart. Contrary to Hennart's assertion that markets are risky for such skills, Kogut shows that such know-how can be revealed with low expected opportunism costs in a market transaction. This condition results from the impossibility of duplicating implicit skills without duplicating the organization. Despite low costs, tacit knowledge requires organizational forms for accurate transmission. Equity joint ventures rather than licensing contracts are to be expected when firms plan to acquire implicit organization-specific knowledge from each other, or when the MNC wishes to retain its organizational capabilities but needs specific technical knowledge from the local firm.

The role of organization learning in encouraging equity JVs, whether international or domestic in scope, is tested by Berg, Duncan, and Friedman (1982).

The Berg et al. model is developed from the resource dependence framework of Pfeffer and Salancik (1978). This organization theory model is interpreted to show that firms use equity JVs as alternatives to R & D in acquiring new knowledge about related products. This interpretation results from two studies. Pfeffer and Nowak (1976) found a high degree of horizontality (same industry affiliation) at the 2-digit SIC code level among parent firms in a JV relationship. Berg et al. found much less horizontality at the "2 ½ digit" SIC code level. Firms appear to form equity JVs within their industry group, but seek ventures in product areas outside their specific major product line, presumably to acquire new skills.

Both the organizational learning and the transaction cost perspectives were developed to explain the activities of large firms based in ICs. This paper attempts to apply these perspectives to a sample of NIC-based firms in order to explain their strategic plans toward international cooperative ventures. We expect that both perspectives will provide some relevant insights, but that neither will be completely satisfactory when applied to this sample. Wells (1977) and Kumar and Kim (1984) find that NIC firms possess only older technologies which they adapt to non-industrialized environments and then apply in LDCs, often through JVs, in contrast to IC multinationals which often specialize in the latest technology. We will finish by deriving a model of ICV activity for NIC firms which will be sensitive to established theory and more appropriate to the firms investigated.

Hypotheses

Certain hypotheses about ICVs can be constructed from the assertions of the theoretical models described above. These can then be tested on patterns of strategic planning for outward ICVs found in a sample of small and medium sized Korean firms. By testing planned ventures, we are observing strategic priorities without interference from exogenous environmental conditions. Most studies observe only those ventures which are actually completed, after locational and competitive pressures have compromised the original intentions of strategic planners. Observing initial intent eliminates, for instance, the effect of specific host government limits on types of inward foreign investment. From a transaction cost perspective, we suggest the following:

Hypothesis 1: NIC firms planning ventures in high technology industries should prefer equity JVs over contractual ventures, especially in less developed regions.

This hypothesis suggests that equity ventures are chosen to protect explicit technologies from possibly opportunistic licensees. We can also say:

Hypothesis 1a: NIC firms planning ventures in lower technology industries should favor contractual forms over equity JVs.

This hypothesis suggests that in the absence of high opportunism costs, lower transaction costs will result from licensing activity due to the lower costs of managing the ICV.

The organizational learning perspective and the related concept of resource dependency suggest somewhat different expected patterns of ICV plans. We except the following:

Hypothesis 2: NIC firms planning ventures in industrialized regions should favor equity JVs over contractual forms, especially in high tech industries.

This hypothesis results from the assumption that NIC firms seek knowledge through IC ventures, especially in fields high in explicit technology. We also suggest:

Hypothesis 2a: NIC firms planning ventures in industries with lower levels of explicit technology should favor equity JVs over contractual forms.

This hypothesis is based on the assumption that such firms seek to apply implicit organizational skills in the absence of easily codified technologies. On the other hand, we can say:

Hypothesis 2b: NIC firms planning ventures in industries with high levels of explicit technology would prefer contractual means over equity JVs.

This last hypothesis suggests that if equity forms are chosen to transmit implicit knowledge due to its non-specific nature, then contractual forms will be selected when information is explicit.

Sample

The sample consists of 340 small and medium sized Korean manufacturing firms listed in the 1987 version of *Business Partners from Korea*. Compiled by the Small and Medium Industry Promotion Corporation (SMIPC) of South Korea, this survey was designed to identify the needs of smaller firms of foreign partners to engage in cooperative ventures outside of Korea. The venture types included equity joint ventures, plant exports, and technology transfers. The firms also indicated preferred areas of the world for their activities, the product proposed for the venture, and firm data to include the primary industry(ies) in which the firm competed.

The data source does not indicate the response rate for the survey. As most international business activities in Korea are still conducted by a small number of large multinational firms (Kumar and Kim 1984), we would not expect a large population of small internationally oriented companies. Small Korean firms have few means of contacting foreign partners, so that an opportunity to be listed in such a document would provide unique and valuable exposure, and would probably attract a high rate of response among firms with international plans. The sample of 340 firms looking for overseas cooperative ventures in 1987 compares well to be small number of investments of all types by smaller firms, 31 in 1987, again implying a sample representing a large portion of the population.

The data base also does not indicate how many similar firms might be attempting wholly owned overseas ventures. However, Wells states that 87% of developing country firms use joint ventures for overseas investment (Wells 1977). In addition, while large Korean firms have the resources for wholly-owned investment, the small firms represented here would generally lack the resources for wholly-owned overseas ventures.

Findings

Industry Patterns

Table 1 presents a breakdown of the observations by industry based on the product categories proposed by Hladik (1985), which contain one or two 2-digit SIC classifications.

Table 1 and subsequent comparisons involving industry affiliation are based on the industry of the proposed venture. The data base is organized by this measure, and it appears to be most closely associated with the question at hand. The small firms in this study show a high degree of horizontality at both 2 and 3-digit SIC code levels. At the industry level, only 11 of 340 observations (3.24%) show different SIC codes for the cooperative venture and the primary industry of the firm. At the 3-digit SIC code level only 28 of 340 observations (8.24%) show different primary industry and cooperative venture codes. The close correlation of primary industry of the firm and industry of the proposed venture indicates that organizing the data by primary industry would have no

Table 1. Cooperative Venture Industry Affiliation

Industry	Tech Level	# Firms	%
1 Food & Tobacco Products (SIC 2000–2199)	Low	14	4.12
2 Textiles & Apparel (SIC 2200–2399)	Low	42	12.35
3 Wood Products & Furniture (SIC 2400–2599)	Low	5	1.47
4 Paper, Allied Products, Printing (SIC 2600–2799)	Low	11	3.24
5 Chemicals, Pharmaceuticals & Allied Products (SIC 2800–2899)	High	19	5.59
6 Petroleum & Energy Products (SIC 2900–2999)	High	1	0.29
7 Rubber & Plastic Products (SIC 3000–3099)	High	30	8.82
8 Leather products (SIC 3100–3199)	Low	1	0.29
9 Stone, Clay & Glass Products (SIC 3200–3299)	Low	1	3.53
10 Metals & Metal Products (SIC 3300–3499)	Low	47	13.82
11 Machinery, Except Electric (SIC 3500–3599)	High	55	16.18
12 Electric & Electronic Equipment (SIC 3600–3699)	High	49	14.41
13 Transport Equipment (SIC 3700–3799)	High	26	7.65
14 Scientific Instruments (SIC 3800–3899)	High	11	3.24
15 Miscellaneous Mfg. (SIC 3900–3999)	Low	17	5.00
Total		340	100.00

impact on subsequent comparisons. It also indicates that cross-industry learning (Berg et al. 1982) is not a significant factor here.

We see a wide range of industries represented, in consonance with the findings of Kumar and Kim (1984) for large Korean firms. The largest areas of interest are in textiles, a traditional Korean export industry, and in metals, machinery, and electrical equipment, industries where large Korean firms are becoming major world players. These smaller firms seem to reflect the strengths of Korea's major companies, possibly due to domestic supplier relationships (an area not addressed in the database).

Table 1 also includes a classification of the observations by high or low technology industry groups. This was done on the basis of similar divisions in Buckley and Casson (1976) and Pearce (1983), and is based on R&D/Sales ratios for the same industry in the United States. Obviously, this measure says little about the specific technology commitment of the sample firms of individual ICV plans. Kumar and Kim (1984) show that large firms from Korea have lower technology levels than IC firms in the same industry, with advantages in LDC-appropriate adaptations of mature technologies. The small firms in our sample probably depend also on adapting mature technology in technology-intensive industries.

Tests of transaction cost type models have relied heavily on relative industry levels of technologies (Buckley and Casson 1976, Fagre and Wells 1982, Kogut 1988), and U.S. levels of R&D spending have been used to rank foreign firms by industry affiliation (Lall and Siddharthan 1982). In an exploratory study of small foreign firms, industry affiliation seems to be the only practicable means of assigning relative technology levels.

One-way Investment Patterns

Regional. We see in Table 2 that a majority of the firms are seeking partners in LDCs (primarily Asia and Latin America).

Ventures in countries at a lower level of development than Korea are not likely to be major sources of new knowledge. The purpose of ICVs for most of these firms therefore seems to be to exploit existing skills in a wider market rather than to gain new knowledge, contrary to the results of Berg et al. (1982). The small number of investments in IC regions might be for market access or to gain access to new technology. This pattern conforms to Wells' (1977) finding

Table 2. Distributions of ICVs

	# Firms	%	Z	P>Z
Target Region Development Level				
Low	290	85.3	18.4	0.00
High	50	14.7		
Total	340	100.0		
Technology Level of Venture				
Low	149	43.8	−2.3	0.01
High	191	56.2		
Total	340	100.0		
Type of Cooperative Venture				
Equity Joint Venture	109	32.1		
Plant Export	49	14.4		
Technology Transfer	124	36.4		
2 or More	58	17.1		
Total	340	100.0		

or large LDC firms, which aim most of their outward ventures at countries with even lower levels of development than their home countries. Given that Korea hosts much foreign investment and licensing (a similar SMIPC source for planned inward ventures lists over 800 firms), Wells' (1977) description of MNCs from developing countries as intermediaries in the international flow of technology from ICs to LDCs appears to apply in Korea.

Technology. Table 2 shows the number of firms in each technology intensiveness group. We see that a significant majority of the firms are interested in ventures in high technology industries. This implies that explicit technological know-how is an important factor for firms seeking outward ICVs. The transaction cost perspective would predict a preponderance of equity ventures for IC firms under similar conditions.

Investment Type. Table 2 also shows the relative proportions of firms using each of the three types of cooperative investment related to the study. We see that large groups of the firms are interested in equity JVs and in pure technology transfers. Fewer firms are interested in the market for embodied technology via plant exports.

We can consider both plant exports and outward technology transfers to be contractual ventures in which the Korean partner would lose control of its technology once it was in place abroad. From the transaction cost perspective, this implies that 68% of the firms are willing to risk compromising their core technologies through contractual ventures in LDCs. The organizational learning perspective might suggest that these findings imply a low rate of dependence on implicit skills.

However, these findings, like those of Kumar and Kim (1984) cited above, may suggest that NIC firms, like those in lower technology industries in ICs, might be willing to use licensing extensively due to a lack of any proprietary intellectual property to protect. If technology in technology intensive NIC industries comes from the ICs rather than internal R&D, and is mature in nature, the opportunism costs of market transactions would be low and a greater number of contractual ventures would be expected.

Cross Comparisons

Two-dimensional comparisons of the observations permit direct testing of the hypotheses proposed above.

Technology and Location. Table 3 indicates that the relative interest levels of sample firms in IC ventures versus LDC ventures is not significantly different

Table 3. Cross Tabulation of Area of Investment and Technology Level of Venture

Area	Technology Level		
	Low	High	Total
LDC	127	163	290
Total	37.35%	47.94%	85.29%
Row	43.79%	56.21%	
Column	85.23%	85.34%	
IC	22	28	50
Total	6.47%	8.24%	14.71%
Row	44.00%	56.00%	
Column	14.77%	14.66%	
Total	149	191	340
	43.82%	56.18%	100.00%

Chi-square with continuity correction factor = 0.016, Prob. = 0.8989; Chi-square without continuity correction factor = 0.001, Prob. = 0.9783 D.F. = 1.

between high tech and low tech industries. The firms in High Tech industries do not appear to see great potential for exploiting their technologies in more technologically advanced nations. Again, this supports the role of the NICs as intermediaries in the international flow of technology (Wells 1977). We would expect NIC firms, especially smaller firms without an independent technology development capacity, to have little technology which is marketable in the ICs. Korean firms in low technology industries may have process skills which are exploitable in LDCs, but which are not unique in IC markets.

Technology and Venture Type. Table 4 shows that firms in low tech industries seek equal numbers of equity JVs and contractual ICVs while firms in high tech industries seek relatively more contractual ventures. This appears to be inconsistent with the expectations of Hypothesis 1. Firms in high tech industries do not seem to be seeking equity positions to protect their technology. Rather, they are using direct (technology transfer) or indirect (plant exports) contractual means to seel their explicit technologies. This is consistent with Hypothesis 2b. Firms in low tech industries have a greater interest in equity ventures, consistent with the expectations of Hypothesis 2a, but contrary to the transaction cost interpretation in Hypothesis 1a.

This pattern does not reflect the transaction cost model's position that equity investment results from firms internalizing market transactions for high technology due to the potentially high costs of compromising technological know-how. Again, it is possible that these smaller NIC firms only have access to older technologies and that they do not expect to incur high costs from comprising their core technologies. These small firms may feel that they are

Table 4. Cross Tabulation of Investment Type and Technology Level of Venture

Investment Type	Technology Level		
	Low	High	Total
Equity Investment	61	48	109
Total	17.94%	14.12%	32.06%
Row	55.96%	44.04%	
Column	40.94%	25.13%	
Plant Export	16	33	49
Total	4.71%	9.71%	14.41%
Row	32.65%	67.35%	
Column	10.74%	17.28%	
Technology Transfer	47	77	124
Total	13.82%	22.65%	36.74%
Row	37.90%	62.10%	
Column	31.54%	40.31%	
More Than One	25	33	58
Total	7.35%	9.71%	17.06%
Row	43.10%	56.90%	
Column	16.78%	17.28	
Total	149	191	340
	43.82%	56.18%	100.00%

Chi-square = 10.786, D.F. = 3, Prob. = 0.0129.

better off gaining maximum short term returns on skills which are obsolescent while acquiring new technologies from IC sources or from larger Korean firms for the long run, rather than protecting existing technologies with limited lifespans. In high tech ventures, firms sell technology or plants. In low tech ventures, firms with no marketable technology seek more equity ventures, through which they can potentially market their implicit organizational skills in low cost manufacturing.

Location and Investment Type. Table 5 indicates that equity JVs comprise 50% of the proposed investments in the IC markets, but only 29% in the LDC markets. Some degree of ownership interest is emphasized in industrialized markets as compared to a higher proportion of contractual activity in LDCs. If Korean firms (in high or low tech industries) do not have technology to protect or to market in the ICs, we must question the need for equity positions in these countries. A possible explanation is that this indicates the one condition where firms may be seeking knowledge in accordance Hypothesis 2. An equity position in a venture with a more advanced firm would provide ownership rights to improved technology. Previous research (Beamish 1985, Killing 1983) indicates that local partners improve market access for investing firms. However, the

Table 5. Cross Tabulation of Investment Type and Area of Investment

Investment Type	Area		
	LDC	IC	Total
Equity Investment	84	25	109
Total	24.71%	7.35%	32.06%
Row	77.06%	22.94%	
Column	28.97%	50.00%	
Plant Export	47	2	49
Total	13.82%	0.59%	14.41%
Row	95.92%	4.08%	
Column	16.21%	4.00%	
Technology Transfer	106	18	124
Total	31.18%	5.29%	36.47%
Row	85.48%	14.52%	
Column	36.55%	36.00%	
More Than One	53	5	58
Total	15.59%	1.47%	17.06%
Row	91.38%	8.62%	
Column	18.28%	10.00%	
Total	290	50	340
	85.29%	14.71%	100.00%

Chi-square = 12.011, D.F. = 3, Prob. = 0.007345.

sample firms seem to have little to offer in IC markets which would require FDI. We must keep in mind, though, that the total number of IC proposals is small, so learning is a minor incentive for cooperative venturing overall.

Three-Way Analysis

Table 6 presents a simultaneous cross-tabulation of technology level, area of interest, and desired venture type for firms seeking only one venture type. The three panels offer alternative views of the three-dimensional table to better present the results.

Panel 6a indicates that for ventures in low tech industries the proportions of equity to contractual venture proposals are not significantly different in LDC and IC regions of interest. Neither Hypothesis 1a nor Hypothesis 2a is supported. In high tech industry ventures, contractual ventures are significantly more popular in LDCs, while equity and contractual ventures are equal in IC venture proposals. These results confirm the results in Table 4, showing that the high technology emphasis on contractual ventures in LDCs is the primary source of

Table 6. Comparison of Single Strategy Firms and Three Dimensions

a) (Venture Type × by Area) by Technology Level

Technology Level	Venture Type	Area		
		LDC	IC	Total
Low[a]	Equity	49	12	61
	Contractual	56	7	63
	Total	105	19	
High[b]	Equity	35	13	48
	Contractual	97	13	110
	Total	132	26	

[a] $\chi^2 = 1.15$ (0.28); [b] $\chi^2 = 4.61$ (0.03).

b) (Venture Type × Technology Level) by Area

Area	Venture Type	Technology Level		
		Low	High	Total
LDC[a]	Equity	49	35	84
	Contractual	56	97	153
	Total			
IC[b]	Equity	12	13	25
	Contractual	7	13	20
	Total	19	26	

[a] $\chi^2 = 9.52$ (0.002); [b] $\chi^2 = 0.329$ (0.566).

c) (Area × Technology Level) by Venture Type

Venture Type	Area	Technology Level		
		Low	High	Total
Equity[a]	LDC	49	35	84
	IC	12	13	25
	Total	61	48	
Contractual[b]	LDC	56	97	153
	IC	7	13	20
	Total	63	110	

[a] $\chi^2 = 0.47$ (0.49); [b] $\chi^2 = 0.01$ (0.91).

significant differences. This is contrary to Hypothesis 1 and supports Hypothesis 2b.

Panel 6b shows that, for firms interested in LDC ventures, the numbers of equity and contractual ventures are nearly equal in low tech industries, but that contractual ventures are significantly more likely in high tech industries. Again, the large number of high technology contractual ventures is noticeable. In IC oriented ventures, the numbers of firms interested in each venture type is not significantly different across industry types. This refines and confirms the results in Table 5. These results are contrary to Hypothesis 1 and support Hypothesis 2 to some degree.

Panel 6c shows that, for the firms interested in equity ventures, the ratios of LDC to IC ventures are similar for low and high tech industries. The pattern of contractual ventures is also similar between ICs and LDCs for both high and low tech industries. This does not support Hypothesis 1a.

Results, Conclusions, and Future Research

Results

The results tend to support the organizational learning perspective (Hypotheses 2, 2a, 2b) over the transaction cost perspective (Hypotheses 1 and 1a). Firms in high tech fields emphasize contractual ventures in LDCs, offering their explicit core technologies for sale. This supports Hypothesis 2b but not Hypothesis 1. Equity ventures are relatively more popular in high tech industries in IC venture proposals, although the numbers of IC ventures are much lower than for LDC ventures. This is consistent with Hypothesis 2. We infer from this that firms in high tech fields seek ownership rights to knowledge through equity ventures in the ICs.

Firms in low technology industries tend to offer relatively more equity ventures in LDCs, indicating that equity ventures are tied more to selling im-plicit skills than to protecting high technology. This result supports Hypothesis 2 and seems to be most consistent with learning models.

These patterns are consistent with learning perspectives, but not the usual interpretation of transaction cost models. Only the added assumption of an intermediary role in technology transfer for NIC firms makes the results compatible with transaction cost interpretations. This step is directly related to learning and transmittal of knowledge and brings organizational learning into the middle of transaction cost concepts.

Conclusions

This paper has analyzed the characteristics of strategic proposals for ICVs by small and medium sized Korean firms in the light of models developed from studies of large firms from developed countries. We see that most such ventures are aimed at countries with even lower levels of development, compared to large multinationals which usually conduct their activities within the community of industrial states. This is a similar pattern to that found by Wells (1977) for large firms from developing nations. Indeed, this study supports the findings of Wells and of Kumar and Kim (1984) that position NIC firms as intermediaries in the flow of technology from ICs to LDCs. Ventures in ICs appear to favor the collection of knowledge, although this function is primarily supported through inward ventures in Korea. Most activity in LDCs appears to be oriented toward selling technology while it is still valuable. This is done efficiently in high tech industries by contractual means. However, low tech ventures do not have valuable explicit technology, so they emphasize equity ventures to transmit implicit skills. Figure 1 shows these relationships graphically.

Neither of the two theoretical perspectives is fully supported. The transaction cost perspective, as expressed in concepts such as the internalization model, is least applicable in its standard form. Protection of knowledge from opportunistic behavior is the theoretical key to equity ventures in this model. This does not conform to the results. Adding the technology flow concept makes internalization theory a contingency model, reducing the expected transaction costs of contractual ventures by minimizing the value of explicit technology. Mature or obsolescent technology which will be replaced from IC firms rather

Figure 1. A Model of ICV Activity in Small NIC Firms.

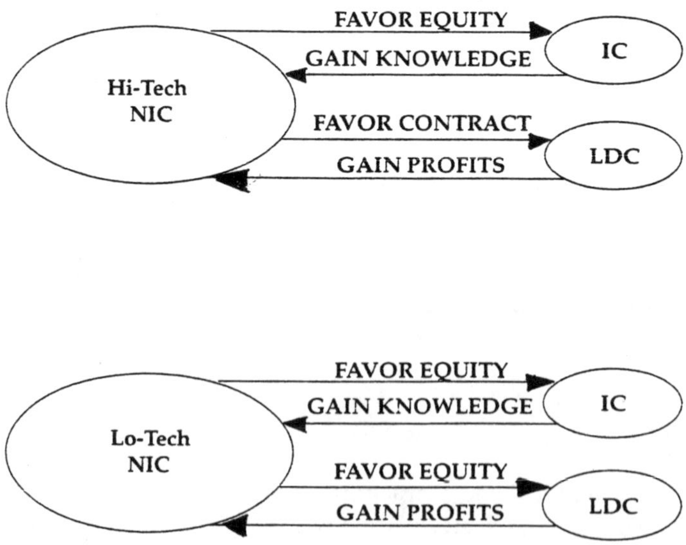

than by internal means has low value. Under this regime, transaction costs would permit the observed results, though we have added an assumption with strong overtones of resource dependency.

The organizational learning perspective, with its similarity to resource dependency concepts, fares better. The specific resource dependency concepts, fares better. The spedific resource dependency finding that equity JVs are primarily used to gather knowledge is supported only in part. However, Kogut's proposal that tacit organizational skills will require the use of more equity ventures is supported if we assume that high technology is likely to involve more explicit, saleable technology. The "technology flow" picture is in accord with organizational learning models of firm activity. Firms use more equity in ICs where they may learn. When transmitting skills, they favor contracts to sell explicit high technology, but use equity ventures in low tech fields where the only saleable skills are organizationally bound.

Studies of new sources of international activity will be crucial to the refinement of existing models of the MNC. Incorporation of such concepts as the "technology transfer mediator" role of NIC firms into present models enhance our framework for analyzing international cooperative ventures. Adding perspectives such as resource dependency to transaction cost models of the multinational firm may assist in explaining patterns of international activity which remain anomalies.

Future Research

Since the present study raises some important questions regarding the universality of current theoretical frameworks of the international firm in relation to cooperative ventures, it seems that further research is warranted. Technology seems to enter Korea through inward investment in most cases, so a study of flows into and out of Korea is planned. We hope to follow up this study of secondary data with primary research into the specifics of firm strategies which are only inferred here. We also plan to investigate the ventures which have been successfully completed by these firms to compare planned and actual strategies. If time series data can be gathered, we will investigate the impact of environmental changes on planned and actual ICVs. Finally, similar studies of ICVs from other NICs would be most useful in verifying the generalizability of our findings.

Notes

1 Research for this paper was carried out at the College of Business Administration, University of Hawaii at Manoa, Honolulu, Hawaii, U.S.A.

References

Beamish, P.W. (1985): The characteristics of joint ventures in developed and developing countries. *Columbia Journal of World Business*, Fall, 13–19.

Berg, S.V./Duncan, J./Friedman, P. (1982): *Joint Venture Strategies and Corporate Innovation*. Oelgeschlager, Gunn & Hain, Publishers, Cambridge.

Buckley, P.J./Casson, M. (1976): *The Future of the Multinational Enterprise*. MacMillan, London.

Buckley, P.J./Casson, M. (1988): A theory of cooperation in international business. In: Contractor & Lorange, eds., *Cooperative Strategies in International Business*. Lexington Books, Lexington.

Calvet, A.L. (1981): A synthesis of foreign direct investment theories and theories of the multinational firm. *Journal of International Business Studies*, Spring/Summer, 43–60.

Casson, M. (1987): *The Firm and the Market*. Basil Blackwell, Oxford.

Caves, R.E. (1971): International corporations: the industrial economics of foreign investment. *Economica*, 38, February, 1–27.

Fagre, N./Wells, L.T., Jr. (1982): Bargaining power of multinationals and host governments. *Journal of International Business Studies*. Fall: 9–23.

Franko, L.G. (1971): *Joint Venture Survival in Multinational Corporations*. Praeger Publishers, New York.

Graham, E.M. (1974): *Oligopolistic Imitation and European Direct Investment in the United States*. Doctoral dissertation, Harvard Business School.

Ghoshal, S. (1988): Environmental scanning in Korean firms: organizational isomorphism in action. *Journal of International Business Studies*, 19, Spring, 69–86.

Hennart, J.F. (1982): *A Theory of the Multinational Enterprise*. Ann Arbor, MI: University of Michigan Press.

Hennart, J.F. (1988): A transaction cost theory of equity joint ventures. *Strategic Management Journal*, 9, 361–374.

Hladik, K.J. (1985): *International Joint Ventures*. Lexington Books, Lexington.

Hymer, S.H. (1960): *The International Operations of National Firms: A Study of Direct Foreign Investment*, Ph. D. dissertation, MIT (published by MIT Press, 1976).

Killing, J. P. (1983): *Strategies for Joint Venture Success*. Praeger, New York.

Kobrin, S.J. (1988): Trends in ownership of American manufacturing subsidiaries in developing countries: an inter-industry analysis. *Management International Review*, Special Issue.

Kogut, B. (1988): Joint ventures: theoretical and empirical perspectives. *Strategic Management Journal*, 9, 319–332.

Kumar, K./Kim, K.Y. (1984): The Korean manufacturing multinationals. *Journal of International Business Studies*, Spring/Summer, 45–60.

Lall, S./Siddharthan, N.S. (1982): The monopolistic advantages of multinationals: lessons from foreign investment in the U.S. *The Economic Journal*, 92, 668–683.

Pearce, R.D. (1983): Industrial diversification among the world's leading multinational enterprises. In: Casson, ed., *The Growth of International Business*. George Allen & Unwin, London.

Pfeffer, J./Nowak, P. (1976): Joint ventures and interorganizational interdependence. *Administrative Science Quarterly*, 21, September, 398–418.

Pfeffer, J./Salancik, G.R. (1978): *The External Control of Organizations: A Resource Dependence Perspective*. Harper & Row, New York.

Small & Medium Industry Promotion Corporation (1987): *Business Partners from Korea*. SMIPC, Seoul.

Stopford, J.M./Wells, L.R. Jr. (1972): *Managing the Multinational Enterprise*. Basic Books, New York.

Teece, D.J. (1981): The market for know-how and the efficient international transfer of technology. *The Annals of the American Academy of Political and Social Science*, 458, November, 81–96.

Wells, L.T., Jr. (1977): The internationalization of firms from developing countries. In: Agmon & Kindleberger, eds., *Multinationals from small countries*. MIT Press, Cambridge.

[4]

Joint Ventures: No Longer a Mysterious World for SMEs from Developed and Developing Countries

by Rik Donckels and Johan Lambrecht

At present, we are seeing increasing numbers of alliances between firms. They are working together more closely, both to strengthen their competitive position on their domestic market and to move into or expand in international business. Joint ventures are one of the forms of co-operation which has been thoroughly investigated by researchers. However, they have rarely focused on SMEs. If the joint venture also happens to be in a developing country and entrepreneurs from the industrialised countries and Third World countries are the main actors, there is even less specialised literature on the subject of SMEs.

This paper sheds the light on the mysterious matter of joint ventures between SMEs from the North and South. Joint ventures in this context are defined as a business in a developing country, where the capital is owned by entrepreurs from a developed and a developing country.

1. CONCEPTUAL MODEL

In Figure 1, we identify the entrepreneurs involved in their SME. Their characteristics are obviously decisive for the direction their business will take. The company's development in turn exerts an influence on the entrepreneur. We also observe an interdependence between small businessmen and their company on the one hand and the external environment on the other hand. The entrepreneurs and their SME have to face environmental factors which may help or hinder their business activities. They can also send out signals and have an impact on the outside world. The shaded concentric sections illustrate that co-operation causes the bodies from the industrialised country and the developing country to intertwine. In this article, our attention is devoted to the inter-relationship between small businessmen and the SMEs themselves.

Figure 2 illustrates that entrepreneurs are the linchpin of the co-operation agreement. They need to develop mechanisms to make sure that their objectives coincide. It will be shown that joint ventures are the most suitable means to fit the motivations for co-operation. We shall also identify the way in which the external environment can lead to joint ventures being set up.

Figure 1
The Bodies Involved in a Joint Venture

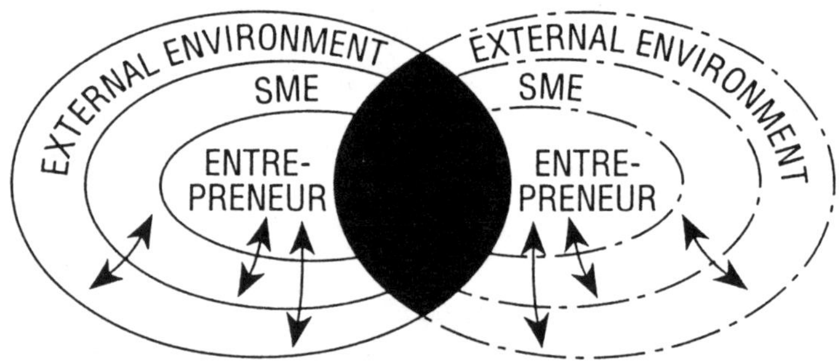

2. HYPOTHESES

The hypotheses have been written from the point of view of the entrepreneurs and SMEs from the industrialised countries, though they do also take account of the developing countries and the SMEs there.

Introductory transactions

A survey held in France by the United Nations Industrial Development Organisation shows that most of the French business first want to sell their products before considering a closer association (Pasquet, 1988). During that loose alliance, the partners examine whether they can get onto the same wavelength. Once they have succeeded in doing so, they can begin rehearsing the joint venture.

Hypothesis 1: A joint venture is preceded by other types of transactions with developing countries.

Network formation

The growth of a business can be significantly influenced by its network position. A growth-oriented company, for instance, appears to tap external sources

Figure 2
Motives for Co-operation

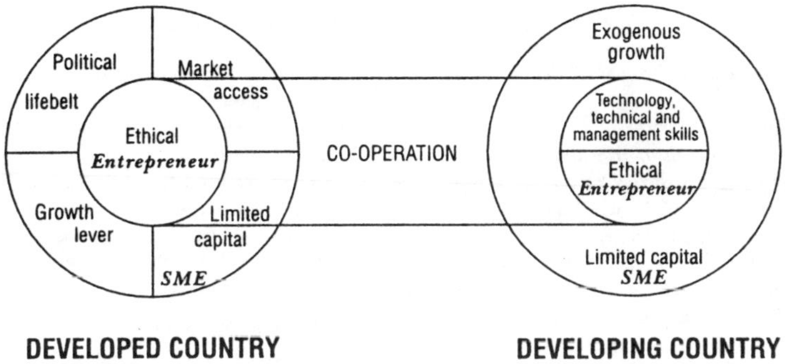

of information (Jarillo, 1989; Donckels, Hoebeke, 1990). Since a joint venture opens up prospects for growth, an entrepreneur will need sound network equipment to make the most of this form of association.

Hypothesis 2: Setting up a joint venture in a developing country must necessarily involve full attention to network formation.

Greater problems

A joint venture in a developing country is a difficult and fragile agreement (Newman, 1992). The partners have to create a melting pot of a traditional and non-traditional entrepreneurial culture in the formal economy. Those setting up a joint venture are therefore likely to encounter greater problems.

Hypothesis 3: Entrepreneurs working on a joint venture face greater problems.

Detailed written plan

Ferdows (1980) examined the investments in Iran by 40 SMEs from industrialised countries. He found that the entrepreneurs who had set up successful projects had not followed any written plan. Ferdows attributes the lack of such plans to the uncertain environment, the novelty and mutual dependence of the activities.

Hypothesis 4: A detailed written plan is not regarded as a decisive factor for a successful joint venture in a developing country.

External lever

Samuels, Greenfield and Mpku (1992) observed that small firms in the West Midlands (England) did good business with developing countries. One-fifth of the businesses quoted the developing world as their main export market: 37 per cent and 21 per cent respectively mentioned the EC and North America as most important. Since a joint venture offers the best view of the local and neighbouring markets, we assume that entrepreneurs who enter into such an associati... are more successful in their business dealings with developing countries.

Hypothesis 5: A joint venture constitutes an external lever for the SME's performance.

Entrepreneur-related factors

Research into the internationalisation of Belgian SMEs has shown that the internationally active business managers speak significantly more languages (Donckels, Aerts, 1992). The Belgian small businessmen who were examined also have more business dealings with developing countries as the level of education and knowledge of languages increase (Lambrecht, 1992). Finally, a study of Belgian entrepreneurs and their environment has clearly shown that the network position is more intensive if the level of education is higher (Donckels, Elshout, 1992). From the foregoing we may conclude that entrepreneur-related factors play a crucial role in joint ventures in developing countries.

Hypothesis 6: Entrepreneur-related factors have an impact on the decision-making process of a joint venture in a developing country.

Larger businesses

Setting up a joint venture in a developing country requires a great deal of effort from the entrepreneur and his business. We therefore assume that mainly larger SMEs venture into such an association.

Hypothesis 7: Mainly larger SMEs take the plunge into a joint venture in a developing country.

3. METHODOLOGY

3.1 Objectives

The objectives of the present article are three-fold:

- Empirical verification of the hypotheses that were formulated.
- Elaboration of a theoretical framework that is designed to show that entrepreneurs from both developed and developing countries benefit most from a joint venture.
- Proposing the conditions for a successful birth of the joint venture.

3.2 Compilation of data

The study began in 1992 with an in-depth study of specialised literature and carrying out interviews with 65 prime witnesses of the supporting infrastructure in Belgium. Both supplied sufficient ingredients to draw up the survey to be carried out with entrepreneurs. Five hundred Belgian entrepreneurs who have business connections with a developing country were contacted by telephone and surveyed by a specialised marketing consultancy. They were chosen at random from catalogues and databases. The definition of a Belgian SME is a company with less than 100 employees. The definition of developing countries is the low and lower middle income nations of Africa, Asia and Latin America. Their GDP amounts to less than US$ 2,450 per capita in 1989 (criterion used by the World Bank). Before the telephone survey, the entrepreneurs received an introductory letter and list of developing countries. Finally, there were 480 valid responses to the survey. Face-to-face interviews with 27 entrepreneurs who have set up a joint venture in a developing country or are planning to do so formed the final phase of the study.

Their motives for setting up a joint venture, the way it came about and hints from the specialised literature for a successful start-up of a joint venture were discussed with them.

3.3 Statistical processing

The results of the telephone study are presented descriptively and analytically. In the descriptive section, relative frequencies are indicated. The hypotheses are tested in two analytical steps. First of all, subsamples are compared with each other. This enables us to identify significant differences between enterpreneurs who have or want to have a joint venture in a developing country and those who do not wish to employ this mechanism. Our understanding of this was strengthened by using non-linear principal component analysis. This technique was used with the assistance of the computer program PRINCALS which is ideally suited to analyse variables at every level of measurement (for more technical details, see Gifi (1981) and van den Berg (1988)).

4. PROFILE OF THE ENTREPRENEUR HAVING OR PLANNING A JOINT VENTURE IN A DEVELOPING COUNTRY

In this section, a profile is established for the 89 entrepreneurs surveyed who have established a joint venture in a developing country or wish to do so. We portray them therefore next to the 385 entrepreneurs who do not want to use this form of co-operation. First, the significant differences are detected for the two subsamples by placing them side by side (the p-value is given in brackets). We combine the various components under the titles: relationship pattern with developing countries; exploratory work; experience; personal characteristics; and role of the size of the SME. Then they are charted together via non-linear principal component analysis.

4.1 Comparison of subsamples

4.1.1 Relationship pattern with developing countries

In Figure 3, the relationship pattern with developing countries is shown for joint venture entrepreneurs and non-joint venture entrepreneurs. We emphasise that all small businessmen who are involved in a joint venture now or will be in the future have at least one of the economic ties mentioned with developing countries. Furthermore, 72 per cent of those who are now in a joint venture had first started off with such a looser association. Hypothesis 1 is therefore confirmed by the present and future joint venture entrepreneurs. From the charts, it can be seen that exports to Third World countries figure prominently for both groups, while imports are at a much lower level. This is characteristic of the fact that most SMEs limit their imports to neighbouring coutries. Dagevos and De Groot (1990) showed that in Brabant businesses in the Netherlands, there was a sharp discrepancy between exports to and imports from developing countries. As far as the other activities are concerned, we note that there are significant differences between the two groups. The joint venture entrepreneurs work to a significantly greater extent as subcontractors ($p<0.01$) and for an organisation ($p<0.05$), grant significantly more licences to developing countries ($p<0.01$) and allow significantly more to be produced with their own trade marks (franchising, $p<0.01$). We also mention,

Figure 3
Relationship Pattern with Developing Countries (several answers possible)

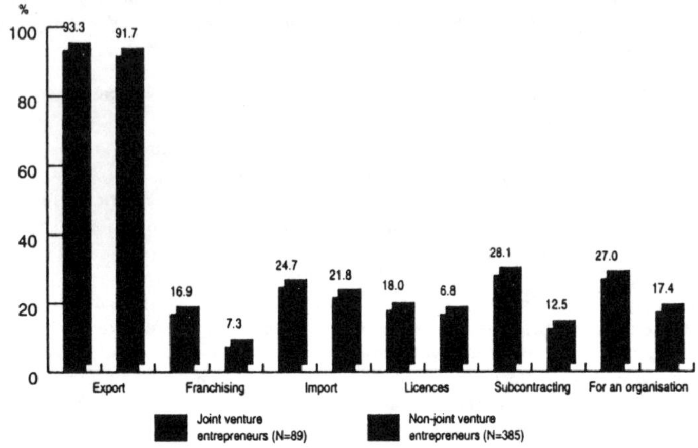

by the way, that 10.6 per cent of the non-joint venture entrepreneurs are or wish to be 100 per cent owners of a commercial branch in a developing country. For a production plant, this percentage is 6.2.

Table 1
Exploratory Work when Setting up in a Developing Country

		Joint venture entrepreneurs (%)	Non-joint venture entrepreneurs (%)	Chi-square test
Market research carried out (N=432)	Yes	65.5	42.5	p < 0.01
	No	34.5	57.5	
Seminars attended (N=429)	Yes	41.0	22.3	p < 0.01
	No	59.0	77.7	
Information obtained from institutions in the developing country (N=427)	Yes	50.6	27.9	p < 0.01
	No	49.4	72.1	
Information obtained from EC Institutions (N=423)	Yes	30.5	19.4	p < 0.05
	No	69.5	80.6	

4.1.2 Exploratory work

Table 1 shows that the joint venture entrepreneurs explore far more information sources before they go to a developing country. This is also clearly demonstrated in the sources of financing which they use. Approximately 60 per cent of the joint venture entrepreneurs, as compared with 46.4 per cent of the others ($p<0.05$), financed their activities in developing countries by other means than their own capital. In particular, they make more use of the possibilities of government support at a regional, national and EC level. As suggested by hypothesis 2, the network machine of the joint venture entrepreneurs clearly operates at a higher speed.

4.1.3 Experience

Significantly more joint venture entrepreneurs indicate that they have experienced problems with setting up their business in a developing country (80.7 per cent compared with 69.3 per cent, $p<0.05$). Local staff problems arise more frequently for them (20.6 per cent compared with 7.7 per cent, $p<0.01$). The discrepancies show that a joint venture in a developing country cannot be set up instantly. Such an alliance involves a holding in a local company, which often employs personnel.

As far as the determination of success in Third World countries are concerned, the joint venture group attaches significantly greater importance to a detailed written plan (62.4 per cent considered this important, versus 47.9 per cent of the non-joint venture entrepreneurs, $p<0.05$). This finding does not agree with that of Ferdows (1980) and therefore refutes hypothesis 4.

Finally, the relationship of the joint venture entrepreneurs with developing countries seems to be more fruitful. Over half of them (52.5 per cent) derive at least 30 per cent of their turnover from exports to developing countries. In the group of non-joint venture entrepreneurs this figure is 36.3 per cent ($p<0.01$). Hypothesis 5, in which we assume that a joint venture constitutes an external lever for the SME's performance, is therefore endorsed.

Given the very good results in developing countries, it is hardly surprising that the majority of the Belgian SMEs studied wanted to expand their activities to other developing countries. There are significantly more joint venture entrepreneurs who anticipate such a development (85.2 per cent compared with 73.7 per cent ,$p<0.05$).

4.1.4 Personal characteristics

The joint venture entrepreneurs are significantly older ($p<0.05$). Almost 80 per cent of them are aged over 39, compared with 68.2 per cent in the other category. The second marked difference concerns the level of education ($p<0.01$). In the joint venture section, there are a much higher number of university graduates (80.2 per cent versus 62.4 per cent). As is suggested in hypothesis 6, entrepreneur-related factors influence the decision to enter into a joint venture.

4.1.5 Role of the size of the SME

As regards company size, we did not find any significant difference between joint venture and non-joint venture entrepreneurs. In both groups, about 25 per cent of the SMEs employed at least 50 staff. Hypothesis 7 therefore has to be refuted.

Figure 4
Analysis of Joint Ventures Via Non-linear Principal Component Analysis

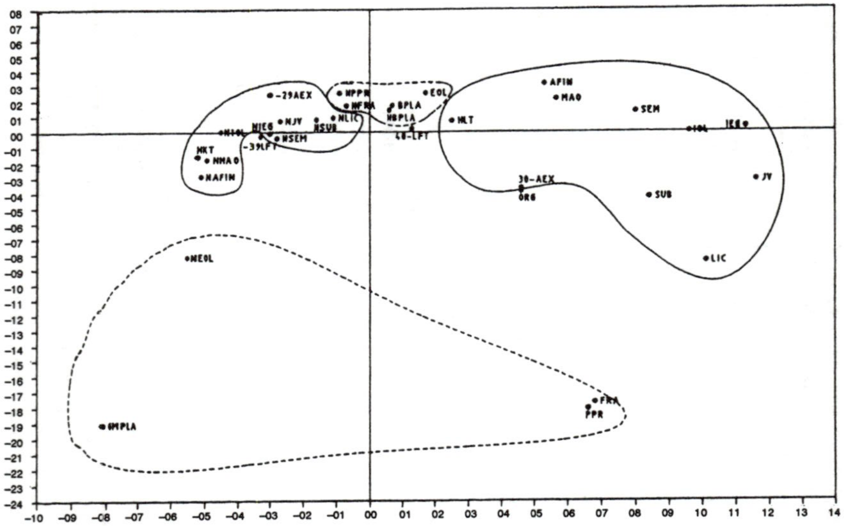

The category co-ordinates of the variables that have high component loadings on the horizontal axis (first principal component) belong together and are encircled with a continuous line. The category co-ordinates of the variables that load highly on the vertical axis (second principal component) are encircled with an interrupted line. There are two variables (age with the categories -39LFT/40-LFT and working for an organisation with the categories NORG/ORG) of which the component loadings are too low to be attributed to one of the two principal components. We will focus on the categories of the variables that load highly on the horizontal axis, because the joint venture variable (categories NJV/JV) belongs to that group.

NLIC coincides with NORG.

- GMPLA/NBPLA/BPLA = no opinion about detailed written plan/finds plan unimportant/important.
- NEOL/EOL = no planned/planned expansion to other developing countries.
- NAFIN/AFIN = no use/use of other financing sources than own capital.
- HKT/HLT = no university/university education.
- NMAO/MAO = no market research/market research carried out.
- NIOL/IOL = no information/information obtained from institutions in the developing country.
- -39LFT/40-LFT = entrepreneur aged under 40/40 or more.
- NIEG/IEG = no information/information obtained from EC Institutions.
- NSEM/SEM = no seminars/seminars attended.
- NJV/JV = no joint venture/joint venture now or in the future.
- -29AEX/30-AEX = less than/at least 30% of sales via exports to developing countries.
- NSUB/SUB = no subcontracting/subcontracting work in developing countries.
- NLIC/LIC = no licences/licences granted in developing countries.
- NORG/ORG = not working/working for an organisation in a developing country.
- NFRA/FRA = no franchising/franchising in developing country.
- NPPR/PPR = no personnel problem/personnel problem in developing country.

Figure 5
Importance of Network Formation for a Joint Venture, for Success in Developing Countries and for Other Business Relations

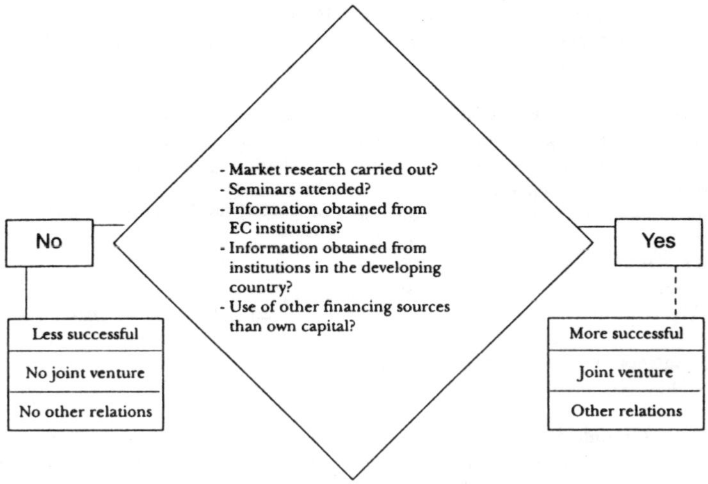

4.2 Non-linear principal component analysis

Via non-linear principal component analysis, a relationship is defined between the above-mentioned variables which show significant differences and the existence or planning of joint ventures in developing countries. The results of this technique are shown in Figure 4 where the category co-ordinates of the variables are plotted.

We observe a strong connection between an unsteady network position and the absence of a joint venture. The variables that suggest the inactivity of the network machine (NMAO, NSEM, NIOL, NIEG and NAFIN) cluster around NJV. The joint venture entrepreneurs, on the other hand, got their network mechanism working. The connection between networks and joint venture is less strong, though, than in the case of no joint venture. This emerges from the distance between the network variables (MAO, SEM, IOL, IEG and AFIN) and JV. The principal component analysis also shows us that there is a strong relationship between an unused network instrument and the absence of other forms of business relations with developing countries (NLIC and NSUB). Finally, we see that a smoothly running network control has a stimulating effect on the turnover derived via developing countries. Hypothesis 2 concerning the necessity of networks for a joint venture is therefore unequivocally endorsed. Since network formation enhances the SME's performance and joint venture entrepreneurs are more actively engaged in their network, hypothesis 5 is confirmed here too.

In Figure 5 we show the importance of network formation for a joint venture, for success in working with developing countries and for other business relations (the broken line shows a weaker link).

5. WHY A JOINT VENTURE?

In this section, we attempt to provide evidence that the joint venture pays off, both for the entrepreneurs from the industrialised countries and those from developing countries. In doing so, we take a look at their objectives for co-operation and those of their SME, shown in Figure 2.

5.1 Entrepreneur from an industrialised country: ethical principles

Notwithstanding the fact that business considerations must take precedence, entrepreneurs from industrialised countries can be guided by ethical principles in their co-operation. This means that for cementing a relationship with a developing country, they are often prepared to make a greater effort to ensure it works. One can sense their disappointment if knowledge transfer dies out or if plant is poorly used, or even not used at all (Dagevos, De Groot, 1990). Buckley and Casson (1988) also emphasise that the more socially worthwhile the project, the more commitment increases. Dawson (1982) stresses that the entrepreneur from the industrialised country experiences a moral satisfaction from helping to alleviate the need of the underprivileged of this world.

The form of co-operation which small businessmen can really put their ethical heart into is undoubtedly the joint venture. This is because it is a kind of association in which both partners are most likely to combine their strengths and resources to the full (Harrigan, 1988). For Kogut (1988) joint ventures are the ideal vehicle for exchanging information and technology and for reaping rich rewards. According to him, this is a consequence of being "mutually held to ransom" via the pooling of assets and sharing of costs and profits.

5.2 SME from the industrialised country

5.2.1 Market access

For an SME from an industrialised country, it is extremely difficult to penetrate markets in developing countries. There is not only a geographical distance, but a psychological distance to be bridged. On the other side of that bridge there is a totally different culture. Assimilating this culture is the key to opening the locks on the market in the developing country. However, the entrepreneur from the industrialised country runs the risk of using the wrong key, or spending far too much time looking for the right one, if he tries to discover the possibilities of that market by himself. It is therefore a good idea to find a local partner. They have better knowledge of the competition, consumer behaviour, the sector and the distribution system there (Schillaci, 1987). Moreover, a local entrepreneur is an excellent guide through the administrative jungle which often prevails in developing countries.

The next question which arises is whether joint ventures are a more advantageous ticket for access to that market than other forms of association. Licences permit a very fast representation in that market, with a relatively limited investment (Lei, Slocum, 1991). But there is specific knowledge, such as that of the characteristics of the country, which can be transferred virtually only through joint ventures (Hennart, 1988). This is certainly the case where there are major cultural differences between the partner countries. Kogut and Singh (see Kogut, 1988) found that there was a greater incidence of joint ventures where cultural differences were most pronounced. The Belgian companies which were surveyed, and which planned to set up a joint venture in the future, also referred in the first instance to a more effective canvassing of the local and neighbouring markets.

5.2.2 Limited capital

The majority of SMEs have neither the financial nor the organizational resources to set up their own sales branch in a deleveloping country, let alone a production plant (Berlew, 1984). A joint venture gives a boost to the SME in the industrial country, since the capital investment is shared with a local entrepreneur. Nevertheless, it will still need considerable financial muscle for this form of co-operation. The joint venture group of entrepreneurs cited payment and financing difficulties (64.8% of them) as the second largest obstacle on the route to developing countries. The high costs and great risk involved were the most frequently recurring reasons for the other group declining to set up a joint venture.

5.2.3 A lever for growth

In section 4, we saw that exports to developing countries account for a considerable proportion of the turnover. It can be inferred from this that an economic link with a developing country can be a very useful tool to achieve growth. Three-quarters of the joint venture entrepreneurs confirm that doing business with developing countries is an attractive lever for growth. The joint venture is once again the most appropriate route for SMEs which want to expand. This alliance ensures that a market can be effectively occupied. Expansion of capacity, vertical integration or diversification also make the joint venture a source of growth (Schillaci, 1987).

5.2.4 Political lifebelt

Entrepreneurs with business activities in developing countries should take account of the fact that they may end up in turbulent political waters. Joint venture entrepreneurs actually consider the political and economic instability in the developing countries as the major obstacle (81.4 per cent cited this difficulty). In a sea with so many political eddies, a local partner can function as a lifebuoy. He may be able to use his political influence to avoid sudden government actions affecting his joint activities with his partner (Contractor, Lorange, 1988). However, prudence is required with a partner who is too ready to go with the prevailing political current.

A joint venture is undoubtedly the safest lifeboat. The financial contribution by the local entrepreneur offers the best protection against political risks. Very often, the authorities in the developing country require a local partner to be brought in, which provides an additional guarantee.

5.3 Entrepreneurs from the developing country

5.3.1 Technology, technical and management skills

Entrepreneurs in the developing country wish to acquire technology, technical and management skills through co-operation. All these elements are, however, encapsulated in individuals, and exchanging these skills therefore depends on close human contact (Hennart, 1988). This is abundantly present in joint ventures between SMEs, where co-operation occurs more between entrepreneurs than between companies.

For the small businessmen from the developing country, a joint venture is therefore the most effective means of learning. He must be willing and able to learn, and he and his partner both need to put all their cards on the table (Hamel, 1991).

5.3.2 Ethical principles

For the entrepreneur in the developing country, an entrepreneur of an SME in an industrialised country is simply the best possible team-mate. SMEs operate namely in market niches and consequently a local entrepreneur is not seen as a necessary evil, but rather as an essential link in the chain. In a global strategy, however, there is a real possibility that the local entrepreneur will be regarded as merely a political alibi. In that case, the activities in the developing country are part of a worldwide, standardised network. This requires a strict control and a partner can soon become a millstone around the other's neck in those circumstances (Harrigan, 1988, Gomes-Casseres, 1989). Multinationals with a moderately performing joint venture in developing countries do indeed appear to use a local man purely for political reasons (Beamish, 1987). By comparison, SMEs from an industrialised country, because they have made a considerable investment in time and money, will make every effort to ensure that their joint venture is a success. Multinationals, because their operations are worldwide, will probably not breathe any new life into ailing subsidiaries (Simiar, 1983).

To summarise, via a joint venture with an SME from an industrial country, there is a very real chance that the entrepreneur of the developing country will receive an injection of management and technology. This injection may enable him to contribute to a socio-economic renaissance of his country. Thriving entrepreneurs and SMEs in developing countries will also attract microbusinesses away from the informal economy into the formal sector. Through this transition, the missing middle, the gaping abyss between very small and large companies, can be bridged.

5.4 SME from the developing country: exogenous growth and limited capital

Thanks to sounder technical and management structure, the local SME will not only be better equipped to compete on the local stage. In international competition too, the company will be better able to hold its own (Datta, 1988). This makes growing pains easier to withstand, because they are of an exogenous nature. In other words, there is a partner to strengthen its precarious financial position.

6. THE FIVE CONDITIONS FOR SETTING UP A SUCCESSFUL JOINT VENTURE IN A DEVELOPING COUNTRY

We conclude this article by indicating five conditions for setting up a successful joint venture in a developing country, as indicated by the theoretical research and our own empirical findings. These are mainly addressed to small businessmen from the industrialised countries, but indirectly also to their colleagues from developing countries.

1. Get engaged before getting married

Entering into a joint venture in a developing country is like getting married to a partner who lives a long distance away. Therefore it is advisable for partners to 'get engaged' first via other forms of co-operation. In this way, they can learn to understand each other's culture, improve communication and develop confidence (Cascio, Serapio, 1991). Another major advantage of setting up a looser association to start with is that the local SMEs can go through the learning process gradually. Joint ventures will always remain a pipe-dream, if the skills of the partners differ too much (Hamel, 1991). The local entrepreneur needs to know most of all how his partner has developed. Our research shows that small businessmen do start with looser co-operation agreements. As we saw, these continue to exist alongside joint ventures.

2. Careful preparation, appetite for network formation and patience

Nobody should rush into a joint venture in a developing country. Proper preparation should start with an internal analysis of the company (Crouse, 1991). If this study results in a go-ahead, a thorough examination of the external environment is the next step. The economic, political, social and cultural scene in the developing country needs to be reconnoitred in detail (Datta, 1988). For this purpose, it is important that the entrepreneur should put out feelers locally and develop a ravenous appetite for networking. Market research, seminars, gathering information from various institutions, etc., should belong to his network.

By preparing the joint venture carefully, the entrepreneur from the industrialised country learns to be patient, as in developing countries this is a fundamental requirement. Waiting is a specific feature of their culture. Once a joint venture is operational, the patience of the entrepreneurs from the industrialised countries will be put to the test. The investment will probably only show a return after a few years. Disappointing results should not just be blamed on the local entrepreneur. Otherwise the small businessman from the industrialised country risks hastening something which he absolutely needs to avoid: a confrontation with an unhappy and disillusioned partner (Ohmae, 1989).

3. Develop a blueprint

The difficulty of founding a joint venture makes it imperative to have a blueprint, which the partners need to draw up beforehand (Gyenes, 1991). The first ingredient in this is what the mission statement of the joint venture should be. This should answer the question: 'Who are we?'. This vocation will plot out the course ahead for the joint venture and should involve responses from the entrepreneurs, their employees and the external environment. Furthermore, this should enable the objectives of the joint venture to be outlined. These must answer the question: 'What do we want to achieve?', and should be grafted onto the reasons why each partner wants to co-operate. A subsequent compoment of the blueprint should contain the means to achieve those objectives.

Gyenes also finds it important that the conditions under which any of the partners can leave the joint venture should be included in the logbook. Of course, the partners must endeavour to make the co-operation agreement last as long as possible, but at the same time, they should also consider the possibility of an unexpected end to the co-operation. Sensitive issues like share transfers, valuation of a partner's contribution, etc. should not be side-stepped.

Finally, various entrepreneurs argue in favour of incorporating financial and technical safety nets into the planning. This should include written agreements on drawing up a budget and financial reports, and contain provisions about protection of the technology transferred.

4. Enthusiastic entrepreneurs

A joint venture can only get off to a good start if both partners take care of its choreography. They may not delegate the design of this multicultural dance figure. Only through their personal effort, a melting pot of traditional and non-traditional entrepreneurial culture in the formal economy can be created. Moreover, their passion must be based on more than purely financial reasons. This mutual dedication also implies that the entrepreneurs are prepared to share one of their most valued assets, namely their independence with each other. The local entrepreneur in particular will need to show a great deal of tolerance in terms of independence, if the joint venture involves a shareholding in his existing SME.

5. Well-informed and trained employees

Setting up a joint venture in a developing country involves changes in the business, which are mainly centred around the human factor. Considering that this is where things can really break down when a small business changes, it is absolutely vital to inform the workforce. They must be fully informed beforehand about the purpose of the joint venture. Furthermore, those who will be closely involved in the co-operation agreement should be well-versed in local customs. For this reason, it is advisable to send them to the developing country during the negotiations. In this way, the entrepreneur from the industrialised country can find out whether his employees will be able to get along with the potential partner and his employees, and vice-versa.

Acknowledgements

The authors would like to thank the Belgian Administration for Development Co-operation for funding the research on which this article is based. They would also like to express their sincere gratitude to Professor Léopold Bragard and Isabelle Leboulle of the SME Research and Documentation Centre of the University of Liège for their most helpful co-operation in the research.

References

Beamish, P. W. (1987), 'Joint Ventures in LDCs: Partner Selection and Performance', *Management International Review*, 1, pp23–37.

Berlew, F. K. (1984), 'The Joint Venture — A Way Into Foreign Markets', *Harvard Business Review*, July–August, pp48–51.

Buckley, P. J., and Casson, M. (1988), 'A Theory of Co-operation in International Business', *Management International Review*, Special Issue, pp19–38.

Cascio, W. F., and Seramio, M. G. (1991), 'Human Resources Systems in an International Alliance: The undoing of a Done Deal?', *Organisational Dynamics*, Winter, pp63–74.

Contractor, F. J., and Lorange, P. (1988), 'Competition vs. Co-operation: A Benefit/Cost Framework for Choosing Between Fully-owned Investments and Co-operative Relationships', *Management International Review*, Special Issue, pp5–18.

Dagevos, J., and De Groot, G. (1990), *Brabants Bedrijfsleven en Ontwikkelingslanden (Enterprises in Brabant and Developing Countries)*, Tilburg, Development Research Institute.

Datta, D. K. (1988), 'International Joint Ventures: A Framework for Analysis', *Journal of General Management*, 2, pp78–79.

Dawson, L. M. (1982), 'Opportunities for Small Business in Third World Markets', *American Journal of Small Business*, July–September, pp19–26.

Donckels, R., and Hoebeke, K. (1990), *Network-induced Growth of SMEs, Experiences from Two Regions in Belgium*. Paper presented at the Rencontres de St. Gall, Neuchâtel.

Donckels, R., and Elshout, G. (1992), *KMO'ers en hun Omgeving, een Studie Over de Netwerkpositie in Vlaanderen (Small Businessmen and their Environment; A Study on the Network Position in Flanders)*, Brussels, BAC, Small Business Research Institute.

Ferdows, K. (1980), 'Start-up of Small Manufacturing Ventures in Developing Countries', *American Journal of Small Business*, October–December, pp12–22.

Gifi, A. (1981), *Non-linear Multivariate Analysis*, Leiden, Department of Data Theory, University of Leiden.

Gomes-Casseres, B. (1989), 'Joint Ventures in the Face of Global Competition', *Sloan Management Review*, 3, pp17–26.

Gyenes, L. (1991), 'Build the Foundation for a Successful Joint Venture', *Journal of Business Strategy*, November–December, pp27–32.

Hamel, G. (1991), 'Competitions for Competence and Interpartner Learning Within International Strategic Alliances', *Strategic Management Journal*, Special Issue, pp83–103.

Harrigan, K. R. (1988), 'Joint Ventures and Competitive Strategy', *Strategic Management Journal*, 2, pp141–158.

Hennart, J. F. (1988), 'A Transaction Costs Theory of Equity Joint Ventures', *Strategic Management Journal*, 4, pp361–374.

Jarillo, J. C. (1989), 'Entrepreneurship and Growth: The Strategic Use of External Resources', *Journal of Business Venturing*, 2, pp133–147.

Kogut, B. (1988), 'Joint Ventures: Theoretical and Empirical Perspectives', *Strategic Management Journal*, 4, pp319–332.

Lambrecht, J. (1992), *Co-operation Agreements Between Entrepreneurs from Developed and Developing Countries, Theoretical Considerations and Empirical Evidence from Belgium*. Paper presented at rent-VI-Research in Entrepreneurship, Barcelona.

Lel, D., and Slocum, J. W. (1991), 'Global Strategic Alliances: Payoffs and Pitfalls', *Organisational Dynamics*, pp44–62.

Newman, W. H. (1992), ' 'Focused Joint Ventures' in Transforming Economies', *The Executive*, 1, pp67–75.

Ohmae, K. (1989), 'The Global Logic of Strategic Alliances', *Harvard Business Review*, March–April, pp143–154.

Pasquet, P. (1988), 'Co-operation Industrielle — la 'Joint Venture' '

(*Industrial Co-operation — the Joint Venture*), Le MOCI, January 25, pp15–38.

Samuels, J., Greenfield, S., and Mpuku, H. (1992), 'Exporting and the Smaller Firm', *International Small Business Journal*, January–March, pp24–36.

Schillaci, C. E. (1987), 'Designing Successful Joint Ventures', *Journal of Business Strategy*, 2, pp59–63.

Simiar, F. (1983), 'Major Causes of Joint Venture Failures in the Middle East : the Case of Iran', *Management International Review*, 1, pp58–67.

van den Berg, G. M. (1988), *Princals voor Beginners (Princals for Beginners)*, Leiden, Department of Data Theory, University of Leiden.

[5]

THE CHARACTERISTICS AND PERFORMANCE OF KOREAN JOINT VENTURES IN LDCS

Chol Lee*
Hong Ik University

Paul W. Beamish**
University of Western Ontario

Abstract. Little has been reported on joint ventures between firms from newly industrialized countries and developing countries. This paper examines twelve characteristics of a sample of Korean firms with partners in developing countries (LDCs) and contrasts them with existing research where (a) developed country firms have linked with firms in other developed countries, and (b) developed country firms have linked with local firms in developing countries. As part of the analysis, ten hypotheses were formulated and tested.

Relative to previous findings on joint ventures from developed countries in LDCs, differences were found in terms of stability, venture creation rationale, satisfaction level with performance, and the relationship between control and performance and between ownership and control.

INTRODUCTION

A joint venture is the investment form used by nearly half of all multinational corporations (MNCs) from developed countries to enter developing countries [Austin 1990; Kobrin 1988]. Recently, there has been an increasing rate of foreign direct investment from developing countries, by the so-called third-world multinationals. One of their characteristics is the frequent use of joint ventures in entering foreign markets [Wells 1983].

Despite the growing importance of joint ventures from newly industrialized countries (NICs), little research has been reported on them [Tallman and Shenkar 1990]. Until recently, most studies of joint ventures have focused on joint ventures from developed countries, particularly U.S. firms in other developed countries or in developing countries. Findings from the work on joint ventures from developed countries have not been verified on the experiences of newly industrialized countries' joint ventures, and thus fail in

---

*Chol Lee is an Assistant Professor at the College of Business, Hong Ik University, 72–1 Sangsu-Dong, Mapo-Ku, Seoul, Korea 121.

**Paul W. Beamish is the Royal Bank Professor in International Business, Western Business School, University of Western Ontario, London, Ontario, Canada N6A 3K7.

Received: November 1992; Revised: August 1994 & March 1995.

providing a complete managerial understanding of joint ventures. This also presents a significant obstacle for establishing a general theory on joint ventures [Tallman and Shenkar 1994], which has been an important objective of scholarly research.

The first objective of this research is to ascertain the characteristics of joint ventures from a newly industrialized country – South Korea – that has rapidly increased its foreign direct investments in recent years. This study assesses the characteristics of South Korean (hereafter Korean) joint ventures in terms of ownership, stability, partner form, venture-creating rationale, performance, ownership-control, and control-performance relationships. In particular, the findings on the characteristics of Korean joint ventures are compared with previous findings on joint ventures in developed countries and developing countries.

The newly industrialized countries are unique as sources of foreign direct investment. In the case of Korea with 1993 per capita GNP of $7670, it is too economically developed to be considered a less developed country (LDC), but too recently developed to be included among the traditional ranks of the industrialized or developed countries (DC). Korea is the most economically important of the Asian NICs, with a larger national GNP and population than the other three Asian "Tigers," Singapore, Hong Kong, or Taiwan.

A second objective is to identify determinants of superior performance in Korean joint ventures. Performance is an important issue in joint ventures, because performance difficulties are costly not only for the parent firms, many of which have fragile financial structures, but for the recipient country itself due to the social costs and economic disturbances associated with performance problems.

This study was motivated in part by a concern that our existing JV frameworks and models are not applicable outside a developed-to-developed country context. This article is part of a tradition of recent JV research that has adopted a more contingent, situational perspective, one that reflects an emphasis on the particular environment. Streams of work within this tradition include developed versus developing country JV studies, equity versus non-equity JV studies, planned versus market economy JV studies (e.g., Shan [1991]; Beamish [1993]), international versus domestic JV studies, and so forth.

BACKGROUND

Most joint venture research has a developed country orientation. However, some researchers [Artisien and Buckley 1985; Beamish 1988; Daniels, Krug and Nigh 1985; Lecraw 1983; Schaan 1983; Simyar 1983] have focused their attention on joint ventures in developing countries. The relationship between ownership, control and performance has been the focus of most previous research. Some studies have attempted to identify predictors of both satisfactory and unsatisfactory joint venture performance.

Much of the previous research on joint ventures has been from a developed-country perspective, particularly U.S. MNEs, but more recently Japanese MNEs [Sohn 1994; Woodcock et al. 1994; Negandi et al. 1987]. It has shown that certain characteristics of joint ventures differ when located in developed and developing countries. Specifically, joint ventures from developed countries into developing countries are characterized by: (a) a higher instability rate and greater managerial dissatisfaction than those in developed countries, (b) equal ownership being more frequent in DC joint ventures, and minority ownership most common in LDC joint ventures, (c) a strong relationship between ownership and control in DC – but not LDC-based – joint ventures, and (d) an inconclusive relationship between joint venture performance and dominant management control in DC joint ventures, and shared control showing more satisfactory performance in LDC joint ventures [Beamish 1985; Reynolds 1979; Killing 1983; Franko 1971; Tomlinson 1970].

With respect to the predictors of joint venture performance, Beamish [1988] found that partner need and commitment were good predictors of both satisfactory and unsatisfactory performance. MNE executives from the low-performing joint ventures regarded their local partners' contributions as unimportant, while those from the high-performing ventures considered their partners' contributions important. Also observed was a strong correlation between commitment and joint venture performance. The indicators of commitment included the MNE's willingness to visit and offer assistance, adapt products, employ nationals, voluntarily use the joint venture structure, and hold regular meetings.

Theoretical contributions towards the development of a rationale for equity joint ventures (see Hennart [1988]; Kogut [1988b]; Beamish and Banks [1987]; and others) have shown how internalization theory can be extended to joint ventures using the transaction cost paradigm developed by Williamson [1975]. Within the context of internalization theory, joint ventures have been shown to be more efficient than wholly owned subsidiaries for the MNE investing in foreign countries under some circumstances. Under particular arrangements the transaction costs incurred by opportunism, a small-numbers condition and uncertainty can be dealt efficiently within a joint venture, and thus, joint ventures become a more efficient means of dealing with environmental uncertainty and maximizing the profit potential of the MNE's firm-specific assets.

HYPOTHESES ON JOINT VENTURES FROM KOREA

This study compares previous findings on the characteristics of joint ventures from developed and developing countries with those from a newly industrialized country, Korea. The characteristics examined include reasons for creating the venture, stability, performance, frequency of government partners, and ownership. Particular emphasis is placed on relationships among ownership, control and performance because this has been the main focus of most previous research. As with many previous studies, our focus is on two-partner ventures.

Venture-Creating Rationale

External environments, including industry structure, competitive behaviour, technology, and government policies differ between countries and these differences influence the initial configuration of a joint venture [Harrigan 1984]. Previous research has shown that joint ventures are created for different reasons in developed and developing countries. In a sample of joint ventures in developed countries, Killing [1983] found that the major reasons for creating the ventures were, in a rank-order of importance: need for other partner's skills, needs for the other partner's attributes or assets, and government suasion or legislation. Beamish's [1985] sample of joint ventures in developing countries showed that government suasion or legislation was the primary reason for creating the venture. However, the two major motivations for most Korean foreign direct investment are expansion into local markets and the utilization of cheap labour costs to circumvent high protectionistic trade barriers of developed countries [Min 1985]. Unlike firms from developed countries, most Korean firms rarely have the monopolistic advantages to compensate for the inherent disadvantages of being a foreign company. They are willing to form joint ventures to reduce the cost of "foreignness," regardless of whether there are regulations on ownership rates. Thus, it is hypothesized that joint ventures from Korea will be created primarily because of a need for the other partner's knowledge of the local market or local business practices rather than government regulations.

> **H1**: Korean joint ventures in LDCs will be created primarily due to a need for the other partner's knowledge of the local market and business practices rather than government regulations.

Stability

Joint venture instability is defined as equity changes or major reorganizations that were unplanned from one or both partners' perspective. Previous research on joint ventures has demonstrated that for joint venture partners from developed countries, the joint venture instability rate is higher in less developed countries than in developed countries [Beamish 1985; Reynolds 1979; Killing 1983; Franko 1971]. This is due to the size of the gap in the foreign partner's knowledge of the local economy, politics and culture. Developing countries represent a more uncertain environment to which they must adjust.

For firms from newly industrialized countries moving into less developed countries, the foreign knowledge gap should not be as wide as the gap that exists for firms from developed countries. This is because the NIC partner is more familiar with, and realistic about, the type of economic situation and national context [Parkhe 1991] they are likely to confront.

> **H2**: Stability rates of joint ventures from Korea in LDCs will be higher than those from developed countries.

Stability rates are higher in joint ventures involving local private partners than those with local government partners. This has been observed in both the aluminum industry [Stuckey 1983] and in manufacturing [Beamish 1985].

> **H3**: Korean joint ventures in LDCs will have higher stability rates with local private partners than with local government partners.

Ownership

Killing [1983] found that equal ownership (50%) was most common in DC joint ventures. However, in the LDC samples of Blodgett [1991], Reynolds [1979], and others, most foreign firms held a minority equity position. Most developing countries have aspirations for local dominance in the shareholdings of local joint ventures. They set up regulations on ownership or provide local tax advantages for foreign partners taking minority equity positions.

> **H4**: Most Korean partners in joint ventures in LDCs will have a minority equity position.

Performance

Managers of MNEs from developed countries assess their joint ventures in LDCs as unsatisfactory performers more frequently than those in DCs [Beamish 1985]. However, the Korean firms that first invested in Southeast Asia (i.e., Singapore, Indonesia and Thailand) found the cultural environment, traditions and behaviour patterns to be similar to Korea, about which Korean firms possessed information and understanding [Kumar and Kim 1984]. The Korean firms entering LDC markets also do not confront as large a foreign knowledge gap regarding the economic situation. They may not have the same level of hesitancy in entering such markets as has been observed elsewhere [Agarwal and Ramaswami 1992] because they do not perceive as much risk as other foreign investors do. This is due in part to the fact that many Korean managers feel that the socioeconomic conditions of southeast Asian developing countries are similar to those that they had faced in Korea in earlier periods. Thus, in addition to the reasons discussed in the stability section, the similar cultural systems lead us to expect Korean joint ventures in

LDCs to be better performers than joint ventures from developed country partners in LDCs.

H5: The performance of Korean joint ventures will be more satisfactory in LDCs than are developed country joint ventures in LDCs.

Ownership-Control Relationship

Researchers in the past have found mixed results on the relationship between ownership and control. Killing [1983] found that there were strong relationships between ownership and control in developed countries with 70% of the dominant-management control ventures majority owned. However, Sohn [1994] observed that with social knowledge, investing firms may reduce their dependency on ownership as a means of control over their subsidiaries.

In research on joint ventures in developing countries [Beamish 1985], no correlation was found between ownership and control. With most Korean joint venturers in developing countries, goals include not only expansion into local markets, but the increase of exports (average export/sales ratio of Korean joint ventures is almost 50%). In addition, the average lifespan of Korean joint ventures is somewhat short. For these reasons, we expect that managers of Korean firms investing abroad will tend to participate actively in the management of joint ventures rather than remain as passive shareholders.

H6: Korean joint ventures in LDCs will have a positive relationship between ownership and control.

Control-Performance Relationship

In studies of joint ventures in developed countries, inconclusive results have been obtained in the relationship between control and performance [Geringer and Hébert 1989]. Some studies have found that dominant-parent ventures perform better, while others have shown more satisfactory performance with shared control ventures. However, Beamish [1985] and Tomlinson [1970] found a strong correlation between unsatisfactory performance and dominant foreign control in LDC joint ventures while shared control ventures obtained higher performance levels.

As noted earlier [Min 1985], one important function of Korean joint ventures in developing countries is to export their products to third countries. With the need to meet third-country market requirements most Korean managers favor a strong decisionmaking role and feel more comfortable with the performance of dominant-control ventures than shared control ventures, where their roles are minor.

H7: There will be a positive relationship between Korean control and superior performance in Korean joint ventures in LDCs.

Ownership and Performance

In Beamish's [1985] sample of LDC joint ventures from developed countries, when the MNE owned less than 50% of the equity there was a greater likelihood of satisfactory performance. Also, when MNEs were a minority or equal partner joint venture, performance was better than in those cases where the MNE was the single largest shareholder. However, in Korean joint ventures in both developed and developing countries, Lee [1989] found no relationship between ownership and performance. Despite this, for several reasons we hypothesize that there will be a positive relationship between ownership levels and performance in Korean joint ventures.

First, an hypothesized relationship between ownership and control is consistent with Hypotheses 6 and 7 which emphasize the ownership-control and control-performance relationships. Second, due to the owner-manager system that is so prevalent in Korean companies, increased ownership tends to bring about increased effort on the part of the Korean firm towards the JV.

H8: In Korean joint ventures in LDCs there will be a positive relationship between Korean ownership levels and performance.

Partner Need and Performance

Firms establishing joint ventures typically need partners for a variety of potential contributions. Several researchers have examined the effect of partner need on joint venture performance. Raveed and Renforth [1983] have shown that the two most important objectives of joint ventures were to obtain local market knowledge and local management. Beamish and Banks [1987], in a sample of sixty-six joint ventures in LDCs, found that greater need between partners resulted in more satisfactory performance. This study demonstrated a pattern that managers in high-performing ventures looked to their local partners for greater contributions than did managers in low-performing ventures. Thus, in Korean joint ventures we expect a positive relationship between the extent of desired partner need and satisfactory performance.

H9: A positive relationship between partner need and satisfactory performance will exist in Korean joint ventures in LDCs.

Commitment and Performance

One of several constructs found to be relevant to joint venture performance is commitment. Several researchers [Tomlinson and Willie 1982; Schaan 1983; Cullen, Johnson and Sakano 1995], have emphasized the role of commitment to joint venture success. Beamish [1988] found a strong correlation between commitment and performance in joint ventures, noting that most of the commitment characteristics in the high-performing venture were related to the MNE's willingness to do something: adapt products, increase employment of nationals, visit and offer assistance, or supply special skills. Lee [1989] also found in his work on joint ventures from Korea that mutual confidence and close business relationships between local partners and Korean investors significantly influenced the level of satisfaction that Korean management felt about the performance of their ventures.

H10: There will be a positive relationship between commitment and performance in Korean joint ventures in LDCs.

METHODOLOGY

All international manufacturing joint ventures (108) established by Korean firms before 1988 were originally surveyed to test the hypotheses. This list was obtained from the central bank (Bank of Korea), an organization with which all prospective Korean foreign investors must coordinate. A mail questionnaire (in Korean) was used to collect data from the population. The questionnaire was mailed to the Korean managing director charged with the joint venture project. Before mailing, each company was contacted by telephone in order to enlist cooperation with the research. The first response rate was 28%; thirty-one mail questionnaires were returned. After a second wave of telephone contacts to nonrespondents, the response rate increased to almost 40%. After eliminating incomplete questionnaires, forty-one completed joint venture questionnaires were available to test the hypotheses. Eight of the forty-one Korean joint ventures were located in developed countries, two in newly industrialized countries and thirty-one in developing countries. For reasons of comparability, only the LDC-based venture results are reported.

The average amount of investment in the joint ventures was $1.8 million, and half the ventures had average sales between $1 million and $5 million. Average ratio of exports to sales was 58%, with a low standard deviation. Also, average local market share for the venture was 29% with a high standard deviation. The joint ventures were established between 1973 and 1988 and had been in operation an average of 4.4 years. None were established with a pre-determined duration in mind. Only one joint venture was autonomously managed.

The average equity share of the Korean partner in the venture was 47%. A very high proportion of the announced joint ventures were actually implemented, since Korean firms need formal government permission to obtain the foreign exchange needed for overseas investments.

The types of products produced in the joint ventures included textiles and footwear (22.6%), electric and electronic machines (22.6%), chemical products (16.1%), food and beverages (12.9%), nonferrous metals (9.7%) and lumber

(6.5%). The level of technology was relatively high compared with those of local firms. From the questionnaires, the average technology level for the joint ventures versus the local firms was 5.64 on a seven-point scale ranging from very high (7) to very low (1). This is consistent with the experience of developed country partners in LDC-based JVs (see Beamish [1985]) but stands in contrast to the experiences of developing country partners in other LDCs (see Wells [1983]).

MEASURES OF VARIABLES

The *reasons for creating* the venture were divided into four categories: need for partner's knowledge of local market; need for partner's technology; government regulation on ownership; and need for partner's capital. The importance of each venture-creating rationale was rated on a five-point scale ranging from (5) "very important to" (1) "not at all important".

Performance of the joint venture was measured by manager's overall satisfaction with the joint venture. This subjective measure has been previously used in joint venture research by Killing [1983], Schaan [1983] and Beamish [1985] and has been shown to correlate with such quantitative measures as profitability [Geringer and Hébert 1991]. Overall satisfaction with the joint venture was rated by the respondents on a one-item, seven-point scale ranging from (7) "very satisfied" to (1) "not at all satisfied".

Partner need was assessed in terms of the relative importance of each partner's contribution to the joint venture for ten items (faster entry into local market; inexpensive labour; local political advantage; raw material supply; knowledge of local business practice; local managers; capital; general knowledge of the local market and culture; better export opportunities; and technology or equipment). The importance of each partner contribution was measured on a five-point scale ranging from (5) "very important" to (1) "not at all important". Overall partner need was measured by the average of the importance of the ten partner contributions. In terms of results, the highest scoring items were: inexpensive labour (3.70), knowledge of local business practices (3.24), and general knowledge of the local market (3.21).

To measure *commitment*, respondents were asked to assess how characteristic a total of thirteen statements were of the foreign parent company's attitudes and activities vis-à-vis joint ventures and the particular venture. The thirteen statements assessed the Korean parent in terms of commitment to international business (attitude toward foreign investment; willingness to adapt product to the needs of the local market; and willingness to increase the number of local employees), the joint venture structure (willingness to form a joint venture where there were no regulations on ownership rates; willingness to take a minority-equity position; spending a long time weighing the costs and benefits of using joint ventures; and having a contingency plan for increasing assistance to the venture), the particular venture (willingness to visit regularly and offer assistance to the venture; willingness to commit resources such as people and money to the venture; and willingness to find special skills required by the venture in the parent firm) and the particular partner (willingness to change current working procedures and reporting requirement to accommodate the partner; ensuring through regular meetings that each partner knew what to expect from the venture; and the amount of time spent with the partner working on venture business). Ratings on each statement were over a five-point scale ranging from (1) "not at all characteristic" to (5) "very characteristic".

An iterative procedure was used to refine the set of measures of the commitment construct. The item-to-total correlation, i.e., the correlation between the score of each measure and the total score of those measures used to capture the construct, was examined. Following the steps suggested by Nunnally [1978], those measures with a low item-to-total correlation (i.e., $r < .25$) were eliminated. These were: willingness to take a minority equity position; willingness to regularly visit the venture; willingness to find special skills required by the venture in the parent firm; spending a long time weighing the costs and benefits of using the joint venture form; and having a contingency plan for increasing assistance to the venture. Overall commitment was measured by the average of the rating of the eight statements. The highest scoring items were: willingness to increase the number of local employees (4.09), and attitude toward foreign investment (3.70). The measures of partner need and commitment used were from Beamish [1985].

Control was measured by assessing the degree of the parent firm's influence in decisionmaking regarding fourteen decisions (product pricing; product design; production scheduling; production process; quality control; budgeting; dividend policy; hiring and firing; wage and labour policy; advertising and promotion; capital expenditures; exporting; choosing supplies; and daily management), and by their assessment of the importance of each decision. Parent firm's influence in decisionmaking was rated on a seven-point scale ranging from (7) "very great" to (1) "not at all great". Also, the importance of the decision was rated on a five-point scale ranging from (5) "very much" to (1) "not at all". Overall control was measured by averaging the products of the importance of the decision and the influence of the firm in making the decision. The highest scoring items were: quality control (4.21), product pricing (4.21), and capital expenditures (3.76). Finally, *ownership* was measured by the actual percentage of holdings of the parent firm.

For the three multi-item measures: control, partner need, and commitment, the Cronbach's *alphas* were respectively .91, .80, and .70. All measures used in the research met or exceeded the .70 cut-off point established by Nunnally [1978]. Hence, the reliabilities of these constructs were judged to be sufficient.

RESULTS

Table 1 reports the mean values of the importance attached to each venture-creating rationale.

TABLE 1
Importance of Venture-Creation Rationale

	In LDCs
Need for partner's local knowledge (skills)	3.60*
Government regulation on ownership	3.07
Need for partner's capital (assets)	3.00
Need for partner's technology (assets)	1.53

*value of importance on a five-point scale

For Korean joint ventures in LDCs, the order of importance of reasons for forming joint ventures was: need for local market knowledge; government regulation on ownership; need for partner's capital; and need for partner's technology. These findings for Korean joint ventures are different from those used by investors from developed countries when investing in LDCs, and are consistent with Hypothesis 1 (see Table 4 for a complete summary).

The difference between the relative importance of the need for partner's local knowledge (3.60) and that of government regulation on ownership (3.07) was statistically significant at the .10 level ($t = 1.74$, $p < .10$).

Frequencies analysis was used to test Hypothesis 2. Only 19% of the joint ventures were considered unstable by the Korean partners. However, this figure may be understated because only one of the joint venture partners was surveyed. Nonetheless, the results seem to support the hypothesis that Korean joint ventures in LDCs will be more stable than developed country joint ventures in LDCs.

Chi-square analysis was used to test Hypothesis 3. The *chi*-square value for the relationship between stability and partner type is also significant (*chi*-square = 6.48, $p < .05$). The *chi*-square test shows clearly that a relationship exists between the stability of Korean joint ventures and whether the partner is government (or public shareholder) versus a private firm. This finding is consistent with that from developed countries' joint ventures where stability was observed to be higher in joint ventures involving local private partners rather than government partners.

Frequencies were used to test Hypotheses 4 and 5 about levels of ownership and satisfaction with performance. For H4, in 55% of cases, the Korean partner held a minority equity position. This is consistent with other investments in LDCs and provides support for the hypothesis.

Consistent with H5, the overall satisfaction with the Korean joint ventures was higher than that experienced by developed country partners with joint ventures in LDCs. The average value for the overall satisfaction level in the sample was 4.32 on the seven-point semantic differential scale. Overall, only 29% of those who responded were dissatisfied with the performance of the joint venture.

Pearson correlation analysis was used to test Hypothesis 6 about the relationship between ownership and control. The results show a significant positive relationship between control and ownership (r = .587, p < .01). This contrasts with previous findings on joint ventures in developing countries. As noted earlier, unlike firms from developed countries, Korean firms making direct foreign investments rarely have monopolistic advantages such as technology, marketing or managerial know-how which can be used as control methods to substitute for ownership.

For the control-performance relationship (H7), the correlation analysis shows that there was a positive relationship on the basis of the total sample. This is not consistent with previous findings on joint ventures from developed countries in developing countries. Given the Korean objective of exporting much of the joint venture's production to developed countries as a means of circumventing high protectionist barriers, managers favour a strong decision-making role. Table 2 illustrates the results of correlation analysis of the ownership-control and control-performance relationships.

DETERMINANTS OF PERFORMANCE OF KOREAN JOINT VENTURES IN LDCs

A stepwise multiple regression was performed to test Hypotheses 8, 9 and 10 regarding the determinants of performance of joint ventures from Korea. The dependent variable was overall satisfaction with joint venture performance; the independent variables were four characteristics of joint ventures: ownership rates; control; partner need; and commitment. A stepwise procedure was used because there were high correlations between the independent variables (e.g., the correlation between ownership and control was .587, as in Table 2). The results of the stepwise multiple regression are shown in Table 3.

TABLE 2
Results of Correlation Analysis on Characteristics of Korean Joint Ventures

Relationship	Correlation Value	*p*-Value
Ownership–Control	.587	.000
Control–Performance	.386	.031

TABLE 3
Results of Stepwise Multiple Regression on Joint Venture Performance

Stage	Variable	Parameter Estimate	Partial *R*	*P*-Value
1	Partner Need	.602	.073	.087
2	Control	.524	.308	.000

TABLE 4
Summary of Research Hypotheses and Overall Support

	Hypotheses	Support/Non-Support
1)	Korean joint ventures in LDCs will be created primarily due to a need for the other partner's local knowledge of the local market and business practices rather than government regulations.	+
2)	Stability rates of joint ventures from Korea in LDCs will be higher than those from developed countries.	+
3)	Korean joint ventures in LDCs will have higher stability rates with local private partners than with local government partners.	+
4)	Most Korean partners in joint ventures in LDCs will have a minority equity position.	+
5)	The performance of Korean joint ventures will be more satisfactory in LDCs than are developed country joint ventures in LDCs.	+
6)	Korean joint ventures in LDCs will have a positive relationship between ownership and control.	+
7)	There will be a positive relationship between Korean control and superior performance in Korean joint ventures in LDCs.	+
8)	In Korean joint ventures in LDCs there will be a positive relationship between Korean ownership levels and performance.	NR
9)	A positive relationship between partner need and satisfactory performance will exist in Korean joint ventures in LDCs.	+
10)	There will be a positive relationship between commitment and performance in Korean joint ventures in LDCs.	NR

NR = No Relationship

The model's predictive power is significant with an adjusted *R*-square of .38. According to Table 3, using aggregate measures again, H8 and H10 were rejected. For Korean joint ventures ownership and commitment have no relationship with performance. Instead, control and partner need were found to be the primary determinants of joint venture performance; only these two variables were significant at the .10 level.

The results show that control was the most important factor in determining the performance of Korean joint ventures. As discussed earlier, for Korean joint ventures in LDCs where one of the primary motivations is exporting output to developed countries, taking strong management control plays an important role in raising overall satisfaction with the performance of the ventures. The finding that partner need is significantly related to Korean joint venture's performance, but ownership rates or commitment are not, is consistent with the result of Lee's [1989] previous research on Korean joint ventures. Also, this finding coincides with those from joint ventures from developed countries in LDCs, where greater need between partners resulted in more satisfactory performance.

CONCLUSIONS

This study was designed to ascertain the characteristics of joint ventures from a newly industrialized country (Korea) in developing countries and the determinants of performance of Korean joint ventures. As summarized in Table 5, several findings have emerged that differ from previous findings on joint ventures from developed countries in LDCs. Differences were found in terms of stability, reasons for creating the venture, satisfaction level with performance, and the relationship between control and performance, and between ownership and control. Some similarities were also found: the relationships between ownership rates and stability and partner type; and between partner need and performance.

This study suggests that the characteristics of Korean joint ventures in LDCs are as follows. First, the need for partner's local knowledge is a more important reason for creating a venture than government regulation on ownership. Second, Korean joint ventures are more stable than developed country joint ventures. Third, the stability of Korean joint ventures is related to the type of local partner: government or public shareholder versus private firm. Fourth, the most common ownership level of Korean partners is a minority one. Fifth, overall satisfaction with the performance of Korean joint ventures is higher than that of developed country joint ventures in LDCs.

This study also shows different results than the findings on joint ventures from developed countries for the ownership-control and control-performance relationships, which has been the main focus of past research. For Korean joint ventures, the relationships are direct; ownership has a positive relationship with control, and control has the same relationship with performance. Finally, only control and partner need are found to be the correlates of performance. Other variables such as ownership rates and commitment, which were found to influence performance in joint ventures from developed countries, had no relationship with the performance of Korean joint ventures. The major implication for future research is to suggest that the characteristics of joint ventures differ depending on the development stage of both the originating country and host country.

TABLE 5
Summary of Differences of Joint-Venture Characteristics

Characteristics	JV Partners from developed countries in other developed countries	JV Partners from developed countries in developing countries	JV Partners from a NIC (Korea) in developing countries
Major reason for creating venture*	Skill required	Respond to Government pressure	Skill Required
Frequency of association with government partners*	Low	Moderate	Moderate
Overall use of JVs versus other modes of foreign involvement	Significant	High (but contingent on country, industry and technology level)	High
Proportion of intended JVs actually implemented	High	Relatively high	High
Use of JVs with a pre-determined duration	Low (except in certain industries)	Low	Low
Most common level of ownership for MNE*	Equal	Minority	Minority
Number of autonomously managed ventures	Small	Negligible	Negligible
Ownership-control relationship	Direct	Unclear	Direct
Control-performance relationship in successful JVs*	Inconclusive	Shared or split	Direct
Instability rate*	30%	45%	Low (19%)
MNE managerial assessment of dissatisfaction with performance	37%	61%	Moderate (29%)
Foreign partner's technology level relative to local level	Similar	Higher	Higher

Note: Characteristics indicated with an asterisk in the two left-hand columns were previously summarized in Beamish [1985].

LIMITATIONS

There are a number of limitations to this study. First, it employed a small sample of joint ventures. While we had a relatively high response rate, it may still not be representative of all Korean JVs, or JVs from other NICs. It sought the views of only one of the parent companies (which by definition will overstate the performance and stability levels), and was restricted to joint ventures in manufacturing firms. In addition, some of the measures employed were perceptual in nature, which introduces possible concerns about the subjectivity of response. Thus the conclusions must be considered preliminary and in need of corroboration and extension by future research.

REFERENCES

Agarwal, Sanjeev & Sridhar N. Ramaswami. 1992. Choice of foreign market entry modes: Impact of ownership, location and internalization factors. *Journal of International Business Studies*, 23(1): 1–27.

Artisien, Patrick F.R. & Peter J. Buckley. 1985. Joint ventures in Yugoslavia: Opportunities and constraints. *Journal of International Business Studies*, 16(1): 111–36.

Austin, James E. 1990. *Managing in developing countries*. New York: Free Press.

Beamish, Paul W. 1985. The characteristics of joint ventures in developed and developing countries. *Columbia Journal of World Business*, Winter, 13–19.

______. 1988. *Multinational joint ventures in developing countries*. London: Routledge.

______. 1993. The characteristics and performance of joint ventures in the People's Republic of China. *Journal of International Marketing*, 1(2): 29–48.

______ & John C. Banks. 1987. Equity joint ventures and the theory of the multinational enterprise. *Journal of International Business Studies*, 18(2): 1–16.

Blodgett, Linda. 1991. Partner contributions as predictors of equity share in international joint ventures. *Journal of International Business Studies*, 22(1): 63–78.

Contractor, Farok J. & Peter Lorange, editors. 1987. *Cooperative strategies in international business*. Lexington, Mass.: D. C. Heath.

Cory, Peter F. 1982. Industrial cooperation, joint ventures and the MNE in Yugoslavia. In A. M. Rugman, editor, *New theories of the multinational enterprise*. London: Croom Helm.

Cullen, John B., Jean L. Johnson & Tomoaki Sakano. 1995. Japanese and local partner commitment to IJVs. *Journal of International Business Studies*, 26(1): 91–115.

Daniels, John D., Jeffrey Krug & Douglas Nigh. 1985. US joint ventures in China: Motivations and management of political risk. *California Management Review*, Summer: 46–58.

Franko, Lawrence G., 1971, *Joint venture survival in multinational corporations*. New York: Praeger.

Friedman, Wolfgang G. & J. P. Beguin. 1971. *Joint international business ventures in developing countries*. New York: Columbia University Press.

Geringer, J. Michael & Louis Hébert. 1989. Control and performance of international joint ventures. *Journal of International Business Studies*, 20(2): 235–54.

______. 1991. Measuring joint venture performance. *Journal of International Business Studies*, 22(2): 249–63.

Harrigan, Kathryn Rudie, 1984, *Strategies for joint ventures*. London: D.C. Heath.

Hennart, Jean-François. 1988. A transaction costs theory of equity joint ventures. *Strategic Management Journal*, 4: 361–74.

Hills, Stephen M. 1978. The search for joint venture partner. *Academy of Management Proceedings*. 277–81.

Jo, Sung-Hwan. 1981. Overseas Direct Investment by South Korean Firms: Direction and Pattern. In K. Kumar & M.G. McLeod, editors, *Multinationals from developing countries*. Lexington, Mass.: Lexington Books.

Killing, J. Peter, 1983. *Strategies for joint venture success*. New York: Praeger.

Kobrin, Stephen J. 1988. Trends in Ownership of U.S. Manufacturing Subsidiaries in Developing Countries: An Interindustry Analysis. In F. J. Contractor & P. Lorange, editors, *Cooperative strategies in international business*. Lexington, Mass.: D.C. Heath.

Kogut, Bruce. 1988a. A Study of the Life Cycle of Joint Ventures. In F. J. Contractor & P. Lorange editors, *Cooperative strategies in international business.* Lexington, Mass.: D.C. Heath.

______. 1988b. Joint ventures: Theoretical and empirical perspective. *Strategic Management Journal,* 9: 319–32.

Kumar, Krishna & Kee Young Kim. 1984. The Korean manufacturing multinationals. *Journal of International Business Studies,* 15(1): 45–62.

Lecraw, Donald J. 1983. Performance of transnational corporations in less developed countries. *Journal of International Business Studies,* 14(1): 15–34.

Lee, Jangho. 1989. Study on strategic success of Korean joint ventures overseas. *Song Kok Journal,* 20.

Min, SangKee. 1985. Korean manufacturing FDIs. In B. Hwang, editor, *Korean business management.* Seoul, Korea: Hanwool Books.

Negandhi, Anant R., Edith C. Yuen & Golpira Eshghi. 1987. Localisation of Japanese Subsidiaries in Southeast Asia. *Asia Pacific Journal of Management,* 5(1): 67–79.

Nunnally, Jum C. 1978. *Psychometric theory.* New York: McGraw Hill.

Parkhe, Arvind. 1991. Interfirm diversity, organizational learning, and longevity in global strategic alliances. *Journal of International Business Studies,* 22(4): 579–601.

Patton, Donald J. & Anh-Dung Do. 1978. Joint Ventures in Yugoslavia. *Management International Review,* 51–63.

Peterson, Richard B. & Justin Y. Shimada. 1978. Sources of management problems in Japanese-American joint ventures. *Academy of Management Review,* October: 796–804.

Raveed, S. R. & W. Renforth. 1983. State enterprise – multinational corporation joint ventures: How well do they meet both partners' needs? *Management International Review,* 1(1): 47–57.

Reynolds, John I. 1979. The pinched-shoe effect of international joint ventures. *Columbia Journal of World Business,* 19(2): 23–29.

Schaan, Jean-Louis. 1983. Parent control and joint venture success: The case of Mexico. Unpublished doctoral dissertation, University of Western Ontario, London, Ontario.

______ & Paul W. Beamish. 1988. Joint venture general managers in developing countries. In F. Contractor & P. Lorange, editors, *Cooperative strategies in international business.* Lexington, Mass.: D.C. Heath.

Shan, Weijan 1991. Environmental risks and joint venture sharing arrangements. *Journal of International Business Studies,* 22(4): 555–78.

Simyar, Farhad. 1983. Major causes of joint venture failures in the Middle East: The case of Iran. *Management International Review,* 23: 58–68.

Sohn, Jung Hoon Derick. 1994. Social knowledge as a control system: A proposition and evidence from the Japanese F.D.I. behavior. *Journal of International Business Studies,* 25(2): 295–324.

Stuckey, John A. 1983. *Vertical integration and joint ventures in the aluminum industry.* Cambridge, Mass.: Harvard University Press.

Sullivan, Jeremiah & Richard B. Peterson. 1982. Factors associated with trust in Japanese–American joint ventures. *Management International Review,* 22: 30–40.

Tallman, Stephen B. & Oded Shenkar. 1990. International cooperative venture strategies: Outward investment and small firms from N.I.C.s. *Management International Review,* 30(4): 299–315.

______. 1994. A managerial decision model of international cooperative venture formation. *Journal of International Business Studies*, 25(1): 91–113.

Tomlinson, James W. C. 1970. *The joint venture process in international business: India and Pakistan*. Cambridge, Mass.: MIT Press.

______ & C. S. W. Willie. 1982. Modelling the joint venture process in Latin America: Mexico. *Canadian Journal of Development Studies*, 3(1): 66–94.

Wells, Louis T. 1983. *Third world multinationals*. Cambridge, Mass.: MIT Press.

Williamson, Oliver E. 1975. *Markets and hierarchies: Analysis and antitrust implications*. New York: Free Press.

Woodcock, C. Patrick, Paul W. Beamish & Shige Makino. 1994. Ownership-based entry mode strategies and international performance. *Journal of International Business Strategies*, 25(2): 253–73.

[6]

Business Networks and Transnational Corporations: A Study of Hong Kong Firms in the ASEAN Region*

Henry Wai-chung Yeung
Department of Geography, National University of Singapore, Singapore 119260

Abstract: In recent years, the question of how business firms are embedded in society and space has received serious attention in economic geography. Arising from empirical research into the transnational operations of Hong Kong–based firms in Southeast Asia, this paper is concerned with the organizational processes of transnationalization—that is, how transnational operations are accomplished through networks of personal and business relationships. A network perspective specifies that three dimensions of transnational organizations—extrafirm, interfirm, and intrafirm networks—must be addressed simultaneously. Based on personal interviews with top executives from 111 headquarters and 63 subsidiaries of Hong Kong transnational corporations operating in the ASEAN region, I argue that social and business networks are necessary mechanisms of transnationalization. Political connections at the highest level enable Hong Kong entrepreneurs and business firms to tap into extrafirm networks and to penetrate local markets in Southeast Asia. Business connections and personal relationships are cornerstones of interfirm transactional governance structures through which Hong Kong firms establish their ASEAN operations. At the intrafirm level, personal trust and experience are keys to coordination and control in transnational operations. By showing how these Hong Kong firms and their ASEAN operations are socially and culturally embedded in networks of relationships, this paper serves also as a critique of economistic arguments and transaction cost analysis commonly found in leading international business research.

Key words: Hong Kong transnational corporations, regulatory regimes, social organization, Chinese business networks, personal relationships, social embeddedness, ASEAN region.

Research in international business and production has been dependent largely upon economistic and Western-centric theories developed predominantly in industrial and institutional economics (e.g., Buckley and Casson 1976, 1985, 1991; Dunning 1981, 1988, 1993; Pitelis and Sugden 1991). This paper points to the uncritical acceptance and applications of these theoretical frameworks in the so-called "Third World multinationals" literature (see Yeung 1994a). Typically, empirical studies of transnational corporations (TNCs) from developing countries and Asian newly industrialized economies (NIEs) are based on economistic interpre-

* I am deeply indebted to Peter Dicken for his guidance and encouragement. An earlier version of this paper was presented at the Annual Conference of the Institute of British Geographers, University of Northumbria at Newcastle, 3–6 January 1995; I would like to thank participants for their comments. Constructive comments from two anonymous referees of this journal and Richard Peet are much appreciated. Financial support from the National University of Singapore and the 1993 Postgraduate Award by the Developing Areas Research Group of the Institute of British Geographers is gratefully acknowledged. I have also benefited enormously as Visiting Associate at the Institute of Southeast Asian Studies, Singapore, and Visiting Scholar at the Center of Asian Studies, University of Hong Kong. All errors in this paper are, however, my sole responsibility.

tations (e.g., Agmon and Kindleberger 1977; Kumar and McLeod 1981; Lall 1983; Wells 1983; Khan 1986; Tolentino 1993). They tend to overlook the historical and social formations of these emerging TNCs (e.g., Yeung 1996c). Economic motivations of transnational operations are often ascribed causal status in explaining why domestic firms transnationalize their activities. These mixed motivations are further dichotomized into survey responses classified as either "push" or "pull" factors. The end product of most of these explanations becomes a theoretically infertile description of various *contingent* situations that may account only partially for transnational operations. They fail to stipulate the causal mechanisms through which transnational operations are made possible. A comprehensive theorization of the process of transnationalization, defined as a dynamic process through which TNCs are engaged in a diverse range of cross-border network relations and operations, is urgently required (cf. Yeung 1993, 1994b, 1997a).

On the other hand, recent reappraisals of the state-of-the-art of economic geography have called for a more culturally and socially sensitive approach to the fundamental concept of "the economic" (Thrift and Olds 1996). This paper puts forward a similar argument against prevailing economistic and Western-centric theories of the TNC. I argue that the role of *guanxi*, or personal relationships in social and business networks, is crucial in spearheading foreign direct investment (FDI) from Hong Kong TNCs (HKTNCs) into the ASEAN region.[1] Through personal interviews with top executives from both headquarters and ASEAN subsidiaries/affiliates of HKTNCs, I find that although lower production costs and the search for new markets are typical motivations for large investments made by these Hong Kong firms, *guanxi* or network relationships decide through which countries (locations) and how (mechanisms) these investments are channeled. Arguably, the economic actions undertaken by business enterprises such as HKTNCs are firmly embedded, socially and culturally (Granovetter 1985, 1991; Granovetter and Swedberg 1992), because business executives do not always base their investment actions on economic considerations per se. But network relationships play an equally, if not more, vital role as well. In conjunction with this argument, a deeper understanding of the processes of transnational operations via a network approach can be interpreted as providing a culturally and time-space sensitive perspective. For instance, Wade (1990), Biggart and Hamilton (1992), and Redding (1994) recently have launched critical reappraisals of the Western bias in neoclassical economic interpretations of Asian "economic miracles." This paper follows and expands upon the gist of their arguments, calling for a more socially and culturally sensitive explanation of changing world economic phenomena.

The main argument of this paper has three parts. First, at the macro *extrafirm* level, regulatory barriers and institutional opportunities in host ASEAN countries tend to induce HKTNCs to enter all kinds of extrafirm political relationships. These regulatory barriers arise from unique historical and social contexts, in particular the suspicion displayed by many host ASEAN countries (except Singapore) toward foreign capital, including overseas Chinese capital. Second, at the intermediate *interfirm* level, this paper emphasizes the role of personal and business relationships in transnational operations by looking at the social organization of Chinese business. The question of ethnicity is at the forefront of the discussion because Chinese business networks are socially and culturally specific and because Hong

[1] The Association of South East Asian Nations (ASEAN) was established in August 1967. The six member states are Brunei, Indonesia, Malaysia, the Philippines, Singapore, and Thailand. For the purpose of this paper, however, Brunei is effectively excluded because of its lack of data and inward foreign direct investment.

Kong is predominantly a Chinese society.[2] Third, at the micro *intrafirm* level, coordination and control of networks within HKTNCs are best achieved through trusted family members and close associates. It is also imperative to examine how power relations are manifested in the processes of controlling transnational operations (Dicken and Thrift 1992; Yeung 1994b, 1997a). In fact, the element of control is the key to any definition of the TNC and FDI (Cowling and Sugden 1987; Low, Ramstetter, and Yeung forthcoming). Based on this causal link between power and control, this paper sheds light on the nature of transnational operations through intrafirm network relationships.

Some methodological caveats are appropriate here. First, HKTNCs are defined as domestic business enterprises headquartered in Hong Kong that control assets and/or exert influence in the decision-making process of one or more cross-border subsidiaries and/or affiliates. Second, the original study was based on field research from December 1993 to August 1994 (see Yeung 1995a, forthcoming). In Hong Kong, I contacted some 182 headquarters of HKTNCs from an incomplete master directory that I had compiled from various published sources and validated through telephone interviews. Subsequently, 111 successful personal interviews were conducted, representing a 61 percent response rate. In four ASEAN countries, excluding the Philippines, another 63 personal interviews were completed from a sample of 102 ASEAN subsidiaries/affiliates of HKTNCs (61 percent response rate). This large data base also contains transcripts of personal interviews with top executives from 41 HKTNCs *and* (some of) their ASEAN subsidiaries/affiliates and transcripts of 19 additional personal interviews with top executives from the headquarters only. Third, this paper takes a qualitative analytical approach to the explanation of HKTNCs and their operations in the ASEAN region.[3] Fourth, company and personnel names reported in this paper are disguised in order to protect their confidentiality.

The next section offers a brief overview of an emerging network perspective on the TNC, followed by an excursion into the social and institutional settings of Hong Kong and the ASEAN region to set the context in which HKTNCs operate. Both the social organization of the Chinese business system and the regulatory regimes of ASEAN countries are examined. The penultimate analytical section is concerned exclusively with business networks among HKTNCs operating in the ASEAN region. Three levels of network relationships are presented, from extrafirm to interfirm and finally to intrafirm relationships. Some implications for theoretical development in international business and business developments in the ASEAN region are discussed in the concluding section.

A Network Perspective on Transnational Corporations

Although the concept is not altogether new, interest in the notion of the "network" form of business and industrial organization has reemerged in recent years (Camagni 1991; Dicken and Thrift 1992; Cooke and Morgan 1993; Dicken 1994; Dicken, Forsgren, and Malmberg 1994; Thrift and Olds 1996; Yeung forthcoming). This section discusses "net-

[2] There are many similarities in the transnational experience among minority ethnic groups throughout the world. It is thus possible to extend this analysis of the transnational operations of Chinese firms from Hong Kong to that of Jews, Indians, or other minority ethnic groups.

[3] I have dealt elsewhere with the spatial organization of HKTNCs and their associated FDI flows in the ASEAN region (see Yeung 1994c, 1995b, 1996b, 1996c). This paper therefore concentrates on the qualitative aspects of network relationships in their transnational operations.

works" as an important mechanism through which TNCs and their overseas operations are organized (see Yeung 1994b).

A network perspective views the TNC and its network relations as a *governance structure* through which transnational operations are made possible. Governance structure is conceptualized as the organizational forms and processes through which business activities are directed. The network form of governance in international business may be interpreted as the organizational forms and processes through which *transnational* activities are directed across different fields and geographic locations. The patterns and character of the connections among various relations in networks constitute their structures, because "such structures are conditioned by technical and cultural factors, but, primarily, they are interactive, that is, they are formed and modified through interaction among the actors. The network structure is a result of history" (Håkansson and Johanson 1993, 42).

In contrast to neoclassical economic models of the firm as an abstract economic entity (i.e., the "black-box approach"), this network approach advocates that all TNCs are simultaneously *embedded* in ongoing networks of relationships at three distinct levels: intrafirm, interfirm, and extrafirm networks (Table 1). This network perspective also argues that network relationships, expressed at different levels, are essentially the causal mechanisms of transnational operations—that is, network

Table 1

A Typology of Network Relations and the Sociospatial Organization of Transnational Operations

	Network Relations		
Categories	Intrafirm	Interfirm	Extrafirm
Nature	• Parent-subsidiary relationship • Internalized operations: proprietary rights and economies of scale	• Firm-firm transactional and institutional relationship • Externalized operations: economies of scope and joint production/marketing	• Firm-institution politics and relationship: state and nonstate • Contractual basis: direct business • Legal laws and enforcement
Instruments	• Integration (horizontal and/or vertical) • Coordination (loose vs. tight and centralized vs. dispersed) • Internal arbitration of disputes: labor relations • Transfer pricing	• Competition and cooperation • Contracts and agreements • Flexible production systems: just-in-time	• Conflicts and negotiations • Political bargaining • Social regulation • Propaganda strategy
Concrete dimensions	• Tentative full integration of R&D and production • High quality at reasonable costs • Decentralization of production decisions	• Close and long-lasting ties between producers and users • Networking to reap specialization and coordination gains • Long-term and cooperative subcontracting	• Power relations more than monetary relations • Quest for proprietary rights • Search for social and political legitimacy
Organizational forms	• Quasi-integration • Internalization • Multidivisions • Family business groups • Conglomerates	• Joint ventures • Subcontracting • Cooperative agreements • Strategic alliances • Licensing and franchising • Ethnic and personal networks • Technology financing	• Government contracts • Joint R&D collaboration • Institutional relationship, e.g., memberships

Source: Yeung (1994b, Table 3).

relationships empower the TNC to execute its overall modus operandi. Contrary to the capital-logic approach (cf. Hymer 1972; Palloix 1975, 1977; Harvey 1982; Ietto-Gillies 1992), it places *both* the TNC and its embedded network relations as the central foci of analysis.

Causal mechanisms, however, are subject to dynamic changes in the global capitalist space-economy. When the context in which causal powers in network relationships are realized changes over time, the empirical landscape of transnational operations will be expressed differently. For example, in the context of global technological change, TNCs will continuously reshape their corporate strategy according to their overall modes of rationality. Subsequently, new spatial organizations of their transnational activities will occur (see de Smidt and Wever 1990; Dicken 1992; Carnoy et al. 1993; Dunning 1993; Moran and Riesenberger 1994). The accelerated pace of globalization in the late 1980s and early 1990s has prompted many global TNCs to tighten their coordination and expand their operations among more geographic areas in the Triad regions (Ohmae 1985, 1990; Porter 1986; Bartlett and Ghoshal 1989). This pattern would be impossible if these giant TNCs were not embedded in ongoing network relationships. But these network relationships per se do not stimulate their escalated processes of globalization. It is rather the contextual change that has activated causal powers embedded in ongoing network relationships.

A business network may be defined as "an integrated and co-ordinated set of ongoing economic and non-economic relations embedded within, among and outside business firms" (Yeung 1994b, 476; emphasis omitted). Although this conceptual definition is necessarily broad, its concrete realization may take a very specific form (e.g., joint ventures and strategic alliances). A network is more than just an integrated structure, because it is simultaneously a structure *and* a process. It is a nested structure with emergent power in an abstract sense. Networks are enduring structures emerging from social relations and hence networks represent the sum of all social relations focusing at a particular nodal point—the TNC in this case. The "emergent power" nature of networks also enables them to synergize more than the sum or totality of social relations.

Social and Institutional Settings in Hong Kong and ASEAN

The "overseas Chinese networks of capital" is a predominant mode of business organization in Asia. This form of social and business organization of transnational production has spearheaded a rapid diffusion of economic activities and intraregional FDI flows among various Asian-Pacific countries in which Chinese have significant economic control (see Yeung 1994d, 1997b). Kao (1993, 32) points out that "cross-border investments alone are responsible for turning the de facto network of loose family relationships into today's Chinese commonwealth." Examples of such countries are China, Indonesia, Hong Kong, Malaysia, the Philippines, Singapore, Taiwan, and Thailand. Any serious attempt to probe the processes of transnational operations by Chinese firms must therefore take into account the nature and specificity of so-called "Chinese business systems."[4]

Another important contextual issue is

[4] It should be noted that, in the case of HKTNCs, not only Chinese businesspeople are embedded in complex networks of personal and business relationships, but also long-time foreign business executives who have embedded themselves in the peculiar social and organizational settings of doing business in Hong Kong and the ASEAN region. It is not the intention of this paper to contrast Chinese business and Western managerial practices. Rather, this paper serves to show *how* HKTNCs, whether owned by ethnic Chinese or not, establish their ASEAN operations.

the organizational and institutional settings in which HKTNCs operate. Transnational operations do not occur in a time-space vacuum. Rather, they are embedded in specific historical and geographic contexts, within which the social organization of capital and institutional regulations are obviously important. This explains why many economic theories of international business and production have failed: they assume that the firm—that is, the TNC—is empowered to conduct its business activities according *only* to its internal logic. They forget that TNC activities are necessarily *influenced* by broader organizational and structural forces. For example, although TNCs are exerting greater influences over nation-states, political sovereignty remains essentially in the hands of the nation-state. Government policies toward inward foreign investment, both promotional and restrictive, serve as the "visible hand" reinstating national economic sovereignty and reshaping the geography of transnational operations.

The Chinese Business System

In most Asian economies, the concrete operation of business activities takes place in business systems belonging to specific ethnic groups (e.g., overseas Chinese and Indians). These business systems are socially and culturally reproduced and hence are embedded in specific time-space contexts (Hamilton and Biggart 1988; Clegg 1990; Hamilton 1991; Biggart and Hamilton 1992; Kotkin 1992; Whitley 1992a, 1992b; Yeung 1997a). Culture and society interact to produce a distinctive "way of business" that evolves over time. This "way of business" must also embed itself in a specific historical period and spatial context. Amin and Thrift (1994) call this local embeddedness of business institutions "institutional thickness." To them, local institutional thickness is defined as "the combination of factors including inter-institutional interaction and synergy, collective representation by many bodies, a common industrial purpose, and shared cultural norms and values" (Amin and Thrift 1994, 15). They identify four dimensions of "institutional thickness": (1) strong institutional presence; (2) high levels of interaction among the institutions in a local area; (3) development of sharply defined domination and coalitions through collective representation; and (4) development of mutual awareness (Amin and Thrift 1994, 14–15). Based on these criteria, the Chinese business system is institutionally "thick." It is perhaps one of the most institutionalized systems in world business, giving rise to what Kao (1993) calls "the worldwide web of Chinese business" and "the Chinese commonwealth."

The Chinese business system is traditionally based on interpersonal trust relations and family and business networks; it retains its distinctive characteristics even at a large organizational scale (Redding 1990). In the Anglo-Saxon business world, family businesses tend to break down and to be replaced by public ownership and professional management when they grow beyond a certain size.[5] Redding (1990, 1991) speculates on the strategic predisposition of overseas Chinese entrepreneurs as follows: (1) it is essential to retain control of the firm in the interests of long-term family prosperity; (2) risks should be hedged to protect family assets; (3) key decisions should remain within an inner circle; and (4) dependence on nonbelongers for such essentials as managerial, technical, or marketing skills should be carefully limited. Because of this tradition of family linkages and network relations, Chinese businesspeople find it more rational to exploit these relations across space. One would therefore expect more transnational operations by Chinese firms controlled either by family members or by entrepreneurs with extensive overseas networks. These com-

[5] Exceptions include the Walton, Mars, and Du Pont families in the United States and other top families in the *Forbes* list of the world's billionaires.

plex and extensive interpenetrations of overseas Chinese business networks and entrepreneurs among various Asian countries are well recorded in the literature (Wu 1983; Brown 1990; Hamilton 1991; Smart and Smart 1991; Chan 1992; Kao 1993; Leung 1993; Chan and Chiang 1994; Chen 1994; Mitchell 1995; Olds 1995; Weidenbaum and Hughes 1996).

In Hong Kong, the spirit and ethos of Chinese capitalism produce socially, culturally, and politically specific business systems (Wong 1985, 1988, 1991, 1993; Lau and Kuan 1988; Redding 1990, 1991; Yeung 1995b, 1997b). Chinese industrialists in Hong Kong are known for their entrepreneurship and higher propensity to engage in risky business and overseas ventures. The arrival of industrialists and entrepreneurs from mainland China after the communist takeover in 1949 contributed significantly to the rapid process of industrialization and economic development in Hong Kong (Wong 1988, 1991; Ho 1992). During the early twentieth century, turmoil and foreign occupations in mainland China forced an outward exodus of the Chinese work force, particularly young laborers from southern provinces. Many subsequently became permanent residents in the Chinese diaspora in Southeast Asia. This minority group of the overseas Chinese (except in Singapore, where the Chinese remain the major ethnic group) maintains its century-long contacts and relations with contemporaries elsewhere in the Asia-Pacific region. These contacts and relations form the organizational basis of Chinese business firms. Wong (1991, 24) contends that Chinese "entrepreneurs tend to dominate the market by activating particularistic ties such as regional networks rather than by building large, impersonal corporations." In Southeast Asia, a similar high level of entrepreneurship among the ethnic- and family-based Chinese business networks is observed. This phenomenon partially accounts for Chinese dominance of local business and commercial sectors.

Institutional Settings in ASEAN

Changing Regulatory Issues among ASEAN Countries. With the exception of Singapore, the postindependence ASEAN region was filled with antiforeign and anti-Chinese capital sentiment (Mackie 1988; Yoshihara 1988; Dixon 1991; McVey 1992). During the 1960s, virtually all ASEAN countries were in their embryonic stage of industrialization. Foreign capital was needed only insofar as it could contribute to employment. Domestic sectors, particularly agriculture and services, were mostly closed to foreign participation in order to protect the basic livelihood of indigenous nationals. During this period, anti-Chinese sentiment was rather deeply rooted in Indonesia and the Philippines (Robison 1986; Mackie 1988; Suryadinata 1988). In Thailand, the Chinese were able to assimilate themselves into the Thai economy, and Sino-Thai businesses experienced rapid growth under Thai political and, often de facto, military patronage (Suehiro 1985, 1992; Mackie 1988). In Malaysia, the Chinese managed to establish themselves under a more favorable political and ethnic climate because of the political coalition between the Chinese and the Malays (Jesudason 1989). In Singapore, Chinese capital faced serious competition from foreign TNCs entering one of the most open economies in the region. Although all investment boards had been established by the 1960s, few of them had explicit strategies for luring foreign investors because of stifling domestic economic problems and political instability. Impediments to foreign investment in these ASEAN countries originated not from the regulatory regime per se, but from the still underdeveloped ASEAN economies themselves.

The 1970s saw the emergence of major ethnic backlash in Indonesia, Malaysia, and, to a lesser extent, the Philippines and Thailand. The regulatory regime was much more restrictive. Domestically, pressure was exerted to allow a greater share of national economic wealth to indigenous people, known as *pribumi* in Indonesia and *bumiputra* in Malaysia. In Malaysia, for example, the New Economic Policy (NEP) was launched in 1970 with two key objectives (Jesudason 1989; Yasuda 1991; Taylor and Ward 1994): to eradicate poverty in general, and to strike a better balance in ethnic distribution of wealth. In order to achieve the latter objective, the Industrial Coordination Act of 1975 required all manufacturing establishments above a certain registered capital to be licensed under the Ministry of Trade and Industry. The initial minimum threshold for the shareholders' fund was M$100,000, but this was raised to M$250,000 in 1977 in an amendment to the act and recently increased further to M$2.5 million. It was hoped that through restricting both Chinese and foreign equity ownership, *bumiputra* ownership of the Malaysian corporate sector could eventually be increased from 2.6 percent in 1970 to 30 percent in 1990.

Externally, with the exception of Singapore, all ASEAN countries followed an inward-looking approach to industrialization. The oil boom in the early 1970s provided sufficient foreign exchange to cash-starved countries such as Indonesia and Malaysia to fuel their huge national development budgets and import-substitution industrialization strategies. In the Philippines, the Marcos government favored "cronies capitalism" rather than promoting inward investment. In Thailand, frequent military coups d'état created instability at the expense of foreign investment. In Singapore, foreign TNCs continued to enjoy government promotion; drastic industrial restructuring, however, effectively forced labor-intensive and low-tech manufacturing to relocate outside Singapore (Ho 1993, 1994; Yeung 1994c, 1995b).

From the 1980s onward, the attitudes of these ASEAN-4 countries changed toward more vigorous promotion of inward investments. The ethnicity issue has not disappeared completely, but instead it is supplemented by an increasing influx of foreign capital. Ironically, a large proportion of this foreign capital originates from ethnic Chinese societies—for example, Hong Kong, Taiwan, and Singapore. After decades of debate on the role of foreign capital in economic development, these ASEAN countries are convinced that they can progress and industrialize with the participation of foreign capital, as in Singapore.

Current Regulatory Climate in the ASEAN Region. Most ASEAN countries generate only a meager amount of FDI outflows; instead, they actively seek inward FDI to fuel their economic development processes. All ASEAN countries set up institutions in the early days of their political independence to take charge of investment promotion and approval procedures. These include the Capital Investment Coordinating Board (BKPM) in Indonesia, Malaysian Industrial Development Authority (MIDA), Board of Investment (BOI) in the Philippines, Economic Development Board (EDB) in Singapore, and Office of the Board of Investment (BOI) in Thailand. All have a similar goal: to promote inward FDI through various marketing strategies (Wells and Wint 1993). Singapore's EDB, however, has a dual role, to promote both inward *and* outward FDI (Mirza 1986; Dicken and Kirkpatrick 1991; Perry 1992, 1995; Low et al. 1993; Régnier 1993; Yeung 1996d). Since its establishment in 1967, Singapore's EDB has been wooing investors from all over the world. Today, Singapore prides itself in attracting high value-added and high-technology FDI from mainly developed countries (Yeung 1994c, 1995b).

FDI approvals and regulations in different ASEAN countries significantly shape the orientation and processes of transnational operations. In Indonesia, Malaysia, the Philippines, and Thailand, local participation in the form of equity ownership is required in most industries, except under specific conditions such as investment in export processing zones (EPZs) or special development zones outside primate cities. Network relationships are thus helpful in these transnational operations. Typically, a foreign firm must team up with a local partner in order to get its investment application approved by the boards of investment. In addition, many investment boards enforce a policy of indigenization of foreign investment, so that over a period of time after the initial inception, local equity shareholding of an FDI project must be increased to a certain level, usually above 50 percent. In so doing, these nation-states aim to achieve not only technology and expertise transfer through FDI projects, but also domestic control of the corporate sector (e.g., Malaysia).

On the other hand, some industries and sectors are completely closed to foreign participation under the "negative list for investment." These are usually domestic industries that are small-scale and labor-intensive, such as contracting services in forest logging, casino gambling, utilization and cultivation of sponges, transportation services, retail and advertising, and mass media in Indonesia (Capital Investment Coordinating Board 1993). In Singapore, all industries and sectors are supposedly open to foreign investors, although some sectors are somewhat protected from full-scale foreign participation, such as stockbrokerage. In order to trade in shares and stocks on the Stock Exchange of Singapore, any stockbrokerage firm must obtain a full member license from the Monetary Authority of Singapore. Foreign firms are not normally granted full licenses in order to protect domestic stockbrokerage firms—an infant-industry argument. Instead, many foreign stockbrokerage firms are granted half-licenses so that they can act as intermediaries between their international clients and local brokerage firms; they are not permitted to conclude final trading deals or contracts. This indirect regulation puts foreign stockbrokerage firms in a difficult situation in competing with local firms (interview with the deputy managing director of the Singapore office of a leading Hong Kong stockbrokerage TNC, 18 July 1994).

These restrictions and regulations aside, foreign firms can invest and establish operations in most host ASEAN countries without going through the boards of investment (e.g., Singapore and Thailand). The main drawback is that they do not enjoy investment incentives and privileges. Even in Malaysia, a foreign firm can set up a manufacturing plant or a service company without applying for approval from MIDA, but approval for manufacturing plants must be sought under the Industrial Coordination Act of 1975 and service companies must be registered with the Registry of Companies. Most investors, particularly large TNCs from developed countries, still prefer to go through host country investment boards, not so much because of their incentive packages but largely because of the convenience and protection of these investment incentive schemes (Yeung 1996a). For example, a BOI-promoted Hong Kong firm in Thailand once suffered from low-price (dumping) imports from other countries. On receiving complaints by this HKTNC, the Thai Board of Investment immediately imposed duties and surcharges to protect the company, which is now enjoying good profitability (interview with the director of the Thai Board of Investment in Hong Kong, 25 March 1994).

Business Networks among Hong Kong Firms in ASEAN

This paper validates empirically that the TNC, as a network governance structure, is engaged in transnational operations through its preexisting and newly developed network relations. This view of both the TNC and its dynamic operations abroad contradicts economic theories of international production in which the TNC is conceptualized as a transaction cost economizing institution. More important, the network approach confronts economistic and essentially Western-centric "models" of international production by focusing on the sociospatial embeddedness of the TNC (Yeung 1997a). This argument, however, does not preclude the role of economic benefits (e.g., markets, profits, and diversification) and costs (e.g., cost reduction and minimization) in the calculus of transnational entrepreneurs; such is the "oversocialized" view of the economic (see Granovetter 1985). Rather, these so-called economic "factors" are necessarily contingent historically and geographically because the same set of economic "advantages" are not always replicated elsewhere. On the other hand, network relations are important causal mechanisms of transnational operations, irrespective of their contingent economic motivations.

This section explains the processes in which HKTNCs are engaged in cross-border networks and business operations. Table 2 shows that some 59 percent of respondents from the headquarters (N = 111) choose to set up their ASEAN operations through relationship-based mechanisms: personal relations (18 percent), suitable local partners (25 percent), and intrafirm personnel transfer (15 percent). While the first two mechanisms are largely interfirm relationships, intrafirm coordination and control constitutes the third mechanism. An additional 17 percent of respondents enter into important relationships with state institutions (extrafirm networks). Similarly, responses from ASEAN subsidiaries confirm these observations.

As discussed earlier, business networks of HKTNCs in the ASEAN region may be examined at three levels (see Table 1): extrafirm networks: intermediaries and political connections; interfirm networks: personal and business relationships; and intrafirm networks: coordination and control. These expressions of business networks and social relations by no means exhaust the list. They are merely indicators of the range and extent of network relations (see also Yeung 1997b, forthcoming). These three levels of network relationships are also embedded within each other to form the totality of network relationships.

Table 2

Ways of Establishing Successful ASEAN Operations by Hong Kong Transnational Corporations

Mechanisms of ASEAN Operations	Headquarters Frequency	Headquarters %	Subsidiaries Frequency	Subsidiaries %
Personal relations are important in establishing overseas operations	20	18.0	8	12.7
Stimulation, guidance, and assistance from local government institutions	19	17.1	4	6.4
Able to find a suitable local partner/person to set up the operation	28	25.2	10	15.9
Sent someone over to set up the operation	17	15.3	25	39.7
A well-developed corporate procedure to set up overseas operations	6	5.4	0	0.0
Decision or suggestions from major client	2	1.8	0	0.0
Long history of operation	3	2.7	1	1.6
Direct merger or acquisition	6	5.4	8	12.7
Branch out from existing ASEAN operations	4	3.6	4	6.4
Unknown	6	5.4	3	4.8
Total	111	100.0	63	100.0

Source: Author's survey.

The Politics of HKTNCs and ASEAN Operations: Extrafirm Networks

At the macro level, there are many institutional hurdles in the ASEAN operations of any TNC. It remains to be seen whether these regulations are effective in practice. The existing literature seems to suggest that, because of connections and coalitions between top government officials and businesspeople, *actual* regulations and restrictions are effectively circumvented through successfully cultivated extrafirm relationships at the micro level. Chinese businesspeople, in particular, are well known for cultivating political relationships with government officials. Such an argument defies the contractual basis of transnational operations and is particularly relevant to ASEAN countries such as Indonesia, Malaysia, Thailand, and the Philippines.

Government assistance and even direct involvement are crucial in establishing a firm's market significance in host ASEAN countries. Singapore prides itself in providing positive government assistance through various ministries to prospective foreign investors. Such direct government assistance is not common in those ASEAN countries characterized by red tape and bureaucracy. One way of building up extrafirm relationships in these host countries is to coopt influential politicians in local subsidiaries or to activate political connections available to the parent HK-TNC (see HKElectronics, Table 3). For example, the son of HKElectronics's founder and chair has good connections with one of the sons of the Malaysian prime minister. They worked previously for Salomon Brothers, an international security company, for many years, and since then a strong friendship and personal trust have developed. When HK-Electronics wanted to expand into the ASEAN region to produce cordless and cellular telephones mostly on an original equipment manufacturer (OEM) basis, they were looking for a piece of land and a good place to set up an electronics plant. HKElectronics finally decided to set up in Malaysia because it was thought that the prime minister's son could help overcome the hurdles in application approval and site selection.

The Malaysian prime minister's son, together with a reputable local property developer, subsequently took up 30 percent equity of the Malaysian plant and became its first chair. He is also currently on the board of directors in Hong Kong. Although these Malaysian partners are not involved in HKElectronics's day-to-day operations, they do give advice on what should or should not be done in Malaysia. During the start-up phase, they helped select the location of the manufacturing plant in a suburb of Kuala Lumpur. This assistance is potentially very important because it not only affects the smooth operation of the factory in terms of transportation and labor supply, but also greatly reduces production costs by locating outside the city area of Kuala Lumpur. The prime minister's son also obtained approval for the project and pioneer status[6] from the Malaysian Industrial Development Authority (MIDA), which again helped lower the costs and increase the profitability of HKElectronics's Malaysian operation. His political power was demonstrated by the presence of the Minister for Trade and Industry at the opening ceremony for the Malaysian plant.

A number of other "high-powered" HKTNCs have coopted senior host country civil servants in order to circumvent hostile host country regulations and investment climate. These "political patrons" often play a relatively insignificant role in terms of operational management and control. But they help at the start-up stage to secure critical licenses and approvals. Beyond that, these "political patrons" usually become "sleeping part-

[6] A foreign firm will enjoy tax holidays and investment incentives if it is conferred pioneer status, which refers to manufacturing firms in relatively new or underdeveloped industries promoted by the host country.

Table 3

A Profile of Selected Hong Kong Transnational Corporations

Company Name	Company History	Main Businesses	Sales Value	Profit	Total Assets	Number of Staff	Countries of Operation
HKArch	Established in 1979, it has developed into a niche market firm solely owned by its founding chair, Mr. Lee, an architect, and his partners in Hong Kong.	Architectural, engineering, and development consultancy firm	NA	NA	NA	240 for Group	China. Singapore, Thailand, and United Kingdom
HKCarpet	Established in 1956 by a Shanghainese entrepreneur, Mr. Chiu, who is extensively connected to leading Jewish and Chinese businesspeople in Hong Kong. Now owned by the Chiu family and another Jewish family and managed by the chair's son.	Manufacture, import, export, and sale of carpets, trading of interior furnishings, investment and property holding	HK$258 million (1992)	HK$38 million (1992)	HK$867 million (1991)	200 (HK) and 8,000 (Group)	ASEAN, United States, France, United Kingdom, New Zealand, and China
HKComputer	Founded in 1983 by three parties—Mr. John (Australian), Mr. Chan (a Thai Chinese and director of Bangkok Bank), and IBM—it is owned 25% by IBM and 75% by Mr. John and Mr. Chan. Mr. John is chair and managing director of the holding company in Hong Kong.	Consulting and business solutions in computer software, specializing mainly in IBM systems	US$35 million (1993)	NA	US$3 million (1993)	120 (HK) and 250 (Group)	Indonesia. Malaysia Singapore, Thailand, China, and Macau
HKElectronics	Established in 1971, it is one of the leading electronics manufacturers in Hong Kong, specializing in OEM manufacturing, e.g., for AT&T cordless phones. The founding chair is still CEO of the holding company.	Development, manufacturing, and distribution of telecommunications products; some medical products and vehicle monitoring systems	HK$976 million (1993)	HK$90 million (1993)	HK$445 million (1993)	3,000 (Group)	Malaysia and China

Sources: Author's survey and various company reports.

ners," relinquishing management control to the parent HKTNC. On the other hand, these "political patrons" are often personal friends or associates of key personnel in those HKTNCs, and in exchange for their political connections they often benefit from personal investment opportunities.

HKTNCs tend to enter into extrafirm network relations in order to take advantage of "rent-seekers" in host ASEAN countries. These extrafirm relationships are often embedded in complex networks of personal and business relationships (e.g., the case of HKElectronics). It would be erroneous to view extrafirm network relationships in isolation from other forms of network relationships. The following section addresses interfirm networks which are embedded in other dimensions of network relationships.

The Social Organization of Transnational Operations: Interfirm Networks

HKTNCs enter into interfirm network relationships mainly through personal contacts in business networks and close friends in "family" networks. These interfirm network relationships are predominantly cooperative and mutually beneficial, albeit shaped by unequal power relations over time (Yeung 1997b). Redding (1991, 41) points out that "the large structures of cooperation needed for an economy to flourish and to manage economic exchanges are reliant on a peculiarly effective mechanism for interfirm linkages." But how are these cooperative relationships manifested in the ASEAN operations of HKTNCs? To what extent do they show characteristics of Chinese business relationships? This section outlines two main mechanisms through which HKTNCs enter into cooperative relationships with host country partners and/or business associates: through complementary partnership and reliance on local capital, and by developing interpersonal relationships.

In the first mechanism, an interfirm network can emanate from active participation on the part of local partners in both parent HKTNCs and ASEAN subsidiaries. These network relations are somewhat more formal than personal friendship. Most likely, the original HKTNC is not family-controlled and thus all shareholders contribute to successful operations abroad through their individual business contacts and connections. The level of coordination would likely be higher than in a family-controlled business. When operations are created at the level of business connections—that is, at the interfirm level—not only trust and reputation are important, but business interests and operational coordination are also cornerstones of successful transnational operations.

An example is the HKComputer Group, a computer software services company (see Table 3). HKComputer specializes in IBM systems, and IBM has a 25 percent stake in the company. In this case, individual country general managers do not own any significant equity shares of the company. But they are fully entrusted to set up individual country operations, in collaboration with their local partners, representing a kind of loose intrafirm network relationship. All country general managers have been working for the company for a long time and all have worked previously in Hong Kong for more than five years, except the general manager in Thailand. This form of intrafirm coordination resembles Hedlund's (1986, 1993) concept of "heterarchy," in which individual country managers are given substantial autonomy in decision making and running of the operation.

In compliance with the Board of Investment regulation in Thailand, the Thai operation is owned 49 percent by the HKComputer Group and 51 percent by Mr. Chan, a majority shareholder, and his two Thai brothers. One of the two brothers became the majority local shareholder because he wanted to experience growing a software house. This arrangement of a "virtual joint venture" serves not only to overcome regulatory constraints posed by the host country, but also to strengthen business networks within the company. The Thai operation looks like a joint venture on paper, but the Thai regulatory authority knows little about the complex ways in which shareholding is worked out among key owners of the company in Hong Kong. Such an arrangement also favors future business relationships between the three brothers and the Hong Kong group. From IBM's perspective, the Thai operation is a safe bet because of the strong partnership between the Hong Kong–based company and the Thai brothers. In fact, the role of Mr. Chan is instrumental in the start-up phase, but over time he becomes mainly advisory. According to Mr. John, group chair and managing director, the Chan brothers' connections are not used in the running of the business:

> Believe it or not, not at all, because you find with very influential businessmen, they often won't use their connections unless you prove you are successful. They're not going to recommend us and find that we are too small. They'll leave us alone to grow. It [the connection] didn't help to start with; it's starting to help now though. (interviewed in Hong Kong, 24 March 1994)

Mr. John's comments are echoed by Mr. Louis, general manager of HKComputer Thailand:

> We all agree that because they [the Chan brothers] are such a significant family in Bangkok, it's not wise for them to be involved directly in recommending or trying to push a decision in one way or the other. They are also quite a long way removed from the decision-making process because they are just so senior and they are too high profile. They would compromise themselves if they were to say "Buy this because I say so." Then it will reflect badly on their name if either the solution didn't work or whatever. They restrict themselves to advice when I ask them. They are happy to let me run their business and it seems to work well. (interviewed in Bangkok, 7 June 1994)

The Chan brothers seemingly do not want to involve themselves too much in the "personalization" of the business, representing a relatively more formal approach to interfirm networks.

A more interesting case is HKComputer's Malaysian operation, because it originated from a close and symbiotic relationship among company shareholders as well as customers—a good example of interfirm networks. The former managing director of IBM Hong Kong/China, Mr. Low, introduced Mr. John (HKComputer) to Mr. Ismail, the managing director of MalayComputer, which had been IBM's sole distributor in Malaysia. HKComputer and MalayComputer subsequently went into a joint venture that was favored by IBM because HKComputer could establish itself faster and have a better chance with a recognized local business partner (MalayComputer). Both companies in Malaysia also have complementary business platforms. Mr. John commented:

> Legally you can be in Malaysia and own 100 percent of the operations as an overseas business, which we did for several years. It didn't seem to work; we were legal, but the business didn't seem to work. We evaluated along with IBM and decided to invite [MalayComputer] to take 30 percent, which used to be the old rule in Malaysia. And since they took the 30 percent, the business boomed. You don't have to do it, but people felt more comfortable when they saw that we have a local business partner. (interviewed in Hong Kong, 24 March 1994)

Mr. Andy, the general manager of HKComputer Malaysia, confirmed this:

> It gave us a level of credibility. If we just walk into the country as a subsidiary of a Hong Kong–based company, regardless of the fact that there is IBM ownership, it would have been hard to establish ourselves. But the fact that [MalayComputer] then entered into the partnership gave us credibility from the day we opened. (interviewed in Kuala Lumpur, 11 August 1994)

In brief, the HKComputer case is embedded in trust relationships and cooperative spirit among suppliers and customers—that is, between IBM, HKComputer, and local partners. It is an interfirm business relationship that evolved over time and developed eventually into a strategic partnership. Transnational operations are thus the outcome of these interfirm cooperative and trust relationships.

The second mechanism through which HKTNCs enter into cooperative relationships with host country partners and business associates is through interpersonal relationships, in particular among Chinese family-controlled HKTNCs. These Chinese family-based HKTNCs tend to operate in ASEAN countries through a combination of intricate interpersonal relationships and interfirm cooperation. Personal friendship is perhaps one of the most peculiar modes of business rationality in the Chinese business system. Among family business operations in Hong Kong, reliance on personal trust and social circles is common. Founders and owners of many family-controlled HKTNCs would first exploit their personal networks when going transnational. This tendency works in two directions: the owner will either approach personal friends or business associates whom the owner trusts and has known for a long period of time (anywhere from 10 to 40 years), or personal friends or business associates will approach the owner and ask for joint venture collaborations in a particular host country. In the latter situation, the level of trust and business goodwill of the initiating party will be assessed, and normally personal friends are preferred over "new comers," or complete strangers introduced by business associates or friends. Because personal friends may originate from the host country (e.g., the prime minister's son in the case of HKElectronics), transnational operations are often motivated by personal relationships rather than by purely abstract economic cost and benefit factors. The actual process of establishing oneself in the host country also takes place through personal networks of friends and associates.

Consider the case of HKCarpet (see Table 3), in which personal relationships are involved in the processes of setting up overseas operations. While Hong Kong remains the marketing, R&D, and coordinating center of HKCarpet's world carpet manufacturing activities, all manufacturing facilities have relocated to other countries. Except in Singapore, all ASEAN operations are established through joint ventures with reputable local businesspeople or families. Ethnic and business connections are the single most important mechanism through which HKCarpet set up its ASEAN operations. The present managing director, the son of the founding chair, described the process:

> Typically, the connections are made through friends, referrals. That's very important . . . I think a partner can make or break a venture. In all these countries, but not all of them, at the time when we went into most of these countries, the structure, the system, the laws were all not very clear. So you relied on your local partner to tell you everything about the market, take care of the venture and hopefully not cheat you. So that's why the local partner is very important . . . Well, for us, we were not in the carpet business at the very beginning. You just find someone, through other connections who has other ventures with other people, who has proven to be reliable. All you need them for is their financial support and their business contacts in their countries to set up a new plant . . . Typically, either we would know them or we have close associates who would know them. In any case, the key is to make sure that whoever we pick has a reputation in that local community. Trust and reputation are most important. (interviewed in Hong Kong, 12 April 1994)

My interviews with several directors of HKCarpet's ASEAN operations offer additional insights into the complex ethnic relationships between the company's chair, a Shanghainese, and his ASEAN associates. Some 20 years ago, the Philippine operation was set up by a Shanghainese, Mr. Tso, who went to Hong Kong in the late 1940s and had been a long-standing friend of the chair, Mr. Chiu. Through connections with a reputable Jewish family in Hong Kong that owned large hotel chains and public utility companies, Mr. Chiu was able to find a local partner who was also the partner of a five-star hotel owned by the Jewish family in the Philippines. The managing director in Hong Kong said that "we both relied on the same person because he was reliable. You know then that someone already has experience, that he's a good person" (interviewed in Hong Kong, 12 April 1994).

The personal relationship between the Chiu family and the Jewish family is based on historical contingencies during the Japanese occupation of Hong Kong in the Second World War. The Jewish family was subsequently sent to a Japanese camp in Shanghai, where they met and received substantial help from Mr. Chiu and his family. In the postwar period the Jewish family returned to Hong Kong to resume their hotel and infrastructural business. The same period also saw the emigration of the Chiu family to Hong Kong and the establishment of HKCarpet. Their prior personal relationships in Shanghai, embedded in mutual obligation and sentiments, developed into significant interfirm business relationships in Hong Kong. In fact, the Jewish family is a significant shareholder of the HKCarpet Group, but it is not involved in the management and control of HKCarpet. Meanwhile, there are significant economic complementarities between HKCarpet and the hotel business of the Jewish family. Its five-star hotels need high-quality carpets that HKCarpet is well positioned to supply. Congenial interpersonal relations between the two families are complemented by interfirm business relationships. In theoretical terms, economic action is socially and culturally embedded within specific time-space contexts.

In 1972, the Indonesian operation of HKCarpet was established by an Indonesian family that had been long-associated friends of the chair and of Mr. Tso, the founder of the Philippine plant. Mr. Tso went to Indonesia to assist during the process of establishing the Indonesian plant. He is also a member of the Indonesian and Thai boards. In both countries, partnership with local families is embedded in the personal relationships between Mr. Chiu and his close circle of friends and business associates.

HKCarpet's wholly owned operation in Singapore was set up in 1968 by another Shanghainese, Mr. Chen, who emigrated from Shanghai to Hong Kong and then from Hong Kong to Singapore in the early 1960s. Mr. Chen was a good friend of Mr. Chiu in Hong Kong. The Singapore operation was established to fulfill the wish of Mr. Chen to emigrate to Singapore and the marketing strategies of Mr. Chiu's HKCarpet Group, increasingly focused on the Southeast Asian regional market. The director of the Singapore operation commented:

> The first partner of [Mr. Chiu] in Singapore was a gentleman . . . from Hong Kong; he's a Shanghainese. But he settled in Singapore. So I think that's how he started. [Mr. Chiu] knew people already in the country. So he said: "Come, why don't we do business together?" . . . It's quite different [from Western firms]. It's very important because there is already this element of trust. If you want to set up an operation in a foreign country, it helps if you have a friend staying in the foreign country, knowing what the pitfalls are, rather than going to an independent firm and saying: "Can you do me a market survey of what it would be like for me to set up a factory in such and such place?" But if it's from your old personal friends and contacts, I think the trust is there and the information will be more reliable. (interviewed in Singapore, 15 July 1994)

Intrafirm Networks: Coordination and Control in Transnational Operations

Intrafirm networks in TNCs are governed by coordination and control. There is a continuum of control in decision making and power relations, varying from centralization at one end to decentralization at the other. Any point along such a continuum is dependent upon the relationship between the subsidiaries and the headquarters. If their *guanxi*, or relationship, is weak, it is likely that centralization will follow. For example, a professional employee may be recruited locally to set up a subsidiary. If the headquarters has relatively little experience of or confidence in this local manager through a prior relationship, it is unlikely that he or she will be socialized into the corporate "family." Rather, the headquarters will exercise greater control through inspection, auditing, and reporting mechanisms. On the other hand, if the local manager is trusted for any of various reasons—such as a prior working experience in the headquarters, as in the case of HKComputer, or personal contacts or close friends, as in the case of HKCarpet—it is likely that he or she will be included in the "family." The subsequent intrafirm network between the headquarters and local subsidiaries tends to be closely knit, although decision making may be largely decentralized. Over time, relations between headquarters and subsidiaries may be strengthened or may deteriorate, depending on contingent circumstances such as business performance; the local manager may develop a successful relationship with the headquarters over time, or the local manager may damage the relationship by performing badly. The point is that intrafirm networks, although enduring like any other networks, are dynamic over time and flexible over space.

Survey data reveal interesting patterns of intrafirm coordination and control among HKTNCs. Both headquarters and ASEAN subsidiaries tend to agree that there is a high degree of integration and coordination among them. They differ, however, in their perception of the extent of control. While almost half of the headquarters report controlling their ASEAN subsidiaries, few subsidiaries agree on such a view. Rather, respondents from subsidiaries think that they are more autonomous. This reflects a perception gap between key executives presiding over the headquarters and local managers in charge of ASEAN subsidiaries. The headquarters of HKTNCs perceive their firm control of ASEAN operations because of their direct investment and shareholding arrangements. Often, they send expatriate staff from Hong Kong to manage their ASEAN operations. By putting their own people from the "corporate family" in place, top executives in Hong Kong feel their presence in ASEAN subsidiaries. From the ASEAN subsidiary's point of view, local managers tend to think that they are less controlled by Hong Kong per se because either they are sent by Hong Kong (empowered to make decisions, as in the case of HKComputer) or they have good personal relationships with the Hong Kong headquarters (e.g., HKCarpet).

What then are the mechanisms of intrafirm control? Three major control mechanisms are employed by HKTNCs: periodic reporting (23 percent), periodic inspection (19 percent), and cost control (18 percent) (see Table 4). Responses from ASEAN subsidiaries largely conform to the headquarters' view. Data on channels of marketing and sourcing demonstrate that ASEAN subsidiaries are relatively autonomous. Both marketing and sourcing activities for ASEAN subsidiaries are conducted at the local level, as demonstrated in Table 5. There is thus little intrafirm control by the headquarters through marketing, sourcing, and technology.

The primary mode of intrafirm control exercised by parent HKTNCs is finance. Survey data show that an overwhelming majority of ASEAN subsidiaries are financed by headquarters in Hong Kong. A crude generalization is that many HKTNCs still behave like traditional Chinese businesses, in which finance is tightly controlled by the head of the family (see Limlingan 1986; McVey 1992; Chan and Chiang 1994). Despite a significant number of joint ventures in this study (see Yeung 1995b, forthcoming), financial control still lies with HKTNCs, not with their local partners. This finding further reinforces the idea that "money matters" in the Chinese business system.

HKArch provides an interesting case study of intrafirm control and coordination within HKTNCs. In a period of 15 years, HKArch (see Table 3) developed into one

Table 4

Mechanisms of Control of ASEAN Operations by Hong Kong Transnational Corporations

Mechanisms of Control	Headquarters		Subsidiaries	
	Frequency[a]	%	Frequency	%
Production and marketing planning from headquarters	20	8.6	9	6.1
Inventory and quality control by headquarters	9	3.9	1	0.7
Cost control by headquarters	42	18.0	34	23.1
Provision of broad guidelines by corporate groups	21	9.0	11	7.5
Centralized decision making from headquarters	18	7.7	6	4.1
Employment of expatriate managers and/or executives	12	5.2	4	2.7
Periodic inspection by top management executives from headquarters	43	18.5	6	4.1
Periodic report of local managers to headquarters	54	23.2	40	27.2
Corporate sourcing of information from headquarters	2	0.9	0	0.0
Mutual exchange of information	9	3.9	19	12.9
Annual meetings	3	1.3	17	11.6
Total	233	100.0	147	100.0

Source: Author's survey.
[a] Total number of cases exceeds sample size ($N = 111$) because up to three responses were allowed in the survey.

of the largest and most established architectural TNCs based in Hong Kong. It is also one of the earliest architectural firms to work on projects in China, since 1979. The Singapore office of HKArch was established in 1991 as a response to a specific project request in Singapore. The founding chair and sole proprietor of the company in Hong Kong, Mr. Lee, has close connections with a director in one of the largest property development firms in Hong Kong (HKProperty), whose sister company is a leading property developer in Singapore (SINLand). Because of this connection, HKArch has done many projects for HKProperty in Hong Kong. The director of HKProperty asked Mr. Lee to set up an office in Singapore to serve SINLand in Singapore and related projects in China. Mr. Lee recapitulated:

> Some of our customers asked us to go over; we set up overseas operations because we don't want all our activities in Hong Kong and China alone. Even when we ignore political factors, economic risk is still substantial if we don't diversify . . . We have had this idea of overseas operation for a long time, for seven to eight years; but four years ago, we had a chance to realize it. We had some clients in Hong Kong who originated from Singapore. When we had casual chats, they asked us whether we were interested in operating in Singapore as well. So this is how we went. They gave the project to us. (interviewed in Hong Kong, 8 March 1994)

Although the contact was made, the main difficulty was how to set up an office in Singapore, because HKArch did not have any existing operations in Singapore and Mr. Lee was not granted an architect's license in Singapore. Subsequently, he sent a Singaporean, Mr. Tan, who used to work in their Hong Kong office, to set up the Singapore office (note the similarities with the case of HKComputer). Through two years of working experience with the parent company in Hong Kong,

Table 5

Channels of Marketing and Sourcing among Hong Kong Transnational Corporations in the ASEAN Region

	Headquarters		Subsidiaries	
Channels	Frequency	%	Frequency	%
Marketing				
Through central marketing department in the headquarters	5	4.5	12	19.0
Through local marketing department in subsidiaries and affiliates	77	69.4	51	81.0
Through subcontracting independent marketing services in Hong Kong	1	0.9	0	0.0
Through subcontracting independent marketing services in ASEAN	11	9.9	0	0.0
No such marketing activities	17	15.3	0	0.0
Sourcing				
Through central corporate sourcing from the headquarters	10	9.0	14	22.2
Through local production and supply department in subsidiaries and affiliates	49	44.1	36	57.1
Through subcontracting independent suppliers in Hong Kong	1	0.9	0	0.0
Through subcontracting independent suppliers in ASEAN	8	7.2	0	0.0
No such sourcing activities	43	38.7	13	20.6
Total	111	100.0	63	100.0

Source: Author's survey.

Mr. Tan, now the director of the Singapore office, developed a strong personal trust relationship with the directors in Hong Kong. He reasoned:

> Yes, definitely a trust has to be formulated before anybody goes into business together, whether in the same place or different places. I think a big proportion of the operation is based on trust. Yes, it's true. Well, I did not do anything behind [Mr. Lee's] back which I think I could. I could set up another company and all the jobs would run to that company. [He] would never know about it. I've never done . . . Yes, I think the partner in Hong Kong has to know this person who will take charge. At the same time, the associate company has to know the principal company will actually look after his interest financially as well as give a certain amount of support. (interviewed in Singapore, 18 July 1994)

The trust and confidence of the Hong Kong head office in Mr. Tan is substantial. Clearly, the Hong Kong office has ruled out the possibility of relying upon other executives recruited locally in Singapore because prior trust relationships serve the company best. Trust relationships therefore tend to narrow the choice of intrafirm personnel transfer and to justify preferential reliance upon specific personnel in the transnationalization processes. Trust elements also form the "noncontractual basis of contracts," in Durkheim's terminology (cited in Holton 1992, 189). A strong bond within the corporate "family," for example, exists between Mr. Tan and his chair, Mr. Lee. Mr. Tan explained how such a personal bond enables a closer intrafirm relationship and defies the use of elaborate contractual arrangements in the Singapore operation:

> There is always this nagging feeling of suspicion that will still be there. You know, in Hong Kong our operation is very cautious. Unless you really know the person very well, then otherwise the partnership will form on a different basis. Like, for example, there may be a lot of legal writings

in the lawyer's office and more frequent contact . . . It [the Singapore operation] is some kind of contractual basis, but not so explicit. It's kind of loose, based partially on understanding and partially on written agreements. But the written agreement is still quite loose, subject to a certain amount of interpretation . . . They [directors in Hong Kong] have to feel that this person whom they entrust in running the operation is trustworthy and loyal and has the drive to make the company work. (Interviewed in Singapore, 18 July 1994)

This case study shows that intrafirm personal trust relationships are coupled with interfirm project relations to prompt transnational ventures in professional business services. It is typical that a trusted member is sent over to set up in the host country (see Table 2). Mr. Tan was also given complete autonomy in running the Singapore office. Although the initial capital investment came from HKArch, the Singapore office is now responsible for its own profit and loss. It established itself quickly as a profit center independent of HKArch. This does not mean, however, that HKArch has lost control of its Singapore office. Instead, both operations are closely integrated and coordinated through personal trust relationships between Mr. Lee and Mr. Tan. In order to serve projects secured through interfirm connections with HKProperty and SINLand, HKArch must coordinate its intrafirm networks well enough to serve their friends and clients. Meanwhile, the Singapore office is governed by a complicated budget because there are two separate companies, one owned by Mr. Tan and the other controlled by Mr. Lee in Hong Kong.

Conclusion

In this paper I have shown that Chinese business networks, embedded in host country regulatory regimes and the social organization of "institutional thickness," explain the processes and mechanisms of transnational operations by HKTNCs in the ASEAN region. This finding contradicts the prevailing negative perception of the ability of Chinese family firms to expand into overseas markets. The paper also justifies Wong's (1988, 151) argument that "there is nothing inherent in the Chinese family structure to limit the size of an enterprise." In this study, there is nothing in the Chinese business structure that inhibits the growth of transnational operations (e.g., HKCarpet). Rather, Chinese business structures, particularly their emphasis on networks of personal and business relationships, tend to facilitate transnational operations by providing the "institutional thickness" and social organization of capital. Such support is carried mainly through three network relationships: (1) extrafirm relations with "rent-seekers" within the state bureaucracy through political connections; (2) interfirm relations with business partners through intricate shareholding arrangements and with personal friends through joint ventures; (3) intrafirm control and coordination through the process of "family-ization," that is, socialization of key personnel into the "corporate family."

This conclusion has critical implications for research into international business and production. "Network thinking" serves as an alternative approach to the understanding of transnational operations of firms from all countries. What we must bear in mind is the emerging concept of business organizations as networks of ongoing personal and social relationships embedded in specific geographic contexts. Perhaps it is time to divert *some* attention away from the narrow focus on transaction costs and economic advantages as the sole explanatory variables in international business. We need to examine the embedded power relations and social construction of transnational activities. The TNC is as much a social entity as an economic institution. More important, we need to realize the crucial difference between time-space contingent factors and causal mechanisms in our explanations. This paper shows that network relations are important causal mechanisms of transnational operations.

What are the implications of this study for business development in the ASEAN region? ASEAN countries, in particular Indonesia, Malaysia, Singapore, and Thailand, are likely to continue to benefit from traditional family links and cultural ties with Hong Kong in "overseas circuits of Chinese capital." In view of Hong Kong's reversion to China in 1997, more Hong Kong firms will go transnational; many of them will consider their preexisting network relations in activating such transnational operations (Lam 1990). FDI flows from Hong Kong to the ASEAN region will continue to grow, and HKTNCs will also flourish in many ASEAN countries vis-à-vis their global competitors from developed countries (Yeung 1994d, 1995b, forthcoming). Ethnicity and connections become two critical dimensions to the success of transnational operations in many ASEAN countries. In this regard, HKTNCs will gain the upper hand over many foreign competitors. Increasing attention has recently been paid to this interesting topic of ethnicity and connections in national development and business success (e.g., Jesudason 1989; Kotkin 1992). Future studies of the geography of international business in the Asia-Pacific region are promising. But such an optimism can only be realized if we take a much more open-minded and interdisciplinary approach to such an important topic.

References

Agmon, T., and Kindleberger, C. P., eds. 1977. *Multinationals from small countries*. Cambridge: MIT Press.

Amin, A., and Thrift, N. 1994. Living in the global. In *Globalization, institutions, and regional development in Europe*, ed. A. Amin and N. Thrift, 1–22. Oxford: Oxford University Press.

Bartlett, C. A., and Ghoshal, S. 1989. *Managing across borders: The transnational solution*. London: Century Business.

Biggart, N. W., and Hamilton, G. G. 1992. On the limits of a firm-based theory to explain business networks: The Western bias of neoclassical economics. In *Networks and organizations: Structure, form, and action*, ed. N. Nohria and R. G. Eccles, 471–90. Boston: Harvard Business School Press.

Brown, R. 1990. Chinese business and banking in South-East Asia since 1870. In *Banks as multinationals*, ed. G. Jones, 173–90. London: Routledge.

Buckley, P. J., and Casson, M. 1976. *The future of the multinational enterprise*. London: Macmillan.

———. 1985. *The economic theory of the multinational enterprise: Selected papers*. London: Macmillan.

———. 1991. *The future of the multinational enterprise*. 2d ed. London: Macmillan.

Camagni, R. P., ed. 1991. *Innovation networks: Spatial perspectives*. London: Belhaven Press.

Capital Investment Coordinating Board. 1993. *Investment deregulation 1993*. Jakarta: BKPM.

Carnoy, M.; Castells, M.; Cohen, S. S.; and Cardoso, F. H. 1993. *The new global economy in the information age: Reflections on our changing world*. University Park: Pennsylvania State University Press.

Chan, W. K. K. 1992. Chinese business networking and the Pacific Rim: The family firm's roles, past and present. *Journal of American East Asian Relations* 1:171–90.

Chan, K. B., and Chiang, S-N C. 1994. *Stepping out: The making of Chinese entrepreneurs*. Singapore: Simon and Schuster.

Chen, X-M. 1994. The new spatial division of labor and commodity chains in the Greater South China Economic Region. In *Commodity chains and global capitalism*, ed. G. Gereffi and M. Korzeniewicz, 165–86. Westport, Conn.: Praeger.

Clegg, S. R. 1990. *Modern organization: Organization studies in the postmodern world*. London: Sage.

Cooke, P. N., and Morgan, K. 1993. The network paradigm: New departures in corporate and regional development. *Environment and Planning D: Society and Space* 11:543–64.

Cowling, K., and Sugden, R. 1987. Market exchange and the concept of a transnational corporation: Analysing the nature of the firm. *British Review of Economic Issues* 9:57–68.

de Smidt, M., and Wever, E., eds. 1990. *The corporate firm in a changing world economy: Case studies in the geography of enterprise*. London: Routledge.

Dicken, P. 1992. *Global shift: The internation-*

alization of economic activity. 2d ed. London: Paul Chapman.

______. 1994. Global-local tensions: Firms and states in the global space-economy. *Economic Geography* 70:101–28.

Dicken, P.; Forsgren, M.; and Malmberg, A. 1994. The local embeddedness of transnational corporations. In *Globalization, institutions, and regional development in Europe*, ed. A. Amin and N. Thrift, 23–45. Oxford: Oxford University Press.

Dicken, P., and Kirkpatrick, C. 1991. Services-led development in ASEAN: Transnational regional headquarters in Singapore. *Pacific Review* 4:174–84.

Dicken, P., and Thrift, N. 1992. The organization of production and the production of organization: Why business enterprises matter in the study of geographical industrialization. *Transactions of the Institute of British Geographers* 17:279–91.

Dixon, C. 1991. *South East Asia in the world-economy*. Cambridge: Cambridge University Press.

Dunning, J. H. 1981. *International production and the multinational enterprise*. London: Allen and Unwin.

______. 1988. *Explaining international production*. London: Unwin Hyman.

______. 1993. *The globalization of business*. London: Routledge.

Granovetter, M. 1985. Economic action and social structure: The problem of embeddedness. *American Journal of Sociology* 91:481–510.

______. 1991. The social construction of economic institutions. In *Socio-economics: Toward a new synthesis*, ed. A. Etzioni and P. R. Lawrence, 75–81. Armonk, N.Y.: M.E. Sharpe.

Granovetter, M., and Swedberg, R., eds. 1992. *The sociology of economic life*. Boulder, Colo.: Westview Press.

Håkansson, H., and Johanson, J. 1993. The network as a governance structure: Interfirm cooperation beyond markets and hierarchies. In *The embedded firm: The socio-economics of industrial networks*, ed. G. Grabher, 35–51. London: Routledge.

Hamilton, G. G., ed. 1991. *Business networks and economic development in East and South East Asia*. Hong Kong: Centre of Asian Studies, University of Hong Kong.

Hamilton, G. G., and Biggart, N. E. 1988. Market, culture, and authority: A comparative analysis of management and organization in the Far East. *American Journal of Sociology* 94:52–94.

Harvey, D. 1982. *The limits to capital*. Oxford: Basil Blackwell.

Hedlund, G. 1986. The hypermodern MNC—a heterarchy? *Human Resource Management* 25:9–35.

______. 1993. Assumptions of hierarchy and heterarchy, with applications to the management of the multinational corporation. In *Organization theory and the multinational corporation*, ed. S. Ghoshal and D. E. Westney, 211–36. New York: St. Martin's Press.

Ho, Y. P. 1992. *Trade, industrial restructuring and development in Hong Kong*. London: Macmillan.

Ho, K.C. 1993. Industrial restructuring and the dynamics of city-state adjustments. *Environment and Planning A* 25:47–62.

______. 1994. Industrial restructuring, the Singapore city-state, and the regional division of labour. *Environment and Planning A* 26:33–51.

Holton, R. J. 1992. *Economy and society*. London: Routledge.

Hymer, S. 1972. The internationalization of capital. *Journal of Economic Issues* 6:91–111.

Ietto-Gillies, G. 1992. *International production: Trends, theories, effects*. Cambridge: Polity Press.

Jesudason, J. V. 1989. *Ethnicity and the economy: The state, Chinese business, and multinationals in Malaysia*. Singapore: Oxford University Press.

Kao, J. 1993. The worldwide web of Chinese business. *Harvard Business Review* (March–April):24–36.

Khan, K. M., ed. 1986. *Multinationals of the South: New actors in the international economy*. London: Frances Pinter.

Kotkin, J. 1992. *Tribes: How race, religion and identity determine success in the new global economy*. New York: Random House.

Kumar, K., and McLeod, M. G., eds. 1981. *Multinationals from developing countries*. Lexington, Mass.: D.C. Heath.

Lall, S. 1983. *The new multinationals: The spread of Third World enterprises*. Chichester: Wiley.

Lam, D. K. K. 1990. Hongkong Chinese emigration and investment patterns in response to the 1997 problem. *Journal of Northeast Asian Studies* 9:60–79.

Lau, S. K., and Kuan, H. C. 1988. *The ethos of*

the Hong Kong Chinese. Hong Kong: Chinese University Press.

Leung, C. K. 1993. Personal contacts, subcontracting linkages, and development in the Hong Kong—Zhujiang Delta region. *Annals of the Association of American Geographers* 83:272–302.

Limlingan, V. S. 1986. *The overseas Chinese in ASEAN: Business strategies and management practices*. Manila: Vita Development Corporation.

Low, L.; Ramstetter, E. D.; and Yeung, H. W. C. forthcoming. Accounting for outward direct investment from Hong Kong and Singapore: Who controls what? In *Geography and ownership as bases for economic accounting*, ed. R. E. Baldwin and J. D. Richardson. Chicago: University of Chicago Press.

Low, L.; Toh, M. H.; Soon, T. W.; Tan, K. Y.; and Hughes, H. 1993. *Challenge and response: Thirty years of the Economic Development Board*. Singapore: Times Academic Press.

Mackie, J. A. C. 1988. Changing economic roles and ethnic identities of the Southeast Chinese: A comparison of Indonesia and Thailand. In *Changing identities of the Southeast Asian Chinese since World War II*, ed. J. W. Cushman and G. W. Wang, 217–60. Hong Kong: Hong Kong University Press.

McVey, R., ed. 1992. *Southeast Asian capitalists*. Ithaca, N.Y.: Cornell University Southeast Asia Program.

Mirza, H. 1986. *Multinationals and the growth of the Singapore economy*. London: Croom Helm.

Mitchell, K. 1995. Flexible circulation in the Pacific Rim: Capitalism in cultural context. *Economic Geography* 71:364–82.

Moran, R. T., and Riesenberger, J. R. 1994. *The global challenge: Building the new worldwide enterprise*. London: McGraw-Hill.

Ohmae, K. 1985. *Triad power: The coming shape of global competition*. New York: Free Press.

———. 1990. *The borderless world: Power and strategy in the interlinked economy*. London: Collins.

Olds, K. 1995. World property markets and the global culture economy: Tales from Vancouver and Shanghai via Mammon's Temple. Paper presented at the Institute of British Geographers' Annual Conference, University of Northumbria at Newcastle, 3–6 January.

Palloix, C. 1975. The internationalisation of capital and the circuit of social capital. In *International firms and modern imperialism: Selected readings*, ed. H. Radice, 63–88. Harmondsworth: Penguin.

———. 1977. The self-expansion of capital on a world scale. *Review of Radical Political Economics* 9:1–28.

Perry, M. 1992. Promoting corporate control in Singapore. *Regional Studies* 26:289–94.

———. 1995. New corporate structures, regional offices and Singapore's new economic directions. *Singapore Journal of Tropical Geography* 16:181–96.

Pitelis, C. N., and Sugden, R., eds. 1991. *The nature of the transnational firm*. London: Routledge.

Porter, M., ed. 1986. *Competition in global industries*. Boston: Harvard Business School Press.

Redding, S. G. 1990. *The spirit of Chinese capitalism*. Berlin: De Gruyter.

———. 1991. Weak organizations and strong linkages: Managerials ideology and Chinese family business networks. In *Business networks and economic development in East and South East Asia*, ed. G. G. Hamilton, 30–47. Hong Kong: Centre of Asian Studies, University of Hong Kong.

———. 1994. Competitive advantage in the context of Hong Kong. *Journal of Far Eastern Business* 1:71–89.

Régnier, P. 1993. Spreading Singapore's wings worldwide: A review of traditional and new investment strategies. *Pacific Review* 6:305–12.

Robison, R. 1986. *Indonesia: The rise of capital*. Sydney: Allen and Unwin.

Smart, J., and Smart, A. 1991. Personal relations and divergent economies: A case study of Hong Kong investment in South China. *International Journal of Urban and Regional Research* 15:216–33.

Suehiro, A. 1985. *Capital accumulation and industrial development in Thailand*. Bangkok: Chulalongkorn University Social Research Institute.

———. 1992. Capitalist development in postwar Thailand: Commercial bankers, industrial elites, and agribusiness groups. In *Southeast Asian capitalists*, ed. R. McVey, 35–63. Ithaca, N.Y.: Cornell University Southeast Asia Program.

Suryadinata, L. 1988. Chinese economic elites in Indonesia: A preliminary study. In

Changing identities of the Southeast Asian Chinese since World War II, ed. J. W. Cushman and G. W. Wang, 261–88. Hong Kong: Hong Kong University Press.

Taylor, M., and Ward, M. 1994. Industrial transformation since 1970: The context and the means. In *Transformation with industrialization in Peninsular Malaysia*, ed. H. Brookfield, 95–121. Kuala Lumpur: Oxford University Press.

Thrift, N., and Olds, K. 1996. Refiguring the economic in economic geography. *Progress in Human Geography* 20:311–37.

Tolentino, P. E. E. 1993. *Technological innovation and Third World multinationals*. London: Routledge.

Wade, R. 1990. *Governing the market: Economic theory and the role of government in East Asian industrialization*. Princeton: Princeton University Press.

Weidenbaum, M., and Hughes, S. 1996. *The bamboo network: How expatriate Chinese entrepreneurs are creating a new economic superpower in Asia*. New York: Free Press.

Wells, L. T., Jr. 1983. *Third World multinationals: The rise of foreign investment from developing countries*. Cambridge: MIT Press

Wells, L. T., Jr., and Wint, A. G. 1993. Marketing strategies to attract foreign investment. In *Multinationals in the global political economy*, ed. L. Edan and E. H. Potter, 168–86. New York: St. Martin's Press.

Whitley, R. 1992a. The social construction of organizations and markets: The comparative analysis of business recipes. In *Rethinking organization: New directions in organization theory and analysis*, ed. M. I. Reed and M. Hughes, 120–43. London: Sage.

———. 1992b. *Business systems in East Asia: Firms, markets and societies*. London: Sage.

Wong, S. L. 1985. The Chinese family firm: A model. *British Journal of Sociology* 36:58–72.

———. 1988. *Emigrant entrepreneurs: Shanghai industrialists in Hong Kong*. Hong Kong: Oxford University Press.

———. 1991. Chinese entrepreneurs and business trust. In *Business networks and economic development in East and South East Asia*, ed. G. G. Hamilton, 13–29. Hong Kong: Centre of Asian Studies, University of Hong Kong.

———. 1993. Business and politics in Hong Kong during the transition. In *Hong Kong in transition 1992*, 488–514. Hong Kong: One Country Two Systems Economic Research Institute.

Wu, Y. L. 1983. Chinese entrepreneurs in Southeast Asia. *American Economic Review* 73:112–17.

Yasuda, N. 1991. Malaysia's new economic policy and the Industrial Co-ordination Act. *Developing Economies* 29:330–49.

Yeung, H. W. C. 1993. Critical realism and the transnationalization of transnational corporations: Towards a re-conceptualization. Paper presented at the Annual Conference for Socialist Economists, University of Leeds, 9–11 July.

———. 1994a. Third World multinationals revisited: A research critique and future agenda. *Third World Quarterly* 15:297–317.

———. 1994b. Critical reviews of geographical perspectives on business organisations and the organisation of production: Towards a network approach. *Progress in Human Geography* 18:460–90.

———. 1994c. Hong Kong firms in the ASEAN region: Transnational corporations and foreign direct investment. *Environment and Planning A* 26:1931–56.

———. 1994d. Transnational corporations from Asian developing countries: Their characteristics and competitive edge. *Journal of Asian Business* 10:17–58.

———. 1995a. Qualitative personal interviews in international business research: Some lessons from a study of Hong Kong transnational corporations. *International Business Review* 4:313.

———. 1995b. The geography of Hong Kong transnational corporations in the ASEAN region. *Area* 27:318–34.

———. 1996a. Attracting foreign investment? The role of investment incentives in the ASEAN operations of transnational corporations. *Pacific Review* 9:505–29.

———. 1996b. Sectoral specialization and competitive advantage: Hong Kong investments in the ASEAN region. *ASEAN Economic Bulletin* 13:74–94.

———. 1996c. The historical geography of Hong Kong investments in the ASEAN region. *Singapore Journal of Tropical Geography* 17:66–82.

———. 1996d. Competing for transnational corporations? The regional operations of foreign firms in Hong Kong and Singapore. In *Business, trade and economic development in Pacific Asia*, ed. I. Cook, M. Doel, and R. Li. Aldershot: Avebury.

———. 1997a. The social-spatial constitution of business organisations: A geographical perspective. *Organization* 4, forthcoming.

———. 1997b. Cooperative strategies and Chinese business networks: A study of Hong Kong transnational corporations in the ASEAN region. In *Cooperative strategies: Asia-Pacific perspectives*, ed. P. W. Beamish and J. P. Killing. San Francisco: New Lexington Press, forthcoming.

———. forthcoming. *Transnational corporations and business networks: Hong Kong firms in the ASEAN region*. London: Routledge.

Yoshihara, K. 1988. *The rise of ersatz capitalism in South East Asia*. Singapore: Oxford University Press.

Part II
Impact of the Globalization of Business Firms from Emerging Economies

[7]

Third World Multinationals

A Growing Force in International Relations

KRISHNA KUMAR
East-West Center

This article examines the growth processes of multinational corporations based in Third World states. It is suggested that both ownership and location-specific factors explain the emergence of these firms. The main competitive strengths of these firms lie in their access to manufacturing technologies suitable to the conditions of the developing world: lower operating and overhead costs, familiarity with the business environment of Third World states, and their perceived less threatening nature. The article identifies their advantages and disadvantages to home and host states and indicates that these firms could become a significant factor in the international economic system.

One recent development in international economic relations has been the emergence of multinational corporations based in developing states. During the last decade, a significant number of business enterprises from the Third World have established or acquired foreign subsidiaries and joint ventures. Firms from countries such as Argentina, Brazil, Hong Kong, India, the Philippines, Singapore, South Korea, and Taiwan have taken the lead in this regard, along with firms from other developing states (Kumar and McLeod, 1981). Third World multinationals now operate in almost every major sector of the world economy, and all available indications are that their foreign investments will continue to grow in the future.

AUTHOR'S NOTE: I wish to acknowledge the assistance of Sandy McLeod and Sripada Raju in the preparation of this article. I have profited very much from the suggestions of the anonymous referees and the editors of *International Studies Quarterly*.

INTERNATIONAL STUDIES QUARTERLY, Vol. 26 No. 3, September 1982 397-424

This article examines the growth processes of these multinationals, especially those engaged in manufacturing, and explores their implications for economic relations at the national and international levels. First, the internationalization of Third World firms is discussed in the context of contemporary theory. More specifically, an attempt is made to compare their competitive advantages with those of the multinationals from industrialized countries. Then, a macro-level analysis examines the possible contribution of Third World multinationals to the development of host and home countries and the implications for the existing international system.

Some conceptual definition of Third World multinationals is needed to prevent unnecessary confusion. By Third World states, we mean all nonsocialist states of Africa, Asia, and Latin America which are not members of the OECD. While all these states display marked differences from each other, they nevertheless share a set of common structural properties that justifies their inclusion in a single conceptual category. Following the United Nations (1973: 25), we define a multinational firm as an enterprise that owns production and/or service facilities in one or more countries other than the one in which it is based. This definition is less restrictive than those generally used in the studies of American and European corporations. Thus, the expression "Third World multinational" refers to a firm that is located in one of the Third World states and that owns production and/or service facilities outside its national boundaries. Such enterprises can operate in extractive, agricultural, industrial, or service sectors.

Comprehensive information about the number of Third World multinationals, their overseas subsidiaries and joint ventures, and their total investments is not available for various reasons. First, the phenomenon is too recent, and most of the developing states have yet to take steps to keep adequate and reliable records of their foreign investments. Second, these firms have also used informal channels, such as kinship and ethnic networks, to make overseas investments. Often such investments are not reflected in official statistics. Third, the firms themselves are often reluctant to share vital information. Despite these obvious limitations, a partial picture of the nature, sectoral distribution, and magnitude of overseas investments made by Third World firms can be gleaned from the limited information provided by a few developing countries.

In Asia, Hong Kong, India, South Korea, and Taiwan have emerged as important foreign investors. Hong Kong firms were the first to internationalize their operations in the region. They now have subsidiaries in Indonesia, Malaysia, Singapore, Taiwan, and Thailand in a wide range of industries (Chen, 1981). While the earlier investments were made in garments, textiles, plastics, and rubber products, more recent investments involve chemicals, electronics, heavy machinery, and resource development projects. Hong Kong firms are also venturing into several Middle East, Latin American, and even European countries. It has also been reported that about 500 firms are now operating in the People's Republic of China (Chen, 1981).

The overseas investment made by South Korean firms now exceeds $248 million (Kumar and Kim, 1981). Nearly 59% of their overseas projects are in trading; manufacturing accounts for only 10% of foreign direct investment. Korean firms have also been active in construction, warehousing, transport, fisheries, lumber, and minerals (Kumar and Kim, 1981).

There has also been a slow but steady increase in the foreign operations of Taiwanese firms. By 1978, the Taiwanese government had approved 124 projects, of which 27 were later withdrawn (Kumar and Chi, 1981). While the early investors mainly went to Thailand, Malaysia, and Singapore, later ones have been showing a preference for Indonesia, the Philippines, and the United States. The preferred investment sectors for these firms are manufacturing, trading, and construction. The Philippines, Singapore, and Malaysia are also some of the countries in the Asian region whose firms have started exploring the possibilities of establishing overseas operations.

The total volume of overseas investment made by Indian firms is smaller than that of Hong Kong firms. Data released by the Indian government indicate that by the end of July 1979, Indian firms had established 110 foreign joint ventures, while another 87 were in the implementation stage (FICCI, 1980: 80-95). Most of these ventures are in the manufacturing sector, particularly steel, heavy machinery, plastics and polyethylene products, automotive assembly, chemicals, pharmaceuticals, sugar, cement, and textiles.

In Latin America, Argentine firms had started overseas investment as early as the middle of the present century. Their annual foreign investments totaled around $4 million during 1973-1978, with the exception of 1978 when they totaled $8 million dollars (White, 1981). About half of these investments are in manufacturing, including machine tools, food, and automobiles. Brazil is yet another Latin American country that has been making significant foreign investments. Most of its investments have gone to neighboring countries. It is estimated that in "nine Latin American countries, Brazilian foreign investment amounted to 60 million dollars in 1978" (White, 1981). One notable feature of the Brazilian case has been the foreign expansion of its state-controlled enterprises, such as Petrobras and Bracho de Brazil. Brazilian firms have also started manufacturing operations in several African countries. The rapid growth of the Mexican and Venezuelan economies encourages their firms to move toward multinationalization.

Some general patterns of Third World foreign investment will be briefly noted here. First, most investment has gone to developing countries. Although some Third World firms have also invested in industrialized countries, these investments are predominantly in the service sector or are designed to protect or boost their exports to these countries. Second, at least in the case of Asia, states that have followed the course of export-oriented industrialization have been the major source of foreign investments. Their export orientation has enabled these states to acquire effective international networks and infrastructures that are readily used by entrepreneurs. Third, firms have usually gone to the neighboring states with familiar social and economic systems. And finally, Third World firms have invested in those manufacturing sectors that have standardized operating technologies.

Theories of Multinational Corporations

Before we discuss the internationalization of Third World firms, it is necessary to mention briefly the current theories on the growth of multinationals in economic analyses. The contemporary view starts with the premise that overseas production involves additional costs to a firm arising from legal, linguistic, cultural, and political differences between the home and host countries and the increased cost of transport and communication. Thus, the firm venturing abroad must have some competitive advantage over the national firms in the host country, which could benefit more from direct investment than from exports, licensing, or portfolio investments. Much effort, both at theoretical and empirical levels, has gone into the identification of these competitive assets. Broadly speaking, they can be classified into two categories: ownership-specific and location-specific. The former is related to the structure, possessions, or capabilities of a firm, while the latter concerns the conditions and the system properties of the host country that attract foreign investors. They can also be described as "push" and "pull" factors.

The possession of technology undoubtedly remains the most important ownership-specific advantage of multinational corporations. Technology, in this context, means knowledge and skills regarding products and production processes. Multinationals often enjoy oligopolistic positions in the goods and services produced by them (Kindleberger, 1970). Even when manufacturing simple standardized products, they are able to differentiate them from others by minor physical variations or subjective distinctions created by advertising and marketing skills (Hood and Young, 1979: 48). Còmpanies like Coca-Cola, Kellogg, or Nestle have been able to create worldwide operations partly on the basis of "product differentiation." More importantly, overseas expansion appears to be closely related to the ownership of advanced, operating technologies. It is the ownership of production technologies that leads host countries to attract foreign direct investment. Empirical evidence (Parker, 1974) shows that multinational firms operate largely in research-intensive industries and that research-intensive firms tend to internationalize. American- and European-based multinational firms have been able to acquire or develop product and process technologies through research and development, and also through experience: so-called "learning by doing."

Marketing and managerial skills can also contribute to the internationalization of a firm. Caves (1971) has argued that product differentiation, under which he includes both technological intensity and marketing skills, is the main reason for foreign direct investment. Firms move to foreign countries on the strength of their specific management skills or to exploit managerial potential that remains underutilized at home.

The other two important competitive assets of multinational corporations are their easy access to capital resources and their control of raw materials. Multinationals tend to be large firms with vast assets and good reputations. Therefore, they are able to raise the necessary capital resources both in home and host countries on better terms than single-nation enterprises. Besides, they are in a better position to tap international monetary markets. Control of raw materials can also put a firm in an advantageous position over the firms in host countries. Control can arise out of a firm's advantages in production, processing, transportation, and sales of raw material.

Several other sources of a firm's competitive strength are large size, ability to diversify risks, and favorable government policies. Whatever the specific sources of a firm's competitive strength might be that enable it to cross national boundaries, the fact remains that multinationals are oligopolies that operate under imperfect market conditions. Their monopolistic or oligopolistic advantages are similar to those of leading firms in domestic markets (Kindleberger, 1970).

Ownership-specific advantages are necessary, though not sufficient, conditions for overseas direct investment. They cannot explain why a firm seeks to exploit its competitive assets through direct investments and not by licensing or exports. Nor do they account for the location of foreign subsidiaries and plants. For this purpose, researchers have introduced many "location-specific" variables that include, for example, trade barriers, low labor costs, availability of raw materials, market size and growth, and host government policies. For example, high tariffs, import quotas, product standards imposed by importing countries, and high transportation costs always provide firms with incentives to invest in such countries. The prevailing low level of wages also attracts foreign investors. In the past, American and European firms have established their overseas sourcing operations in many Southeast Asian countries to take advantage of low labor costs. The availability of large and/or growing markets in host countries also attracts many firms. Perceived political and economic stability always remains an important consideration for foreign investors. It should be noted, however, that the location-specific factors are largely the same for national and foreign firms. The complex interaction between these factors and ownership-specific advantages explains the overseas expansion behavior of firms.

The above-mentioned explanatory variables have been identified, developed, and empirically tested by researchers on the basis of their studies of the multinationals based in the United States and Western Europe. The few available studies of Third World multinationals suggest that many of the variables have very limited value in predicting their internationalization.

Ownership-Specific Variables

Third World multinationals do not manufacture new products, but rather sell those products for which technology has been standardized (Wells, 1978, 1979, 1980, 1981; Lecraw, 1977, 1981; Nambudiri et al., 1981; Kumar and Kim, 1981; Kumar and Chi, 1981). In fact, these firms do not have the advantage of familiar brand names and consequent consumer loyalties, although there are exceptions. For example, Tatung, which is based in Taiwan, has acquired good visibility and its brand name is becoming well known in several Asian countries. As a rule, Third World firms do not have access to the latest manufacturing technologies and, in fact, do not operate in technology-intensive industries (Wells,

1978, 1979, 1980; Lecraw, 1977, 1981; Kumar and Kim, 1981; Kumar, 1981; Chen, 1981; White, 1981). The marketing and management skills of these multinationals are not strong either, at least as compared with multinationals from industrialized countries. Differences based on firms' national origins can, however, be delineated. Indian firms, which have long been accustomed to operating in a protected environment, have been weak in marketing (Raju and Prahalad, 1980), while Korean firms, with their strong ties with general trading companies, show good marketing skills (Kumar and Kim, 1981).

Access to capital resources, which has been an important asset of American and European firms, is also an irrelevant consideration in a developing state's firms. Most of the developing states suffer from a persistent shortage of foreign exchange, creating problems for their firms. A recent study of Indian joint ventures in Malaysia, for example, reveals that their cash shortage threatens their very survival (Raju and Prahalad, 1980). India is perhaps the worst case, but the foreign exchange situation of firms from South Korea, Taiwan, or the Philippines is not always entirely satisfactory. Since most firms from developing states do not have privileged access to raw materials, only now have some of them begun to invest in resource development projects (Diaz-Alejandro, 1977; White, 1981; Kumar, 1981; Kumar and Chi, 1981). Thus we find that the ownership-specific variables usually stressed as assets of multinational corporations can hardly explain the overseas expansion of Third World firms.

What, then, are the ownership-specific advantages? These seem to lie in the suitability of their operating technologies, lower overhead and expatriate payments, familiarity with the conditions and problems of developing countries, and their less threatening position. Perhaps the most important strength of Third World firms lies in their less advanced, though not necessarily less efficient, manufacturing technologies, which function reasonably well in other developing countries (Wells, 1977, 1978; Lecraw, 1977; Agrawal, 1981).

Most, if not all Third World multinationals acquire manufacturing technologies from industrialized states under various kinds of arrangements, from collaboration to outright purchases. However, after they are received, these technologies are adapted with respect to the distinctive characteristics of developing economies. Wells (1977, 1978, 1979) has suggested that these adaptations are generally of four kinds. First, firms introduce innovations enabling them to use machinery on a smaller scale without sacrificing efficiency. Since markets in developing states are usually limited, large plants are not economically viable. Second, firms make modifications that permit multipurpose use of the same machinery and equipment. This is again necessitated by the small size of the market and the general scarcity of capital resources. Third, adaptations are sometimes made to enable maximum use of available raw materials. Fourth, operating technologies are made more labor-intensive by substituting manual labor for machines wherever possible, without raising costs. These kinds of adaptations make the technologies at the disposal of Third World firms seem quite attractive to developing host states.

In this connection, Lall (1978) has identified three stages of what he calls "technical learning" by firms. The first stage is "learning within a given technology." Employees contribute to the greater efficiency of the imported technology by minor changes and adaptations dictated by the exigencies of the situation. However, as a firm's workers and engineers grapple with the machinery and equipment (often without the assistance of foreign experts), they gain valuable insights and experience that enable them to manufacture mechanical components which improve the equipment's performance. This stage is labeled by Lall as "learning the embodied technology." Here he distinguishes between learning by imitation and learning by design; the former implies that the firm simply reproduces the machinery's components, while the latter suggests that it is able to modify them. The third and final stage comes, according to Lall, when the firm is able to reproduce the entire technology that it imported earlier in a functional plant. The firms from several developing countries already seem to have reached the third stage of technical learning in many industries.

It is indeed misleading to suggest that all Third World firms compete in international markets on the basis of adapted technologies. Quite a few have been able to develop altogether new products and production processes.[1] For example, countries like Brazil, Korea, Mexico, and even Taiwan have been able to make significant progress in the heavy machinery and tools industry (World Bank, 1979). India has accomplished breakthroughs in agriculture and in both small and large industrial sectors, which its firms have begun to utilize in their overseas expansion drive.

The second and perhaps equally important asset of some Third World multinationals is their lower overhead and expatriate costs, which are passed on to consumers (Lecraw, 1977, 1981; Nambudiri et al., 1981; Kumar and Kim, 1981). The firms from industrialized states usually make huge investments in factory sites, offices, housing, and other amenities for their managerial and technical staff. Moreover, the cost of expatriate staff is usually high for the developed states' multinationals. These firms not only provide remuneration according to the standards of their home countries but also give various kinds of allowances to their expatriate employees to induce them to leave familiar surroundings for some exotic, unknown environment. These firms (Kumar, 1979) also provide slightly higher wages for their local employees compared to the local firms. All these items are reflected in the cost of production. Two studies have indicated that the case is different with Third World firms (Wells, 1978; Lecraw, 1981). They make a minimum investment in posh buildings, imposing offices, and attractive work facilities, and provide moderate wages to their expatriate staff. For example, it is estimated that it costs a U.S. firm about 100,000 U.S. dollars to keep a middle-level executive in Malaysia. The corresponding figure for an Indian employee hired by an Indian firm is about $20,000. Even when Third World firms keep more ex-

1. It is instructive to look at UNIDO (United Nations Industrial Development Organization) Newsletter, which publishes reports about the new product and process technologies developed by Third World states.

patriate staff than their counterparts from the industrialized states, their overall expenditures are lower.

The lower costs of keeping expatriate staff also explain the growth of international consultancy firms based in developing states. Since their manpower costs are modest, these firms are able to compete effectively with those from industrialized states, especially when the technologies involved are not very sophisticated. Thus, consultancy services offered by Indian firms in Middle East states have grown impressively (FICCI, 1980). Many firms from the United States, Europe, and Japan have also been subcontracting to Indian, South Korean, and Filipino firms to take advantage of the latter's lower staffing costs.

Besides the above two assets, Third World multinationals also have an advantage in their familiarity with developing states. Most Third World states share a similar work orientation and ethic, bureaucratic inefficiency at government levels, interpersonal business networks, inadequate economic infrastructures, and a cultural environment that is not always conducive to development. That these firms can operate within such an environment is often an important asset in a host country. They can easily establish rapport with their employees, local businessmen, and governmental authorities.[2] They are also well prepared to deal with the system of patronage and gifts that American multinationals now find exasperating.

Third World firms are perceived as less threatening, politically and economically, by many host countries (White, 1981; Panglaykim, 1979). Politically, their home countries are not as powerful as the industrialized states and are not in a position to intervene effectively on their behalf. Economically, Third World firms possess neither the capital nor the managerial and technological resources of their counterparts from the developed world. Nevertheless, this widely recognized "handicap" of Third World multinationals is perhaps their strength at a time when

2. This point was mentioned to the author by the executives of the Chinese and Indian firms. They stated that they could more effectively operate in the Third World countries than their counterparts from the industrialized countries.

there is widespread concern about world domination by powerful multinationals based in a few industrialized nations. Studies of South Korean and Taiwanese firms have underscored this point. In several cases, their executives stressed that the modest international role of their countries often helped, rather than hindered, their entry into many Asian and African countries.[3] However, a caveat is necessary. When a large, powerful developing country seems to dominate a region, it is quite likely that its small neighbors might prefer investments from distant industrialized countries rather than from their immediate, powerful neighbor.

The above ownership-specific variables explain the assets and capabilities of Third World firms that enable them to enter and then survive in host countries. But they only tell part of the story and do not explain the preference of Third World firms for direct investment over export, or their decisions about the location of their overseas plants. These can be better explained by location-specific factors that motivate a firm to invest in a particular set of countries.

Location-Specific Variables

The barriers imposed on imports in host countries are undoubtedly the most important reasons for foreign direct investment by Third World firms. There is widespread concern about protectionism, both in developing and industrialized states. As their entrepreneurial and technological capabilities grow, developing states typically introduce policies that favor import substitution as a means of encouraging domestic economic activity and improving their balance of payments situation. Industrialized states have started to curb the import of certain types of manufactured goods from developing states that threaten their indigenous production. Third World firms have often responded by establishing subsidiaries and joint ventures in the

3. These conclusions are based on personal interviews.

countries to which they have been exporting, thus protecting their markets. In many cases they can avail themselves of various investment incentives provided by the host government. For example, when textiles exports were threatened, Hong Kong firms reacted by establishing their manufacturing operations in Indonesia (Chen, 1981). Similarly, Taiwanese firms started establishing their subsidiaries in the United States when they noticed growing concern about the import of electrical and electronic products from Asia (Kumar and Chi, 1981). Hence, part of the overseas manufacturing investment by Korean firms has been defensive in nature (Kumar and Kim, 1981).

Firms from Hong Kong that were exporting garments to industrialized states have followed an altogether different strategy. As quotas were introduced on the import of textile products from Hong Kong, these firms established their subsidiaries and joint ventures in developing states whose quotas had not been fully subscribed. Thus, they invested in countries like Thailand, Mauritius, and Sri Lanka (Chen, 1981). In such cases, textiles or semifinished garments are supplied by the firms to their subsidiaries or joint ventures, which do the final processing. The products are then labeled as manufactured in the host country and exported to industrialized states. Only a very limited portion of the output is allowed to be sold in the domestic markets of the host states. Several Korean firms have also formed overseas ventures to bypass quota restrictions (Kumar and Kim, 1981).

Some firms, especially those whose home countries are involved in export-oriented industrialization, initiated their overseas investments for promotional reasons. In such cases, the main objective is not to manufacture abroad but to support the export efforts of home countries. Most of the South Korean direct investment in the United States, for example, has been designed to encourage the country's exports by providing needed support facilities (Jo, 1981; Kumar and Kim, 1981). Several Third World firms have also established subsidiaries and joint ventures in a member-state of one of the regional grouping (Sela, Lafta, the Andean Group, Caricom, Ceao, Asean, and others) so that they can have easy access to the markets of other countries in the group

(White, 1981; Chen, 1981). For example, Hong Kong and Taiwanese firms have been setting up their joint ventures in member-states of Asean for gaining a foothold in the growing Asean market.

The prospects for the sale of manufacturing technologies also attract Third World firms. As mentioned earlier, firms in developing countries are fast accumulating production technologies in a wide range of industries. The firms naturally like to profit from them in the international market. Wherever possible, they sell or lease them through licenses, technical collaborative arrangements, or supply of turnkey projects. However, it is not always possible for these firms to market them in other countries. Firms often lack exclusivity of patented technologies, nor do they have the advantage of familiar brand names. Moreover, an international market has not developed for these technologies since little information about the potential buyers and sellers is available (Wells, 1981). Under these circumstances, it makes sense for these firms to establish joint ventures or subsidiaries for selling/leasing their operating technologies. Usually they partly subscribe their equity shares in the foreign subsidiaries or joint ventures in the form of machines and equipment. Thus, a firm can sell its operating technologies, for which there is a limited international market, and it also gains equity shares in foreign ventures that should turn over a continuous profit.

In India's case, the export of machinery and equipment is one of the principal reasons for overseas expansion (Indian Investment Centre, 1979). Indian entrepreneurs started tapping foreign markets for their joint ventures when the country's capital goods industry was facing a recession. The majority of Indian firms have subscribed their equity shares in the form of machines and equipment (IIFT, 1977: 2). In Hong Kong, South Korea, and Taiwan, a substantial number of firms have sold their operating technologies to their joint ventures (Chen, 1981; Kumar and Kim, 1981; Kumar and Chi, 1981). The situation is similar for many Latin American firms.

Third World firms even sell their old machinery and equipment to other countries in the above fashion. In such cases, firms go to a country where the old operating technologies are still economically viable and politically acceptable. Hong Kong firms have been known for repainting their old machines and selling them at profit to their overseas partners (Wells, 1978). There have been similar complaints about two Indian firms, although the country's regulations prohibit the use of old machinery in foreign joint ventures. In Taiwan, a firm sold its own manufacturing plant to its subsidiary in a South American country (Kumar and Chi, 1981).

Some Third World firms have tried to take advantage of lower production costs in other developing states. Wages have significantly increased in the more industrialized developing states, such as Hong Kong, South Korea, and Singapore (Asian Finance, 1979). Therefore, their labor-intensive products are not always competitive in world markets. Increasing labor costs have caused some South Korean garment firms to seek new venues for manufacturing, and they have already established subsidiaries in many Asian states (Kumar and Kim, 1981). Medium-sized firms from Singapore that have been involved in labor-intensive operations have also been exploring new sites in Bangladesh, Indonesia, Malaysia, Sri Lanka, and Thailand. A recent study has reported that increasing rents and wages led a number of Hong Kong firms to search for overseas manufacturing bases (Chen, 1981), and a similar situation exists in Singapore.

Third World firms have also been attracted by the lure of raw materials. The rising prices of petroleum and the perceived scarcity of raw materials have made many firms acutely conscious of their vulnerability. Their concern is not only the price of raw materials and the cost of importing them, but also their continued availability. The present situation has especially affected the firms from those developing states that have made significant strides toward industrialization but are not rich in vital natural resources. Thus, Brazilian Petrobras and its subsidiaries have set up several ventures for oil exploration (White, 1981), while several Hong Kong firms are increasingly investing in Indonesia, Malaysia, and Thailand in the wood and wood products industry (Chen,

1981). South Korean and Taiwanese firms have recently entered into collaborative arrangements with several OPEC countries for oil exploration and refining (Kumar, 1981; Kumar and Chi, 1981). Several states have been actively encouraging their firms to make overseas investments in resource development projects. For example, South Korea and Taiwan give priority to those projects that invest in vital sources of raw materials, even providing incentives for such investments (Kumar and Kim, 1981; Kumar and Chi, 1981). Some countries are also using their state-controlled enterprises for this purpose. Taiwan Fertilizer Co., a state-controlled firm, has established a joint venture in Saudi Arabia for manufacturing chemical fertilizers. Under the terms of the agreement, part of the output will be imported to Taiwan. And as mentioned, state-controlled enterprises in Brazil have taken a lead in foreign oil exploration. As the general demand for raw materials grows, more and more Third World firms will come under pressure from their governments to establish overseas subsidiaries and joint ventures for gaining access to them.

Two other location-specific variables can be mentioned here. The first is the similarity between the cultural and economic systems of home and host countries. Firms have usually gone to neighboring countries whose social and cultural systems are familiar. While there is nothing new in this pattern, the Asian Third World firms are distinguished by their widespread use of ethnic and kinship networks. Firms from Hong Kong, Singapore, and Taiwan have successfully used the Chinese communities in neighboring states for establishing their joint ventures and subsidiaries. Indian entrepreneurs have been relatively less successful in making use of overseas Indian communities (IIFT, 1977).

A second attracting factor can be the political and economic stability of the host countries as compared to the home environment. Developing states often have a high degree of political upheaval and economic uncertainty. It is therefore understandable that when a state faces economic or political problems, its firms seek investments in countries that are perceived to be more stable (and safer). Argentine firms were reported to have increased their overseas investments during the last years of the Perón regime (White, 1981). Hong Kong firms have sought security in foreign countries as the present lease draws close to its expiration date of 1997. The situation has drastically improved with the recent political changes in China, which have given Hong Kong entrepreneurs a new confidence about their future. Uncertainty persists in Taiwan, however, and its firms have been known to expand their overseas investments through both formal and nonformal channels (Kumar and Chi, 1981).

We discussed earlier the ownership-specific and location-specific variables that explain the internationalization of a firm. The available data suggest that the ownership-specific advantages of Third World firms are usually quite different from those associated with the multinationals from North America and Western Europe. However, there is marked similarity between the two types of multinationals with regard to location-specific factors. We will now examine the possible contribution of Third World firms to the development of host and home countries.

Relevance to Development

Development is a multidimensional process: It implies more than the mere production of goods and services. It also involves laying the foundations for self-generating growth that can satisfy the growing needs and aspirations of the different segments of a society. Therefore, to assess the relative contribution of Third World firms, their overall impact on the economy, society, and polity in the host and home countries must be considered, in addition to their economic output.

Host nations. Some empirical evidence suggests that, as compared to multinationals from industrialized states, Third World firms are content with lower equity participation (Lecraw, 1977, 1981; Kumar and Kim, 1981; Kumar and Chi, 1981). This preference is not necessarily the result of any altruistic concern or benevolent empathy on their part, but is dictated by the exigencies of the situation. As noted earlier, the capital resources of these firms are limited, as are their technical and managerial capabilities. Thus, Third World firms often need partners in host countries who can contribute capital, other resources, and, whenever necessary, serve as brokers with local authorities. Multinationals from industrialized states have shown a marked preference in the past for total ownership or at least majority ownership, which has aroused suspicion in the minds of Third World elites about their economic independence. Some of them feel that foreign investment contributes to their economic dependence by passing the ownership of critical national productive resources into foreign hands. Thus, to the extent that Third World multinationals accept lower equity participation, they help lessen the degree of perceived political and economic dependence of host countries and at least partly fulfill the political aspirations of developing host countries in their search for greater ownership of their productive resources.

In addition, the operating technologies that are transferred by Third World multinationals are generally suited to the conditions of developing states. Some of them can be characterized as "appropriate technologies" inasmuch as they are labor-intensive and can efficiently use locally available input. This in itself can be regarded as a significant contribution by Third World multinationals. Moreover, the terms of technology transfer by Third World firms are more favorable to host countries as compared to those from industrialized states' firms. A study of Indian joint ventures indicated that there were no restrictive clauses in the agreements about technology, supply of spare parts, or experts (IIFT, 1977).

More importantly, the presence of Third World firms improves the bargaining strength of developing host states. That there are alternative sources that can supply needed technologies has "enabled host countries to secure better terms from the developed world." In a way, these ventures can be "said to represent a countervailing force without implying any idea of confrontation vis-à-vis developed countries" (Agrawal, 1975: 16).

On the other hand, Third World firms may bring disadvantages as well as advantages to their hosts. Some concern has been expressed that Third World firms are not likely to provide a continuous flow of upgraded technologies to their subsidiaries and joint ventures (Wells, 1977) because they lack the research and development facilities of multinationals from industrialized states. While there is some substance to this apprehension, we should not overstress it. Most of the large foreign enterprises from developing states have been making significant progress toward the acquisition of new technologies.[4] Moreover, they are likely to continue to procure certain kinds of technologies from industrialized states to survive in the market. Therefore, a good proportion of Third World firms are soon likely to be in a position to upgrade their technologies in overseas ventures.

Furthermore, there is a possibility that the process of employing nationals in management and technical positions might be slow in Third World multinational firms. Developing states insist that nationals of the host country should, as far as possible, occupy all technical and managerial positions, but most of these firms have yet to develop a sophisticated system for transferring management skills and rely heavily on the expatriate staff for maintaining control over their subsidiaries and joint ventures (Kumar and Kim, 1981; Lecraw, 1977). Thus, developing countries might be at a disadvantage in hosting Third World investments. This situation is likely to change in the future, however, as these firms accumulate overseas experience and as host countries begin to exert greater pressure on them.

Closely related to this issue is the growth of local entrepreneurship in developing host countries. Experience shows that local businessmen assume entrepreneurial roles in those industries that do not require sophisticated operating technologies or high technical and managerial skills in the early stages of development (Kumar, 1979: 73-89). They thus go to the industries that have mature technologies and effective demand in the country. Even in these areas, they need protection from foreign firms. Problems arise because considerable investment made by Third World firms is precisely in those areas in which local businessmen can

4. Our data show that most of the South Korean and Chinese firms, which had made overseas investments, were trying either to develop new technologies themselves or were seeking to acquire new machines and equipment from other sources.

assume entrepreneurial roles, given the necessary protection and assistance by their government. For example, these firms have been active in the textile, garment, shoemaking, utensil, sugar, soap, cement, and similar industries. Therefore, there is a real possibility that Third World investments in such industries might discourage the budding entrepreneurs who find themselves unable to compete with foreign firms.

Many of the general effects of Third World multinationals on the development process are likely to be similar to those of multinationals from industrialized nations. That a firm comes from a less developed country should not make much difference to its effects on the economy or the society. Thus, all the advantages and disadvantages associated with direct foreign investment generally accrue to developing host countries.

Home nations. One principal advantage desired by some home countries is increased foreign exchange (Jo, 1981: Kumar, 1981). This may sound paradoxical, since direct investment by definition implies the movement of capital from home to host countries. However, in reality the situation is far from simple. The experience of American and European firms indicates that their actual investments are often much lower than their book values suggest and that they are in a position to siphon off considerable amounts in the form of profits, fees, and prices for raw materials. In the case of developing states, several other considerations make it likely that the home countries get a reasonable foreign exchange return on their investments. First, the equity shares of these companies are either wholly or partly subscribed through the supply of machinery, equipment, and other services. Home governments generally encourage their entrepreneurs to subscribe their equity shares in kind rather than cash (Indian Investment Centre, 1979). It is reasonable to assume that without overseas direct investments, they would not have been able to sell their machinery and services. Second, as suggested earlier, some firms have established overseas subsidiaries or joint ventures only when they perceived a threat to their markets in the host country. Thus, foreign direct investment represents an attempt to protect exports as much as possible. Third, many firms from developing countries have invested in the Third World to export to industrialized states. Finally, as mentioned earlier, these firms have invested in industrialized states to build up an infrastructure that can facilitate the export of goods from home countries.

We do not know how far these expectations are realized in practice. The record is probably a mixed one. In some countries, notably India, the foreign exchange earnings have been meager (IIFT, 1977: 10-14).[5] In others, foreign earnings have been encouraging. The majority of South Korean firms that have established overseas manufacturing operations expect a 15% or higher rate of return on their investments which they hope to send back to Korea (Kumar and Kim, 1981). Taiwanese and Hong Kong firms have also been making reasonable profits (Kumar and Chi, 1981; Chen, 1981), although the percentages of these profits that are reinvested in host countries rather than returned home are not known.

We mentioned earlier that one objective of foreign investment is to gain access to natural resources. It is perhaps too early to evaluate their efforts, but at this point the future of such endeavors is not very clear. To what extent host nations will permit control over their natural resources by Third World firms remains questionable.

There are other benefits to the home country as well. The impetus that direct foreign investment can give to the economy of the home country cannot be totally ignored. In some cases, it helps to utilize idle industrial capacity. Indian efforts at foreign investment started in the wake of sagging domestic demand for capital goods (Raju, 1980). In other cases, a country can gain access to new technologies and skills (Jo, 1981). Some states can also reap some political benefits from their foreign investments. For example, Taiwanese national authorities and entrepreneurs see their foreign direct investment as one way of strengthening their political and economic ties with other countries. Several

5. This has been partly because Indian entrepreneurs have often reinvested their profits in host or Third World countries or have kept them abroad, beyond the watchful eye of the Indian government.

Korean firms claim that their investment led to the establishment of diplomatic relations or strengthening of ties between Korea and host countries (Kumar, 1981).

The main cost to the home country is the migration of its scarce capital, at least during the initial stages. This can be a serious consideration for developing states and explains the general lack of enthusiasm of many Third World countries for the multinationalization of their firms. The Indian government, for example, had been very reluctant in the past to permit overseas direct investment by Indian firms, as it feared that it would be a drain on the limited capital resources of the country. Overall, Third World direct foreign investment is by no means an unmixed blessing for home and host governments. Its developmental effects are bound to differ across countries and industries. This situation implies that each case of investment needs to be evaluated carefully by the governments concerned.

Implications for the International System

Over the last two decades, the economic relationship among developing states has been growing. Together with measures for increasing trade, monetary and fiscal cooperation, multinational marketing agencies, and schemes for complementary production, Third World multinations can promote horizontal cooperation among Third World nations. Several studies undertaken through UNCTAD/UNDP have underscored the critical role that they could play in this regard. For example, an investigation of the fertilizer industry identified 25 possible projects that could be established as joint ventures by developing states (Mukerjee, 1979). These carefully identified projects, if and when implemented, could give a tremendous boost to agricultural production and lessen the dependence of developing states on industrialized countries for their supply of fertilizers.

A second study that focused on the rubber industry has also suggested that joint ventures among natural rubber-producing countries, both at private and public sector levels, would pave the way for more efficient utilization of rubber resources and growth of rubber-related industries (Allen, 1979). Still another investigation also stressed the possible contribution of Third World multinationals to the paper industry (Glenshaw, 1979). In almost every sector of economy (extractive, agricultural, manufacturing, transport, and service), there remain unlimited opportunities for Third World multinationals.

However, it is erroneous to conclude that the growth of Third World multinationals will contribute to a major structural transformation of the world economic order. Their overall effects on the vertical world system are bound to remain minimal for some time to come. Three points can be made in this connection. First, while the volume of overseas investments made by Third World firms will undoubtedly grow, we should not expect phenomenal growth. The infrastructures, both in home and host countries, are hardly adequate to sustain a rapid expansion of Third World firms. In many cases, home countries do not have sufficient banking, transportation, or communication facilities to give the firms needed assistance. Host countries are also cautious, if not skeptical, about them. There is yet to be a cogent policy toward investments made by Third World firms in most host countries. The foreign exchange situation of most developing nations continues to be unsatisfactory and is likely to impede the process of multinationalization of their firms. Factors like these are likely to retard the growth of many Third World investments.

Second, direct investments made by developing states in other Third World states remain largely asymmetrical. The usual pattern has been that the more industrialized developing states invest in the less industrialized ones. Thus, developing host countries are naturally conscious that in the name of Third World cooperation, a new kind of dependency relationship might be created. It is not surprising that Indian firms have encountered innumerable problems in expanding to South Asian countries. Indian investment is less than welcome because her neighbors are concerned about the possible economic hegemony. Mexico is viewed as a giant by many of her neighbors, who voice fear about the country's growing foreign investments (Agmon and Kindleberger, 1977: ix). In any case, economic domination is not an exclusive trait of industrialized states. The growth of Third World multinationals does not necessarily imply that horizontal cooperation is being established among developing nations. Such problems may diminish as developing countries start making cross-investments.

Finally, Third World firms pose little threat at present to the preeminent position of the multinationals from industrialized countries. They are more likely to be dependent on the latter for operating technologies in many areas. Moreover, they operate in those fields in which technologies have already matured and that are not regarded as very attractive by the multinationals from the industrialized world.

The expansion of Third World multinationals could contribute to the emergence of an international middle class comprising those states that are the homes of these firms. There is a distinct possibility that a three-tiered world system might emerge in which the technologically sophisticated and economically most rewarding tasks will be performed by the multinationals from industrialized nations, while less sophisticated manufacturing and other labor-intensive operations are likely to be done by Third World multinationals. Still less technologically sophisticated industrial production might be carried out by national firms in developing states that might have various kinds of working relationships with the firms from the above two categories of states.

Agenda for Research

Many issues can be identified in the foregoing discussion. Only a few are identified here. These are the topics which in my view deserve top priority for formulating appropriate policies toward Third World multinationals:

(1) As indicated earlier, initial research suggests that manufacturing technologies transferred by Third World multinationals are generally labor-intensive, multipurpose, capable of

utilizing locally available raw materials, and can be used on a small scale. This hypothesis needs to be vigorously tested. The research investigations should focus on the characteristics of technologies transferred by these firms.

(2) It has also been suggested that the terms for technology transfer offered by Third World firms are usually more favorable to host countries than those gained by their counterparts from industrialized states. This can be attributed not to the generosity of these firms but to their weak bargaining position vis-à-vis host countries. Research is necessary to analyze the terms for technology transfer insisted on by them.

(3) It is claimed that Third World firms do not possess capabilities for continually upgrading their manufacturing technologies in the host countries. The immediate resolution of this claim is urgently needed, for if this is the case, then host countries ought to exercise extreme caution in negotiating long-term projects.

(4) We have mentioned that the operations of Third World firms could have some adverse effects on the growth of local entrepreneurship in developing host societies, since these firms are likely to operate in sectors where local entrepreneurs could assume leadership roles. This issue needs to be carefully investigated.

(5) The process of indigenization of managerial and technical staff is yet another issue that appears to be problematic. As mentioned earlier, the existing evidence, though by no means conclusive, indicates that these firms usually rely on expatriate staff. Thus we need to examine whether the process of indigenization in Third World firms is likely to be slow.

(6) The issue of the relationship between multinationals from developing and industrialized states also raises a number of questions that need to be answered on the basis of empirical data. To what extent do the former rely on the latter for the supply of manufacturing technologies, marketing networks, and even managerial expertise? What are the effects of such a reliance on the competitive strength of the former? Are the Third World firms

performing a junior role in the international economic system by undertaking those functions that the multinationals from industrialized states are not willing to undertake?

(7) Finally, researchers should examine the structure of economic cooperation being generated among developing countries as a result of the operations of Third World multinationals.

In conclusion, I suggest that comparative, cross-disciplinary research must examine the growth of Third World multinationals and their possible contribution to economic development and international cooperation. Several research enterprises are presently underway on this subject. The Harvard Business School is collecting micro-level data and has even established a data bank on Third World multinationals. Instituto para la Integracion de America Latina has done some work on Latin American firms, and a research project has been initiated at the East-West Center that focuses on the Asian and Pacific regions. The results of these endeavors will further illuminate the issues raised in this article.

Date of receipt of final manuscript: March 22, 1982.

REFERENCES

AGMON, T. and C. P. KINDLEBERGER [eds.] (1977) Multinationals from Small Countries. Cambridge, MA: MIT Press.

AGRAWAL, R. G. (1981) "Third World multinational corporations: Indian experience," pp. 115-132 in K. Kumar and M. McLeod, Multinationals from Developing Countries. Lexington, MA: D. C. Heath.

——— (1975) Joint Ventures Among Developing Asian Countries. Geneva: United Nations Conference on Trade and Development.

ALLEN, P. W. (1979) The Rubber Industry: Present Situation and Prospects for Further Development Through Trade Expansion and Economic Cooperation Among Developing Countries. New York: UNCTAD/UNDP.

Asian Finance (1979) Economic Survey. Hong Kong.

CAVES, R. E. (1971) "International corporations: the industrial economics of foreign investment." Economica 38: 1-27.

CHEN, E.K.Y. (1981) "Hong Kong multinationals in Asia: characteristics and objectives," pp. 79-100 in K. Kumar and M. McLeod, Multinationals from Developing Countries. Lexington, MA: D. C. Heath.

DIAZ-ALEJANDRO, C. (1977) "Foreign investment by Latin Americans," in T. Agmon and C. P. Kindleberger (eds.) Multinationals from Small Countries. Cambridge, MA: MIT Press.

DUNNING, J. (1979) "Explaining changing patterns of international production: in defence of the eclectic theory." Oxford Bull. of Economics and Statistics 41: 269-296.

FICCI (Federation of Indian Chambers of Commerce & Industry) (1980) "Workshop on Indian joint ventures and project exports." New Delhi, February.

GLENSHAW, P. (1979) The Paper Industry: Present Situation and Prospects for Further Development Through Trade Expansion and Economic Cooperation Among Developing Countries. New York: UNCTAD/UNDP.

HEENAN, D. A. and W. J. KEEGAN (1979) "The rise of Third World multinationals." Harvard Business Rev. (Jan.-Feb.): 101-109.

HOOD, N. and S. YOUNG (1979) The Economics of Multinational Enterprise. London: Longman.

IIC (Indian Investment Centre) (1979) Joint Ventures Abroad: Status and Guidelines. New Delhi.

IIFT (Indian Institute of Foreign Trade) (1977) India's Joint Ventures Abroad. New Delhi.

JO, S. H. (1981) "Overseas direct investment by South Korean firms: direction and pattern," in K. Kumar and M. McLeod (eds.) Multinationals from Developing Countries. Lexington, MA: D. C. Heath.

KINDLEBERGER, C. P. (1970) The International Corporation. Cambridge, MA: MIT Press.

KUMAR, K. (1981) "The Korean manufacturing multinationals." Honolulu: East-West Center (mimeo).

——— (1979) The Social and Cultural Impacts of Transnational Enterprises. Sydney: Research Project on Transnational Corporations, University of Sydney.

——— and K. Y. KIM (1981) "Multinational firms from the republic of Korea: a study of overseas investments in manufacturing sector." Honolulu: East-West Center (mimeo).

KUMAR, K. and M. McLEOD (1981) Multinationals from Developing Countries. Lexington, MA: D. C. Heath.

KUMAR, K. and C. SCHIVE (1981) "The Chinese multinationals." Honolulu: East-West Center.

LALL, S. (1979) "Developing countries as exporters of industrial technology," in H. Giersch (ed.) International Economic Development and Resource Transfer. Tübingen: J & B Mohr.

——— (1978) "Developing countries as exporters of technology: a preliminary analysis." Oxford: Oxford Institute of Economics and Statistics (mimeo).

LECRAW, D. J. (1981) "The internationalization of firms LDCs: evidence from the ASEAN region," in K. Kumar and M. McLeod (eds.) Multinationals from Developing Countries. Lexington, MA: D. C. Heath.

——— (1977) "Direct investment by firms from less developed countries." Oxford Economic Papers 29, 3: 442-457.

MAGEE, S. P. (1977) "Information and multinational corporations: an appropriability theory of direct investment," pp. 317-340 in J. N. Bhagwali (ed.) The New International Economic Order. Cambridge, MA: MIT Press.

MUKERJEE, S. K. (1979) The Fertilizer Industry: Present Situation and Prospects for Further Development Through Trade Expansion and Economic Cooperation Among Developing Countries. New York: UNCTAD/UNDP.

NAMBUDIRI, C.N.S., O. IYANDA, and D. M. AKINNUSI (1981) "Third World country firms in Nigeria," in K. Kumar and M. McLeod (eds.) Multinationals from Developing Countries. Lexington, MA: D. C. Heath.

PANGLAYKIM, J. (1979) "Multinational corporations in ASEAN/South Korea/Hong Kong: a descriptive picture." Presented at the East-West Culture Learning Institute's Seminar on Third World Multinational Corporations, Honolulu, September 12-18.

PARKER, J.E.S. (1974) The Economics of Innovation: The National and International Enterprise in Technological Change. London: Longman.

RAJU, M. K. (1980) Internationalisation of Indian Business. Bombay: Forum of Free Enterprise.

——— and C. K. PRAHALAD (1980) The Emerging Multinationals: Indian Enterprise in the ASEAN Region. Madras, India: M. K. Raju Consultants Private, Ltd.

RHEE, Y. W. and L. E. WESTPHAL (1978) "A note on exports of technology from the republics of China and Korea." The World Bank, November (mimeo).

United Nations Department of Economics and Social Welfare (1973) The Impact of Multinational Corporations on Development and on International Cooperation. New York: United Nations.

WELLS, L. T. (1981) "Foreign investors from the Third World," pp. 23-36 in K. Kumar and M. McLeod (eds.) Multinationals from Developing Countries. Lexington, MA: D. C. Heath.

——— (1980) "Multinationals from Latin American and Asian developing countries: how they differ." Harvard Business School (mimeo).

——— (1978) "Foreign investment from the Third World: the experience of Chinese firms from Hong Kong." Columbia J. of World Business (Spring): 39-49.

——— (1977) "The internationalization of firms from the developing countries," in T. Agmon and C. P. Kindleberger, multinationals from Small Countries. Cambridge, MA: MIT Press.

——— and V'E. WARREN (1979) "Developing country investors in Indonesia." Bull. of Indonesian Economic Studies (March): 70-84.

WHITE, E. (1981) "The international projection of Latin American firms," pp. 155-186 in K. Kumar and M. McLeod (eds.) Multinationals from Developing Countries. Lexington, MA: D. C. Heath.

World Bank (1979) "Exports of technology by newly industrialized countries: research proposal." Washington, DC: World Bank (mimeo).

[8]

DEVELOPMENT AND PEACE VOLUME 3, SPRING 1982

MULTINATIONAL JOINT VENTURE COMPANIES OF DEVELOPING COUNTRIES AS INSTRUMENTS OF ECONOMIC INTEGRATION FOR DEVELOPMENT

JEFFREY B. NUGENT

I. Introduction

The purpose of this paper is to draw upon the recent experience of various regions of the world, but especially of the Arab countries, with respect to regional economic integration to argue the relative merits of multinational joint venture companies of developing countries (MJVs) as effective instruments of regional economic and technical cooperation for development among developing countries (ECDC and TCDC).

Almost invariably economic analyses of the different instruments of ECDC and TCDC, such as free trade arrangements, customs unions and other forms of agreements among developing countries, have taken the feasibility of such schemes for granted, focusing statically on whether or not, once in existence and perpetuated, the schemes would generate now and forever net benefits for each individual participant in the scheme. They assume, therefore, that both the information about the indefinite future and the activities involved in obtaining, administering and enforcing agreements among countries are costless. As economists put it, they assume the information and transactions costs of such schemes to be zero.

It shall be argued in this paper that because these assumptions are extremely unrealistic, the existing economic analyses of ECDC and TCDC efforts have been highly misleading, diverting attention from the forms of ECDC and TCDC that are viable and efficient vehicles for attaining long-term economic development toward those that are simply not feasible and to the identification of the villains responsible for the failure of ECDC and TCDC.[1]

The organization of our presentation is as follows: The importance of transactions costs in international agreements, particularly among developing countries (DCs), is emphasized in Section II. Section III argues the advantages of MJVs relative to other instruments of regional economic integration particularly in terms of reduced transactions costs and greater and more active contributions to the long-term economic development goals of the countries involved. The paper is concluded with a restatement of the principal conclusions and some important reservations in Section IV.

II. The Importance of Transactions Costs in Initiating and Preserving International Agreements

The archives of all regional commissions and several of the specialized agencies of the United Nations are well-stocked with studies demonstrating the advantages of various specific schemes of regional economic cooperation and integration which

* I am very grateful to Samar Datta, Nabil Al-Khatib, Nadim Munla and Erfan Shafey for useful comments on an earlier draft.

have never come into existence. Considering that only the largest scale failures ever creep into print in journal articles or in the press, the record of achievement in ECDC and TCDC is no doubt far worse that is generally realized, and even that small part of the record which is known is dismal indeed.

The relatively few schemes that have actually come into being among DCs have done so only after years of off-and-on-again negotiations,[2] substantial subsidization of the negotiation process by international agencies and multinational enterprises, the offering of considerable financial inducements to successful negotiations by donor organizations,[3] and in no small part due to a variety of exceptionally favourable circumstances and good luck.[4]

In view of the size of the investments that would seem to have been made in the various kinds of *ex ante* studies, in international travel, in diplomacy, and in the establishment of regional institutions, it would seem important and appropriate to measure the extent to which the overall benefits relative to costs of such schemes would have been reduced had these elements of transactions and information costs been included in the evaluations of such schemes. Unfortunately, the necessary data to make such calculations are not generally available. The most important component of such costs would, no doubt, be the large number of man-years of time absorbed (a) in the numerous studies of all phases of such schemes and of the available alternatives to these schemes, (b) in all phases of the implementation process from preliminary discussions to final negotiation, and, (c) subsequent to the consummation of the agreement, in public relations, and in monitoring and enforcing the agreement.

Several reasons may be given for why these information and transactions costs are likely to be especially high in the case of DCs. First, given the skill requirements of all the afore-mentioned activities and the extreme shortage of skilled manpower in most DCs, the opportunity costs of the people need for these activities are likely to be extremely high. Second, since many if not most DCs, have only recently and after considerable struggle succeeded in gaining their political independence, they are likely to be extremely reluctant to undertake the sacrifices in autonomy or sovereignty that participation in most such schemes implies. Third, sensitivities of this sort are exacerbated and the possibilities of sticking by agreements made in the past are greatly reduced by the greater degree of political and economic instability that tends to characterize the DCs. Fourth, since transactions costs in making agreements between different countries are raised by country differences, the fact that both the level of price distortions and the structure of those distortions tend to vary more among DCs than among industrial countries makes for higher transactions costs of the traditional instruments of ECDC and TCDC in DCs than among industrial countries. Fifth, the economic structures of DCs are known to change over time to a much greater extent than those of developed countries[5] making it less likely that an agreement which is beneficial at one time will also be beneficial at another time.

In any case, evidence of the greater magnitude of transactions costs of economic cooperation among developing countries than among developed countries can be seen in the smaller proportions of schemes mentioned that come into fruition and of those created which are maintained. By the same token, however, because of the higher transactions costs among DCs their poorer record of achievement should not be held up as evidence that it is their fault or that all efforts are doomed to failure.

On the basis of the experience with various forms of economic cooperation in various parts of the world, several factors influencing the magnitude of the transactions of such schemes can be identified. (1) The fact that bilateral schemes, especially with respect to trade among DCs, are more numerous and more frequently renegotiated than multilateral ones provides evidence to suggest that transactions costs increase with the number of countries involved.[6] (2) The fact that bilateral schemes have more frequently given rise to multilateral schemes rather than *vice versa* suggests that small efforts are likely to generate greater linkages to large efforts (i.e., reduce future transactions costs) than large efforts to small ones[7]. (3) The more homogeneous the countries with respect to tax rates and other policies, the lower the transactions costs may be expected to be, hence, suggesting that ECDC and TCDC may be more successful among similar countries or small subregions than among dissimilar countries or between regions.[8] (4) In the long run, transactions costs are likely to be positively related to the degree of government involvement. (5) Also in the long run transactions costs are likely to be positively related to the amounts of structural change that participating countries are likely to undergo.[9] (6) The greater the extent to which ECDC and TCDC efforts internalize the benefits and costs ot their effects, the lower are the transactions costs.[10] (7) Information costs and transactions costs rise with the comprehensiveness, complexity and permanence of the scheme because more factors become involved and greater certainty with respect to future conditions becomes important. (8) Agreements which are not adhered to raise the transactions costs of future or additional agreements among participating countries.[11] (9) The transactions costs (and also the economic benefits) of ECDC and TCDC efforts are likely to increase with the degree of complementarity in the resource endowments of the countries involved.[12] (10) Transactions costs of ECDC and TCDC are negatively related to both the degree of resource utilization within participating countries, and their overall rates of economic growth.[13]

In the following section we shall use these principles or hypotheses to demonstrate the special advantages of multinational companies of developing countries as forms of ECDC and TCDC in which the transactions costs are minimized and other benefits maximized.

III. A New Strategy for Regional Economic and Technical Cooperation among Developing Countries Featuring MJVs

Because of the importance of transactions costs in ECDC and TCDC efforts and the resulting fragility of economic cooperation and integration efforts and processes that has been noted above both in DCs, in general, and among the Arab countries, in particular, it would seem important that the hypotheses advocated above be referred to and made use of in decisions about how to go about ECDC and TCDC.

One important implication is that it may be much more important to lay a proper foundation for long-run economic cooperation and integration than to create quick and ambitious steps toward regional cooperation and integration that are not likely to endure. For this reason but also because of hypotheses (2), (4) and (6) in contrast to the vast majority of both actual cooperative efforts and the prescriptions of academic and political leaders alike for additional efforts, which rely heavily on what may be called "top-down" approaches to economic integration and for which the political good-will supplied by high-level political leaders is an essental ingredient, we advocate a "bottom-up" approach in which multinational joint ventures among DCs (MJVs) play a pivotal and dynamic role in the achievement of long-run economic cooperation and integration. Indeed, one of the purposes of this "bottom-up" approach is to minimize dependence on political good-will.

Also, in contrast to most traditional forms of cooperation, which tend to be rather inflexible and hence insufficiently adaptable to changing circumstances, the experience with MJVs in various parts of the world but especially in the Arab world[14] suggests that they can be expanded or diminished, redirected or terminated to fit changing conditions. Moreover, despite their relatively recent origins, there is already a wide variety of types of MJVs to choose from. They can be private, public or mixed; they can include extraregional parties or exclude them; they can be holding companies or directly productive enterprises; they can be bilateral or multilateral. In almost all of them, participation is voluntary and countries or firms are generally allowed to divest themselves of all or at least some of their equity shares. They can be, and have been, set up in virtually any kind of activity, with mandates to operate in areas, and with objectives defined, either narrowly or broadly. The greater flexibility of MJVs provides them with considerably better chances not just for survival and growth but also for achieving efficiency and equity than other instruments of regional cooperation and integration.

Another advantage of MJVs is that they are relatively "active" in the sense that they do not simply set the rules of the game which may allow certain things to happen as with the more "passive" traditional instruments of cooperation and integration such as customs unions, but rather they "make things happen". Considering the relative scarcity of decision-making capability, and even more fundamentally the lack of ability to formulate, evaluate and especially implement projects in DCs, the fact that these functions can be designated as priority activities of MJVs by their managers makes their activism especially relevant and useful. MJVs, by making positive investment and production decisions, tend to create the opportunities for trade rather than *vice versa*. The advantage of the MJVs in this respect arises if and when (as seems likely) the pressures they exert for trade and other forms of cooperation among countries of the region are stronger and more durable than those exerted by trade arrangements for production and investment decisions.

Most importantly, MJVs are ideally suited for serving, and taking advantage of, resource complementarity. For example in the Arab world, they provide efficient vehicles for combining the surplus capital of oil-exporting countries with the surplus labour of capital-scare economies and, to some extent, also the human capital and know-how of some of the in-between countries. The fact that most MJVs among Arab countries are profit-oriented and motivated provides the necessary inducement for the capital-surplus countries of the region to invest in them. To the extent that MJVs succeed in joining surplus capital with surplus labour and human capital within the region, they also succeed in achieving an overall better utilization of all resources, which as noted above is itself a condition conducive to regional cooperation. Since MJVs in the Arab world are in general free to hire Arabs of all nationalities, their existence contributes significantly to the mobility of human capital within the region and internalizes in the Arab world the benefits of experience and on the job training.

The experience with MJVs among Arab countries suggests that even the most commercially-oriented MJVs among LDCs are likely to be politically acceptable even in the most socialist countries of the region. Because they are organized along modern corporate lines, with private management that can enjoy considerable independence from ownership, MJVs have the potential to serve as innovating agents in demonstrating how modern management operates and in inducing imitative behaviour on the part of other enterprises, private or public.

The holding-company character of many MJVs and the comparative advantage of

MJVs in being able to identify additional investment opportunities make it probable that MJVs will save and reinvest higher percentages of the incomes they generate than other types of productive enterprises. If so, MJVs can be expected to expand over time in size and scope relative to national activities and enterprises.

MJVs may also exert important linkages to other MJVs, as well as to other productive activities in a given region. This tends to be especially true of "second-generation" MJVs[15] where the participation of government bureaucrats on the board of directors and in management is likely to be diminished relative to that in "first-generation" MJVs. As time goes on, therefore, there would seem to be less and less of a likelihood that participating countries will want to repatriate their share of profits in order to cover the budgetary deficits of their sister national public or private enterprises. MJVs may, therefore, through their own expansion, by the linkages that they exert on other investment activities, and through the expected rise in their own reinvestment rates over time contribute very significantly to an overall increase in the national savings rates. Hence, they may accelerate the overall growth rates of the economies in which they operate, and encourage more diversified and higher-yielding asset portfolios in the primarily capital-surplus countries which invest in them.

As MJVs expand and become more integrally linked with each other and with other productive enterprises in a region through backward and forward linkages, and as they become more influential through the workers they employ and the consumers they serve, they should lay the foundation for broad economic and social interest group support for cooperation and integration. As this broadly-based interest group support spreads throughout participating countries, it should begin to exert pressure on national governments to adopt the policies favouring the free flow of commodities and resources among participating countries that are presumably necessary for their success. Indeed, it is this genuinely pro-regional interest group base that has been conspicuously absent in most regions of developing countries, even in those which have undertaken ambitious schemes of regional cooperation and integration. The creation of this regional interest group base is perhaps the best means of insuring any forms of regional cooperation and integration against disruptive actions of individual national governments, and even of the regional or subregional political organizations in which such governments are represented. Moreover, MJVs would seem to be the appropriate vehicles for identifying the specific instruments of cooperation and integration that matter. This is important for assuring that the time-consuming and sometimes friction-creating process of negotiating agreements, especially those of multilateral character, becomes concentrated on those issues and problems on which concerted action is likely to be most useful and productive.

Preliminary evidence suggests that MJVs have been able to uncouple the parts of foreign TNC packages more succesfully, and to adopt more appropriate technologies and to obtain better terms with foreign TNCs than host governments or local affiliates of the foreign TNCs.[16] Also, experience has shown that, once they have gained governmental permission to exist, MJVs tend to have a relatively free hand to work out regional projects in an efficient manner by themselves and without further recourse to government authorities. This greatly shortens the amount of formal intergovernmental negotiations that would be involved where this to be done instead by higher-level organizations, such as international or regional specialized agencies and development banks.

Last but not least, experience demonstrates that MJVs have a remarkable ability to survive substantial political and other changes. Several interesting examples can be cited from the Arab world of rather remarkable survival power in the face of enormous political changes. The Jordanian–Syrian MJVs, which are perhaps the most directly politically-inspired and high-level politician-initiated MJVs in the Arab world, and are by no means the most rational or potentially profitable ones, are apparently able to operate despite substantial deterioration in political relations between the two countries. Even these MJVs are strongly profit-oriented and eager to compete openly and, therefore, are not dependent on protective and trade-diverting measures that, in the long run, may be divisive as far as regional cooperation is concerned. Another example comes from the politically inspired Federal government proposed by Egypt, Syria and Libya in the early 1970s. Although the Federal government itself never came into existence and political relations between Egypt and both Libya and Syria have since deteriorated to the point of diplomatic break between them, some of the MJVs established under this federation have not only survived but in fact fluorished, as have the Arab Investment Bank in Cairo, Egypt and the Syrian–Libyan Corporation for Agricultural Investments in Damascus, Syria. Still another example is the Egypt–Iran Development Bank set up with the personal involvement of the late Shah of Iran and President Sadat of Egypt. Not only has the bank fluorished in the period subsequent to the Iranian Revolution but other prominent Egyptian enterprises have attempted to merge with it so as to be able to share its advantages in terms of decreased control by the national authorities.[17]

On the basis of the several important advantages of MJVs that have been mentioned above, and most of which seem to be strongly supported on the basis of the early experience with them in the Arab world, MJVs would seem to offer a promising basis for a new, more "bottom-up", "active", and durable approach to regional economic cooperation and integration than the approaches that have been tried in the past. The undeniable fact is that the traditional instruments of or approaches to ECDC and TCDC have not worked, in our opinion for the reasons given in Section II.

IV. Conclusion and Reservation

From the experience with various forms of regional cooperation and integration in various parts of the world, it can be confidently concluded that, despite demonstrations that they provide net benefits to participating countries as a whole, the vast majority of proposed schemes of regional cooperation are never realized. Of the relatively few that do come to fruition, most are either never fully implemented and enforced or are subsequently dropped and repudiated. These facts underscore the importance of transactions costs in creating, sustaining and renegotiating schemes of regional economic cooperation, especially among LDCs. They also suggest the importance of adopting a considerably longer-run perspective in analysing and evaluating such schemes, with careful consideration given also to each of the relevant constraints on or bottlenecks to economic development.

Among the various instruments of regional economic cooperation and integration, multinational joint venture companies among DCs (MJVs) would seem to offer numerous advantages both with respect to reducing transactions costs and in terms of their sizeable potential contributions to long-term economic development.

One important reservation, however, is that the advocacy of MJVs is based on rather limited experience with them. As relatively recent and non-traditional instruments of regional economic cooperation, relatively few of them have been in existence for a sufficiently long time to be very confident about their long-term effectiveness relative to other instruments.

Another reservation that needs to be stated is that since one of their principal advantages is that of facilitating resource complementarities among countries of a region and since most of the experience with MJVs has been among the Arab countries where differences in factor endowments among countries are especially great, it is possible that the rather positive early experience with inter-Arab MJVs may not be entirely generalizable to other regions where resource endowments are less complementary. In the same vein, it should also be admitted that MJVs may be less competitive, progressive and outward-oriented in regions in which *all* (not just some as in the Arab world) countries of the region have substantial tariff and other barriers to trade with the outside world. It is also unlikely that MJVs will possess none of the undesirable features of foreign TNCs with whom some might cooperate rather closely making it difficult to draw distinctions between them in some cases. Finally, there seems little reason to believe that MJVs by themselves can or will do very much to equalize the distribution of incomes within countries or to satisfy basic needs.

NOTES

1. For accounts of such failures see especially Vaitsos (1978), Vargas-Hidalgo (1979), Wionczek (1978), Hazlewood (1979), Salgado Penaherrera (1980 a, b) and Payne (1981). The reader will note in several of these a tendency to want to assign the blame for failures to different agents, in some cases to foreign TNCs, in others to host or foreign governments or to special interest groups.
2. See, e. g., Karnes (1961), Hazlewood (1979), Wionczek (1978) and Vaitsos (1978).
3. Note, for example, the role of U. S. AID in the CACM, that of the Inter-American Development Bank in the Andean Pact, the World Bank, British foreign aid and the African Development Bank in the East African Common Market. See also Vaitsos (1978).
4. Usually, the successes have been recorded during peaks in the international business cycle with relatively full employment, favourable weather in participating countries and an unusual degree of consensus on economic and political matters.
5. The reader should be reminded of the well-known findings of Chenery and Taylor (1968), Chenery and Syrquin (1975) and Chenery *et al.*(1979) demonstrating that the bulk of the various structural changes that all countries go through in the process of economic development occur relatively "early" in the development process, i.e., well before countries leave the ranks of DCs.
6. For example, with respect to trade agreements among the Arab countries of Western Asia, whereas there have been only two multilateral trade agreements of any importance (the Arab Trade Convention and the Arab Common Market), between virtually any given pair of countries numerous bilateral trade or other economic agreements have come into existence and then been reconstituted on several subsequent occasions, e.g., on at least seven occasions between Iraq and Jordan, Lebanon and Saudi Arabia, Syria and Saudi Arabia, Egypt and Iraq, Egypt and Jordan, Lebanon and Egypt, Egypt and Syria, and Iraq and Syria.
7. This would seem to be true not only in the case of the Arab countries, but also in the cases of the Central American Common Market /Wionczek (1970, 1972)/, and ASEAN /Arndt and Garnaut (1979)/.
8. Evidence for this may be seen in the greater longevity and effectiveness of the Central American Common Market than of the East African Common Market or the Latin American Free Trade Agreements. Also, the proposition is supported by the greater success the Arab countries of the Gulf have had at arriving at agreements among each other than with other Arab countries.
9. Evidence in support of this proposition is provided by the greater longevity of the United States as a nation and the EEC than political and economic unions of and among DCs.
10. Hypotheses (4) and (6) are supported by the greater success of multinational corporations in coordinating their activities than governments.
11. Evidence in support of this hypothesis was obtained in interviews with government officials in the Arab world several of whom spoke of their reluctance to take other Arab governments on

faith because of their failure to live by their commitments of the past. See United Nations Economic Commission for Western Asia (ECWA) 1981.

12. This is supported by the greater cooperation between capital surplus countries and capital scarce countries of the Arab region than between one capital scarce country and another.
13. This explains why trade agreements have historically been easier to obtain during periods of prosperity rather than depression and in regions of rapid growth than ones of slower growth for example more recently among Arab countries and ASEAN countries than in Sub-Saharan Africa.
14. For details of this review, see United Nations ECWA (1981). See also Agrawal (1975), Ahmad (1978), Casas-Gonzalez (1975), Little (1966), Mingst (1977), Mateo and White (1975), Mirza (1974), Okigbo (1975), Shihata (1975) and UNCTAD (1979).
15. "Second-generation" MJVs are those MJVs set up by other (first-generation) MJVs.
16. Note especially White (1981).
17. These latter examples were suggested by Prof. Erfan Shafey of Kuwait University.

REFERENCES

Agrawal, R. G. "Joint Ventures among Developing Asian Countries". UNCTAD Trade and Development Board, Expert Group on Economic Cooperation among Developing Countries (27 October, 1975) TD/B/AC. 19/R. 7.

Ahmad, I. N. "The Role of International Joint Ventures in Fostering Economies of Developing Countries, with Special Study of the Arab Countries Experience," Kuwait: The Arab Planning Institute, 1978, unpublished thesis.

Arndt, H. W., and R. Garnaut, "ASEAN and the Industrialization of East Asia", *Journal of Common Market Studies*, No. 3, 1979, pp. 191–212.

Casas-Gonzalez, A. "Joint Ventures among Latin American Countries", UNCTAD Trade and Development Board. Expert Group on Economic Cooperation among Developing Countries (22 October, 1975) TD/B/AC. 19/R. 2.

Chenery, H. B. and M. Syrquin, *Patterns of Development, 1950–1970*, London: Oxford University Press, 1975.

Chenery, H. B. and L. Taylor, "Development Patterns: Among Countries and Over Time", *Review of Economics and Statistics*, November, 1968, pp. 391–416.

Chenery, H. B. *et al. Structural Change and Development Policy*, New York: Oxford University Press, 1979.

Hazlewood, A. "The End of the East African Community: What are the Lessons for Regional Integration Schemes?", *Journal of Common Market Studies*, No. 1, 1979, pp. 40–58.

Karnes, T. L. *The Failure of Union: Central America, 1824–1860*, Chapel Hill: University of North Carolina Press, 1961.

Little, I. M. D. "Regional International Companies as an Approach to Economic Integration", *Journal of Common Market Studies*, No. 2, 1966.

Mateo, F. and E. White, "Public Corporations as a Means of Distributing Costs and Benefits within a Framework of Integration," in *Current Problems of Economic Integration*, New York: United Nations, TD/B/517, 1975.

Mingst, K. A. "Regional Sectorial Economic Integration: The Case of OAPEC", *Journal of Common Market Studies*, No. 2, 1977, pp. 95–113.

Mirza, J. A. "RCD and its Achievements", *The RCD Magazine*, Vol. 1, No. 1, 1974, pp. 28–33.

Okigbo, D. N. C. "Joint Ventures among African Countries", UNCTAD Trade and Development Board. Expert Group on Economic Cooperation among Developing Countries (2 October, 1975), TD/B/AC. 19/R. 3.

Payne, A. "The Rise and Fall of Caribbean Regionalization", *Journal of Common Market Studies*, No. 3, 1981, pp. 255–280.

Salgado Penaherrera, "Viable Integration and the Economic Cooperation Problems of the Developing World", *Journal of Common Market Studies*, No. 1, 1980, pp. 65–76.

Salgado Penaherrera, "Viable Integration and the Economic Cooperation Problems of the Developing World", *Journal of Common Market Studies*, No. 2, 1980, pp. 175–188.

Shihata, I. F. I. "Joint Ventures among Arab Countries", Trade and Development Board UNCTAD, Group of Experts on Economic Cooperation among Developing Countries (21 October, 1975), TD/B/AD. 19/R. 5.

"Mechanisms for Facilitating Agreement on the Establishment of Multinational Industries in Developing Countries: An Approach to Modifying the Distribution of Costs and Benefits in Regional Integration Schemes," in *Current Problems of Economic Integration*, *op. cit.*

United Nations, ECWA, Development Planning Division, "Evolution of Economic Cooperation and Integration in Western Asia", Beirut, 1979, mimeo

United Nations, ECWA, Development Planning Division, "Toward a Feasible Path to Economic Cooperation and Integration in Western Asia", Beirut, 1981.

Vaitsos, C. V. "Crisis in Regional Economic Cooperation (Integration) among Developing Countries: A Survey", *World Development*, No. 6, 1978, pp. 719–769.

Vargas-Hidalgo, R. "The Crisis of the Andean Pact: Lessons for Integration among Developing Countries", *Journal of Common Market Studies*, No. 1979, pp. 213–226.

White, E. "Multinational Companies of Developing Countries: The Issue of Correct Policies", Paper presented to the International Workshop on the Promotion of Economic and Technical Cooperation among Developing Countries, Bled, Yugoslavia, November 1981.

Wionczek, M. S. "The Rise and Decline of Latin American Economic Integration", *Journal of Common Market Studies*, September 1970, pp. 49–66.

Wionczek, M. S. "The Central American Common Market", in *International Economic Integration*, P. Robson (ed.), Middlesex, 1972, Penguin Books.

Wionczek, M. S. "Can the Broken Humpty-Dumpty Be Put Together Again and by Whom? Comments on the Vaitsos Survey", *World Development*, No. 6, 1978, pp. 779–782.

[9]

THIRD WORLD MULTINATIONALS AND SOUTH AFRICA'S DECENTRALIZATION PROGRAMME

C.M. ROGERSON
University of the Witwatersrand, Johannesburg
(Manuscript received 30th September, 1985; in revised form 10th January, 1986)

ABSTRACT

Geographers have accorded considerable attention to the spatial behaviour of developed-country multinationals in host countries. In this analysis the aim is to investigate the location behaviour of a particular category of multinational enterprise which has emerged significantly only in the past decade *viz.*, the developing country or Third World multinational. More specifically, the emergence of the Third World multinational is detailed and their growth and locational behaviour in South Africa is investigated. It is shown that the patterns of manufacturing investment from developing country multinationals are almost exclusively oriented towards peripheral regions of South Africa in contrast to the core region orientation of developed country multinationals.

Introduction

Over the past decade the global expansion of large business enterprises has engendered an enormous volume of literature by industrial geographers. The intense research interest on the growth paths, location patterns and developmental impact of multinationals prompted one observer to suggest that within geography "the multinational corporation has become a focus of study in its own right" (Clarke, 1985, p.5). In terms of the geographical research agenda, it is imperative to emphasize the considerable degree of variety which exists among the population of multinationals (Clark and Massey, 1982; Dicken, 1982; Giddy and Young, 1982; Taylor and Thrift, 1982, 1986). For some scholars, the emergence during the 1970s and 1980s of new or "unconventional" (Giddy and Young, 1982) forms of multinationals radically different from earlier types has led to a distinction between the 'classic multinational corporation' and the newer 'global' corporation (Dicken, 1977; Taylor and Thrift, 1982; Clarke, 1985). Other researchers argue the most important facet of heterogeneity is the country of origin of the parent which accounts for some significant organizational and behavioural differences between multinational enterprise (Dicken, 1982). Increasingly, therefore, geographical scholars of multinational corporations are discarding the old stereotype view of these enterprises as undifferentiated and are instead coming to "recognise that there are different types of organisation and that they will have varied spatial effects" (Clarke, 1985, p.13).

In this paper the aim is to investigate the spatial impact of a particular category of multinational enterprise which has emerged significantly only in the past decade *viz.*, the developing country or Third World multinational. Research on the geography of overseas investment has been a recent popular focus of study at the intra-national scale of analysis (e.g. Blackbourn, 1974, 1982; Dicken and

Lloyd, 1976, 1980; McDermott, 1977; Law, 1980; Watts, 1979, 1980b; Cunningham, 1981; McConnell, 1980, 1983; Edgington, 1984; O hUallachain, 1985). Nevertheless, excepting Forbes' (1986) examination of the spatial aspects of Third World multinationals in Indonesia, the extant literature overwhelmingly deals with location decisions made by enterprises whose parent company is based in developed or First World countries. In the host environments of both developed and developing economies a mass of literature now evidences that the distribution of developed-country multinationals may differ substantially from the aggregate pattern of economic activities (Dicken and Lloyd, 1976; Watts, 1980a, 1980b, 1982; Dicken, 1983; McConnell, 1983; O hUallachain, 1985, 1986). More specifically, that corporations display a preference for expanding along lines of least resistance is reflected in an orientation towards certain locations inside host countries (Clarke, 1985). The consistent locational preference for economic core regions is interpreted as one way that enterprises cope with environmental uncertainty (Edgington, 1984; Clarke 1985). Accordingly, in the United Kingdom there occurs a relative over-concentration of foreign enterprise in the South-East of England (Watts, 1979, 1980b; Mason, 1982), in Canada a pattern of multinationals clustering in Southern Ontario (Ray, 1971) and in Kenya of the concentration of foreign manufacturing investment in Nairobi or Mombasa (Langdon, 1975). The recent spatial dynamics of foreign direct investment within developed countries, however, indicates a possible reversal of this trend with a progressive drift of foreign manufacturers from core regions towards peripheral locations (McDermott, 1977; McConnell, 1980; O hUallachain, 1985, 1986).

Geographers have recognized that an understanding of the location choices and regional impacts of multinationals is essential for interpreting change in modern spatial systems. Moreover, it is possible that in the absence of intervention by national governments, location decisions made by developed-country multinationals may accentuate spatial inequalities by reinforcing existing core-periphery relationships (Blackbourn, 1982; Edgington, 1984). Many observers argue that developed-country multinationals help to perpetuate and even create additional regional imbalances within countries because their economic size and power facilitates their pursuit of locational behaviour contrary to the needs of peripheral regions (Holland, 1976; Blackbourn, 1978; Hamilton, 1978). In the present paper, attention centres upon issues of regional imbalance and the location decisions made by Third World or developing country multinationals in the specific setting of apartheid South Africa. Earlier research on the spatial patterns of developed-country multinationals in South Africa revealed the overwhelming attraction of core regions for foreign manufacturing investors (Rogerson, 1981, 1982a, 1982b). At the time of conducting this research the Third World multinational had not made an appearance on the South African scene. During the past five years, however, a steady stream of investors from several developing countries have established manufacturing facilities in South Africa. The objectives in this paper are therefore to chronicle the emergence of Third World multinationals, to detail their expansion in South Africa and to draw attention to the location behaviour of this new genre of multinational enterprise.

The Rise of Third World Multinationals

Although there is evidence as far back as the late nineteenth century of the existence of a scatter of companies which might fall under the rubric "Third World multinational", it is generally agreed that the emergence of this kind of enterprise has been a phenomenon of the 1960s and, more particularly, the 1970s (Lall, 1983; Wells, 1983; Linge, 1984). In the contemporary world economy no longer is the art of global reach confined merely to corporations based in developed countries for the number of developing countries whose firms qualify for the appellation 'multinational' steadily has risen over the past decade (Wells, 1977; Heenan and Keegan, 1979; Kumar, 1982). Spearheading the drive of multinational investment from the Third World are the broad group of Newly Industrializing Countries, both in Asia and Latin America (Kumar, 1982; Lall, 1983; Linge, 1984). From fragmentary statistical evidence currently available, the leading individual sources are Hong Kong, Brazil and India followed by a second order group composed of Argentina, Mexico, South Korea, Taiwan and Venezuela (Wells, 1978; Lall, 1982a, 1982b, 1983; Wells, 1983; Chen, 1984). In total the volume of global investments deriving from Third World sources is a relatively small total of US $10 billion, a share of perhaps three percent in overall foreign direct investment (Lall, 1983; Linge, 1984; Hamilton, 1986). Notwithstanding this small volume, the rise of Third World multinationals has generated considerable scholarly interest.

The consensus view on Third World multinationals is that their competitive edge rests in small-scale labour-intensive production technologies, in manufacturing undifferentiated price-competitive products and in possessing cheap skilled management which is particularly adept at running businesses in the circumstances of developing countries (Kumar, 1982; Wells, 1983; Linge, 1984; Monkiewicz, 1985). For Wells (1981, 1983) the special assets of these firms follow from the peculiar nature of their home markets which are conducive to innovations markedly dissimilar to those that evolve in advanced capitalist economies. Further, it is maintained that market conditions in Third World countries induce local entrepreneurs to innovate small-scale labour-intensive processes and products and to search out means to substitute available local inputs for imported goods. Accordingly, many Third World multinationals possess 'appropriate technologies' that are multi-purpose, labour- rather then capital-intensive and capable of using locally available raw materials and other inputs (Wells, 1981, 1983; Nambudiri, 1983). Moreover, the fact that these enterprises have much smaller proprietary assets than those of developed country multinationals causes them to display a high propensity for entering into joint venture arrangements with local firms (Lall, 1983; Linge, 1984). Although exceptions to the above caricature undoubtedly exist, Lall concurs that "there is a great deal of validity in this portrayal of Third World MNCs" (Lall, 1983, p. 624).

The rise of Third World multinationals has triggered much debate on their differences with those of developed country multinationals. Their particular attributes of small-scale, low technology, labour-intensity, cheap modes of management and so on appear to mark them off as a special sub-category of multinationals. This viewpoint is further strengthened by the particularly high profile of governments and of state-owned enterprises and agencies in the multinationalization of Third World enterprises (Kumar, 1981, 1982; Monkiewicz, 1985). Indeed, for one observer, the facilitating role played by government and of the weight of public sector Third World multinationals is one of the major distinguishing features of this group of enterprises (Linge, 1984). A further striking trait of the Third World multinational concerns the spatially circumscribed sphere of their international operations, with the majority of investments taking place in other developing countries at low levels of industrialization (Nambudiri, *et al.*, 1981; Nambudiri, 1983; Linge, 1984). Behind this geographical spread of Third World multinationals is the critical importance of ethnic ties especially amongst Indian and Chinese communities in various parts of Asia (Chen, 1981; Lall, 1982a, 1982b; Wells, 1983). The salience of ethnic connections is evident, for example, in the initial overseas path of Hong Kong and Taiwanese multinationals expanding in Asia (Wells, 1978; Chen, 1981; Linge, 1984; Chen, 1985). Finally, as compared to developed country multinationals, Third World firms are perceived as less threatening, in both economic and political senses, by many host countries, an attribute which can be turned to advantage in circumstances of widespread concern about world domination by powerful multinationals based in a few developed countries (Kumar, 1982).

If the differences between developed and developing country multinationals suggest that the latter constitute a separate genre of enterprises, it is important not to overlook their commonalities. Initial writings on Third World multinationals often portrayed them as having benevolent motivations in terms of their international expansion, leading mutual support to other developing countries. This view is now replaced by an emphasis upon a recognition by capitalists in developing countries of markets abroad for their products and of the taking of steps to exploit those opportunities in much the same fashion as capitalists elsewhere (Linge, 1984). Hong Kong firms, for example, have ventured abroad for defensive reasons similar to those that caused firms from developed countries to internationalize their operations (Wells, 1978; Chen, 1981). More specifically, the spread of Hong Kong multinationals is linked to a desire to maintain and whenever possible to extend the level of their exports to industrialized nations, an objective identical to developed country multinationals establishing production facilities in Third World export processing zones. The particular international geography of Hong Kong investors is heavily influenced by import quotas imposed in North America and Western Europe causing production to be relocated to countries which are not affected by such restrictions (Wells, 1978; Chen, 1981, 1985). In many respects, these commonalities suggest that multinationals from the Third World may not differ substantially from those from developed countries (Lall, 1983; Linge, 1984).

Third World Multinationals in South Africa

The appearance of Third World multinationals in South Africa is of recent moment, beginning as late as the close of the 1970s. Strikingly, no mention appears of the issue of Third World investors in the avalanche of writings which surfaced during the 1970s debating foreign enterprise as a force for eroding or buttressing the structures of apartheid. The first stirrings of Third World investment occurred in the late 1970s when a campaign was launched to attract Taiwanese investors to Transkei, against a backdrop of general reluctance by developed country multinationals to invest within the Bantustans (Rogerson, 1982a). Information on contemporary investment flows into South Africa from the Third World is veiled in secrecy and no official data exists to enable researchers accurately to monitor such flows. Nevertheless, information gleaned from a range of published secondary souces (newspapers, trade journals) and from unpublished data made available by official chambers of trade permits the construction of the broad lineaments concerning Third World multinationals in South Africa.

It is evident that the sources of Third World investment into South Africa do not mirror the global picture. The leading Third World sources of manufacturing investment into South Africa in order of importance are Taiwan, Israel and Hong Kong. Together these three sources account for at least fifty manufacturing operations either in operation or currently under construction. In terms of the number of enterprises, it is clear that Taiwan is by far the major investor with some 35 firms which have collectively generated 6 000-7 000 employment opportunities. Third World investors are engaged in a wide spectrum of manufacturing activities spanning the production of cane furniture, radios, toys, printing, pharmaceuticals, cutlery, bicycles and plastic bags. The majority of investment occurs, however, in the production of an array of clothing and textile goods, an activity in which manufacturers from Taiwan, Hong Kong and Israel are all presently engaged. Indeed, of the current tally of 35 Taiwanese enterprises, 23 or almost two-thirds fall into the category of clothing, textiles and footwear. Characteristic of the Third World multinational is the small size of capital commitment by Taiwanese investors; information for 21 enterprises reveals that for 15 companies the capital commitment was less than R1 million, and for 11 enterprises less than R500 000. Despite their global significance in terms of Third World multinationals, no evidence is recorded of substantive investment in South African manufacturing by companies based in Brazil, Argentina, Mexico, Venezuela, South Korea or India. The geographical origins of Third World investors into South Africa reflects the impress of international politics with the grouping of pariah states — the South Africa-Israel-Taiwan axis — which are politically ostracised by much of the rest of the world.

Behind the stream of Third World investors into South Africa are sets of economic and political considerations. The arrival of the Third World clothing and textile manufacturers is inseparable from the imposition of import quotas by developed countries upon such exports from Taiwan and Hong Kong and of corresponding attempts to benefit from an under-utilized South African quota. Accordingly, the entry of Taiwanese and Hong Kong multinationals into South African manufacturing is part of a long-established defensive investment strategy to retain export markets particularly in the United States and Western Europe (see Wells, 1978; Chen, 1981, 1984; Amsden, 1984; Chen, 1985). Illustratively, the Hong Kong based Amigo International clothing factory at Newcastle is geared to export its entire output of jeans and jackets to the U.S. and E.E.C. markets (*Growth,* October 1983). Similarly, the Tally (Pty) Ltd. Butterworth factory constitutes the latest move to defend the market position of a Taiwanese company which is the largest single clothing exporter to the United States; all the company's Transkei production is targeted for the U.S.A. (*Sunday Times,* 12/2/1984). It is alleged that many of these Third World clothing operations based in South Africa undertake only minimal manufacturing as they import nearly complete clothing for local finishing and RSA labelling prior to export (*Sunday Times,* 19/5/1985). The growth of Third World clothing and textile multinationals is evidenced in the rocketing levels of South African exports from a static total of R24 million for the years 1981-83 to R49 million in only the first nine months of 1984 (*Sunday Times,* 10/2/1985; *Manufacturing Review of South Africa,* 30 May-7 June 1985). Apart from export markets other Third World investors have been attracted to South Africa by the possibilities of a share of the home market. Typical of this kind of investor is the Taiwanese company, Ricky Shoes, whose first venture in international manufacturing consists of a factory at Lebowakgomo producing women's and children's shoes for the South African market (*Momentum,* January 1984).

Beyond the imperative of defensive investment it may be conjectured that the decision of Hong Kong and Taiwanese enterprise to establish affiliates in South Africa is linked, at least in part, to the spreading of risk in situations of political uncertainty (cf Linge, 1984). Certainly, the recent multinationalization of many Hong Kong firms is tied to the political instability surrounding the colony's future with the expiration in 1997 of the lease from China (Chen, 1985). Although one cannot lay too much stress upon political uncertainty as a factor in the entry of Hong Kong firms into South Africa, it remains that interest in the promotional lures offered by Bantustan development corporations was greatly heightened in the wake of diminished business confidence in the colony following the decision of Jardine, Matheson & Co. — Hong Kong's oldest, largest and most prestigious firm — to relocate its world headquarters to Bermuda (*Financial Mail,* 11 May 1984). Uncertainties concerning future political developments in Taiwan over the succession to the present political leadership and the threat from Mainland China, are factors also underpinning the emergence of Taiwan as a seedbed for multinational enterprise (Kumar, 1982; Chen, 1985). That said, the degree to which political uncertainties are a notable influence upon the investment drives of Taiwanese — or, for that matter, Israeli — enterprise into South Africa must remain an issue for speculation.

The surge of Taiwanese firms into South Africa is connected more firmly to the political benefits that accrue from overseas investment to the home country. Kumar (1982, p. 417) argues that "Taiwanese national authorities and entrepreneurs see their foreign direct investments a one way of strengthening their political and economic ties with other countries". In this regard, it is significant that government-owned firms are a major component in the contingent of Taiwanese firms presently in South Africa (Copping, 1983, p. 85). Since 1980 the Taiwanese government has adopted a policy of actively encouraging foreign investment particularly directed towards 'friendly' resource-rich countries (Copping, 1983). In the 1980s the whole of the Southern African sub-continent became a prime investment area for Taiwanese investors, with ventures not only in South Africa but also Botswana, Lesotho and Swaziland. The international politics of two Chinas, however, served to narrow the sphere for prospective Taiwanese investors. For example, in May 1983 Lesotho decided to terminate diplomatic relations with Taiwan and instead to recognize Mainland China (*Africa Research Bulletin,* May 1983, p. 6851). This decision led to the withdrawal of Taiwanese investment from Lesotho with the relocation of at least one concern to the Qwa Qwa Bantustan.

In addition to the important factor of strengthened political ties between Taiwan and South Africa, other advantages have flowed subsequent to the growth of Taiwanese investors. Most important, perhaps, is the improved conditions of residence rights of the Chinese community in South Africa, which, until recently, was accorded diminished rights relative to White South Africans. In addition, Taiwanese investors coming to South Africa were issued with residence permits valid only for a maximum period of five years and subject to annual renewal (Copping, 1983, p. 84). During 1984 these regulations were altered so as to waive both the five year maximum residence ruling and the yearly renewal of permits for Taiwanese industrialists and their key personnel (de Klerk, 1984). Nevertheless, it was made clear that one important consideration governing the continuing operation of these regulations would be "the locality of new ventures" established by Taiwanese investors (*Rand Daily Mail,* 27/6/1984). Indeed, these new residence regulations forged a direct link between the future admission of Taiwanese personnel and the geography of Third World investment in South Africa.

TABLE 1: *Approvals for Foreign Investors in Decentralized Areas.*

	No. of Approved Applications	**Average Capital Investment (R)**
Taiwan	21	1 185 000
United Kingdom	10	2 160 000
Israel	10	2 030 000
Italy	5	762 000
Zimbabwe	4	521 000
Hong Kong	3	1 076 000
West Germany	2	3 157 000
United States	2	2 196 000
Peru	1	1 255 000
Belgium	1	804 000
Australia	1	367 000

Source: *Manufacturing Review of South Africa,* 30 May-7 June 1985.

In terms of their location decisions within South Africa, Third World investors have played a notable role in succouring manufacturing expansion in decentralized areas generally and those growth points in the Bantustans in particular. The emerging strength of Third World multinationals in the decentralization programme is indexed most dramatically in Table 1 recording new approvals by foreign investors in decentralized areas. Of a total of 60 new factories planned by foreign enterprise, 39 or 65 percent derive from Third

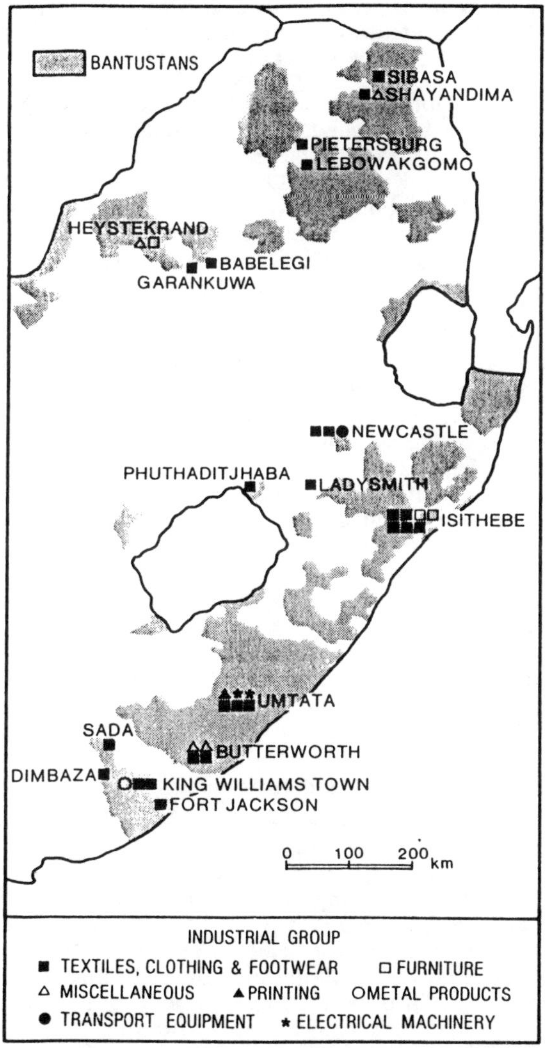

Fig. 1: Location of Taiwan Multinationals in South Africa.
Source: Information provided by press reports and the Commercial Office, Taiwan.
Note: Some companies are operating more than one plant.

World countries. The single importance of Taiwan is highlighted by its role of accounting for 35 percent of new ventures. Almost without exception, the factories of Third World multinationals are situated either at decentralized locations within 'White' South Africa or, more commonly, at Bantustan growth points. In the case of Taiwanese and Hong Kong concerns the picture emerges of *all* manufacturing investment being confined to decentralized locations. Less clear is the position surrounding Israeli ventures; an enquiry directed to the Israel-South Africa Chamber of Trade, however, drew the response that "99 percent" of Israeli investors were taking advantage of the concessions offered at decentralized locations (Joison, 1985).

The spatial distribution of Taiwanese investment in South Africa is presented on Figure 1 revealing their representation in all four of the so-called 'independent' Bantustans (Bophuthatswana, Ciskei, Transkei and Venda), Lebowa, KwaZulu, Qwa Qwa as well as at the 'White' growth points of Pietersburg, Newcastle and Ladysmith. Clearly, the mass of Taiwanese ventures are located at Bantustan growth points, a pattern which reflects the influence of their assiduous courting by Bantustan leaders and individual development corporations with the frequent exchange of trade delegations and parties of prospective industrialists. In addition, the nature of Third World multinationals is such that they bring into South Africa considerable knowhow in terms of low-skill, labour-intensive production as well as a proven product range, a set of characteristics which places them in a good position for taking advantage of the specific locational advantages of decentralized locations (Bell, 1985). The obvious attractions of Bantustans for new plants by Third World investors are the lucrative package of concessions and investment incentives on offer and the large supplies of relatively cheap labour which is kept in a subjugated condition by the repressive state apparatuses of both South Africa and the Bantustans (Hirsch, 1984, 1985). The combination of rising levels of incentives and the ability of paying poverty wage levels underpin the competitive strength of these concerns both in terms of the South African market and for international exports (*Sunday Times*, 16/2/1985, *Finance Week* 25/4/1985).

Concluding Remarks

The locational behaviour of Third World multinationals in South Africa exhibits a sharp contrast to the geographical pattern of investment which emanates from developed countries. Whereas the spatial pattern of manufacturing investment from the United Kingdom, United States or West Germany is predominantly core region in focus, the corresponding patterns of Third World investment is almost exclusively oriented towards periperal regions. In this respect, it might be argued that the Third World multinational, unlike the developed country multinational, is a vital force contributing towards "balanced regional growth" in South Africa, a role which it assumes in some parts of Asia (Thee, 1981). Nonetheless, the contrasting locational behaviour of developed and developing country multinationals in South Africa should be viewed with some caution. It must be emphasized that a synoptic picture of the geography of foreign manufacturing investment is inevitably a composite of not only original location decisions concerning new plants but also derived location decisions surrounding, *inter alia,* relocations, branch plants, acquisitions and *in situ* expansions. Further, these decisions have been aggregated over differing time periods, in which there existed far more constrained spatial environments for locational choice than confronts the latterday Third World multinational. In the final analysis, the locational preference of Third World investors for peripheral decentralized locations is scarcely surprising if placed against the backdrop of their defensive investment motives and the particular characteristics and genesis of the Third World multinational.

REFERENCES

Amsden, A.H., 1984: Taiwan, *World Development,* 12, 491-503.

Bell, T., 1985: Is decentralisation a thing of the past?, unpublished paper presented at the Workshop on South Africa's Regional Strategy with special reference to industrial decentralisation, University of the Witwatersrand, Johannesburg, 5-6 September.

Blackbourn, A., 1974: The spatial behaviour of American firms in Western Europe, in F.E.I. Hamilton (ed.) *Spatial Persepectives on Industrial Organization and Decision-Making,* John Wiley, London, 245-264.

Blackbourn, A., 1978: Multinational enterprises and regional development: a comment, *Regional Studies,* 12, 125-127.

Blackbourn, A., 1982: The impact of multinational corporations on the spatial organisation of developed countries: a review, in M. Taylor and N. Thrift (eds.), *The Geography of Multinationals,* London, Croom Helm, 147-157.

Chen, E.C.Y., 1981: Hong Kong Multinationals in Asia: characteristics and objectives, in K. Kumar and M.G. McLeod (eds.), *Multinationals from Developing Countries,* Lexington, Mass., D.C. Heath, 79-100.

Chen, E.C.Y., 1984: Hong Kong, *World Development,* 12, 481-490.

Chen, E.C.Y., 1985: *The Newly Industrializing Countries in Asia: Growth Experience and Prospects,* Hong Kong, University of Hong Kong Department of Economics Discussion Paper No. 55.

Clark, G.L. and Massey, D., 1982: A research agenda on multinational enterprises and the spatial division of labour, in B.T. Robson and J. Rees (eds.) *Geographical Agenda for a Changing World,* London, Social Science Research Council, 78-85.

Clarke, I.M., 1985: *The Spatial Organisation of Multinational Corporations,* London, Croom Helm.

Copping, P., 1983: South Africa — Republic of China Trade, unpublished M.B.A. Report, University of the Witwatersrand, Johannesburg.

Cunningham, S., 1981: Multinational enterprises in Brazil: locational patterns and implications for regional development, *Professional Geographer,* 33, 48-62.

de Klerk, F.W., 1984: Address by the Honourable F.W. de Klerk, Minister of Internal Affairs, Annual General Meeting, S.A.-Republic of China (Taiwan) Chamber of Economic Relations, Johannesburg 25 June, 1984, unpublished mimeo.

Dicken, P., 1977: A note on location theory and the large business enterprise, *Area* 9, 138-143.

Dicken, P., 1982: Recent trends in international direct investment, with particular reference to the United States and the United Kingdom, in B.T. Robson and J. Rees (eds.), *Geographical Agenda for a Changing World,* London, Social Science Research Council, 118-161.

Dicken, P., 1983: Japanese manufacturing investment in the United Kingdom: a flood or mere trickle?, *Area,* 15, 273-284.

Dicken, P. and Lloyd, P., 1976: Geographical perspectives on United States investment in the United Kingdom, *Environment and Planning A,* 8, 685-705.

Dicken, P. and Lloyd P., 1980: Patterns and processes of change in the spatial distribution of foreign-controlled manufacturing employment in the United Kingdom, 1963 to 1975, *Environment and Planning A*, 12, 1405-1426.

Edgington, D.W., 1984: Some urban and regional consequences of Japanese trans-national activity in Australia, *Environment and Planning A*, 16, 1021-1040.

Forbes, D., 1986: Spatial aspects of Third World multinational corporations' direct investment in Indonesia, in M. Taylor and N. Thrift (eds.), *Multinationals and the Restructuring of the World Economy: The Geography of Multinationals, Volume 2*, London, Croom Helm, 105-141.

Giddy, I.H. and Young, S., 1982: Conventional theory and unconventional multi-nationals: do new forms of multinational enterprise require new theories?, in A.M. Rugman (ed.), *New Theories of Multinational Enterprise*, New York, St Martin's Press, 55-78.

Hamilton, F.E.I., 1978: Multinational enterprise and the European Economic Community, in F.E.I. Hamilton (ed.), *Industrial Change: International Experience and Public Policy*, London, Longman 24-41.

Hamilton, F.E.I., 1986: The multinationals: spearhead or spectre?, in C. Dixon, D.W. Drakakis-Smith and H.D. Watts (eds.), *Multinational Corporations and the Third World*, Beckenham, Croom Helm, 1-24.

Heenan, D.A. and Keegan, W.J., 1979: The rise of third world multinationals, *Harvard Business Review*, 57, 101-110.

Hirsch, A., 1984: Bantustan industrialization with specific reference to the Ciskei 1973-1981, unpublished M.A. thesis, University of Cape Town.

Hirsch, A., 1985: The industrialisation of Dimbaza: population relocation and industrial decentralisation in a Bantustan, unpublished paper presented at the Workshop on South Africa's Regional Strategy with special reference to industrial decentralisation, University of the Witwatersrand, Johannesburg, 5-6 September.

Holland, S., 1976: *Capital Versus the Regions*, London, Methuen.

Joison, J.I., 1985: Personal communication, South Africa-Israel Chamber of Commerce, Johannesburg, 12 August.

Kemper, N.J. and de Smidt, M., 1980: Foreign manufacturing establishments in the Netherlands, *Tijdschrift voor Economische en Sociale Geografie*, 71, 21-40.

Kumar, K., 1981: Multinationalisation of Third World public-sector enterprises, in K. Kumar and M.G. McLeod (eds.), *Multinationals from Developing Countries*, Lexington, D.C. Heath, 187-201.

Kumar, K., 1982: Third World multinationals: a growing force in international relations, *International Studies Quarterly*, 26, 397-424.

Lall, S., 1982a: The emergence of Third World multinationals: Indian joint ventures overseas, *World Development*, 10, 127-146.

Lall, S., 1982b: Third World multinationals: the Indian case, in J. Carlsson (ed.), *South-South Relations in a Changing World Order*, Uppsala, Scandinavian Institute of African Studies, 128-164.

Lall, S., 1983: The rise of multinationals from the Third World, *Third World Quarterly*, 5, 618-626.

Langdon, S., 1975: Multinational corporations, taste transfer and underdevelopment: a case study from Kenya, *Review of African Political Economy*, 2, 12-35.

Law, C., 1980: The foreign company's location investment decision and its role in British regional development, *Tijdschrift voor Economische en Sociale Geografie*, 71, 15-20.

Linge, G.J.R., 1984: Developing-country multinationals: a review of the literature, *Pacific Viewpoint*, 25,173-195.

McConnell, J.E., 1980: Foreign direct investment in the United States, *Annals, Association of American Geographers*, 70, 259-270.

McConnell, J.E., 1983: The international location of manufacturing investments: recent behaviour of foreign-owned corporations in the United States, in F.E.I. Hamilton and G.J.R. Linge (eds.), *Spatial Analysis, Industry and the Industial Environment Vol. 3: Regional Economies and Industrial Systems*, Chichester, John Wiley, 337-358.

McDermott, P., 1977: Overseas investment and the industrial geography of the United Kingdom, *Area,* 9, 200-207.

Mason, C., 1982: Foreign-owned manufacturing firms in the United Kingdom: some evidence from South Hampshire, *Area,* 14, 7-17.

Monkiewicz, J., 1985: *Multinational Production Enterprises: A Preliminary Overview,* Vienna, United Nations Industrial Development Organization UNIDO/PC.121.

Nambudiri, C.N.S., Iyanda, O. and Akinnusi, D.M., 1981: Third World country firms in Nigeria, in K. Kumar and M.G. McLeod (eds.), *Multinationals from Developing Countries,* Lexington, D.C. Heath, 145-154.

Nambudiri, C.N.S., 1983: *Third World Multinationals: Technology and Employment Choice in Nigeria,* Geneva, International Labour Office.

O hUallachain, B., 1985: Spatial patterns of foreign direct investment in the United States, *Professional Geographer,* 37, 155-163.

O hUallachain, B., 1986: The role of foreign direct investment in the development of regional industrial systems: current knowledge and suggestions for a future American research agenda, *Regional Studies* 20, 151-162.

Ray, D.M., 1971: The location of United States manufacturing subsidiaries in Canada, *Economic Geography,* 47, 389-400.

Rogerson, C.M., 1981: Spatial perspectives on United Kingdom investment in South Africa, *South African Geographical Journal* 63, 85-106.

Rogerson, C.M., 1982a: Multinational corporations in Southern Africa: a spatial perspective, in M.J. Taylor and N. Thrift (eds.), *The Geography of Multinationals,* London, Croom Helm, 179-220.

Rogerson, C.M., 1982b: Patterns of indigenous and foreign control of South African manufacturing, *South African Geographer,* 10, 123-134.

Taylor, M.J. and Thrift, N.J., 1982: Models of corporate development and the multinational corporation, in M.J. Taylor and N.J. Thrift (eds.), *The Geography of Multinationals,* London, Croom Helm, 14-32.

Taylor, M.J. and Thrift, N.J., 1986: Introduction: new theories of multinational corporations, in M.J. Taylor and N.J. Thrift (eds.), *Multinationals and the Restructuring of the World Economy — the Geography of Multinationals, Vol. 2,* Beckenham, Croom Helm, 1-20.

Thee, K-W., 1981: Indonesia as a host country to Indian joint ventures, in K. Kumar and M.G. McLeod (eds.), *Multinationals from Developing Countries,* Lexington, Mass., D.C. Heath, 133-144.

Watts, H.D., 1979: Large firms, multinationals and regional development: some new evidence from the United Kingdom, *Environment and Planning A,* 11, 71-81.

Watts, H.D., 1980a: *The Large Industrial Enterprise: Some Spatial Perspectives,* London, Croom Helm.

Watts, H.D., 1980b: The location of European direct investment in the United Kingdom, *Tijdschrift voor Economishe en Sociale Geografie,* 71, 3-14.

Watts, H.D., 1982: The inter-regional distribution of West German multinationals in the United Kingdom, in M.J. Taylor and N.J. Thrift (eds.), *The Geography of Multinationals,* London, Croom Helm, 61-89.

Wells, Jr., L.T., 1977: The internationalization of firms from developing countries, *Multinationals from Small Countries,* M.I.T. Press, Cambridge, Mass., 133-156.

Wells, Jr., L.T., 1978: Foreign investment from the Third World: the experience of Chinese firms from Hong Kong, *Columbia Journal of World Business,* 13, 39-50.

Wells, Jr., L.T., 1981: Foreign investors from the Third World, in K. Kumar and M.G. McLeod (eds.), *Multinationals from Developing Countries,* Lexington, Mass., D.C. Heath, 23-36.

Wells, Jr., L.T., 1983: *Third World Multinationals: The Rise of Foreign Investment from Developing Countries,* Cambridge, Mass, M.I.T. Press.

[10]

OUTWARD DIRECT INVESTMENT BY INDONESIAN FIRMS: MOTIVATION AND EFFECTS

Donald J. Lecraw*
Institute Pengembangan Manajemen Indonesia
and The University of Western Ontario

Abstract. As part of Indonesia's opening to the world economy, over the past several years Indonesian firms have begun to invest abroad. This study compares Indonesian firms that have invested abroad and those that have not and with Third World Multinationals and other MNEs. It found that the performance of Indonesian firms that invested abroad improved dramatically after their investment in terms of management expertise, exports, quality, and costs relative to their past performance and relative to the other firms in the sample. These results support a conclusion that Indonesian multinationals have gone abroad not only to exploit their ownership advantages but also to access and develop ownership advantages they did not previously possess.

Over the period 1977 to 1985, there was a stream of research concerning foreign direct investment (FDI) by firms based in developing countries, Third World multinationals (TWMNEs).[1] Since the books by Wells [1983], Lall [1984], and Ting [1985], however, little work has been done on this interesting topic.[2] This paper once again addresses the topic of Third World multinationals. The paper is based on data gathered from a sample of firms in Indonesia, both domestic and multinational Indonesian firms and foreign firms.

REVIEW OF THE LITERATURE AND THEORY OF TWMNEs

Past research on Third World multinationals reached several conclusions in three areas: (1) the firm-specific advantages that allowed these firms to compete with both domestically owned firms and other multinationals abroad (the ''how'' of investment abroad); (2) the factors that motivated them to invest abroad (the ''why'' of investment abroad); and (3) the factors

---

*Donald J. Lecraw is a Professor in the Finance/Economics Area Group at Western Business School, The University of Western Ontario. His research interests center on multinational enterprises in developing countries and industrial organization. He has taught at Harvard, Western, INSEAD, and the Institut Pengembangan Manajemen Indonesia (IPMI). This article was written while he was on a leave of absence at IPMI. This is his fourth article in *JIBS* since 1984.

Received: April 1991; Revised: November 1991, March & June 1992; Accepted: June 1992.

that influenced the geographical location of their investments (the "where" of investment abroad). These results can be summarized as follows:

Third World multinationals invested abroad based on firm-specific advantages in product and process technologies that were appropriate to the factor costs, input characteristics, and demand conditions in the host countries in which they invested [Lall 1984; Wells 1983; Lecraw 1977, 1981]. Third World multinationals usually utilized smaller scale, more labour-intensive, more flexible (among inputs and outputs) technology than did other MNEs and often domestically owned firms [Lecraw 1977, 1979, 1981]. Their output was generally of lower quality than that of other MNEs and they competed based more on lower price than on product differentiation [Wells 1983; Lecraw 1977, 1981].

In the early 1980s, Third World multinationals based in upper middle income developing countries, such as Singapore, Taiwan, and Hong Kong, began producing more technology-intensive and marketing-intensive products in other countries. These products, however, were largely confined to such items as rice cookers, and products such as consumer electronics, the initial technology for which had been developed in high income countries (Ting [1985]; but see Lecraw [1986] for a critique of this research).

Third World multinationals, except for their quota-hopping investments, tended to export less of the output from their foreign subsidiaries than did other MNEs or domestically owned firms [Lecraw 1977, 1981]. Their exports were most often to markets other than those in their home countries. On the other hand, they tended to import a lower proportion of their inputs than did other firms, especially other MNEs.

Several factors were identified as motivating Third World multinationals to invest abroad: market protection and development in host countries; avoidance of quotas in high income countries; and risk diversification by locating assets outside their home countries [Lecraw 1977]. Third World multinationals in some instances also began to invest abroad in heavy, dirty industries due to rising land costs and environmental constraints in their home countries [Chen 1981].

Third World multinationals undertook outward investment through FDI, rather than via portfolio investment, due to foreign exchange constraints in their home countries and in order to utilize their firm-specific advantages in process and product technology. Their technological advantages tended to be impacted in their human capital and could not easily have been unbundled through licensing. Third World multinationals chose to access markets in the host countries via FDI, rather than through exports or licensing. Exports of their products were often blocked by tariffs and nontariff barriers in the markets of other developing countries.

Third World multinationals invested in neighbouring, "downstream," developing countries with lower levels of industrialization and technological capabilities. In host countries, demand conditions, market size, factor costs, and input characteristics were similar to those in their home countries.

FDI BY FIRMS BASED IN INDONESIA

In order to place the results of this research on Indonesian multinationals in perspective, a brief description of the Indonesian economy and industrial structure is useful. Indonesia's industrial structure, resource base, and factor costs have several implications for the competitive advantages and conduct of Indonesian firms at home and abroad. Over the period 1966 through 1991, the Indonesian economy grew quite rapidly, on average well over 5% per year. Indonesia has abundant and relatively inexpensive natural resources in agriculture products, timber, fisheries, minerals, and energy. The economy has been highly regulated both internally and on its external interface. Prior to the mid-1980s, Indonesia followed an import substitution policy to foster the growth of the manufacturing sector. It employed high tariffs and non-tariff barriers to trade. By 1985, 1,780 out of 5,229 imported items (30% of import value) were covered by special licenses or quotas. Despite low wages, in many industries Indonesian firms are high cost due to their small scale and lack of technology and due to the high costs of imported and domestically produced inputs.

Starting from the mid-1980s, there has been a slow but continuous government initiative to deregulate the domestic economy and its interface with the world economy. After a sharp devaluation of the rupiah in 1986, the real effective exchange rate of the rupiah against the dollar has been maintained more or less constant in order to accelerate export growth. Indonesia's foreign exchange regime is very open: the rupiah is freely convertible and there are few restrictions on international capital flows. Over the period from 1986 to 1991, Indonesia's regulations on foreign direct investment were progressively liberalized. Over this period, approvals of foreign investments increased from $300 million to over $4 billion. Over the same period, approvals for domestic investors increased five times.

Despite these measures, by the early 1990s much of the Indonesian manufacturing sector was still "inward looking," scale, technology, and management inefficient. There was still heavy government regulation and ownership in many industries. The private sector was dominated by ten to twenty large conglomerates spread across all sectors of the economy. Groups such as the Salim Group, Bimantara, Astra/Summa, Genung Sewu, and Sinar Mas owned well over one hundred companies each.

Market entry and expansion in Indonesia is often difficult due to industry overcapacity, oligopolistic response by existing competitors, and the limited size of the domestic market. Under these conditions, one way for firms to expand is to extend their operations abroad through foreign direct investment or through exports. From 1986 to 1991, exports of non-energy products expanded by 20% to 30% per year. Outward FDI also grew rapidly, not only in the manufacturing sector, but also in the banking and finance, real estate, and domestic trade sectors.

Export-Enhancing FDI

The devaluation of the rupiah in 1986 (and its constant real rate through 1991), and Indonesia's plentiful natural resources and low wages presented potential opportunities to export. Falling trade barriers and industrial deregulation also placed pressures on Indonesian firms to become larger, more efficient, and lower cost. This pressure may have been particularly strong on newer, smaller, scale-inefficient firms with small market shares. One means for these firms to expand to reduce costs was to export part of their output abroad.

To do so, however, they had to gain access to foreign product and process technology and management expertise, and access channels of distribution in export markets. One way to access these firm-specific advantages was through purchasing firms in their export markets. This type of FDI can be called ''export-enhancing'' FDI.

Prior to the investment, we would expect ''export-enhancing'' multinationals to be relatively small (and have small market shares) and to be scale and cost inefficient. Subsequent to the investment, they should gradually have become more like export-oriented Third World multinationals and multinationals based in high income countries. These firms should largely invest in ''upstream,'' higher income countries.

Operations-Extending FDI

Firms without export capabilities, those whose output was sold only on the domestic market, may have been able to invest abroad to serve domestic markets there. Indonesian multinationals undertaking this type of FDI can be called ''operations-extending'' multinationals. ''Operations-extending'' multinationals should be older, established firms that were relatively large, with large market shares. They should have been relatively efficient compared to other Indonesian-owned firms in their industries.

Operations-extending Indonesian multinationals should more closely resemble other import-substituting Third World multinationals. Their investments should have tended to be in other developing countries where factor and market demand conditions were similar to those in Indonesia.

The Role of Managerial Expertise in FDI

Some firms in Indonesia have responded to competitive pressures by expanding abroad through ''operations-extending'' and ''export-enhancing'' FDI. This raises the question of why other firms in their industries did not undertake overseas investment. Part of the answer may lie in the managerial and international expertise, experience, and formal management education of the management personnel of different firms, and at the corporate group level of these firms. This set of factors may have given Indonesian multinationals the international orientation and expertise necessary to invest abroad. Firms whose managers did not possess this international orientation and expertise may have remained uninational enterprises. This viewpoint of the motivation and the ability of Indonesian multinationals to invest abroad combines the structural approach of research on multinationals by economists with the behavioral approach often used by researchers from Scandinavia (Johanson and Vahlne [1977]; Welch and Luostarinen [1988]; but also see, Root [1987]; and Goodnow [1985]).

Management expertise of all kinds is in short supply in Indonesia. One possible motivation for investing abroad by acquiring an existing foreign firm might have been to acquire management expertise in marketing, technology, and general management.

Stages of Internationalization

A number of classification systems have been advanced concerning the entry strategies of firms into international operations [Johanson and Vahlne 1977; Cavusgil 1980, 1982; Root 1987]. Typically these classification systems are along the dimensions of resource commitment, market commitment, and control over foreign operations. Resource commitment here is taken to mean not just capital, but, more importantly, management and technological resources.

The amount of control is seen to increase as the firm's resource commitment increases. When faced with risk, however, firms tend to reduce their resource commitment [Aharoni 1966; Mascarenhas 1982]. Usually, when a firm first enters a market, its knowledge of the market and of operations in the host country is low and the risks of operations are perceived to be high. Hence past research has found that firms tend to enter a host country with a low level of resource commitment. Over time, they work their way up the scale to direct exports, an export subsidiary, a minority joint venture, a majority joint venture, and finally a wholly owned subsidiary. (See Erramilli and Rao [1990], for one such classification system; see Anderson and Gatingnon [1986] for another perspective.) Recent research by Millington and Baylis [1990], however, has found that U.K.-based firms when they entered the European market most often engaged in "jumps" from no involvement or simple export operations to "Transnational Operations" with a producing subsidiary in the market.

Several factors should have influenced Indonesian multinationals to engage in similar jumps. Due to the size of their corporate groups and the convertibility of the Indonesian rupiah, capital availability may not have been a binding constraint for them. Large Indonesian firms also had experience in owning highly diversified subsidiaries over which they had little direct operating control. Export-enhancing Indonesian multinationals may have been motivated to undertake FDI to access the entire package of advantages of the acquired firm. They may also have desired to transfer some of those advantages back to the parent in Indonesia. Hence for these firms, it is likely they have acquired an existing firm rather than started a new operation. From this viewpoint, they most likely acquired 100% ownership of the operation in order to facilitate the transfer of broadly defined technology, including management skills.

Operations-extending Indonesian multinationals must, of course, have made "jumps" into some sort of equity position, since, by definition, they had little involvement through exports in the host country prior to the investment. Previous research [Lecraw 1977; Wells 1984] found that Third World multinationals generally took minority positions in joint ventures abroad. They had low bargaining power with firms and governments in host countries and they lacked certain advantages needed to operate there [Lecraw 1983, 1984]. Operations-extending Indonesian multinationals should be more similar to other import-substituting Third World multinationals. They should be expected to enter into joint ventures abroad.

THE SAMPLE AND DATA

There are a number of features of the sample and the type of data collected that need to be mentioned. In general, there is a lack of publicly available statistics and data at the firm level in Indonesia. Most firms are privately owned and there are no government reporting requirements that would enable outsiders to assemble data profiles based on various government sources. There is, however, a wide variety of what might best be described as "informal data" concerning the operations of firms. This qualitative data is readily available and managers are quite willing and able to provide qualitative data on their own and rival firms.

For these reasons, the data on the various aspects of the firms in the sample were scaled on a range of "much higher, somewhat higher, about the same, somewhat lower, much lower" basis. These qualitative ratings were then assigned values of 5 (much higher) to 1 (much lower). Managers in each of the firms in the sample were asked to rank their own firm as well as all the others on each of the characteristics.

Twenty-four industries were selected. Each industry contained an Indonesian multinational that had made either an export-enhancing or operations-extending investment abroad over the 1986-1990 period. Each industry also contained at least one Indonesian uninational, one Third World multinational and one multinational based in a high income country. In all, there were fourteen export-enhancing Indonesian multinationals and ten operations-extending Indonesian multinationals in the sample.

The data were collected during interviews using a questionnaire. Data were collected for Indonesian multinationals, Indonesian uninationals, Third World multinationals, and other multinational enterprises.

RESULTS AND INTERPRETATION

The small size of the samples of the two types of Indonesian multinationals precluded sophisticated statistical analysis. In particular, multiple regression analysis to isolate the variables that were significant in determining investment behaviour was not possible.

Tables 1 and 2 display the results of simple pair-wise comparisons between the average scores on various characteristic dimensions (quality, export intensity, and so on) of the different types of firms. For example, in Table 1, column 1, row 1, the average quality rating prior to investment of the export-enhancing Indonesian multinationals in the sample was .53 *below* that of Indonesian uninationals. The significance level of the differences in the means is displayed below the differences in the means to the nearest 5% [Wonnacott and Wonnacott, 1984, p. 232].

The results of the comparisons in Table 1 give some support to the hypotheses concerning the competitive advantages and the motivation of Indonesian export-enhancing multinationals in undertaking investments abroad. Prior to the investment, they were relatively scale, cost and technology inefficient. Their quality, however, was somewhat above Indonesian uninational firms; they used relatively more of Indonesia's inexpensive domestic inputs; but they were somewhat less export intensive than Indonesian uninational firms. To expand, they would have had to increase exports, which in turn meant that they would have to reduce costs and increase quality. One means to do this would be to invest abroad. At the corporate group level, management had relatively high formal management training and international experience through other joint ventures, trade, and licensing.

At the time of the study, the performance of export-enhancing Indonesian multinationals had improved substantially in terms of size, exports, quality, cost, and the use of domestic inputs. This result seems to suggest that, by acquiring firms abroad, these firms had been able to access the advantages they needed to compete abroad. They were not only able to operate their subsidiaries abroad, but they also became export-intensive, low-cost producers of high quality products. This is a remarkable example of the transfer of broadly defined technology via investment. In this case, however, the transfer was from the acquired subsidiary to the parent.

The data in Table 2 show the similarity of operations-extending Indonesian multinationals to Third World multinationals, and their dissimilarity with other multinationals. These firms, however, generally produced at lower quality, used fewer domestic inputs, had a higher capital-labour ratio, and produced at higher costs than did other Third World multinationals. Their

TABLE 1
Characteristics of Indonesian Export Enhancing Multinationals Compared to Indonesian Uninational Enterprises (IUNE), Third World Multinationals (TWMNE), and Other Multinational Enterprises (MNE)

	Before Investment			Present		
	IUNE	TWMNE	MNE	IUNE	TWMNE	MNE
1. Quality	-.53	-.92	-2.32	+1.12	+.78	-.62
	(.70)	(.80)	(.98)	(.95)	(.80)	(.75)
2. Domestic inputs	+.21	-.53	+1.33	-1.58	-2.38	-.48
	(.60)	(.90)	(.85)	(.90)	(.98)	(.70)
3. Unit size	-1.03	-.86	-3.22	+1.66	+1.73	-.63
	(.85)	(.70)	(.95)	(.90)	(.90)	(.60)
4. Group size	+2.41	N.A.	N.A.	+3.37	N.A.	N.A.
	(.98)			(.98)		
5. Capital/labour	+.96	+1.35	-1.40	+2.44	+2.89	+.09
	(.80)	(.95)	(.95)	(.98)	(.98)	(.55)
6. Costs	+.43	+1.84	+1.20	-1.33	+.31	-.33
	(.60)	(.95)	(.90)	(.95)	(.60)	(.65)
7. Exports unit	-1.25	-1.43	-.88	+2.42	+2.24	2.79
	(.85)	(.70)	(.70)	(.90)	(.85)	(.95)
8. Trade group	+1.30	N.A.	N.A.	+1.75	N.A.	N.A.
	(.90)			(.95)		
9. JV group	+1.28	N.A.	N.A.	+1.85	N.A.	N.A.
	(.85)			(.90)		
10. Licensing group	+.65	N.A.	N.A.	+.67	N.A.	N.A.
	(.70)			(.70)		
11. Expatriate managers unit	-1.65	-4.20	-3.33	+1.11	-1.42	-.60
	(.90)	(.98)	(.98)	(.95)	(.95)	(.55)
12. Expatriate managers group	+1.30	N.A.	N.A.	+1.45	N.A.	N.A.
	(.85)			(.85)		
13. MBA ed. group	+.75	N.A.	N.A.	+1.16	N.A.	N.A.
	(.70)			(.90)		
14. International experience group	+1.43	N.A.	N.A.	+1.56	N.A.	N.A.
	(.95)			(.95)		

N.B. percentile values for the *t*-statistic below the differences

performance on these dimensions, however, was superior to that of Indonesian uninationals. The formal business training and international experience of the management of the corporate groups of operations-extending multinationals was greater than that of Indonesian uninationals. There was no significant improvement in the operations-extending Indonesian multinationals relative to other firms from their positions before undertaking investment to the present.

Both types of Indonesian multinational enterprises tended to leap over the stages of internationalization. They most often had little involvement in the

TABLE 2
Characteristics of Operations-Extending Indonesian Multinationals Compared with Those of Indonesian Uninational Enterprises (IUNE), Third World Multinational Enterprises (TWMNE) and Other Multinational Enterprises (MNE)

	Before Investment			Present		
	IUNE	TWMNE	MNE	IUNE	TWMNE	MNE
1. Quality	+2.11 (.95)	-1.02 (.80)	-.83 (.85)	+1.23 (.95)	-.95 (.50)	-1.45 (.80)
2. Domestic inputs	+1.59 (.90)	-.55 (.90)	-2.33 (.95)	+1.69 (.90)	-.63 (.80)	+2.90 (.95)
3. Unit size	+1.20 (.80)	+.80 (.70)	-1.11 (.90)	+1.32 (.85)	+.85 (.70)	-1.22 (.90)
4. Group size	+2.29 (.95)	N.A.	N.A.	+2.50 (.95)	N.A.	N.A.
5. Capital/labour	-1.24 (.90)	+1.32 (.90)	-1.75 (.90)	-1.30 (.85)	+1.37 (.90)	-1.80 (.90)
6. Costs	-1.97 (.90)	+1.11 (.80)	+1.42 (.90)	-2.04 (.90)	+1.32 (.85)	+1.52 (.85)
7. Exports unit	-1.50 (.85)	-1.31 (.90)	-1.21 (.75)	-1.40 (.90)	-1.30 (.90)	-1.25 (.80)
8. Trade group	+1.34 (.85)	N.A.	N.A.	+1.40 (.90)	N.A.	N.A.
9. JV group	+.86 (.85)	N.A.	N.A.	+1.21 (.90)	N.A.	N.A.
10. Licensing group	+.21 (.80)	N.A.	N.A.	+.31 (.90)	N.A.	N.A.
11. Expatriate manager unit	+.68 (.70)	-1.56 (.98)	-.77 (.95)	+.70 (.90)	-1.42 (.95)	-.65 (.95)
12. Expatriate managers group	+1.67 (.90)	N.A.	N.A.	+1.75 (.90)	N.A.	N.A.
13. MBA ed. group	+.85 (.80)	N.A.	N.A.	+.87 (.80)	N.A.	N.A.
14. International experience group	+2.45 (.90)	N.A.	N.A.	+2.84 (.95)	N.A.	N.A.

host country prior to the investment. And they most often took majority or full ownership in their subsidiaries abroad (Table 3). In results not reported in the tables, operations-extending multinationals tended to invest in other developing countries. Export-enhancing multinationals tended to invest in higher income countries.

The results of this study shed some light on the question of foreign investment by firms based in developing countries. Due to limitations in the data, however, the conclusions of the pape" can only be viewed as indicative and

TABLE 3
Stages of Internationalization of Indonesian Multinational Enterprises

	Export-Enhancing		Operations-Extending	
	Before FDI	After FDI	Before FDI	After FDI
1. No involvement	0	N.A.	5	N.A.
2. Export agent	2	0	4	0
3. Export distributor	5	0	1	0
4. Direct exports	7	0	0	0
5. Minority JV	0	2	0	2
6. 50-50 JV	0	1	0	1
7. Majority JV	0	2	0	1
8. Wholly owned subsidiary (acquired)	0	9	0	6
9. Wholly owned subsidiary (new venture)	0	10	0	0

suggestive rather than as statistical confirmation of an accepted body of theory. Despite these caveats, some insights can be drawn.

Managerial experience, training, and international orientation would seem to have had a strong influence on the behaviour of the firms in the sample. Indonesian firms with greater expertise in international operations tended to engage in outward investment to a greater extent than did other firms.

An argument can be made that export-enhancing Indonesian multinationals undertook investment to gain access to advantages in technology, access to channels of distribution, and management. In doing so, they improved their operations in Indonesia and were able to expand their exports.

For operations-extending Indonesian multinationals, however, the picture was different. They had developed advantages that enabled them to invest abroad in import-substituting industries. In general, however, their ability to utilize labour-intensive technologies, domestic inputs, and produce quality products at low cost was not as high as those of other Third World multinationals. Perhaps, over time, as the Indonesian economy grows and deepens, this type of firm will be able to match the skills of other Third World multinationals. But, at present, these skills do not seem to be well developed.

The results for export-enhancing Indonesian multinationals raise an interesting conceptual issue. Typically, multinationals based in high income countries are viewed as possessing a package of firm-specific advantages in such areas as management, marketing, technology, and access to capital. They then utilize these advantages to operate abroad to seek markets or low-cost natural resources or factors of production. The advantages of export-enhancing Indonesian multinationals, however, were in their access to low-cost natural resources and labour. They then used their capital to buy management, technology, and marketing advantages through foreign direct investment.

NOTES

1. See Wells [1983]; Lall [1984]; Chen [1981]; Kim and Terpstra [1984]; Lecraw [1977, 1981]; Ting [1985]; and articles in Kumar and McLeod [1981].

2. But see Monkiewicz [1986]; Khan [1986]; Aggarwal and Agmon [1990]; Han and Brewer [1987]; and Potts [1988].

REFERENCES

Aggarwal, Raj & Tamir Agmon. 1990. The international success of developing country firms: Role of government-directed comparative advantage. *Management International Review*, 30(2): 163-80.

Anderson, Erin & Hubert Gatignon. 1986. Modes of entry: A transactions cost analysis and propositions. *Journal of International Business Studies*, 17(3): 1-26.

Cavusgil, S. Tamer. 1980. On the internationalization process of firms. *European Research*, 8(6): 273-81.

______. 1982. Some observations on the critical variables for internationalization stages. In Michael Czinkota, editor, *Export Management*. New York: Praeger.

Chen, Edward. 1981. Outward investment from Hong Kong. In Krishna Kumar & Malcolm McLeod, editors, *Multinationals from developing countries*. Lexington, Mass.: D.C. Heath, Lexington Books.

Erramilli, M. Krishna & C.P. Rao. 1990. Choice of foreign entry modes by service firms: Role of market knowledge. *Management International Review*, 30(2): 135-50.

Goodnow, James D. 1985. Developments in international mode of entry analysis. *International Marketing Review*, 2(3): 17-30.

Han, C. Min & Thomas L. Brewer. 1987. Foreign direct investments by Korean firms: An analysis with FDI theories. *Asia Pacific Journal of Management*, 4(2): 90-102.

Johanson, Jan & Jan-Erik Vahlne. 1977. The internationalization process of the firm: A model of knowledge development and increasing foreign market commitment. *Journal of International Business Studies*, 8(1): 23-32.

Khan, Kushi, editor. 1986. *Multinationals from the south*. New York: St. Martins Press.

Kim, W. Chan & Vern Terpstra. 1984. Interregional foreign direct investment in the Asia Pacific region. *Asia Pacific Journal of Management*, 2(1): 1-9.

Kumar, Krishna & Malcolm McLeod, editors. 1981. *Multinationals from developing countries*. Lexington, Mass.: D.C. Heath, Lexington Books.

Lall, Sanjaya. 1984. *The new multinationals: The spread of Third-World multinationals*. New York: John Wiley.

Lecraw, Donald J. 1977. Direct investment by firms from less developed countries. *Oxford Economic Papers*, 29(3): 442-57.

______. 1979. Choice of technology in low-wage countries: A non-neoclassical approach. *Quarterly Journal of Economics*, 93(4): 631-54.

______. 1981. The internationalization of firms from LDCs: Evidence from the ASEAN region. In Krishna Kumar & Malcolm McLeod, editors, *Multinationals from developing countries*. Lexington, Mass.: D.C. Heath, Lexington Books.

______. 1983. Performance of transnational corporations in less developed countries. *Journal of International Business Studies*, 14(1): 15-33.

______. 1984. Bargaining power, ownership and profitability of subsidiaries of TNCs in developing countries. *Journal of International Business Studies*, 15(1): 27-43.

______. 1985. Some determinants and effects of foreign direct investment in Singapore. *Asia-Pacific Journal of Management*, 2(2): 71-80.

______. 1986. *Book review* (Wenlee Ting, Business and technological dynamics in newly industrializing Asia, Westport, Conn.: Quorum Books). Wall Street Review of Books, Spring: 104-106.

Mascarenhas, Briance. 1982. Coping with uncertainty in international business. *Journal of International Business Studies*, 13(2): 87-98.

Millington, Andrew I. & Brian Baylis. 1990. The process of internationalization: U.K. companies in the EC. *Management International Review*, 30(2): 151-61.

Monkiewicz, Jan. 1986. Multinational enterprises of developing countries: Some emerging trends. *Management International Review*, 26(3): 67-79.

Potts, Philippa. 1988. Andean multinational enterprises: A progress report. *Multinational Business*, 1(Spring): 50-52.

Root, Franklin. 1987. *Foreign market entry strategies*. New York: AMACOM.

Ting, Wenlee. 1985. *Business and technological dynamics in newly industrializing Asia*. Westport, Conn.: Quorum Books.

Welch, Lawrence & Reijo Luostarinen. 1988. Internationalization: Evolution of a concept. *Journal of General Management*, 14(2): 34-55.

Wells, Louis T., Jr. 1983. *Third world multinationals—The rise of foreign direct investment from developing countries*. Cambridge, Mass.: MIT Press.

Wonnacott, Thomas H. & Ronald J. Wonnacott. 1984 (third edition). *Introductory statistics for business and economics*. New York: John Wiley & Sons.

[11]

Direct Investment and Economic Integration in the Asia Pacific: The Case of Taiwanese Investment in Xiamen

Qi Luo and Christopher Howe

The Asia–Pacific region, and particularly its East Asian core, has achieved an impressive record of growth, export expansion and regional economic integration that now spans more than three decades and a wide variety of world economic environments. A key indicator of these achievements is the changing level of intra-regional foreign trade. This indicator is positive for the region as a whole over the period, although trends since 1980 are quite sensitive to the precise definition of the region employed. However, for the NICs (Hong Kong, Taiwan, South Korea and Singapore) and the ASEAN group (Thailand, Malaysia, Indonesia, Philippines and Brunei) in isolation, intra-regional trade increased by approximately 25 per cent over the decade 1980–90.[1]

Trade within the Asia–Pacific as a whole has been driven by the exceptionally diverse endowments of the region's constituent economies in terms of natural resources, relative labour–capital proportions and technological capabilities. These complementarities have been far more important than regionally-biased policy factors or institutionalized preferential arrangements although, in the case of Japan, the intensity of regional trade is also a reflection of Japan's export credit and aid policies.

Within the Asian sub-group, the patterns of trade have become even more interesting and complex since the mid-1980s. As incomes have risen and development deepened, new patterns of increasing specialization have led to a distinct rise in intra-industry trade. Initially, this was a result of a deepening division of labour between Japan and neighbouring economies; more recently there have been signs of a growth in intra-industry trade both between and within the NIC and ASEAN groups. A major stimulus to these changes has been the combination of Japanese trade liberalization and exchange rate changes consequent upon the upward valuation of the yen against the U.S. dollar. While this change involved only the dollar and the yen at first, leaving the NICs in an exceptionally favourable competitive position, under pressure the NICs have been forced to appreciate their currencies strongly against the dollar (with the exception of Hong Kong which is tied to the dollar for political reasons), and this has helped to open their markets to other, new Asian industrializers.

Apart from trade, the major factor in Asian–Pacific integration has

1. Valuable surveys of these trends are in FAIR, *Interim Report of Asia Pacific Economic Research* (Tokyo, 1989) and Koichi Ohno (ed.), *Regional Integration and its Impact on Developing Countries* (Tokyo: Institute of Developing Economies, 1993, Part 1). An excellent survey of the development of south China with a valuable chapter and data survey on Taiwan–Fujian relations is Maruyama Nobuo (ed.), *Kanan keizaiken (The South China Economic Region)* (Tokyo: Ajia Keizai Kenkyujo, 1992).

been the cross flow of foreign direct investment (FDI). Prior to 1980, there were some substantial flows of investments from Japanese firms seeking to secure reliable supplies of raw materials, access to protected markets, or locations where pollution-intensive industries would find lower costs and less political opposition than was the case in Japan. However, during the course of the 1980s, a series of developments accelerated FDI flows and transformed their impact on trade structures.

First, Reaganite policies took the dollar to levels that forced American-based multinationals to seek low cost locations from which output could be re-exported back to the United States and to other markets. The Asian NIC group, with relatively low wages, well-educated labour forces and strongly motivated business environments, was an ideal solution to this problem. In addition, American multinational FDI flows were accompanied by technology flows to Asia which enabled local producers to take advantage of the opportunities created by the newly favourable cost and exchange rate levels. As a result, the American share of NIC exports expanded from 25 per cent in 1980 to 40 per cent in 1984 – an extraordinarily rapid change.

Secondly, between 1985 and 1988 the revaluation of the yen, designed to alleviate U.S.–Japan trade frictions, profoundly affected Japanese corporate attitudes to FDI. Faced with a rapid reduction in the value of the dollar from 250 to 125 yen by 1988, Japanese businessmen were taking the view that they must plan their business strategies on the assumption of a rate of 100 yen to the dollar. Although this level was never quite reached, the shift in resources was enormous. Between 1984 and 1989 world-wide Japanese FDI rose from US$10 billion to US$70 billion.[2] Of this, in the years 1986–90, more than a third was for investment in manufacturing and 12 per cent of the total went to Asia. The Asian share may seem small, but in relation to the size of some of the favoured Asian economies, the flows were large.

The impact of these flows on the economies of the NICs has been striking, and strongly supported by the slow upward adjustment of their exchange rates against the yen and their consequent gain in competitiveness vis-à-vis Japan. As a result, output, employment, exports and prices increased rapidly, providing strong incentives for government-supported upgrading of domestic and trade structures. In the cases of Taiwan, South Korea and Singapore, upgrading policies were reflected in a significant jump in R & D expenditures. In Hong Kong, where no appreciation against dollar was permitted by the dollar-link system, adjustment mainly took the form of a sharp increase in domestic prices and a rapid relative increase in the size of the service sector. In industry, although official Hong Kong policies had hitherto been strongly against any form of industrial policy, a shift of attitude could also be detected.

Rapidly rising labour and land costs in the NICs had important consequences for ASEAN, which found itself the beneficiary of further

2. All references in dollars ($) in this paper are, unless specified otherwise, to United States dollars (US$).

restructuring FDI, sourced not only from Japan and the United States but also from the NICs themselves. Data problems make the quantification of these changes difficult, but according to Japanese estimates, in 1988 FDI accounted for no less than 48.5 per cent of total ASEAN fixed capital formation, and flows of direct investment to Asian regional partners accounted for about half of all Asian investment outflows. These trends have begun to transform ASEAN trade structures. Traditionally primary producers, the ASEAN group have diversified into industrial exports, with Thailand as a striking example of development that has reached the stage where such exports are predominant. Further, since 1990 there have been signs that a new group, including Vietnam and the Philippines, is moving into the circle of FDI-led development. The overall strength of these recent changes has been so strong that while world-wide inflows of direct investment fell by 28 per cent between 1990 and 1992, total Asian inflows actually rose by 51 per cent.[3]

As for the Greater China economies, it is clear that while Hong Kong and China are to some extent special cases, Taiwan fits precisely into this analysis. An archetypal NIC, Taiwan has grown at about 9 per cent per annum for 40 years and during this period it has become the 14th largest trading economy in the world. A major factor in Taiwanese growth has been an active policy to encourage inflows of direct investment – especially from the United States and Japan. In recent years, moreover, Taiwan has been a major recipient of technology flows unrelated to investment in physical capital.

The events of the past five to six years have required a major re-evaluation of Taiwanese economic strategy. Wages and land prices have risen, exchange rate trends have been adverse, and ASEAN economies have become serious competitors in the more labour-intensive and less technologically demanding industries. As a result, Taiwan has been forced to make major efforts to upgrade its economic structure. This has been reflected not only in the massive plans for infrastructure investment, but also in a sharp rise in R & D expenditure. At the same time, Taiwan's exceptional trade surpluses have reflected the macro-economic shift to a rich and mature surplus savings stage of development. This has been evident since 1981. According to estimates by the Ajia Keizai Kenkyujo (Tokyo), the average gap between savings and investment as a percentage of national product during 1981–91 inclusive was an astonishing 11 per cent. These savings have provided the resources to attempt further economic restructuring through outflows of FDI. By investing abroad, Taiwanese companies can combine their own competitive advantages in management, trading and technology with the lower land and labour costs of neighbouring Asian economies. In addition, the impact of these flows on visible trade means that some of the surpluses that are an embarrassment for Taiwan vis-à-vis the United States can be shifted to those economies in which the Taiwanese companies locate.

The data on the size of the outflow of direct investment from Taiwan

3. Bank for International Settlements, *63rd Annual Report* (Basle, 1993), pp. 90–91.

are very imprecise. Taiwanese companies only report a part of their activities and a great deal of the flow goes through intermediary companies (often located in Hong Kong, where capital flow data is unavailable anyway). However, the general level of estimates suggests that between 1987 and 1992 Taiwan directly invested $25 billion abroad. Of that, $12 billion went to local Asian economies and about $6 billion (indirectly) to the PRC. Although the general level of outflow has been falling off, the flow to the PRC increased to flood levels in 1992/93, so that the accumulated stock of investment grew by about 50 per cent in a single year.[4]

The development of Hong Kong and China does not precisely fit this pattern for several reasons. In China's case, the critical difference is that its behaviour as a recipient of direct investment is strongly affected by the nature of the domestic administrative system, planning and legal arrangements, the nature of its industrial enterprises, and its political problems. All these tend to limit FDI from market economies and modify its impact. In Hong Kong's case, the impending reunification in 1997 creates many forces unique to that economy.

This article, therefore, will examine the effects of Taiwanese investment on the PRC economy, through a case study of the Xiamen Special Economic Zone (SEZ). This will throw light on ways in which Taiwanese FDI flows may influence the *overall pattern* of economic integration in the Asia–Pacific Region. These are issues of interest to both the PRC and Taiwan, as well as to scholars, traders and industrialists who have invested, or are planning to invest, in the PRC. After outlining the trend and characteristics of Taiwanese investment in Xiamen, the major effects of Taiwanese investment on the Xiamen economy are analysed and the problems and wider issues arising from the utilization of Taiwanese capital in the PRC discussed. The article ends with some conclusions on the prospects of the PRC–Taiwan relationship and implications for the formation of the so-called "Greater China Economic Community" within the Asia–Pacific region. It is hoped that the underlying issues can be revealed, in spite of the fact that FDI data are scarce and unreliable, and that changes in the policies and measures of the PRC and Taiwanese authorities are so frequent that research is often outdated before publication.

The Special Features of Taiwanese Investment in Xiamen

The upsurge of Taiwanese investment has been one of the most prominent developments in PRC foreign economic relations in recent years. According to official Chinese sources, by the end of 1992 about 10,000 contracts had been concluded, calling for Taiwanese commitments

4. These estimates are based on figures quoted in *The Far Eastern Economic Review* (*FEER*), *China Daily* and the *Asian Wall Street Journal*. According to some commentators, all official numbers should be doubled. Judging by the discoveries made in the UK when serious enquiries were made into illicit post-war direct investment flows from the UK, this view should be taken quite seriously.

of more than $8 billion.[5] In 1992 alone, Taiwanese capital accounted for 13.19 per cent of total FDI projects in China, 9.54 per cent of total foreign capital commitments.[6] As a result, Taiwan has now surpassed Japan and the United States and become the second largest investor, behind Hong Kong, in the PRC.

Most Taiwanese projects are concentrated in the south-eastern coastal areas, with Fujian province accounting for nearly 65 per cent of the total. The Xiamen SEZ in southern Fujian has emerged as the front runner in attracting Taiwanese capital in the country, accounting for approximately a fifth of total projects and half of total pledged and invested capital.[7]

The Xiamen SEZ was opened in 1980 as one of China's five Special Economic Zones. The city faces Taiwan across 140 nautical miles of the Taiwan Straits. It has close historical, political, economic, social and lineage ties with Taiwan. Taiwanese and southern Fujianese speak the same dialect (*Minnanhua*), share the same culture and customs, and have an intimate historical relationship. Merchandise trade between southern Fujian and Taiwan was active as early as the 16th century and, with fluctuations, continued to thrive until 1949. Thereafter the Nationalists severed all links with the Communist mainland.

Today, Xiamen is a typical, small industrial city, containing an under-developed but all-embracing industrial system with some 620 largely outmoded enterprises. With the growing influx of Taiwanese investment, the SEZ authorities have attempted to transform their old industries as their top reform priority. According to the Eighth Five-Year-Plan (1991–95) for Xiamen, Taiwanese firms will generate almost 55 per cent (or 12 billion *yuan*) of total GNP (22 billion *yuan*) by 1995.[8] Thus, the significant involvement of, and the crucial role played by, Taiwanese investment in Xiamen's economic development clearly merit a detailed analysis.

The large-scale influx of Taiwanese capital into mainland China did not start until 1988. The political relaxation in Taiwan and, in particular, the removal of the ban on its citizens on travel to the mainland, triggered a steady stream of visitors to the PRC, especially to Xiamen.[9] Many combined private visits with a search for business opportunities. In response to this new development, the Xiamen authorities, apart from promulgating a series of laws, regulations and rules to encourage Taiwanese investment, opened up three investment zones (*Haicang*, *Xinglin* and *Jimei*) and one high-tech park (*Yazhou*) exclusively for the Taiwanese. As a result, the inflow grew at a staggering speed. The total annual investment amount peaked in 1989 ($454.15 million) and the number of projects in 1990 (172). More significantly, in 1989 the Taiwanese projects accounted for 76.62 per cent of all FDI projects and

5. BBC, *Summary of World Broadcasts*, FE/W00278, 19 May 1993, p. 7.
6. *Guoji maoyi* (*Intertrade*), April 1993, p. 58.
7. *Beijing Review* (*BR*), 27 January–2 February 1992, p. 17.
8. *Ibid.* p. 18.
9. It was estimated that the number of Taiwanese visitors to Xiamen had exceeded 1.3 million by the end of 1992.

87.06 per cent of all foreign committed capital in Xiamen (see Table 1). Today, Taiwanese projects play an increasingly important role in the development of export-oriented activity in Xiamen, with more than $300 million invested and over 200 projects under operation. These produce about one-fifth of the SEZ's total gross value of industrial output (GVIO) and nearly 15 per cent of total exports.[10] Without doubt, once direct communication, transport and business links with Taiwan commence, Xiamen will be the beach-head for further Taiwanese investment in the PRC.

Motives

There are several important reasons for the recent flows of Taiwanese capital to the PRC. First, as noted above, is the consistent and steady appreciation of the New Taiwan dollar (NT$). Over the last decade this has seriously weakened Taiwan's export competitiveness. Since 1985 the NT$ has appreciated by more than 40 per cent against the US$ to NT$25 to $1 at mid-1992.[11] As the majority of exporters in Taiwan are small and medium-sized manufacturing firms, selling standardized products in highly competitive conditions, the rise of the NT$ has left them unprofitable or, at best, only marginally profitable.

Secondly, other production costs have risen sharply in recent years. Manufacturing wages have been increasing by about 15 per cent per year, pushing the latest minimum wage up to NT$12,365 ($494.6) per month, equivalent to NT$51.5 ($2.06) per hour.[12] This rate, which applies to both native and foreign workers in Taiwan, is about 13–14 times higher than that prevailing in most parts of the PRC.[13] Rising land cost adds another problem and pollution-control expenses have also gone up steeply.[14] All this has made the manufacture of labour-intensive products no longer competitive.

A third factor has been the deterioration of social order in Taiwan in recent years. Violent political demonstrations, various forms of public disorder and, especially, gangland extortion of businessmen by threats of kidnapping or other criminal actions, have all contributed to businessmen's lack of confidence in the local investment environment.[15]

Fourthly, many Taiwanese firms are following the strategy of using FDI to expand their exports by opening up the mainland market, potentially

10. *Jingji ribao* (*Economic Daily*) (*JJRB*), 8 January 1992, p. 4.

11. *Free China Journal* (*FCJ*), 18 August 1992, p. 3. According to Osman Tseng, there are four reasons for the continued appreciation. The large surplus generated by Taiwan's foreign trade, its extraordinarily large sums of foreign exchange reserves and its higher interest rates have all created a growing demand for the NT$. Also, the economic recession in the U.S. has weakened the US$ and thus further raised the NT$. For more details, see Osman Tseng, "Unappreciated appreciation," *Free China Review* (*FCR*), February 1992, pp. 40–43.

12. *Ibid.*

13. The average wage in the mainland is only about one-tenth of that prevailing in Taiwan. For a typical Taiwan operation in the mainland, wages account for about 11% of the total production costs while in Taiwan it is about 36%. See *Jingji daobao* (*Economic Report*) (*JJDB*), No. 9 (9 March 1992), p. 33.

14. *FCR*, June 1990, p. 60.

15. *FCJ*, 6 October 1992, p. 7.

Table 1: **Development of Taiwanese Investment in Xiamen (1983 to September 1992)**

	1983–87	*1988*	*1989*	*1990*	*1991*	*1992 (Jan.–Sept.)*	*Total*
No. of contracts signed	16	57	154	172	94	105	598
% of total FDI contracts	5.42	31.67	76.62	65.65	44.13	39.92	42.29
Capital committed by Taiwan investors ($m.)	21.50	82.19	454.15	370.00	195.68	204.21	1,327.73
% of total foreign capital commitments	4.19	52.80	87.06	67.40	37.65	27.73	44.25

Sources:
1983–87: *Xiamen tongji* (*Xiamen Statistics*), No. 8 (1990), p. 23. 1988: Xiamen Statistical Bureau (XSB), *Xiamen tongji nianjian 1989* (*Almanac of Xiamen's Statistics 1989*) (Xiamen: Xiamen tongji ju, 1989), p. 362. 1989: XSB, *Xiamen jingji tequ nianjian 1990* (*Almanac of the Xiamen Special Economic Zone 1990*) (Beijing: Zhongguo tongji chubanshe, 1990), p. 329. 1990: ACE Editorial Board, *Zhongguo jingji nianjian 1991* (*Almanac of China's Economy 1991*) (Beijing: Jingji guanli chubanshe, 1991), p. IV–89. 1991–September 1992: XSB, *Tongji jianxu* (*Statistical Summary*) (Xiamen: Xiamen tongji ju, 1992), p. 13.

the largest in the world. Expressing the general mood of the Taiwan business community, Wang Chien-shien, Taiwan's former Finance Minister, was quoted as saying: "the mainland is a market for Chinese people, and Chinese people from Taiwan should not lag behind Japanese and Koreans in penetrating the mainland market."[16]

A fifth factor is that in industries subject to heavy international restrictions, some Taiwanese businessmen try to make use of PRC export quotas, especially to the North American and EEC markets.[17] Finally, although Taiwanese appear to have been the leading NIC investors in ASEAN (especially Malaysia and Thailand), the very predominance of these investments has meant that they have not only served to raise local wage costs making them less attractive, but have also caused anti-Taiwanese "frictions" that have encouraged diversification to China and Vietnam.

Special Features

The basic pattern of Taiwanese investment in Xiamen is that investors provide capital, technology and management expertise while Xiamen supplies cheap and abundant labour and land. However, in contrast to other investors in Xiamen, Taiwanese investors prefer wholly owned ventures to other forms of investment and, in many cases, emphasize their independence by supplying their own raw materials and export markets.

Predominance of wholly owned ventures. There is a growing tendency for Taiwanese investors to set up wholly owned ventures in Xiamen, instead of joint equity ventures or contractual management projects. Table 2 shows that the share of wholly owned ventures in the total number of Taiwanese firms climbed steeply, from 37.50 per cent in 1983–87 to a peak of 85.47 per cent in 1990, with an average percentage of 77.52 for the whole period 1983–91. Investment in wholly owned ventures amounted to nearly $1 billion, making up 90 per cent of the total Taiwanese investment in Xiamen.[18] Such a high proportion is unusual in the history of FDI in developing countries.

Predominance of labour-intensive and light industries. Because most Taiwanese investors go to the mainland to take advantage of the low labour costs there, the industries they bring in tend to be those producing light industrial/consumer goods, with low capital/technology-labour ratios. About 75 per cent of Taiwanese firms in Xiamen use only simple and, in many cases, second-hand machines imported from Taiwan, manufacturing goods such as footwear, clothing, toys, umbrellas, handicrafts,

16. *Ibid.* 18 August 1992, p. 3.

17. *Yuanjian* (*Global Views*) (*YJ*), May 1992, p. 47. According to a survey report published in Taiwan in 1992, the export prices for the products manufactured by the Taiwanese firms in the mainland, i.e. those "made in China," are estimated to be 10% cheaper than those "made in Taiwan." See *ibid.* p. 44.

18. *BR*, 27 January–2 February 1992, p. 17.

Table 2: **Shares of Wholly Owned Ventures in the Total Number of Taiwanese Firms in Xiamen (1983–91)**

	1983–87	*1988*	*1989*	*1990*	*1991 (Jan.–Nov.)*	*Total*
No. of wholly owned ventures	6	32	125	147	59	369
Total no. of Taiwanese firms	16	57	154	172	77	476
Share (%)	37.50	56.14	81.17	85.47	76.62	77.52

Sources:
No. of wholly owned ventures: *Xiamen tongji*, No. 8 (1990), p. 26 and *Jingji ribao* (*Economic Daily*), 8 January 1992, p. 4. Total number of Taiwanese firms: Table 1.

luggage and sports equipment.[19] Indeed, some Taiwanese firms even used *less* capital per unit of labour than their local state-owned counterparts.[20]

Prominence of chemical industry. Relocation is crucial for Taiwanese chemical manufacturers because many of their customers have moved to the PRC.[21] Thus it is not surprising that Xiamen, as the focus of Taiwanese investment in the mainland, has a strong presence of chemical projects, including plastics and textile processing branches. As shown in

Table 3: **Composition of Taiwanese Firms in Xiamen by Industry (1990)**

	No. of projects	*%*	*Amounts involved ($ million)*	*%*
Chemical	48	17.27	284.70	48.76
Paper and stationery	67	24.10	69.44	11.89
Sewing and leather	49	17.63	66.88	11.45
Electric machinery	26	9.35	61.89	10.60
Textile	21	7.55	38.41	6.58
Building material	23	8.27	30.03	5.14
Food processing	20	7.19	13.37	2.29
Electronic	10	3.60	10.91	1.87
Engineering	14	5.04	8.25	1.41
Total	278	100.00	583.88	100.00

Source:
Xiamen tongji, No. 8 (1990), p. 24.

19. *Xiamen tongji* (*Xiamen Statistics*), No. 8 (1990), p. 25.
20. One of the findings of the field visit in Autumn 1991. This is particularly true in umbrella and luggage manufacturing.
21. The plastic footwear industry is a good example. The total number of factories in Taiwan dropped from a peak of 1,400 to only 700 in 1990, primarily because of moves to the mainland. See *FCR*, June 1990, p. 60.

Table 3, although they make up only 17.27 per cent of all Taiwanese manufacturing projects in Xiamen in 1990, the amount involved ($284.70 million) accounts for a remarkable 48.76 per cent – nearly 37 per cent ahead of its closest rival, the paper and stationery industry. At the beginning of 1992 it was still at 40 per cent.[22]

High ratio of export. As most Taiwanese firms' finished goods are placed by their parent corporations in Taiwan, they tend to have very high ratios of export.[23] For example, in 1990 Taiwanese firms exported 86.12 per cent of their total output valued at 799.83 million *yuan*, in contrast with only 35 per cent for non-Taiwanese FDI firms in the same period.[24] The exports from Taiwanese firms accounted for 22.65 per cent of Xiamen's total exports. About three-quarters of these went to Europe and North America and 10 per cent to Japan.[25] A survey carried out in 183 Taiwanese firms in 1990 reveals that 107 of them (58.47 per cent) exported more than 80 per cent of their outputs, and that only eight (4.37 per cent) exported less than half (see Table 4).

Table 4: **Composition of Taiwanese Firms in Xiamen by Export Ratio (1990)**

Export ratio (%)	*Number of firms*	*Share (%)*
100	56	30.60
80–99	51	27.87
50–79	68	37.16
Below 49	8	4.37
Total	183	100.00

Source:
Hu Peizhao *et al.*, "Report on the Taiwan investment in Xiamen," *Zhongguo jingji wenti* (*China's Economic Problems and Issues*), April 1990, p. 16.

Diversification of investment structure. Taiwanese investment in Xiamen tends to concentrate on manufacturing industries producing light industrial/consumer goods. In 1990, for example, 86 per cent of Taiwanese firms were engaged in manufacturing operations, making up 78 per cent of the total Taiwanese investment funds. Since 1991, however, service industries, particularly real estate, have become the new focus of Taiwanese investment. At present, they account for 12 per cent of all

22. *BR*, 27 January–2 February 1992, p. 18.
23. Caves argues that foreign investors having a competitive edge in overseas marketing are likely to play an active role in the export marketing of their subsidiaries. See R. E. Caves, "International corporations: the industrial economics of foreign investment," *Econometrica*, No. 149 (February 1971), pp. 1–27.
24. Kong Zhang, "Assessment of Taiwan investment in Xiamen," *Gang-Ao jingji* (*Hong Kong and Macau Economies*), June 1991, p. 34.
25. Xiamen Statistical Bureau (XSB), *Xiamen jingji tequ nianjian 1991* (*Almanac of the Xiamen Special Economic Zone 1991*) (Beijing: Zhongguo tongji chubanshe, 1991), p. 58.

Taiwanese projects and 20 per cent of investment capital. Indeed, real estate has become the second largest investment sector, after the chemical industry.[26] Two-thirds of property developers are known to come from Taiwan, and they, together with thousands of contracted builders, have created a booming property business in Xiamen.[27]

Growing average size of investment. Before mid-1988, Xiamen did not have a single Taiwanese project involving more than $10 million and average capitalization was only $736,355 per project.[28] Most were the same scale as local rural or township enterprises. Since the second half of 1988, however, the situation has changed as a result of the political initiative taken by the Taiwanese authorities. More than half of Taiwan's Top 100 Companies (including the Formosa Plastic Group) have sent delegations to Xiamen to explore the possibility of investment. As a result, a total of 11 big contracts involving $10 million each had been signed by the end of 1990, with the largest investment worth $200 million.[29] This has increased the average capitalization to $3.469 million per project, compared with only $1.35 million for the non-Taiwanese FDI projects.[30]

Furthermore, many existing Taiwanese firms have expanded their operations in Xiamen by re-investing their profits. For instance, the Sandexing Industry Co. Ltd., set up in 1985, has increased its production capacity 11-fold and is planning to build a new industrial park housing 16 other Taiwanese firms. The Xianglu Chemical Co. Ltd., in addition to considering the establishment of weaving projects, has asked to build new plants to produce related high-pressure packaging containers.[31]

Taiwanese investors have shown increased willingness to extend the length of their investment term. Table 5 shows that from July 1987 to June 1989 the shares of the firms having an investment term of over 20 years increased substantially, while those below dropped sharply. By the beginning of 1992 some firms had extended their investment terms to 70 years.[32]

Thus a new investment pattern seems to be emerging. It is gradually shifting from single investments in manufacturing made by small or medium firms to joint investments (or developments) in both manufacturing and service industries by several companies, company groups or even conglomerates. There has also been a shift from renting workshops or buildings to buying them and, more recently, to leasing or buying a piece of land to develop it into an exclusive Taiwanese investment zone or industrial park.

26. *BR*, 27 January–2 February 1992, p. 18. The total Taiwan investment in mainland real estate stood, at the beginning of 1992, at $100 million. See *ibid.*

27. Xu Caixue, "Xiamen builds her dream on Taiwan," *YJ*, February 1992, p. 121.

28. Hu Peizhao *et al.*, "Report on the Taiwan investment in Xiamen," *Zhongguo jingji wenti (China's Economic Problems and Issues)*, April 1990, p. 14.

29. *BR*, 27 January–2 February 1992, p. 17.

30. Zhang Fenqing, "Analyses of Taiwan investment in the Xiamen SEZ," *Duiwai maoyi yanjiu (Research on Foreign Trade)*, p. 3.

31. *BR*, 27 January–2 February 1992, p. 18.

32. *Ibid.* p. 17.

Table 5: **Composition of Taiwanese Firms in Xiamen by Length of Investment Term (July 1987–June 1989)**

	July 1987–June 1988		*July 1988–June 1989*	
Length (year)	*No. of firms*	*%*	*No. of firms*	*%*
Over 30	9	12.68	45	36.00
20–29	17	23.94	35	28.00
10–19	43	60.56	45	36.00
Below 10	2	2.82	0	0.00
Total	71	100.00	125	100.00

Source:
Hu Peizhao, "Report on the Taiwan investment in Xiamen," p. 16.

Generally good performances. In contrast to the less satisfactory situation in all FDI projects, the financial performance of Taiwanese firms appears good.[33] Since many of them are small, light and self-equipped manufacturing ventures, they have the flexibility to plan for short gestation periods, and are normally able to sign contracts, go into operation and get returns within a year. According to a sample survey carried out by the Chinese Academy of Social Sciences, about 95 per cent of Taiwanese firms in Xiamen were profitable.[34] This ratio is considerably higher than the 53 per cent for the non-Taiwanese FDI firms. The footwear factories, for example, were reported to make 10–15 per cent more profits in Xiamen than in Taiwan.[35] Because of good performance, many firms start to play an important role in their parent corporations or their fields. Cankun Electric Appliance Co. Ltd. now produces two-thirds of the total output value of its general corporation,[36] while the Sandexing Industry Co. Ltd. has become the world's second largest manufacturer of conductive rubber.[37]

Major Effects of Taiwanese Investment on the Xiamen Economy

Since it was opened as an SEZ in 1980, Xiamen's economy has grown rapidly, fuelled mainly by the inflow of FDI. In 1992 the SEZ's GDP rose to 7.8 billion *yuan*, a 5.1-fold increase over 1980. Exports hit $3.53 billion, jumping by 53 per cent over 1991 – the largest increase among all the SEZs. The overall indicator of economic efficiency was 5.4 percentage points higher than the national average.[38]

33. However, the scale of losses in all FDI projects in the PRC is rising, and, in some areas, about 50% of FDI firms are reported to run at a loss. This has already become the focus of attention both within and outside China. See *JJDB*, 6 April 1992, p. 18.
34. *Jing bao* (*The Mirror*), January 1992, p. 79.
35. Kong Zhang, "Assessment of Taiwan investment," p. 34.
36. *BR*, 27 January–2 February 1992, p. 17.
37. Xu Caixue, "Xiamen builds her dream," p. 120.
38. *Renmin ribao* (*People's Daily*) overseas edition, 14 April 1993, p. 1; *JJRB*, 20 February 1993. p. 3.

Taiwanese investment, as the largest source of FDI in Xiamen, has played a crucial role in its economic development in recent years. The most evident contributions made by Taiwanese firms to Xiamen seem to be the creation of employment, increase in exports and expansion of tourism.

Reducing importance of the state-owned sector. As in other parts of China, Taiwanese firms in Xiamen grow much faster than local Chinese enterprises, especially state-owned ones (SOEs). At present, there are several Taiwanese firms producing more than $30 million worth of GVIO monthly.[39] As a result, the share of the state-owned sector in the economy has declined steadily, while the private sector (including Taiwanese and other foreign-owned firms) has risen. By the end of 1991, for example, the GVIO and exports of some 200 Taiwanese firms in Xiamen accounted respectively for one-fifth and 22.65 per cent of the SEZ's totals.[40] Together with all other FDI firms, they make up about 52 per cent of the SEZ's total GVIO and 80 per cent of its exports.[41] It is thus clear that the role played by the state-owned sector in Xiamen's economy has diminished significantly. Facing stiff competition from Taiwanese and other foreign firms, some inefficient local enterprises, especially SOEs, find it hard to survive. For instance, the Xiamen Mechanical Engineering Plant, one of the leading SOEs in the SEZ, was forced to close down in 1991.[42]

Over-riding local industrial development plan. In the 1985–2000 Socio-economic Development Plan, the Xiamen authorities (like their counterparts in other SEZs) decided to put the development of the electronic industry as their top priority in the hope that it would, through FDI, become the leading industrial sector by 1995. This decision was made on the grounds that "the electronic industry will pioneer Xiamen's industrial transformation through its extensive linkage effects."[43] However, the growing influx of Taiwanese capital since 1988 has swept the plan aside. As shown in Table 3, Taiwanese investment in Xiamen is dominated largely by the chemical industry (48.76 per cent of total investment), and the share of electronics is almost negligible (1.87 per cent). Thus the structure of Taiwanese investment does not coincide with Xiamen's own industrial transformation plan. Faced with this divergence, the Xiamen authorities apparently abandoned their original goal and declared petrochemicals to be their new "investment emphasis."[44] Indeed, a great deal of work has been done to accommodate more and bigger chemical projects from Taiwan.

39. *JJDB*, 16 March 1992, p. 10.
40. *JJRB*, 8 January 1992, p. 4; *BR*, 27 January–2 February 1992, p. 17.
41. *JJDB*, 1 January 1992, p. 28.
42. Xu Caixue, "Xiamen builds her dream," p. 120.
43. Research Office of Development Strategy of the Xiamen SEZ Government, *Xiamen jingji shehui fazhan zhanlue 1985–2000* (*The Strategy of Xiamen Socio-Economic Development 1985–2000*) (Xiamen: Lujiang chubanshe, 1989), p. 139.
44. *BR*, 27 January–2 February 1992, p. 19.

Linkage effects. Most Taiwanese firms are characterized by what local people call the "five self-responsibles" (*wuge ziwofuze*), that is, they are responsible for their own capital, technology, raw materials, management and export markets. This means that, apart from making use of cheap labour and land in Xiamen, all other inputs are brought from Taiwan. For example, more than three-quarters of all raw materials, components and parts needed by Taiwanese firms in Xiamen come from Taiwan, and about 85 per cent of their finished products are exported to existing overseas markets. Some midstream factories have even invested with upstream and/or downstream factories, and formed a self-sufficient, self-sustained operational system, almost wholly independent of the local economy.[45]

Moreover, as most of the ventures are wholly owned (77.52 per cent, see Table 2), top and middle-level managerial personnel are normally sent from their parent corporations in Taiwan and control all aspects and stages of their operations in Xiamen. Xiamen employees with low-level management responsibilities account for less than 30 per cent of the total number of managerial staff and play only a minor role in the decision-making process.[46]

Clearly, these enclave operations have little linkage effect (forward or backward) or demonstration effects on the local economy. As a result, the plan to make use of Taiwanese investment to transform local industrial enterprises and to stimulate the development of other related industries is still far from being reality.

Technology transfer. As already shown, many Taiwanese firms are small-scale and labour-intensive enterprises, producing light industrial/consumer goods. Thus in most cases the technologies employed are simple, mature and standardized. A considerable amount of their capital equipment is second-hand, imported from factories in Taiwan. Of the 200 identified technologies introduced so far, "very few" could really be regarded as sophisticated.[47]

On the other hand, according to another survey, about 65 per cent of technologies introduced by the Taiwanese are judged as appropriate to Xiamen's conditions. The Taiwanese shoe-manufacturing technology in Xiamen, for example, has been carefully studied and then copied by the Fujian Mechanical Engineering Bureau, with a view to equipping all the mainland shoe-making factories with the same technology. Also, several Taiwanese firms have brought in some practical technical know-how and/or Western manufacturing standards, such as the American "UL," Canadian "CSA," Japanese "JIS" and German "RDEF-TUV," to manufacture products with well-known brands such as "Philips" and "Esars."[48]

45. *Xiamen tequ yanjiu* (*Research on the Xiamen SEZ*) (*XMTQYJ*), March 1991, pp. 17–18; Kong Zhang, "Assessment of Taiwan investment," p. 34.

46. *XMTQYJ*, March 1991, pp. 17–18.

47. *China–Britain Trade Review*, January 1992, p. 14; Yan Zhiping, "The constraints on and counter-measures for Taiwan investment in Xiamen," *Fujian jingji* (*Fujian Economy*), p. 28.

48. Yan Zhiping, "Constraints and counter-measures," p. 34.

Increasing employment. The total number of people working in Taiwanese firms is now around 45,000. Many more are self-employed in the service industries which flourish in the periphery of the enterprises. The Xiamen authorities spent only 140 million *yuan* on facilitating these employment opportunities. It was estimated that if the jobs had been created solely by the authorities it would cost them at least 700 million *yuan*.[49]

External effects. As well as taxes, rents and charges paid to the local authorities, Taiwanese investment has had a number of advantageous effects. First, it has stimulated real estate business and greatly improved the utilization of local infrastructure. Before 1988 only about 50 per cent of a large number of standard factory buildings (which cost the authorities 420 million *yuan* to build) had been leased out. Since then, however, all the empty buildings have been rented to or bought by the Taiwanese. Many late arrivals had to settle in makeshift buildings or rent empty space in local factories. As a result, the authorities claim to have recovered all the buildings' construction costs by 1989, and to have achieved a rate of return of 162 per cent.[50]

Secondly, Taiwanese investment has created a desirable social effect on Xiamen and the neighbouring areas by generating employment. The average annual salary for a worker in a Taiwanese firm is about 5,000 *yuan*, which is four times higher than the local annual living costs (1,250 *yuan*). Thus a worker employed in a Taiwanese firm can support another three people in his or her family, compared with only 0.87 people in the case of a worker employed by a local Chinese factory. As 80 per cent of the 45,000 employees came from poorer rural regions around Xiamen, the income effects created by Taiwanese firms are far-reaching.[51]

Thirdly, it has promoted the development of tourism in Xiamen. During 1989–90, the number of foreign tourists visiting the PRC dropped sharply because of the Tiananmen Square violence. In Xiamen, however, the number of Taiwanese "tourists," many actually looking for business opportunities, reached record highs of 73,000 in 1989 and 136,000 in 1990.[52] Indeed, Xiamen hotels had unusually high occupancy rates at that time. Tourist numbers continued to grow in 1991 and 1992, when taxes paid by the tourist industry to the SEZ authorities were reported to have "climbed to new heights."[53]

Finally, it has induced investment from more than 30 Japanese firms, business partners of Taiwanese firms currently operating in Xiamen.[54]

However, the massive influx of Taiwan capital and personnel has also brought some unwelcome changes to the local population and economy. First, it has contributed to inflation and social dualism. In 1988 and 1989,

49. Kong Zhang, "Assessment of Taiwan investment," p. 34.
50. Hu Peizhao, "Report on the Taiwan investment in Xiamen," p. 17.
51. Kong Zhang, "Assessment of Taiwan investment," p. 34.
52. XSB, *Xiamen jingji tequ nianjian 1990* (*Almanac of the Xiamen Special Economic Zone 1990*) (Beijing: Zhongguo tongji chubanshe, 1990), p. 333.
53. Xu Caixue, "Xiamen builds her dream," p. 121.
54. *Ibid.* p. 120.

the price index of living costs for local people rose by 28.9 and 24.0 per cent respectively, leading to the deterioration of living standards for 17 per cent of families in Xiamen.[55] Thus while families benefiting from Taiwanese investment have greatly improved their welfare, some outside this group have clearly lost.

Secondly, the growing number of immigrants working in Taiwanese firms has exerted great pressure on housing, city-wide transport, schooling and entertainment facilities. It has also led to an increase in crime and other illegal activities in Xiamen. This problem has been aggravated by the fact that many Taiwanese investors by-passed the local Labour Management Bureau to employ even cheaper labour from the rural areas around Xiamen. Taiwanese real estate speculation has also pushed up property prices to an unduly high level.

In addition, the perceived superiority of employment in Taiwanese firms has seriously affected the morale (and hence probably the productivity) of employees in local Chinese enterprises, particularly SOEs. The wages and salaries of the former are about 2.14 times higher than those of the latter. As a result, many talented professionals and skilled workers have left their Chinese units for Taiwanese firms, leaving the local ones in decline.[56]

In short, the effects of Taiwanese investment on the Xiamen economy are profound, but they are by no means as influential and indeed crucial as those of Hong Kong investment on the Shenzhen SEZ, where a close economic integration between the two economies is taking place. Despite the achievement of attracting a greater inflow of Taiwanese capital, Xiamen seems to have failed to integrate Taiwanese investment into its economy, in particular to establish extensive economic and technological links between Taiwanese and local firms to transform its old, outmoded industry.

Taiwanese Investment and the PRC Economy

Taiwan is the PRC's second largest source of foreign investment, so its impact on the PRC economy as a whole is significant. The scale of the investment is growing and its structure is becoming more diversified. More importantly, the capitalization per project in 1992 rose from $560,000 to $781,000, up by nearly 40 per cent over 1991.[57] According to a survey report released recently in Taiwan, Taiwanese-funded firms made up 19 of 500 top foreign-funded firms on the mainland in 1991. Professor Kao An-pang of Taiwan's National Chengchi University estimates that Taiwanese capital accounts for $8.6 billion of the mainland's GNP and $7.2 of its per capita income.[58] Another report, released by Taiwan's Council for Economic Planning and Development (CEPD)

55. XSB, *Xiamen tongji nianjian 1989* (*Almanac of Xiamen's Statistics 1989*) (Xiamen: Xiamen tongji ju, 1989), p. 352; XSB, *Xiamen jingji tequ nianjian 1990*, p. 305.
56. Kong Zhang, "Assessment of Taiwan investment," p. 35.
57. *FCJ*, 4 September 1992, p. 3.
58. *Ibid.* 30 November 1992, p. 3.

indicated that a 0.28 per cent increase in Taiwan's trans-shipment to the mainland would lead to a growth of one percentage point in mainlanders' per capita income.[59]

Perhaps the most important contribution of Taiwanese investment to the PRC economy has been its impact on exports. As most Taiwanese firms in the PRC have very high export ratios, they play an important part in boosting PRC exports.[60] Indeed, as a result of this investment, the PRC is increasingly becoming a foreign trade rival to Taiwan, especially in the American market. In 1991, Taiwan's market share in the United States rose by only 0.1 per cent from 1990's 4.6 per cent. The PRC, on the other hand, closed the gap by increasing its share markedly from 3.1 to 3.9 per cent.[61] In 1992, PRC exports rose to a staggering $165.6 billion, outstripping Taiwan's $153.48 billion.[62] Thus 1992 will go down in history as the first year the PRC out-traded Taiwan, which has long been praised for its successful, export-oriented economy. The Taiwanese authorities attributed the growth to Taiwanese investment, especially in labour-intensive, light industrial sectors. For example, mainland toy exports hit $810 million with an annual growth rate of 41 per cent, while footwear exports expanded at a speed of 44.3 per cent per year to $2.31 billion.[63]

Problems and Wider Issues

In spite of the positive effects above, several serious problems and issues have emerged from the utilization of Taiwanese capital in the mainland, and these are now considered.

Conflict between the structure of Taiwanese investment and the mainland plan of industrial transformation. China's present industrial priority must now be to raise the technological level through, *inter alia*, the development of the engineering and electronic sectors. At the micro-level, it is crucial to improve the performance of tens of thousands of SOEs through radical reform programmes (including privatization). The role of FDI should be to assist the development of the industries which have extensive linkages to other manufacturing sectors, including machine tools, motor, iron and steel, heavy chemical, new material, equipment and instrument, and non-ferrous metal industries.

However, it is clear from the previous sections that the level and structure of Taiwanese investment generally do not match this strategy. In

59. *Ibid.* 20 November 1992, p. 3.
60. Trade between the PRC and Taiwan is growing sharply. Total trade volume with the mainland accounts for 4.6% of Taiwan's global trade (exports account for 7.3% and imports for 1.6%). See *FCJ*, 30 October 1992, p. 3. The same CEPD report also reveals the close trade linkage between the two in the sense that when PRC total exports expand by HK$1 million, Taiwan's exports to the PRC increase by 0.02%; while a decrease of $1 million in the PRC foreign exchange reserves result in a 0.01% drop in Taiwan's trans-shipments. See *ibid.*
61. *Ibid.* 24 July 1992, p. 3.
62. *Ibid.* 2 April 1993, p. 3.
63. *Ibid.* 18 September 1992, p. 3.

Xiamen's case, as has been seen, there is a conflict between the main interest of Taiwanese investment (chemical industry) and the local development priority (electronic industry). As well as the motives of investors, the policy of the Taiwanese authorities is also responsible for this conflict. According to the MOEA's new proposal, Taiwanese businessmen are automatically allowed to invest indirectly (via a third place) in 3,764 labour-intensive, low-tech products in the PRC. Applications for investment in some of the more capital/technology-intensive industries such as petrochemicals, cement and industrial parks will be considered on individual merit.[64] The authorities still firmly ban investment in what they see as high-tech products, projects "related to Taiwan's defence or economic security." A new law now requires that Taiwanese firms register their mainland operations with the authorities in order to facilitate "effectively guiding and ensuring the soundness of Taiwan investment on the mainland." Those failing to comply are subject to fines ranging from $115,000 to $576,000 and will be ordered to close down their project(s).[65]

Thus the role played by Taiwanese investment in the PRC economy is quite limited, despite the lower-level functions of increasing Chinese employment and exports. To rely on Taiwanese investment to restructure local industry and develop high-technology sectors, as Xiamen hopes, is, at least for the moment, unrealistic.

Small-scale and enclave-type operations. One of the legacies of the Maoist economy is the compartmentalization of industry by tens of thousands of local, small, self-sufficient enterprises. The current industrial reform has tried to eradicate this problem by reorganizing enterprises along economic lines, by mergers and by the formation of horizontal economic associations. As a result, many large enterprises, such as enterprise groups, are appearing. It is therefore essential for the PRC to integrate into the economy some advanced foreign multinationals which have extensive links with these enterprises.

However, the Taiwanese authorities' policy toward Taiwanese investment in the mainland is a major obstacle to this plan. Kao Koong-lian, a vice-chairman of Taiwan's Mainland Affairs Council, was recently quoted as saying that Taipei is "certainly not willing to see too many large firms go across the Straits."[66] It is reported that they wanted to use the indicator of output value as the criterion of approving investment projects. Thus a private firm will be allowed to invest in the mainland only if its output value per person per year is *below* Taiwan's average level by a certain margin. The standard set for 1992 is $50,000. Later, seven qualitative criteria were laid down to define the industries as labour-intensive, linkage-free, utilizing mainland resources, non-competitive, non-energy-consuming, non-polluting and achieving an appropriate

64. *Ibid.* 4 September 1992, p. 3.
65. *Ibid.* 21 July 1992, p. 8; 4 June 1993, p. 3; 15 June 1993, p. 3.
66. *Ibid.* 1 December 1992, p. 3.

ratio of local sales.[67] More recently, the authorities require manufacturers to retain part of their businesses, or "leave roots," in Taiwan. In other words, their mainland investments "cannot exceed a designated proportion of their domestic investments."[68] Taiwan's Investment Commission has already suspended approval of applications by ten companies listed on the island's stock market.[69] Without doubt, all these measures are intended to prevent or restrict large Taiwanese companies from investing in the mainland and thus to minimize the possibility of enhancing the mainland's industrial competitiveness.

Regional limitation. At present, Taiwanese investment is largely confined to China's south-eastern coastal areas, especially Fujian province, which reflects the economic and political considerations of both parties. One consequence of this high concentration, however, is severe overlapping of investment in the region. For example, a small rural town in Jinjiang county, southern Fujian, overwhelmed by 19 Taiwanese shoe-making factories has been dubbed as the "Taiwan shoe town." Indeed, the whole of southern Fujian will soon become a Taiwanese export processing zone.

In fact, with Taiwanese investment becoming larger and more diversified, other places in the Chinese interior may prove to be more suitable for Taiwanese investment. The MOEA's survey shows that Taiwanese firms situated in North-east China, Jiangsu and Zhejiang are the most profitable, followed by those in the Xiamen SEZ and Shanghai, while those in Fujian, Guangdong and the Shenzhen SEZ are the least.[70] Indeed, locations such as Shanghai, Tianjin, Liaoning, Jiangsu, Hubei and Sichuan are certainly better locations in terms of attracting large-scale or capital/technology-intensive industrial projects. Since these regions are generally more developed than South-east China, economic co-operation between the two sides will be at a higher and more sophisticated level. It will also be easier for Taiwanese investors to build up linkages with the local economy.

Dual economy. The expansion and, especially, enclave-type operation of Taiwanese investment has resulted in some dualistic phenomena in the PRC economy. It has become almost commonplace in some parts of Fujian, for example, to see fast-growing, capitalist Taiwanese firms coexisting side by side with stagnant or even declining socialist local enterprises.

From the national point of view, the influx of Taiwanese investment has aggravated the disparity of economic development between the south-eastern coastal areas and the inland regions. Since the PRC started to implement the open-door policy in the late 1970s and the early 1980s,

67. *JJDB*, 1 June 1992, p. 31.

68. *FCJ*, 4 September 1992, p. 3. As more than 90% of Taiwan firms are small and medium-sized, few have the ability to conduct simultaneous investment on both sides of the Taiwan Straits.

69. *Ibid.* 15 June 1993, p. 3.

70. *YJ*, May 1992, p. 44.

the economic growth in the south-east has persistently and substantially outpaced that inland, owing largely to the huge injection of foreign investment. As a result, the country is now divided by the more marketized, export-oriented economy in the south-east and the more centralized, inward-looking one in the vast hinterland. Both GNP and national income per capita of the former region are more than double those of the latter,[71] which has caused a large-scale migration from the poor inland to the more affluent south-east, destabilizing the inland economy. The inequality has already given rise to strong opposition from certain factions within the CCP leadership, as well as widespread resentment on the part of the inland authorities and people.

Clearly, these phenomena are potential causes for social unrest. If the Chinese authorities do not take action to narrow the divergence, they will soon face serious economic, social, cultural and, eventually, political consequences.

Opening domestic market and attracting high-tech investment. The PRC and Taiwan do have some high-technology industries which are complementary to each other. For example, the PRC is strong in space technology, micro-biology, medicine, optics and nuclear engineering, while Taiwan has computer manufacture, information technology, aviation, motor industry and electrical appliances. The PRC's strengths, coupled with its mighty heavy industrial base, could serve Taiwan's objective to upgrade its industries, while those of Taiwan, together with its experiences in industrialization, seem to suit the PRC's priority to develop electronic, automation, telecommunications and engineering industries.

Despite the fact that Taiwan, together with another 23 countries/regions, has been chosen by the PRC as a partner for high-technology co-operation, the general technology level of Taiwanese investment attracted so far is, as shown above, disappointingly low. As well as the above-mentioned factors of the investment environment and Taiwan's official policy, the PRC's so-called Special Policy toward high-technology investment should be blamed. The policy has not been backed by effective tax, price and financial mechanisms and hence has had little influence on Taiwanese investors.[72] The PRC authorities ought to understand that insistence on export quotas for FDI may be inappropriate for high-technology investment, at least in the short term. In fact, those investors carrying advanced technologies or new products tend to take a longer-term view and are hence more interested in opening a new market in the PRC. Although the authorities have gradually come to realize the importance of "exchanging domestic markets for advanced foreign technology," no specific policy measures have been worked out.[73]

71. *JJDB*, 15 June 1992, p. 12.
72. *Ibid.* 24 February 1992, p. 16.
73. Recently, the PRC offered to help Taiwan dispose of waste from its three atomic energy plants, which the PRC will not normally do for a "foreign" country. In exchange, Taiwan was to

Funding of Taiwan firms. Like other FDI firms on the mainland, Taiwanese firms suffer from the difficulty of raising local funds. The mainland banks, all owned by the state, lend most of their money to SOEs, in many cases to prop up the inefficient ones. Hence there is little left for Taiwanese firms. In addition, because of the lack of mortgage law in the PRC, it is very hard for a newly-established Taiwanese company (without credit record) to obtain a loan there. This situation has been exacerbated by the non-existence, up till now, of Taiwanese banks on the mainland and by the prohibition of foreign banks in the PRC to lend or deposit money in PRC currency.

Thus Taiwanese firms have to raise most, if not all, of their funds from outside the mainland.[74] According to a recent survey conducted by Taiwan's Chung-Hua Institution for Economic Research, 72.25 per cent of Taiwanese firms on the mainland get their funds from Taiwanese financial institutions, 17.2 per cent from mainland banks, 7 per cent from banks in a third country, and only 1.45 per cent from foreign banks operating on the mainland.[75] It was reported that, in the first five months of 1993 alone, Taiwan's capital outflow to the mainland soared to 700 per cent annual growth to a total of $511.4 million. This figure exceeds, for the first time, Taiwan's outward investment in all other sites.[76]

In the light of this, the Taiwanese authorities have recently reaffirmed their ban on Taiwanese banks setting up branches or directly financing Taiwan firms across the Straits.[77] A warning has been issued to banks involved in such financing that they will not receive support from BOT, the central bank, if they suffer from a shortage of funds.[78] At the same time, the authorities still ban direct remittances between the two sides and, instead, ask investors to remit their funds to a third place first in order to be considered as "indirect investment."[79] Moreover, they again ruled out the use of the NT$ and RMB *yuan* in any operation involving banks from both sides. Obviously, all these measures are designed to curb the outflow of Taiwanese capital and therefore will do nothing to ease the difficulty of raising funds or to cut costs of operation for Taiwanese firms on the mainland.

The PRC authorities, to encourage FDI, should relax their restrictions

---

footnote continued

co-operate in high-technology areas. At the same time, influential people in Taiwan made the suggestion that Taiwan should use its foreign exchange resources to buy the mainland's technology to support high-technology researches there. See *FCJ*, 28 August 1992, p. 3. Plans have reportedly been made to co-operate in such areas as aerospace, superconductivity and computers. See *ibid.* 6 October 1992, p. 7.

74. Some mainland scholars maintain that the acute difficulty of raising funds in the mainland is one of the major reasons why Taiwanese entrepreneurs prefer wholly owned ventures to mainland–Taiwan joint ventures. See Yan Zhiping, "Constraints and counter-measures," p. 29.

75. *FCJ*, 3 August 1992, p. 3.

76. *Ibid.* 15 June 1993, p. 3.

77. *Ibid.* 18 August 1992, p. 3; *Jiushi niandai* (*The Nineties*), September 1992, p. 67.

78. *Ibid.* 14 August 1992, p. 8.

79. *Ibid.* 1 September 1992, p. 3.

on issuing loans to Taiwan firms, promulgate mortgage and other related laws as soon as possible, and consider allowing foreign banks in the PRC to handle their businesses in RMB *yuan*.

Host policy. Driven partly by long-term political considerations and partly by compatriot emotion, the PRC authorities offer more financial incentives to Taiwanese than to non-Taiwanese foreign investors. In addition, local authorities compete fiercely with each other in offering even more concessions to the Taiwanese, in order to boost the quantity of FDI in their regions. This has two consequences: first, as shown above, an unusually large number of low-level or "sunset" projects were attracted, many of which are overlapping; and secondly, the double standards have not only created confusion in the incentive policy but, more importantly, seriously damaged the prospect for non-Taiwanese foreign investors, particularly those from the industrialized West or with advanced technology, to come to the PRC. In fact, it is not necessary to offer extra financial concessions to Taiwanese investors. Many of them would rather see an increase in the ratio of local sales, relaxation of credit controls, and/or opening more sectors to them.[80]

Prospects and Implications

In the light of the levels of economic development on both sides of the Taiwan Straits, it appears to be an ideal combination if Taiwan and the mainland's south-eastern coastal areas can restructure, at least partly, their economies and form a vertical economic integration, with the former focusing on R & D and design of products, manufacturing technologies, business management and international marketing, and the latter on massive production, especially of labour-intensive, light industrial exports. At present, both sides seem to work hard to maximize benefits from investment links and avoid negative impacts on their economies and states. At the same time, they try to achieve political ends by economic means. The failure to sign a bilateral investment protection agreement in the historic Singapore Talks earlier this year is a good case in point.

By actively promoting close economic links and interdependence across the Taiwan Straits, Beijing clearly hopes to achieve two political objectives: to counterbalance the growing tendency in Taiwan toward independence, and, eventually, to force the Taipei authorities to come to the negotiating table on Beijing's terms, if necessary by cutting off, or threatening to cut off, the linkages. On the other hand, by allowing the development of Taiwan businesses in the PRC, Taipei, too, could achieve two political gains: it could create powerful interests in certain groups of mainlanders and certain parts of the mainland which want to avoid the use of force against their business partners, and it could introduce "Taiwan experiences" and the culture of Asian capitalism to the mainland to expedite the process of "peaceful evolution."

80. *JJDB*, 25 May 1992, p. 22.

Of course, Taiwan has to prevent its economy from becoming too dependent on the mainland's, which, in a different context, is now the fate of Hong Kong and Macau. Taipei's view is that it must not give Beijing undue leverage in its dealings with Taiwan. It has made it clear that it will allow trade and investment links to develop more freely only when Beijing shows "gestures of goodwill" towards Taiwan. Based on this principle, Taiwan's CEPD has urged the government to implement a policy which would encourage trade with, instead of investment in, the mainland.[81] Clearly, Taipei is using economic assistance in the political bargaining process with Beijing.

Thus, how far and how fast PRC–Taiwan economic links will develop seems to depend more on political than economic factors. The persistent refusal by both to meet the other's demands has become the major obstacle to close economic integration. There is very little prospect, at least in the foreseeable future, of either changing their stance. It is this uncertainty in PRC–Taiwan political relations which will overshadow the development of economic links for a considerable time. Indeed, it also casts doubt on the formation of the so-called "Greater China Economic Community," comprising mainland China, Hong Kong (and Macau) and Taiwan.[82]

Among the three inter-relationships, the PRC–Hong Kong one has no really insurmountable problem from Hong Kong's impending return to the PRC's sovereignty. In fact, the two economies are already in a process of integration. There can be no doubt that after 1997 this process can only be faster and smoother. With regard to the Hong Kong–Taiwan relationship, as they have reasonably compatible economic systems, linkage between them should not be more difficult than that between any two market economies.[83] It is the PRC–Taiwan relationship which stands out as the most problematic and decisive of the three.

However, whatever happens in PRC–Taiwan political relations in the future, the economic ties between them will continue to grow in some form, because the structural conditions favouring co-operation are so powerful. It is possible that market forces may yet drive the economic links across the Taiwan Straits to an extent that neither Beijing nor Taipei can control the pace of development. If so, the formation of the "Greater China Economic Community" will come about in spite of the political obstacles.

Against this rather popular view, two points should be borne in mind. First, the future of Taiwan–China regional links will depend on global shifts in the pattern of trade liberalization and regional protection and integration. Thus, if the global shift is to greater regional and bi-lateral arrangements, this will tend to reinforce the PRC–Taiwan links within

81. *FCJ*, 4 June 1993, p. 3.

82. The World Bank, referring to the three entities as the "Chinese Economic Area," predicts that the area's economic boom will continue, making it the world's fourth growth pole. See *ibid.* 20 April 1993, p. 1.

83. In fact, the PRC–Taiwan relationship could affect Hong Kong's ties with Taiwan since the bulk of trade between the mainland and Taiwan goes through Hong Kong.

the broader framework of the regional arrangements. Secondly, the commercial case for Taiwan to avoid too much reliance on China is as strong as the political one. China has benefited precisely from the Taiwanese diversification away from other Asian locations and, given China's record of economic and political instability, no rational investor will become too dependent on it, either as a market or as a location for direct investment. Hong Kong's lack of room for flexibility on this issue is its major problem of economic strategy; Taiwan is fortunate in that it can enjoy strong benefits from its natural links with China, while retaining significant options to integrate its economy in other directions.

[12]

The Journal of International Trade & Economic Development 4 (2) 1995 153–170

The turning point of the Hong Kong manufacturing sector

Impact of outward investment to the Pearl River delta

Chyau Tuan and Linda F.-Y. Ng

Department of Decision Sciences and Managerial Economics, The Chinese University of Hong Kong

Abstract

Relocation and cross-border operations of Hong Kong manufacturing since early 1980 have induced significant restructuring of the sector. This study investigates the issue in terms of industrial concentration and input–output relations. The findings of the study suggest that structural adjustment in manufacturing employment and production has occurred and that the year 1987 is probably the critical point that marks the beginning of this restructuring. Significantly different contributions attributable to labour and capital were observed. The study also suggests that the manufacturing sector in Hong Kong has become especially management oriented since 1987 in coordinating the division of labour between operations performed in the Pearl River delta and Hong Kong.

Keywords

Manufacturing restructuring, foreign direct investment, industry concentration, productivity, Hong Kong manufacturing, Guangdong economic development.

1. INTRODUCTION

The open-door policy adopted by Mainland China since 1979 induced a rapid increase in both Hong Kong investment in China and trade activities between the two regions. Hong Kong's export and re-export trade with China increased more than eleven-fold and six-fold respectively from 1980 to 1986, and three-fold and six-fold respectively from 1986 to 1991. The opening up of the nearby Pearl River delta (PRD) and special economic zones in 1986, and the beginning of indirect trade/investment between Taiwan and the People's Republic of China (PRC) after the mid-1980s resulted in re-exports exceeding domestic exports from the fourth quarter of 1987 (Tuan, 1992b).

Address for correspondence
Dept of Decision and Managerial Economics, The Chinese University of Hong Kong, Shatin, N.T., Hong Kong.

 ISSN 0963–8199

During the 1980s with intensive outward investment to the PRC, manufacturing contribution to GDP and employment declined from 30.9 per cent and 47 per cent respectively in 1970 to 23.7 per cent and 42 per cent in 1980, and further declined to 13.7 per cent and 23.9 per cent in 1992. The Hong Kong Trade Development Council (1992) reported that in 1992 3 million labourers in the proximate regions worked for Hong Kong-based manufacturing industries, while employment in the territory's manufacturing sector was only 650,000. This continuous outward investment has considerably altered Hong Kong's industrial structure.

For the period 1981–87 (the period when Hong Kong manufacturers started direct investment to the PRC), the number of manufacturing establishments, value of assets and value-added achieved positive real annual growth rates of 0.70 per cent, 10.47 per cent and 11.19 per cent respectively, although manufacturing employment already showed a decrease of 0.76 per cent. Manufacturing employment has declined continuously since 1987. The local unemployment rate, however, averaged 3.6 per cent from 1981 to 1986 and has been held to below 2 per cent since 1987 (Tuan, 1992b).

The opening up of the PRD in the 1980s accelerated the decline of manufacturing in number of establishments (–2.86 per cent per annum) and employment (–7.15 per cent), and a slower growth in value of fixed assets (9.47 per cent) and value-added (4.12 per cent) between 1987 and 1991. In terms of factor use and average productivity, labour made real gains in average productivity of 12.03 per cent and 12.15 per cent per annum between 1981, 1987 and 1991 respectively. The opposite was observed for capital (0.66 and –5.16 per cent respectively).

1.1 Cross-border operations in the PRD

In 1985 the 'Little' PRD was formed from three cities and thirteen counties to include an area of 10.1 per cent of Guangdong Province and 15.4 per cent of its population. The 'Little' PRD quickly evolved into the 'Large' PRD in two years, with an addition of three cities and eight counties, which covered about 24.9 per cent in area and 27 per cent of the population.

Of the total amount of direct foreign investment made by Hong Kong manufacturers in China and South-east Asian countries in 1987–91, 69.2 per cent went to the PRC.[1] A sampling survey of Hong Kong manufacturing firms conducted in 1993 (Tuan and Ng, 1994) reported that 84.8 per cent of Hong Kong manufacturers had engaged in outward foreign direct investment (FDI), 58.6 per cent of which was to China.[2] Further, 88 per cent of the firms reported that they started their overseas operations after 1985; 1988 and 1989 were the peak years of outward investment, comprising 34 per cent of the total (Tuan and Ng, 1994). Findings consistent with these were reported by annual manufacturing surveys conducted by the Industrial Department (1992a, 1992b) on factories having plant/production facilities outside Hong Kong on the timing of the movement. Inward FDI to Hong Kong also took advantage of the colony's strategic location as a stepping stone to the market of PRC. According to a study on operations of local multinational corporations (MNCs) (Tuan and Wong, 1993), more than half of the MNCs sampled established their regional headquarters or local business in Hong Kong in the late 1980s.

More than 75 per cent of the outward FDI made by Hong Kong manufacturers in the PRC was in Guangdong Province, the proximate PRD cities, and Shenzhen in particular. The majority of the manufacturing investment in the PRD was to establish relatively labour-intensive operations. Cheap labour and land costs, and geographical proximity to Hong Kong, were the major reasons reported by Hong Kong manufacturers for choosing the PRD as their production base (Tuan and Ng, 1994). Most of the outward investment to the PRD was found in the form of sole proprietorships, producing by means of original equipment manufacture (OEM), and subcontracting substantial parts of the manufacturing process. The findings were consistent with those obtained from other major surveys conducted previously.[3]

The increasing outward investment in the PRD fostered outward processing trade between the two regions. According to the Hong Kong trade statistics, the estimated proportion of outward processing trade as a percentage of total trade value with China for imports, domestic exports, and re-exports of China origin in 1992 were 72, 74 and 78 per cent respectively. The export of raw material and parts to, and the re-import of processed and assembled products from, Guangdong by Hong Kong firms constituted a substantial part of the trade between Hong Kong and China. This was largely the result of the shifting of the production base to China, and specifically to Guangdong Province and the PRD, where more than 94 per cent of the imports from outward processing investment were produced.[4]

1.2 Objective of the study

It is reasonable to assume that the relocation process of moving the manufacturing production base of Hong Kong to the PRD and the induced division of labour between the two regions will affect the nature and content of manufacturing operations, and hence their structure, in the territory.[5] It is the aim of the present study to investigate the restructuring in manufacturing in terms of evolving industry organization and the change in manufacturing operations reflected by input–output relationships. Specifically, the study examines and identifies any turning points which can be found in (i) the pattern of industry concentration via entropy analysis; and (ii) the utilization behaviour of labour and capital over time. It also examines the pattern of output elasticities and factor intensities which have resulted from the extensive outward investment generated during the study period by means of production function analysis.

2. MANUFACTURING RESTRUCTURING MEASURED BY ENTROPY

2.1 Employment entropy

Entropy measurement will be used to measure industrial concentration as one feature of industrial structure because it reflects both the number of firms in the industry and the inequality of market shares. It aims to measure the degree of industrial concentration through information described by the shape of the probability distribution of market shares (Theil, 1967; Horowitz, 1970). The entropy index is inversely related to industry concentration and, it may be argued, directly related to industry competition (Horowitz and Horowitz, 1968; Horowitz 1970). Industry structure in terms of concentration may be studied through the changing concentration pattern over time.

Using an employment entropy measurement, Ng (1990) first studied industry concentration in Hong Kong manufacturing for 1976–87 when the size of outward processing in the sector was limited and its impact had not fully materialized. The study concluded that in a small open economy with free trade, manufacturing industry concentration decreases over time. However, heavy cross-border operations in Hong Kong's proximate area and outward investment to China, especially to the PRD, led to a drastic adjustment in the structure of the manufacturing sector in the 1980s. Further investigations into changing industry distribution between manufacturing and non-manufacturing revealed that a structural change between the two sectors might have occurred (Ng, 1991). The almost unchanging industrial concentration in manufacturing was accompanied by a decreasing concentration (increasing participation) in services, which seemed to suggest that the economy was moving away from manufacturing to become more service oriented. The results of the study also implied a change in the structural mix of industry, mostly caused by manufacturing firms relocating to mainland China to exploit cheap labour and land costs (Tuan and Ng, 1994); this produced a further inequality of market share.

A study of the competitive patterns of industries in both manufacturing and non-manufacturing for the period 1976–91 confirmed that a structural change had occurred between the two sectors (Ng, 1995). Industrial concentrations in both sectors had changed over time. In addition, a structural change in the pattern of industrial concentration seemingly came over both sectors in 1987.[6] Research results showed that the decreasing employment entropies in manufacturing after 1987 were accompanied by a rapid increase in employment entropies in the service sector, which implied that manufacturing had become more concentrated in terms of number of firms and market shares, while services exhibited the opposite behaviour (Ng, 1995).

2.2 Correlation analysis

To further understand the coincidence of the turning points in industry concentration in both manufacturing and non-manufacturing sectors in 1987 and their opposite trends, it is important to investigate the restructuring linkages between the two sectors. Limitations of data availability prevented the application of Leontief input–output analysis in the study of sectoral interdependence in the economy.

Table 1 presents the simple (Pearson's) correlation coefficients between employment entropies of manufacturing with manufacturing subgroups and with services. The aggregate entropies of the two sectors are negatively correlated at $r = -0.86$ ($p<0.01$). Seven industry groups in the service sectors were found to be significantly and negatively correlated with manufacturing measured by entropy: these were wholesale ($r = -0.77$), restaurants ($r = -0.69$), hotel/boarding houses ($r = -0.88$), import/export (–0.73), transport ($r = -0.55$), communications (–0.66) and business services ($r = -0.82$). The decreasing concentration in manufacturing was found to be associated with increasing concentration in these service groups after 1980 (Table 1).

This finding suggests that the increase in outward investment in the PRD, and hence the cross-border processing of manufacturing firms, encouraged more services related to trade in manufactured or semi-finished goods between the two regions and created more investment opportunities for Hong Kong entrepreneurs. It is therefore not surprising that wholesale, import/export trade and business services that directly support trading activities expanded in number of establishments and employment to achieve a more equal market share. Further, given the increasing outward investment and processing to the PRD and a rapid decrease in both employment and the number of establishments in manufacturing, other industry groups in the service sector (restaurants, hotel/boarding houses, transport and communications) also showed moves to the opposite direction by increasing the number of persons engaged and in the number of firms. This may well indicate an absorption by the service sector of labour redeployed from manufacturing, or an indirect impact generated by increasing outward investment into the PRD. The service sector achieved its expansion by, in effect, replacing manufacturing as an employment source in the territory.

In manufacturing 11 industry groups significantly dominated the change in structural patterns in overall manufacturing during the study period (namely, ISIC 320/322, 324, 331, 332, 355, 371, 382, 383, 384, 385 and 389) (Table 1), with significant positive correlations (at least $p<0.1$) between the entropies of these industry groups and aggregate manufacturing entropy. The majority of these industries were identified as industries involving relatively heavy outward processing activity (wearing apparel, footwear, rubber and plastic products, metal products, consumer electrical and electronics, electrical and electronics parts and machinery, and professional and scientific equipment:

Table 1 Correlation coefficients between employment entropy in manufacturing with manufacturing subgroups and services (1978–91)

ISIC	*Industry*	*Correlation estimates All manufacturing*
All manufacturing		1.000
311/312	Food manufacturing	0.173
313	Beverages	0.377
314	Tobacco	−0.361
320/322	Wearing apparel	0.560**
323	Leather/leather products	0.257
324	Footwear	0.816****
325/329	Textiles	0.176
331	Wood and corks	0.797***
332	Furniture and fixtures	0.775***
341	Paper/paper products	−0.020
342	Printing/publishing	−0.080
351/352	Chemical and chemical products	0.374
355	Rubber products	0.645***
356	Plastic products	0.336
361/369	Non-metallic minerals	0.223
371	Basic metals products	0.463*
380/381	Fabricated metal products	0.290
382	Machinery	0.452*
383	Consumer electrical and electronic products	0.603**
384	Electrical/electronics parts/machinery	0.629**
385	Professional/scientific equipment	0.463*
389	Transport equipment	0.347
390	Other manufacturing	0.631***
Non-manufacturing		−0.860***
61	Wholesale	−0.777***
62	Retail	−0.254
631	Restaurants	−0.691**
632	Hotels/boarding houses	−0.868***
64	Import/export	−0.739***
71	Transport	−0.586*
72	Storage	−0.013
73	Communications	−0.674*
81	Financing	−0.335
82	Insurance	0.487
83	Business services	−0.827***

Source: Data of employment entropies were computed by and obtained from Ng (1995).

Notes: ****, ***, **, * indicate significance at $p<0.001$, $p<0.01$, $p<0.05$, and $p<0.1$ respectively; 1978–91 for manufacturing; 1980–91 for ISIC 61 to 64, 1981–91 for ISIC 71, and 1982–91 for ISIC 82 to 83; ISIC 353 is an industry recorded since 1988 and is excluded because of the small number of observations available.

(Tuan and Ng, 1994)). Although 9 of the other 12 industry groups showed insignificant correlations with overall manufacturing they still exhibited the same (positive) sign. The remaining three industry groups, though negatively correlated with all manufacturing entropy, were statistically insignificant. Major manufacturing industries with outward processing experienced a reduction in number of firms and an increase in market share inequality, as measured by employment entropy.

3. MANUFACTURING RESTRUCTURING MEASURED BY INPUT–OUTPUT RELATIONS

To study further the nature of the restructuring of the manufacturing sector during the period of heavy outward FDI to the PRC, the production function approach is used to explore whether the manufacturing sector experienced any restructuring in input–output relations, and hence factor productivity, during the period.

3.1 Production relations

We assume a two-factor case of separable production technology:

$$Q = A(t)\, F(L, K)\, \varepsilon \tag{1}$$

where Q represents value-added, $A(t)$ stands for technology, L for labour, K for capital stock and ε for the stochastic shocks to production.

Following a Solow type of production with disembodied technological progress and competitive factor markets, equation (1) can be written in the form of a Cobb–Douglas production function:

$$Q = A\, L^{\alpha}\, \mathrm{K}^{\beta}\, \varepsilon \tag{2}$$

where A is Solow's autonomous neutral technological factor, and α and β are labour and capital shares respectively (Solow, 1957). Capital stock is computed by the following relation:

$$K_t = I_t + (1 - \delta)\, K_{t-1} \tag{3}$$

where K_t is capital stock in time period t, I_t is investment in time t and δ is the depreciation rate.

A disadvantage of a Cobb–Douglas production function, although it is still the most popular type, is that it assumes constant factor elasticities for all observations (firms/industries) during the period. To overcome this difficulty and to ensure validity of the estimators, a translog production function was also used to obtain the returns to factors (output elasticities) and the productivity of the production factors (Christensen *et al.*, 1971; Corbo and Meller, 1979). The function is written as:

Table 2 Cobb–Douglas and translog production function estimations, 1978–91 (dependent variable: *LVA*)

	Cobb–Douglas			*Translog*	
Variable	*(A)*	*(B)*	*(C)*	*(D)*	*(E)*
Intercept	3.970***	3.852***	4.095***	14.220***	6.621**
	(0.601)	(0.433)	(0.487)	(2.468)	(1.920)
L*NP*	0.604***	0.814***	0.838***	0.474	0.895**
	(0.052)	(0.040)	(0.041)	(0.364)	(0.274)
L*CAPI*	0.300***	0.129***	0.092**	−1.225***	−0.354
	(0.030)	(0.024)	(0.029)	(0.291)	(0.226)
1/2*L*NP**L*NP*				0.107	0.107*
				(0.064)	(0.048)
1/2*L*CAPI**L*CAPI*				0.176**	0.104**
				(0.051)	(0.038)
L*NP**L*CAPI*				−0.073	−0.088**
				(0.045)	(0.034)
*D*87		0.354***	0.208		0.348***
		(0.021)	(0.199)		(0.023)
*D*87*L*NP*			−0.079**		
			(0.028)		
*D*87*L*CAPI*			0.071*		
			(0.029)		
Industry dummies (23)	23	23	23	23	23
Adj R^2	0.971	0.985	0.985	0.973	0.985
F-ratio	407.593	765.554	726.120	401.107	697.360
Root MSE	0.217	0.156	0.154	0.207	0.155
DF	284	283	281	281	280

Notes: Columns (A)–(C): estimates of Cobb–Douglas function; columns (D)–(E): estimates of translog function; L*VA* = log (value-added), L*NP* = log (number of persons), L*CAPI* = log (capital); *D*87 is a dummy variable where *D*87 = 1 if year > = 1987; otherwise, *D*87 = 0; 23 dummies were used for the 24 industry groups. Coefficients were not reported for simplicity because they affected the intercept only. ***, **, * indicate significance at $p<0.0001$, $p<0.01$, and $p<0.05$ respectively. Standard errors in parentheses.

$$\ln(Q) = \ln(A) + \alpha_L \ln(L) + \alpha_K \ln(K) + (1/2)\,\alpha_{LL}\,(\ln(L))^2 + (1/2)\alpha_{KK}(\ln(K))^2 + \alpha_{LK}\ln(L)\,\ln(K) + \varepsilon \quad (4)$$

Constant returns to scale requires $\alpha_L + \alpha_K = 1$, $\alpha_{LL} + \alpha_{LK} = 0$, and $\alpha_{KK} + \alpha_{LK} = 0$. If $\alpha_{LL} = \alpha_{KK} = \alpha_{LK} = 0$, the output elasticities are simply α_L and α_K.

3.2 Estimation results

Both the Cobb–Douglas form (equation (2)) and the translog form (equation (4)) of production functions were fitted by pooling three-digit-level industry data for the period of 1978–91.[7] Estimation results are given in Table 2 with columns (A) to (C) for the Cobb–Douglas form and columns (D) and (E) for the translog form.

Cobb–Douglas production estimation

In Table 2, column (A) presents the estimated Cobb–Douglas production function for the whole period of study (1978–91). The equation had a high R^2 (0.97) and a highly significant F-ratio. Both regression coefficients of labour (0.60) and capital (0.30) were found to be statistically significant at $p<0.0001$. Dummy variables (23) were used to represent the 24 groups of manufacturing industries to filter any effects associated with industry characteristics. Industry dummies of eight industry groups (ISIC 314, 323, 331, 332, 341, 353, 355 and 383) were statistically significant at $p<0.05$ and two (ISIC 324 and 361) were significant at $p<0.1$.

In order to test whether a change in the structural relation of the production relation was taking place during the period of study, a dummy variable method was used to differentiate two subperiods (1978–86 and 1987–91) by means of an intercept (Table 2, column (B)) and by both intercept and slope of the regression line (Table 2, column (C)). It was found that a shift in intercept (represented by the dummy variable $D87$, where $D87 = 0$ for 1978–86 and $D87 = 1$ for 1987–91) of 0.35 was significant at $p<0.0001$ (Table 2, column (B)). The effects of dummy variables assigned to 1985 or 1986 were found insignificant.[8]

To test for a possible change in the structure of the production relation, the interaction effects between the time dummy variable ($D87$) and labour and capital can be studied. Interaction effects measured by a change in the slope of the regression with respect to labour ($D87*LNP$) ($= -0.079$) and with respect to capital ($D87*LCAPI$) ($= 0.071$) were significant at $p<0.01$ and $p<0.05$ respectively (Table 2, column (C)), which suggested the validity of an interaction effect between time and factors of production. With the addition of the dummy variable, the root MSE was reduced to 0.16 and the goodness-of-fit was further improved (0.99). Industry dummies were also used to represent industry effects; 17 industry groups showed statistically significant dummy effects (the six industry groups with insignificant dummies were ISIC 311, 320, 325, 356, 383 and 385). While the time dummy of the intercept effect in this specification was insignificant, the significant changes in the slopes of both labour and capital confirmed a structural change in the production regression relation beginning in 1987.[9]

The study period was further divided into two subperiods (1978–86 and

1987–91) with two distinct regressions fitted to the data. The results showed that all regression coefficients are statistically significant and Chow's test reconfirmed the significant difference between the two regression relations.[10] Industry dummies were used in both regressions to absorb the industry effects.[11]

Output elasticities (factor shares at competitive equilibrium) computed by all estimated relations for different periods yielded the result that labour had higher output elasticities than capital. For the whole study period (Table 2, column (C)), labour and capital shares were found to be 0.84 and 0.09 respectively for the first subperiod, and 0.76 and 0.16 respectively for the second subperiod.

When considering the scale factor, column (C) shows that the sum of labour and capital shares was 0.93 in the first subperiod and 0.92 in the second subperiod. Constant returns to scale of production were confirmed by the unity test.[12] According to Ng and Tuan (1991), using cross-section data, manufacturing in Hong Kong was found to exhibit constant returns to scale in production for the period of 1978–87. The average scale factor reported was 0.96. Using disaggregated *Industrial Census Survey* data in 1978, Tuan (1982) also confirmed that constant returns to scale existed in Hong Kong's manufacturing.[13] The results of this research study further suggested that the manufacturing sector decreased slightly in its scale factor in the second subperiod; this was attributable to a decrease in the output elasticity of labour and an increase in that of capital.

Translog production estimation

Table 2 (columns (D) and (E)) also presents the results of the estimations with a translog production function, where column (E) incorporates a time dummy effect ($D87$). From column (D) it was found that for the entire period under study (1978–91) the translog function with labour and capital and their higher orders explained 97.3 per cent of the variation of output. Regression coefficients related to capital were statistically significant ($p<0.005$), but those of labour were not (F-ratio = 401.1, $R^2 = 0.97$, and root MSE = 0.207) (Table 2, column (D)). Dummy variables were also used to represent the effects due to individual industry groups.

A time dummy ($D87$) was also used to represent a shift in the intercept term over time (Table 2, column (E)). Testing the existence of structural change in 1987 showed that time effect ($D87$) was also statistically a significant ($p<0.0001$). The goodness-of-fit increased slightly to 98.5 per cent and root MSE was reduced to 0.16 with this specification (Table 2, column (E)). Industry dummies were used to represent industry effects and 14 industry groups showed significant results.[14]

The estimated translog regression illustrated that a shift in the intercept of the estimated production function was found to occur in 1987.[15] Such a result is consistent with the result when a Cobb–Douglas form of production function is assumed. Since all higher-order terms in the functional relations were found statistically significant, the translog relation could not be reduced statistically to a Cobb–Douglas form (that is $\alpha_{LL} \neq \alpha_{KK} \neq \alpha_{LK} \neq 0$ and $\alpha_L + \alpha_K \neq 1$). Further, a Chow test also confirmed separable regression relations for each of the two subperiods with the use of the translog form of estimation.[16]

4. MANUFACTURING RESTRUCTURING: PRODUCTION ELASTICITIES

4.1 Output elasticities and factor productivities (1978–91)

In order to ascertain whether there was a change in output elasticities between the two subperiods, elasticities of production for both labour and capital for 1978–91 were computed from the translog function[17] (Table 3). When comparing the results of the two subperiods using 1987 as the turning point, labour output elasticities decreased from an average of 0.81 in 1978–86 to 0.76 in 1987–91; and capital output elasticities increased from 0.12 to 0.16 respectively.[18] These results are consistent with the findings from the Cobb–Douglas production estimation.

Labour showed higher output elasticities than capital during the whole period under study. The magnitude of output elasticities of labour decreased over time from 0.80 in 1978 to 0.75 in 1991 (the minimum among all years), while that of capital increased from 0.12 to 0.17 (second highest among all years) (Table 3). The output elasticity of labour reached its peak in 1981 and showed a rapid decrease from 1984. This movement was closely matched by the output elasticity of capital in an opposite direction; capital elasticity was at minimum during 1979–82 and started to show a rapid increase after 1983.

Marginal and average productivities for labour and capital were also computed from the translog form of production relation (Table 3). Both average and marginal productivities of labour displayed U-shaped in the study period, with the minima in 1981. Average and marginal productivities of capital showed slight decreasing and increasing trends respectively (Table 3). Most important, when the means of the average and marginal productivities for both labour and capital for the two subperiods (1978–86 and 1987–91) were computed and tested for differences, the results showed statistically significant difference between all means, except that of average productivity of capital.

Summary results for the simple annual real growth rates of factors and factor productivities for the two subperiods, given technology progress, are provided in Table 4. The output elasticity of labour grew at 4.4 per cent per year for the first subperiod but contracted at 1.6 per cent per year for the second subperiod, while output elasticity of capital, in contrast, changed by –5.6 and 5.1 per cent for the respective subperiods. In terms of factor

Table 3 Output elasticities and factor productivities from translog production function for 1978–91

	Output elasticities		*Productivities*			
			Average		*Marginal*	
	Labour	*Capital*	*Labour* (HK$000/ person)	*Capital* (HK$000/ HK$000)	*Labour* (HK$000/ person)	*Capital* (HK$000/ HK$000)
1978	0.808	0.116	66.562	2.474	53.810	0.286
1979	0.818	0.109	54.363	2.203	44.475	0.241
1980	0.817	0.112	51.778	2.094	42.319	0.235
1981	0.820	0.112	44.495	2.205	36.485	0.246
1982	0.810	0.119	45.097	2.009	36.535	0.240
1983	0.812	0.119	47.619	2.207	38.661	0.263
1984	0.812	0.119	51.756	2.338	42.026	0.279
1985	0.806	0.125	52.831	2.181	42.577	0.272
1986	0.790	0.144	58.672	1.964	46.377	0.282
1987	0.782	0.154	67.753	1.884	52.961	0.290
1988	0.772	0.157	77.291	1.987	59.674	0.312
1989	0.753	0.176	85.968	2.753[a]	64.772	0.485
1990	0.763	0.162	92.730	1.925	70.749	0.312
1991	0.750	0.170	101.590	1.842	76.141	0.314
Average						
1978–91	0.794	0.135	64.179	2.147	50.540	0.290
	(0.025)	(0.024)	(18.541)	(0.250)	(12.886)	(0.062)
1978–86*	0.810	0.119	52.575	2.186	42.585	0.260
	(0.008)	(0.010)	(6.920)	(0.156)	(5.403)	(0.020)
1987–91*	0.764	0.164	85.066	2.078	64.859	0.343
	(0.013)	(0.009)	(13.160)	(0.381)	(9.088)	(0.080)

Notes: All productivity values are in real terms (1980 = 100).
* indicates significant difference at $p<0.01$ (except average productivity of capital) for t-tests between means
[a] ISIC 313 in 1989 was omitted due to the extreme negative value.
Standard errors in parentheses.

Table 4 Real annual growth rates of major statistics in manufacturing by subperiods

Variable	*1978–87 (%)*	*1987–91 (%)*
Labour	2.126	–8.794
Capital	4.632	2.202
Labor productivity	3.906	5.067
Capital productivity	1.270	–6.233
Value-added	5.972	–4.199
Total factor productivity	5.780	7.159
Factor intensity	2.962	12.213
Labour share	4.424	–1.562
Capital share	–5.608	5.134

Note: Total factor productivity, labour share and capital share are computed from the Cobb–Douglas form of production function.

productivities, average labour productivities showed an increase between the two subperiods (3.9 and 5.1 per cent respectively) and average capital productivities had a significant decrease (1.3 and –6.2 per cent respectively). Increasing growth in factor intensity (capital–labour ratio) and total factor productivity were also observed. In terms of factor use, however, both labour and capital showed a decrease in growth between the two subperiods from 2.1 to –8.8 per cent for labour, and 4.6 to 2.2 per cent for capital. Manufacturing output in value-added also contracted from a rate of 6 per cent to –4.2 per cent (Table 4).

It seems reasonable to put forward the following characteristics in factor productivities and use in view of the restructuring of the manufacturing sector with its turning point in 1987: (i) a decline in local production with less labour and capital employment; (ii) reduced labour output elasticities (shares) and increased capital output elasticities (shares) in production; (iii) increase in factor intensity (capital–labour ratio) and total factor productivity; and (iv) a gain in labour productivity.

4.2 Output elasticities by industry groups

Output elasticities of the 24 industry groups in manufacturing for the two subperiods were computed from the translog production function estimated (Table 5). Half of the 24 industry groups were found to conform to the overall manufacturing behaviour of decreasing labour elasticities and increasing capital elasticities between the two subperiods. The 12 industry groups with decreasing labour elasticities were ISIC 314, 320/322, 325/329, 341, 342, 356, 380/381 to 390; and the 12 groups with increasing capital elasticities were ISIC 314, 325/329, 341, 342, 351/352, 356, 380/381 to 390. Therefore, 11 of the groups showed consistent behaviour.

Table 5 Output elasticities by factors from translog production function by ISIC and by subperiods

		Labour		*Capital*	
ISIC	*Industry*	*1978–86*	*1987–91*	*1978–86*	*1987–91*
311/312	Food manufacturing	0.515	0.644	0.384	0.324
313	Beverages	0.175	0.845	0.539	0.062
314	Tobacco	–0.088	–0.620	0.696	1.665
320/322	Wearing apparel	1.068	0.950	0.093	0.045
323	Leather/leather products	0.469	0.820	0.466	0.085
324	Footwear	0.586	1.032	0.414	–0.143
325/329	Textiles	0.802	0.444	0.202	0.593
331	Wood & corks	0.513	1.019	0.444	–0.138
332	Furniture and fixtures	0.565	0.905	0.412	0.003
341	Paper/paper products	0.509	0.201	0.404	0.815
342	Printing/publishing	0.593	0.249	0.329	0.783
351/352	Chemical and chemical products	0.349	0.357	0.463	0.624
353	Products of petroleum and coal	—	0.878	—	–0.057
355	Rubber products	0.350	0.599	0.522	0.307
356	Plastic products	0.793	0.319	0.225	0.716
361/369	Non-metallic minerals	0.224	—	0.518	—
371	Basic metals products	0.277	0.756	0.516	0.152
380/381	Fabricated metal products	0.779	0.525	0.235	0.485
382	Machinery	0.578	0.524	0.363	0.476
383*	Consumer electrical and electronics products	0.817	0.277	0.222	0.759
384*	Electrical/electronics parts/machinery	0.664	–0.012	0.295	1.073
385	Professional/scientific equipment	0.728	0.636	0.280	0.347
389	Transport equipment	0.489	1.070	0.394	–0.161
390	Other manufacturing	0.704	0.614	0.303	0.365

Note: Only 1987–9 average is available for the period 1987–91 due to recoding of the industries since 1990.

The majority of these industries were dominating industries in manufacturing, including wearing apparel, textiles, consumer electrical and electronics products, electrical and electronics parts and machinery, professional and scientific equipment and plastic products. These industries were also found actively engaging in cross-border operations (Tuan and Ng, 1994).

5. CONCLUDING REMARKS

Manufacturing export-led growth stimulated the Hong Kong economy after World War II. The economy's success is perhaps attributable to the conscious decision of the Hong Kong government to avoid adopting any positive industry policy, a policy which is quite prevalent in other newly industrialized economies as a way of coping with rising factor costs and becoming competitive in the world market. Such a *laissez-faire* policy, together with the economic opening of the PRC in the late 1970s, induced manufacturers in Hong Kong to commit themselves to cross-border processing and outward investment to China, which enabled the territory to compete better with other newly industrializing economies in the market for labour-intensive products (Tuan and Ng, 1995).

Numerous pieces of evidence point to changes in Hong Kong's industrial structure during the last decade (Tuan, 1992a). The downward trend in manufacturing employment and the facts that re-exports exceeded domestic exports from 1987–88 on are just two among many. To explore the evolution of the manufacturing sector and the timing of the accumulation of the critical mass of structural change, this study investigated the issues with reference to changes in industrial concentration and input–output relationships. The findings of the study suggest that the year of 1987 was probably the critical turning point in the evolution of manufacturing of Hong Kong.

The degree of industrial concentration in manufacturing was found to be fairly constant from 1981 to 1987, and sharply decreasing after 1987. This pattern was accompanied by continuous increasing concentration in the major service industries. The phenomenon is consistent with the observation that the local unemployment rate has been kept low during the economic restructuring of the last decade. A change in input–output relationships has also been confirmed to happen in 1987 in terms of the significantly different contributions attributable to labour and capital.

A rapid growth in labour productivity was observed in the period after 1987. Given decreases in the growth of the total value of assets in manufacturing, and stagnant growth in capital productivity for the period 1987–91, the increase in the capital–labour ratio caused by a steady decrease in local manufacturing employment thus appears to be the primary contributory factor, among others, to such growth.[19] This increase in factor intensity (capital–labour ratio) implies a problem of labour underestimation (due to the neglect of 'hidden labour' in the PRD) rather than the adoption of more capital-intensive techniques of production in the manufacturing process. New investment is probably technology embodied, and cross-border operations may engage in a higher degree of specialization, which would also contribute to the increase in labour productivity.

In other words it is the outward FDI from Hong Kong and the millions of inland labourers working for Hong Kong manufacturers over the border that have made the reduction in local manufacturing labour possible and enhanced/increased labour productivity for the manufacturing sector in Hong Kong during the study period.

In this connection, the findings derived from the analysis of the production function suggest that the manufacturing sector in Hong Kong has become management oriented since 1987 in coordinating cross-border processing in PRD and the remaining operations performed in Hong Kong.[20] Taking the city as a unit of observation, 'industrial hollowing' has been taking place since the early 1980s and has been intensified after 1987. Taking Hong Kong and the PRD as an integral neighbourhood, this 'hollowing' is the natural outcome of division of labour between a core city and its suburban industrial locations (Tuan and Wong, 1993; Tuan and Ng, 1994). The mature stage of such a labour division, therefore, was most probably arrived at in 1987.

In order to enrich the findings of the study, it will be useful to investigate in detail major industries within the manufacturing sector in order to observe the change in total factor productivity, in labour movements between manufacturing and the major service sectors, and to analyse the impacts of indirect investment from Taiwan to the PRD, and FDI from other MNCs to the PRD, upon the de-industrialization of Hong Kong. These are interesting topics to be investigated in further studies.

NOTES

The authors thank Professor Ira Horowitz for helpful comments on an earlier draft of this paper. All errors remaining are ours.

1 According to Chung (1992), other outward investment to Malaysia was 17.1 per cent and to Indonesia was 11.2 per cent for the same period.

2 A thousand manufacturing firms were surveyed through a random sequential sampling method. The response rate was 16.9 per cent.

3 For example, findings of the 1991 *Survey of the Federation of Hong Kong Industries* also indicated that mixed forms of investment included wholly foreign-owned enterprise and subcontracting, equity joint venture and subcontracting, and cooperative joint venture and subcontracting. Other forms of less importance included consignment and licence agreement.

4 Maruya (1992) and Tang (1993) studied the relationship between the recent Hong Kong–China trade structures. Hong Kong had served to link China with the world economy by importing capital, raw materials and parts from mainly Asian countries; they were then sent into Guangdong Province for assembling and processing, and the finished goods were exported to other Western countries.

5 The relationships between manufacturing evolution, outward FDI and the passive industry policy of Hong Kong were first questioned by Tuan and Ng (1995).

6 A dummy variable used to test if a structural change beginning in 1987 was found to be statistically significant. The slope of the trend of entropy in or after 1987 was decreased by 0.31 ($p<0.0001$) in manufacturing and increased by 0.026 ($p<0.005$) in non-manufacturing (Ng, 1995).

7 Output (value-added) is the net production output due to labour and capital. Labour is measured by the number of persons engaged. Because no book value of fixed assets was reported by the Hong Kong government except in the census year 1978, capital stock was computed with a 15 per cent rate of depreciation (Ng and Tuan, 1991); that is, $K_t = K_t + (1 - \delta) K_{t-1}$, where K_t is capital stock in time period t (K_0 is book value of fixed assets in 1978) and δ is the depreciation rate. Further, all variables used for the regression estimations were deflated to real terms by the GDP deflator (1980 = 100).

8 Dummy variables used to represent years after 1987 (specifically 1988 and 1989) to

test for a shift intercept were statistically significant at $p<0.0001$.

9 Dummies used to test for significance in the change in slopes for labour and capital in 1985 and in 1986 were insignificant. There was no effect on the shift in the intecept terms. Significant intercept shifts were confirmed starting 1987 and onwards.

10 A Chow test (Chow, 1960) ($F(3, 303) = 147.28$) confirmed the inequality of regression coefficients of the two regression relations between the two subperiods.

11 Industry groups showing significant dummy effects in the first subperiod were ISIC 314, 323, 324, 331, 332, 341, 355 and 382; in the second subperiod ISIC 313, 314, 323–332, 342, 351, 355 and 384.

12 The sum of factor shares was tested for unity and was found to be insignificantly different from one.

13 Tuan (1982) used other forms of production functional relations, including CES and VES, and confirmed constant returns to scale in all forms.

14 The industry groups with significant industry dummies were ISIC 313, 314, 323, 324, 331–351, 355, 371, 382, 384 and 389.

15 Testing time dummy effects for changes to occur in 1985 and in 1986 yielded insignificant results. Significant time dummy effects were confirmed since 1987 and onwards.

16 When two separate translog production functions were estimated for each of the two sub periods (1978–86 and 1987–91), the root MSE was in each case reduced to 0.16 and 0.14 respectively. However, all regression coefficients except that of labour were found insignificant. A Chow test also confirmed significant statistical difference between the two relations.

17 Output elasticities of labour and capital for the translog form of the production function are respectively:

$$\delta \ln (Q)/\delta \ln (L) = \alpha_L + \alpha_{LL} \ln (L) + \alpha_{LK} \ln (K)$$

$$\delta \ln (Q)/\delta \ln (K) = \alpha_K + \alpha_{KK} \ln (K) + \alpha_{LK} \ln (L)$$

The translog form of the production function has the advantage in allowing different output elasticities of factors for different time periods and different industries, while the Cobb–Douglas form assumes constant elasticities for all periods and observations.

18 t-tests between means indicated that they were significantly different at $p<0.001$.

19 In its simplest form, average labour productivity is decomposed into the product of the capital–labour ratio and average capital productivity; that is, $Y/L = K/L * Y/K$. Using logarithms, $\ln (Y/L) = \ln (K/L) + \ln (Y/K)$. Further, the derivative with respect to time of the expression yields the growth in labour productivity attributable to growth in the capital–labour ratio and capital productivity.

20 Such a conclusion is not intended to make any correction with de-industrialization, which is mainly associated with cross-country comparisons.

REFERENCES

Chow, G.C. (1960) 'Tests of equality between sets of coefficients in two linear regressors' *Econometrica* 28, 591–605.

Christensen, L.R., Jorgenson, D.W. and Lau, L.J. (1971) 'Conjugate duality and the transcendental logarithmic production function (abstract)'. *Econometrica* 39, 255–6.

Chung, C. (1992) *Export-led Industrial Policy in PRC and its Impacts on Taiwan International Trade and Taiwan's Policy*. Chung Hwa Institution for Economic Research.

Corbo, V. and Meller, P. (1979) 'The translog production function: some evidence from establishment data'. *Journal of Econometrics* 10, 193–9.

Guangdong Statistical Yearbook (1986, 1988) China Statistics Publisher.

Hong Kong Trade Development Council (1992) *Status Report on China's Economic Reforms*.
Horowitz, A. and Horowitz, I. (1968) 'Entropy, Markov processes and competition in the brewing industry'. *Journal of Industrial Economics* 17, 196–211.
Horowitz, I. (1970) 'Employment concentration in the Common Market: an entropy approach'. *Journal of Royal Statistical Society (B)* Part 3, 463–79.
Industry Department (1991) *Departmental Reports, 1990–91, 1991–92*.
——— (1992a) *Report on the 1991 Survey of Overseas Investment in Hong Kong's Manufacturing Industry*, February.
——— (1992b) *Report on the 1992 Survey of Overseas Investment in Hong Kong's Manufacturing Industry*, November.
Kim, H. Youn (1992) 'The translog production function and variable returns to scale'. *The Review of Economics and Statistics*, 546–52.
Maruya, T. (ed.) (1992) 'Economic relations between Hong Kong and Guangdong'. In *Guangdong 'Open-door' Economic Development Strategies*. Tokyo: Institute of Developing Economies.
Ng, Linda F.Y. (1990) 'An analysis of the degree of competition in a small open economy: the case of Hong Kong's manufacturing'. *Proceedings Academy of International Business* 6, 35–40.
——— (1991) 'Structural changes and industrial competitive patterns of manufacturing and non-manufacturing in a small open economy: an experience from Hong Kong'. *Fourth International Conference on Comparative Management Proceedings* 4, 249–56.
——— (1995) 'Changing industrial structure and competitive patterns of manufacturing and non-manufacturing in a small open economy: an entropy measurement. *Managerial and Decisions Economics*, forthcoming.
Ng, Linda F.Y. and Tuan, C. (1991) 'A comparative study of productivity in the textiles and electronics industries in Hong Kong and Taiwan'. *Journal of International Economic Studies* 5, 31–55.
Solow, R.M. (1957) 'Technical change and the aggregate production function'. *Review of Economics and Statistics* 39, 312–20.
Tang, K.Y. (1993) 'Outward processing in China and its implications for the Hong Kong economy'. In Lin, T.B. and Tuan, C. (eds) *The Asian NIEs: Success and Challenge*. Hong Kong: Lo Fung Learned Society, 103–20.
Theil, H. (1967) *Economics and Information Theory*. Amsterdam: North Holland.
Tuan, Chyau (1982) 'Aggregate production functions of manufacturing industries in Hong Kong: a cross-section analysis'. *Academia Economic Papers*, 10, 35–75.
——— (1987) 'Changing trade environments and business strategies: the textiles industry in the Asia–Pacific region'. In Romaguera, J.M. (ed.) *Proceedings of the 4th Symposium on Hispanic Business and Economy*. Puerto Rico: University of Puerto Rico, 200–17.
——— (1992a) *Challenges and Responses in Economic Development and Management in Taiwan and Hong Kong*. Beijing: Economic Management Publisher.
——— (1992b) 'Hong Kong as an economic medium and its policy implications on Mainland–Taiwan relations'. *Essays on Conference of Mainland China Studies*. Taiwan: National Sun-Yet-Sen University, 443–55.
Tuan, Chyau and Ng, Linda F.Y. (1994) 'Economic liberalization in China and structural adjustment in Hong Kong's manufacturing'. *Seoul Journal of Economics* 7, 141–60.
——— (1995) 'Manufacturing evolution under passive industrial policy: the case of Hong Kong'. *Journal of Asian Economics*, forthcoming.
Tuan, Chyau and Wong, C.S. (1993) 'Evolution of FDI patterns and management of transnational corporations in Hong Kong'. Regional Development Dialogue (UNCRD) 4, 125–45.

[13]

TYING THE FIRM TO THE REGION OR TYING THE REGION TO THE FIRM?

EARLY OBSERVATIONS ON THE CASE OF LG IN SOUTH WALES

Nicholas A. Phelps, John Lovering and Kevin Morgan
University of Wales, Cardiff

Abstract

In 1996 the Korean conglomerate LG announced plans to create up to 6100 jobs at a new greenfield electronics manufacturing operation in Newport, South Wales. The investment would have been unthinkable without the unique institutional capacity involved with inward investment attraction and development which exists in Wales. However, the scale of the LG investment has placed enormous demands on this institutional capacity and raises questions regarding the way in which major investments effectively capture the strategic orientation and resources of local institutions and service-providing organizations. In this article we explore some of the main dimensions of such institutional capture as revealed by an initial examination of the LG case.

Introduction

In July 1996 the Korean conglomerate LG announced a £1.7bn investment by two of its subsidiary companies on a site at Newport in South Wales. LG Electronics is to develop a factory producing picture tubes, televisions, and related components employing up to 4400 people. Alongside this, LG Semicon (54 percent owned by LG Electronics) will establish a plant to produce wafers for multimedia chips, employing up to 1700 people. The two operations will serve the entire European market. The monitor assembly line came on-line in 1997, and the semiconductor plant is due to come on-line the following year. Several factory units will be built, creating 3.5m square feet of new production space. Final figures regarding the total value of financial assistance for the project have been hard to come by, but the only exact figure which has been quoted to date is £247m (Tucker, 1997).[1]

LG's South Wales project is the largest single instance of Foreign Direct Investment (FDI) in the UK in terms of promised employment. It is also the largest in terms of land use. It was won at the cost of the biggest aid package ever given to a foreign company investing in Britain (Burton et al., 1996). The company estimates that 6100 jobs will be created. Some local commentators, including the then director of the Welsh Development Agency (WDA), asserted that the total number of jobs created in South Wales as a result would be more than 20,000. At the signing in Seoul, the then Welsh Secretary, William Hague, said the LG announcement was 'the biggest vote of confidence the Welsh economy has ever had' (Adburgham, 1996a).

In this article, we discuss the LG investment highlighting some aspects of its impact, especially on the apparatus of economic development and planning in South Wales. Our aim is partly to offer an early account of this development, and partly to identify some trends which may be of relevance beyond the case of Wales. The article draws upon diverse sources, including press reports, material gathered at various public meetings, and interviews with individuals involved with the LG project. We begin by outlining some of the practical issues associated with the current phase in inward FDI in Britain. Next we review the recent growth of Korean FDI, before focusing on LG's decision to set up in Newport. We then look at the relationship between LG and institutions and service-providing organizations in South Wales. We highlight major aspects of the LG project and the institutional response, noting the danger of corporate capture of

European Urban and Regional Studies 0969-7764 (199804) 5:2 Copyright © 1998
SAGE Publications, London, Thousand Oaks and New Delhi, Vol. 5 (2): 119–137; 003695

economic development institutions and debates.[2] The article closes with a more general consideration of the potential for corporate capture of institutional capacity.

The academic and policy debate over large-scale FDI

The role of FDI in the British economy has received considerable attention. British affiliates of overseas firms have demonstrated higher productivity than UK firms in general, and are argued to have had advantageous impacts on the host economy (Hill and Munday, 1994). Michael Heseltine pointed out that the UK has a higher ratio of inward direct investment to gross domestic product than any other leading global economy, and remains ahead of other EU members in the race to attract and retain FDI. The national effort to attract FDI has become more cohesive, heightening the role of the Invest in Britain Bureau (IBB) (Cassell, 1996).

The belief that multinational firms are often more 'advanced' in technical, organizational and employment terms, and that FDI would provide a demonstration of best practice to British industry, underpinned an 'open-door' strategy towards inward FDI under the Thatcher administrations. More recently, a somewhat more nuanced approach has emerged at the national level, which emphasizes targeting those FDIs which are likely to bring the greatest benefits (Cassell, 1996; Gripaios et al., 1997). Thus the IBB has focused its promotional efforts on particular sectoral and geographical sources of FDI as well as giving priority to repeat investments within the foreign-owned sector in the UK.

This national predisposition in favour of FDI has imposed a similar bias at the regional level. As a result, FDI has acquired a hegemonic place in most regional and local development strategies (Collis and Noon, 1994; Fynes and Ennis, 1997; Gripaios et al., 1997; Hill and Munday, 1994; Hudson, 1995; Phelps, 1997). This bias towards FDI as the focus of regional development strategies is increasingly echoed in other European countries, as they adopt broadly neo-liberal economic development strategies (Amin and Tomaney, 1995). It is implied that FDI can provide a unique boost to the local economy, in both quantitative and qualitative terms. This may operate through the impact of FDI on local suppliers (especially where FDI is accompanied by deliberate regional supply-chain development policies), the demonstration effect on local management (especially when the incoming company is Japanese), or the skills-generating nature of the employment provided, and the relatively good remuneration levels compared to local SMEs or the service sector. Versions of these claims have been made explicitly in relation to FDI in Wales (see Alden, 1996; Cooke et al., 1995a; Hill and Munday, 1994; Institute of Welsh Affairs, 1996; Mainwaring, 1995; Morgan, 1997a, b; Osmond, 1995; Roberts, 1994).

New forms of corporate governance and the rise of 'quality' investments

It is widely held that new corporate dynamics have led to the emergence of qualitatively new and essentially superior forms of manufacturing investment by multinationals (e.g. Amin et al., 1994; Fynes and Ennis, 1997; Rugman and D'Cruz, 1997). Such quality investments are the product of a number of changes in the organization of multinationals. Amin et al. (1994) identify a gradual change from geographical to product-based divisional structures of multinationals and a corresponding shift at the level of individual plants giving rise to 'quality' investments. Others agree that there has been a gradual shift away from defensive and offensive export-substituting investment towards rationalized efficiency-seeking and asset-seeking investment by multinationals (UNCTAD, 1994) which is closely related to regional economic integration (Yannopoulos, 1990). More precisely still, Hood and Young, drawing upon UK experience, have detailed a shift away from the 'marketing satellite' investments of the 1950s through the 'miniature replicas' of the 1950s and 1960s to the rationalized investments of the 1970s and 1980s (Hood and Young, 1988). As such, new FDI inflows into the UK are perceived to be composed of a greater proportion of larger scale, high-technology, strategic investments. To an extent, this perception is borne out by changes in the stock of FDI in the UK peripheral regions

(Stone and Peck, 1996). In-situ expansions have assumed greater importance as a component of change within the foreign-owned manufacturing sector in these regions and are suggestive of the rise of larger scale, multiphase investments being undertaken by multinationals. Such repeat investments have assumed a special significance within academic and policy circles within Wales (TUC in Welsh Affairs Committee, 1995; Rees and Thomas, 1994).

New incentives to FDI: customized incentives and 'after-care'

The shift in global FDI flows, and in UK policy, towards what the promotion industry likes to term 'quality investments' has been accompanied by a growing interest in the design of appropriate FDI-oriented institutions and strategies in receiving regions (e.g. Campbell, 1994; Castells and Hall, 1994; Cooke et al., 1995a; De la Mothe and Paquet, 1996; Ohmae, 1993; Porter, 1990; Young et al., 1994). Indeed, somewhat of an orthodoxy has emerged that 'drawing down benefits from companies into the social and economic life of a place in environmentally sensitive ways requires a capacity for locally-informed, place-based governance . . .' (Healey, 1997: 202). If regions are to be able to attract such companies, and handle their requirements effectively, their institutions need to be well resourced and flexible.

In all British regions the repertoire of policies related to FDI has been broadened. Under the rubrics of 'customization' and 'after-care', regional and local FDI strategies increasingly stress the provision not only of a portfolio of sites, start-up grants and tax incentives, but the flexibility to devise a mix of financial and other incentives tailored to the client firm, along with an on-going assistance with expansion. The fact that these are increasingly seen as imperatives reflects both the increased interregional and international competition for inward investment but also the increasing volatility of the inward-investment sector as successive rounds of investment fail to replace closures and rationalizations among existing firms from earlier rounds (e.g. Morris, 1987).

Formally, the scope for regional autonomy over provision is very limited in the UK, as is local and regional autonomy more generally (Keating and Jones, 1995). Consequently, the regional competition for FDI is increasingly fought out on the terrains of the aggregate grant (involving creative exploitation of the various sources), and customized variations in the wider and 'softer' aspect of the incentive package. As Peck notes, 'once all other criteria have been satisfied, success in levering-in new investment can still depend critically on the ability of public authorities, regional organizations and development agencies to produce and reproduce an infrastructure which is customized to the requirements of incoming firms' (Peck, 1996). According to Malcolm Frazer, Chief Executive of the Invest in Britain Bureau, indirect aid, such as offers of help in finding land, improving access roads and other services such as help with recruitment and training, is 'where the real internal competition is' (Wagstyl, 1996). Such measures imply an extensive and enduring commitment on the part of the relevant institutions, both immediately and through time. Various forms and degrees of such 'customization' of provision are now common in all regions (Gripaios et al., 1997; Hudson, 1995; Peck, 1996).

Embedding and the potential for corporate capture

The increased opportunity for host-region agencies to influence the development of incoming companies to establish fruitful linkages with firms and workforces in the local economy has generated an extensive literature. Much of this focuses on the idea that if FDI is to realize its full potential for the host region it should be induced to act as a catalyst for the development of territorially proximate industrial 'clusters' (Hudson, 1995; McKinnon, 1996; Morgan, 1997a; Porter, 1990; Twomey and Tomkins, 1996). With the aim of increasing the embeddedness of FDI, host-region agencies increasingly attempt to influence the development of an 'economic space' around incoming firms, especially through supply-chain and labour-market policies (Hudson, 1995; Peck, 1996; Turok, 1993). The 'customizing of physical space' in terms of the site for an incoming FDI can thus form the leading edge of a wider strategy 'to match the specific requirements of particular private companies to broader regional development objectives' (Peck, 1996: 331).

In the UK at least, there is very little evidence of much 'embedding' to date (Gripaios et al., 1997; McKinnon, 1996; Phelps, 1993a, 1993b) but it is increasingly emphasized as a desirable policy goal for regions (Cooke et al., 1995a; De la Mothe and Paquet, 1996; Institute of Welsh Affairs, 1996). Yet, measures aimed at embedding FDI can be advantageous for the firms concerned because they mean that their regional impact can be substantially greater than the investment they themselves make. 'The major corporations may find much that is advantageous to them in the development of community-based industrial strategies capable of raising the economic dynamism of any particular locality, a dynamism which cannot be achieved within the transnational organisation of production' (Cowling and Sugden, 1996: 305). Almost by definition, such 'embedding' entails the commitment of local capital and public resources in the service of the competitive goals of the incoming company, and therefore reduces the burden on the incoming firm of the costs of establishing an infrastructure of suppliers and distributors, and training and staff retention.

One effect of the current policy emphasis on broadening the relationship between FDI and institutions may therefore be an inflation of the net public subsidy to the inward investor. The United Nations recently noted that 'many incentives packages for foreign investors more than cover the wedge between private and social benefits to correct for market failures, they can introduce distortions in the production structure similar to those caused by restrictions in trade' (UNCTAD, 1996a: 181). Similar concerns have been expressed in the EU. A second effect is that, the bigger the inward investor and the larger the elements of after-care, the greater the potential for corporate capture not only of immediate financial aid, but also the strategic orientation and resources of local institutions. Rugman and D'Cruz's (1997) analysis of flagship investments in Canada suggests that such investments are designed with a sensitivity to the politics of local economic development in a way that their predecessors may not have been. Typically, for example, 'the flagship will prescribe the areas for research inquiry of its university partners, set the terms of reference for human capital development projects with unions, and provide leadership for business–government initiatives' (Rugman and D'Cruz, 1997: 46). Seen in this light, as Peck and Burdis (1996: 77) note, 'the idea of after-care as a form of after-sales service is ... potentially hazardous ... the agenda for regional development could be set by the demands made by powerful foreign firms who are treated as "customers" by agencies which are capable of moulding regions to their requirements' (Peck and Burdis, 1996: 77).

This leads us to the main question posed in this article: Does the emergence of the 'embedded branch plant' imply that otherwise 'footloose' companies are now being tied to the regions? Or does it mean instead that regions are being remoulded around the interests of such companies with the effect that they have less need to be footloose? Such questions create a rather unrealistic opposition between embeddedness and capture. Indeed, embeddedness and local economic development entail a degree of local dependence or capture (Cox and Mair, 1988). However, in posing these questions we wish to raise the level of debate regarding the building of institutional capacity and its contribution to local economic development. Specifically, early observations on LG suggest that institutional capacity without a coherent and long-term strategy for the use of that capacity can result in elements of corporate capture.

The arrival of LG in Wales

Scotland, Wales, and the Northern and West Midlands regions of England have received disproportionate shares of the FDI arriving in Britain since the 1980s (Hill and Munday, 1994). Many commentators argue that Wales and Scotland enjoy a particular advantage by virtue of their unique economic-development institutions (Keating and Jones, 1995; Thomas, 1996). These are said to be 'better able to understand, articulate, engage with and act upon regional problems and opportunities than their counterparts in England' (Evans and Harding, 1997: 24). This is a common complaint in English regions (Gripaios et al., 1997) but it can be overstated. The North Region has been remarkably successful with far fewer resources than either Wales or Scotland, and many English regions may be advantaged through other channels. Nevertheless, the idea that Wales in particular is well equipped to maximize the potential of FDI is widely accepted. Some have gone further to claim that as a result Wales has enjoyed an 'economic renaissance' over the past decade, driven primarily by FDI (Cooke et al., 1995a, 1995b; Institute of Welsh Affairs, 1996; Osmond, 1995). In themselves such claims have undoubtedly been overstated (Lovering, 1995, 1997b; Thomas, 1996). Furthermore, these accounts are part of a more general tendency in some of the recent regional economic development literature to slip into a celebratory account of local boosterism, juxtaposing local institutional missions against descriptions of economic 'successes'. Economic gains in areas of 'institutional thickness' may not be caused by those institutions (Amin and Thrift, 1995; Evans and Harding, 1997; Lovering, 1997a; Staber, 1996).

Wales is thick with institutions. The LG investment would have been unthinkable without them, but it remains to be seen whether the relationships that they have established with each other and LG will be conducive to significant economic development in Wales beyond the company itself. We now look at the background to the arrival of LG in Wales.

Korean FDI and the globalization strategies of the Chaebol

The growth of Korean FDI in Britain in the mid-1990s is a product of the adoption of globalization strategies in the leading 'Chaebol' (conglomerate companies) in preceding years. The term 'globalization' conceals wide variations in national and corporate strategies and geographical outcomes (Hirst and Thompson, 1996; Ruigrok and Van Tulder, 1996). Accordingly, the wave of Korean outward direct investment, of which the LG case is a leading instance, reflects a number of specificities of the Korean economy (Amsden, 1989; Chang, 1993; Lee, 1993).

The strategies of the Korean Chaebol are more accurately depicted as ones of selective internationalization than of literal globalization. To date, the EU is some way behind the US and Asia as a destination for Korean FDI, possessing around one-tenth of the stock of Korean FDI (UNCTAD, 1996b). The initial defensive export-substituting investment flowing into the EU has given way to offensive investment on a potentially much larger scale. In the first instance, each of the Chaebol reacted to protect established export markets in the EU by setting up small-scale operations. In comparison, the LG investment in Newport is the largest in a sequence of larger scale offensive Korean FDI projects in Britain.

In the 1960s and 1970s Korean economic development policy was dominated by an emphasis on labour-intensive light industries oriented to exports (Chang, 1993). In the 1970s the government's emphasis shifted to heavy industry, and designated 'strategic industries' including electronics (Park, 1990). The concentration of industry grew sharply, and with it the political and economic centrality of the government-supported Chaebol, the three largest of which were Samsung, Hyundai, and Lucky Goldstar. This pattern of domestic capital formation created a distinctive business system in which there was intense rivalry among the Chaebol (Burton, 1995), an emphasis upon economies of scale and hierarchical structures of authority and management, and an underdeveloped small-firm sector (Whitley, 1992). The rapid growth generated by 'late industrialization' created a number of pressures within the domestic economy which were exacerbated by hasty attempts at economic liberalization and deregulation of domestic labour and financial markets as a condition of OECD membership. By the mid-1990s, rising domestic incomes and land prices and overstretched infrastructure (resulting in higher transport and distribution costs than in the US and Japan) were already creating pressures on the Chaebol to contain costs, and to seek out new markets and sources of technology overseas (Burton, 1996c, 1996d).

The LG Group was formed from the Lucky chemical company, founded in 1947, and the Goldstar electronics company, founded in 1958. By the mid-1990s LG was the third largest Korean Chaebol behind Samsung and Hyundai. In 1993 the LG Group inaugurated its 'Leap 2005' strategy to overcome three structural problems: excessive dependence on down-market consumer niches;

over-reliance on the stagnating Korean domestic market, and poor productivity. 'Leap 2005' sets out the goal of producing an eightfold increase in turnover over the ten-year period 1995–2005, raising overseas turnover from 20 percent to 50 percent of the total, and shifting into higher-profit product ranges (Adburgham et al., 1996). Until the 1990s LG's constituent companies had invested overseas only cautiously. LG's first European plant for VCRs was opened in Germany in 1986, followed in the late 1980s by a microwave oven and TV plant in Newcastle and a refrigerator plant in Milan, and now the Newport investment. Most of LG Group's expansion in manufacturing operations up to the mid-1990s took place in Asia, but with the new corporate strategy of the mid-1990s more attention has been focused on Europe and the US.

The location decision

The broad reasons for the concentration of Korean investment into the UK within Europe – like that of Japan and Taiwan (Hill and Munday, 1994; Phelps, 1997; Taylor, 1996) – are fairly well known. The UK offers good access to the EU market, along with relatively low costs, low risk of industrial-relations disturbance, flexible employment conditions, well defined mechanisms for negotiation over FDI, and the use of English (taught in Korean schools). While evidence of the connection between labour costs and labour-market flexibility and patterns of FDI within the EU is far from clear (Barrell and Pain, 1997), these do appear important to the internationalization of Korean Chaebol given their emphasis on economies of scale. As noted above, LG began its entry to Europe in Germany, but has distanced itself from the country as a production location, complaining about high wage and tax costs (Adburgham et al., 1996). There has also been a marked 'herding' tendency within the sequence of waves of FDI from Asian countries, as early pioneers demonstrate to their national rivals the viability of a UK location.[3]

Having chosen a UK location, LG focused on the three regions able to generate significant incentives: Scotland, Wales, and northern England (where it already operated a factory). It was expected in the latter region that it would be preferred for any subsequent investment by LG, but in the event, the North East was ruled out because it lacked a sufficiently large site (Adburgham et al., 1996). Another factor may have been a wish to avoid locating in areas where rival Korean companies have a major presence; it is noticeable that Korean FDI is spread around the 'peripheral' regions of the UK. According to one commentator on the Hyundai investment in Scotland, its Korean competitors 'had already claimed other areas in the UK as their own, with LG in Wales, Samsung in northern England and Daewoo in Northern Ireland' (Burton, 1996a). The spreading of Korean FDI may in part reflect regional labour-market constraints but it may also reflect a desire to be seen as a unique high-profile 'visitor'.

The choice between Scotland and Wales triggered a particularly vigorous competition (Cassell, 1996). Scotland apparently nearly succeeded in splitting off the LG Semicon factory until the overarching LG management decreed that the two plants should be on the same site. As noted above, it is at this 'regional' level that the incentive portfolio plays a critical role. Notionally, the incentives available to incoming foreign companies are identical in all assisted areas in the UK. In practice, since the policies which impact on the package of provisions is complex and uncoordinated, local variations can be significant, especially when it comes to on-going commitments of assistance rather than one-off grants or tax concessions (Wagstyl, 1996). 'The fundamental difficulty in the UK, as in the EU, is that the rules governing state subsidies are chaotic: they derive from many unconnected schemes, from which ingenious agencies could in theory put together subsidies worth three-quarters of a project's total cost' (*Financial Times*, 1996). The competition between the Welsh and Scottish secretaries of state, and between the Welsh Development Agency (WDA) and Locate in Scotland, to attract LG was particularly fierce (Wighton, 1996). In the process it exposed the gap between the formalities and the realities of regional competition.

UK government officials insist that the grants to LG did not breach UK Treasury guidelines, and denied that LG encouraged any kind of auction between competing regions (Burton and Wagstyl, 1996). Yet 'government officials who observed the negotiations said that the South Korean group exploited differences among the regions competing for the project to get the best deal . . . LG played it for all it was worth' (Adburgham et al., 1996). The lack of central control over public spending on foreign firms, and the untidy package of incentives, provides significant space for negotiation and bargaining. As a result, William Waldegrave, then Chief Secretary to the Treasury, proposed reducing the autonomy of the Welsh and Scottish secretaries in this area, and placing UK inward-investment policy firmly within the Department of Trade and Industry's Invest in Britain Bureau to prevent another de facto subsidy race between competing UK regions. In the event, he was defeated by the regional interests (Blitz, 1996). LG received a £247m package comprising grants, a free and fully serviced 250-acre large site, commitments to provide training for employees, and an 'after-care' programme which includes help with the sourcing of components, and other regional measures to promote innovation and technology transfer (Adburgham, 1996b).

From the point of view of the local authority, the attraction of LG to Newport represented the culmination of a strategy lasting almost a decade. The Newport area was badly hit by the run-down of employment in the coal and steel industries (although an important plant in the restructured steel industry lies a couple of miles to the east of the town). Lying between the retail and service-centre magnets of Cardiff and Bristol, Newport missed out on much of the office expansion and relocation of the 1980s. However, in recent years it appears to have been relatively successful in attracting inward investment compared to both those cities, possibly at the expense of Cardiff, due largely to the greater availability of land and grant assistance (Gripaios et al, 1997: 597), and lower property costs.

From the mid-1980s, economic development planning in Newport focused on attracting inward investors, both from abroad and the rest of the UK. By the late 1980s, Newport Borough Council had developed ambitions to attract a major large-scale inward-investment project. This became embedded in the local economic development strategy which foresaw the Usk barrage and waterfront improvements raising the attractiveness of Newport to inward investors. The barrage scheme did not materialize but a goal of attracting £100m of private investment and 5000 jobs over 10 years remained. In the event, this target was exceeded by a generous margin, despite an initial setback when the plan to attract Toyota to the location now chosen by LG was unsuccessful.[4]

By the early 1990s the gearing of economic development in Newport to FDI had therefore gained considerable legitimacy. Against this background, senior officers and councillors continued to press for a higher-profile effort to attract a large-scale 'quality' investment, in collaboration with the Welsh Development Agency. This was translated into the need to provide a large 'quality' site, which was seen as a key lesson of the failure to attract Toyota.

Capacity building and the potential for corporate capture

The forum within which the project for 'embedding' LG is being addressed consists of a complex set of networks coordinated by the Welsh Development Agency. Given the diversity of institutions, public and private, and the political and economic contingencies which they each face, the development of a meaningful nexus for policy development and implementation is likely to be complex and slow. In the meantime, LG has come to command the strategic attention and resources of institutions. To some extent this is inherent in the methods of attracting major inward investors. James Turner, Managing Director of the WDA's international division, was recently quoted as saying:

> 'The international investor is faced with a huge amount of choice . . . The market has become more competitive and more complex. To respond to that, one raises one's game plan and becomes even more professional.' That game plan hinges upon 'the ability to demonstrate to businesses that we can provide a solution to their needs, and to focus very specifically on particular companies in particular sectors. We do not set out to present to companies the 10 best reasons to come to Wales, but to take their needs and present them with a solution – albeit a Welsh solution. What distinguishes the men from the boys is the whole question of deliverability – it is a case of translating promises into concrete action.'
>
> (Adburgham, 1996b)

This is very much the approach in the LG case. As we illustrate below, the 'Team Wales' approach was

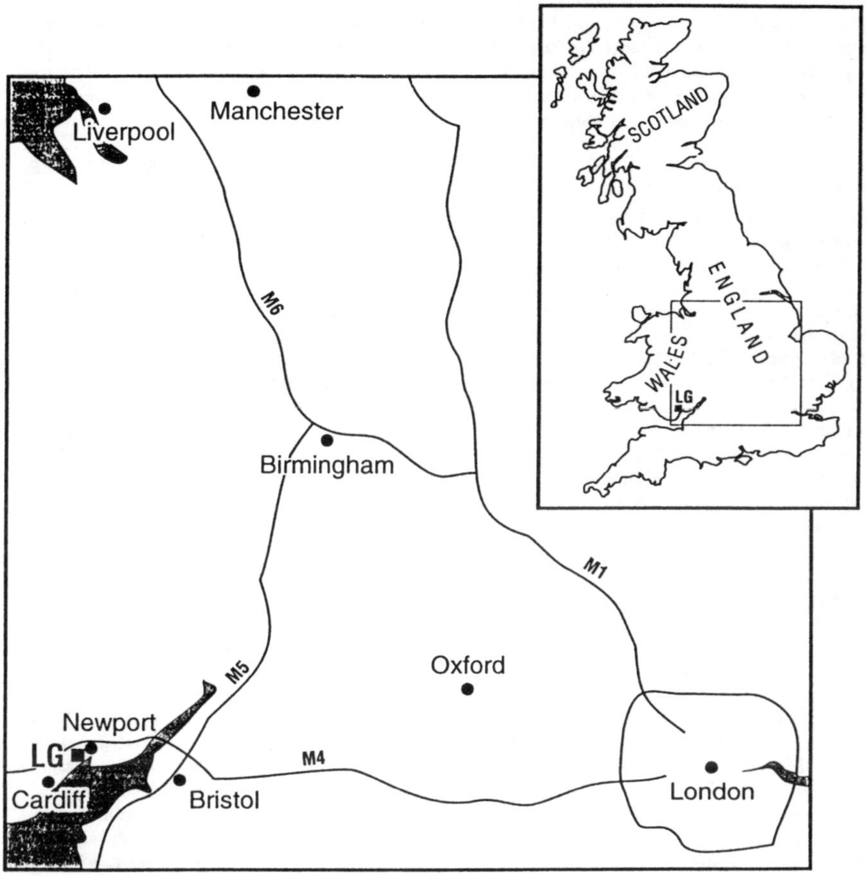

Figure 1 Location of the LG site

particularly effective in delivering a customized space for LG but questions remain about the 'deliverability' of the wider package of support for LG and the creation of an economic space around the investment.[5] In what follows we illustrate aspects of the firm–institution nexus in relation to the creation of a customized space for LG, the tensions on an established discourse regarding inward investment in Wales, and the capture of key institutions and service-providing organizations in Wales.

A customized physical space for LG: a quality site for a quality investment?

The 'Imperial Park' site adopted by LG covers over 250 acres, lying a half mile south east of the M4, just to the west of Newport. It has been developed as a joint venture by the WDA, Newport Council, and Imperial College. The site is one of the best in Wales (although it could equally well be described as lying on Severnside, being within 10 minutes of the new Severn bridge). The WDA and Newport agreed that it should not be sold short. The firm intention was to reserve the entire site for a single major investment, bringing a substantial number of jobs, especially if these involved skills above the level of the kind of assembly jobs which have predominated in the firms attracted to Wales in recent years.

LG's present plans account for 150 of the 250 acres of the site. Newport Council spent £1.5m landscaping part of the site to create 'Celtic Lakes' – a technology park in which Imperial College operates a technology-transfer unit – to further enhance the value of the site and its attractiveness to a major international company. The site was sold on the basis of not only its external locational advantages, via the M4 to the West Country, the Midlands, and Europe (see Figure 1), but also its internal design features, including streams with waterfalls, and walkways planted with shrubs and flowers, in the Celtic Lakes park. According to one closely involved local-authority officer, the latter features were important in creating the 'right feel' for the Koreans. However true this may be, a major factor in drawing the attention of LG, and ruling out competitor English regions, was simply the scale of the site.

Some indication of the determination to attract a major investor such as LG can be gauged by the way in which potentially significant planning issues were overcome without controversy. Specific provision in both the structure and local plans (Borough of Newport, 1993; Gwent County Council, 1992) allowed for inward investment to override other uses and environmental considerations if required. Nevertheless, several major issues were raised by LG's proposed investment. The site falls within a formerly unbroken stretch of green land which has hitherto been maintained by local authorities in Newport and Cardiff as a barrier to urban sprawl. The granting of planning permission for LG places the future of this green area in some doubt, especially since its arrival is likely to generate further development pressures associated with roads, suppliers and housing (Jones, 1997). Two new roads are planned to service the LG electronics factory, local villagers fearing that these will carve a huge slice through their rural neighbourhood (Barding, 1996). The WDA owned half the site and had to purchase the other half. LG's demand that the whole site be free from public access necessitated the rerouting of electricity pylons and a public footpath. Part of the site falls within a Site of Special Scientific Interest (SSSI) which required particularly sensitive handling of potential objections and the rerouting of reens (man-made irrigation ditches).

An expensively produced presentation package was used to market the Newport site to LG. This has been described as a glossy but technical document which, among other things, contained details of how the various planning issues involved with the site would be addressed. As early as December 1995 the WDA started consultations with the likes of environmental groups and utility companies which were vital to the smooth passage of the eventual planning application. This preparatory work ensured that the planning application, complete with environmental statement, was made the day following the final confirmation of the LG investment at Newport and was approved within four weeks.

The politics of an economic space for LG

LG's arrival has undoubtedly caused a major stir in a subregion where there has been a vacuum concerning strategic land-use and transportation issues, and even more concerning industrial development and employment. Partly by virtue of the investment's sheer scale, and partly as a result of its enormous political and ideological significance in the context of Welsh economic development institutions and discourses, it has precipitated new interactions between a range of local and regional institutions which had previously scarcely been in regular contact with each other. The relationships between the incomer and the institutions which have responsibility for the host regional economy are in the process of being defined. The provision of a piece of customized physical space, though potentially problematic, has been remarkably uncontroversial compared to the creation of a mutually advantageous economic space centred on LG. Here the central role accorded to collaborative planning and shared discourses in the creation and deployment of institutional capacity (Healey, 1997) may be misplaced. In contrast, the arrival of LG appears, for the time being, to have foreclosed some

Figure 2 Constituents of the Inward Investment Service Class in South Wales

- leading politicians (the Secretary of State for Wales, and the leading Conservative and Labour MPs)
- the 'Friday Group' in the Welsh Office
- WDA networks: 'Team Wales', 'Source Wales', the LG project team
- Gwent TEC, The Wales TEC national coordination group
- development bodies such as Cardiff Bay Development Corporation
- Land Authority for Wales
- local authority economic development departments, and ad hoc groupings across local authorities
- consultants, notably local representatives of global companies such as Price Waterhouse and Coopers & Lybrand
- ad hoc collectivities among South Wales FDI businesses – prominently the 'Electronics Forum'
- ad hoc/sporadic networks and gatherings such as Cardiff Business Club
- Wales TUC
- diverse Innovation and Technology Transfer organizations
- individual academics, especially at Cardiff and Newport Universities, and Imperial College
- individuals in the Cardiff-based media

emergent lines of thought on – and yet created divisions within – an otherwise hegemonic set of beliefs regarding the value of inward investment to economic development in Wales.

Inward-investment strategies are never purely technical devices and are inextricably bound up with the local politics of economic development (Cox and Mair, 1988; Phelps, 1997: 57). This is particularly evident in South Wales. One effect of the extensive experience of inward investment into Wales has been the emergence of a new stratum of managers of foreign-owned plants (many of whom are locally born and/or have worked for a sequence of FDI companies) (Cooke et al., 1995a; Roberts, 1994). Long before the arrival of LG, this group interacted regularly if unsystematically with a stratum of economic development practitioners, especially in the Welsh Office, the Welsh Development Agency, Local Authorities and TECs. These parties also interact through various technology-transfer and local economic development networks with a cohort of locally based academics and consultants. This nexus forms what could be described as an Inward Investment Service Class (IISC).[6] Figure 2 outlines the main constituent organizations. The move to establish a corporate-led forum for the de facto management of the local labour market, in response to the arrival of LG, may turn out to be particularly significant for the future consolidation of this grouping.

A distinctive feature of the IISC in South Wales, as compared to similar groupings in English regions, is that it is largely regulated from above by the institutions of the devolved British state; the Welsh Secretary, the Welsh Office, and the WDA. Also, many of the actors (consultancies, financial-service firms, property developers, etc.) are employed by Welsh branches of firms which operate internationally (and it is not uncommon for key members of the institutions involved, including the WDA, to live outside Wales). The IISC would therefore seem to be very much an entity built around the state's disposition towards FDI, rather than an organic grouping arising from locally oriented businesses and local communities, as described in the literature on growth coalitions (e.g. Logan and Molotch, 1987; see also Imrie et al., 1995). 'Boosterist' groups and growth coalitions in South Wales have been largely subsumed into a nexus around FDI.

The long-term impact of LG on South Wales will depend in part on whether the institutional shock waves it has caused will trigger a transformation of the IISC from a loose network united by an agenda imposed from above, to an operationally effective grouping oriented to local economic development in a more general sense. Here the signs are contradictory. On the one hand, the growing emphasis on indigenous industry within the strategic thinking of the WDA (see for example the Regional Technology Plan) appears to have lost ground to established ideas regarding inward investment with the arrival of LG. The voice of the 'indigenous lobby' within the WDA was greatly diminished when the Executive Director of the Business Services division left and was not replaced. Whereas in the recent past there has been a parity in the respective budgets of the International and Business Services Divisions, these have diverged markedly in the current financial year with the former being allocated £16m and the latter just £8m. In this way the institutional and strategic adaptation to the arrival of LG has not transformed the IISC-legitimated FDI-focused regional 'subsidy machine' into an apparatus which is capable of optimizing the contribution of FDI to the wider local economy (particularly the provision of employment of appropriate kinds, and in the right places). On the other hand, the arrival of LG may yet open up significant fissures within the IISC as debate over the precise economic impact of LG is generated. Thus ideas surrounding the impact and definition of an economic space around LG are themselves contradictory.

On the one hand, LG and institutions in South Wales have argued that the Newport investment fits into an economic space covering not just South Wales but also encompassing the West Midlands, the South West and London. The definition of this economic space is a product of the desire to win the semiconductor investment for Newport. Until quite late on in negotiations the semiconductor element of the investment may have been bound for Scotland, with its greater tradition of electronic engineering and existing semiconductor industry and supply infrastructure. However, the WDA managed to persuade LG that, despite the lack of skills and suppliers currently available in Wales, the semiconductor operations could draw on inputs from further afield, notably London's Imperial College which has been involved with the company's semiconductor project. Thus one press report noted that there had been concerns over skills shortages in Wales but that 'this obstacle was overcome by emphasising the geographical location of Newport next to two Severn bridges and near the intersection of the M4 and M5, which makes movement into and out of England, especially Bristol, London and Birmingham, relatively painless' (Wilkinson, 1996). Yet this definition of an economic space, so important to attracting LG to Newport, is one which, on occasion, is denied due to the political sensitivity of perceived leakages from the Welsh economy.[7]

On the other hand, and for the purposes of enhancing its perceived impact, the LG investment has been situated within a more narrowly defined economic space. For instance, the site chosen by LG falls within an area designated as 'intermediate' status for the purposes of grant aid. Yet the project has received development-area grant-aid levels because of the wider impact of the project on industrial South Wales (notably the Valleys), parts of which are designated as development areas. This is perhaps the dominant idea regarding the impact of LG in Newport. However, it is one which is propagated and shared perhaps only by LG, the WDA and to a lesser extent the Welsh Office since it has promoted divisions between these three organizations on the one hand and both other inward investors and service-providing organizations and institutions on the other. So, for example, although around two-thirds of those currently unemployed in Wales are within the travel-to-work area of LG, as yet there has been little thought as to how these populations might access these job opportunities – not least in terms of the transportation planning issues (Thomson, 1996). Similarly, the concerns of existing inward investors are at odds with those of LG and centre on rising levels of competition in the labour market within South Wales (see below).

The arrival of LG has undoubtedly renewed and heightened the frequency of contact between institutions and raised interest in strategic planning for South Wales, a project which hitherto had little impetus. Among the organizations closely involved with LG, it is said that LG has galvanized local institutions in a way that would not otherwise have happened and in a way that many hope will be of lasting value, especially for the attraction of future inward investment. Yet the substance of the new interactions is restricted and there are as yet few signs that they are leading to the development of a coherent strategic context capable of utilizing these partnerships to ensure the optimal embedding of inward investors more generally.

After-care and the capture of institutional capacity

The LG case illustrates the distinctiveness of Wales in contrast to English regions, in that coordination is predominantly imposed from above by state bodies (Gripaios et al., 1997). The central role is played by the WDA-led 'Team Wales' network. As we have seen, a distinctive feature of the LG Newport investment was the preparatory work by the WDA and the local authority within the 'Team Wales' approach. But these addressed mainly land-use issues and the incentives package. The details of longer-term aspects of the local economic impact, including questions concerning suppliers and the labour market, have been left largely until after the investment decision was made, to be gathered under the umbrella of 'after-care'. It was only at this stage that other public authorities and local actors were brought on board. Moreover, most have been required to take some responsibility for handling the effects of LG, without increased resources (a particularly pressing issue in the Local Authorities, Training and Enterprise Councils and Further Education Colleges).

Funding for the WDA has been in decline for some time, with an increasing proportion of its spending having to be generated from the sale of assets (Morgan, 1997b; Thomas, 1996). In the months immediately after the LG announcement, it was widely rumoured that the WDA itself would be financially exhausted by the deal for up to three years, and was relying on additional funding from the existing or an incoming Labour government. The implication was that the LG project would preempt resources, implying a reduction in other economic-development activities. For the financial year 1997/98 the WDA's budget stands at £150m (£85m in grant-in-aid and £65m receipts), of which £30m has been ring-fenced for LG – a further £39m being ring-fenced for the financial year 1998/99. Despite an increase in the 1997/98 budget, the WDA has had to divert funds toward the LG cause. For instance, £1m worth of WDA funding for a research centre at Swansea was withdrawn, resulting in the loss of matching EU funds (Jones, 1996). The WDA's land reclamation programmes – vital to attracting inward investment beyond the relatively prosperous South East of Wales and into West Wales and the Valleys – were cut by £11m as one immediate consequence of LG's arrival (*Western Mail*, 1996b). Here the full implications of the LG investment upon the distribution of inward investment in Wales become apparent. First, the diversion of funds means that the WDA is poorly placed to contribute to securing EU funding for the Industrial South Wales Programme bid (for Objective 2 funding), which had to be revised with a greater emphasis on support for indigenous industry and inward investment only in, or directly serving, the Valleys. Second, West Wales and the Valleys are being doubly penalized since they have not attracted much inward investment in the first place and will be unable to do so as long as advance sites are not in place.

The labour market dimension

As we saw earlier, the effective local labour supply ranges from west of Cardiff to Bristol, Swindon, and Gloucester. In the face of this, the mechanisms to ensure maximum take-up by Welsh jobseekers are being put in place only slowly. Perhaps the greatest pressures on local institutional capacity are being felt in relation to the local supply of electronics and semiconductor-related skills. With nine staff devoted to LG, Gwent TEC, whose turf includes the LG site, has perhaps the largest of a number of small teams within the Team Wales network surrounding LG.

A Semiconductor Training Centre has been established at Imperial Park adjacent to the LG site to help provide for operator, technician and graduate-level skills. This has been financed in the main by the WDA, Welsh Office and Gwent TEC, with some modest funding from neighbouring TECs in South and Mid Glamorgan. The training centre was triggered by LG but of necessity has been designed to meet the skill requirements of a number of other local semiconductor firms (a similar initiative, but led by the private sector, is underway in the North East – Tighe, 1996b). The University of Wales at Newport, Swansea and Cardiff are all expected to develop and expand courses for microelectronics graduates with the latter two reportedly receiving financial assistance from LG for this purpose.

The problem of what is generally (if often misleadingly) called skills-mismatch among lower-grade recruits is to be addressed primarily by Gwent Training and Enterprise Council. Yet this organization was not privy to the initial discussions with LG before the investment was finalized. For the next few years a large part of the resources of Gwent TEC and local colleges will be tied up in administering the supply of up to 1500 people per year trained to NVQ1 level in electronics assembly skills. To this end, an Electronics Training Centre has been established which is specifically designed for LG alone. The centre has been jointly funded by the WDA, Welsh Office and Gwent TEC with LG contributing all the technical kit and teaching staff. To date, organizations like the WDA and Gwent TEC have been remarkably successful in keeping to the ambitious deadlines of LG. However, this may conceal the way in which institutional capacity may be stretched to breaking point among lower-tier service-providing organizations such as FE Colleges. Changes from input to output-related funding by TECs coupled with budget cuts made by the Welsh Office (Dalingwater, 1997), mean that FE Colleges may not be able to deliver on their share of the burden of training for LG.

These are essentially medium to long-term measures. In the meantime, anxieties about the 'poaching' of staff have been expressed throughout the South Wales manufacturing sector. The companies concerned include a number of earlier FDI arrivals such as Sony, Bosch, and Matsushita (Panasonic) and Newport Wafer-Fab. One FDI manager complained that the shortage of information technology and electronic design skills in Wales 'has been exacerbated by LG's decision to set up its manufacturing operation in Newport and the considerable resources that the Welsh Office and its agencies have put at LG's disposal' (quoted in Parkin, 1997). Fears have been expressed over both the potential 'churning' of scarce staff, and general upward pressure on local wage rates (Parkin, 1997). These led to the formation of the 'South Wales Electronics Forum' at the instigation of Matsushita (a company which has a reputation locally for being one of the most persistent in complaining about the lack of qualified staff in South Wales – Gripaios et al., 1997: 600). The success of this corporate attempt to impose some coherent management of the local electronics labour market organization remains to be seen.

The supplier dimension

Labour market impacts remain the main source of anxiety among local employers. Supplier impacts are viewed more optimistically, at least by the agencies involved with the attraction of LG. As in the North East, the growth of electronics FDI in South Wales has drawn attention to the possibility of encouraging a local supplier base. In the North East, incoming firms such as Samsung and Nissan appear to have deliberately brought suppliers with them from their home country. In South Wales, despite the build-up of a second wave of Japanese manufacturing investment (Munday, 1995), this model is less familiar. Nevertheless, inquiries from suppliers wishing to locate close to LG have been received from Asia, California and Europe (Smith, 1996).

As far as the consumer electronics element of the investment is concerned there may be relatively few problems in finding and developing acceptable Welsh, UK and European suppliers. One major Japanese inward investor in Cardiff – NEG – will supply LG with glass for monitors assembled at Newport. However, the development of a Welsh-based supply infrastructure for the semiconductor element of the LG investment is more problematic. There are only a few Wales-based firms which serve the semiconductor industry – though one has recently announced an £11m expansion of its Bridgend photo-masking operations (Smith, 1996).

The development of regional supply-chains is the goal of the WDA's 'Source Wales' initiative. Soon after agreeing the project, LG gave the 'Source Wales' team their entire supplier list and asked them to identify three local suppliers in each category. Reports of progress on this front are imprecise and contradictory. Initially the WDA claimed to have identified 100 potential suppliers in the UK. By May 1997, LG buyers had visited 40 potential suppliers in Wales. By July of that year, the WDA was speaking of having identified 45 potential suppliers of which 25 were 'Welsh' (Groves, 1997), with four Welsh companies being the first to gain contracts with LG (*Western Mail*, 1997). Supply initiatives around LG are likely to benefit a number of Welsh companies, and may draw in further inward investment from both Korea and the UK. However, it must be borne in mind that Wales does not constitute a territorially integrated supply structure, despite the growth of such initiatives. The SME sector is under-represented in Wales (Morgan, 1996), and in recent years new-firm death rates have exceeded birth rates. As such even the modest levels and turbulent record of indigenous spinoffs centred on the Scottish semiconductor industry (Phelps, 1992) may be out of reach. And although many existing overseas-owned electronics plants aim to maximize local sourcing, they still draw the overwhelming majority of their key inputs from England or beyond. Matsushita, for example, claims 70 percent EU content, but 'very little is bought within Wales with the exception of bulky goods, plastic and metal pressings, and selected electronic components'. Similarly, at Bosch, supposedly one of the most 'embedded' local FDIs, 'true Welsh content is minimal' (Gripaios et al., 1997: 600).

The sheer scale of the LG investment suggests that it could eventually have a significant impact on the regional supply infrastructure – certainly the greatest supply potential in Wales centres on the engineering industries (Twomey and Tomkins, 1996) but this will not emerge without a deliberate and well resourced policy.[8] A number of initiatives have been set up in Wales with the goal of improving linkages in the longer term, including a Regional Technology Plan part-funded by DG16, but there is as yet no explicit linking of this to the LG project. The suggestion by a local Labour MP that the blighted former coal communities of South Wales could be revitalized as industrial villages based on components companies supplying the LG group met with no response (*Western Mail*, 1996a).

Conclusions: tying up the region to tie down the global

In this preliminary examination of LG in Wales we have been able to identify some important instances of institutional capture. LG has been successful in recruiting South Wales institutions to its radical experiment in corporate restructuring.[9] It is less clear both that those institutions will be able to deliver all of what LG requires of them, and that LG will be able to realize the ambitious scenario on which the future of the Newport investment depends.

It appears the strategic orientation and resources of many South Wales institutions have become tied up with attracting and attempting to embed LG in the region. The stakes are high. Failure to meet LG's requirements is unthinkable for at least two reasons. First, it would have seriously deleterious effects upon other existing inward investors in South Wales – most notably, as we have seen, in terms of the tightening of the labour market. Secondly, it could have a negative impact on future FDI inflows. Some have suggested that so great are the drains on institutional capacity by LG that for the time being major inward investors are likely to be deterred in any case. One businessman asserted that 'the LG situation has highlighted a number of major deficiencies in the infrastructure of the Welsh economy which might prove a deterrent to future inward investors' (quoted in Parkin, 1997). There are a number of imponderables surrounding the institutional adjustment to the arrival and development of LG. The turbulence of these adjustments, and their indeterminate effects, reveal much about the lack of advance planning – in the broadest sense – in South Wales.

Capture of the orientation and resources of institutions by a major inward investor like LG may itself be a product of the way in which the apparatus oriented to FDI in Wales is adjusting to new forms of FDI characterized by a shift towards 'quality' FDI, characterized by a greater scale of investments, land-use, subsidies, and requirements of regional institutions. In effect, this is a story of adjustment at the local and regional levels to a context which is set at the national (and indeed EU) levels and beyond. But as our account and recent debate on globalization has illustrated, it would be wrong to read this as a 'top-down' process, as if the region were a mere recipient of influences originating elsewhere. The engagement between local institutions and FDI is a constitutive feature of the regional economy of Wales and has resulted in the dominance of an Inward Investment Service Class and its ideas regarding the value of inward investment to economic development in Wales. Within this context major inward investors, like LG, have been able to exert considerable influence over the strategic orientation and resources of a number of key institutions and service-providing organizations. In the medium term, the arrival of LG may provoke a concern to spread the available institutional capacity in Wales more broadly among the range of inward investors, as appears to be happening in the North East (Peck and Burdis, 1996), but for the time being this debate is, of necessity, foreclosed.

The LG case raises questions of general importance for regions and localities seeking to develop through FDI. The first of these concerns the general wisdom of the ubiquitous predisposition towards FDI as a key element in regional development strategies. It is noticeable that even after two decades of significant FDI in the UK's 'peripheral regions', the recipient areas remain relatively economically disadvantaged. Despite a remarkably successful record in attracting FDI since the 1970s, the Welsh economy remains the least successful in the UK in terms of providing jobs – apart from Northern Ireland (Lovering, 1997b). Despite attracting a new car industry, the North East remains the poorest region in England. There is little evidence that success in attracting FDI has reduced regional susceptibility to economic fluctuations.[10] If large-scale FDI of the LG kind represents a dominant trend, as some observers claim, the commitment to FDI carries with it the additional problem of creating major economic and institutional dependence on a single company. In this respect the 'new regional policy' centred on FDI is turning out to be much more similar to the 'old regional policies' of the 1960s than many have recently claimed.[11] Yet the growth in scale poses new problems of degree. The attempt to attract 'new wave' FDI projects seeking very large sites, for example, raises new questions concerning environmental sustainability. In the North East of England, English Partnerships has recently argued that up to another 5000 acres will be required to attract the next generation of 'quality' inward investment (Tighe, 1996a). There must be a limit to which – and the locations in which – allocating very large areas of land to possible FDI projects is justifiable.

The second question concerns the dynamics of the sociological and political-economy dimensions of FDI-focused development strategies. Our account reveals the hegemonic position of, what we have termed, an Inward Investment Service Class within policy debate in South Wales. This hegemony is evident in the 'Catch-22' character of much of the regional economic policy debate. The failure of the present policy bias towards FDI to generate adequate employment or other spin-offs has tended merely to refuel the assumption that further efforts are needed to enable the region to compete more effectively for FDI (for example see Institute of Welsh Affairs, 1996; for criticisms see Lovering, 1997a; Thomas, 1996). Hudson notes a similar foreclosure of the policy debate in the North East of England (Hudson, 1995: 92). The particular nature of the local Inward Investment Service Class and its impact on the strategic discourse and concrete provision in UK and EU regions deserves further research.

Finally, because efforts to embed inward investors by definition entail a degree of institutional capture or local dependence, greater attention should be paid by both researchers and practitioners to the institutional structures and strategies which might forge a sustainable link between development *in* a region and the development *of* it (Sayer, 1985). There is enough evidence to suggest that the institutional adjustment to LG in South Wales is far from an optimal model. More precisely, the LG case indicates that the effort spent in attracting major inward investments needs to be matched by a coherent strategy and mechanisms for strategy implementation in order to: maximize the contribution of a given inward investor; balance its needs against the competing claims of existing inward investors and indigenous industry; ensure that the burden of after-care is suitably distributed among the agents of local governance.

Acknowledgements

The authors would like to thank referees for their comments on the initial draft of this article.

Notes

[1] The figure of £247m includes Regional Selective Assistance of up to £104.5m (including the second phase of the project), £17.6m financial assistance with training, with the remainder presumably accounted for by the value of the site and infrastructure costs such as rerouting of pylons and sewers.

[2] In this article we use the term 'institutional capacity' (as an alternative to the term 'institutional thickness' – Amin and Thrift, 1995) to refer to the number, power and resources of institutions and service-providing organizations in a given region or locality. Capture of that capacity implies some significant orientation of the strategies and resources of such institutions and organizations to a single client or limited number of clients.

[3] The 'herd effect' among inward investors is evident in the wave of FDI from Japan, now being followed by a wave from South Korea. According to a UK official in Seoul, 'the Samsung decision was the turning point that

encouraged other Korean companies to invest in the UK' (Burton and Wagstyl, 1996). Hyundai's decision to invest in Scotland was a direct response to the LG decision to invest in Newport (Burton, 1996a).

[4] Other major investments include: Panasonic, which moved to Newport in 1986 creating 300 jobs (promising an eventual 1000); the expansion of locally based electronics company Newbridge Networks; the reopening of the old Inmos factory by Newport Wafer-Fab, subsidiary of Hong Kong-based QPL, which has subsequently expanded into a new £230m semiconductor plant nextdoor. There have also been a number of back-office relocations to Newport. The Patent Office was followed in the early 1990s by the TSB insurance and phone bank divisions, bringing 1000 jobs. By moving in to a high-quality new building, TSB had an important impact on the business image of Newport, marking a clear break with the 'heritage era' of coal and steel, and manual labour.

[5] 'Team Wales' brings together staff from the Welsh Office, WDA, local authorities, Land Authority for Wales, TECs and others with functions bearing on FDI reception or after-care. As a method of working, Team Wales was reinvigorated in 1995 after the Taiwanese company Chung Hwa chose Scotland over Wales for its £260m TV tube factory (Adburgham, 1996a).

[6] On the concept of the Service Class in general, see Urry (1995: ch. 6). Despite three decades of significant FDI in UK regions, there has been no research into the make-up and performance of the network of individuals and institutions servicing it (although see Blackhurst and Cope, 1993; Lovering, 1997a).

[7] The company was quick to distance itself from reports that up to 60% of applicants to one recruitment agency involved with initial construction work were from outside Wales (Coleman, 1997).

[8] There have been a number of different estimates of the impact of LG. Hill and Roberts's (1996) estimate, using the recently constructed input–output tables for Wales, suggests an eventual total of 14,514 jobs created in Wales. Gwent TEC, using Cambridge Econometrics's model suggests an eventual total of only 11,600 jobs across the UK as a whole, of which 800 would be created in Gwent (Gwent Training and Enterprise Council, 1997).

[9] LG's Newport project takes place against the background of not only a major restructuring in the company, but also severe short-term financial problems. LG Semicon is expected to make a loss in the year in which the investment begins. It is investing (globally) around 90% of annual sales, raising the net debt/equity ratio from 60% to 200% (Burton, 1996b). The semiconductor industry and to a lesser extent the electronics industry are likely to remain extremely volatile into the new century. Semiconductor prices plummeted in 1995–6, forcing postponements of investment by National Semiconductor (Greenock), Fujitsu (Newton Aycliffe) and Samsung (Wynyard) in the UK alone. The massive LG investment at Newport therefore represents a particularly aggressive strategy.

[10] During the recent recession (1991–3), capital investment in the most FDI-dependent regions – Wales and the North of England – collapsed more severely than in any other UK regions (see Office of National Statistics, 1996: Table 12.11).

[11] As Hudson (1995: 82) points out, many of the issues arising from reliance on FDI have an air of 'back to the future'.

References

Adburgham, R. (1996a) 'South Wales Euphoric about Flood of New Jobs', *Financial Times* (11 Jul.): 9.

Adburgham, R. (1996b) 'Survey – Inward Investment into the UK: Springboard into Europe', *Financial Times* (18 Jul.): 6.

Adburgham, R., Burton, J. and Wagstyl, S. (1996) 'Making all the Right Connections: Korean Team Chose Region after Closely Examining All the Options', *Financial Times* (11 Jul.): 9.

Alden, J. (1996) 'The Transfer from Problem to Powerful Region: the Experience of Wales', in J. Alden and P. Boland (eds) *Regional Development Strategies*, pp. 129–58. London: Jessica Kingsley.

Amin, A. and Thrift, N. (1995) 'Globalisation, Institutional "Thickness" and the Local Economy', in P. Healey, S. Cameron, S. Davoudi, S. Graham and A. Madani-Pour (eds) *Managing Cities: the New Urban Context*, pp. 91–108. London: Wiley.

Amin, A. and Tomaney, J. (1995) 'The Regional Dilemma in a Neo-liberal Europe', *European Urban and Regional Studies* 2 (2): 171–88.

Amin, A., Bradley, D., Howells, J., Tomaney, J. and Gentle, C. (1994) 'Regional Incentives and the Quality of Mobile Investment in the Less Favoured Regions of the EC', *Progress in Planning* 41: 1–112.

Amsden, A. (1989) *Asia's Next Giant*. New York: Oxford University Press.

Barding, A. (1996) 'Villagers in Protest' *South Wales Echo* (22 Aug.): 26.

Barrell, R. and Pain, N. (1997) 'The Growth of Foreign Direct Investment in Europe', *NIESR Review* 160: 63–75.

Blackhurst, C. and Cope, N. (1993) 'The New Barons', *The Independent on Sunday* (3 Jan.): 10.

Blitz, J. (1996) 'Rival Bids for Inward Investment Continue', *Financial Times* (25 Nov.): 8.

Borough of Newport (1993) *Local Plan (Consultation Draft)*. Newport: Borough of Newport.

Burton, J. (1995) 'Reforms Running Fast Forward – Changes at Korea's LG Electronics have led to a Sharp Reversal in Fortunes', *Financial Times* (25 Sep.): 13.

Burton, J. (1996a) 'Koreans Gamble on Recovery with Big Bite into Europe', *Financial Times* (9 Oct.): 8.

Burton, J. (1996b) 'LG Semicon Shares Fall in First Full Day's Trading', *Financial Times* (12 Nov.): 28.

Burton, J. (1996c) 'Business Beckons on Foreign Shores', *Financial Times* (15 Nov.): 4.

Burton, J. (1996d) 'Structural Inefficiencies Persist', *Financial Times* (15 Nov.): 1.

Burton, J. and Wagstyl, S. (1996) 'EU is the Lure for Koreans in Regions', *Financial Times* (10 Jul.): 7.

Burton, J., Adburgham, R., Tighe, C. and Wagstyl, S. (1996) 'Hague Defends £200m Grants to LG Group', *Financial Times* (11 Jul.): 9.

Campbell, D. (1994) 'Foreign Investment, Labour Immobility and the Quality of Employment', *International Labour Review* 133: 185–204.

Cassell, M. (1996) 'Survey – Inward Investment into the UK', *Financial Times* (18 Jul.): 6.

Castells, M. and Hall, P. (1994) *Technopoles of the World: the Making of 21st Century Industrial Complexes*. London: Routledge.

Chang, H-J. (1993) 'The Political Economy of Industrial Policy in Korea', *Cambridge Journal of Economics* 17: 131–57.

Coleman, C. (1997) 'Sixty Per Cent of LG Job Bids from Outside Wales', *South Wales Echo* (5 Mar.): 1.

Collis, C. and Noon, D. (1994) 'FDI in the UK Regions: Recent Trends and Policy Issues', *Regional Trends* 28: 843–8.

Cooke, P., Morgan, K. and Price, P. (1995a) 'The Welsh Renaissance', Papers in Planning Research No. 157. Cardiff: Department of City and Regional Planning, University of Wales.

Cooke, P., Price, A. and Morgan, K. (1995b) 'Regulating Regional Economies: Wales and Baden-Wurttemberg in Transition', in M. Rhodes (ed.) *The Regions and the New Europe*, pp. 105–35. Manchester: Manchester University Press.

Cowling, K. and Sugden, R. (1996) 'Capacity, Transnationals, and Industrial Strategy', in J. Michie and J. Grieve-Smith (eds) *Creating Industrial Capacity: Towards Full Employment*, pp. 289–307. Oxford: OUP.

Cox, K. and Mair, A. (1988) 'Locality and Community in the Politics of Local Economic Development', *Annals of the Association of American Geographers* 78: 307–25.

Dalingwater, A. (1997) 'Colleges Nearer Breaking Point, Hague Warned', *Western Mail* (6 Mar.): 10.

De la Mothe, J. and Paquet, G. (1996) 'Evolution and Inter-creation: the Government–Business–Society Nexus', in J. De la Mothe and G. Paquet (eds) *Evolutionary Economics and the New International Political Economy*, pp. 9–34. London: Pinter.

Evans, R. and Harding, A. (1997) 'Regionalisation, Regional Institutions and Economic Development', *Policy & Politics* 25: 19–30.

Financial Times (1996) 'Comment & Analysis: Jobs for the Boyos' (11 Jul.): 23.

Fynes, B. and Ennis, E. (eds) (1997) *Competing from the Periphery: Core Issues in International Business*. London: Dryden Press.

Gripaios, P., Gripaios, R. and Munday, M. (1997) 'The Role of Inward Investment in Urban Economic Development: the Cases of Bristol, Cardiff and Plymouth', *Urban Studies* 34 (4): 579–603.

Groves, P. (1997) 'Business is Geared up to Reap the Rewards', *Wales 2000* July (Issue 11, *Western Mail*): 24–5.

Gwent County Council (1992) *Gwent Structure Plan 1991–2006*. Newport: Gwent County Council.

Gwent Training and Enterprise Council (1997) *Future Skills Needs in Gwent*. Newport: Gwent Training and Enterprise Council.

Healey, P. (1997) *Collaborative Planning: Shaping Places in Fragmented Societies*. London: Macmillan.

Hill, S. and Munday, M. (1994) *The Regional Distribution of Foreign Manufacturing in the UK*. London: Macmillan.

Hill, S. and Roberts, A. (1996) 'The Economic Impact of LG in Wales', *Welsh Economic Review* 9 (1): 6–7.

Hirst, P. and Thompson, G. (1996) *Globalization in Question*. Oxford: Polity Press.

Hood, N. and Young, S. (1988) 'Inward Investment and the EC: UK Evidence on Corporate Integration Strategies', in J.H. Dunning and P. Robson (eds) *Multinationals and the European Community*, pp. 91–104. Oxford: Blackwells.

Hudson, R. (1995) 'The Role of Foreign Inward Investment', in L. Evans, P. Johnson and B. Thomas (eds) *The North Region Economy*, pp. 79–95. Aldershot: Mansell.

Imrie, R., Thomas, H. and Marshall, T. (1995) 'Business Organizations, Local Dependence and the Politics of Urban Renewal in Britain', *Urban Studies* 32 (1): 31–48.

Institute of Welsh Affairs (1996) *Wales 2010: Three Years On*. Cardiff: Institute of Welsh Affairs.

Jones, N. (1996) 'Anger as WDA Pulls out of Scheme to Establish £3m Research Centre', *Western Mail* (17 Dec.): 11.

Jones, N. (1997) 'New Town Planned to House LG Staff', *Western Mail* (19 Feb.): 1.

Keating, M. and Jones, B. (1995) 'Nations, Regions and Europe: the UK Experience', in B. Jones and M. Keating (eds) *The European Union and the Regions*, pp. 89–114. Oxford: Clarendon Press.

Lee, Y-S. (1993) 'Industrial Subcontracting and the Labour Movement: the Korean Automotive Industry', *Journal of Contemporary Asia* 23: 25–40.

Logan, J.R. and Molotch, H.L. (1987) *Urban Fortunes: the Political Economy of Place*. Berkeley: University of California Press.

Lovering, J. (1995) 'Creating Discourses Rather than Jobs: the Crisis in the Cities and the Transition Fantasies of Intellectuals and Policy Makers', in P. Healey, S. Cameron, S. Davoudi, S. Graham and A. Madani-Pour (eds) *Managing Cities: the New Urban Context*, pp. 109–26. London: Wiley.

Lovering, J. (1997a) 'Global Restructuring and Local Impact', in M. Pacione (ed.) *Britain's Cities: Geographies of Division in Urban Britain*, pp. 63–87. London: Routledge.

Lovering, J. (1997b) 'Misleading and Misreading Wales: The New Regionalism', *Papers in Planning Research*, No. 166. Cardiff: Dept. of City and Regional Planning. University of Wales.

McKinnon, A. (1996) 'Logistics, Peripherality and Manufacturing Competitiveness', in B. Fynes and S. Ennis (eds) *Competing from the Periphery: Core Issues in International Business*, pp. 47–82. London: Dryden Press.

Mainwaring, L. (1995) 'Catching Up and Falling Behind: South-East Asia and Wales', *Contemporary Wales* 8: 9–28.

Morgan, B. (1996) 'Economic Development from Within – the Next Phase', *Agenda: The Journal of the Institute of Welsh Affairs* (Summer): 29–31.

Morgan, K. (1997a) 'The Learning Region: Institutions, Innovation and Regional Renewal', *Regional Studies* 31 (5): 491–503.

Morgan, K. (1997b) 'The Regional Animateur: Taking Stock of the Welsh Development Agency', *Regional and Federal Studies* 7: 70–94.

Morris, J. (1987) 'Industrial Restructuring, Foreign Direct Investment and Uneven Development: the Case of Wales', *Environment & Planning A* 19: 205–24.

Munday, M. (1995) 'The Regional Consequences of the Japanese Second Wave: a Case Study', *Local Economy* 10: 4–20.

Office of National Statistics (1996) *Regional Trends*. London: HMSO.

Ohmae, K. (1993) 'The Rise of the Region State', *Foreign Affairs* 72: 78–87.

Osmond, J. (1995) *Welsh Europeans*. Bridgend: Seren.

Park, S.O. (1990) 'Government Management of Industrial Change in the Republic of Korea', in D.C. Rich and G.J.R. Linge (eds) *The State and Management of Industrial Change*, pp. 74–87. London: Routledge.

Parkin, D. (1997) 'LG Accused of Cherry-picking Welsh Skills', *Western Mail* (12 Apr.): 1.

Peck, F. (1996) 'Regional Development and the Production of Space: the Role of Infrastructure in the Attraction of New Inward Investment', *Environment & Planning A* 28: 327–39.

Peck, F. and Burdis, C. (1996) 'After-care for Inward Investors: Implications for Regional Development in the European Union', in C. Collis and F. Peck (eds) *Industrial Restructuring: FDI and Regional Development*, pp. 67–83. London: Regional Studies Association.

Phelps, N.A. (1992) 'From Local Economic Dependence to Local Economic Development? The Case of the Scottish Electronics Industry', Papers in Planning Research No. 136. Cardiff: Department of City and Regional Planning, University of Wales.

Phelps, N.A. (1993a) 'Branch Plants and the Evolving Spatial Division of Labour: a Study of Material Linkage Change in the Northern Region of England', *Regional Studies* 27: 87–102.

Phelps, N.A. (1993b) 'Contemporary Industrial Restructuring and Linkage Change in an Older Industrial Region: Examples from the North East of England', *Environment and Planning A* 25: 863–82.

Phelps, N.A. (1997) *Multinationals and European Integration: Trade, Investment and Regional Development*. London: RSA/Jessica Kingsley.

Porter, M. (1990) *The Competitive Advantage of Nations*. New York: Free Press.

Rees, G. and Thomas, M. (1994) 'Inward Investment, Labour Market Adjustment and Skills Development: Recent Experience in South Wales', *Local Economy* 9: 48–61.

Roberts, A. (1994) 'The Causes and Consequences of Inward Investment: the Welsh Experience', *Contemporary Wales* 6: 73–86.

Rugman, A. and D'Cruz, J. (1997) 'Strategies of Multinational Enterprises and Governments: the Theory of the Flagship Firm', in G. Boyd and A. Rugman (eds) *Euro–Pacific Investment and Trade: Strategies and Structural Interdependencies*, pp. 248–72. Cheltenham: Edward Elgar.

Ruigrok, W. and Van Tulder, R. (1996) *The Logic of International Restructuring*. London: Routledge.

Sayer, A. (1985) 'Industry and Space: a Sympathetic Critique of Radical Research', *Environment and Planning C: Society & Space* 3: 3–29.

Smith, I. (1996) 'Jobs Galore for Valleys', *The Times* (12 Nov.): 35.

Staber, U. (1996) 'Accounting for Variations in the Performance of Industrial Districts: the Case of Baden-Wurttemberg', *International Journal of Urban and Regional Research* 20: 299–315.

Stone, I. and Peck, F. (1996) 'The Foreign-owned Manufacturing Sector in the UK Peripheral Regions, 1978–1993: Restructuring and Comparative Performance', *Regional Studies* 30: 55–68.

Taylor, R. (1996) 'South Koreans Eye European Prospects: Big Industrialists See Investment in EU as Means to Gain Larger Market Share', *Financial Times* (3 Dec.): 9.

Thomas, D. (1996) 'Winner or Loser in the New Europe?: Regional Funding, Inward Investment and the Prospects for the Welsh Economy', *European Urban and Regional Studies* 3 (3): 225–40.

Thomson, R. (1996) 'Valleys Gear up to Cope with Jobs Problems', *Western Mail* (2 Sep.): 6.

Tighe, C. (1996a) 'North Takes Steps to Maintain Inward Investment', *Financial Times* (10 Oct.): 8.

Tighe, C. (1996b) 'Centre to Deal with Skills Crisis in Chip Industry', *Financial Times* (4 Nov.): 10.

Tucker, E. (1997) 'LG Wales Gets £247m Aid', *Financial Times* (3 Apr.): 14.

Turok, I. (1993) 'Inward Investment and Local Linkages: How Deeply Embedded is Silicon Glen', *Regional Studies* 27: 401–18.

Twomey, J. and Tomkins, J.M. (1996) 'Supply Potential in the Regions of Great Britain', *Regional Studies* 30: 783–90.

UNCTAD (1994) *World Investment Report: Transnational Corporations, Employment and the Workplace*. Geneva: UN.

UNCTAD (1996a) *World Investment Report: Trade and Investment Policy*. Geneva: UN.

UNCTAD (1996b) *Sharing Asia's Dynamism: Asia Direct Investment in the European Union*. Geneva: UN.

Urry, J. (1995) *Consuming Places*. London: Routledge.

Wagstyl, S. (1996) 'Grants Help Trap Foreign Moneyspinners: Fight for LG Complex Highlights Britain's Skill at Attracting International Investment', *Financial Times* (25 May): 5.

Welsh Affairs Committee (1995) *Wales in Europe*, Vol. 2., pp. 81–4. London: HMSO.

Western Mail (1996a) 'Industrial Villages Idea for Valleys' (25 Jul.): 9.

Western Mail (1996b) 'WDA Cutback a Threat to Lottery Cash' (1 Aug.): 11.

Western Mail (1997) 'Four Companies Win First Contracts from LG', *Western Mail Business Supplement* (9 Jul.): 1.

Whitley, R. (1992) *Business Systems in East Asia: Firms, Markets and Society*. London: Sage.

Wighton, D. (1996) 'Regional Bodies Face Controls', *Financial Times* (6 Jun.): 4.

Wilkinson, S. (1996) 'Lucky for Wales?', *Western Mail* (13 May): 10.

Yannopoulos, G. (1990) 'Foreign Direct Investment and European Integration: the Evidence from the Formative Years of the European Community', *Journal of Common Market Studies* 28: 235–60.

Young, S., Hood, N. and Wilson, A. (1994) 'Targeting as a Competitive Strategy for European Inward Investment Agencies', *European Urban and Regional Studies* 1 (2): 143–59.

Part III
Sectoral Studies of Business Firms from Specific Emerging Economies

[14]

Hong Kong firms lead developing countries into foreign investment, once the domain of industrialized nations.

Foreign Investment from the Third World: The Experience of Chinese Firms from Hong Kong

Louis T. Wells Jr.

MOST STUDIES OF international business have focused on the foreign investments of companies based in the industrialized nations. The reason is apparent: these firms have accounted for the bulk of the international transfer of capital and technology by private enterprise. However, transfers from the richest of the developing countries are rapidly growing in importance.[1] One of the principal sources of this investment is Hong Kong.

Hong Kong-based firms account for the second largest source of foreign investment in nonmineral industries approved by the Indonesian foreign investment authorities between 1967 and 1972.[2] An adequate accounting of Hong Kong-owned firms that have not registered as foreign investors would increase the figures significantly. In the Philippines, overseas Chinese investors account for 15% of foreign investment.[3] Many of these Chinese investors operate out of Hong Kong. In Singapore, the growth has been impressive. From 1971 to 1972, Hong Kong investment increased by 85% to account for almost 6% of all foreign investment in Singapore.[4] An ex-government official from Hong Kong claimed that in 1977 Hong Kong firms ran more than 50 factories in one export area alone of Singapore.

Although the foreign investments of Hong Kong firms are concentrated in Southeast Asia, their activities extend much further. In West Africa, Hong Kong investors are involved in manufacturing items that range from umbrellas to steel. Most of the textile manufacture in Nigeria and Ghana, for example, is done by Hong Kong companies. In fact, the activities of Hong Kong enterprises are not limited to the developing countries; Hong Kong businessmen have a few plants in Europe and the United States.[5]

Hong Kong seemed an appropriate place to undertake a study of the strategies and drives behind the overseas activities of firms from developing countries. It is in some ways typical of certain other developing countries that serve as homes for foreign investors; but it also has some unique characteristics. Keeping in mind the risks of facilely generating from the experience of Hong Kong's firms, I set out in the summer of 1977 to conduct structured interviews with the managers of a sample of Hong Kong's firms with overseas subsidiaries.

Casual observers have suspected that the large investment flows reported as originating in Hong Kong actually represent subsidiaries of firms based in the industrialized nations. Indeed, the traditional Hong Kong holding companies owned by Australian, British and other industrialized countries' enterprises do have interests in other South-gest that for every such holding company reported
gest that for every such holding company reported
by host countries as a Hong Kong investor, there may be several Hong Kong investments not reported. In Indonesia especially, a large number of Hong Kong firms have projects not registered as foreign investments at all.

Louis T. Wells Jr. is Professor at the Harvard Graduate School of Business Administration. His research interests include the activities of U.S. and European multinational firms in developing countries, as well as the international activity of firms from the developing nations.

Observers also point out that some of the Hong Kong firms are really not Chinese. John Swire and Sons (H.K.) Ltd., Hutchison International, Ltd., Jardine Matheson and Company and the Hong Kong and Shanghai Banking Corporation were founded and are still largely managed by the British. Although one cannot deny the importance of these firms in a study of Hong Kong's development, they do not seem to account for a significant portion of Hong Kong's foreign investment and were not included in this research. In Indonesia, for example, these firms account for only two of the registered Hong Kong investment approvals.[6]

It is not yet possible to make reasonable estimates of the total volume of the foreign investments of Chinese Hong Kong firms. The government of Hong Kong imposes no restriction on outgoing capital and collects no data on the foreign direct investments of its companies. One is left with only the piecemeal data reported by host countries. Indonesia, for example, reports $214 million of realized investment from Hong Kong.[7] The same ex-government official mentioned earlier suspected that the annual outflow of investment by Hong Kong firms in 1977 exceeded foreign investment coming into the country.

Investment Strategies

Hong Kong firms have ventured abroad for reasons similar to those that led firms from the industrialized countries to internationalize their operations. Like their multinational counterparts headquartered in the industrial nations, the largest number of Hong Kong firms appear to have invested abroad for defensive reasons. However, Hong Kong investors have also been driven by factors that do not have obvious analogs in the activities of firms from the industrialized nations.[8]

Defensive Drives

Consider the overseas manufacturing investments undertaken by Hong Kong firms to serve the markets in which the plants were located. It appears that about three quarters of these were made in countries that the Hong Kong parent had served with exports a short time before the investment was made.[9] In these cases, the managers explained the foreign investments as reactions to higher tariffs or to import quotas. Like many American, European or Japanese firms, the companies invested abroad to defend a market gained earlier through exports.

Defensive investments of this type have, not surprisingly, followed Hong Kong export patterns. In the late 1950s, Hong Kong firms found their exports of simple items, such as kerosene lanterns, flashlights and umbrellas, threatened by tariffs and quotas designed to encourage local production in the poorer countries.[10] In the 1960s, textile exports were under siege. By the mid-1970s, there was evidence of threats to more sophisticated exports, such as electronics. Foreign investment from Hong Kong has followed a similar pattern: from the manufacture of simple household goods and simple food processing (biscuits, flour, etc.) to the production of textiles, and now to the manufacture of more sophisticated items.

But defensive investments by Hong Kong firms have a twist uncommon to foreign investments by firms from industrialized nations. Hong Kong has long exported manufactured goods to the richer countries as well as to the poorer ones. For the richer markets, Hong Kong's comparatively cheap labor was an important factor. In the early 1960s, the richer countries began to impose quotas on exports from Hong Kong. Moreover, by the late 1960s labor costs in Hong Kong were rising sharply. In response, Hong Kong firms sought production sites in other, lower-wage countries and in countries where quotas had not yet been set. The goal, of course, was to continue to supply the markets in the advanced countries. The textile manufacturers, for instance, set up plants in Singapore (some 15 plants in 1963 and 1964), Taiwan, Macao and Thailand.[11]

Those firms that have gone abroad to manufacture products for the industrialized nations provide a more complex story. Although the early investors went abroad primarily to escape quotas being imposed on Hong Kong, investors today cite diversification of risk as a reason for spreading their production sites. The lessons from export quotas certainly underlie some of the desire for multiple sources. Increasingly, high wage costs and factory rents in Hong Kong are causing exporting firms to look for other manufacturing bases. In the Southeast Asian area, Taiwan and particularly Indonesian wages have appeared increasingly attractive. Further afield, Mauritius has successfully attracted export firms with low wages, special incentives and access to the EEC market.

Aggressive Strategies

Like some of the industrialized countries' multinationals, a number of Hong Kong firms have actively sought overseas investment opportunities. In a few of the cases, the Hong Kong firm had not recently exported to the country in which it set up a factory to serve the local market. Even in those cases, however, these markets were typically not unknown to Hong Kong managers. In most of them, the markets had been supplied many years earlier by the Hong Kong manufacturer or they had bought Hong Kong products from another firm.

Less like the traditional multinationals, several Hong Kong firms were motivated to search for foreign opportunities to make use of equipment no longer suitable for Hong Kong conditions. Many plants in Hong Kong had been established at least a decade earlier with simple, labor-intensive machinery. As wages rose in Hong Kong, the costs of operating with this equipment grew to the point where the companies could no longer compete abroad. With poorly developed international markets for secondhand machinery, a number of Hong Kong companies sought opportunities to use their equipment elsewhere.[12] In a few cases, a Hong Kong businessman would learn of an opportunity and purchase an outdated factory for use overseas. Indonesia, with its very low wage costs, was a favorite place for such equipment; it could continue to be used competitively there. But second-hand plants went as far as West Africa. Much of this equipment was repainted, labeled as new and imported illegally into foreign markets.

A Comparison with Multinationals

Unlike the multinationals from Europe and the United States, Hong Kong firms have not gone abroad to use consumer marketing skills developed for the home market. In fact, few Hong Kong firms have developed well-known trade names. Most have relied instead on undercutting the prices of potential competitors.

That was not the only difference. I identified no Hong Kong firm that was, on its own, attempting to build a system of several affiliates that were integrated to gain economies of scale and lower costs. The usual Hong Kong-based foreign investment seems designed to serve the domestic market, with little or no integration with other affiliates. Some integration exists for the subsidiaries established to escape quotas, but operations are integrated only to the extent that the Hong Kong offices allocate export orders to particular plants.[13] There were efforts to establish vertically integrated enterprises to procure raw materials or to provide sales outlets. These special cases will be dealt with once the advantages of the more common types of investors are understood.

Hong Kong's Competitive Edge in the Developing Country Markets

It has been pointed out by researchers that a foreign investor must have some kind of competitive advantage to survive outside his home country, no matter what motivation takes him overseas. In foreign markets, the Hong Kong investor must be able to compete with local firms and with multinationals from the industrialized nations. If the Hong Kong firm has no advantage over local enterprises, then its unfamiliarity with the local market, the higher overhead costs associated with extended lines of communication and the use of foreign managers will place it in an untenable position vis-à-vis domestic companies.

Competing Against the Local Firm

The principal advantages of many of the Hong Kong firms over potential local competitors appear to derive from two areas: experience and the imperfections in international machinery markets.

Hong Kong, as one of the richer of the developing countries, has provided its businessmen with the opportunity to manufacture for local consumption certain items not yet in sufficient demand in poorer countries to support local production. Like U.S. firms, Hong Kong enterprises have typically supplied those foreign markets first by exporting. As exports were threatened, the exporters invested in plants overseas. The advantages gained from extensive production experience were transferred in part to the new, overseas facility. Potential local competitors must start without the accumulated experience of the exporting firm.

The pattern of manufacture for local consumption, export and then foreign production describes rather well the process in the early and, perhaps, the very recent waves of Hong Kong investment. However, the whole story for Hong Kong is more complicated than that simple pattern. Hong Kong textile firms, for example, have had an advantage out of proportion to the size of the Hong Kong market. Virtually all of today's spinning and weaving firms began operations in Shanghai; some, several generations ago. They had a much larger home market there, and a few had established export markets in Asia. As it became clear that the Communists would control the mainland, the textile managers moved to Hong Kong, taking with them knowhow based on experience and some access to export markets. These strengths served them well when they went abroad.

Some elements of manufacturing knowhow are embodied in the machinery; others are in the minds of the managers and engineers who have long been solving problems in the factories. Even in the cases when knowhow is largely embodied in the machinery, the Hong Kong firm can usually retain an advantage when it ventures overseas. A potential new producer would have to purchase machinery. New equipment available on the well-developed international machinery market is generally designed for the long production runs typical of manufacturers in the advanced nations. Little new equipment is available for the small-volume production required in most developing countries where Hong Kong firms have invested. On the other hand, some secondhand equipment is quite suitable for low-volume manufacture. In contrast to the new equipment market, however, the market for secondhand machinery is rather poorly developed. A potential manufacturer views the opportunities to purchase secondhand machinery as being very limited and entailing a great deal of risk.

The Hong Kong manufacturer often has at his disposal secondhand equipment he would like to deactivate in Hong Kong. The poorly developed markets make it difficult for him to sell the equipment. But he knows the machinery well and can use it abroad more profitably than someone else buying used machinery with which he has no experience. Thus, many Hong Kong investors have access to appropriate machinery without the uncertainties facing a local investor.

Note that the advantages of access to machinery derive not only from familiarity with the secondhand machinery. In some cases, Hong Kong firms have designed special pieces of equipment for low-volume production. Their foreign operations are outfitted with new machinery based on these designs. In most cases, that machinery is built in Hong Kong. In one, perhaps unique, case, I discovered a group of Hong Kong firms that had made a special deal with a foreign machinery manufacturer to supply a large quantity of new but outdated (for the wage rates of the industrialized countries) machinery. Part of the machinery was to be used in Hong Kong; part, in foreign subsidiaries of the Hong Kong group. The Hong Kong group had the advantage of being able to purchase enough of the machinery to make it worthwhile for the foreign manufacturers to produce it.

A Hong Kong manufacturer of aluminum household utensils illustrates the more typical case. Production in Hong Kong at approximately a third of the volume of a medium-sized Japanese manufacturer involves the hand-pouring of molten aluminum into small moulds. Rolling is done on hand-fed equipment that has no automatic device to return the slab for the second pass. Punching of pieces from sheets of aluminum is done with foot-operated equipment. Other operations are similarly scaled down for small production runs. When the firm set up operations in another Southeast Asian country to produce aluminum household utensils at about 80% of the volume of its home factory, it exported some of its used equipment. It also sent simple new machinery it had made in Hong Kong according to the designs it was already using for low-volume manufacture. A potential local manufacturer would have to design and build from scratch the machinery required for small-scale production.[14]

The small-scale facility was very labor-intensive. In the Southeast Asian market, the low wage rates meant that costs were bearable. In an industrialized nation, the higher wage rates would almost certainly have imposed costs such that the technology could not be competitive.

Like those investors producing for the local market, the advantage of Hong Kong export firms over potential local competitors rests partly on their experience. One manager explained, for example, that there are skills in organizing a large-scale garment operation that are not easily learned. To drive the point home, he asked, "You know many textile schools in the United States; how many garment schools do you know?"

Perhaps more important than manufacturing experience is the relationship with foreign buyers. It is difficult to establish the reputation for reliability that Hong Kong firms have already built with buyers in the advanced countries. The difficulty for new entrants is illustrated by what happened in Indonesia. In the early 1970s, Indonesian authorities did not accept Hong Kong applicants for permits to operate free-trade zones and make garments for export from Indonesia. One of several reasons for this action was the hope that Indonesian entrepreneurs would pick up the export opportunities. They did not.

Competing Against the Multinational

If experience and access to appropriate machinery enable many Hong Kong firms to survive against potential local competitors, one must still explain how the Hong Kong firms survive against the competition of the multinational firms from the industrialized nations. These firms have long experience as well as access to secondhand machinery. The answer, it seems, lies in the appropriateness of the experience of the multinationals and in their cost structures.

The experience of multinationals has typically been based on large-scale manufacture. For most, it has been many years since they have produced at volumes as small as those appropriate for manufacture in developing countries. Thus, when they do set up factories in developing areas, they tend to build large plants. In many cases, they are not able to utilize the full capacity of their plants.[15] If they do scale down operations, they lose the advantages of experience. Consider the example of a Hong Kong firm that operates a plant abroad to produce about 20,000 units of household refrigerators per year. A U.S. factory would make some 500,000 units per year to obtain reasonable economies of scale. The Hong Kong firm has developed appropriate (albeit simple) techniques for small-scale production. Sheet metal bending is done on equipment that can be used for several bends; the U.S. manufacturer would typically use one piece of specialized equipment for each bend. U.S. engineers could develop such technologies, but they would then begin without the advantage of experience with the process.

The illustrations do not quite capture all the adjustments being made by Hong Kong firms to small-scale manufacture. The flexibility built into the plants of Hong Kong firms is said by managers to be very important. Rather than design a plant to manufacture a limited number of items, they design for the production of a wide range of models or products. In some cases, this involves having certain pieces of equipment standing idle part of the year, but the plant is set up so that machines can be compatible with each other in many ways and the plant can produce different items if the market for certain products is saturated. Again, multinationals could also design such plants, but the advantage of experience would be lost.

An additional cost advantage of Hong Kong investors, according to many of the firms interviewed, is found in the area of expatriate managers and technical specialists. Although Hong Kong firms tend to send a large number of Chinese technicians to start up their overseas plants, the costs of these technicians are considerably less than those of engineers sent by the multinationals. In 1977, according to the estimates of Hong Kong firms, a Chinese engineer stationed in another Southeast Asian country could cost up to $14,000 a year plus bonus, depending on the company's performance. An engineer from an advanced country employed by a multinational would cost several times this. Moreover, the salary structures for Chinese managers sent abroad typically do not saddle the firm with the high fixed costs facing a company that sends managers from the industrialized nations. Hong Kong firms reported, in many cases, that they paid managers stationed abroad a very small base salary and that much of the salary of overseas management depended on the performance of the subsidiary. Thus, if the market remained small and profits were low, management costs would also remain low. In other cases, the managers were relatives whose income from the enterprise was fairly fixed.

Why don't the multinationals simply hire Chinese technicians and managers to capture the advantages of relevant experience and low cost? Part of the answer lies in the nature of organizational skills. One or two people from a factory can rarely provide the total gains from experience.[16] In addition, if such managers were hired, they would not be intimately familiar with the processes and business techniques of the multinationals. Most multinationals have concentrated their activities in areas in which they have an advantage: high technology, sophisticated marketing, large-scale production. Low-cost production for small markets appears to be considered an inefficient allocation of management attention.

Some of the Chinese interviewed claimed an additional advantage for the Hong Kong investors. Hong Kong firms are, they say, accustomed to operating out of cramped, unattractive quarters. When they go abroad, those firms invest little in buildings compared to the multinationals, which are concerned with image. Although I have no data to support this contention, it is consistent with impressions I gathered on my visits to foreign factories of both types of investor in Indonesia.[17]

Lower costs, whether from appropriate production techniques, lower personnel costs or lower building costs, can be used to gain market share in several ways. One possibility is to exploit the cost advantage by selling at lower prices. Another is to spend more on marketing while maintaining the price structure of high-cost competitors.

Price competition appears to be the strategy favored by most Hong Kong firms. Since few have followed marketing-intensive strategies at home, they have little experience with marketing as a competitive tool. Moreover, many of the products with which they have had manufacturing experience appeal primarily to consumers who, by the standard of industrialized countries, have low incomes. Thus, price becomes a suitable means for gaining market share.[18]

If a marketing-intensive strategy is called for, the Hong Kong firm seems to prefer to join forces with a multinational experienced in that strategy.

Complementary Skills

Several Hong Kong firms have invested abroad as a part of an arrangement with a firm from an industrialized country. In these cases, a matching of skills and strategies has led to the joint operation.

Consider, for example, the arrangement between one Hong Kong firm and a Japanese enterprise. The Hong Kong company had served for some time as the import agent for the products of the Japanese company in Singapore and Malaysia. When Singapore and Malaysia, in about 1965, took steps to encourage local assembly of the products, the Hong Kong firm began manufacture of the products in both countries, with the technical assistance of the Japanese exporter. At that time, according to the Hong Kong manager, large Japanese firms were reluctant to undertake direct investment abroad.[19] More recently, the same Hong Kong firm and the Japanese company have made joint investments in third countries. The Japanese firm provided some technical expertise and its well-known trade name; the Hong Kong firm provided rather special production skills. Out of its experience in Singapore and Malaysia, the Hong Kong firm learned to manufacture efficiently at production levels that are a small fraction of those to which the Japanese firm was accustomed. In fact, the Hong Kong firm mastered the technology so well that it was beginning, by 1973, to go it alone in some markets where it thought the well-known trade name of the Japanese firm unnecessary.

Lack of an established trade name and a shortage of consumer marketing skills have led other Hong Kong companies to integrate their activities with firms from the industrialized nations. One paint manufacturer, for example, joined with an American firm in a Southeast Asian country in order to gain its trade name. The Hong Kong firm had already proved its technical ability in a third country where it had made paint without international help (and sold it successfully in that market, which was protected from competitors with international trade names).

In still another case, a Japanese synthetic fiber manufacturer obtained a 45% interest in a large Hong Kong textile firm that had been having financial difficulties. The Japanese used that enterprise to expand operations in Asia. The Hong Kong spinning and weaving operations required synthetic fibers produced by the Japanese firm. Keeping such a customer in business was certainly of some significance. Then, when the Hong Kong firm went abroad, it was used by the Japanese as a vehicle to establish a vertically integrated network throughout Southeast Asia. The overseas operations set up by the Hong Kong firm continued to require fibers produced in Japan or in the host country by the Japanese company. The integration eventually extended to garment manufacture, a skill in which the Hong Kong firm had a considerable edge over the Japanese, according to managers familiar with the situation.

Joint projects in the textile industry may serve a role beyond that of gaining the advantage of complementary skills. Some observers suggest that many of the projects involving Japanese and Hong Kong textile interests aim to blur the national identity of participating textile export plants. If the Japanese and Hong Kong manufacturers face quotas in the West on textiles from their home plants, they may be tempted to set up plants in some other country, say, Malaysia. If a project is jointly owned by a Hong Kong investor and a Japanese investor, perhaps even with a Malaysian, textiles from the plant may not be identified as Japanese or Hong Kong products. Needless to say, the Hong Kong businessmen did not mention this as a reason for joint projects.

A Vertical Structure

There is, the reader will remember, a special class of Hong Kong firms that have attempted to build a vertically integrated structure. Some Hong Kong companies have established foreign raw material operations to supply their home plants.

The Hong Kong firms that source raw materials abroad are apparently relatively few in number. Most are in timber. Like some of their counterparts from the industrialized nations, their ability to survive overseas depends on the advantages they gain from vertical integration. Market prices for tropical timber are rather unstable. Once a tropical timbering operation is established in Indonesian or Malaysian Borneo (the source of much of Hong Kong's hardwoods), the costs are relatively fixed for the medium term. Infrastructure is in place and machinery has been purchased. Crews cannot be easily laid off, partly because of Indonesia's restrictive labor legislation. Additionally, the lumbering crews are largely imported, from the Philippines or Malaysia. When demand for timber falls slightly, production continues and prices drop dramatically, since the demand is not very price-elastic. When supply varies, as it does frequently with the fluctuating market and the lumpy investments required for new timber developments, prices also swing. In fact, according to buyers, there are sometimes periods of actual shortages during which adequate supplies cannot be obtained regardless of price.

Moreover, since many of the timber producers are not considered reliable by the manufacturers, long-term contracts will not solve the problem of fluctuating prices and availability.

The market is not only unstable, but prices are generally much higher than costs, according to timber users. This is so because few Indonesian entrepreneurs have the money and skill to respond to high profits by developing more timberland. And foreigners have been excluded from official participation in most timbering in Indonesia.

To stabilize their costs and supply and to gain monopoly rents, some Hong Kong firms have established timber operations in Borneo. In Indonesia, much of this investment is not registered as foreign. (Six registered investments amount to some $22 million.) The unregistered investment consists of informal joint ventures with Indonesian military officials or with Indonesians of Chinese extraction. Hong Kong businessmen explain that they are better able to work out such arrangements than are their multinational competitors from the advanced countries. The small size of the firm, the few public reporting requirements and the ethnic ties enable them to carry out the informal agreements and to provide the payments required to smooth the way.

In another approach to vertical integration, some of the firms that export to the industrialized countries have integrated forward into their markets in the advanced nations. They do so generally to secure markets for goods made in Hong Kong or at other low-wage producing sites. A furniture manufacturer illustrates. Rather than incur higher shipping costs and tariffs on furniture, the firm decided to ship the components. To assure proper assembly, it set up assembly operations in the

United States. One might argue that Hong Kong investment was not required—an American firm could assemble the furniture equally well. But the relationship between the Hong Kong supplier and the American assembler would appear to both parties as one fraught with risk.[20] The assembler would be dependent on a single supplier, and the manufacturer on a single assembler. The risks could be eliminated with common ownership. The Hong Kong firm gained additional advantages from the U.S. operation, in that it was able to get feedback from furniture shows in the United States. The information helped the firm to estimate demand and to recognize the need for design changes.

A similar case of integration into the market involves the acquisition of production facilities in England by a Hong Kong textile manufacturer. The primary purpose, it seems, was to obtain the marketing channels of the failing British company.

In these cases, the basic advantage of the Hong Kong investor depends on its ability to produce cheaply in Southeast Asia. The assembly and marketing outlets serve only as vehicles to help exploit that advantage.

Conclusions

Some special characteristics of Hong Kong should temper any generalization one might be tempted to make from this study. But there are lessons that will be useful in looking at the foreign activities of firms from other developing countries.

The most important special characteristic of Hong Kong has probably been its large volume of manufactured exports. There are many explanations for this: the immigration of Shanghai entrepreneurs who had been exporting in the past, the ties with foreign markets through the Overseas Chinese, the openness of the Hong Kong economy which kept domestic costs to international levels, the lack of bureaucratic red tape, the trading ties of the old British enterprises and so on. Whatever the cause of the export performance of Hong Kong firms, it has meant that an unusually large number of Hong Kong firms were likely to have their import markets threatened. In few other developing countries would so many local firms be motivated to go abroad to defend export markets. However, with the rapid expansion of manufactured exports from the developing countries, one would anticipate that more manufacturers will follow the Hong Kong example and invest abroad.

Hong Kong has probably differed from other developing nations in the degree to which its businesses faced pressure to send old equipment abroad. Wages have also risen rapidly in other developing areas. However, without the important export markets and without the open borders that have characterized Hong Kong, firms elsewhere have typically faced less pressure to respond to higher wages by replacing old equipment.

Hong Kong, and Indian, managers have had special ethnic ties to overseas communities that have been important in helping them to establish foreign operations. For many other countries, such ties have not been available to help in overcoming the uncertainties inherent in overseas investment.

On the other hand, Hong Kong is similar in many ways to some other developing countries. Many of the elements of strength that characterize Hong Kong firms appear to be like those that describe firms from Argentina, Mexico, Brazil, India and other developing areas with a large industrial sector. The firms of these countries have acquired experience in the small-scale, flexible production facilities needed later by their poorer neighbors. When they go abroad to their poorer neighbors, they probably have an advantage in manufacturing know-how. In addition, like Hong Kong firms, they face cheaper overhead than their multinational competitors and are better able to deal with "off-book" payments and informal investment arrangements.

Impressionistic evidence suggests that firms from other developing countries share Hong Kong firms' weaknesses in marketing. There are, of course, a few well-known exceptions, such as Incacola from Peru (with plants in Puerto Rico and Ecuador), F and N from Singapore (with plants in Indonesia and Malaysia), San Miguel beer from the Philippines (with plants in Spain, Indonesia and Hong

Kong). But the majority of the firms from developing countries appear to depend on special production abilities that enable them to compete on price. Perhaps some will also find opportunities to combine their production skills with the marketing skills of the multinationals in joint arrangements in third countries. These arrangements may be similar to those observed for Hong Kong-based investors.

NOTES

1. For a few rough measures, see Louis T. Wells, Jr., "The Internationalization of Firms from Developing Countries," in Tamir Agmon and Charles P. Kindleberger, eds., *Multinationals from Small Countries* (Cambridge: MIT Press, 1977), anl Eduardo White *et al., Las Empresas Conjuntas Latinoamericanas* (Buenos Aires: INTAL, 1977).

2. Indonesian Foreign Investment Board, "Investment Applications and Approvals, 1967 through 1973," mimeographed (Jakarta, n.d.).

3. Government of the Republic of the Philippines, *Four-Year Development Plan: 1974-1977* (Manila, 1973).

4. *Singapore Trade and Industry,* May 1973, p. 13.

5. These data and others about Hong Kong firms were collected by the author in interviews conducted in Hong Kong in July 1977.

6. From records of the foreign investment authorities in Indonesia.

7. From records of the foreign investment authorities in Indonesia. Information about realization is not available for an almost equal amount of proposed Hong Kong investments.

8. For summaries of the motivations of the multinationals from the United States, see Raymond Vernon, *Sovereignty at Bay* (New York: Basic Books, 1971); for European firms, see Lawrence G. Franko, *The European Multinationals* (Stamford, Conn: Greylock, 1976); for Japanese enterprises, see Michael Yoshino, *Japan's Multinational Enterprises* (Cambridge: Harvard University Press, 1976), and Yoshi Tsurumi, *The Japanese Are Coming* (Cambridge: Ballinger, 1976). For the importance of defensive motivations, see Robert B. Stobaugh *et al., Nine Investments Abroad and Their Impact at Home* (Boston: Harvard Business School Division of Research, 1976).

9. No statistical significance should be attached to the proportions reported in this section on motivations. They are based on direct interviews with only 12 Hong Kong-based Chinese firms with some 50 foreign manufacturing investments. However, most managers described the activities not only of their own firms but also of several competitors. In addition, some subsidiaries of Hong Kong firms were interviewed in Indonesia and in the Philippines. Thus, the findings are based on impressionistic evidence from several dozen foreign investors.

10. Some clues to the shifting makeup of Hong Kong exports can be gathered from Theodore Geiger and Frances M. Geiger, *Tales of Two City States* (Washington, D.C.: National Planning Association, 1973), pp. 84-92, and from James Riedel, *The Industrialization of Hong Kong* (Tuebingen: J. C. B. Mohr, 1974).

11. For an account of the investments of this type in Singapore, see Paul Luey, "Hong Kong Investment," in Helen Hughes and You Poh Seng, eds., *Foreign Investment and Industrialization in Singapore* (Madison: University of Wisconsin, 1969).

12. For a study of the markets and the appropriateness of secondhand equipment, see James D. Dilmus, *Used Machinery and Economic Development* (East Lansing: Michigan State University, 1974).

13. For a description of control in the textile plants, see Luey, "Hong Kong Investment," pp. 126, 134.

14. A careful study of investment in Thailand demonstrates that foreign investors from developing countries typically use more labor-intensive, smaller-scale equipment than do local Thai firms. See Donald Lecraw, "Choice of Technology in Low-Wage Countries: The Case of Thailand" (Ph.D. diss., Harvard University, 1976). Riedel, *The Industrialization of Hong Kong*, discusses the plastic injection machinery built in Hong Kong.

15. The study of Lecraw, just cited, also demonstrates that firms from other developing countries use techniques that are more labor-intensive and smaller-scale than firms from the advanced countries. A similar conclusion is tentatively supported by the data from Indonesia in Louis T. Wells, Jr., "Economic Man and Engineering Man," *Public Policy*, Summer 1973, pp. 319-42.

16. See Vernon, "Organization as a Scale Factor in the Growth of Firms," in Jesse W. Markham and Gustav F. Papanek, eds., *Industrial Organization and Economic Development* (Boston: Houghton Mifflin, 1970), pp. 47-66.

17. See also R. Hal Mason, "The Transfer of Technology and the Factor Proportions Problem," *UNITAR Research Report No. 10* (New York: United Nations Institute for Training and Research, n.d.), for suggestions that multinationals might spend more on building than do local firms in the Philippines.

18. For evidence of this strategy in Indonesia, see Wells, "Economic Man and Engineering Man."

19. For corroborating evidence of the reluctance of Japanese firms to invest abroad during this period, see Yoshino, *Japan's Multinational Enterprises*, pp. 67-111.

20. This is similar to the "horrors of bilateral monopoly" which, according to Jürg Niehans, has been an inducement to Swiss firms to set up overseas operations. See his "Benefits of Multinational Firms for a Small Parent Economy: The Case of Switzerland," in Agmon and Kindleberger, eds., *Multinationals from Small Countries*.

[15]

Journal of Common Market Studies
Volume XXI, No. 4 June 1983

Andean Multinational Enterprises: A New Approach to Multinational Investment in the Andean Group

RACHELLE L. CHEROL* and JOSÉ NUÑEZ DEL ARCO

Introduction

For thirteen years now, five of the intermediate-size nations of South America[1] have been working together under the Andean Pact, or Cartagena Agreement, to achieve their shared goal of economic integration. As the years have progressed, they have developed several corporate models for companies or businesses which are formed with capital from both Andean Group and non-Andean Group sources.

Soon after the Andean Group was created, for example, all business enterprises in the Andean countries were defined under Decision 24 of the Andean Pact's Commission[2] as being of one of three distinct types (national, mixed, or foreign), according to the exact ratio of "national" or "foreign" capital invested in them; they were then assigned different treatments according to their specific category.

Foreign capital in those early days was taken to mean capital from any other country, even if that country was a fellow member of the Group. A few years later, the Andean Countries began to distinguish between capital from non-Andean Group countries (true "foreign" capital) and capital from fellow member countries (or "subregional" capital) – so much, in

* Ms. Cherol is a member of the District of Columbia Bar and consultant for the Latin American Integration Institute (INTAL), Buenos Aires, Argentina. Mr. Nuñez del Arco is a Senior Economist in the Integration Division of the Inter-American Development Bank (IDB) in Washington, D.C. The views expressed in this paper are those of the authors and not necessarily those of the IDB or INTAL.

[1] The five countries which form the Andean Group are Bolivia, Colombia, Ecuador, Peru and Venezuela.

[2] The Commission is the highest body of the Cartagena Agreement and is composed of a plenipotentiary representative from each member country. The Commission expresses its opinions through "Decisions." For a brief description of the Cartagena Agreement *see below*

fact, that the latter, or so-called "subregional" capital, began to be given the very same favourable treatment by the Andean host countries as that received by their own national capital (Decision 103), provided that the subregional capital was invested in a mixed company or in one of the new "multinational" enterprises defined in 1971 by Decision 46.[3] The multinational enterprises of the Andean countries are not to be confused with the well-known large transnational corporations which originate in industrialized countries.

These new multinational enterprises, with their attendant advantages, incentives and special treatment, were to operate only within a limited and predefined set of economic activities. However, as things turned out, their implementation was more problematic than was originally anticipated; to date, very few multinationals have actually been formed under Decision 46, and fewer still of these have been successful.

For this reason, and others which will subsequently be discussed in detail, the countries were obliged to create an alternate type of Andean corporate structure to help further their economic integration goals, one which would be more flexible and practical, more attractive to investors and, most importantly, one which would be allowed to operate in all areas of economic activity. In 1982, the Andean Group gave its seal of approval to the structure of the Andean Multinational Enterprise[4] (AME) (Decision 169), which joins the company of the other possible corporate structures available to investors as defined earlier by Decision 24 and Decision 46, and which is meant to complement, rather than supersede, these earlier Decisions. (See Table 1).

The AME is the subject of the present paper which seeks to describe its principal features, to make a comparative analysis of the AME with the original multinational enterprise defined in Decision 46 and to predict the possible impact of the new regulations on the Andean integration process itself. However, before entering into an analysis of the characteristics and scope of the AME, a brief discussion of the Cartagena Agreement and its operative provisions, as well as the events that led to the approval of this new AME regime, would be helpful.

The Cartagena Agreement and a History of the Andean Group

In 1969 Bolivia, Chile, Colombia, Ecuador and Peru signed the Cartagena Agreement with the intention of accelerating their economic and social development and improving the standard of living of their peoples. (In

[3] Multinational enterprises refer to particular types of enterprises located within the Andean Group and are defined as companies 60% of whose capital comes from investors of two or more Andean countries with the optional participation of foreign investors. For a more detailed discussion of multinational enterprises *see below*.

[4] For a more detailed discussion of AME's *see below*.

Table 1
*Comparison among enterprises in the Andean Group**

Categories	*Mixed Enterprises (Decision 24)*	*Multinational Enterprises (Decision 46)*	*Andean Multinational Enterprises (Decision 169)*
Ownership Requirements	51–80% national and 20–49% foreign	60% national** 40% foreign	80% national** 20% foreign
Profit remittance	Up to 20%	No limit to the country of the origin of the capital	No limit
Access to Domestic Credit	No restrictions	No restrictions	No restrictions
Reinvestment	Above 7% must be authorized	No restrictions	No restrictions
Acquisitions	Foreign investors prohibited from acquiring shares owned by national or subregional investors except in cases of bankruptcy	Foreign investors prohibited from acquiring shares of subregional investors. Subregional investors need authorization to buy other subregional shares	Same as Multinational enterprises
Areas of Participation of Foreign Investment	No foreign investment in public sectors, insurance, banking and other financial institutions, transportation and communications	Possible participation in public sectors, insurance, banking and other financial institutions, transportation and communications with authorization	Same as Multinational enterprises

* The table represents the three main ways for foreign and subregional investors to participate in the Andean region.
** For purposes of this chart, national participation includes subregional.

1973 Venezuela entered into the Agreement and in 1976 Chile withdrew). The creation of this scheme of integration, the so-called "Andean Group," came basically from the desire of the member countries with small to medium-size markets to accelerate their development through the creation of a larger economic unit. It was thought that this would allow them to benefit from certain resultant economies of scale and to compete more effectively with the three largest economies of Latin America – Argentina, Brazil and Mexico.

The Cartagena Agreement was also the result of the Andean countries' dissatisfaction with the overall achievements of the Andean Pact's "mother" organization, the large but often ineffective Latin American Free Trade Association (LAFTA). LAFTA's performance had left much to be desired because of the ultimately unequal participation of its member countries in the benefits of the integration process.

The Cartagena Agreement was based on the integration experience of LAFTA and on the Central American Common Market, but it also incorporated certain new and original mechanisms which quickly established it as a unique model of economic integration for developing countries.

Table 2
Main Economic Indicators of the Andean Group and Argentina, Brazil and Mexico in 1980

	Andean Group	*Argentina*	*Brazil*	*Mexico*
Population (millions of inhabitants	72.2	27.7	120.3	69.9
Gross domestic product (billions of 1980 dollars)	91.4	53.6	200.1	107.2
Gross investment (billions of 1980 dollars)	25.4	12.7	48.0	30.9
External sector (billions of dollars)				
Exports in 1980	30.2	8.0	20.1	15.0
Imports in 1980	23.6	10.0	22.9	18.5

Source: Inter-American Development Bank, *Economic and Social Progress in Latin America, 1980–81 Report.*

The principal characteristics and mechanisms of the Cartagena Agreement are as follows:

(1) The principle of balanced and harmonious development among the member countries as a way of lessening the existing differences in development levels and ensuring an equal distribution of the benefits of integration.

(2) Joint industrial development programming accomplished through two mechanisms: Sectorial Programmes of Industrial Development, designed to create new large-scale basic and Intermediate Andean subregion-wide industries' and Industrial Rationalization Programmes, designed to revitalize and give a subregional dimension, if possible, to existing industries.

(3) The coordination of development plans and the harmonization of economic and social policies.

(4) The Common Rules on the Treatment of Foreign Capital in order to regulate the behaviour of foreign investment and foreign business within the subregion so as to guide foreign capital into those sectors which the member countries consider the most appropriate.

(5) The creation of margins of preference through: (a) the trade liberalization programme (the total elimination of intrasubregional duties and other trade restrictions on imports from other member countries); and

(b) the gradual adoption of a Common External Tariff on imports from non-Andean Group sources.

(6) A system of agricultural programming and the integration of the nations' communications and transportation infrastructure based on specific multinational actions in these areas.

(7) The granting of special treatment to Bolivia and Ecuador to ensure their effective participation in all aspects of the integration process.

(8) The unique and vital role played by the Junta of the Cartagena Agreement[5] which acts not only as the technical secretariat but also as a guiding and unifying force for the entire integration process.

Most of these mechanisms may be roughly divided into two groups based on the simultaneous existence of: (1) a "development strategy," in which public enterprises will seek an active participation in industrial programming and rationalization and in which the public sector will set the basic rules for the harmonization of policies and development plans of the member countries; and (2) a "trade strategy," in which the internal trade liberalization programme and the establishment of a Common External Tariff allow free competition to create an expanded subregional market for Andean businesses. The simultaneous application of both the development and the trade strategies depends on the countries being able to construct a skilful balance among the various mechanisms provided for in the Agreement; for example, the establishment of successful and equitable sectorial programmes of industrial development is closely linked to the prudent application of the Common Rules on the Treatment of Foreign Capital and to the harmonization of the various industrial development and trade competition laws of the different Andean nations.

Once the Common Rules on the Treatment of Foreign Capital, the Minimum Common External Tariff and the intrasubregional tariff reduction programme had been adopted, the main efforts of the Andean integration process during its first decade (1969–1979) began to centre on the "development" aspect of its two-part strategy. The efforts to design the Sectorial Industrial Development Programmes, to get them approved by the member countries and, finally, to implement them dominated the integration process throughout most of that difficult and eventful time.

Unfortunately, in the final analysis, neither the strong support of the Andean governments for the principle of industrial programming nor the best efforts of the Junta and the Commission were enough to bring about the advanced levels of agreement necessary for attaining approval of all of the Andean industrial development programmes. This was largely the

[5] The Junta is the technical organ of the Cartagena Agreement. It is made up of three members and acts in the interest of the subregion as a whole. The Junta has different functions; on the one hand, it serves as a regional organ and, on the other hand, it acts as a secretariat. Its duties are principally directed towards ensuring the application of the Agreement and the execution of the Decisions of the Commission.

result of the countries' lack of understanding of what was really involved in the development of Andean-wide industries. Each country seemed to be interested mainly in having as many aspects of the industry as possible assigned to it alone, with little regard for whether or not it would actually be able to follow through and produce the part or the goods in question once it had been granted the assignment. As a result of this time-consuming competition for assignments, the countries approved only three sectorial programmes of industrial development, i.e., the metalworking, petrochemical and automotive programmes. Although discussions were held at the Commission level on the proposals presented by the Junta concerning the establishment of programmes in the chemical, pharmaceutical, electronic, fertilizer and iron and steel industries, no final action was taken on them during this first decade (1969–1979).

The approval of the first three programmes involved complex discussions which were not completed until the end of the 1970's. Meanwhile, there were serious delays in implementing the metalworking and petrochemical programmes as well as the projected spin-off of the smaller auxiliary integration projects. Moreover, the countries were not able to comply with the schedule adopted for two important aspects of these sectorial programmes (the establishment of a Common External Tariff and the implementation of the internal trade liberalization programme). In addition, they often failed to honour their pledge not to encourage within their national borders the production of any parts or components which had been assigned to another member country through the Sectorial Programmes for Industrial Development.

These factors created serious problems for industrial programming and, therefore, for the creation of the original multinational enterprise of the Andean countries, which was dependent, by definition, on the successful establishment of the industrial development programmes through member countries' *ab initio* compliance with assignments and other basic contractual obligations.

Decision 46, which set forth the rules which were to govern the first multinational enterprises, was based on the supposition that industrial programming was a *sine qua non* element of the integration process. The Decision provided that multinational enterprises were to be used to establish decision centres in the subregion for those sectors of production which were viewed as the most dynamic or strategically important and which were, therefore, subject to industrial programming. The multinational enterprise should also contribute to the principle of balanced and harmonious development, the equitable distribution of the benefits of integration and the reduction of the differences in development which exist between the countries.[6] As can be seen, much was expected of these

[6] G. Fernández, "El Régimen Uniforme de la Empresa Multinacional en el Grupo Andino," *11 Revista Derecho de la Integración* 20 (1972). [hereafter cited as Fernandez].

multinational enterprises as defined in Decision 46. However, because of the largely unsatisfactory development of industrial programming to date, as well as the member countries' delay in formally ratifying Decision 46, the establishment of these multinational enterprises among the Andean Group countries has failed to materialize.

During 1980 the Andean Group was undergoing a serious institutional crisis due to the temporary abstention of Bolivia from the Commission meetings. In this context, the process was driven almost to the breaking point in 1981 by the boundary conflict between Ecuador and Peru. The Junta and the Commission agreed upon the urgent need to review the whole process of Andean integration if it was to continue despite this conflict and despite the serious changes in the economic policies and priorities of many of its member countries. They also agreed upon the need to: (1) broaden the base of the Andean integration effort through increased participation by management and labour; (2) give a more balanced orientation to the Andean model by placing less emphasis on industrial programming; and (3) place greater emphasis on trade competition among the member countries. On the basis of a more liberal interpretation of integration which calls for the free movement of capital within the subregion, Decision 169 was created, allowing for the operation of the innovative and more flexible AME within the full spectrum of economic activity.

Historical Development of Multinational Enterprises within the Andean Group

The countries' interest in encouraging the establishment of some type of multinational enterprise can be traced back to August 1966 when Colombia, Chile, Venezuela, Ecuador and Peru signed the Declaration of Bogota.[7] This document calls for the adoption of projects in which enterprises and capital of several Latin American countries can participate in order to facilitate the process of integration. Later, when the Cartagena Agreement was signed, it contained a provision to approve a uniform regime for multinational enterprises (Article 28); to recommend the establishment of multinational enterprises for the implementation, expansion or complementation of certain industries in the area of industrial programming (Article 38); and to establish multinational enterprises which facilitate the development of infrastructure projects in the fields of energy, transportation and communications (Article 86).

The importance of joint projects in promoting and developing the subregion is also emphasized in other provisions of the Cartagena

[7] The Declaration of Bogota expressed the political desire of the Andean presidents to promote economic development through integration and was the basis for the Cartagena Agreement. *See* Junta del Acuerdo de Cartagena, *Historia Documental del Acuerdo de Cartagena* 245 (1974). [hereafter cited as Junta del Acuerdo de Cartagena].

Agreement[8] which serve as the basis for Decision 24.[9] Decision 24 was the first juridicial standard adopted within the Andean Group in order to formulate a policy for incentives and controls on foreign and domestic investment and the transfer of science and technology. Decision 24 reaffirms the position taken in the Declaration of the Presidents of America[10] by recognizing that integration must fully serve the goals of Latin America which are achieved through the strengthening of Latin American enterprises. While acknowledging that foreign investment can play an important complementary role in assuring the fulfillment of the goals of integration,[11] Decision 24 calls for the gradual divestment of wholly-owned foreign enterprises and encourages a transition to national or mixed enterprises which can then enjoy the benefits of the expanded market.[12]

While Decision 24 only discussed the treatment of national, mixed or foreign enterprises, it set the stage for Decision 46 and a discussion of the treatment of subregional investments and, therefore, multinational enterprizes. Article 1 of Decision 46 defines capital as that owned by national investors of any member country other than the host country. Since mixed enterprises only involved the participation of foreign investors and national investors of the country where the business was located, investments by national investors of other member countries were, up to this point, considered foreign and therefore subject to the regulations of Decision 24.[13]

[8] Article 26: The Member Countries shall immediately begin a process of coordinating their development plans by specific sectors and of harmonizing their economic and social policies for the purpose of attaining a stage of joint planning for the integrated development of the area.

This process shall be accomplished in conjunction with the establishment of the subregional market through the following mechanisms: (a) an industrial programming regime; (b) a special regime for the agricultural sector; (c) the planning of the physical and social infrastructure; (d) the harmonization of exchange, monetary, financial and fiscal policies, including the treatment of subregional and foreign capital; (e) a common trade policy towards third coutries; and (f) the harmonization of planning methods and techniques.

Article 27: Before December 31, 1970, the Commission, on the proposal of the Junta, shall approve and submit to the consideration of the member countries a common regime on the treatment of foreign capital and trademarks, patents, licensing agreements and royalties.

The member countries agree to undertake the necessary measures for enforcing this regime within six months of its approval by the Commission. *Id.* at 24–25.

[9] Decision 24, the "Common Treatment of Foreign Capital, Trademarks, Patents, Licensing Agreements and Royalties," was approved near the end of 1970 and implemented six months later.

[10] The Declaration promotes the establishment of a Latin American Common Market through the convergence of the Latin American Free Trade Association and the Central American Common Market.

[11] F.V. Garcia-Amador, *The Andean Legal Order: A New Community Law* 334 (1978).

[12] F. Vinces and A. Kuljevan, *Estructura Jurídica del Acuerdo de Cartagena* 262 (1974). [hereafter cited as Vinces and Kuljevan]. Article 1 of Decision 24 defines a national enterprise as one with more than 80% of the capital belonging to national investors. A mixed enterprise is one whose capital belongs to national investors in an amount which varies between 51% and 80%.

[13] When Decision 24 was first approved subregional capital was treated as foreign. In 1976 Decision

Thus, when Article 1 of Decision 46 was drafted, it proposed to treat subregional investments the same as national investments[14] as long as the investments were made in a multinational enterprise. Since the multinational enterprise could be made up of contributions from two or more member countries as well as contributions of up to 40% by foreign investors, it was viewed as an institutional mechanism which met the needs of joint development, directed subregional financial resources towards priority sectors, created opportunities for more economic interrelation and and helped subregional businesses create new industrial markets designed for the harmonious and joint development of the subregion.[15] Due to the limited mobility of capital among the Andean countries at the time Decision 46 was approved, the establishment of these multinational enterprises was thought to be the most viable means of facilitating the movement of capital towards the most dynamic sectors.

Decision 169, approved more than ten years after Decision 46, was not meant to supersede Decision 46, but rather to broaden the areas of economic activity in which multinationals could engage. Due to the fact that Decision 46 was unable to stimulate the process of integration, contained complex and time-consuming rules for the formation and operation of multinational enterprises and imposed restrictions on their areas of activity, Decision 169 was approved in an attempt to eliminate the rigidity of Decision 46 and encourage economic integration.

Elements of a Multinational Enterprise (Decision 46)

In Articles 8, 10, 11 and 12 of Decision 46 the principal elements of a multinational enterprise are set forth. They include the following:

(1) Subregional participation in a multinational enterprise must comprise at least 60% of the total capital of the enterprise with optional foreign participation not exceeding 40%.

103 amended Decision 24 by stating that subregional capital can be treated as national capital if the following conditions are fulfilled: (1) the approval of the country of origin of the capital is obtained if so required by the national legislation; (2) the approval of the host country is obtained and the investment is registered in the host country; (3) the remittance of profits or the re-exportation of capital is only to the country of origin of the capital; and (4) there is no subregional investment in companies which produce products reserved for the sectorial programmes unless the companies are located in those member countries which are the beneficiaries of the reservation. Thus, whereas Decision 46, which was approved in 1971, treats subregional capital as national only if such capital is invested in a multinational enterprise, Decision 103 holds that all subregional capital will be treated as national whether it is invested in a multinational, mixed or national enterprise. Junta del Acuerdo de Cartagena, *Decision 24, Régimen común de tratamientos de los capitales extranjeros sobre marcas, patentes, licencias y regalias* 33 (1981).

[14] Vinces and Kuljevan, p. 374.

[15] J. Galves and A. Llosa, *Dinámica de la Integración Andina* 142 (1974).

(2) The capital participation of national investors from member countries in a multinational enterprise may not be less than 15% of the total subregional participation.

(3) The majority subregional capital must be reflected in the technical, financial, administrative and commercial operation of the enterprise.

(4) The principal office of the enterprise must be located within one of the member countries.

(5) There must be capital contributions from national investors of two or more member countries.

(6) Investors from Bolivia and Ecuador may pay their capital contribution corresponding to their percentage of participation within five years from the date other national investors pay their capital contributions.

(7) The enterprises must have as a corporate objective the intent to participate in any one of the following projects or programmes: (a) Sectorial Programmes for Industrial Development; (b) infrastructure projects designed to solve problems which affect the process of subregional integration; (c) industrial rationalization programmes designed to revitalize and give a subregional dimension to existing industries; or (d) joint agricultural development programmes.

At the time Decision 46 was approved, the idea of combining capital contributions of two or more member countries with those of foreign investors was believed to be an improvement over the formation of the mixed enterprise of Decision 24, in part because of the more favourable treatment accorded Andean investors. Although Decision 46 reduced the participation of foreign investors from 49% (Decision 24) to 40%, it was expected to induce more development projects for the region because the foreign investment was subject to fewer restrictions and was to be channeled toward more dynamic sectors. In other words, Decision 46 appears to be a trade-off for the foreign investor between a lower level of participation in capital and broader investment opportunities.

Special Treatment of Multinational Enterprises (Decision 46)

All multinational enterprises located in the Andean countries are granted special treatment inasmuch as their products enjoy the benefits of the trade liberalization programme. However, only those multinational enterprises which are located in member countries where the nationals participate in at least 15% of total subregional capital (9% of all subregional and foreign capital) may enjoy the following special treatment:

(1) Member countries shall adopt measures which facilitate the transfer of capital intended for the operation of multinational enterprises.

(2) Multinational enterprises shall enjoy the same treatment as that established for national enterprises regarding the State's acquisition of goods or services.

(3) Investors in a multinational enterprise are not required to transfer their shares or rights to national investors of the country where the enterprise is located.

(4) Multinational enterprises shall enjoy the same treatment as that established for comparable national enterprises regarding national taxes.

(5) Multinational enterprises are not required to obtain authorization from the appropriate national agency in order to reinvest their profits.

(6) Multinational enterprises shall have access to domestic credit and, in general, to the same financial treatment as that established for comparable national enterprises.

(7) With the authorization of the appropriate national agency, subregional investors have the right to transfer to their country the net profts of their direct investment.

(8) With the authorization of the appropriate national agency, multinational enterprises can participate in those sectors of economic activity which the member countries had reserved for national enterprises as long as they receive 15% of the subregional capital from investors of the countries solicited.

Elements of an Andean Multinational Enterprise (Decision 169)

The main characteristics of an AME are set forth in Articles 1 and 2 of Decision 169 and include the following:

(1) AME's must receive contributions from national investors of two or more member countries and they must total more than 80% of the capital of the enterprise.

(2) Contributions from foreign investors must be less than 20% of the capital of the enterprise.

(3) When the enterprise is capitalized with contributions from only two member countries, the sum of the contributions from the investors of each member country may not be less than 15% of the capital of the enterprise. If there are investors from more than two member countries, the contributions from at least two countries shall meet the above-mentioned requirements. In both cases, investors from the country where the principal place of business is located shall contribute 15% or more of the capital of the enterprise.

(4) The principal place of business shall be located in one of the member countries.

(5) The majority of subregional capital shall be reflected in the technical, administrative, financial and commercial operation of the enterprise.

(6) AME's located in Bolivia and Ecuador may consist of subregional capital contributions amounting to 60% and foreign capital contributions

amounting to 40% for a period of ten years from the establishment of the enterprise, or fifteen years from the time Decision 169 becomes effective.

Special Treatment of Andean Multinational Enterprises (Decision 169)

All AME's may enjoy the following benefits:[16]

(1) The products of an AME shall enjoy all the benefits of the trade liberalization programme.

(2) The enterprise shall receive the same tax treatment as an equivalent national enterprise.

(3) The AME shall have access to domestic credit and the same financial treatment as a national enterprise.

(4) The enterprise shall not be required to obtain prior authorization from the appropriate national agency to invest or reinvest in the same country as the principal office. Also in such cases, the net profits of the AME's shall be transferable in freely convertible currency.

(5) AME's may establish branch offices in member countries other than the one where the principal office is located.

(6) With the authorization of the appropriate national agency, the AME, or its branch, may participate in sectors reserved for national enterprises.

(7) The branches, with the authorization of the appropriate national agency, may transfer all net profits in freely convertible currency to the principal office.

(8) Foreign and subregional investors in an AME may transfer abroad, with the authorization of the appropriate national agency, all net profits in freely convertible currency.

(9) To avoid double taxation, shareholders of an AME will not be required to pay taxes on the profits received from the branch office which are redistributed to them as dividends by the main office, nor will investment companies which are shareholders in AME's be required to pay taxes on the income they derive from the redistribution of the AME's profits.

(10) Member countries shall treat subregional employees of an AME as national employees for purposes of the application of foreign labour quotas.

(11) Member countries shall facilitate the entry into their territories of promoters, investors and executives of such enterprises.

(12) Member countries shall facilitate the contracting of technology, patents and trademarks within the region where the AME's operate.

Differences Between Decision 46 and Decision 169

A. *General Differences*

While the AME of Decision 169 resembles the multinational enterprise of

[16] *Cf.* above (special treatment of multinational enterprises).

Decision 46 regarding subregional control and location, the amount of capital contributions from national and foreign investors, as well as the special treatment of Bolivia and Ecuador, differ considerably.[17]

The change in the ratio of national (or Andean) capital contribution to foreign (or non-Andean) capital contribution from 60/40% to 80/20% appears to be based on certain implicit assumptions. One of these is that the greater the ratio of national capital, the more influence nationals will be able to exert over decisions of the enterprise.

National investors have always questioned the presence of foreign investors in their enterprises even when they do not represent majority ownership. Minority foreign investors can gain actual control of an enterprise by forming a cohesive group while national, or Andean, investors are often dispersed throughout the region; minority foreign investors may also use nationals as intermediaries, thus creating artificial minority foreign participation. The likelihood that minority foreign investors will be able to exert such control over an enterprise, however, is clearly lessened if their participation is restricted to a rather small percentage.

Thus, the requirement in Decision 169 that foreign participation in AME's be limited to 20% appears to be based on the belief that the influence of such investors will be substantially lessened as compared to the Decision 46 criterion allowing 40% participation.

Reduced capital participation by non-Andean investors is a result not only of the desire of the nationals to maintain control of the enterprise, but also of their apprehension concerning foreign competition. Since Decision 169 permits the freer movement of capital (subregional as well as foreign) within the subregion, and given the existence of the Common External Tariff and the lack of duties within the Andean market, it is believed that foreign capital will be attracted to the Andean Group. However, the introduction of this new foreign capital could bring stiff competition and conceivably hinder the development of local markets by subregional industrialists. Thus, when Decision 169 was drafted, national businessmen insisted on maintaining a high level of capital participation in AME's. Increased Andean participation was also enthusiastically supported by Venezuela and Colombia, two of the more developed Andean countries which have the capital necessary to develop AME's and which are understandably anxious to invest it in enterprises in which they can have relatively greater control.

Another assumption related to the change in the capital contribution

[17] It is worth noting that the 80/20 AME of Decision 169 represents the most extreme type of mixed enterprise in terms of capital participation since the mixed enterprise can have anywhere from 51% to 80% national participation and 20% to 49% foreign participation. The AME is not, however, restricted in terms of profit remittances, reinvestment of capital and areas of operation as is a mixed enterprise.

requirement of AME's is that capital is not a scarce resource in the Andean countries. The Latin American experience during the 1970's was that subregional industrialists and governments found it relatively easy to borrow from capital markets. Therefore, the requirement for an overwhelming subregional majority in the capital composition of AME's set forth in Decision 169 did not seem unreasonable.

Another difference between Decision 46 and Decision 169 is the decision to grant a different type of special treatment to Bolivian and Ecuadorian AME's due to the fact that investors from these countries are more limited than other subregional investors in terms of their access to technological, managerial and capital resources. Unlike Article 12 of Decision 46, which allows the Bolivian and Ecuadorian investors to pay their contributions to Bolivian or Ecuadorian multinational enterprises as much as five years after the other subregional and foreign investors pay their contributions,[18] Article 2 of Decision 169 provides that a Bolivian or Ecuadorian AME may be capitalized with 60 rather than 80% subregional capital and as much as 40% foreign capital for a period of ten years from the establishment of the enterprise or fifteen years from the time Decision 169 is implemented.[19] Under these conditions, the enterprise will still enjoy the same treatment as a regular AME, except that it will not yet be able to establish branches in Colombia, Peru and Venezuela. At the end of the ten or fifteen years, the enterprise must comply with the general regulations, i.e., it must have at least 80% subregional capital and less than 20% foreign capital or it will lose its Andean Multinational status. Thus, the establishment of AME's in Bolivia or Ecuador not only affords these countries the opportunity to develop despite their own limited resources, but also enables foreign investors with better access to development resources to receive greater participation rights.

What is clearly not included in the definition of an AME is a corporate purpose clause as found in Decision 46. Article 8(e) of that Decision states that the corporate purpose must be directed towards subregional interests and that the projects of such enterprises must include one of the following: industrial development programmes, infrastructure projects, industrial rationalization programmes or joint agricultural development programmes.[20]

Decision 46 is based on the assumption that the process of subregional integration can best be achieved by orienting subregional and foreign capital towards only those sectors which are deemed the most important for the joint development of the Andean Group. Decision 46 illustrates the

[18] Article 12, Decision 46.

[19] La Comisión del Acuerdo de Cartagena, *Decision 169* 2 (March 1982) (Unpublished, but copies available in the Economic Integration Subdepartment, Inter-American Development Bank.) [hereafter cited as La Comisión del Acuerdo de Cartagena].

[20] Vinces and Kuljevan, p. 377.

need to distinguish between a transnational corporation controlled by non-Andean investors and often concerned with the advantages offered by the expanded market and a Decision 46 multinational enterprise, which could be a useful instrument of economic integration. The multinational enterprise, because of its subregional control, was thought to be capable of promoting the equitable and planned development of countries of the subregion, something which the transnational corporation would be less likely to do.[21] As stated previously, despite an implementation period of ten years, few multinational enterprises have actually been established because of the difficulties in implementing industrial programming, the absence of industrial rationalization and agricultural programmes to date and the lack of support by the Andean member countries' governments. Therefore, Decision 169 defines a new type of multinational enterprise that can be established in any area of economic activity.

Although lacking a corporate purpose clause, Decision 169 does contain the following general objectives which are to be viewed as guidelines, and not requirements:

(1) To work towards perfecting the process of integration and the fulfilment of the objectives of Andean subregional integration.

(2) To utilize subregional savings and facilitate the implementation of joint projects.

(3) To help strengthen subregional financial and technological capacity as well as subregional participation in third-country markets.

(4) To generate employment opportunities in the subregion.[22]

B. *Special Treatment Differences*

The special treatment of AME's clearly resembles that granted to multinationals in Decision 46. Both types of enterprise enjoy: (1) the benefits of the trade liberalization programme; (2) the same tax treatment as national enterprises; (3) the same access to domestic credit and the same financial treatment as national enterprises; and (4) the ability to reinvest their profits without authorization.

However, the special treatment of AME's goes one step further. Not only does Article 21 of Decision 169 allow them to reinvest their profits without obtaining authorization, they may also invest their profits in the country where the principal office is located without obtaining authorization from the appropriate national agency.[23] If the AME wishes to invest in another member country, it then must register its investment as well as obtain authorization. However, in either case, the net profits of the investments of the enterprise are transferable in freely convertible currency. Thus, not

[21] Fernandez, p. 24.

[22] La Comisión del Acuerdo de Cartagena, p. 1.

[23] *Id.* p. 5.

only are both AME's and multinational enterprises immune to the 7% reinvestment limit of Decision 24,[24] but the AME investing in the same member country may also do so without obtaining authorization from the appropriate national agency as required by Article 2 of Decision 24.[25]

Further, the ability of foreign and subregional investors of AME's to transfer abroad, with authorization, all net profits not only releases such investors from the 20% limit placed on such transfers by Decision 24[26] but also does not restrict such transfers to the country of origin of the capital, as does Decision 46.

Decision 169, in addition to maintaining some of the special treatment clauses of Decision 46 and restructuring others, also sets forth new clauses. For example, the establishment of branch offices in all member countries is first discussed in Article 23 of the new Decision.[27] This is due to the fact that Decision 169 promotes the greater movement of capital among member countries, in addition to establishing a new provision concerning an investor's ability to contribute tangible goods, rather than currency only. Thus, existing enterprises, which contribute machinery, equipment and parts to an AME in return for shares in the enterprise, can be transformed into branch offices quite easily. The legal representation, allocation of capital and operation of the branches are subject to the national legislation of the member country in which they are located. Further, Article 24 of Decision 169 states that such offices are permitted to transfer all their net profits to the principal office with the authorization of the appropriate national agency.[28]

Another important and distinctive feature of Decision 169 concerns double taxation. For the purpose of avoiding double taxation, Decision 40[29] provides that the profits of enterprises that are remitted from one country to another, i.e., a branch office sending its profits to the principal office, are only taxed in the country where the enterprise which distributes them is located, i.e., where the branch office is located. Decision 40 does not, however, exempt from tax the redistribution of these profits, i.e., when the

[24] Article 13 of Decision 24 required that the reinvestment of profits in excess of 5% of capital be explicitly authorized and registered. This percentage was subsequently raised to 7% in October of 1973 by Decision 103.

[25] Vinces and Kuljevan, p. 260.

[26] Article 37 of Decision 24 allowed foreign investors, with prior authorization, to transfer abroad up to 14% of the net profits of the foreign direct investment. This limit was subsequently raised to 20% by Decision 103.

[27] La Comisión del Acuerdo de Cartagena, p. 5. *Cf.* Article 13 of Decision 46 referring to the establishment of manufacturing, marketing or other types of enterprises in those member countries where their nationals participate in the capital stock of the enterprise.

[28] *Id.*

[29] Vinces and Kuljevan, p. 346. By means of Decision 40, the member countries of the Andean Group approved a model agreement to avoid double taxation among the member countries and third countries outside the subregion.

principal office redistributes the profits of its branch as dividends to its shareholders. Nor does Decision 40 exempt from tax the income derived from the redistribution of the branch profits by investment companies located in the same or different member country as the principal office. Therefore, Decision 169 contains a provision exempting from tax the redistribution of profits as well as the income derived from the redistribution. Thus, the double tax provision of Decision 169 benefits shareholders of an AME which has branch offices as well as investment companies which invest in AME's.

Other Differences

In addition to the provisions concerning the special treatment of AME's and multinational enterprises, both Decisions also include provisions on the general operation and management of the enterprises. The following is a brief summary of some of the most notable differences between these provisions:

(1) While Decision 46 gives the Commission of the Cartagena Agreement the power to regulate the functions of the enterprise,[30] Decision 169 places this responsibility with the appropriate national agencies or the legislatures of the member countries. This change reflects the countries' desire to play a more active role in implementing the regulations adopted by the Commission as well as the need to simplify the operation of these enterprises.

(2) Article 8 of Decision 169 states that AME's producing goods reserved within any of the subregional programmes can only be established in those member countries which are the beneficiaries of the reservation agreements although branch offices may be established for the purpose of marketing the assigned or reserved products.[31] This is a more liberal standard than that given in Article 5 of Decision 46, which provides that the investment can be authorized only when it is made in an enterprise which produces goods reserved for industrial programming, and then only once the programme has been adopted by the Commission.[32]

(3) Article 2 of Decision 46 substantially modified Decision 24 by treating subregional investors as national investors if they invest in

[30] For example, see Article 9, Decision 46 which provides that the Commission may declare the desirability and establish the specific conditions of multinational enterprises in order to implement subregional projects, while Decision 169, in Article 5, provides that subregional investments in an AME shall be authorized by the appropriate national agency of the host country. Also see Article 27 of Decision 46 which places the responsibility of revoking the multinational status of a multinational enterprise which has committed a breach with the Commission, while the same function, described in Article 34 of Decision 169, is performed by the member country.

[31] La Comisión del Acuerdo de Cartegena, p. 2.

[32] Vinces and Kuljevan, pp. 375–376.

multinational enterprises.[33] However, since multinational enterprises are restricted in their activities, i.e., to Sectorial Industrial Development Programmes, the movement of capital within the subregion is still restricted. Thus, when Decision 169 was approved, it not only continued to treat subregional investors alike, but it also liberalized the movement of capital by allowing AME's to be established in any economic sector in which there was a joint interest.

(4) According to Article 25, Decision 169 is to take effect within the Andean Group when two or more member countries deposit their respective instruments with the Junta.[34] Temporary Article (c) of Decision 46, on the other hand, requires all member countries to deposit their instruments of implementation before the regime becomes effective.[35] This difference is the result of the countries' desire to facilitate the establishment of AME's and is related to Decision 169's independence of the approval of industrial development programmes along with its orientation towards any project which would be of common interest to at least two member countries.

Conclusions

By the beginning of the 1980's, the Andean countries' terms of trade with other countries had deteriorated as a result of the worldwide recession; their foreign debt had increased substantially in relation to their gross domestic product; their economic growth rate had decreased considerably; and they faced serious unemployment problems. As a result of these economic problems and the 1981 border conflict between Ecuador and Peru, it was decided that new mechanisms had to be found to make the subregional integration process more dynamic. The countries agreed that the private sector should play a more active role in the integration process, less emphasis should be placed on industrial programming and more on intraregional trade competition.

The approval of Decision 169 reflects this search for new mechanisms as well as the countries' interest in AME's based not only on already programmed industries, but also those to be created in other areas of economic activity which benefit from the trade liberalization programme.

The Andean private sector (business and labour) has actively collaborated with the Junta on the structuring of the AME, generously sharing its expertise and producing many innovative and practical ideas as to how subregional investors might best ensure their optimum participation in such an enterprise. In general, the new regime consists of a set of specific structural rules and direct incentives for investing in such enterprises.

[33] *Id.* at 375.
[34] La Comisión del Acuerdo de Cartagena, p. 8.
[35] Vinces and Kuljevan, p. 387.

AME's, like multinational enterprises do not represent a new type of legal entity for the Andean countries but are simply a special kind of corporation, i.e., one with a multinational purpose. Since they are structured just like any other Andean corporation, many undercapitalized Andean enterprises, as well as those with little access to technological and managerial resources, will find it relatively easy to merge with other more developed Andean enterprises to form AME's in order to compete effectively in the Andean market.

There are other factors which will encourage not only subregional but also foreign enterprises and investors to participate in the formation of AME's. These factors include: (i) the absence of restrictions and limits on the transfer of profits and the repatriation of capital; (ii) the absence of limits on investment or reinvestment; (iii) the incentives derived from the exemption from tax of redistributed AME profits as well as the income derived from the redistribution; and (iv) the increase in the number of sectors in which foreign investors can participate through investments in such enterprises.

Some areas in which the AME's could have great impact are: (i) the traditional Andean manufacturing sector (foodstuffs, textiles and apparel, shoes, etc.) many of whose products, because of their inability to face strong competition, were included on the list of exceptions to tariff reductions in 1970 and are now undergoing the process of being removed from the protected lists; (ii) the wholesale and retail marketing sector, which is at an ideal stage for development by AME's; and (iii) the transportation sector, which is characterized by high costs due to the limited number of participating firms.

The delineation of appropriate regulations and adequate incentives is essential if the countries wish to ensure the creation of AME's in the Andean Group. However, other equally vital factors exist, such as: (i) the implementation of adequate and stable margins of preference for products of the enterprises; (ii) the financial participation of national investment companies and national, regional and subregional banks; and (iii) government cooperation in regard to the creation of enterprises, the movement of capital, the avoidance of double taxation and the establishment of branch offices.

The creation of AME's could be facilitated also by establishing an Andean Trust Fund within the Andean Development Corporation.[36] The Fund would be oriented towards the development of private enterprises

[36] The Agreement establishing the Corporation was signed in February 1968 and entered into force on January 30, 1970. The Corporation is the "financial organ" of the subregional integration process. As such its functions include the undertaking of studies to determine investment opportunities, the supplying of technical and financial assistance necessary for the preparation and implementation of multinational or complementary projects, the acquiring of domestic or foreign credit, the granting of loans and issuance of securities and the encouragement of the attraction and mobilization of resources.

through the identification and promotion of possible projects and would help to provide: (i) long-term equity capital loans; (ii) working capital loans; and (iii) loans to national investment companies which promote the establishment of AME's. This Fund would be composed of contributions from the governments of the member countries and would serve as a catalyst for participation in AME's by national investors while encouraging the creation of AME's in Bolivia and Ecuador in particular.

Finally, in order to encourage the formation of AME's, it might be wise to increase the participation of foreign investors in the capital of these enterprises so as to be similar to the level set forth in Decision 46 (40% of total capital). Financial projections for the 1980's show that there will be relatively less international commercial financing available to subregional investors, implying that direct foreign investment will have to play a greater role. Due to this and to the fact that subregional savings have lately been attracted to capital markets because of high yields, the Andean countries may find that subregional capital is scarce and that the goal of promoting their development through the creation of AME's will be more difficult than they expected when the 80/20 capital ratio was set. The suggestion to increase foreign participation would also permit greater participation on the part of non-Andean, but nonetheless, Latin American investors, whose present treatment is no different than that of U.S., European or other foreign investors.

To conclude, the AME could, with the proper support, become an effective tool for revitalizing the Andean integration process. It is more flexible and pragmatic than the multinational enterprise created by Decision 46, and its adoption provides an unmistakable sign that the Andean Group is willing and able to adapt to the rapidly changing economic and social realities of today's world.

[16]

THE KOREAN MANUFACTURING MULTINATIONALS

KRISHNA KUMAR*
International Business Consultant

KEE YOUNG KIM**
Yonsei University

Abstract. As an extension of the export-led growth of national economy overseas, direct investment by Korean multinationals has been rapidly increasing. This article explores the development of the overseas manufacturing direct investment by Korean firms and the relationship between parent firms and overseas affiliates. Three main issues are discussed: the ownership-specific assets, location-specific factors, and government policies are the important sets of variables that help to explain the internationalization of the Korean firms in the manufacturing sector, the nature of technology transfer by Korean multinationals to their subsidiaries, and the benefits as a result of its overseas investment to Korea. The data for this study were gathered through structured interviews with the parent companies of 18 out of 21 manufacturing overseas subsidiaries and joint ventures formed by Korean firms.

INTRODUCTION

■ The Republic of Korea (henceforth called Korea) is no longer only a recipient of foreign direct investment (FDI). It is also emerging, slowly but steadily, as a source. The country now occupies a prominent place among a small group of Third World nations (Argentina, Brazil, Hong Kong, India, Mexico, Singapore, and Taiwan) whose firms have been establishing foreign direct investment, thereby earning the label of "multinational."[1] The total number of overseas joint ventures and subsidiaries established by Korean multinationals was 298 by the middle of 1980, and their total volume of overseas investment was $246 million (U.S.).[2] Korean multinationals have invested in trading, warehousing, transportation, mining, forestry, and construction.

Manufacturing accounts for only 12 percent of the overseas projects and of the total volume of FDI by Korean multinationals. The authorized Korean FDI in manufacturing was $31,266,000 by June 1980.[3] This volume of investment is not a large sum considering the size of overseas investments by firms from industrialized nations, but is also not an insignificant amount in the context of the size, resources, and state of economic development of Korea. The Korean government has authorized 24 overseas manufacturing investments in a wide range of industries including garment, cement, electric cables, motors and diesel engines, paper, plywood, artificial chemicals, and shoes. Three of the 24 have been abandoned for various reasons. The details of the existing projects (at the time of interview) are given in Table 1. The overwhelming majority of these projects are located in developing countries, particularly Asia and the Middle East.

The main purpose of this paper is to discuss overseas manufacturing direct

---

*Krishna Kumar received his M.A. and Ph.D. from Michigan State University. He has held many academic and administrative positions and has published extensively in professional journals. His most recent books include *Ethics and Politics of International Collaborative Research* (co-author), *Multinationals from Developing Countries* (co-editor), *Transnational Enterprises: Their Impact on Third World Societies and Cultures* (editor), and *The Social and Cultural Impacts of Multinational Enterprises*. Currently, Dr. Kumar is completing a volume on the monitoring and evaluation of development projects.

**Kee Young Kim is a Professor of Management at the School of Business and Economics, Yonsei University, Seoul, Korea. He holds a B.A. from Yonsei University; an M.B.A. and a Ph.D. from Washington University; and was at MIT and the East-West Center as a research fellow. His published books include *Production and Operations Management*, and *Quantitative Methods for Business Decisions*. His recent research interests lie in the areas of technology innovation, technology transfer, and foreign direct investment from developing countries.

The data for this paper were collected as a part of a 3-nation study of foreign direct investment by developing nations, under the direction of Krishna Kumar. The authors have very much profited from the comments and suggestions of the anonymous referees.

TABLE 1

Korean Foreign Direct Investment in Manufacturing*
(U.S. Dollars)

Year	Subsidiary/ Joint Venture	Country	Volume of Investment+	Equity Share (in percent)	Value of Exports to Subsidiary/Joint Venture (till end of 1980)##
1973	Food chemicals	Indonesia	1,200,000	80	2,181,000
1973	Cement	Singapore	1,316,362	40	18,298,000
1974	Cement	Indonesia	1,220,000	80	5,907,000
1974	Fountain pen	Thailand	1,047,500	76-99	1,060,000
1975	Printing	Japan	25,000	50	870,000
1977	Garment	El Salvador	410,000	100	4,364,000
1977	Pulp	New Zealand	1,368,200	10	0
1978	Garment	Honduras	449,899	100	606,000
1978	Agricultural implements	Thailand	367,500	49	57,000
1978	Tire	Sudan	7,000,000	50	#
1978	Soldering	Thailand	100,000	50	157,000
1978	Shoe	Philippines	678,300	70	3,017,000
1978	Cement	Philippines	1,000,000	25-64	#
1978	Garment	Sri Lanka	118,193	50	235,000
1979	Bakery	Qatar	193,058	49	255,000
1979	Electric cables	Thailand	140,000	27	670,000
1980	Garment	Sri Lanka	#	25	#
1980	Plywood	Indonesia	235,200	60	#
1980	Steel pipes	Saudi Arabia	2,133,000	30	#
1980	Jewelry	Philippines	63,450	30	#
1980	Cement pipes	Saudi Arabia	#	49	#

* These figures are for those projects which have not been abandoned.
\+ Investment includes transferred amount of loan, capital by local financing, cultural projects, and loans to the partners in joint ventures.
\# Data not available.
\## These figures are for only these firms which invested by the end of 1979.

investment by Korean firms. The focus is on 3 issues: (1) What are the important sets of variables that help to explain Korean FDI in the manufacturing sector? (2) What is the nature of technology transfer by Korean multinationals to their subsidiaries/joint ventures? (3) What are some of the benefits which have accrued or are likely to accrue to the country as a result of its FDI?

The data for this paper were collected from the parent companies of 18 out of 21 foreign subsidiaries/joint ventures formed by Korean firms in manufacturing sectors at the time of the study.[4] In all, 16 Korean multinationals were covered by this study. Interviews were held with the senior executives in charge of the overseas investment projects, and, in most of the cases, with the chief executives of the firms as well. Interviews were based on a structured questionnaire, and were conducted in Korean. Company reports, documents, and other relevant information were also procured. In addition, interviews were held with the officials of various government agencies and the Bank of Korea, which supervises overseas investments.

This paper begins with a brief discussion of the theory of multinational firms, especially the conceptual framework developed by John Dunning [1979]. Next, the firm-specific assets of Korean firms are examined, along with the host-country-specific factors which attract them, and the role of Korean government in foreign direct investment. Finally, some aspects of technology transfer to host countries and the benefits to Korea from its overseas direct investments are mentioned.

EXPLANATORY VARIABLES

Contemporary theory on multinational enterprises is based on the assumption that they operate and thrive under the conditions of imperfect competition. [Kindleberger 1970; Hymer 1960]. A firm has little or no incentive to make overseas investments if the conditions of pure competition prevail in all goods and factor markets at home and abroad, because the firm will not enjoy any competitive edge over the local firms in the host country. The focus of research, therefore, has been on the identification of those monopolistic or oligopolistic advantages that enable a firm to establish overseas business operations despite the additional costs involved in crossing national boundaries and the incentives to make investments abroad.[5] These advantages, often known as "ownership-specific," are similar to those stressed in the literature on industrial economics about the barriers to the entry of new firms in a market.

The theorists of multinationals generally agree that the most important ownership-specific advantage of multinational corporations lies in their possession of patented or unpatented technology, which is variously described as "information," "knowledge," "skills and expertise," and "intangible capital goods." Their production technology is as important as their capacity to produce new goods and services. Even when they do not produce new goods, multinationals are in a position to differentiate their products from others having similar functional value through product variations, brand names, and subjective distinctions created by advertising. Product differentiation is closely related to the marketing skills and research and development capabilities of a firm. Multinational firms tend to be strong in both areas. They invest more resources in R&D than the mononational firms, and possess efficient marketing skills and experience.

In addition to technology, another strength of multinational firms is their capital resources. Size has been an important predictor of the multinationality of a firm. The reputation of a firm and its large capital assets often enable its subsidiaries in the host countries to secure capital on more favorable terms than those available to local firms. It is widely recognized that multinational firms are able to raise capital resources in international markets.

The third competitive advantage which has been associated with some multinationals is their access to needed raw materials. This access can be attributed to their control over their production, processing, transporting, or marketing. In addition to these 3 main advantages, a firm can have a competitive edge over others because of large size, economies of scale, capacity to diversify risks, governmental protection, and access to export markets, particularly in its home country.

These ownership-specific variables by themselves do not explain why a firm seeks to exploit them through direct investment rather than through licensing, the sale of technology, or exports. No definitive answer can be given to this question, although many explanations have been propounded. Caves [1971], for example, has argued that direct investment is often preferred because know-how cannot be always transferred independently of the firm and its management. Buckley and Casson [1976] and Rugman [1980] have developed the concept of internalization, and have pointed out that imperfect competition induces a firm to internalize activities such as research and development, training of employees, and marketing. Magee [1977] has stressed the fact that firms opt for direct investments over other forms of gaining rent for their knowledge, skills, or information, thereby ensuring full "appropriability" of their investments in the production of technology. All these explanations are complementary rather than exclusive of one another.

Recent theories on multinational corporations have also incorporated several location-specific variables of the host country in an attempt to explain internationalization of a firm [Hood and Young 1979; Dunning 1979]. These are considered as "pull" factors which may attract foreign firms to a country; these factors may include trade barriers, low labor costs, availability of raw materials, market size and growth, and host government policies. For example, high tariff duties, import quotas, product standards imposed by importing countries, and high transportation costs often provide incentives to a firm for investing in another country. The prevailing low wages in many countries also attract foreign investors. Several U.S. and Japanese firms have invested in labor-intensive industries in Southeast Asia for this very reason.

The large or growing markets in host countries also may pull multinational firms toward them. Such markets are better served by direct investments rather than exports because of tariff and non-tariff barriers to trade. Perceived political and economic stability always remains an important consideration for foreign investors. It should be noted, however, that the location-specific factors are same for both mononational and multinational firms. It is the complex interaction between the ownership-specific and location-specific factors that sheds light on overseas direct investment. Also important in this interaction are the advantages of internationalization itself.

These explanatory variables have been identified, developed, and tested by researchers on the basis of the studies of North American and West European multinationals. It is perhaps premature to suggest that such variables are equally applicable to the multinational firms which are springing up in other parts of the world under different political, economic, and social systems.

There is, in fact, some evidence that generalizations concerning multinationals from Western countries are of limited validity in describing the growth of multinationals from developing nations or from Japan. Several students of Japanese firms [for example, Kojima 1977; Ozawa 1979] have suggested that Japanese overseas investors were mainly small firms that were producing standardized products, and that have invested abroad to gain access to relatively cheap labor and raw materials. The majority of the Japanese firms that have engaged in FDI in Asia have been small- and medium-sized firms that invested with the help of large general trading companies. It should be noted, however, that all these studies largely focused on early investors in developing countries. It is indeed doubtful that the conclusions of such studies are relevant for the large Japanese conglomerates that have more recently been investing in many industrialized countries.

The information about the socialist multinationals that are based in the Soviet Union and Eastern Europe is also limited [Wilezynski 1976]. Anecdotal evidence suggests that their strength is both technological and political. They receive various kinds of assistance from home governments, which gives them a competitive edge over firms based in free market economies.

Several studies of the multinationals from developing countries (DC multinationals) indicate that the competitive assets of these firms are different from those of their counterparts from industrialized countries.[6] These firms usually do not have the advantage of brand names or consumer loyalties. Nor do they manufacture new or exclusive products. In most cases, they operate in industries using standard technologies [Wells 1977, 1980, 1981; Lecraw 1977, 1981; Wells and Warren 1979]. The capital resources of these firms are also limited. Moreover, they face problems in transferring capital resources from home to host nations, as home countries usually put restrictions on capital outflows. Although some DC multinationals can have proprietary access to raw materials, such cases are few.

Studies on these firms indicate that their sources of competitive strength follow from a different set of conditions and factors. These firms have come to acquire or have been able to develop labor-intensive, multipurpose operating technologies that can use locally available inputs and that can operate at a lower scale of production [Wells 1978, 1980; Wells and Warren 1979]. Such technologies are often more efficient in developing countries. The cost of the production of these firms is usually low because of their use of appropriate technologies, and they are able to provide goods and services at prices below those of other multinationals or locally owned firms [Kumar and Kim 1981; Wells 1978; Lecraw 1981].

In addition, researchers have pointed out that the product technology of these firms is also appropriate. Such firms sometimes manufacture simple, low quality consumer goods that can be used by a large segment of the populace, and that are usually not manufactured by the firms from industrialized countries [Nambudiri, Iyanda, and Akinnusi 1981; Lecraw 1981]. It has been also noted that DC multinationals have the experience of operating in the conditions of underdeveloped infrastructure and thus are able to adjust themselves quickly to the environment of host developing countries [Nambudiri, Iyanda, and Akinnusi 1981]. In addition, because of their small size and lack of political clout, DC multinationals are not perceived as threatening to the political sovereignty of the host countries. In many cases, their activities are viewed as an example of growing economic cooperation among the Third World nations. Such perceptions can be an important asset of the DC multinations in the countries in which popular apprehensions and concerns exist about the political and social effects of the activities of the multinational firms.[7]

The findings about the Korean manufacturing multinationals seem to be more or less in accord with these conclusions about DC multinationals.

KOREAN MULTI-NATIONALS: Firm-Specific Assets

The self-perceived ownership-specific assets of Korean multinationals are given in Table 2. These assets are: their ability to initiate and operate overseas projects at relatively low costs; suitability of their operating technology; lower costs of their expatriate staff; suitability of their products; and their skills in marketing.

The most important asset of the Korean firms is their ability to establish and start overseas manufacturing projects at costs lower than those cited by their competitors. The majority of the firms in the sample stated that they could secure the approval of the host government for this very reason. Many firms also observed that their projections had been 10 to 20 percent lower than those of other firms, and equally important, they were able to fulfill their commitments within the stipulated budgets.[8] Korean firms have been able to accomplish this by careful planning, lower costs of expatriate staff, minimum spending on infrastructure, and by supplying necessary inputs at low prices.

TABLE 2

Perceived Firm-Specific Assets of Parent Firms*
(N = 18)

Assets	Number of Firms	Percentage
Price advantage	12	66.7
Suitability of operating technology	7	38.9
Lower cost of expatriate staff	4	22.2
Suitability of the product	3	16.7
Skills in marketing	2	11.1

*Firms mentioned more than one perceived competitive asset.

The suitability of the manufacturing technology is also an important factor. The Korean firms generally stated—and were perhaps able to convince their overseas partners—that their manufacturing technologies were suitable to the conditions of the host countries. The subject of manufacturing technology will be discussed further on; suffice it to mention that Korean firms do not use highly capital-intensive technologies in their overseas manufacturing plants.[9] Some firms also stated that their manufacturing technologies were simple to use. By a process of trial and error they have been able to simplify complicated production processes and reduce time involved in production. Table 2 indicates that 39 percent of the firms cited suitability of manufacturing technology as one of their major assets.

Another asset of Korean firms which seems to give them an edge over the firms from industrialized nations is the commitment of their expatriate staff. The executives of Korean companies often observe that their overseas expatriate staff are highly committed to their work and are prepared to do everything within their capabilities to keep the name of the company and of Korea high in the international business community.[10] In addition, they seem to be content with relatively low remuneration. Of course, as compared to the salary and benefits given in Korea, expatriate staff do receive better treatment. The salaries that they receive are lower, however, than what European and American firms have to pay to their overseas employees. This asset has been of greater value to Korean firms in trading and construction than to those in manufacturing. Even so, it emerges as the third most important asset in Table 2.

The international marketing networks that Korean firms have built up during the past 15 years also help them to establish overseas manufacturing operations.[11] Nearly 33 percent of the Korean overseas manufacturing projects have been primarily involved in exports to third countries. In these cases, it is obviously the ability of these firms to market the merchandise in international markets which facilitated their entry in the host nations. Another 33 percent have started or are expected to start exporting a part of their products. To most developing nations any prospect for manufactured exports is indeed attractive.

Two other variables which appear to be worth mentioning are the suitability of the products and skills in marketing. Only 3 firms out of 18 regarded their products to be more suitable to the conditions of host countries, and only 2 stated that they could enter and survive in the host country because of their skills in marketing alone.

Location-Specific Factors

The geographical distribution of the Korean FDI in the manufacturing sector can be explained with reference to location-specific factors in the host countries. The most important factor has been the availability of relatively cheap inputs for manufacturing. The countries which possess an abundant labor force and have wages lower than Korea have attracted Korean investors in export-oriented industries. Moreover, the availability of the necessary raw materials, such as, lumber, limestone, pulp, and molasses, has also induced Korean firms to invest in host countries.

The general business environment and the incentives provided by the host government are also important factors. Korean firms have been keen to avail themselves of the various incentives, such as, tax holidays, exemption of import duties on the import of machinery and equipment, and unlimited expatriation of profits, dividend, and capital. In several cases, before establishing their subsidiaries/joint ventures, Korean firms asked for and were promised protection against imports for a limited duration of time. Korean firms have shown a marked preference for countries which impose relatively few restrictions on economic activities or in which governmental regulations are not strictly enforced.

The cultural systems of the host countries and their geographical proximity to Korea have undoubtedly influenced the decision of the firms with regard to the location of overseas manufacturing projects. The Korean firms first invested in countries such as Singapore, Indonesia, Thailand, and the Philippines, where the cultural environment, traditions, and behavior patterns are least different from those of Korea and about which the Korean firms possessed information and understanding. Political ties also played an important role at the early stage. Only later did the Korean firms start moving to the Middle East, Africa, or Latin America.

Finally, Korean firms prefer the countries which, in their view, offer good prospects for mutually advantageous economic activities. Like the Japanese firms, they take a long-term view of their overseas investments. They generally aim at the expansion of their operations to other industries as well. This explains why countries with rapidly growing domestic markets are preferred by Korean firms. The 2 regions that are seen as good hosts are the fast-developing countries of southeast Asia and the rich nations of the Middle East.

It is interesting to note here that, as predicted by the theories of international investments, Korean firms have generally invested in "down-stream" countries, that is, countries that are relatively less industrialized than Korea itself. There are only 2 exceptions: a printing plant in Japan, and a pulp project in New Zealand in which a Korean firm has a minority share. In "down-stream" countries, both process and product technologies possessed by Korean firms are regarded as appropriate.

Two other points are obvious from the above discussion. First, the ownership-specific advantages of the Korean multinationals are not the same as those which are usually associated with North American and European multinationals. Korean firms do not offer either new products or capital-intensive technologies that have been developed through research and development activities. Instead, these firms are able to compete on the basis of their lower costs of production and, to a limited extent, on the suitability of their operating technologies to the conditions of developing countries. Second, there is marked similarity between the Korean firms and the multinationals of industrialized nations with regard to location-specific factors.

Government Policies

The discussion of explanatory variables is not complete without reference to the Korean government policies for the country's overseas investments. Like other developing nations, the Korean government defines the objectives of FDI and even specifies the sectors in which overseas investments are permitted, prohibited, or encouraged.

The Korean government has clearly outlined the policies for overseas investments by its firms. It has specified the following 4 areas in which "overseas investment shall be promoted and supported": (1) "investment for development and import of raw materials essentially required at home"; (2) "investment for overcoming any bottleneck in exports"; (3) "fisheries investment to secure fishing grounds"; and (4) investment in industries in which "competitiveness in the world market has been weakened under the nation's industrial structure."[12] The government strictly prohibits investments "which have serious adverse effects on Korean economy." Investments in the form of "emigration funds" are also prohibited by the Korean government.

The 2 main objectives that the government seeks to accomplish are quite obvious from the above guidelines. First, it seeks to protect and expand its exports. The country has opted for export-oriented industrialization and has been successfully widening its industrial base by expanding its manufactured exports. The government expects that its FDI will remove any "bottlenecks" or will directly or indirectly facilitate fresh exports of goods and services. Second, the government seeks to assure the supply of raw materials needed for the nation's industries, or foodstuff (fisheries) for domestic consumption and exports. Korea lacks raw materials and minerals to sustain its industrial production and depends heavily on foreign countries for a steady supply. The government therefore encourages its firms to establish subsidiaries/joint ventures in resource development projects.

The Korean government has sanctioned only those overseas manufacturing projects that serve either of the 2 objectives. Most of the overseas projects have been devised to protect the existing markets or explore new opportunities. In at least half the cases, the Korean firms had been exporting to the host countries before establishing their subsidiaries/joint ventures. The firms realized, however, that there was some threat to their markets, or that there would be new opportunities for expansion if they started indigenous production. Only on these grounds were the exporting firms authorized to establish overseas manufacturing operations.

Korean companies have also been permitted by the government to start foreign subsidiaries and joint ventures for serving the markets of third countries. As the guidelines imply, Korean firms were losing their comparative advantages in many labor-intensive industries, such as, garments, artificial jewelry, electric and electronic goods, bags, and so on. There are several reasons for this state of affairs. The wages in Korea have been steadily increasing over the past decade, making labor-intensive products less competitive in world markets. In addition, many industrialized countries have imposed quota restrictions on the import of textiles and electric and electronic products. Shipping costs have also increased. Firms in these industries have been permitted by the Korean government to locate part of their manufacturing operations in such countries as the Philippines, Sri Lanka, Thailand, El Salvador, and Honduras. The wages in these countries are usually ½ to ⅓ those paid in Korea. In addition, the quota for textile products from these countries was undersubscribed, permitting Korean firms continual access to the markets of North America and Western Europe. Seven out of 21 overseas joint ventures of Korea are located in export processing zones. Many executives of garment firms indicated that ideally they would like to move their whole plants to other developing countries if suitable opportunities were forthcoming. The government of Korea is likely to authorize such overseas investments as long as the parent firms export semi-processed raw materials to their subsidiaries and make a profit that is remitted back to Korea.

The second objective of FDI, that is, the supply of the needed raw materials, is only marginally fulfilled by overseas manufacturing investment. Only in a few cases have Korean firms started overseas manufacturing activities for the importation of the semi-processed raw materials. A good example is provided by Sun Kyong Company, which manufactures plywood in Indonesia and exports part of its output to Korea. The company established its Indonesian subsidiary because Korea is planning to prohibit the export of lumber. Yeung Wha, which has formed a joint venture for manufacturing solder in Thailand, also expects to sell part of the output in Korean markets.

The government, then, largely determines the objectives of FDI by Korean firms. The Korean government has been able to accomplish this by regulation and inducement as well as by putting pressure on large business houses, which have a close working relationship with the government.[13] This does not mean that individual firms have no motives for making overseas investments other than the 2 main objectives identified by the government. In fact, at least 3 other motivations can be identified: sale of technology, prestige associated with foreign operations, and acquisition of new skills and expertise [Kumar and Kim 1981]. These motivations are at best of secondary importance, however, as far as the government is concerned. In the case of Korea, it is the government decision which ultimately counts in overseas investments.

TECHNOLOGY TRANSFER TO HOST COUNTRIES

The subject of technology transfer by the Korean multinationals to their overseas subsidiaries/joint ventures is important for 2 reasons. First, one of the main reasons for seeking FDI by host nations is to gain access to new product or process technologies. Second, the technology transfer by the Korean multinationals is in itself an indicator of the technological and industrial progress made by the country. Practically all the technologies transferred by the Korean firms are process and not product technologies.

Table 3 identifies the sources of operating technologies for the overseas affiliates of the Korean multinationals. The table indicates that 72 percent of the firms stated that they were the exclusive suppliers of operating technologies to their affiliates. Another 22 percent stated that they provided partial operating technologies. Only one firm in the sample did not make any such claim, though it stated that it did give some technical assistance. All these statements should be taken with care, because process technologies in the industries established by Korean multinationals are quite standardized, and these firms have been using them for some time. Even in those cases where the parent company did not manufacture the particular product, it could draw upon the resources of its sister firms within a group or from outside. An interesting example is provided by Daewoo, which does not manufacture tires but started a tire manufacturing project in Sudan. The company could do this by hiring the services of engineers, technicians, and even skilled workers from another Korean firm which had to curtail its domestic production for various reasons.

The supply of operating technology does not necessarily imply the supply of machinery and equipment to the overseas subsidiaries. Table 4 presents data on

TABLE 3

Sources of Operating Technology for Affiliates*

Sources	Number of Affiliates	Percentage
Operating technology from Korea	13	72.2
Operating technology from industrialized nations	1	5.6
Operating technology from Korea and from industrialized nations	4	22.2
Total	18	100.0

*The above categories are based on the following question: Who were the main suppliers of the operating technology? Please identify the relative shares of the following: (1) parent company, (2) other firms from Korea, (3) firms from industrialized nations, and (4) firms from developing countries.

TABLE 4

Sources of Machinery for Affiliates

Sources	Number of Affiliates	Percentage
Mainly from Korea	2	11.1
Mainly from industrialized nations	4	22.2
Both from Korea and industrialized nations	12	66.7
Total	18	100.0

the sources for machinery for the affiliates. Here the picture becomes more complex. Only in 2 cases did the entire machinery come from Korea. In the other 12 cases, it was jointly supplied by Korea and by industrialized countries. The dominant pattern is thus that the parent firm procures machinery partly from Korea and partly from other countries. Such an arrangement is usually more acceptable to many host countries which may harbor reservations about Korea's technological capabilities.

The relative amount of the machinery and equipment supplied by Korean multinationals varied from case to case. For example, while Daedong, manufacturer of tractors and diesel engines in Thailand, supplied only 20 percent of the machinery to its affiliate, Sun Kyung Group was responsible for 85 percent of the machinery and equipment used in its plywood plant in Indonesia. Several factors, such as, the state of technology in a particular industry, the preference of the host country partners (in the case of joint ventures) for some countries or brands, and the experience of the parent company in that particular industry, appear to affect the relative share of the Korean-made machinery in overseas manufacturing plants.

The main supplier of machines and equipment to the Korean overseas affiliates is Japan, followed by European countries and the United States. Two reasons explain the predominance of Japan in this regard.[14] First, Korean firms have been using Japanese machinery in several industries, such as, textiles, plywood, cement, and so on, and hence they are quite familiar with the machines and equipment made in Japan. Second, Japanese firms have been able to offer better terms through their general trading companies.

The comparison between the manufacturing technologies used by parent firms and those used by their subsidiaries reveals that there are differences between them with regard to the scale of operation and labor intensity. Some Korean firms tend to scale down the production capacity of their overseas projects mainly because of the small size of the markets. For example, Gold Star Instrument Company's joint venture in Thailand has lower production capacity than the company's plant at home. Dukseung, a garment manufacturer, has 8 production lines in Korea and only 5 in Sri Lanka. The majority of the Korean overseas operations are of recent origin and the firms are understandably cautious at this stage. Several firms, however, indicated that they planned to scale up their production capacity in the near future. The labor intensity of the overseas ventures is higher or, at most, equal to that of the parent firms.[15] In only 2 cases, the overseas ventures have low labor intensity as compared to the parent firm, one of which is a printing operation in Japan and the other a pulp project in New Zealand.

The labor intensity of the overseas projects seems to be the function of 2 variables: the prevalent wages, and the productivity of the labor. Wages in the countries to which Korean FDI has gone are usually low. The exceptions are

Middle East countries, Japan, and New Zealand. Low wages in the host countries attract Korean firms to labor-intensive operating technologies. Sometimes the host governments also encourage the Korean multinationals to follow such a course. On the other hand, the majority of the companies in the sample stated that the labor productivity in the host countries is low, and this pulls them towards introducing capital-intensive machineries.[16] Among the factors responsible for low productivity—a problem stressed by the companies—are a lack of desire to work, high rates of absenteeism, a strong labor movement, physical climate, and, above all, a widespread indifference among the local employees towards the interests of the firm. Several firms indicated that they would like to make their overseas plants more capital-intensive in the future partly because of the low productivity of labor in host countries and partly to upgrade their operating technologies. Sun Kyung Company, which manufactures plywood in Indonesia, has already made its plant more capital-intensive because of the perpetual labor problems. Daewoo, too, is planning to make its tire plant in Sudan more capital-intensive, partly because of low productivity but mainly because it wants to introduce new product lines in the future.

The overall picture of technological diffusion that emerges from the experience of the Korean firms is in some respects similar to that suggested by the growing literature on south-to-south technology transfer.[17] It can be summarized as follows. Originally, a Korean firm secures some manufacturing technology from an industrialized country through licensing, outright purchase, or even joint venture arrangements. During the initial stage, the firm's main concern is the implementation of the operating technology. It does not yet possess capabilities to introduce modifications in the imported technology. After production has started, however, the skills and expertise of the firm begins to improve. Its engineers and technicians are able to assimilate the operating technology through "learning by doing" and through research and development. They first acquire the skills to introduce minor changes in their operating technologies and later major modifications. In some cases firms are able to manufacture all or part of the machinery and equipment used, while in others they are able to provide assistance to other firms in manufacturing them.[18] Korean firms tend to form overseas subsidiaries/joint ventures only when they have assimilated the technology and are confident that they can introduce it in host countries. As a result, what they usually transfer to their overseas affiliates is not the originally imported operating technology but its modified version.

In other words, there is a 3-tier system for the diffusion of manufacturing technology in which Korean multinationals play an intermediary role. They are the middle parties which absorb, modify, and improve the manufacturing technologies originally developed in industrialized countries, and pass them on to other developing nations. The major contribution of the Korean multinationals lies at present not in developing new product or process technologies but in modifying and adapting the existing technologies and in making the latter available to other developing countries.

The most interesting example in this regard is provided by Mahajak International Electric Company, a joint venture of the Gold Star Instrument and Electric Company.[19] The parent company, in which Fuji Electric Company of Japan has a minority share, secured its manufacturing technologies for WHM from Fuji, which in turn acquired it from Siemens of Germany. It is the adapted version of this technology that has been supplied to the Thai subsidiary by the Korean parent company as well as by Fuji directly. In other words, the manufacturing technologies used by the Thai subsidiary have passed not one but 2 intermediaries—Fuji and Gold Star.

The question can then be raised: why did Mahajak not acquire its manufacturing technology directly from Siemens? One possible answer is that the Thai partners did not establish the joint venture simply to gain that particular technology.

Several other considerations—sources of finance, mode of training, possibilities for future collaboration, and terms of technology transfer—must have also affected their decision in this regard. More importantly, Gold Star and Fuji provided adapted operating and product technologies that were perceived as more appropriate than those that could be secured from Siemens by the Thai government.

The overall capability of the Korean multinationals to upgrade the technologies in their overseas ventures continually is undoubtedly limited at present. There are reasons to believe, however, that the conditions will change in the future. First, the Korean firms are highly competitive and continue to procure new machinery and equipment from industrialized nations for their home plants. They could thus be in a position to transfer the new technologies which they acquire, after modification. Second, research and development activities by Korean firms have been growing. [See, for example, Westphal and Rhee 1981.] Several firms in the sample have research and development departments. The Korean government is also exerting pressure on the firms to invest more on R&D activity. The recent 5-year plan places a great emphasis on the country's capability to produce sophisticated machines and equipment for exports.

BENEFITS TO KOREA

Finally, some possible benefits to Korea from overseas direct investment in manufacturing by its firms should be discussed. It need hardly be stressed that the phenomenon of FDI from Korea is too recent and the data too meager to permit definitive conclusions or viable generalizations.

Exports

As explained earlier, one of the main objectives of FDI has been to boost national export efforts. The Korean firms are successfully accomplishing this objective. Almost all the firms in the sample exported some kind of goods or services to their affiliates as shown in Table 5. All the firms provided some kind of technical assistance, and an overwhelming majority provided managerial expertise to their overseas affiliates. It is not clear, however, if all these firms charged their overseas subsidiaries for their technical assistance and management expertise. In some cases the parent company entered into separate management contracts with their overseas joint ventures and was paid for them. Table 4 shows that about 78 percent of firms exported machinery and equipment to their overseas affiliates. Besides, 66.6 percent of companies provided or continue to provide raw or semi-processed materials. Nearly ⅓ of the Korean overseas manufacturing projects are

TABLE 5

Goods and Services Provided by Parent Companies*

Items	Number of Subsidiaries	Percentage of firms
Technical assistance (including operating technologies)	18	100
Management expertise	15	83.3
Raw materials	13	72.2
Marketing channels	12	66.6
License, patents, and so on	6	33.3
Others (training, finance, and so on)	2	11.0

N = 18

*Each of the firms was asked which of the listed goods and services it provided to its subsidiaries.

located in export processing zones and import most of the needed raw or semi-processed material from Korea.

The dollar values of the exports by parent firms to their subsidiaries are quite impressive. Table 1 presents data about the value of exports to subsidiaries/joint ventures for all those firms whose overseas investments were approved by the Korean government by the end of 1979. It shows that only one firm did not make any exports to its affiliate. This firm has only 10 percent equity shares in the joint venture, which imported its operating technology from Sweden and which depends on local sources for raw materials. The dollar values of exports of the other firms ranged from $57,000 to $18,298,000. The largest exporter has been Ssang Yong which has a joint venture for manufacturing cement in Singapore. This venture is dependent on Korea for the supply of clinker for the plant.

Besides these direct exports, several companies stated that the establishment of overseas subsidiaries led to new business for Korean firms. Daewoo's officials suggested that they were able to conclude several business deals in Sudan after the successful completion of their tire manufacturing plant. Ssang Yong Group won 2 contracts in Singapore partly as a result of networks established due to their cement joint venture.

Return on Investments

The return on overseas investments in the form of profits, dividends, and interest on loans advanced is also an important benefit to the company and the country. The guidelines issued by the Korean government stipulate that all overseas investments should normally be recovered within 10 years. In practice, most of the Korean firms plan and expect on the basis of much shorter time horizon [Kumar and Kim 1981].

The data presented by Kumar and Kim [1981] show that only 3 Korean firms did not expect to make any profit or expected losses for the year 1980. All these were new projects, however, and the firms had started their operations recently. Long-term prospects appeared to be bright for all the firms. Nearly ⅔ of the firms (out of 16) expected a 15 percent or above rate of return, while another expected between 10 to 14 percent. The expected rate of return for the Korean firms is thus quite satisfactory.

Other Benefits

Several other benefits also accrue to the Korean companies and the country.

First is the experience of operating in a new environment. It is not possible to identify the precise content of this learning process. There is little doubt, however, that as a result of their overseas experiences many firms have come to possess a small but effective corps of young executives who are familiar with the customs, traditions, business practices, labor laws, governmental regulations, and market conditions of host countries. Some of these employees can be effectively used by these companies for initiating, managing, and administering new projects. In addition, there are indications that the foreign experience is contributing to some structural differentiation within the Korean multinationals. Although most of them have not established separate international divisions, they have already started thinking about it.

Second, the overseas investments have some political pay-off for Korea. In many cases these investments have directly or indirectly contributed to the growth of stronger political relationships. Daewoo stated that its many activities were instrumental in upgrading political ties between Korea and Sudan. The firm's chief executive was given a goodwill award by the Sudanese President on the successful completion of the tire project. The officials of Sampoong stated that because of their project in El Salvador, political contacts between the 2 countries are being initiated.

Two major concerns can be expressed about the overseas manufacturing investments by Korean firms. First, they contribute to the migration of capital from a capital-scarce country. Second, they may generate short-term unemployment because Korea no longer exports to the host country those items that its firms have started manufacturing in it. The above discussion indicates that these concerns do not appear to be fully justified. Although it is true that overseas manufacturing investments do involve (in most of the cases) the migration of the capital, it is equally true that Korea is able to earn foreign exchange because of its FDI. It has been able to export raw materials, machines and equipment, and technical skills which it could not have otherwise exported. Moreover, the rate of return on investment is high, and nearly half of the firms expect to recover their investments within 3 to 5 years.

It also needs to be recognized that in most of the cases, foreign markets would have been lost or would not have been fully developed had the firms not invested abroad. In reality, then, the unfavorable effect of FDI on the employment situation is likely to be minimal, or nonexistent. Moreover, Korea does not have an unemployment problem. In fact, the overseas investments might have created additional employment opportunities by promoting export of machinery, raw materials, and technical skills. These jobs are likely to be in higher skill categories.

CONCLUSIONS

An attempt has been made in this paper to raise and answer 3 questions about the overseas direct investment by Korean multinationals. In response to the first question—what are the important sets of variables that help to explain Korean FDI in the manufacturing sector?—it has been noted that both ownership-specific and location-specific factors explain the internationalization of the Korean firms. Their competitive assets, however, are different from those of their counterparts from industrialized countries. Also, in the case of Korea, the government policies play a significant role in defining the objectives and goals of the nation's FDI.

The second question asked: what is the nature of technology transfer by Korean multinationals to their subsidiaries? It has been found that, barring some exceptions, Korean firms stated that they have provided operating technologies to their subsidiaries. They tend to procure part of the machines and equipment for their overseas plants from industrialized countries, particularly Japan and partly from Korea itself. The labor intensity of the Korean overseas plants is at par or even higher than that of the parent companies. Korean companies tend to scale down the production capacity in foreign plants.

It is too early to answer the third question about the benefits to Korea from its overseas investments in manufacturing. The limited available data show that the country and its firms are harvesting many benefits. The overseas investments seem to boost exports and assure a return on investment. In addition, they promise fresh business opportunities for Korean firms.

The volume of Korean investment in overseas manufacturing is likely to grow in the near future. The government has shed its initial reservations and is more sympathetic to foreign ventures. The technological and managerial capabilities of the country are also growing. The country has started investing heavily in research and development. The Korean companies themselves are becoming more enthusiastic and seem to have been encouraged by the experience of those firms that have ventured abroad. Moreover, the Korean multinationals have, in the view of Korean government officials, earned a good name in many host countries, particularly in Asia and the Middle East. Their image has improved in these countries which offer excellent prospects for direct investments. All this augurs well for Korea and its firms.

FOOTNOTES

1. For the current status of study and research on Third World multinationals, see Kumar and McLeod [1981].

2. Figures supplied by the Bank of Korea.

3. Ibid.

4. Parents of 3 subsidiaries/joint ventures were not interviewed. These projects were at the planning stage at the time of the study.

5. For the best review of literature on multinationals, see Neil Hood and Stephen Young [1979].

6. See Wells [1977, 1980, 1981]; Wells and Warren [1979]; Lecraw [1977, 1981b]; O'Brien [1980]; Chen [1981]; Nambudiri, Iyanda, and Akinnusi [1981]; Agrawal [1975, 1981]; Heenan and Keegan [1979]; White [1981]; and Raju [1980].

7. This point has been discussed by White [1981], Panglaykim [1979], and Kumar [1982]. Kumar, however, has suggested that when a large, powerful country seemed to dominate a region, it was quite likely that its small neighbors might prefer investments from distant industrialized countries rather than from their immediate, powerful neighbor.

8. Kumar and Kim [1981]. The host governments are also involved in these negotiations about budget and so on.

9. It should be noted that we refer to the relative "height" of capital intensity compared to other MNEs.

10. The importance of national identity and pride in motivating Korean managers and entrepreneurs has been stressed by several observers [Hedberg 1978]. In fact, the success of Korean construction firms in the Middle East has been partly attributed to the national commitment of the Korean workers and supervisors.

11. This point was often stressed by Korean executives. Moreover, it should be noted that Korean General Trading Companies, which are affiliated to several leading business groups, have been instrumental in establishing necessary contacts between Korean firms and their collaborators in host countries.

12. Overseas Investment Guidelines issued by the Korean government. Article 15-6.

13. See Jones and Sakong [1980] about the relationship between business and government in Korea.

14. This predominance was revealed in the authors' interviews with company executives.

15. The managers of the Korean multinationals stated this fact. We have elaborated this point elsewhere.

16. In this respect, the notion of cultural proximity does not apply. In interviews, Korean executives expressed their concern about the productivity of the local employees in host countries.

17. See studies by Wells [1977, 1980, 1981]; Wells and Warren [1979]; Lecraw [1977, 1981b]; O'Brien [1980]; Lall [1978, 1979]; and Rhee and Westphal [1978].

18. This assistance was highlighted in in-depth interviews with company executives.

19. This example is a case study by Professor Kee Young Kim.

REFERENCES

Agmon, T., and Kindleberger, C. P., eds. *Multinationals from Small Countries*. Cambridge, MA: MIT Press, 1977.

Agrawal, Ram Gopal. *Joint Ventures Among Developing Asian Countries*. Geneva: United Nations Conference on Trade and Development, 1975.

________."Third World Multinational Corporations: Indian Experience." In *Multinationals from Developing Countries*, edited by K. Kumar and M. McLeod. Lexington, MA: Lexington Books, 1981, pp. 115-132.

Buckley, P. J., and Casson, M. *The Future of Multinational Enterprise*. London: Macmillan, 1976.

Caves, R. E. "International Corporations: The Industrial Economics of Foreign Investment." *Economica*, February 1971, pp. 1-27.

Chen, Edward K. Y. "Hong Kong Multinationals in Asia: Characteristics and Objectives." In *Multinationals from Developing Countries*, edited by K. Kumar and M. McLeod. Lexington, MA: Lexington Books, 1981, pp. 79-100.

Dunning, J. "Explaining Changing Patterns of International Production: In Defence of the Eclectic Theory." *Oxford Bulletin of Economics and Statistics*, November 1979, pp. 269-96.

Encarnation, Dennis J. "The Political Economy of Indian Joint Industrial Ventures Abroad." *International Organization*, Winter 1982, pp. 31-59.

Hedberg, Hakan. *The New Challenge: South Korea*. Seoul: Chongno Book Center, 1978.

Heenan, David A., and Keegan, Warren J. "The Rise of Third World Multinationals." *Harvard Business Review*, January-February 1979, pp. 101-109.

Hood, Neil, and Young, Stephen. *The Economics of Multinational Enterprise*. London: Longman, 1979.

Hymer, S. *The International Organization of National Firms*. Ph.D. dissertation. Massachusetts Institute of Technology, 1960.

Jones, L. P., and Sakong, I. L. *Government, Business and Entrepreneurship in Economic Development: The Korean Case*. Massachusetts: Harvard University Press, 1980.

Kindleberger, C. P. *The International Corporation*. Cambridge, MA: MIT Press, 1970.

Kojima, K. "Transfer of Technology of Developing Countries—Japanese Type versus American Type." *Hitotsubachi Journal of Economics*, February 1977, pp. 1-14.

Kumar, Krishna. "Third World Multinationals: A Growing Force in International Relations." *International Studies Quarterly*, September 1982, pp. 397-424.

Kumar, Krishna, and Kim, Kee Y. "Multinational Firms from the Republic of Korea: A Study of Overseas Investments in Manufacturing Sector." Hawaii East-West Center, 1981. Mimeo.

Kumar, Krishna, and McLeod, Maxwell, eds. *Multinationals from Developing Countries*. Lexington, MA: Lexington Books, D. C. Heath & Company, 1981.

Lall, Sanjaya. "Developing Countries as Exporters of Technology: A Preliminary Analysis." Oxford Institute of Economics and Statistics, June 1978. Mimeo.

________. "Developing Countries as Exporters of Industrial Technology." In *International Economic Development and Resource Transfer*, edited by H. Giersch. Tubingen: J&B Mohr, 1979.

Lecraw, Donald J. "Direct Investment by Firms from Less Developed Countries." *Oxford Economic Papers*, November 1977, pp. 442-457.

________. "The Internationalization of Firms from LDCs: Evidence from the ASEAN Region." In *Multinationals from Developing Countries*, edited by K. Kumar and M. McLeod. Lexington, MA: Lexington Books, 1981a, pp. 37-52.

________. "Technological Activities of Less-Developed-Country-Based Multinationals." *Annals of the American Academy of Political and Social Science*, November 1981b, pp. 163-174.

Magee, S. P. "Information and Multinational Corporation: An Appropriability Theory of Director Investment." In *The New International Economic Order*, edited by J. N. Bhagwati. MIT Press, 1977, pp. 317-360.

Nambudiri, C. N. S.; Iyanda, O.; and Akinnusi, D. M. "Third World Country Firms in Nigeria." In *Multinationals from Developing Countries*, edited by K. Kumar and M. McLeod. Lexington, MA: Lexington Books, 1981, pp. 145-155.

O'Brien, P. "The New Multinationals: Developing Country Firms in International Markets." *Futures*, 1980, pp. 303-16.

________. "The Argentinian Experience in Export of Technology: Retrospect and Prospect." Vienna: UNIDO, 1981. Mimeo.

Ozawa, T. "International Investment and Industrial Structure: New Theoretical Implications from the Japanese Experience." *Oxford Economic Papers*, March 1979, pp. 72-92.

Panglaykim, J. "Multinational Corporations in Asia/South Korea/Hong Kong: A Descriptive Picture." A paper presented to the conference on "Third World Multinationals" held at the East-West Center, 12-18 September, 1979.

Raju, M. K. *Internationalization of Indian Business*. Bombay: Forum of Free Enterprise, 1980.

Rhee, Yung W., and Westphal, Larry E. "A Note on Exports of Technology from the Republics of China and Korea." The World Bank, November 1978. Mimeo.

Rugman, A. M. "Internalization as a General Theory of Foreign Direct Investment: A Re-Appraisal of the Literature." *Welwirtschaftlickes Archiv*, Band 116, Heft 2, 1980, pp. 365-379.

Wells, Louis T. Jr. "The Internationalization of Firms from the Developing Countries." In *Multinationals from Small Countries*, edited by T. Agmon and C. P. Kindleberger. Cambridge, MA: MIT Press, 1977.

________. "Foreign Investment from the Third World: The Experience of Chinese Firms from Hong Kong." *Columbia Journal of World Business*, Spring 1978, pp. 39-49.

________. "Multinationals from Latin American and Asian Developing Countries: How They Differ." Harvard Business School, 1980. Mimeo.

________."Foreign Investors from the Third World." In *Multinationals from Developing Countries*, edited by K. Kumar and M. McLeod. Lexington, MA: Lexington Books, 1981, pp. 23-36.

________, and Warren, V'Ella. "Developing Country Investors in Indonesia." *Bulletin of Indonesian Economic Studies*, March 1979, pp. 70-84.

Westphal, Larry E., and Rhee, Yung W. "Korean Industrial Competence: Where It Came From." World Bank Staff Working Paper. No. 469, 1981.

White, Eduardo. "The International Projection of Latin American Firms." In *Multinationals from Developing Countries*, edited by K. Kumar and M. McLeod. Lexington, MA: Lexington Books, 1981, pp. 155-186.

Wilezynski, J. *The Multinationals in East and West Relations*. Boulder, CO: Westview Press, 1976.

[17]
Singapore Multinationals

Pang Eng Fong
and
Rajah V. Komaran

Singapore-owned multinationals have greatly expanded their international involvement during the last two decades, reflecting that Asian city-state's rapid economic development. This article describes the characteristics of Singapore's multinationals and compares their foreign activities to those of Hong Kong.

THIS PAPER ANALYZES Singapore-owned multinationals, a subject that has attracted little scholarly attention compared to multinationals from such countries as Brazil, Hong Kong, India, and South Korea.[1] It describes their characteristics and discusses the factors that have activated Singapore firms to internationalize their activities. The paper also compares the foreign activities of Singapore-owned firms with those from Hong Kong, a rapidly industrializing city-economy with firms that have a longer and greater involvement in international investment activities.

OUTWARD INVESTMENTS OF ASEAN AND HONG KONG

To place Singapore's outward investments in regional perspective, it is useful to compare the city-state's flow of outward investments with those from the ASEAN countries and Hong Kong. Estimates of the volume of outward investments by ASEAN- and Hong Kong-owned firms are based on foreign investment data released by the firms' host countries. This is because the ASEAN countries and Hong Kong do not collect data on the foreign activities of their firms. They provide only a partial picture of their firms' activities for three reasons. Firstly, foreign investment statistics are neither comprehensive nor comparable. Host countries that provide foreign investment figures often prepare them differently. Some include only promoted investments (i.e. investments that enjoy tax incentives); others release figures on certain industry sectors only, for example, manufacturing and extractive industries. Indonesia assigns investment data by "Chinese," irrespective of their nationalities, in one category. Separate figures on investment in Indonesia by Chinese-owned firms from different ASEAN countries and Hong Kong are not available.

Secondly, it is often difficult to identify the original source of investments in ASEAN countries. For instance, an investment in Malaysia by a developed-country multinational based in Singapore is classified as a Singapore investment.

Thirdly, in most cases, the available data cover only direct investments in the manufacturing sector. There is little official information on indirect investments in the form of licensing and technical assistance agreements, turnkey projects, management contracts, and minority joint ventures.

The estimates of outward investments by ASEAN and Hong Kong firms in Table 1 are low because they exclude substantial non-manufacturing investments (especially for Hong Kong and Singapore), and cover only some host countries. Compared with other ASEAN countries (excluding oil-rich Brunei which has considerable foreign portfolio investments but an insignificant manufacturing sector), the two city-states, Hong Kong and Singapore, have the most foreign manufacturing investments. Hong Kong companies have invested over $1 billion abroad compared with less than $400 million for Singapore-based companies. For both city-states, their outward manufacturing investments are greatly understated because their recent and fast-growing investments in China are excluded. Singapore firms, for example, are involved in a wide variety of projects with a total value of over $400 million in China.[2]

The data in Table 1 support the hypothesis that outward investments are directly related to the stage of development of a country. Indonesia, the least industrialized of the six countries in Table 1, has the least manufacturing investments abroad, while Hong Kong and Singapore have the most. Hong Kong investments are sizeable in all ASEAN countries and Sri Lanka, while Singapore investments are mainly in Malaysia and, to a lesser extent, in Indonesia and Thailand. Malaysian manufacturing investments are mostly in Singapore, a reflection of the close historical and commercial ties between the two countries. Indonesian, Philippine, and Thai manufacturing investments abroad are small, in part because manufacturing companies in these countries are inward-looking and have little incentive to venture abroad.

Pang Eng Fong and Rajah V. Komaran are both Associate Professors at the School of Management at the National University of Singapore.

FOREIGN INVOLVEMENT OF SINGAPORE MULTINATIONALS

Origins and Characteristics of Singapore Multinationals

Singapore-owned multinationals are diverse, with different origins and orientations. They fall into two main groups: those involved largely in manufacturing activities, and those involved in various activities, including manufacturing, real estate, hotels, etc. These two broad groups of Singapore multinationals can be further classified as follows:

- home-grown, family-owned/managed;
- home-grown, government-owned/managed;
- other home-grown;
- transferred from abroad; and
- ex-foreign companies.

This classification of Singapore-owned multinationals is broader than that used by Agarwal Raj (1984), whose recent study covers only companies listed on the Singapore Stock Exchange. Listed companies comprise only a small portion of Singapore firms that have international investments or interests. Also, many of the listed companies are not headquartered in Singapore nor owned by Singapore nationals. Of the thirty Singapore-owned firms that have projects in China, only eleven are listed companies.[3]

Singapore-owned firms known to have foreign manufacturing investments or interests include Intraco, a government-owned trading company; Acma, a manufacturer of refrigerators and home appliances; Keppel Shipyard, another largely government-owned company; Yeo Hiap Seng, formerly a family-owned food and beverage company that is now a public company; Wah Chang International, a conglomerate with interests in construction, shipbuilding, and engineering; and Jack Chia-MPH, a diversified conglomerate with interests in pharmaceuticals, perfumeries, publishing, and real estate. All these companies have gross fixed assets of over $50 million but, unlike many multinationals from developed countries, they are not in vertically integrated industries.

These companies can be classified in the two distinct groups discussed earlier. The first includes firms like Acma, Yeo Hiap Seng, and Keppel Shipyard. These companies have developed ownership-specific advantages in manufacturing and are expanding abroad in areas related to their businesses. The second are conglomerates like Jack Chia-MPH and Wah Chang International, which are involved in highly diversified activities including manufacturing, construction, finance, real estate, trading, insurance, hotel management, and en-

TABLE 1

Foreign Manufacturing Investments of Asean and Hong Kong Companies in Selected Countries
(US dollars, in millions)

	Indonesia a (1967-1982)	Malaysia b (end 1977)	Philippines c (1968-1978)	Singapore d (end 1979)	Thailand e (1970-1980)	Hong Kong (end 1983)	Sri Lanka f (end 1983)	Taiwan (end 1983)
Investor Country								
Indonesia	-	0.3	..	6.9*	2.0	5.0*	..	..
Malaysia	5.3	-	..	92.6*	12.0	3.0*	..	..
Philippines	35.7	0.9	-	1.4*	2.0	1.0*	..	..
Singapore	64.5	197.1	1.5	-	70.0	20.0*	16.0	10.0
Thailand	13.2	0.7	0.6	2.8*	-	2.0*	..	..
Hong Kong	461.1	121.2	10.0	101.9†	110.0	-	50.0*	310.0†
Total	579.8	320.2	12.1	205.6	196.0	31.0*	66.0*	320.0

* Estimate.
.. Negligible.
NOTES:

a: Indonesia: Investments between June 1967 - June 1982.
Source: Bank of Indonesia, **Indonesian Financial Statistics**, December 1982.

b: Malaysia: Foreign investment in approved projects as of end of 1977.
Source: Malaysia, Federal Industrial Development Authority, **Annual Report**, various issues up to 1978.

c: Philippines: Foreign equity investment in BOI-Approved projects, 1968-78.
Source: Philippines, Board of Investment.

d: Singapore: Foreign investment in gross fixed assets as of end 1979.
Source: Department of Statistics (Singapore), unpublished data.
† Chen, Edward K.Y., "Hong Kong Manufacturing Multinationals," in Lall, S. (ed.), **Third World Multinationals**, London: Wiley (forthcoming).

e: Thailand: Net inflow of direct investment, 1970-80.
Source: Bank of Thailand.

f: Sri Lanka: Singapore, **Business Times**, 4 July 1983 and Singapore, **The Straits Times**, 1 October 1983.

gineering services. Some Singapore multinationals like Jack Chia-MPH, Wah Chang and Prima are not home-grown; they are companies established elsewhere by Chinese families who moved their operations to Singapore in the 1970s.

Of the home-grown multinationals, several (including Yeo Hiap Seng, Lam Soon Oil, The Soap Manufacturing Company and Khong Guan Flour) are still largely owned by Chinese families. Others like Acma, Keppel Shipyard, Sembawang Shipyard, Intraco, and National Iron and Steel Mills are substantially government-owned. Besides these family-controlled and state-owned multinationals, there are a number of Singapore-based multinationals which were owned by the British and bought out in the 1960s by local companies, for example, Wearne Brothers (originally a distributor of motor vehicles and heavy equipment) and Fraser & Neave Ltd. (a soft drink company). Both Wearne Brothers and Fraser & Neave Ltd. are significantly owned by the Overseas Chinese Banking Corporation, one of the four largest banks in Singapore.

Geographical Spread

Most Singapore multinationals, whether home-grown or relocated from abroad, were until recently involved mainly in the Southeast Asian region and Hong Kong. Because of close historical ties, many Singapore-owned companies have large investments in Peninsular Malaysia. In fact, many were well established there before the separation of Singapore from Malaysia in 1965. Other multinationals like Jack Chia-MPH and Wah Chang, which originated from abroad, have maintained their business interests in Southest Asia while expanding their activities beyond the region.

Since the early 1970s, Singapore-owned firms have ventured further abroad. Singapore-owned firms have set up plants or are planning to invest in Bangladesh, Sri Lanka, Pakistan, India, Mauritius, Fiji, Hong Kong, China, Taiwan, Africa, Papua New Guinea, and Australia. In China, these firms are involved in a growing number of oil exploration, manufacturing, hotel, and construction projects. These projects capitalize on the expertise and technology developed by Singapore companies, and at the same time allow Singapore a role as an intermediary in China's quest for modern technology.

For example, in 1984, Intraco (a government-owned trading company) and seven other Singapore-based firms signed an agreement with China for a joint-venture investment in China's Chiwan supply base. The Intraco-led consortium has a 30% equity share in the joint-venture; its aim is to prolong the useful life of Singapore's acquired expertise in the offshore oil-supply field.[4]

Singapore investments in Sri Lanka increased sharply in the late 1970s after Sri Lanka began welcoming foreign investment. Singapore firms and individuals have invested $114 million in Sri Lanka, of which $16 million is in the free trade zone, where investors enjoy a 10-year tax holiday. Singapore investment in the free trade zone is mainly in labor intensive activities, including flour milling, polypropylene, socks, carbon film resistors, jewelry, and printing.[5] Although Sri Lanka allows wholly-owned subsidiaries in the free trade zone, most Singapore investments there are minority joint ventures, including the largest ($40 million) by Prima Flour, which has a 40% equity stake in Prima Ceylon Limited. Outside the free trade zone, Singaporeans have invested in civil engineering, construction, sewing threads, rubber bands, sewing machines, and a commercial refrigerator assembly plant.[6]

Little is known of the activities of Singapore-owned firms in India; however, the Pan Electric group is reported to have formed a minority joint venture to provide construction, engineering, and support services related to shipping and oil production.[7]

In Australia and North America, Singapore-owned firms are involved mostly in trading or real estate development activities. In Africa, two home-grown Singapore multinationals have licensing and contractual arrangements but no manufacturing facilities. In the Middle East, Singapore firms have undertaken construction and engineering projects.

Motivation and Types of Foreign Involvement

Unlike some multinationals from developed countries, Singapore firms internationalize not to obtain raw materials and intermediate inputs but to find new markets and investment opportunities and to sell their technological expertise. The prime factor motivating the foreign involvement of Singapore-owned companies is the limited size of the Singapore and Malaysian markets. Many large Singapore-owned firms are in mature industries and can no longer depend upon growth in these markets. As export markets shrink because of growing protectionist policies in many countries, Singapore firms have adopted strategies which emphasize direct and indirect investment abroad.

Acma, a partly government-owned and listed company, is a good example of a home-grown Singapore multinational that had to seek foreign markets. Protected by tariffs in the 1960s and 1970s, Acma developed ownership-specific advantages in the production of refrigerators. In the late 1970s, when tariffs for refrigerators were removed, its price advantage over competing imports disappeared, forcing it to seek foreign markets and sell its acquired technology. In Pakistan and Sri Lanka, Acma has secured technology contracts to produce refrigerators. In China, it has completed a refrigerator plant in Guangzhou, and will build another three factories in other provinces there. In Nigeria and Kenya, it is providing technological assistance in the assembly of refrigerators and air-conditioners.

Besides the limited growth potential in Singapore and Malaysia, another important factor that has induced Singapore-owned firms (especially the cash-rich ones in mature industries) to internationalize is diversification, particularly into high-technology areas like computers, microelectronics, robotics, biotechnology, and genetic engineering. The Singapore government has identified these industries as development priorities.

An example of a diversifying multinational is National Iron and Steel, which has invested $3 million in a few small venture-capital companies in California. It is hoped these venture capital investments will afford National Iron and Steel a window to new technologies and their applications. The Economic Development Board, the government's investment promotion agency, is assisting other Singapore-owned firms in similar investments.[8]

Modes of Foreign Investment

Singapore multinationals generally prefer to be minority partners in foreign joint ventures, except in Malaysia where, because of close historical ties, they have a substantial number of wholly-owned subsidiaries. As Table 2 shows, over half of the 117 Singapore-owned firms with foreign operations are involved in minority joint ventures. Only thirty-five have wholly- or majority-owned foreign subsidiaries. The relative importance of minority joint ventures and other forms of indirect investment is attributed to the risk-averse approach of Singapore firms, rather than a relative shortage of funds or host country restrictions. Even where wholly-owned subsidiaries are permitted, as in the free trade zone of Sri Lanka, Singapore firms have preferred minority joint venture. Indeed, the more unfamiliar the territory, the more likely the Singapore-owned firm will engage in contractual resource transfers such as licensing and turnkey projects.

TABLE 2

Foreign Involvement of Singapore-Owned Firms by Mode of Investment, 1985

Type of Company	Mode Of Investment							
	Wholly-owned subsidiaries	Majority-owned joint ventures	Minority-owned joint ventures	Licensing agreements	Turnkey projects	Technical contracts	Portfolio investment	Total
A. Manufacturing Companies								
(1) Home-grown, largely family-owned/managed	4	4	15	—	2	—	—	25
(2) Home-grown, largely govt.-owned	—	1	7	—	1	4	1	14
(3) Other home-grown firms	3	5	11	—	—	—	2	21
(4) Transferred from abroad	1	—	2	—	—	—	—	3
(5) Ex-foreign companies	1	1	1	—	—	—	—	3
B. Conglomerates								
(1) Home-grown, largely family-owned/managed	1	1	5	—	—	—	—	7
(2) Home-grown, largely govt.-owned	—	—	4	—	—	—	—	4
(3) Other home-grown firms	3	—	11	—	—	—	1	15
(4) Transferred from abroad	1	1	5	—	2	—	3	12
(5) Ex-foreign companies	2	6	5	—	—	—	—	13
Total	16	19	66	—	5	4	7	117

Note: Data show number of firms with a particular mode of foreign investment; a firm with several wholly-owned subsidiaries in one country is counted only once.

Sources: Stock Exchange of Singapore, **1983 Companies Handbook,** vol xvii, 1984/85. Straits Times and Business Times.

Unlike Sri Lanka, China has defined specific modes of participation by foreign firms. These modes include processing and assembly, compensation trade, co-production and joint ventures. In processing and assembly, the foreign investor provides the production equipment, raw materials and intermediate inputs, and has the responsibility of marketing the finished products. The Chinese carry out the processing and assembly functions, and the fees charged are offset against the installment payments for the capital equipment. In compensation trade, the foreign investor providing the capital and technology is paid in the form of the finished products. Recent Singapore investments in China have included not only minority joint ventures but also technology contracts, compensation trade, and joint production.

Most home-grown Singapore multinationals are in industries with mature technologies. Although they have developed some ownership-specific advantages, they have no internalization advantages. As a result, they have no strong reason to set up wholly-owned foreign subsidiaries. Their investment mode is shaped primarily by locational factors. Where locational advantages arise from geographical proximity or historical or ethnic ties, Singapore-owned firms have gone into joint ventures, though mostly on a minority basis. But where there are no locational advantages, firms with ownership-specific advantages prefer contractual resource transfers. Thus Acma decided on a joint venture in Indonesia but sold its technology to Nigeria and Kenya. Acma has technology contracts in Pakistan and Sri Lanka as well.

While the mode of investment preferred by Singapore-owned manufacturing firms seems clear, the mode of investment preferred by conglomerates is not. The conglomerates' mode of investment varies with technology and location. Wearne Brothers' acquisition of a Florida-based agro-technology firm not only made the firm a majority shareholder but also a franchiser in some countries as well. Wah Chang has several minority joint ventures in energy exploration with China because its participation was limited by Chinese foreign investment regulations.

Finance

Several factors influence the way Singapore multinationals finance their overseas operations. These include the type and size of the firms' investments, the size of their cash reserves, their credit standing, and the riskiness of the investment. Where the investment is small, Singapore multinationals prefer to finance their involvement from their own cash reserves. National Iron and Steel financed its purchase of several million dollars worth of equity in California high-tech companies with its reserves, as did Wearne Brothers.

Where Singapore firms are involved in exporting only expertise or technology, finance is not a critical issue. Many firms (e.g. Acma, Yeo Hiap Seng) which license their mature technologies or provide only expertise and training to foreign operations do not need large cash reserves or loans. Singapore-owned multinationals which have had to raise loans in addition to risking their own capital are involved in large overseas operations, mainly hotels and real estate development and, to a lesser extent, manufacturing. But unlike many Korean or Japanese firms, they do not have financial support from the government nor from banks owned by or affiliated with their parent companies.

Typically, the Singapore multinational involved in a large overseas project obtains the funds to finance its overseas operations from banks. In less frequent cases, it may depend on joint venture partners for financial assistance. For example, banks have financed many of the hotel development projects of Singapore-owned firms in China. Pung Toh, a fairly small Singapore company with excellent Chinese connections, is building a $40 million 200-room hotel in Guangdong, China. It is investing only a few million dollars, raising the rest of the funds it needs from two foreign banks in Singapore.[9]

Apart from risking their own capital or raising capital, Singapore-owned firms have tried other ways of raising the funds to finance their overseas activities. Chuan Hup, a marine company involved in several oil drilling projects in China and Australia, is raising funds by selling shares in Australia through its newly-bought Australian subsidiary, Rocklea Consolidated. Others are seeking cash-rich joint venture partners in the ASEAN Countries and the Middle East in order to finance their overseas ventures.

While they are keen to finance the foreign activities of Singapore-owned firms, banks in Singapore (and also those in Hong Kong which have been involved in financing some of Singapore's investments in China) have been careful not to increase their foreign exposure. For instance, they typically limit their involvement to a small proportion of the total cost of a project, especially if the project is large and located in China (where, notwithstanding official reassurances, there is still much uncertainty about official rules on foreign investment and joint ventures). This has caused many Singapore-owned firms, especially those in highly competitive sectors like construction, where financing arrangements are crucial in winning bids, to complain that local banks are not sufficiently innovative or forthcoming in providing financial backing for their tenders for overseas contracts.

Control and Risk

Singapore-owned companies have attempted to ensure their control over their foreign investments. The degree and extent of control, as in the case of the investment's financing, is determined largely by two variables—the size and type of investment. When the investment is small, consisting mainly of a licensing arrangement or some other contractual transfer, the main instruments of control are periodic visits by company officials and periodic reports filed by the foreign venture. In only a few cases of contractual transfers are skilled manpower from Singapore involved in managing the foreign venture for an extended period. Initially, the Singapore multinational may send its key managers to set up the foreign operation and train workers for the operation, but they are usually quickly withdrawn. The reason is simple: Singapore firms have a scarcity of talented, experienced manpower. They cannot spare their key managers for a long period of time to run overseas operations that constitute only a small proportion of their total corporate activities. The Lam Soon group of companies is a case in point. It relies heavily on local managers wherever it operates.[10]

With large projects of long duration, especially those in countries like China where there is insufficient local expertise, the need for control is great. Singapore-owned firms exert this control in three ways: by ensuring the close involvement of its own top managers in the operation; by loaning staff from the parent company to the foreign venture; and/or by hiring professional and technical staff to manage the overseas operations. Thus Singapore-owned firms are known to send their officials on frequent visits to China, and to recruit international staff to run their foreign ventures.

The degree of risk Singapore-owned firms run when they become involved in international activities varies with the size and type of investment, the financing arrangement, and the foreign country in which they operate. In contractual transfers, the firm does not so much risk its own capital; rather, it risks its own scarce ownership-specific advantages. It may sell its technology to a firm that might one day turn out to be its competitor. Its reputation may diminish if the technology transfer is not successful, resulting in a product or service that is below customer expectations.

The larger and more concentrated by country its foreign involvement, the more the firm risks. Thus Singapore-owned firms investing mostly in China and using mainly their cash reserves are more at risk than similar firms which have spread their investments geographically and funded them with loans from banks.

Singapore-owned firms which have invested in joint ventures with Chinese partners in China are highly exposed. Pung Toh, the Singapore-owned firm with a large hotel project in China, assumes most of the risk of the project. Its Chinese partner, a Chinese farmers' cooperative which gave up its land for the project, will not be liable for any losses from the project for thirty years. During the first twenty years, Pung Toh will pay the cooperative for the use of the land, and in the next ten years, 10% of the profits from the hotel operation. Wah Chang, a Singapore conglomerate involved in a number of oil exploration projects in China, also assumes most of the risk in its joint venture projects in China.[11] Wah Chang's Chinese partners bear none of the risk in the projects' exploration stages. Only in the development and production stages will the Chinese risk their own capital. Although it offers an increasing number of business opportunities, China still poses an enormous risk for most Singapore firms. But it is a risk many Singapore multinationals, as well as those from other countries, are only too willing to take.

Prospects

The trend towards increasing foreign involvement by Singapore-owned firms will continue. Domestically, growth opportunities in many mature industries such as food, beverage, basic metals, electrical and electronics, plastics, textiles and garments, are limited. Internationally, export markets will be increasingly hard to penetrate owing to protectionist policies in both developed and developing countries. So Singapore-owned firms, particularly those that have developed ownership-specific advantages, must internationalize as well as diversify. While they will consider foreign operations outside the region, they will continue to look for regional opportunities first because of locational advantages. Given their relative inexperience, risk aversion, and inability to capture rents because of their lack of proprietary knowledge, Singapore-owned manufacturing multinationals will continue to choose indirect investment modes and contractual resource transfers rather than set up majority-owned foreign subsidiaries.

As for Singapore-owned conglomerates, their strategy in regard to the mode of foreign involvement will continue to be eclectic, reflecting particular circumstances of the investment and the host country. While some cash-rich conglomerates may buy enough equity to gain control of foreign firms, most internationalizing firms will prefer indirect investments and contractual resource transfers.

FOREIGN INVOLVEMENT OF HONG KONG-OWNED FIRMS

Hong Kong-owned firms have invested over $1.8 billion in manufacturing activities abroad, mostly in low-technology, labor-intensive, and mature industries like textiles, garments, footwear, paints, chemicals, pharmaceuticals, food, plastics, rubber, basic metals, and electronic goods. Some have developed ownership-specific advantages as a result of joint ventures with partners from Europe, Japan and the United States. Others like the textile and garment firms have built on technology and expertise brought to Hong Kong from mainland China after 1949. In recent years, as uncertainties increased over the long-term future of Hong Kong, Hong Kong-owned firms and individuals have made significant investments in non-manufacturing sectors, including real estate development, hotels, shipping, tourism, banking and portfolio investment. Though there are no reliable figures, it is probable that foreign non-manufacturing Hong Kong investments far exceed those in manufacturing.

Characteristics and Motivation

Historically, because of cost and cultural factors, Hong Kong-owned manufacturing firms have invested mainly in the ASEAN region and/or China and Taiwan. In recent years, Hong Kong-owned firms have begun investing in India, Pakistan, Sri Lanka, and even some African countries. They have also invested large sums in industrial countries like the United States, Canada, and Australia. Most of this investment is not in manufacturing but in real estate related fields.

Three key factors—labor shortages, the need to circumvent quota restrictions on exports of textiles and garments from Hong Kong, and rising domestic costs—have induced Hong Kong-owned manufacturing firms to internationalize. Compared with other developing Asian countries, Hong Kong had a relatively early start in industrialization, thanks partly to the skills and capital brought to Hong Kong by refugees from China. By the mid-1960s it had developed into a major exporter of textiles and garments, toys and electronic goods. Hong Kong was faced with rising wages and other costs, as well as quota restrictions in its main export markets. Using ownership specific advantages they had acquired in Hong Kong, Hong Kong firms began investing abroad to reduce costs and secure new export platforms. Hong Kong-owned textile firms invested in Singapore and Indonesia to circumvent quotas. Since the late 1970s, Hong Kong-owned firms have subcontracted production of labor-intensive parts and components to China. Like developed country multinationals of the traditional type, these Hong Kong firms are vertically integrating their manufacturing operations, using China as an offshore location.

Though most Hong Kong-owned firms invest abroad to escape quota restrictions or to reduce production costs, there are also a few Hong Kong firms that have invested abroad mainly to acquire technology or to secure raw materials for domestic production. Hong Kong investments in chemical plants in Malaysia, Singapore, and Taiwan are examples of investments made with the primary aim of acquiring technological expertise, while Hong Kong investments in plastics and wood in Southeast Asia provide raw materials for production purposes in Hong Kong.

Hong Kong manufacturing investments abroad are mostly in labor-intensive industries with mature technologies. This means most Hong Kong-owned firms do not possess proprietary information that they can either license or protect through wholly-owned subsidiaries. Consequently, licensing or wholly-owned subsidiaries are unlikely to be common modes of investments among Hong Kong firms abroad. Data from Hong Kong investments in Singapore support this thesis. Of the 225 manufacturing firms with Hong Kong

TABLE 3

Hong Kong-Owned Manufacturing Firms in Singapore, 1981

Industry	Number of Manufacturing Firms	Ownership Structure MNFO	MJFO	WFO
Food	18	12	4	2
Textiles	18	11	6	1
Wearing Apparel (except footwear)	38	24	8	6
Paints, Pharmaceuticals and Other Chemical Products	11	4	3	4
Machinery (except electrical and electronic)	11	7	3	1
Electrical Machinery Apparatus, Appliances, and Supplies	4	3	1	–
Electronic Products and Components	14	5	5	4
Others	95	63	13	19
Total	225	139	46	40

SOURCE: Singapore, Department of Statistics, unpublished data.
MNFO = Minority foreign-owned, i.e. 50% or less equity held by foreigners.
MJFO = Majority foreign-owned, i.e. 51-95% equity held by foreigners.
WFO = Wholly foreign-owned, i.e. 96-100% equity held by foreigners.

equity in Singapore in 1981, 139 (or 60%) are minority-owned, and only 40 are wholly-owned subsidiaries (Table 3). Hong Kong multinationals' preference for minority equity participation holds in all industries.

Finance, Control, and Risk

By and large, Hong Kong multinationals investing in small overseas manufacturing projects use their own reserves, with banks playing only a small role. These firms control their operations mainly through periodic visits and reports and the short-term loan of key engineering staff to their overseas joint ventures. Their large joint venture projects in China appear to be funded mostly by Hong Kong-based banks. Hong Kong-based multinational banks are not as heavily involved in making loans to small Hong Kong companies or individuals who have successfully negotiated sizeable projects in China. As with Singapore-owned companies with joint ventures in China, Hong Kong-owned firms and banks assume most of the risk when they operate in China.

Prospects

Though the Chinese government agreed in negotiations with the British that Hong Kong will retain its economic system for fifty years after 1997, there is still much doubt and uncertainty about Hong Kong's future. This uncertainty will reinforce the strong internationalizing trend among Hong Kong-based firms. While some Hong Kong manufacturing firms have invested in adjoining Chinese provinces, many will seek to transfer production facilities further abroad.

SINGAPORE AND HONG KONG MULTINATIONALS COMPARED

Singapore and Hong Kong investments abroad are similar in many respects. They are concentrated in labor-intensive industries, reveal a preference for Southeast Asian locations and minority equity participation, show a strong trend towards increased nonmanufacturing investments and illustrate a disregard of vertical integration as a motive for foreign investments. However, their investments also make evident important differences, differences which largely reflect these city-states' patterns of industrial development.

First, Hong Kong foreign manufacturing investments are much larger than Singapore's. This is because Hong Kong-owned firms, for cost-control and other reasons, ventured abroad earlier. Also, there are simply more Hong Kong owned firms than Singapore-owned firms. Singapore's industrial development was spurred by foreign capital, unlike that of Hong Kong, which owes much of its development to the influx of capital and entrepreneurship from China after 1949. As a result, there are few large Singapore-owned manufacturing firms. Locally-owned manufacturing firms are generally small, and they mostly provide parts and supporting services to the large developed country firms that account for the bulk of Singapore's manufacturing exports.

Second, Singapore multinationals are more likely than Hong Kong multinationals to have diversified business and manufacturing interests. Only a handful of Singapore multinationals restrict their foreign activities to manufacturing; most are involved in real estate development, construction and engineering consultancy services. In contrast, a sizeable number of Hong Kong firms, especially those involved in garments and textiles, confine their foreign activities to manufacturing, capitalizing on their ownership-specific advantages.

Third, many Singapore multinationals are either state-owned (e.g. Intraco), or have substantial government equity (Keppel Shipyard, National Iron and Steel Mills), while almost all Hong Kong multinationals are privately owned. This difference in ownership influences the way Singapore and Hong Kong multinationals look at international involvement. When investing abroad, Singapore multinationals with substantial government participation take into account the island's development priorities, in addition to other business considerations. Thus, National Iron and Steel Mills views its involvement in California venture capital companies as helpful to the island's effort to upgrade its industrial base. In Hong Kong, this perspective is absent: multinational firms there seek the best investment opportunities, which may not necessarily benefit Hong Kong's industrialization. Because outward investments are more sensitive to national priorities in Singapore than in Hong Kong, they are more likely to have a much greater impact in the long term on the Singapore economy than on the Hong Kong economy.

Fourth, because they are sizeable and largely in labor-intensive industries, Hong Kong manufacturing investments abroad have contributed more to increased employment and technology transfer in Southeast Asia. Hong Kong investments in textiles and garments in Singapore, Malaysia and Indonesia during the 1960s and 1970s created many unskilled jobs in these countries. In contrast, Singapore manufacturing investments abroad (excluding those made by developed country firms based in Singapore) have had little impact on employment or technology transfer in host countries.

Finally, both Singapore and Hong Kong multinationals invest or sell technology in the same countries in the Southeast Asian region. For the most part, however, they do not compete in host countries primarily because the two city-states have different industrial bases and therefore invest in different industries abroad. Hong Kong's exports are concentrated in textiles, garments, plastics, toys and watches, while Singapore depends more on petroleum products, electronic components and products, oil rigs, construction, and engineering.

Not only do they not directly compete; in fact, Hong Kong and Singapore firms have cooperated in joint investment projects. One recent example is the joint venture between Singapore's Khong Guan Group (a biscuit company) and the Hong Kong Far East Consortium to establish a biscuit manufacturing plant in China. Hong Kong and Singapore firms have also cooperated in providing engineering services for China's oil exploration activities. In many ways, Singapore's industrial and service skills complement those of Hong Kong; Singapore is strong on construction, oil-related engineering and computer services while Hong Kong's strengths are marketing and entrepreunership.

As Southeast Asia and especially China industrialize, opportunities for Singapore-Hong Kong collaboration in such areas as electronics, computer and engineering services, construction, and tourism will expand. Both Hong Kong and Singapore-owned firms will also enlarge their roles as middlemen in China's quest for technology. China, for example, has approached two Singapore firms "to act as matchmakers to help it attract foreign investments and expand trade".[12] These two firms will organize conferences and trade exhibitions to help the Chinese authorities meet potential foreign investors, negotiate joint ventures, and establish licensing and technology transfer agreements.

CONCLUSIONS

In the last two decades, Hong Kong and Singapore firms have expanded their international involvement. To a great extent, the rise in foreign involvement by firms from these two city-states reflects their rapid economic development. In the case of Hong Kong, the need for additional export platforms for textiles and garments and other light industrial goods has been a powerful factor inducing firms to internationalize. In the case of Singapore, where the domestic market is small and many large firms are in mature industries, diversification and the need for new markets are key factors. Unlike developed countries, both Singapore and Hong Kong have developed very few vertically integrated international firms.

Both Hong Kong and Singapore manufacturing multinationals show a distinct preference for minority equity participation and/or contractual resource transfers. Partly because they are risk-averse and lack proprietary expertise, they do not insist on wholly or majority-owned subsidiaries, even when such modes of investments are permitted by the host country.

Though Hong Kong and Singapore multinationals share similar characteristics, they also show important differences. These differences—the larger role of state-owned enterprises in Singapore's internationalization, the greater employment and technology transfer contribution of Hong Kong firms in host countries, the greater concentration of Hong Kong multinationals in textiles and garments, etc.—will probably not disappear. In both city-states, however, conglomerates rather than manufacturing multinationals will likely emerge as the main actors in international involvement. Their impact on home and host countries will not only be felt in manufacturing but also in other economic sectors including finance, consultancy, real estate, and tourism. The extent and nature of this impact, of which little is yet known, is a subject which deserves further study.

NOTES

1. These studies include Agmon and Kindleberger (eds.), 1977, Kumar and McCleod (eds.), 1981, Lall (ed.), forthcoming, and Wells, 1983.
2. *Business Times* (Singapore), February 6, 1985.
3. Rajah Komaran, "Singapore Investments in China," MBA Advanced Study Project, National University of Singapore (in progress, July 1985).
4. *Business Times* (Singapore), December 17, 1983.
5. *Business Times* (Singapore), July 4, 1983.
6. *Business Times* (Singapore), July 4, 1983.
7. *Business Times* (Singapore), August 28, 1984.
8. *Business Times* (Singapore), May 4, 1984.
9. *Straits Times* (Singapore), February 8, 1985.
10. *Business Times* (Singapore), July 24, 1984.
11. *Straits Times* (Singapore), April 16, 1984.
12. *Business Times* (Singapore), February 9, 1984.

REFERENCES

1. Agmon, Tamir and Kindleberger, Charles P. (eds.), *Multinationals From Small Countries*, Cambridge, Massachusetts: MIT Press, 1977.
2. Kumar, Krishnan and McCleod, Maxwell G. (eds.), *Multinationals from Developing Countries*, Lexington, Mass., D.C. Heath and Co., 1981.
3. Lall, Sanjaya (ed.), *Third World Multinationals*, London: Wiley, forthcoming.
4. Raj, Agarwal, "Multinationals from the Newly-Industrializing Countries: A Study of the Foreign Operations of Listed Singapore Firms," in *Proceedings of the Academy of International Business International Meeting in Singapore*, June 14-16, 1984, pp. 1015-1034.
5. Wells, Louis T., Jr., *Third World Multinationals: The Rise of Foreign Investment from Developing Countries*, Cambridge, Massachusetts, MIT Press, 1983.

APPENDIX TABLE 1

Foreign Activities of Singapore Multinationals by Country and Mode of Investment, 1985

Country of Foreign Investment	Mode Of Investment							
	Wholly-owned subsidiaries	Majority-owned joint ventures	Minority-owned joint ventures	Licensing agreements	Turnkey projects	Technical contracts	Portfolio investment	Total
Malaysia	10	3	24	-	-	–	–	37
Indonesia	–	1	9	-	1	1	–	12
Thailand	–	2	2	-	1	–	–	5
Philippines	–	1	–	-	-	–	–	1
Brunei	1	1	1	-	-	–	–	3
ASEAN (sub-total)	11	8	36	-	2	1	–	58
Hong Kong	3	4	7	-	-	–	3	17
India	–	–	1	-	-	–	–	1
Pakistan	–	–	–	-	-	1	–	1
Bangladesh	–	1	–	-	-	–	–	1
Sri Lanka	–	–	3	-	-	–	–	3
China	–	–	11	-	2	–	–	13
New Zealand	–	–	1	-	-	–	–	1
Australia	–	4	3	-	-	–	2	9
Papua New Guinea	–	1	–	-	-	–	–	1
Tahiti	–	–	1	-	-	–	–	1
Britain	2	–	1	-	-	–	1	4
USA	–	1	1	-	-	–	1	3
Mauritius	–	–	–	-	1	–	–	1
Kenya	–	–	–	-	-	1	–	1
Nigeria	–	–	–	-	-	1	–	1
Oman	–	–	1	-	-	–	–	1
Rest of World (sub-total)	5	11	30	-	3	3	7	59
Total	16	19	66	-	5	4	7	117

Sources: Same as Table 2

[18]

Journal of Development Economics 20 (1986) 381–397. North-Holland

THIRD WORLD MULTINATIONALS

The Characteristics of Indian Firms Investing Abroad

Rajiv LALL*

Florida Atlantic University, Boca Raton, FL33431, USA

Received May 1984, final version received October 1984

This paper uses models of dichotomous choice to distinguish the characteristics of Indian firms that invest overseas from those that do not. It seeks to shed light on the motivations underlying foreign investment by Indian firms and on the nature of the perceived competitive advantage of these firms in their overseas operations.

1. Introduction

Increasing attention has recently been directed to the phenomenon of firms from less developed countries (LDCs) seeking to set up manufacturing operations overseas. Such firms (for which we shall henceforth use the acronym LDCFI) come from the more industrialized countries of South and South-East Asia and Latin America and tend to have subsidiaries that are located almost exclusively in other LDCs.

The literature on the subject of LDCFIs has dealt with two main issues. First is the question of why such firms from LDCs invest abroad. Second is the question of what enables these firms, in their overseas ventures, to withstand competition from local host country firms and multinationals from developed countries (for which we shall henceforth use the acronym MNC).[1]

It appears, from the literature [e.g., Busjeet (1980), Lecraw (1977)], that LDCFIs invest overseas for a variety of reasons. While some venture abroad to take advantage of lower labor costs in other LDCs, others are motivated by the need to circumvent a threat to existing or potential export markets. Still others go overseas in order to escape the constraining effects of domestic government policy.

*This paper upon my research for a dissertation submitted in January 1984, in partial fulfilment of a Ph.D. in Economics at Columbia University. I am grateful to Professors James Albrecht, Michel Amsalem, Jagdish Bhagwati, Carlos Diaz-Alejandro and John Ruggie for comments and suggestions. Thanks are also due to Sanjaya Lall for earlier discussions on the subject and to an anonymous referee

[1] I.e., Multinational Corporations. These are defined, as for instance, by Horst (1972), as firms from developed countries, engaged primarily in manufacturing with several subsidiaries overseas.

Regarding the characteristics of LDCFIs it seems that unlike MNCs, these firms, in their overseas ventures in general, operate at small scales, avoid competition based on advertising, product differentiation and brand names, do not engage in competition based on sophisticated up-to-date technology, and display ownership patterns that are more inclined towards limited equity participation.

It is suggested that the competitive advantage of LDCFIs derives from the fact that they operate almost exclusively in LDC host countries. It is argued that LDCFIs are able to exploit a cost advantage emanating from their extensive use of machinery brought over to the subsidiary from their respective home countries. Such machinery and personnel, it is believed, is cheaper, more flexible and better adapted to LDC conditions than that employed by MNCs. The nature of technical progress does not allow the latter to compete on this turf – a total reorientation of management ideology and marketing strategy along with a process of relearning of long forgotten skills would be necessary for an MNC to offer a technological package similar to that of LDCFIs [Busjeet (1980)]. On the other hand, the local host country firms often do not have access to the entrepreneurial or technical skills to exploit a similar advantage. The popular image of LDCFIs thus suggests that these firms are able to carve out a competitive niche for themselves by offering a technological package that is somehow more appropriate for LDC conditions.

Two comments are in order about these findings. First, they are based mostly on qualitative information collected through inerviews of limited samples of firms. Mainly for lack of data, statistical/econometric analyses have been very limited.[2] Second, the analyses have focused almost exclusively on comparisons between the characteristics of LDCFI subsidiaries and their competitors in the host LDC environment. No attention has been focused on the nature of LDCFIs in relation to other firms in their respective home countries. Such a comparison could extend our understanding of the nature of LDCFIs. Further, since data are usually more easily available for the domestic operations than for their overseas operations, this approach would be more amenable to econometric analysis.

This paper presents such an alternative approach to the analysis of the characteristics of LDCFIs. It is argued that each firm is potentially a foreign investor, i.e., it faces the choice of investing or not investing overseas. In this context, it is possible to describe firm behavior analytically using models of dichotomous choice. The parameters of such models, estimated using maximum likelihood techniques, help distinguish the characteristics of firms that invest abroad vis-à-vis those that do not, and thus to shed light on the nature of LDCFIs. The exercise is here conducted to shed some light on the

[2]The only exception, to my knowledge, is Lecraw (1977, 1981).

nature of Indian LDCFIs. The findings indicate Indian LDCFIs may not conform in some respects to the popular picture of LDCFIs in general.

2. Model and estimation techniques

The literature, it was noted earlier, suggests that LDCFIs invest abroad for a variety of reasons ranging from a need to circumvent threats to exports to a desire to escape the constraining effects of domestic government policy. Whatever the specific reasons for foreign direct investment (FDI) in each case, it is true that firms invest abroad only if they expect to realize some sort of economic gain from doing so. To this extent, a firm's choice to invest abroad must be based on some criterion of rational choice, i.e., on expectations of being able to realize, directly or indirectly, in the short run or long run, some kind of profits from the venture.

In this context, it is hypothesized that each firm can be described by a set of several attributes, each of which may, over time, have evolved differently for different firms. Each firm has, ex-ante, a perception as to which of these attributes might confer upon it a competitive advantage overseas, and thus help it to realize profits from FDI. It follows, in this view, that a firm which possesses more of these attributes is also more likely to be a foreign investor. The purpose of our analysis is to isolate the set of firm attributes that enhance the likelihood of foreign investment by Indian firms, and thus to shed some light on the nature of the 'perceived competitive advantage' of these firms in their overseas operations. Such an approach can indirectly be translated into a model of dichotomous choice.

Consider a dichotomous choice model[3] wherein the two alternatives are to invest abroad or not to invest abroad. The agents of this choice are the individual firms.

Let

$$P(X;\beta) \tag{1}$$

be an expected gain function where X is a vector corresponding to the attributes of individual companies.[4] X does not change over alternatives. β is a vector of unknown parameters.

Let

$$P(X;\beta) = X\beta + \varepsilon, \tag{2}$$

where $\varepsilon \sim N(0, \sigma^2)$.

[3]This model is a slightly modified version of that presented by Dhrymes (1978).

[4]More specifically, the 'expected gain' is defined as the net expected gain to the firm from choosing the location for its marginal unit of investment.

The decision to invest abroad is taken if and only if

$$P(X;\beta)>0, \qquad (3)$$

or, for the ith firm, if and only if

$$X_{i.}\beta+\varepsilon_i>0. \qquad (4)$$

The probability that the firm will invest abroad can easily be determined from the distribution of ε_i and is given by $F(X_{i.}\beta)$ where $F(\cdot)$ is the cumulative distribution function of a $N(0,\sigma^2)$ random variable. If β is estimated imposing the identifying normalization of $\sigma^2=1$, we in fact have a probit model of the form

$$P_i=F(X_{i.}\beta), \qquad (5)$$

where P_i is the probability of success or, in our case, the probability that the ith firm chooses to invest abroad.

In this model the parameters, β, can be interpreted as the impact of various firm attributes on the decision to invest abroad and can be estimated using maximum likelihood methods.

Further, it needs to be noted that estimates of β from (5) are consistent only if $X_{i.}$ is exogenous (or pre-determined). This is not likely to be the case. In particular it is likely that $X_{i.}$ will be correlated with the error term in (2). Since (2) and (5) are interrelated, it follows that the estimates of β in (5) will also be inconsistent. To overcome this problem, it is hypothesized that (2) is one structural equation in an otherwise unobserved model of several simultaneous equations describing the behavior of a firm. If the exogenous variables of such an hypothesized model can be identified, then it is possible to use these as 'instruments' to get consistent estimates for β by simply replacing, in eq. (5), the endogenous members of the vector $X_{i.}$ with their predicted values obtained from regressing each endogenous variable against the complete vector of instruments [Johnston (1972)].

The above analysis of the firm's decision to invest abroad can be extended into the mold of a tobit model [Amemiya (1973)]. While in the probit model, 'success' or 'failure' depends upon a vector of firm attributes, in the tobit model the following situation is hypothesized for the ith firm:

$$\begin{aligned} y_i&=X_{i.}\beta+u_i \quad \text{if} \quad X_{i.}\beta+u_i>0,\\ y_i&=0 \qquad\qquad\ \ \text{otherwise,} \end{aligned} \qquad (6)$$

where y_i is some index of the extent of the ith firm's involvement overseas, $X_{i.}$, β are as before, and u_i is a random variable distributed $N(0,\sigma^2)$.

As in the case of probit, consistent estimates for β can be obtained in the tobit case using maximum likelihood techniques once the endogenous variables of the vector $X_{i.}$ have been replaced, as before, using instrumental variables.

We now have a complete framework for analyzing the perceived competitive advantage of Indian firms in their overseas operations.[5]

3. Sample characteristics

Our sample is drawn from a population of public limited[6] companies on which the Reserve Bank of India has annual balance sheet data for the years 1977–78 and 1978–79.[7] Firms for which data was not available for both years, or for which information was otherwise incomplete, were excluded from our purview. We ended up with a sample of 162 companies of which 24 are foreign investors, i.e., with a sample of 162 observations of which 24 are non-zero. The overseas ventures of these companies span a total of 16 industry groups. The 24 firms are fairly representative of Indian LDCFIs. Together, they account for over 1/3 of the 86 Indian overseas joint ventures in manufacturing industries in production as of July 1982 and almost 2/3 of the industry groups from which FDI has originated [Ministry of Commerce (1982)].

The fact that balance sheets treat firms as financial units restricts our analysis. The problem is that while most of the firms in the sample are multiproduct firms (i.e., their operations cut across several industry groups), the information gathered from balance sheets cannot be meaningfully broken down according to type of industrial activity. This restricts the analysis mainly for the reason that it is not possible to isolate the industry-specific characteristics from the firm-specific characteristics that might affect the decision to invest abroad. In particular, it is not possible to answer the question of why a particular multiproduct firm chooses to invest abroad in one of its industrial activities and not in another.

4. Hypotheses and variables

In order to suppress the effect of possible random shocks and measurement error, all variables are averaged over the two years for which data were available (i.e., 1978–79 and 1979–80). Each variable and its hypothetical impact on the likelihood of foreign investment is discussed in turn.

[5] In actual fact for the purpose of estimation we ended up with a log-linear version of (5) and (6). For details, see R. Lall (1984).

[6] Public limited companies are joint stock companies with a listing in the Stock Exchange Directory of India.

[7] This data was made available to me upon special request – it is not published. I am grateful to the Statistical Analysis Wing of the Reserve Bank of India, Bombay.

Marketing. Earlier studies reveal that LDCFIs, in their overseas operations, avoid competition based on marketing. It would thus seem reasonable to expect that aggressive marketing ability at home would not make a firm more likely to invest overseas. Using expenditures on advertising as a percentage of total manufacturing expenses as our measure (A) of a firm's reliance on marketing, it is expected that our data on Indian firms will reject the hypothesis that A has a positive significant impact on the likelihood that an Indian firm is a foreign investor.[8]

Technological sophistication. Historically, Indian firms have relied on external sources (mainly collaborations with foreign companies) for their technological development. We therefore use the proportion of total manufacturing expenses spent on royalties as a proxy ($RLTY$) for the infusion of up-to-date technology in Indian firms. The evidence suggests that LDCFIs in general do not rely on their technological sophistication for competing in their overseas operations. For the Indian firms to conform to this popular image of LDCFIs we would expect our data to reject the hypothesis that firms spending a large proportion of their manufacturing expenses on royalties are significantly more likely to be foreign investors than other firms not doing so.[9]

Embodied technological adaptation. There are several studies which indicate that the purpose of research and development (R&D) in India is very different from that in developed countries [S. Lall (1981)]. It seems that R&D in India is frequently directed towards changes to imported production/engineering design for the purpose of raw material substitution. Often, the research effort may also involve making minor modifications to product design to take account of the requirements of local consumers. By and large, the R & D effort of individual Indian firms is not geared towards advancing any technological frontiers but rather towards technological adaptation of various kinds that requires making minor changes to machine, process, or product design to make them more suitable for local conditions, i.e., towards 'embodied technological adaptation'.[10] We therefore use the proportion of

[8]Because our data do not permit us to distinguish the impact of industry-specific from firm-specific characteristics on the decision to invest abroad, it is not possible for us to test the stronger hypothesis that Indian firms from industries that require intensive advertising are less likely to invest abroad than firms from industries that do not.

[9]Again, the nature of our data do not allow us to examine the proposition that Indian firms from technology-intensive industries would be less likely to invest abroad than firms from less technology-intensive industries.

[10]The adaptive effort need not be embodied in machine/process design. It could, for example, just be reflected in a changed plant layout or different management orientation. The Indian firms' ability for such disembodied technological adaptation is hard to quantify. For some qualitative evidence on the impact that such an ability has on the incidence of foreign investment by Indian firms, see R. Lall (1984).

total manufacturing expenses spent on R&D as an index (*R*) of an Indian firm's ability to adapt machine and/or process to LDC conditions.

The literature suggests that an important source for the competitive advantage of LDCFIs in general is their ability to use machinery that is better suited to LDC conditions. If Indian firms conform to the popular picture of LDCFIs, our data should support the hypothesis that Indian firms irrespective of their industry of operation, that have a greater capacity for embodied technological adaption are significantly more likely to be foreign investors than other firms with smaller capacities for the same.

Capital–output ratios. The ratio of the value of plant and machinery (undepreciated) to the value of production is used as an index (*K*) of capital-output ratios for individual firms. Given the theoretical and practical difficulties of measuring capital stock and the fact that our data pertains to the overall operations of different firms rather than to specific plants, care must be exercised in interpreting this variable. The index can be viewed as a measure of the fixed cost of capital (plant and machinery) per unit of output, i.e., as the average fixed cost of capital corresponding to a firm's output level. To the extent that average fixed costs must be some function of technology, *K* must reflect the nature of the technological mix used by different firms in their domestic manufacturing plants. To the extent that foreign investors from India set up overseas subsidiaries with plants similar to those operated at home [R. Lall (1984)], some link between *K* and the decision to invest abroad can be hypothesized.

It should, however, be emphasized that this variable is a more reliable indicator of the financial rather than the scale aspects of the technological mix used by different firms.[11] The literature has often neglected the issue of the link between the ability of LDCFIs to raise finances and the nature of technology used by them in their overseas operations. Reports [Raju (1980) and R. Lall (1984)] indicate that severe liquidity constraints prevent Indian firms from investing in projects requiring heavier initial capital investment. From this perspective it can be expected that firms, irrespective of their industry of operation, with plants characterized by technologies requiring heavier average fixed cost investments would be less likely to invest abroad than firms with technologies requiring lower average fixed cost investments.

Firm size. The firm's gross sales receipts are used as a proxy (*GS*) for firm size. An index of firm size could capture the technological and/or non-technological aspects of firm size. The former entails the link between costs

[11]Since differences in the average fixed cost of investment cannot be an accurate reflection of differences in the scale of operation between firms, *K* cannot be used to test the hypothesis that firms using technologies of small scale are more likely to invest abroad.

and the technology of large scale production. The latter refers to such advantages as financial leverage, political contacts, accessibility to information, etc., normally associated with large firms. Inasmuch as large sale receipts do not necessarily imply the use of large scale technology, *GS* is probably a better index of the non-technological aspects of firm size than of its technological aspects.

There is evidence [Raju (1980), Financial Express (1983)] to indicate that Indian LDCFIs have been handicapped, in their overseas operations, by their relatively unknown names and small international presence – this has affected the ability of these firms to gain access to adequate finances in overseas markets. It is therefore likely that the non-technological aspects of large firm size would be of considerable advantage to Indian firms seeking to invest abroad, irrespective of their industry of operation. It is hypothesized that large firm size will, at least for non-technological reasons, have a significant impact on the likelihood that an Indian firm invests abroad.

Managerial and technical personnel. We use the proportion of the total wages bill (salaries, wages and bonus) that goes to 'highly paid employees'[12] as an index (*MAN*) for the extent to which individual firms use highly trained managerial and technical personnel.

The literature suggests that home country personnel is an important source for the competitive advantage of LDCFIs in their overseas operations because they are relatively less expensive, more flexible and better attuned to LDC conditions than the high level personnel used by competing firms. If Indian firms are similar then it can be expected that, in our sample, firms with greater access to highly trained personnel in their domestic operations would be better equipped for foreign investment than other firms in the same industry. It is further possible, for the same reason, that Indian firms in industries that require more highly skilled personnel would be likelier candidates for foreign investment than firms from industries that do not need very skilled personnel (the implicit argument being that firms in skill-intensive industries would have a greater opportunity to exploit a competitive advantage overseas based on the use of highly trained Indian personnel). Our index, *MAN*, reflects both the access of individual firms to highly trained personnel and also the skill requirements specific to each firm's industry of operation. However, the nature of our data is such that it is not possible to distinguish the proportion of the variation in *MAN* that may be due to differences in the access of individual firms to highly trained personnel and that which is due to differences in the skill requirements of each firm's industry. Should our data indicate that *MAN* has a significant impact on the

[12]Indian firms have, by law, to report the earnings of all employees earning in excess of Rs 36,000 (about $3,500) per annum, separately.

decision to invest abroad, the result could support either or both the above hypotheses – it is not possible for us to test each hypothesis separately.

Export performance. The literature suggests that an important reason for foreign investment by LDCFIs is the need to overcome protection in targeted markets. Also within the Indian context, high domestic production costs resulting from government regulatory policy make exports uncompetitive and the option of investing abroad, therefore, more attractive [R. Lall (1984)].

We take the ratio of export earnings to sales as an index (*XS*) of a firm's export performance. In theory, poor export performance could be the result of several factors such as slack demand overseas that need not make foreign investment any more attractive than the option of exporting. There is reason to expect a causal negative link between *XS* and the likelihood of foreign investments only if poor export performance is the result of protection in targeted markets and/or problems related to the domestic production environment that make the option of exporting less attractive than that of investing abroad. Thus, if our data support the hypothesis that *XS* has a negative impact on the likelihood of foreign investment, at acceptable levels of significance, then we can interpret that result as support for the hypothesized trade off for firms, irrespective of their industry of operation, between the option of exporting and that of investing abroad.[13]

Dependence on imported raw materials. It was indicated above that Indian firms may, due to government regulatory policy, find the option of investing abroad more attractive than that of exporting from India. In particular, the evidence suggests that the Government of India's tariff policy makes the cost of imported inputs so high that it has a significantly deleterious impact on the competitiveness of India's exports of manufactured goods [R. Lall (1984)]. In this context it is likely that firms, irrespective of their industry of operation, that are relatively more dependent on imported raw materials would have greater incentive to invest abroad than other firms that are less dependent on the same, and thus can be expected to be likelier candidates for foreign investment. The proportion of manufacturing costs spent on imported raw materials is used as our index (*IMPRAW*) of a firm's dependence on imported raw materials and it is hypothesized that *IMPRAW*

[13]*XS* could, arguably, also have a positive impact on the likelihood of foreign investment – superior export performance might reflect on a firm's superior competitiveness overseas and hence encourage it to invest overseas. Interviews with Indian LDCFIs, however, show that this is unlikely to be the case. The important impulse for foreign investment by Indian firms seems to be the need to overcome difficulties with exports. See R. Lall (1984).

will have a significant positive impact on the likelihood that an Indian firm is a foreign investor.[14]

5. Statistical findings

The results are summarized in four sets of tables, each corresponding to a different set of instrumental variables. The various sets of instruments correspond to different assumptions about the unobserved system of equations assumed to describe the behavior of each firm. A brief outline of the selection criteria for the various instruments is presented in the appendix.

There is a fairly stable discernable pattern in the results across all runs. The results of the probit and tobit are, as they should be, very similar. The variables that consistently perform best are the size and capital–output

Table 1

Summary results: With instrumental variables V.I, size of sample = 162, no. of non-limit observations = 24.[a]

Explanatory variable	Probit $\hat{\beta}$	Tobit[c] $\hat{\beta}T$
A	−0.120 (−0.14)	−4.780 (−0.52)
GS	0.546 (1.21)	4.252 (0.93)
K	−0.380 (−0.44)	−1.577 (−0.18)
R	−0.122 (−0.027)	−12.995 (−0.29)
RLTY	1.620 (0.39)	28.933 (0.69)
IMPRAW	0.395 (1.29)[b]	5.245 (1.60)[b]
MAN	0.192 (0.33)	1.962 (0.334)
XS	−0.807 (−1.48)[b]	−9.508 (−1.67)[b]
Percentage of predictions correct at critical probability of 0.5[d]	85.19	n.a.

[a]Figures in brackets are t-statistics; other figures are estimated coefficients.

[b]Significant at least at the 10% level.

[c]Hurd (1979) shows how estimation from truncated samples could yield inconsistent estimates if the population disturbance term is not homoscedastic. The estimates from the tobit run presented in all tables derive from a likelihood function that takes account of this problem. For methodological details of how the problem of heteroscedasticity was dealt with, see R. Lall (1984).

[d]I.e., in what percentage of cases was the prediction that a firm is a foreign investor correct when estimated probability exceeded 0.5.

[14]In theory a positive statistical relationship between *IMPRAW* and the likelihood of foreign investment could be the result of the desire of firms dependent on raw materials imported from abroad, to integrate vertically by going overseas. Of all the Indian overseas joint ventures in operation as of July 1982, there is not one that, to my knowledge, was set up for the purpose of providing the Indian parent with a necessary raw material. On the other hand, for evidence about the cost of imports having a deleterious impact on the Indian firm's incentive to export, see R. Lall (1984).

Table 2

Summary results: With instrumental variables V.II.

Explanatory variable	Probit $\hat{\beta}$	Tobit $\hat{\beta}T$
A	−0.079 (−0.087)	−1.300 (−0.14)
GS	0.845 (1.77)[a]	8.721 (1.78)[a]
K	−0.949 (−1.44)[a]	−9.747 (−1.47)[a]
R	2.209 (0.60)	23.589 (0.65)
RLTY	−0.191 (−0.06)	−2.588 (−0.085)
IMPRAW	0.030 (0.98)	3.029 (1.01)
MAN	0.339 (0.80)	3.621 (0.86)
XS	−0.754 (−1.25)	−7.478 (−1.29)[a]
Percentage of predictions correct at critical probability of 0.5	87.04	n.a.

[a]Significant at least at the 10% level.

Table 3

Summary results: With instrumental variables V.III.

Explanatory variable	Probit $\hat{\beta}$	Tobit $\hat{\beta}T$
A	0.160 (0.20)	1.224 (0.15)
GS	0.696 (1.85)[a]	6.790 (1.75)[a]
K	−0.356 (−1.19)	−3.900 (−1.30)[a]
R	0.098 (0.069)	2.902 (0.21)
RLTY	0.963 (0.70)	7.936 (0.60)
IMPRAW	0.056 (0.31)	0.785 (0.43)
MAN	0.339 (0.98)	0.847 (0.31)
XS	−0.030 (−0.11)	−0.847 (−0.31)
Percentage of predictions correct at critical probability of 0.5	85.19	n.a.

[a]Significant at least at the 10% level.

indices. These are followed by the indices of export performance and dependence on imported raw materials, in that order. The coefficients of the proxies for a firm's marketing intensity, technological sophistication, capability for embodied technical adaptation and use of highly trained personnel are all insignificant throughout.

It can be shown that the coefficient β_{GS} of our size variable is an estimate of the impact of increasing firm size on the likelihood that a firm invests abroad under the assumption of constant returns to the scale of plant and

Table 4

Summary results: With instrumental variables V.IV.

Explanatory variable	Probit β	Tobit βT
A	0.202 (0.35)	0.570 (0.200)
GS	0.976 (2.98)[a]	5.970 (3.500)[a]
K	−1.085(−1.95)[a]	−6.265(−2.230)[a]
R	3.503 (1.31)[a]	16.327 (1.27)
RLTY	−1.407(−0.70)	−3.679 (−0.37)
IMPRAW	0.189 (1.19)	2.046 (2.27)[a]
MAN	0.165 (0.69)	1.538 (1.23)
XS	−0.579(−1.23)	−3.964 (−1.57)[a]
Percentage of predictions correct at critical probability of 0.5	85.80	n.a.

[a]Significant at least at the 10% level.

machinery used.[15] To this extent the coefficient is likely to be an indicator of the impact of the non-technological aspects of firm size on the likelihood of foreign investment. Our estimates for β_{GS} are consistently positive across all runs and are significant at least at the 10% level in most. We therefore conclude that at least the non-technological aspects of large size significantly enhance the likelihood of foreign investment by Indian firms irrespective of their industry of operation.

It can also be shown that the coefficient β_K of our index of capital–output ratio isolates the impact of an increasing capital–output ratio on the likelihood of foreign investment under the assumption that the level of output remains unchanged.[16] Our estimates for β_K are consistently negative across all runs and are also significant at the 10% level in most of them. Our data seems, therefore, to support the hypothesis that Indian firms, irrespective of their industry of operation, that require high fixed costs of plant and machinery to generate a given level of output are significantly less likely to invest abroad than other firms with plants requiring smaller fixed costs to produce the same level of output. Although this result does not shed any light on the link between the scale aspects of a firm's technological mix and the likelihood of its investing abroad, it does suggest that the financial aspects of the technology used by Indian firms have significant bearing on

[15]In the tobit case, for instance, the result follows by totally differentiating the log-linear version of eq. (6) and then determining what assumptions are necessary to ensure that $\beta_{GS}=(\mathrm{d}y/y)/(\mathrm{d}GS/GS)$.

[16]Totally differentiating the log-linear (6), it can be shown that $\beta_K=(\mathrm{d}y/y)/(\mathrm{d}K/K)$, if it is assumed that firm size and all the other firm characteristics remain fixed as the capital/output ratio changes.

their decision to invest abroad. In particular, this result is consistent with the impression gathered from independent reports that liquidity constraints severely restrict the ability of Indian LDCFIs to invest in projects requiring heavy initial capital investment.

The importance of financial considerations is an issue that has been ignored in the literature and merits further attention. The literature tends to assume that, in a given industry, LDCFIs operate their subsidiaries at smaller scales than their competitors because of a technological preference for small scale technology. Based on the above result, we speculate that financial considerations may play an important part in determining what type of plants are set up by Indian LDCFIs in their overseas operations. Thus, it is possible that Indian LDCFIs tend to operate small plants overseas not because they perceive small scale technology to be more appropriate for their host country markets, but because they lack the finances and liquidity to set up larger operations.

It was argued earlier that only if a firm's poor export performance were the result of protection in targeted markets and/or chronic problems associated with the domestic production environment is there any a priori reason to expect a causal link between poor export performance and the likelihood of foreign investment. The estimates of the coefficient, β_{XS}, of our export performance index are negative across all runs and although their performance is not as impressive as that of the coefficients of our indices for size and capital–output ratios, they do attain significance at least at the 10% level in several of the runs. It appears, therefore, that our data provide some support for our hypothesized incentive for foreign investment arising from poor export performance.

Although the coefficient estimates $\hat{\beta}_{IMPRAW}$ of our index for dependence on imported raw materials are significant in a fewer number of runs, they are consistently positive across all runs. This result is at least consistent with, even if it does not provide very strong support for, the hypothesis that firms that are more dependent on imported raw materials are also more likely candidates for foreign investment. It was argued that, in the Indian context, such a link probably reflects the fact that government tariff policy tends to raise the production costs of firms more dependent on imported raw materials quite significantly, making the prospect of exporting, for such items, less attractive than that of setting up a manufacturing operation overseas.

Elsewhere, $\hat{\beta}_{MAN}$ and $\hat{\beta}_{R}$, the coefficient estimates for our indices for a firm's use of highly trained personnel and its capability for embodied technological adaptation respectively, are throughout insignificant. The non-performance of *MAN* indicates that our data reject the proposition that firms that make relatively greater use of highly trained personnel are more likely to invest abroad than firms that do not. However, this result is not open to precise interpretation. The problem arises because, given the nature of our data, it is not possible to ascertain what proportion of the variation in *MAN* is due to differences in the access of different firms to managerial and technical expertise and what proportion is due to differences in the skill requirements of the industry of each firm's operation. Thus, while Indian firms in skill intensive industries may not be significantly more likely to invest abroad than firms from industries that are not as skill intensive, it is still possible that within the same industry, firms with greater access to managerial and technical expertise are the more likely candidates for foreign investment. Since it is not possible for us to examine such an hypothesis, it would be inappropriate to draw any specific conclusion about the link between *MAN* and the decision of Indian firms to invest abroad.

The non-performance of *R* would seem to indicate that our data reject the hypothesis that Indian firms, irrespective of their industry of operation, that are better equipped for undertaking embodied technological adaptation are more likely to invest overseas than firms not as well equipped for the same. However, it should be emphasized that the process of technological adaptation is very complex and it is possible that the proportion of total sales allocated for R&D may not be an adequate index for an Indian firm's capability for embodied technological adaptation. In this context, it is useful to present our findings from an independent survey of the technological capability of a sample of Indian LDCFIs [R. Lall (1984)]. The survey indicated that aside from raw material substitution and product development, changes to machinery and process design are also undertaken for the purpose of 'trouble-shooting'. Trouble-shooting takes place continuously through a process of learning-by-doing on the shop floor. Unlike raw material substitution and product development, the process does not require formal R&D and so is excluded from our index of a firm's capability for embodied technological adaptation. However, the survey also indicated that all forms of embodied technological adaptation notwithstanding, Indian LDCFIs, in their overseas operations, tend to use Indian machinery only to the extent that it is 'as good as' foreign equipment or to the extent that government regulations force them to do so. The bulk of Indian LDCFIs would prefer that they be allowed, for the purpose of equity participation, to remit cash overseas rather than be forced, as they are almost without exception, by the Government of India, to export capital goods [Indian Investment Centre (1980)] – such a move would reduce the 'forced' dependence on Indian machinery and enable these firms to use foreign equipment more easily [R. Lall (1984)]. Thus, even if a better index of a firm's capability for embodied technological adaptation could be constructed, it is doubtful that it would perform any better than the existing one. We can be reasonably confident that the non-performance of our R&D variable indicates that Indian firms do not perceive their capability for embodied technological adaptation as a source for a competitive advantage overseas and in this respect our evidence pertaining to LDCFIs would seem to contradict the popular notions about LDCFIs in general.[17]

Finally, the estimates of the coefficients of our indices for a firm's marketing intensity and level of technological up-to-dateness are, as expected, insignificant in all runs. Although these results are consistent with the notion that Indian LDCFIs do not, in their overseas operation, compete on the basis of advertising and/or technological sophistication, they do not allow us to draw any strong conclusions. Our data do not permit us to examine the stronger proposition (a) that Indian firms in industries requiring greater advertising would be less likely to invest abroad than firms from other industries that are not as advertising intensive, and (b) that firms from more technology-intensive industries would be similarly less likely candidates for foreign investment than firms from less technology-intensive ones.

6. Conclusions

This paper has attempted to shed some light on the nature of Indian LDCFIs, on why they invest abroad and what characteristics are perceived by them as contributing to their competitiveness overseas.

The statistical findings lend support to the notion that impediments to export performance provide a definite incentive for Indian LDCFIs to venture overseas and are consistent with the hypothesis that these firms do not perceive their competitive strength overseas as deriving from advertising or technological sophistication.

The results also underline the importance of non-technological considerations in the decision to invest abroad. Our evidence suggests that at least the non-technological advantages of large firm size are important to potential foreign investors from India and that these firms may, for reasons of financial stringency, be restricted in their overseas operations to projects involving small fixed costs per dollar of output. It would appear possible, therefore, that the overseas operations of Indian LDCFIs are small not so much because of a technological preference for smaller scale technology (as the existing literature indicates) but because of non-technological constraints. This is an important question that warrants further research. Finally, another question which our analysis raises is the possibility that in the case of Indian LDCFIs, the role of indigenously adapted technology may have been overemphasized in the literature. Our evidence suggests that an Indian firm's capability for embodied technological adaptation is not perceived as a source for competitive strength overseas. It needs to be emphasized however that

[17]This conclusion pertains only to the adaptation effort that is embodied in Indian machinery. A great deal of technological adaptation, as remarked earlier, is 'disembodied'. See R. Lall (1984).

detailed research into the phenomenon is required before a firm conclusion can be reached in this regard.

Our analysis facilitates the testing of a number of hypotheses concerning Indian LDCFIs in a more systematic manner. Even so, it remains deficient in several respects. The principal deficiency arises from the nature of the available data which do not permit us to isolate industry-specific from firm-specific factors affecting foreign investment by Indian firms. Although some of our hypotheses test reasonably well despite this problem, (a) our results do not yield any meaningful interpretation for the link between a firm's access to trained personnel and its decision to invest abroad, and (b) with regard to the role of advertising and technological sophistication, it was not possible to test the stronger hypotheses that Indian firms from industries that are advertising and/or technology intensive are less likely to invest abroad than firms from industries that are not.

Appendix: Outline of criteria for selection of instrumental variables

To select a vector of instruments for the endogenous members of our vector $X_{i.}$, eq. (2) of the text is hypothesized to be part of a larger (albeit unobserved) system of equations describing the behavior of a firm. The exogenous variables of such an hypothesized model can serve as a viable set of instruments.

The following set of variables V.I were considered to be exogenously given to all firms across our sample at time t and thus, suitable for use as 'instruments' in table 2:

(i) value of plant and machinery (PM),
(ii) gross fixed assets (GF),
(iii) net worth (share capital plus reserves) (NW),
(iv) paid-up capital (PC),
(v) energy consumption per unit of output as proxied by energy costs per dollar of output produced ($FUEL$),
(vi) spare parts used per unit of plant and machinery as proxied by expenditure in the former as a proportion of the value of the latter (SP),
(vii) proportion of imported raw materials to total raw materials used ($IMPRAW$),
(viii) the rate of depreciation as proxied by the difference between gross and net value of fixed assets deflated by value of gross fixed assets (DEP), and
(ix) the rate of excise duty as measured by the expenditure on such duties as a proportion of gross sales revenues ($ETAX$).

Having hypothesized this set of 'instruments', there is only one variable *IMPRAW*, in eq. (2) and, therefore, also in (5) and (6), that can be identified as exogenous. The rest are taken as endogenously determined. The set of instruments (i)–(ix) comprise our set V.I corresponding to table 1. The instruments for the remaining tables correspond to assumptions that become progressively more stringent.

For table 2 our set of instruments V.II, includes aside from instruments (i)–(ix), also the variable *MAN*, the share in total sales of salaries to management. Table 3 uses the same instruments as table 2, but in addition, it is assumed that value of output (*VALPR*), sales (*GS*) and hence the capital–output ratio (*K*), are all given exogenously to the firm as well. This could be the case if the firm were operating in conditions in which it was obliged to meet predetermined output and sales targets. Finally for table 4, aside from all the instruments of table 3, the firm's corporate tax bill as a proportion of its value of output (*T*), is used as an additional instrument to comprise V.IV. Firms could make a-priori provisions for taxes on the basis of output and sales targets. In this context, *T* could be considered to be exogenously given for a firm for which its output and sales levels are predetermined.

For further methodological details on the selection of 'instruments', see R. Lall (1984).

References

Amemiya, T., 1973, Regression analysis when dependent variable is truncated normal, Econometrica 41, 997–1016.

Busjeet, V., 1980, The internationalization of firms from LDCs, Unpublished doctoral dissertation (Harvard Business School, Cambridge, MA).

Dhrymes, P., 1978, Introductory econometrics (Springer, New York) 330–331.

Financial Express, 1983, Indian joint ventures abroad: A Financial Express Symposium (New Delhi) July 15.

Horst, T., 1972, Firm and industry determinants of the decision to invest abroad: An empirical study, Review of Economics and Statistics 54, 258–266.

Hurd, M., 1979, Estimation in truncated samples when there is heteroscedasticity, Journal of Econometrics 11, 247–258.

Indian Investment Center, 1980, Indian joint ventures abroad: Government policies (Government of India, New Delhi).

Johnston, J., 1972, Econometric methods, 2nd ed. (McGraw-Hill, Tokyo) 278–281.

Lall, R., 1984, Multinationals from the Third World: The competitive advantage of Indian firms investing abroad, Unpublished doctoral dissertation (Columbia University, New York).

Lall, S., 1981, Exports of technology from India, Draft report (World Bank, Washington, DC).

Lecraw, D., 1977, Direct investment by firms from less developed countries, Oxford Economic Papers 29, 442–457.

Lecraw, D., 1981, Internationalization of firms from LDCs: Evidence from the Asian region, in: Kumar and McLeod, eds., Multinationals from developing countries (Lexington Books, Lexington, MA) 37–52.

Ministry of Commerce, 1982, Indian joint ventures abroad (Government of India, New Delhi).

Raju, M.K., 1980, The emerging multinational – Indian enterprise in the Asian region (M.K. Raju Consultants, Madras).

[19]

Vol. XVII, No. 2 *Journal of Southeast Asian Studies* *September 1986*

Singapore Corporations Go Transnational

LIM MAH HUI and
TEOH KIT FONG

Introduction

The title of this paper is influenced by that of Lee Soo Ann's book, *Singapore Goes Transnational.*[1] However, the subject matter of this paper though related, is quite different. By Singapore "going transnational", Lee was referring to how Singapore's economy became dominated by foreign transnational corporations (TNCs). During that process and period, local Singaporean companies declined in importance.[2] This paper deals with the resurgence of Singaporean companies to the extent that some have spread their operations to other countries and have attained the status of TNCs.

Even though a few Singaporean companies have been operating as TNCs since the sixties, it was not until after the mid-seventies that the transnationalization of Singaporean companies began to gather momentum. In fact in the first half of the seventies, one of the major concerns of many writers[3] was how the growing dominance of foreign companies had displaced and contributed to the decline of local industries. Yoshihara showed that between 1966–72, foreign firms in Singapore increased their share of the number of manufacturing establishments from 10 per cent to 17 per cent, their share of employment from 25 per cent to 44 per cent, and their share of total output from 42 per cent to 60 per cent, while the share of local manufacturing firms declined concomitantly.[4] However, Yoshihara observed that even though Singaporean firms declined in their relative position, they managed to make some progress in establishing industries either on their own or as partners with foreign firms in joint ventures.[5] Most of Singapore's industrial firms (both pioneer and non-pioneer) were established after 1961, when the first serious effort at industrialization was undertaken.[6] Nevertheless, Yoshihara concluded his book with a note of concern and identified some of the difficulties facing Singaporean companies. In particular, he noted that the growth of domestic

[1]Lee Soo Ann, *Singapore Goes Transnational* (Singapore: Eastern Universities Press, 1977).

[2]The definitions of foreign and local (Singapore) firms follow that of the Singapore Statistics Department. Foreign-controlled firms are those where 50 per cent or more of equity is owned by foreigners and local-controlled firms are those where 50 per cent or more of equity is owned by Singaporeans.

[3]Kunio Yoshihara, *Foreign Investment and Domestic Response* (Singapore: Eastern Universities Press, 1976); Lee Soo Ann, *Singapore Goes Transnational.*

[4]These statistics are based on the *Report of Census of Industrial Production* published by the Singapore Statistics Department. The Census covers only manufacturing establishments which employ 10 or more workers. Yoshihara, *Foreign Investment and Domestic Response,* p. 180.

[5]Of the 435 foreign-controlled firms, half had Singapore equity participation. Yoshihara, *Foreign Investment and Domestic Response*, p. 148.

[6]Yoshihara, *Foreign Investment and Domestic Response*, p. 148.

industrial exports has been borne mainly by foreign firms; that Singapore needs to reduce her dependence on foreign investments; and that Singaporean firms would face stiff barriers in their attempts to establish overseas markets.[7] Lee also shared the same concern when he concluded that "There are many lessons which domestic companies can learn from transnationals and what would be disturbing is the total withdrawal of such companies as if there is no role for them to play in the future."[8]

More recent data indicate that some of these fears have been attenuated. Though the relative position of Singapore's companies have not improved, they have not declined further. Furthermore, a number of Singaporean companies have been successful in penetrating export markets, not only through direct exports but also through direct investments and the sale of technology. In other words, it can now be said that a significant number of Singapore's leading companies have gone transnational. Hitherto, this phenomenon has scarcely been studied.

This paper seeks to analyze the emergence of Singaporean TNCs. It is divided into three sections. The first section sketches the changes in the general economic conditions of the country and the government policies which influenced the regeneration of Singapore companies. The second part estimates the overall value of Singapore's overseas investments and their industrial and geographical distribution. The last part is a case study of some of these Singapore TNCs: it examines the characteristics of such firms, the reasons they invest abroad, the advantages and disadvantages they face, and compares these characteristics with those of TNCs from First World countries.

Changes in the Economy, 1960–80

As late as 1960, the Singaporean economy was still predominantly based on trade: 31 per cent of its gross domestic product (GDP) was accounted for by trade and only 13 per cent by manufacturing.[9] Singapore's first serious attempt at industrialization was rooted in the idea of servicing the domestic market. This was particularly influenced by the prospect of Singapore's entry into the Federation of Malaysia and the availability of the common market of Malaysia. The Economic Development Board was established in 1961 as the principal vehicle to spearhead this industrialization process. It provided infrastructural facilities as well as incentives for firms to invest in manufacturing activities. In 1959, the Pioneer Industries Ordinance and the Industrial Expansion Ordinance were passed granting tax exemptions to firms involved in selected manufacturing industries and products. During this time, Japanese and American firms began to move into Singapore in anticipation of the Federation of Malaysia's expanded market as well as the regional market of Southeast Asia.[10] Between 1960–65, import substitution industrialization was the basic strategy for industrial growth. But this proved to be short lived, for by 1965 Singapore had separated from Malaysia and, given her small domestic market, Singapore's industrial growth had to rely on the export market.

From 1965 onwards, Singapore embarked on an aggressive path of export-oriented industrialization based mainly on foreign investments. Various laws were introduced towards this end: the Economic Export Incentive Act of 1967 for example granted tax concessions on profits from export of domestic products. Concessions were given to

[7]Ibid., pp. 164–65.

[8]Lee Soo Ann, *Singapore Goes Transnational*, p. 40.

[9]Singapore, Statistics Department, *Economic and Social Statistics 1960–1982* (Singapore: Statistics Department, 1983), Table 4.3.

[10]Lee Soo Ann, *Singapore Goes Transnational*, chapter 3.

encourage the inflow of foreign capital and technology and supporting changes in labour and educational policies encouraged the inflow of foreign investments. In 1968 the Employment Act and the Industrial Relations Act were amended to reduce the cost of labour as well as the economic and political power of labour.[11] The educational system was restructured with more emphasis given to vocational and technical training to create a more skilled labour force.

The emphasis given to foreign investment was based on the belief that foreign firms would provide the bulk of the capital, technology and markets for industrial growth, which they did. Between 1966–75, foreign capital accounted for 42 per cent of the total Gross Domestic Capital Formation;[12] and in 1970 foreign firms made up 84 per cent of the direct exports of domestic manufacture.[13] Measured by other indicators, the position of foreign firms rose dramatically while that of local firms declined. Between 1966–76, the amount of foreign investment (measured by Gross Fixed Assets) rose sixteen fold — from S$239 million to S$3,739 million (see Table 1). Comparing the position of foreign to local firms during the period of 1968–76, we find that foreign firms increased their share of the number of manufacturing establishments from 12 per cent to 22 per cent; their share of the manufacturing employment from 26 per cent to 54 per cent; and that of total manufacturing output from 46 per cent to 73 per cent, while that of local firms declined proportionately (see Table 2).

A number of factors were responsible for the relative decline of local firms: most of the incentives given by the government tended to favour the larger companies which also happened to be foreign companies;[14] the Economic Development Board concentrated its attention on attracting foreign rather than local investments; and government infrastructures tended at times to undercut the smaller local industries.[15]

The above policies produced rapid economic growth (GDP tripled between 1965–75) but it was clear that Singapore's economy was highly dependent on foreign investments and painfully vulnerable to international economic forces, its fortunes rising and falling in lock step with world recovery and recession. Table 3 shows that even though foreign investment commitments increased in the long run and in absolute terms, they dropped during the world recessions of 1974 and 1982. The drastic drop in foreign investment commitment in 1974 to S$169 million made it necessary for local investment, particularly government investments, to take up the slack. It was perhaps this realization of the need to reduce Singapore's over-dependence on foreign investment, and that the decline of local industries could pose long-term problems for more self-sufficient growth that prompted the government to pay more attention to the development of local industries. In 1977, Goh Chok Tong, the then Minister of State (Finance) stressed that "if we are going to make it on our own steam ... we should have our own expanding pool of

[11]The critical need for cheap and docile labour was forcefully articulated by a leading Japanese investor, Mr. Isobe, president of the Japanese Chambers of Commerce: "There are ... certain barriers to foreign investment in Singapore. Firstly, Singapore's domestic market is small. Japanese investors will have to be attracted to Singapore on the competitiveness of her export oriented industries. And the biggest deterrent to international competitiveness is labor cost ..." cited in Frederic Deyo, *Dependent Development and Industrial Order* (New York: Praeger, 1981), p. 57.

[12]Lee Soo Ann, *Singapore Goes Transnational*, p. 15.

[13]Chia Siow Yue, "Export Performance of the Manufacturing Sector and of Foreign Investment", in *Singapore in the International Economy*, ed. Wong Kum Poh and Maureen Tan (Singapore: Singapore University Press, 1972), p. 45.

[14]For example, pioneer status was granted only to companies with more than S$1 million capital. This quota was however reduced a few years later.

[15]Deyo, *Dependent Development and Industrial Order*, pp. 65 ff.

TABLE 1
FOREIGN INVESTMENT IN MANUFACTURING INDUSTRY OF SINGAPORE (GROSS FIXED ASSETS) 1965–82
(in S$ million)

	1965	1966	1967	1968	1969	1970	1971	1972	1973	1974	1975	1976	1977	1978	1979	1980	1981	1982
Food & Beverage	9	25	26	29	31	31	54	70	93	113	123	130	143	176	211	241	301	363
Textile & Garments	7	14	14	46	47	45	116	156	175	220	235	230	255	256	342	366	341	173
Paper & Wood	3	6	6	9	33	35	97	124	172	206	201	195	209	222	309	351	385	267
Chemicals	5	12	22	28	30	61	107	124	126	141	171	202	176	188	250	295	443	587
Petroleum	99	115	145	195	265	555	752	1,158	1,267	1,336	1,426	1,520	1,617	2,304	2,627	3,160	3,490	3,903
Metal Engineering, Machinery & Equipment	19	34	44	64	78	34	56	89	176	258	327	435	509	617	661	823	1,012	1,278
Electrical & Electronics	1	4	7	9	21	82	149	215	249	316	354	412	505	620	938	1,212	1,498	1,868
Others	14	29	39	74	95	152	244	347	401	464	543	615	731	859	1,011	1,072	1,169	1,214
Total	157	239	303	454	600	995	1,575	2,283	2,659	3,054	3,380	3,739	4,145	5,242	6,349	7,520	8,639	9,653

Sources: Singapore, Economic Development Board, *Annual Reports 1982/3*; Chia Siow Yue, "Export Performance of the Manufacturing Sector and of Foreign Investment", in *Singapore in the International Economy*, ed. Wong Kum Poh and Maureen Tan (Singapore: Singapore University Press, 1972), p. 67.

TABLE 2
PRINCIPAL STATISTICS OF MANUFACTURING INDUSTRY IN SINGAPORE, BY CAPITAL STRUCTURE, 1968, 1976, 1982

	1968				1976				1982			
	Number Establishments (%)	**Number of Workers (%)**	**Output (%)**	**Direct Exports (%)**	**Number Establishments**	**Number of Workers**	**Output**	**Direct Exports**	**Number Establishments**	**Number of Workers**	**Output**	**Direct Exports**
Wholly Local	80.5	58.7	41.1		66.7	31.3	17.1	8.5	63.8	30.1	17.3	9.3
More than half local	7.8	15.1	12.7		11.3	14.9	9.8	6.7	10.7	14.0	8.9	7.1
Local Controlled	88.3	73.8	53.8		78.0	46.2	26.9	15.2	74.5	44.1	26.2	16.4
Less than half local	5.7	13.7	13.4	N.A.	9.5	20.1	14.6	15.4	9.0	13.8	19.0	18.7
Wholly foreign	6.1	12.4	32.7		12.5	33.7	58.5	69.3	16.4	41.6	54.8	64.9
Foreign Controlled	11.8	26.1	46.1		22.0	53.8	73.1		25.4	55.4	73.8	83.6
Total %	100.0	100.0	100.0		100.0	100.0	100.0	100.0	100.0	100.0	100.0	100.0
Total (Actual Values)	1,586	74,833	2,176		2,505	207,234	15,317	9,575	3,586	275,450	36,476	21,858

Note: The actual values for output and direct exports are in S$ million.
Source: Singapore, Statistics Department (SSD), *Report of Census of Industrial Production*, various years.

TABLE 3
INVESTMENT COMMITMENTS IN SINGAPORE BY COUNTRY OF ORIGIN
1972–82
(in S$ Million)

	1972	1973	1974	1975	1976	1977	1978	1979	1980	1981	1982
USA	25	9	65	46	93	154	147	260	506	677	514
Japan	79	151	45	24	76	129	158	319	140	225	94
Europe	22	44	28	167	50	48	419	161	360	258	403
Others	31	20	32	10	41	32	42	83	215	170	150
Total Foreign	157	224	169	247	260	363	766	823	1221	1330	1160
Total Local	38	72	123	60	43	34	47	120	205	599	592
GRAND TOTAL	195	296	292	306	303	396	812	943	1426	1929	1752

Note: Totals may not add up due to rounding errors.
Source: Singapore, Economic Development Board, *Annual Report 1982/3*, p. 12.

local entrepreneurs.... We must identify the reasons for the slow emergence of local industrialists...." This concern was echoed in the following year by Finance Minister Hon Sui Sen, who noted that "we have yet to see any substantial development of local entrepreneurial ability in the manufacturing sector".[16]

Recognizing the decline in domestic investment after 1973 and the discontent of local industrialists, the government began to take steps to encourage the development of local industries. In November 1976, a Small Industries Finance Scheme was instituted to provide loans at low interest to assist small industries (those with fixed assets of less than S$200,000) to modernize, upgrade and diversify their operations. Between 1976–83, a total of S$248 million of loans were granted under this scheme.[17] In 1978 the Product Development Assistance Scheme (PDAS) was introduced to assist local manufacturers to develop new products and processes so as to improve their competitive ability in the export market. Under this scheme, local firms could apply for a grant to cover up to 50 per cent of the direct development cost of their products (but not exceeding S$200,000 per project).[18] In the same year, two Singaporean manufacturers were given such grants to develop high resistance metal film resistors and hydraulic shears.[19] Two other schemes introduced were the Skills Development Fund (SDF), which provided financial assistance to local companies to upgrade their manpower resources;[20] and the Small

[16]Cited in Deyo, *Dependent Development and Industrial Order*, p. 71.
[17]Singapore, Economic Development Board, *Annual Report 1982/3*, p. 6.
[18]Singapore, Economic Development Board, *Annual Report 1982/3*, p. 42.
[19]Singapore, Economic Development Board, *Annual Report 1978/9*, p. 3.
[20]As of March 1983, S$16 million have been awarded to 319 local companies. Singapore, Economic Development Board, *Annual Report 1982/3*, p. 6.

Industries Technical Assistance Scheme (SITAS) which assisted local companies in acquiring foreign technology. Under the latter scheme, up to 90 per cent of the approved cost of engaging foreign technical assistance and consultancy would be reimbursed.[21] In 1981, another scheme was introduced to upgrade the technological capabilities of foreign as well as local firms in Singapore. The government made available a fund of S$50 million to be used for supporting major research and development projects to companies which collaborated with public institutions in conducting research and development.[22]

Given the rather modest sums of money allocated to the development of local industries, it is difficult to assess the exact impact of such programmes on the development of technological capabilities of local firms or the growth of local investments. Local firms are still mostly concentrated in the low level technology industries. In 1982, of the 4,674 locally controlled manufacturing establishments, 21 per cent were in wood and paper, 19 per cent in textile, garments and leather, 12 per cent in fabricated metal, 10 per cent in food and beverage, and 9 per cent in transport equipment industries.[23] In terms of other indicators, local investors have either stabilized or improved their positions. The investment commitments of local firms increased three-fold between 1980 to 1981, constituting about 40 per cent of the total investment commitments (Table 3). Comparing the position of local with foreign firms, we find that after their initial decline between 1968–76, their position stabilized between 1976–82. They accounted for 26 per cent of the manufacturing output, 44 per cent of the manufacturing employment, 75 per cent of the manufacturing establishments and 16 per cent of the direct exports (Table 2).

It was also in the late part of the 1970s that Singapore's companies began to spread their wings and ventured abroad more aggressively.[24] It is to the examination of these Singapore TNCs that we now turn our attention.

Value of Singapore's Overseas Investments

According to Table 4, the value of Singapore's overseas investments around 1982 within Asia was US$469 million, making it the second largest Third World Asian investor in Asia, after Hong Kong. However, two-thirds of these investments are concentrated in Malaysia. Mutual investment between Singapore and Malaysia may not be the best representation of true foreign investment because Singapore was once part of Malaysia. But it is also clear that most of Singapore's investments flowed into Malaysia long after their separation. Although Singapore's investment in Malaysia amounted to only US$44 million in 1974, in 1978 it rose to US$95 million and then to US$309 million in 1980.[25]

Singapore's investments in the rest of Asia amounted to US$164 million of which US$111 million and US$21 million flowed into Indonesia and Hong Kong respectively. The Philippines and Sri Lanka each received US$12 million, and Thailand accepted US$5 million. A comparison of these estimates with figures cited from other sources indicate

[21]Singapore, Economic Development Board, *Annual Report 1982/3*, p. 6.

[22]Singapore, Economic Development Board, *Annual Report 1982/3*, p. 41.

[23]Singapore, Statistics Department, *Report of Census of Industrial Production, 1982* (Singapore: Statistics Department, 1983), Table 29.

[24]A number of older and more established Singapore companies such as Fraser and Neave, Lam Soon, Yeo Hiap Seng and Malayan Breweries (all food and beverage companies) have had manufacturing operations in Malaysia since the 1960s.

[25]Malaysia, Federal Industrial Development Authority (FIDA), *Annual Reports, 1974, 1978, and 1981*. FIDA was later renamed MIDA — Malaysian Industrial Development Authority.

TABLE 4
DISTRIBUTION OF STOCK OF DIRECT OVERSEAS INVESTMENT, BY COUNTRY & INDUSTRY (in US$ million)

HOST COUNTRY	INDONESIA		MALAYSIA		THAILAND		HONG KONG		SRI LANKA		PHILIPPINES		TOTAL
	(1982)		(1980)		(1981)		(1981)		(1982)				
	$	%	$	%	$	%	$	%	$	%			
Industry													
Manufacturing	64.5	(58)	—	—	2.3	(47)	20.5		—	—			
Food & Beverage	N.A.		110.8	(36)	—	—	5.6	(27)	9.3	(80)	N.A.		
Textile & Leather	N.A.		32.5	(11)	0.8	(16)	3.6	(17)	0.8	(7)	N.A.		
Wood & Paper	N.A.		23.7	(8)	—	—	—	—	0.15	(1)	N.A		
Chemicals & Petroleum	N.A.		34.1	(11)	0.1	(2)	0.3	(1)	0.3	(3)	N.A.		
Non-metal	N.A.		43.2	(14)	1.3	(27)	—	—	—	—	N.A.		
Metal	N.A.		34.2	(11)	—	—	10.6	(51)	0.01	*	N.A.		
Electrical & Electronic	N.A.		10.2	(3)	—	—	0.2	(1)	—	—	N.A.		
Transport Equip.	N.A.		18.7	(6)	—	—	—	—	0.02	*	N.A.		
Other Mfdg	N.A.		0.3	*	—	—	0.1	(1)	0.1	(1)	N.A.		
Agriculture & Forestry	10.9	(10)	N.A.		1.5	(31)	N.A.		—	—	N.A.		
Mining	—	—	N.A.		—	—	N.A.		—	—	N.A.		
Construction	1.1	(1)	N.A.		—	—	N.A.		—	—	N.A.		
Trade	28.2	(25)	N.A.				N.A.		—	—	N.A.		
Hotel	—	—	N.A.				N.A.		—	—	N.A.		
Finance & Insurance	—	—	N.A.				N.A.		—	—	N.A.		
Real Estate	6.7	(6)	N.A.		1.1	(22)	N.A.		0.2	(2)	N.A.		
Other Services	—	—	N.A.				N.A.		0.7	(6)	N.A.		
Others	—	—	N.A.		—	—	N.A.		—	—	N.A.		
TOTAL	111.4	(100)	308.7	(100)	4.9	(100)	20.5	(100)	11.7	(100)	11.8	(100)	469.0

Source: ESCAP/UNCTC, "Survey of Activities of Transnational Corporations from Asian Developing Countries" (mimeo, 1984).

that they under-estimate the amount of Singapore's investments abroad.[26] According to more recent newspaper reports, Singapore's investments in Indonesia, for example, rose from US$112 million to US$140 million between 1979 and 1981. The bulk of this capital was invested in the manufacturing sector, and primarily in the chemical industry, followed by metal, food, and timber industries.[27]

In another case, Singapore's investment in Thailand was reported by the Board of Investment of Thailand to be US$5 million while another source showed the net inflow of direct investment from Singapore for the period between 1970–80 to be worth 1,485 million baht (roughly US$70 million).[28]

A recent visit to Singapore by a team of Sri Lanka officials further illustrates the problem of under-estimation. The team reported that Singaporeans have invested more than US$300 million in about 60 projects in that country, placing Singapore among the top 10 investors in that country.[29]

Industrial Distribution

An examination of the industrial distribution of Singapore's investments, in countries where data permit comparison across all sectors, suggest that more than half of her investments are made in the manufacturing sector: 47 per cent for Thailand, 58 per cent for Indonesia and 92 per cent for Sri Lanka (Table 4). For Malaysia, even though such data are not available, we can surmise that Singapore holds a critical position in Malaysia's manufacturing sector: Singapore is the largest foreign investor in that sector, surpassing Japan which invested $257 million and the United Kingdom, $232 million.[30]

Most of Singapore's investments in neighbouring countries, such as Malaysia, Indonesia, Thailand, and the Philippines, are aimed at serving the local markets rather than exporting to third countries. The food and beverage sector is the most important industry in Singapore's overseas investment, forming 36 per cent of her investments in Malaysia, 27 per cent in Hong Kong, and 80 per cent in Sri Lanka. The textile and non-metal sectors are also considerable in most of these countries. Even in the case of the investments in textile industry, production is geared toward the local market rather than for export. It is only recently, with Sri Lanka and Bangladesh, that Singapore's overseas investments have concentrated on exportation to a third country.

In summary, from the scattered pieces of information available, one finds that Singapore is a major investor in Asian developing countries. It is ranked as the largest foreign investor in Malaysia, among the top 10 investors in Sri Lanka, and second in terms of intended capital investment in Indonesia for 1981. In terms of industrial distribution, manufacturing forms more than half of her overseas investments in many of these host countries. The two most important manufacturing industries are food and textile, both of which are also the most developed industries locally.

---

[26]The value of Singapore's investments in Table 4 refers only to investments made through the Board of Investment of the respective countries. This often applies only to protected industries. However this could be substantially less than the total investments in the receiving country, accounting for the differences in some of the figures cited.

[27]*Business Times* (Singapore), 7 October 1982.

[28]It should be noted that investments reported by the Board of Investment represents only the pioneer industries and forms a small portion of the total industry.

[29]*Straits Times* (Singapore), 27 November 1983.

[30]FIDA, *Annual Report 1981*.

Case Studies

To what extent are some of these generalizations based on aggregated data supported by case studies of Singapore TNCs and what are some of the distinctive features of these TNCs? What follows is an attempt to shed some light on these issues with a brief analysis of 18 Singapore TNCs. It should be noted from the outset that these 18 companies do not represent a random sample of Singapore TNCs. The selection of this sample was done in the following manner: a list of Singapore's corporations with overseas operations was first constructed from two publications — the Singapore Stock Exchange Handbook and the Directory of the Singapore Manufacturers' Association. This was then supplemented by information provided by knowledgeable journalists and officials from the Manufacturers' Association. A short questionnaire was then sent to these companies, 30 per cent of which responded. This was then followed up with interviews. There were seven firms which granted us personal interviews. Further information was collected from these and other firms, from newspapers, business magazines, and company reports. Based on these different sources of information, we present a preliminary analysis of 18 Singapore TNCs, most of which are among the largest companies in Singapore.

The corporations under study can be divided into two categories: industrial/manufacturing companies and conglomerates. The first refers to companies whose activities are concentrated in a few products or services such that it is possible to identify them unambiguously as belonging to a particular industry or sector. This type of corporation resembles the traditional transnational corporations from the First World which originated as manufacturing companies and acquired competitive advantage as they grew. This enabled them to expand overseas in fields which were closely related to their main product line. In our sample, 12 companies fall under this category; 6 are in the food and beverage industry, 2 in the electrical/electronics fields, and 1 each in publishing, plastics, glass, and shipping. Some of the more well known of these companies are Yeo Hiap Seng, Gold Coin Ltd., Acma Electrical Industries Ltd., and Times Publishing Ltd.

Conglomerates

The second category, conglomerates, consists of companies whose subsidiaries and associates are engaged in a wide variety of industries and sectors so that it is difficult to classify them as belonging to a particular industry. We have classified 6 of the companies on our list as conglomerates: Haw Par Brothers International Ltd., Wah Chang International Ltd., Jack Chia-MPH Ltd., Intraco Ltd., Joo Seng Group, and Keck Seng Group. These companies share one common characteristic: they began not as manufacturing firms but as trading concerns and then over a period of time accumulated enough capital and connections to diversify into different sectors which may or may not be vertically related to their original activity. This is well illustrated in the case of Jack Chia-MPH Ltd. This company began as a partnership venture between Jack Chia, who immigrated from China to Thailand after the World War, and Sakol, a Chinese Thai. In 1948 they started two small companies (with a dozen employees) which were engaged primarily in trading and secondarily in the production of toiletries and local pharmaceutical products. After 1959 the company expanded into Malaysia and Singapore. In 1962 a company was established in Malaysia for importing pharmaceutical products from Western multinationals to sell locally and eventually this firm expanded all over Malaysia and Singapore. By 1969 Chia and Sakol shifted their headquarters from Malaysia to Singapore and in 1972 they took a major step by acquiring MPH Ltd., a public company which in turn bought out their own private company, Jack Chia Co. (Singapore) Pte. Ltd. Through this reverse takeover process, the private company became public overnight and stepped up its expansion and diversification program regionally as well as sectorally. In a matter of about 10 years the Jack Chia group had moved beyond trading and pharmaceutical manufacturing into mining, logging, hotels, property development, garment manufacturing, book publishing and distribution, finance, insurance, and management of sports and recreational complexes. Presently, the group has operations in Singapore, Malaysia, Thailand, Hong Kong, Indonesia, the Philippines, Taiwan, Australia and the United Kingdom. It has over 3,000 employees and a group turnover of US$33 million (not including the group sales of Jack Chia International Ltd., a separate company based in Hong Kong but ultimately owned by Jack Chia).

The history and structure of this Singapore based transnational corporation is noteworthy because it reveals a number of features peculiar to Third World Asian TNCs. The most salient of these is the conglomerate structure. The conglomerate structure deserves special mention not only because it is characteristic of Asian TNCs (including the Japanese ones) but because it represents a trend that has begun to affect First World TNCs. In the last 10 years we find traditional transnational corporations like Exxon, and DuPont diversifying into activities that bear little relationship to their original product line. But perhaps the best example is R. J. Reynolds, a cigarette manufacturer that has ventured into different industries through the acquisition of Del Monte (fruits), Heublein (alcohol), Seal and Services (shipping), Kentucky Fried Chicken (food retailing), and Aminoil (petroleum).[31]

Conglomerates are also desirable because they offer a strategy to escape market size limitation (characteristic of small Asian markets) and enable companies to better withstand any rough business tides by shifting resources into whatever sector is most profitable at any given time. As Jack Chia himself declared, "diversification is the philosophy of not putting all your eggs in one basket".[32] Conglomerates also increase the ability of companies to undermine their competitors through the practice of cross-subsidization, whereby they shift profits from one product line to subsidize another and can therefore underprice their competitors.[33] Most of the literature written on transnational corporations has thus far not come to grips with this phenomenon, but it should be taken into account as one of the important competitive advantages that Asian transnationals possess and is worthy of more study. Some of the features of Singapore TNCs will be examined next.

Size

It is conventionally observed that the TNCs tend to be large companies enjoying economies of scale, market leadership, financial resources, and technological capabilities which provide them with a competitive edge over their smaller counterparts.[34] This characteristic is borne out in our sample: 10 of the companies were listed among the top 40

[31]John Cavanagh and Frederick Clairmonte, "From Corporations to Conglomerates: A Review of Multinationals over the Last Twenty Years", in *Multinational Monitor* (Jan. 1983): 16–19.

[32]*Management Journal*, Jan./Feb. 1982: 5.

[33]Richard Barnet and Ronald Muller, *Global Reach* (New York: Simon and Schuster, 1974); Cavanagh and Clairmonte, "From Corporations to Conglomerates".

[34]Stephen Hymer, "The International Operations of National Firms: A Study of Direct Investment" (Ph.D. diss., Massachusetts Institute of Technology, 1960); Charles Kindleberger, *American Business Abroad: Six Lectures on Direct Investment* (New Haven, Conn.: Yale University Press, 1969).

companies in Singapore.[35] These large corporations tend to be conglomerates with total assets ranging from US$60 million (Intraco) to US$163 million (Haw Par Brothers). Measured in total assets Haw Par Brothers was ranked 9th, Jack Chia-MPH 24th, and Intraco 28th among the top companies in Singapore in 1981. The total assets of the other three conglomerates are not available, but in the case of Wah Chang, total sales for the group reached US$200 million, placing it within the top five companies in Singapore when ranked by sales. This is all the more spectacular considering the fact that Wah Chang is still a privately owned company. Conversely, the size of the manufacturing companies are relatively small, although a few of them have assets of over US$100 million (Malayan Breweries and Pan Electric, before its collapse in Nov. 1985).

A number of the manufacturing firms such as Malayan Breweries, Gold Coin, Prima Flour, Acma Electrical, Yeo Hiap Seng, Lam Soon, and Times Publishing are market leaders in their respective industries and enjoy monopolistic advantages that enable them to move into international territories through exports, direct investments and technological licensing. For example, Prima Ltd. first began production of flour in the early sixties when Singapore embarked on import substitution industrialization. Limited by a small domestic market (of which Prima controlled 60 per cent), it soon began to export to Malaysia, Indonesia, and other parts of Asia. This was followed by the establishment of factories in Malaysia and Indonesia and most recently in Sri Lanka. In Sri Lanka, Prima is Singapore's largest investor. Its two principal ventures are Prima Ceylon (four mill) and Ceylon Grain Elevators (animal feed), which reflect a total investment exceeding US$50 million. Yeo Hiap Seng is another case in point of a leading manufacturer (this time of canned food) that expanded overseas. Initially, Yeo's expansion took the form of export, but this was soon followed by direct investments and more recently with technological licensing. Instead of equity investments Yeo provides technology to establish manufacturing plants which will produce and sell products under their brand name.

One important exception where size was not a significant advantage was Lamipak Industries; until it was wound up in January 1986, Lamipak was a relatively small company with paid-up capital of US$0.9 million and total sales of US$13.6 million in 1978. Due to extensive resources invested in research and development, Lamipak managed to make some significant technological breakthroughs in the plastics industry; it had set up a plant in Ireland where it would have manufactured multilayer plastic film for the European market and licensed its technology to a number of European firms.

In sum, when viewed from the point of size, many of Singapore's prominent TNCs are market leaders in their home country or large conglomerates that are industrially diversified with vast resources at their disposal. These huge corporations enjoy monopolistic advantages which facilitate their ability to expand overseas. There are, however, a few exceptions to this trend.

Ownership and Organizational Structure

All of the companies in this study, with the exception of Wah Chang International, have become limited public companies. But it is also the case that they are controlled by a few major shareholders: families or government agencies. For example, Prima Ltd. is controlled by the Chang family, Jack Chia-MPH Ltd. by Jack Chia, and Yeo Hiap Seng Ltd. by the Yeo family. In at least two of the companies, Intraco and Keppel Shipyard, the Singapore government has controlling interests. There also exist significant cross-

[35] *Asian Finance*, Dec. 1982.

holdings among some of these companies: the Jack Chia group owns over 10 per cent of Haw Par Brothers, Ltd., Prima Ltd. owns 15 per cent of Intraco Plantation, a subsidiary of Intraco; and Acma Electrical owned 33 per cent of Pan Electric Industries Ltd.

The overwhelming and continued dominance in many of these corporations by a few individuals or families shape the organizational structure of the companies which in turn affect their growth and stability. The Jack Chia group which represents well the organizational mode of other Asian Third World TNCs effectively illustrates this point. Organizationally, this group can be divided into three independent segments although they are ultimately controlled by Jack Chia through his personal holding company (see Chart 1). The first part is Jack Chia-MPH Ltd. based in Singapore which owns companies in Malaysia, Indonesia, Australia, etc.; the second part is Jack Chia International, a Hong Kong based TNC in which Jack Chia-MPH Ltd. has no equity holdings. The two parent companies, however, jointly own some of the group's overseas ventures. An example is Jack Chia properties (Australia) Pte Ltd., whose ownership is equally divided between these two parent companies. Finally, the third part consists of a number of privately owned companies operating in Thailand which are legally and organizationally separate from the other two TNCs.

The existence of different organizational entities, the concentration of decision making power in the hands of one individual, and the management of a diversified and internationalized conglomerate along the methods of a traditional family enterprise are quite characteristic of Third World Asian TNCs. These factors, however, present formidable obstacles to the rationalization and growth of these corporations. The problem is even more acute in the case of some Asian TNCs (e.g., the Liem Brothers group in Indonesia, Wah Chang International of Singapore, and Charoen Pokphand group of Thailand) that have not yet become public limited corporations. The dominance of family ownership and management will limit the future expansion of these corporations. In the early stage of corporate development, such family-managed corporations were useful, allowing for flexibility in growth. However, as these corporations expand, they require more financial resources and managerial talents than can be provided by family members and friends. There is a need for these corporations to become publicly incorporated. Unless the owners of these family enterprises are willing and able to make such a transition, their future may not be bright.

The diverse organizational centres of the Jack Chia group reflects another quality of Third World Asian TNCs, i.e., the ethnic connections among Chinese businessmen in Asia. In many developing Asian countries, Chinese businessmen form an important sector of local business communities. It is often their linguistic, ethnic, personal, and family connections that enable the Chinese to establish business ventures in different countries more freely — a set of competitive advantages not available to others. In these case studies of Singapore TNCs, three companies started their operations outside Singapore and eventually moved their base to Singapore while retaining their operations in the place of origin. In these cases, the ethnic background of the owners was more salient than their national origin. For instance, Jack Chia, a Chinese Thai, operates out of Singapore but continues to have substantial interest emanating from Thailand and Hong Kong. In the case of Prima Ltd., the company was started by Chinese-Indonesians, the Chang family, who moved to Singapore in the 1960s to establish their business. They retained substantial business concerns in Indonesia, until the early 1980s when they were forced to divest their interests in Indonesia. Finally, the Wah Chang group which is owned by the Ho family (Singaporeans) began most of their business in Thailand and

CHART 1
OWNERSHIP STRUCTURE OF JACK CHIA GROUP

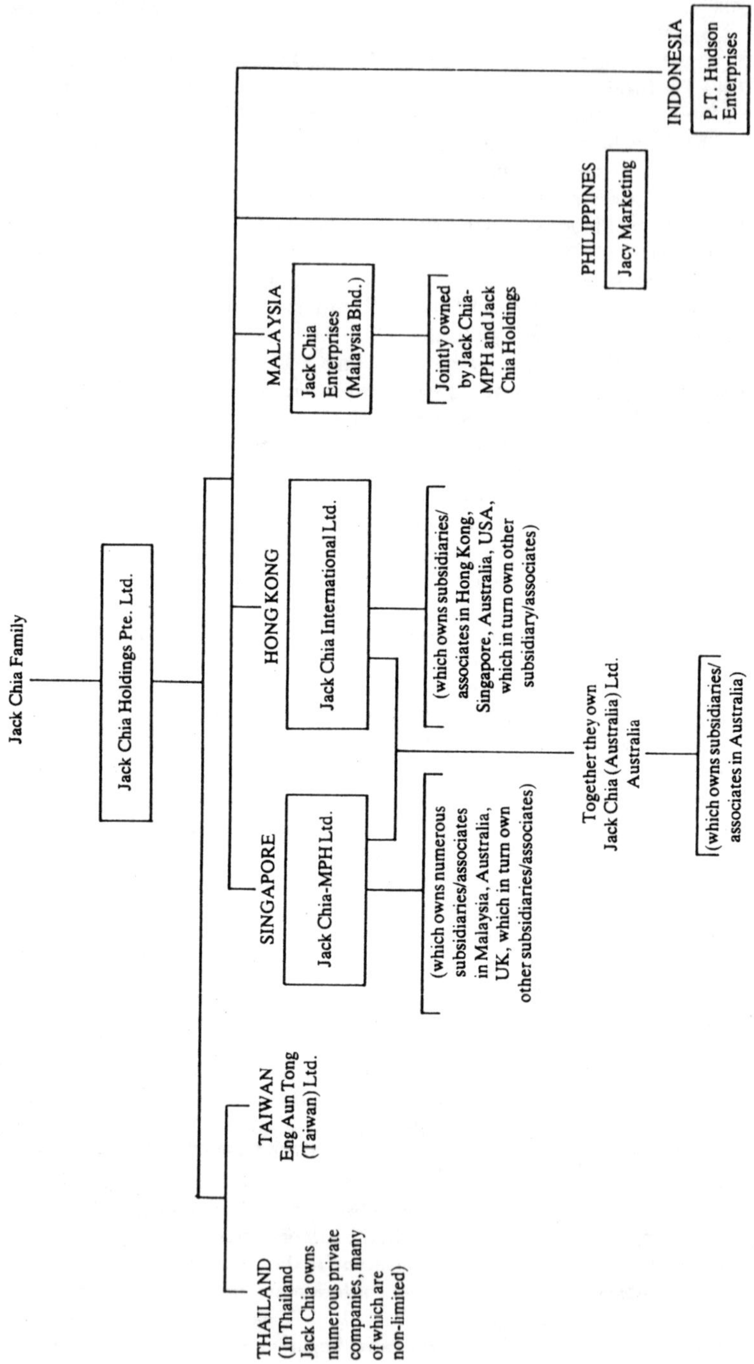

only subsequently moved to Singapore. The group still retains substantial interests in Thailand. This clearly indicates ethnic connections as an important advantage which facilitates the diversification of Chinese business throughout Asia; a factor which has not been adequately studied.

Geographical and Industrial Distribution of Affiliates of 18 Singapore TNCs

A simple way of getting an idea of the geographical and industrial activities of Singapore's TNCs is to examine the number of ventures (affiliates) that these companies have abroad. Tables 5 and 6 contain selected information on affiliates of these companies. It should be emphasized that these include only those companies for which we have public information. Unfortunately, information on the value of their investments abroad are difficult to obtain, and often confidentiality is warranted even when available. Table 5 shows that an overwhelming number of overseas affiliates in this sample of Singapore TNCs are located in Asia. Of the 126 overseas affiliates known to exist, only 16 are situated outside Asia: 4 in the United Kingdom, 7 in Australia, and 5 in the U.S.

Malaysia alone hosts 51 of these ventures and Hong Kong 34 (these include subsidiaries of the overseas affiliates). Of the 51 companies in Malaysia 15 are manufacturing concerns, with 10 in the food and beverage industry. This distribution concurs with the pattern from the aggregate data in Table 4. Trading companies followed manufacturers in frequency (a total of 14) and they were primarily involved in the distribution of goods produced by Malaysian plants.

The overseas ventures in the other parts of Southeast Asia are evenly distributed, with 5 in Indonesia, 5 in the Philippines and 4 in Thailand. In Indonesia, the companies predominantly represent the electrical and food industries, whereas in the Philippines 2 companies are involved in agricultural plantations and 2 in services, and in Thailand of the 2 manufacturing firms 1 produces textiles and the other chemicals.

In East Asia, Hong Kong is the most important base for Singapore TNCs. Most of the large companies have either trading, finance, or investment holding companies there. The large number of service oriented companies in Hong Kong is exaggerated by the chartering and marine service companies of Pan Electrical Industries (see Table 6). Significantly, most of Singapore's TNCs do not have manufacturing firms in Hong Kong as Hong Kong's import substitution industries are highly developed. Furthermore, Hong Kong is no longer considered an attractive base for export promotion. Only Yeo Hiap Seng, Haw Par Brothers, and Jack Chia have manufacturing concerns in Hong Kong.

In contrast to Hong Kong, China is fast becoming an important recipient of Singapore's industrial investments — both in the form of direct investment and technological agreement. At least 5 of the companies in this sample have sizeable manufacturing projects in China. In 1980 Wah Chang built a turnkey factory in Hunan to manufacture televisions and provided China with new technology, equipment and components to establish a consumer electronics factory. Through its subsidiary, Wah Chang International Marine Industry Co. (WIMIC), an equitable joint venture between Wah Chang and Guangdong Shipbuilding Corporation will finance the building of jack-up rigs under a license from Bethlehem Steel, USA. Another company, Zhong Chang Offshore Marine Service Co. Ltd. — a joint venture between Wah Chang, a U.S. company and China's Nan Hai Oil Joint Service Group — will be formed to supply oil vessels for oil exploration in the South China Sea.

Gold Coin Ltd. has a joint venture, Far East Gold Coin Feedmill (China), in which the

TABLE 5
DISTRIBUTION OF OVERSEAS AFFILIATES OF 18 SINGAPORE TNCs BY INDUSTRY & REGION

COUNTRY/ REGION/ INDUSTRY	Elec- trical	Food	Textile	Chemical	Mining	Agricul- ture	Other Mfdg.	Trading	Invest- ment	Property	Hotel	Services	Total
Indonesia	3	1	—	1	—	—	—	—	—	—	—	—	5
Malaysia	2	10	—	2	1	8	2	14	2	2	1	7	51
Thailand	—	—	1	1	—	—	—	1	1	—	—	—	4
Philippines	—	—	—	—	—	2	—	1	—	—	—	2	5
Hong Kong	—	1	1	2	—	—	—	4	3	2	—	21	34
China	—	1	—	—	—	2	—	—	—	—	—	—	3
Taiwan	—	—	—	1	—	—	—	—	—	—	—	—	1
Sri Lanka	—	2	—	—	—	—	—	—	—	—	—	—	2
Bonnei	—	—	—	—	—	—	—	—	—	—	—	1	1
S. Pacific	—	1	—	—	—	—	—	—	1	—	—	—	2
U.K.	—	—	—	2	—	—	—	1	1	—	—	—	4
Australia/N.Z.	—	—	—	—	—	—	—	1	1	3	—	2	7
U.S.	1	—	—	—	—	—	—	—	—	4	—	—	5
Others	—	—	—	—	—	—	—	—	—	—	—	2	2
Total	6	16	2	9	1	12	2	22	9	11	1	35	126

Source: ESCAP/UNCTC, "Survey of Activities of Transnational Corporations from Asian Developing Countries" (mimeo, 1984).

TABLE 6
SELECTED INFORMATION ON 18 SINGAPORE TRANSNATIONAL CORPORATIONS

Company (Parent)	Activities	Paid-up Capital	Total Assets	Total Turnover	Country	Overseas Subsidiaries/Associated Companies: Name of Company	% share by parent	Activities/Products
		(US$ million)						
1. ACMA Electrical Industries Ltd (Established 1961)	Manufacture of refrigerators & air-conditioners	$11 (1981)	$47.7 (G) (1981)	$52.7 (G) (1981)	Indonesia	P.T. Jaya Ital	40%	Mfd of electrical appliances
					Malaysia	OYL	20%	As above and technological licensing
					China	Turnkey project — agreement with Guangzhou Refrigerator factory to set up pilot plant		
					Philippines	Technical licensing agreement with Silicor Management Corp.		
					Thailand	Technical assistance agreement with Compact International		
					Nigeria, Kenya, Pakistan, Sri Lanka	Technological agreements for manufacture and sale of refrigerators and air-conditioners		
2. Amoy Canning Corp (1927)	Food canning	N.A.	N.A.	N.A.	Hong Kong, Philippines, Malaysia			
3. Gold Coin Ltd (1975)	Manufacture of animal feed & pharmaceutical distributor	$13.6 (1981)	$10.2 (1982)	$144.5 (1982)	Malaysia	Gold Coin (Malaysia) Bhd	100%	Mfd of feedmill
						Gold Coin Saranak Bhd	100%	Mfd of feedmill
						F.E. Zuelling (Msia) Bhd	100%	Marketing
						Wang Emas Sdn Bhd	100%	Dormant
						Bintawa Fishmeal Factory	63%	Dormant
						Gold Coin Sabah Sdn Bhd	100%	Dormant
					Hong Kong	Gold Coin Hldgs (HK) Pte Ltd	100%	Investment
					Indonesia	P.T. Subur Gold Coin Indonesia	80%	Mfd of feedmill
					China	Far East Gold Coin Feedmill (China)	55%	Poultry and pig feeding & feedmill

TABLE 6 (*Cont'd*)

Company (Parent)	Activities	Paid-up Capital	Total Assets (US$ million)	Total Turnover (US$ million)	Country	Overseas Subsidiaries/Associated Companies: Name of Company	% share by parent	Activities/Products
4. Haw Par Brothers International	Conglomerate — trading, manufacturing of textile & pharmaceutical, financial & travel services	$56.4 (1981)	$162.7 (G) (1981)	$142.3 (G) (1981)	Malaysia	Setron (M) Bhd	58%	Mfd & distribution of TV & electrical goods
					Malaysia	Haw Par Consumer Prdts SB	58%	Distribution of above products
					Malaysia	Setron Sales & Svcs (M) SB	58%	Same as above
					Malaysia	Drug Houses of Aust (M) SB	58%	Marketing pharmaceutical products
					Malaysia	Asian Computer Svcs SB	58%	Data processing services & software products
					Malaysia	Scott & English (M) SB	58%	Trading in engineering & electrical equipment
					Malaysia	Robert Wilson Jamil (M) SB	44%	Trading of sportswear
					Malaysia	Setron Electronics (M) SB	51%	Trading electrical products
					Hong Kong	Haw Par Bros Int'l (HK)	100%	Holding company
					Hong Kong	Venmor Estate	51%	Property leasing
					Hong Kong	Mandaria Textile	100%	Trading of garments
					Hong Kong	Ying Tai (Far East)	100%	Mfd of garments
					Hong Kong	Dynasty Salons	100%	Distribution of garments
					Hong Kong	Robertson Wilson & Co	60%	Trading sportswear
					Hong Kong	Haw Par Tiger Balm Int'l	50%	Mfd & distribution of pharmaceutical
					Thailand	Haw Par Brothers Int'l (Thailand)	100%	Investment
					Indonesia	D.T. Sanyo Industries (Indonesia)	32.5%	Mfd & distribution of consumer goods
5. Intraco	Conglomerate involved in: —Trading —Manufacture of garments, roofing material, furniture	$13.6m	$87m (G)	$60m (G)	Malaysia	Kedah Marble	20%	Marble Quarrying
					China	Palm oil plantation & milling in joint venture with Guthries and China		
					Sri Lanka	Palm oil plantation, joint venture with Guthries (project stalled)		

(cont'd overleaf)

TABLE 6 (*Cont'd*)

Company (Parent)	Activities	Paid-up Capital	Total Assets (US$ million)	Total Turnover (US$ million)	Country	Overseas Subsidiaries/Associated Companies: Name of Company	% share by parent	Activities/Products
	—Plantations —Timber & marble extraction —Shipping —Property —Services— insurance, tourism					Bangladesh Garment manufacture (not yet in operation)		
6. Jack Chia-MPH Ltd	Conglomerate involved in: —Manufacture of pharmaceutical & confectionary, textile —Book publishing & distribution —Hotel —property —Services— finance —Recreation	$27.3m (1982)	$31.4 m (G) (1982)	$90m (G) (1982)	Malaysia	Jack Chia Enterprises (Malaysia) Bhd	N.A.	Investment holding
						Subsidiaries & associates of Jack Chia (Malaysia) Bhd:		
						—Hudson Malaysia SB	100%	Mfd of pharmaceutical confectionary
						—Jacy Metal Industries SB	100%	Mfd sprinkler corks
						—Jack Chia & Co (Msia) SB	100%	Distribution of consumer products
						—MPH Bookstore SB	100%	Retailing of books & publishing
						—MPH Distributors SB	100%	Wholesaling of books & publishing
						—MPH Magazine SB	100%	Publishing
						—Punjab Tin Dredging SB	100%	Investment
						—Eastern & Oriental Htl SB	87.5%	Hotel & property dev.
					Philippines	Jacy Marketing (Philippines) Inc.	100%	Distribution
					Indonesia	P.T. Hudson Indonesia	100%	Pharmaceutical mfd.
					Taiwan	Eng Ann Tong (Taiwan) Ltd	100%	Pharmaceutical mfd.
					Thailand	Chi Seng Co	100%	Trading
						Thai Enterprise Ltd	100%	Pharmaceutical mfd.
						Design Thai	100%	Garment mfd.
					Australia	J.C. Properties (Australia) Pty Ltd	100%	Property development
						Jacy Investment (Australia) Pty Ltd	100%	Property development

TABLE 6 (*Cont'd*)

Company (Parent)	Activities	Paid-up Capital	Total Assets	Total Turnover	Country	Overseas Subsidiaries/Associated Companies: Name of Company	% share by parent	Activities/Products
		(US$ million)						
					U.K.	J.C. Hudson Ltd	50%	N.A.
					Hong Kong	Jack Chia & Co (Hong Kong) Ltd	100%	N.A.
						Jack Chia Industries (Asia) Ltd	100%	N.A.
						Tsuen Wan Shing On Estate Co Ltd	100%	N.A.
						Apollo Finance & Invst.	100%	N.A.
						Medipharma Ltd	100%	Pharmaceutical mfd
						Antoner Ltd	100%	
						Claymore Investment Ltd	50%	Investment
						Artamus (HK) Ltd	50%	N.A.
						Lesbury Enterprise Ltd	50%	N.A.
						Star of Siam (HK) Ltd	50%	N.A.
						Design-Thai (HK) Ltd	N.A.	N.A.
7. Joo Seng	Conglomerate — trading, manufacturing, hotel, property	N.A.	N.A.	N.A.	Malaysia	Malaysian Feedmills	N.A.	Mfd & distribute animal feedmills
					Malaysia	Tong Kwang Feedmill	79%	As above
					Malaysia	Ben (Johore) SB	100%	
						Hatchery (M) SB	41.7%	
8. Keck Seng & Co Ltd (1943)	Conglomerate — trading in agricultural products & plantations, property development	N.A.	N.A.	N.A.	Malaysia	Keck Seng (Malaysia) Bhd	N.A.	Agricultural plantation & housing development
					Malaysia	Subsidiaries of Keck Seng (Msia) Bhd		
						— Johore (Masai) Plantation SB	100%	Oil palm estate
					Malaysia	— Kota Tinggi Oil Palm Plantations SB	100%	Oil palm estate

(*cont'd overleaf*)

TABLE 6 (*Cont'd*)

Company (Parent)	Activities	Paid-up Capital	Total Assets (US$ million)	Total Turnover (US$ million)	Country	Overseas Subsidiaries/Associated Companies: Name of Company	% share by parent	Activities/Products
					Malaysia	—Lian Huap Oil Palm Plantation SB	100%	Oil palm estate
					Malaysia	—Sin Lian Oil Palm Plantation SB	100%	Oil palm estate
					Malaysia	—Plantation & development (M) SB	100%	Oil palm estate
					Malaysia	—Keck Seng Development Pte Ltd	100%	Investment & housing developer
					Philippines	Agusan Plantation Industr.	40%	Oil palm estate
						Another plantation project in Agusan del Sur	40%	Oil palm estate
					China	Nanhai Plantations Pte Ltd	N.A.	Oil palm estate
						(joint venture with China and other groups: Sim Lim group & Guthrie)		
9. Keppel Shipyard Ltd	Marine Conglomerate	$68m (1983)	N.A.	N.A.	Philippines	Keppel-Philippines	93.4%	Ship-repairing
						Shing Loong Credit (Pte) Ltd	100%	Leasing
					Malaysia	Sobrin-Kapal SB	49%	Shipping
					Hong Kong	Solid Pacific Finance	39%	Finance
					Cayman Islands	Kep Corporation Inc.	100%	Finance
10. Lamipak Industries Pte Ltd (1970–86)	Manufacturer of plastic products	$0.9m (1978)	N.A.	$13.6m (1978)	U.K.	Lamipak Industries (Europe) Ltd	100%	Manufacture of plastic products & technological licensing
11. Lam Soon Soap & Oil Manufacring (1971)	Manufacturer of oil, soap, detergent, canned food	N.A.	N.A.	$18–23m (1981)	Malaysia, Thailand, Indonesia	Lam Soon Ras manufacturing plants in these countries		

TABLE 6 (*Cont'd*)

Company (Parent)	Activities	Paid-up Capital	Total Assets (US$ million)	Total Turnover (US$ million)	Country	Overseas Subsidiaries/Associated Companies: Name of Company	% share by parent	Activities/Products
					Malaysia	Syarikat Ladang Tenggara SB (joint venture with Pahang Tenggara Development Authority)		Cocoa plantation and processing factories
12. Malayan Breweries (1931)	Beer manufacturer	$29m	N.A.	N.A.	Malaysia	Malayan Breweries (Malayan) SB	100%	Beer manufacturing
					Malaysia	Malaya Glass Factory	21.4%	Glass manufacturing
					Papua New Guinea	Pacific Holdings Ltd	100%	
						Malayan Breweries through SP Holdings will acquire San Miguel (PNG) for $1.3 million		
13. Pan Electric Industries Ltd (1960–85)	Manufacturer of electrical appliances, engineering equipment and supply of marine products	$14m	N.A.	N.A.	Brunei	Alpha Marine Ltd	100%	Vessel owning & charter
					Brunei	Kuala Belait Shipyard Ltd	58%	Service of vessel
					Brunei	Marine Services Ltd	67%	Vessel owning & charter
					Brunei	Khidmat Laut (B) Co Ltd	40%	N.A.
					Malaysia	Anrite Communications (SB)	95%	N.A.
					Malaysia	Selco (Malaysian) SB	26%	N.A.
					Malaysia	Selco Shapada (M) SB	25%	N.A.
					Bermuda	Asian Marine Ltd	100%	Vessel owning & charter
					Bermuda	Eastern Marine Ltd	67%	Vessel owning & charter
					Bermuda	Selco International Ltd	100%	Holding company
					Hong Kong	Celosmarine Ltd	100%	Vessel owning & charter
					Hong Kong	Coselmarine Ltd	100%	Vessel owning & charter
					Hong Kong	Coselocean Ltd	100%	Vessel owning & charter
					Hong Kong	Coselsalvage Ltd	100%	Dormant
					Hong Kong	Escolmarine Ltd	100%	Vessel owning & charter
					Hong Kong	Maritime Emergency Consortium Ltd	100%	Marine consultancy
					Hong Kong	Selco (HK) Ltd	100%	Vessel servicing

(*cont'd overleaf*)

TABLE 6 (*Cont'd*)

Company (Parent)	Activities	Paid-up Capital	Total Assets (US$ million)	Total Turnover (US$ million)	Country	Overseas Subsidiaries/Associated Companies: Name of Company	% share by parent	Activities/Products
					Hong Kong	Selco Salvage Ltd	100%	Marine salvage
					Hong Kong	Valetmarine Ltd	100%	Vessel owning & charter
					Hong Kong	Victormarine Ltd	100%	Vessel owning & charter
					Hong Kong	Vigourmarine Ltd	100%	Vessel owning & charter
					Hong Kong	Vipermarine Ltd	100%	Vessel owning & charter
					Hong Kong	Vistamarine Ltd	67%	Vessel owning & charter
					Hong Kong	Viscountmarine Ltd	100%	Vessel owning & charter
					Hong Kong	Vixenmarine Ltd	100%	Vessel owning & charter
					Hong Kong	Vortemarine Ltd	100%	Vessel owning & charter
					Hong Kong	Khidmat Laut (HK) Co Ltd	40%	N.A.
14. Prima Ltd. Flour Mills (1961)	Flour milling Shipping Restaurant Finance Real estate	$13.6 (1982)	$78.6 (G)	$22.7 (G)	Indonesia	P.T. Prima Indonesia (sold out)	100%	Flour milling
					Sri Lanka	Ceylon Grain Elevators Ltd	40%	Flour milling
						Prima Ceylon	40%	Flour milling
					Australia	Prima Holdings	100%	Investment & Property Development
15. Times Publishing Bhd	Printing & distribution of newspapers and books	N.A.	N.A.	N.A.	Malaysia	Federal Publs. SB	100%	Book & Magazine Publshg.
						STP Distr. (M) SB	100%	Service
						Berita Book Centre SB	30%	Book retail
						Berita Pub. SB	30%	Publishing
						Penerbitan Inthomas SB	49.9%	Holding investment
					Hong Kong	Asian Pacific Press (HK) Ltd	100%	Publishing
						Far East Publications Ltd	100%	Publishing
						Federal Pubs (HK) Ltd	100%	Publishing
						Times Distrbtrs (HK) Ltd	100%	Servicing
						Far East Trade Press Ltd	77.4%	Trade magazines
						Asia Bulletin Ltd	50.0%	Research Publication
						Asia Magazines Ltd	30.1%	Magazine publication

TABLE 6 (*Cont'd*)

Company (Parent)	Activities	Paid-up Capital	Total Assets (US$ million)	Total Turnover (US$ million)	Country	Overseas Subsidiaries/Associated Companies: Name of Company	% share by parent	Activities/Products
15. Times Publishing Bhd					Brunei	Brunei Press Ltd	100%	Newspaper
					Australia	Times Entrp. (Aust) PL	100%	Investment
						Macquarie Library Pty Ltd	50%	Publishing
						Rainbow Products Ltd	30%	Book distribution
					U.K.	Marshall Cavendish Ltd	100%	Investment
						STP (London) Ltd	100%	Servicing
					New Zealand	A.H. & A.W. Reed Ltd	46.5%	Publishing
					Tahiti	Hachette Pacifique SA	30%	Publishing
					Oman	Mazoon Printing Press	20%	Printing
16. United Industrial Corporation	Manufacturer of detergent products, property development and trading	$8m	N.A.	N.A.	USA	Has 4 companies in US involved in real estate with GPA of $7m		
					Malaysia	United Detergent SB	45%	Manufacturer of detergent & toiletries
17. Wah Chang International Corp. (S) Pte Ltd.	Conglomerate — —manufacturing of tapioca flour, electronic components —TV assembly —engineering & construction —trading —oil rigs —real estate	N.A.	N.A.	$200m (G) (1982)	Malaysia	Wah Chang Intern'1 (Malaysia) Corp	100%	Trading & Eng Svc
					Malaysia	Syarikat Hitec SB	N.A.	TV Assembly
					Thailand	6 companies — combined GFA $4.7m — engaged in trading & manufacturing of jute, vermicelli, starch, tapioca flour. Engaged in joint ventures with Americans and Chinese in supply of oil vessels and rigs for oil exploration. Wah Chang also built a turnkey factory in Hunan and supplied technology for manufacture of TVs.		
					Taiwan	Engaged in trading, engineering and construction		
					USA	Companies involved in trading & manufacturing of computer colour printers		
18. Yeo Hiap Seng Ltd (1955)	Manufacturer of soft drinks & canned food	$35 (1981)	$66.4 (1981)	$105 (1981)	Malaysia	Yeo Hiap Seng (Malaysia) Bhd	34.1%	Manufacture of food and beverage
						Subsidiaries of Associates of Yeo Hiap Seng (Msia) Bhd		

(cont'd overleaf)

TABLE 6 (*Cont'd*)

Company (Parent)	Activities	Paid-up Capital	Total Assets (US$ million)	Total Turnover (US$ million)	Country	Overseas Subsidiaries/Associated Companies: Name of Company	% share by parent	Activities/Products
					Malaysia	—Leong Sin Mam Farms Bhd	100%	Livestock rearing & meat processing
						—Yeo Hiap Seng (Sarawak) SB	100%	Food & beverage mfd
						—Yeo Hiap Seng (Perak)	100%	Food & beverage distr
						—Wahtai Realty SB	100%	Property investment
						—Yeo Hiap Seng (Malacca)	100%	Food & beverage distr
						—Permanis SB	35%	Beverage mfd & distr
						—Senawang Edible Oil SB	23.9%	Palm oil processing
					Hong Kong	General Bottling Co	68%	Beverage mfd
					USA	Banly Food Inc (sold out)		
						Operations in USA & Canada are limited to trading and promoting exports		
					Indonesia Mauritius	In both countries Turnkey projects and provision of technical and management expertise for setting up food and beverage plants		

Note: G refers to consolidated group accounts.

Source: ESCAP/UNCTC, "Survey of Activities of Transnational Corporations from Asian Developing Countries" (mimeo, 1984).

company has 55 per cent interest in the company with the remaining equity held by Far East Flour Mill, Hong Kong. The company is engaged in the breeding of poultry and pigs and in the production of animal feed in the Shekou Industrial Zone. Acma Electrical won a five-year agreement to set up a turnkey plant for the Guangzhou Refrigerator Factory (GRF). GRF has already ordered Acma's machinery, costing more than US$1.5 million though the sum may eventually exceed $10 million.

Finally, Keck Seng, Intraco, and other partners (Guthries Bhd. and the Sim Lim group) are involved in oil palm planting and milling in China through their associated company Nanhai Plantations Pte. Ltd. This company reportedly will provide US$30 million for the Chinese venture called Chiengmai Oil Palm Plantation Ltd. for the cultivation of 9,340 hectares of oil palm on Hainan Island and for establishing a milling plant. Intraco, a trading company, is interested only in the end product — edible oil, for trading purposes.

South Asia is becoming a more important investment outlet for Singapore's TNCs. The role played by the South Asian countries is primarily one of export platform, though some of the ventures do serve the local market. In this region Sri Lanka is the most important base for Singapore's TNCs. Prima Ltd. set up Prima Ceylon to maintain its market share which was threatened by the import barrier imposed by Sri Lankan authorities. Acma Electric has activities in Sri Lanka and Pakistan which produce refrigerators based on technological contracts. In Bangladesh, Intraco plans to establish a garment factory to produce jeans for export to Third World countries.

Outside Asia, most of these companies, with few exceptions, confine themselves to trading. Jack Chia-MPH has in recent years shifted its emphasis to property investment with Australia as its prime site. Its importance in Australia is reflected in a recent decision by the Australian government to grant the company a waiver for the purchase of Australian property of up to A$30 million.[36] Wah Chang is the only company in this sample with manufacturing activities in the U.S. This is partly because of its links with its forerunner company, Wah Chang Corp., which was engaged in tungsten production in the U.S. Yeo Hiap Seng established a food canning plant in California, but after one unsuccessful year the operation ceased. Lamipak had a subsidiary in Ireland to produce plastics and to license technology to other European countries. And Malayan Breweries has expanded into the South Pacific region by buying San Miguel Papua New Guinea.

Singapore TNCs have not made direct investments in Africa. But companies such as Acma Electrical are active in supplying technological know-how and components for the assembly of refrigerators and air conditioners to Nigeria and Kenya while Yeo Hiap Seng has undertaken a turnkey project to build a food factory in Mauritius.

In sum, Singapore TNCs concentrate their overseas activities around the Asian region where they possess advantages in terms of their knowledge of the region and the close ethnic, personal, and family ties that the Chinese business community enjoy throughout Asia. In China, investments by overseas Chinese are actively encouraged and this had led to a flurry of Singapore investments into China. In only a few cases have Singapore TNCs ventured into manufacturing operations in the West. Those TNCs that have expanded into other developing countries outside of Asia have preferred to do so in the form of technological licensing which entails less financial risks.

[36] *Business Times*, 3 September 1982.

Reasons for Overseas Expansion

Motives for Singapore TNCs undertaking overseas investments can be grouped under two broad categories: investments aimed at securing resources for the home country and investments to promote exports of the home country. In the latter category, the company can either produce in the host country to serve the local market, or use the host country as a production base for export to a third country. The particular reasons vary from firm to firm.

For the seven firms interviewed, the dominant reason for overseas expansion is to serve the local markets of the host countries. Singapore embarked upon import substitution industrialization in the early 1960s, but the process soon ran out of momentum when her own domestic market was saturated, particularly after the separation of Singapore from Malaysia in 1965. By the late sixties the country turned to export-led industrialization. Three manufacturing companies which were interviewed demonstrate how each progressed through these two stages.

Acma Electrical Industries was started in 1965 to produce refrigerators and air conditioners for the home (Singapore) market; up to 1975 the production was for domestic consumption. After capturing the local market and acquiring the technological know-how, Acma began to turn to export production. By 1982 it was exporting 80 per cent of its production and presently it is regarded as one of the world's largest exporters of refrigerators.[37] From exporting, the company expanded into direct production when its markets were threatened by tariff barriers. The company invested in countries such as Indonesia and Malaysia where it felt it had a good knowledge of the economic and political conditions in these countries. However, in Africa and the Middle East, where Acma lacks the knowledge and connections, it feels the risks are too high and the company serves its markets through exportation of its products and technological know-how. The establishment of overseas plants in Malaysia, Indonesia and Sri Lanka by Prima Ltd. illustrates the same process described above.

Yeo Hiap Seng's strategy for overseas investment consists of two steps. First, the overseas market is penetrated through exports and then, when a certain volume is reached, the company moves into production either by establishing its own plant (as in Malaysia), or by buying an existing plant as it did in Hong Kong. But more recently the company has resorted to technological agreement to boost its exports. In Indonesia and Mauritius, Yeo Hiap Seng arranged technological contracts to build plants and provide technology for the production and sale of food products under its own brand name. According to the General Manager of the company, this will provide them with a stronger foothold to expand their sales in the two countries.

Intraco is one of the few companies that has gone into overseas investment to secure material and to promote exports to third countries. In Malaysia, the company is involved in a marble extraction venture with other Malaysian partners; in Indonesia it is sourcing timber for trading; and in China it is engaged in oil palm cultivation and milling to obtain edible oil for trading. This company plans to produce garments in Bangladesh for export to other countries.

A final motive for overseas investment is the diversification of risks. While this may be a less compelling reason for pursuing manufacturing operations abroad, it is more important in explaining overseas investment in real estate and property for companies such as Jack Chia-MPH Ltd.

---

[37] *Business Times*, 14 September 1982.

Competitive Advantage

It is an assumption in conventional theories of foreign investment that foreign investors possess certain advantages which enable them to compete effectively with local producers who are advantaged in other ways when operating in their home ground. In the case of transnational corporations from First World countries, these advantages usually consist of technological superiority, a high level of research and development capability, marketing and management skills, economies of scale, product differentiation, and brand name preference.[38] Third World TNCs, it is observed, tend to have a different set of competitive advantages.[39]

In this sample, the most frequently mentioned advantage of the Singapore TNCs is lower cost of production which arises from the lower cost of management and labour when compared to that of First World TNCs. Another significant advantage is the greater dynamism and flexibility that these Singapore TNCs possess because they are smaller and younger. The executives of some of these firms stressed that First World TNCs resemble well established giants burdened with inertia, whereas Singaporean corporations are younger, smaller in size, and constantly seeking fresh ideas and input in order to stay ahead. For example, Yeo Hiap Seng Ltd. was mindful that they were the first company to introduce Tetra-pak for packaging soft drinks, a move which has reaped benefits for other industries. Acma Electrical exhibits the dynamism of a young and growing corporation willing to entertain a wide variety of demands in order to capture the market. They pointed out that many of the First World TNCs are large corporations that operate huge plants; compete on the basis of economies of scale and are unwilling to entertain smaller markets or to make adaptations to fit local requirements. Acma, on the other hand, is eager to make changes in order to satisfy local tastes. In Nigeria it produces air-conditioners and refrigerators which are smaller, require better insulation and are resistent to corosion. In China, Acma competed with Japanese, European and American firms to win a turnkey contract to build a refrigerator plant because it was able to offer the Chinese a more labour intensive method of production.

Yet another advantage that Singapore TNCs enjoy is their familiarity with the economic, social and political conditions of the neighbouring countries in which they operate. In many of these countries, bureaucratic and political considerations enter into economic decisions and policies. Therefore, knowledge and possession of the appropriate social and political ties are necessary for successful economic transactions. It was revealed by one company that First World TNCs that refuse to take account of these extra economic considerations face a severe handicap in their operations. Furthermore, Singapore's TNCs emerging from the environment of a developing economy are more sensitive to the needs and difficulties of other developing economies of which the First World TNCs are often unaware.

The general observation regarding competition faced by Singapore's TNCs is that it does not come from First World TNCs but rather from other Third World TNCs and local

---

[38]Hymer, "The International Operations of National Firms"; Kindleberger, *American Business Abroad*; Richard E. Caves, "International Corporations: The Industrial Economics of Foreign Investment", in *International Investment*, ed. John Dunning (Harmondsworth: Penguin, 1972).

[39]Louis T. Wells, Jr., "The Internationalization of Firms from Developing Countries", in *Multinationals From Small Countries*, ed. Agmon and Kindleberger (Cambridge, Mass.: MIT Press, 1977); Donald Lecraw, "Direct Investments by Firms from Less Developed Countries", *Oxford Economic Papers* 29, No. 3 (1977): 442–57; Krishna Kumar and Maxwell McLeod, ed., *Multinationals from Developing Countries* (Lexington, Mass.: D.C. Heath, 1981).

companies. As the foregoing discussion reveals, First World TNCs are uninterested in smaller and lower quality markets and are happy to leave the Singaporean TNCs to serve these sectors. Singapore's TNCs also tend to specialize and carve out market shares in products which cater to local tastes. Yeo Hiap Seng for example, pioneered and captured the non-carbonated and herbal drinks markets in Asia.

Some Singaporean TNCs claim that their products are equivalent in quality to those of First World TNCs but they admit to being handicapped on the side of marketing. They therefore manufacture products for First World TNCs which then market the products under the latter's brand name. Two examples are Acma Electrical which manufactures refrigerators for Frigidaire, and Intraco which produces garments for Sears-Roebuck and Macy's.

Research and Technology

While the production of advanced technology is not a *forte* of Third World TNCs they are credited with the ability to adapt technology to fit different local requirements. This was amply demonstrated by Acma Electrical Industries which originally acquired the technology to manufacture refrigerators and air-conditioners from Sanyo and Frigidaire on the basis of a licensing agreement. Subsequently, the company established a small research and development (R & D) unit beginning with one full-time engineer assisted by personnel from other departments. The unit then expanded and became a full-fledged R & D department. By 1982, this department had twenty-four Singaporean engineers, more than half with Ph.D's. The staff of this department now design their own products and components including the moulds, dyes, cabinets, and cooling systems although they continue to import the compressor — the most basic component in a refrigerator. A large part of the R & D department's activities are geared to making necessary changes in their products to suit the requirements of their clientele. The company believes in investing substantially in R & D because the limited domestic market forces them to compete in the international market which requires high quality products. The company, having acquired significant technological know-how, has been able to export turnkey products to other developing countries, a strategy which helps to lower their R & D overhead costs.

Two other manufacturing companies, Yeo Hiap Seng and Prima Ltd., have travelled the same path in their acquisition, adaptation and ultimate sale of technology. Both corporations began by buying machines and technological assistance from First World TNCs and continue to do so. But they were far-sighted enough to establish their own R & D departments to adapt the acquired technology to local needs (in the case of Yeo Hiap Seng most of the innovation is in the product line whereas for Prima they modify the machines for local production). Both companies have developed enough technological capabilities to sell their technology to other developing countries. The R & D department of Prima Ltd. has branched into developing new product lines related to their present activity. One of these is the manufacture of animal feed which makes use of bran, a by-product of flour milling. As we saw earlier, the Singapore government is providing encouragement and assistance for Singapore's companies to strengthen their technological capabilities.

Finally, the most impressive case of the successful development and sale of technology by a Singaporean TNC came from Lamipak. This company developed a plastic film that was three times stronger than any other known polyethylene film. Lamipak has been approached by 12 European and U.S. firms for licensing rights and had started a plant in the U.K. which was intended for production for the European market. The Irish Industrial

Development Authority is looking into the failed Lamipak's operations in Ireland to see how much of it can be rescued.

Conclusion

Among the Asian developing countries, Singapore has the second largest amount of overseas investments within Asia. Two-thirds of this, however, is concentrated in Malaysia, with another 24 per cent in Indonesia. Hong Kong comes third in line. In the last few years, Sri Lanka and China have become major recipients of Singapore's investments.

Upon examination of the pattern of investment for 18 Singaporean TNCs, it seems that an overwhelming number of their overseas affiliates are also within Asia; only 16 out of 126 ventures are outside of Asia and only two companies have manufacturing operations in the West. Singapore's involvement in Africa and the Middle East has been confined to technological agreements.

While most of Singapore's TNCs have not reached the technological level of TNCs from Korea, Hong Kong, or India, in the short period of about 10 years some of Singapore's TNCs have acquired a fair degree of technological know-how and have even begun to export this know-how to other developing countries in Asia, Africa, and the Middle East.

In contrast to the Malaysian TNCs, most of the Singaporean TNCs did not become transnational through the takeover of foreign companies operating locally. Rather, they grew up indigenously and over the years acquired enough financial and technological capabilities to expand abroad. The majority of these TNCs are not small or medium-sized firms but are among the largest corporations in the Singaporean economy.

The issue of the indigeneity of Singapore's TNCs is complicated by the fluidity of Chinese capital in East and Southeast Asia. Ethnic and personal connections among Chinese businessmen in Asia are significant factors in the internationalization of corporations in Asia. This is demonstrated in the case of a few of the Singapore TNCs that were studied. For some of these companies their business started in Thailand and Indonesia. They then moved to Singapore where they established their base and headquarters but they still retained an interest in their countries of origin. This mobility is made possible by the network of relationships among Chinese businessmen throughout Southeast Asia and East Asia. It represents one of the advantages which Singaporean TNCs enjoy.

Most of Singapore's investments in other countries are still aimed at serving the local markets rather than using the companies as platforms for export to third countries, though the latter is becoming more common in some of the Southeast Asian countries. The sourcing of raw materials has not figured significantly as a motive for Singapore's overseas investments.

Finally, the organizational and corporate structure of some of Singapore's largest TNCs, particularly the conglomerate form that they assume, is a characteristic which they share with other Third World Asian TNCs. The origins, nature, and effect of this organizational form present interesting questions for further investigation.

[20]

INTERNATIONAL ECONOMIC JOURNAL
Volume 1, Number 3, Autumn 1987

THE REVERSE DIRECT INVESTMENT: THE CASE OF THE KOREAN CONSUMER ELECTRONICS INDUSTRY

YONGWOOK JUN
Korea Institute for Economics and Technology

This paper discusses the nature of foreign direct investments by firms from developing countries in industrialized country markets, which is coined as "reverse direct investment." On the basis of the experiences of the Korean consumer electronics firms operating in the U.S., this paper identifies the nature of the investment as "defensive" and "premature" strategic moves of firms in their internationalization process. There investments are made not to exploit firms' monopolistic firm-specific advantages, but to protect their export markets at an earlier time than economic forces might have led them to do. However, in the process, firms try to convert their home country-specific advantages (e.g. low labor cost) into firm-specific ones as much as possible. [440]

1. INTRODUCTION

One of the most significant changes in international trade and investment in the past decade has been the rise of firms originating from less-developed countries (LDCs), especially newly industrializing countries (NICs) such as Korea, Taiwan, Hong Kong, Singapore, and Brazil, and their increasing penetration of developed country (DC) markets.[1] They have not only increased their penetration into the industrialized markets through aggressive export activities, but also started to invest in local manufacturing in those markets. A case in point is the foreign direct investments of Korean consumer electronics firms in the U.S. and European markets (see Appendix Table 1).[2] This phenomenon, which the author refers to as "reverse (LDC to DC) direct investment" was unthinkable only a decade ago.

Though many interesting issues can be raised with respect to the emergence of third world multinational corporations (MNCs) in general and Korean firms in particular, this paper will discuss the nature of the reverse direct investment. It aims specifically to show that the reverse direct investment phenomenon is an event which is not clearly explained by conventional theories of foreign direct investment (FDI) and thus requires a new interpretation that is different from the ones implied in the general literature of FDI.

[1] See Scott (1985). According to Scott, by 1982 the four NICs (South Korea, Taiwan, Hong Kong, Singapore) exported almost twice as much to the U.S. as did West Germany and four times as much as France.

[2] Besides Korean firms, Taiwanese firms are also active in foreign operations. Some of the examples are investments by Tatung (electronics) in the U.S. and the U.K., by Sampo (electronics) in the U.S. and by Formosa Plastics (chemicals) in the U.S.

Conventional FDI theories, whether product life cycle theory, the industrial economics based Hymer-Kindleberger theory, internalization theory, or eclectic theory, normally assume that firms investing in foreign markets should have some monopolistic firm-specific advantages which they can exploit over local firms. Otherwise, it is argued that it does not make sense for firms to invest in foreign countries because they face the disadvantage of "cost of foreignness" in terms of cultural, legal, and managerial unfamiliarity. The conventional theories based on this market imperfection have been successful in explaining U.S. and Western European MNCs. They are even persuasive, though not quite as extensively as for U.S. and European cases, in accounting for Japanese MNC behavior. In terms of types of investment, these theories have been quite successful in explaining cross-investments among firms from developed countries, investments of firms from developed countries in less developed countries, and investments of firms from advanced LDCs in other LDCs.[3]

However, once we get into the task of explaining the new phenomenon of reverse direct investment by LDC firms into developed countries, the explanatory power of conventional theories tends to get weakened. How can firms from low labor cost countries set up labor-intensive assembly plants in developed countries, especially when labor cost is their major competitive weapon? To answer the question, we will first review major conventional FDI theories in the following section to identify their limitations as well as applicability in explaining this new phenomenon. The issue will be discussed in the context of Korean consumer electronics firms' investments in the U.S. market.[4] We will then present a new interpretation on the basis of the Korean experience in Section 3. Section 4 presents the summary and conclusion.

2. THE FAILURE OF CONVENTIONAL FDI THEORIES

A. Hymer-Kindleberger Theory

As the pioneers of industrial economics approach in explaining the FDI phenomenon, they have emphasized the presence of monopolistic firm-specific advantages as the condition for FDI. Hymer even went so far as to claim that "unequal" ability of firms deriving from these firm-specific advantages is a sufficient condition for international operations [Hymer (1976: 46)]. The rent yielding

[3] In the case of investments of firms from advanced LDCs in other LDCs, the conventional theories have extended the concept of monopolistic firm-specific advantages to include such items as skills in small scale operations, lower overhead, technology adapted to Third World conditions, ethnic ties, host government preference, and conglomerate group ownership. Two contrasting views on the nature of firm-specific advantages of Third World multinationals can be found in two recent studies: Wells (1983) and Lall (1983).

[4] Korean consumer electronics firms have been selected because they are one of the most active groups among LDC firms in terms of their market activities in industrialized countries. Although individual Korean consumer electronics firms still remain minor players in the global market they have been growing quite rapidly and are currently a strong force as a collective unit in the world consumer electronics industry along with Japanese and Taiwanese firms.

firm-specific advantages they have mentioned are patented technology, product differentiation (e.g. brand name), special access to inputs and distribution channels, and advantage in raising capital [Kindleberger (1969), Hymer (1976)]. Especially, product differentiation has been emphasized as the major factor for the horizontal foreign investment by Caves (1971). Besides the general criticism of their theories that the existence of monopolistic firm-specific advantages *per se* does not explain why the FDI mode is chosen over other market entry methods, such as exports or licensing, to exploit the same advantages, their theory has a limitation in explaining the reverse investment phenomenon, too.

In the case of the Korean consumer electronics industry, Korean firms did not have the above mentioned monopolistic advantages when they ventured their foreign direct investments in the U.S. market. Their brand name was not known very well because they had been dependent mostly on the buyer brand business, such as O.E.M. and importer brands. Their technological skill was unmatched by that of Japanese or U.S. firms as manifested by their low-end market strategies. Their R&D expense had also been very low by international standards.[5] Furthermore, their access to marketing channels or inputs were also very limited. Due to the absence of a strong domestic parts industry, they had to depend on foreign parts.[6] Moreover, access to marketing channels was not in the hand of the Korean firms. Instead, it was mostly under the control of U.S. buyers who maintain established marketing networks in the local market. Korean firms did not have any advantage in raising capital either because they did not possess a superior credit rating in the international capital market. Given this lack of monopolistic firm-specific advantages *vis-a-vis* local U.S. and Japanese competitors, it is very hard to apply the rationale of the H-K theory to explain the Korean reverse investment in the U.S.

B. Internalization Theory

Following the basic line of the industrial economics approach, the internalization theory or transaction cost theory of FDI also emphasizes the market imperfection of both factor and goods markets to explain the FDI [Buckley and Casson (1976); Rugman (1980); Teece (1982)]. However, it has extended the H-K theory one step further. As the possession of firm-specific advantages *per se* does not explain why a domestic firm should choose to exploit its monopolistic advantage by FDI, the theory has identified the nature of market imperfections in terms of transaction costs and suggested reasons for the preference for internalization (i.e. FDI) to external market mechanisms (e.g. licensing or exporting) in exploiting the advantages. Especially, the failure or absence of the factor market

[5] R & D expenditure as a percentage of sales in the electronics industries of three major countries are as follows: Korea (3.5% in 1984; 3.9% in 1985); Japan (4.6% in 1984); U.S. (5.6% in 1985).

[6] The Korean electronics industry depends heavily on Japan for both parts and technology. The proportions of imports from Japan in the total parts import are 49.7% in 1984, 52.2% in 1985 and 61.5% in 1986. Accumulated number of technology acquisitions from Japan as of 1986 counts 479 cases which are almost twice as large as the number of cases from the U.S. (265 cases). Given the total accumulated acquisitions of 843 cases up to 1986, the Japanese proportion is about 56%.

for knowledge (or information) has received most attention because the rent yielding firm-specific advantages are mostly of intangible nature (e.g. technological knowhow, marketing skills, brand name, managerial skills). According to Teece (1982), the internal market is preferred for exploitation of those advantages because external market mechanisms for knowledge are expensive and inefficient due to transactional difficulties in terms of recognition, disclosure and transfer costs.

Though this theory is very convincing in explaining the FDI by firms with firm-specific advantages of high knowledge content (e.g. firms in R&D intensive or marketing intensive industries), its ability to explain reverse investment is very doubtful. As LDC firms in general and Korean firms in particular do not possess such monopolistic advantages of high knowledge content to exploit in the industrialized markets, the issue of choice between licensing and FDI does not occur. In this sense, the theory has a limitation in its explanatory power. However, this theory sheds some light on the new phenomenon when it points out the internalization incentive of firms to bypass goods market imperfection initiated by governments, such as trade barriers [Rugman (1980)]. However, still the issue of firm-specific advantage remains.

Within the framework of the internalization theory of foreign direct investment, another Reading School scholar in the U.K., Dunning (1977), has proposed an eclectic theory of FDI which expanded the internalization theory a little further by emphasizing the location-specific advantages as key factors to choosee FDI over exporting. Besides recognizing three main forms of foreign involvement (i.e. exporting, licensing, foreign investment) to exploit the firm-specific advantages, Dunning proposes an eclectic framework which explains which route of exploitation is preferred.[7] In comparison to previous internalization theories which have placed most emphasis on the condition for the preference of FDI to licensing, this theory suggests the condition under which FDI is preferred not only to licensing but also to exporting by recognizing the importance of location-specific factors such as factor costs, transport and communication cost, control on imports, and infrastructure. According to him, the more a country's enterprises possess firm-specific advantages, the greater is the incentive to internalize them; and the more these enterprises find it profitable to exploit the advantages outside their national boundaries, the more likely they are to engage in foreign direct investment [Dunning (1981)].

This theory offers a very logical three dimensional approach in explaining the FDI phenomenon in general. Its explicit recognition of the location-specific advantages provides a partial explanation for the reverse investment phenomenon. In the case of the Korean electronics firms in the U.S. market, location-specific factors such as trade barriers of the U.S., closer and better communication with the local U.S. market, and local availability of financing for the investment have induced or facilitated the reverse investments. However, its

[7] The framework is called "eclectic" because it explains the conditions for choosing each of the three main forms of foreign involvement, not just that of FDI.

assumption about the types of firm-specific advantages encounters the same problems as previous theories in explaining reverse investments.

C. Product Life Cycle Theory

Vernon's product life cycle theory provides a dynamic framework which relates three different stages of product life cycle (i.e. innovative, mature, and standardized stages) to a product pioneering firm's locational decision of foreign production and to its choice between exporting and overseas production. This theory has explained well the pattern of FDI from an initiating DC to other DCs, and then to LDCs based on the changing nature of technology and the changing economic environment of other countries in terms of income and tastes. Vernon is also insightful in pinpointing the threats of competition as a triggering event for FDI. His projection of eventual supply by LDC firms to DCs in the form of exports to DCs proves to be very correct.

However, the theory has stopped there and does not mention anything about the possibility of reverse investment by LDC firms in DC markets. This may be theoretically contradictory, if we follow his logic, because his original theory implies that nations seem to be ordered in terms of economic hierarchy and that the FDI flow is a down-flowing one from advanced DCs to other DCs and finally to LDCs. In this sense, Vernon's original theory of FDI is a very *situation-specific* one which can be best applied when there is an apparent economic hierarchy among countries. In fact, the theory has well explained the early post-war expansion of U.S. investment into Europe, and still has some applicability for FDI movements from DCs to LDCs and for those from advanced LDCs to other LDCs. Even the cross investments among DCs can be accommodated by his revised theory which recognizes the shrinking gap in incomes and labor costs among developed countries as well as widespreading multinational networks with global scanning capability [Vernon (1979)]. However, this theory is not comprehensive enough to cover the new phenomenon of reverse investment by LDC firms in DC markets. Furthermore, the firm-specific advantages assumed in his model were those of high technology nature which help to save labor and meet the needs of high income consumers in the home country. These advantages are quite different from what LDC firms (or Korean firms) possess (i.e. low technology and labor-intensive skills).

D. New Theories of FDI

Recently a few new approaches have been suggested to explain the foreign investment phenomenon by firms with non-R&D based advantages. Giddy (1982) has tried to see whether or not conventional theories are adequate to explain the overseas expansion of the "non-conventional" MNCs which are relatively small, produce low-technology undifferentiated goods and direct their investments to poorer and smaller neighboring countries (e.g. Japanese and Third World MNCs). By using Freeman's (1974) typology of the strategies open to firms under technological change (e.g. offensive, defensive, dependent, imitative), Giddy argues that firms following particular strategies (i.e. *imitative* or *dependent*) which do not require heavy research expenditures can still make foreign direct investment by utilizing their own transferable firm-specific advantages. Especially, firms adopting the imitative strategy introduce products well after their first appearance in the market by the market leader and have particular advantages in production engineering, labor cost, or skills in adapting products to special market requirements. Or the firm may be strong in marketing.[8] Giddy has found that the unique firm-specific advantages of non-conventional MNCs identified by other studies such as adaptive marketing skills and general production expertise tend to be closest to this imitative strategy. He thus concludes that the foreign investment phenomenon by non-conventional MNCs can be explained within the conventional framework by expanding the scope of firm-specific advantages which include general production and adaptive marketing skills as transferable monopolistic advantages. He has also noticed correctly that those monopolistic advantages of non-conventional MNCs are relatively small or temporary by their nature of low technological content. Thus, the successful transplant of manufacturing to a foreign environment depends heavily on location-specific factors of the host country which may "subsidize" the relative weakness of firm-specific factors..

Though his approach provides an interesting interpretation for foreign direct investment by non-conventional MNCs in general, it is still incapable of explaining the reverse investment in the developed markets. It seems that he has discussed the issue of non-conventional investment in the context of investments made by non-conventional MNCs in other LDCs rather than in DCs. Though the general production expertise and adaptive marketing skills may be valuable monopolistic advantages in LDC markets, it is doubtful whether they can be exploitable assets in the industrialized markets. Furthermore, in the case of Korean firms, Giddy's argument for the marketing adaptability of firms adopting imitative strategies as a source for foreign investment may not hold well. Though it is well known that Japanese firms are very skillful at imitation on the basis of their applied R&D capability, the same ability does not hold strongly for Korean firms due to their lack of design capability.[9]

Another approach to non-R&D intensive investment phenomenon has been presented by Dunning and McQueen (1982). Their basic argument is that FDI is made to maintain the quality of a product or service. They argued that in some industries such as the hotel industry, firms try to maintain the quality image of their services by using their brand name internationally and adopting worldwide reservation systems. They also maintain this quality image by manning their own trained management in foreign operations. Though this is a good explanation for service-oriented industries, it is hard to use it to explain the reverse invest-

[8] The firms adopting "dependent" strategies are mainly subcontractors to finished goods manufacturers. Their firm-specific assets are their expertise and familiarity built up over the years in serving the particular needs of the dominant firms.

[9] Foreign buyers noted a weakpoint in design of Korean products as one of the major obstacles to their international competitiveness. See Korea Trade Association (1982-85).

ment of LDC manufacturers in DC markets.

Another author [Baranson (1981)] has provided some environmental reasons for the investment by non-conventional MNCs in industrialized countries in the context of the Japanese investment in the U.S. consumer electronics industry in 1970s. Besides the trade barriers, he has cited the rising Japanese yen and increasing Japanese production costs as the major reasons for their entry.[10] However, these reasons are not appropriate to explain Korean cases because the Korean Won(*W*) has not experienced a significant real appreciation vis-a-vis U.S. dollars when Korean electronics firms invested in the U.S. in the early 1980s and there has been a big gap in the relative prices of both skilled and unskilled labor between the U.S. and Korea.

3. A NEW INTERPRETATION

In the preceding section we have examined major theories of FDI and seen their weakness in explaining the phenomenon of reverse investment by LDC firms in general and Korean firms in particular in developed countries. The question is, then, how we can explain this phenomenon. This author contends that the foreign direct investment by LDC firms in industrialized markets has to be understood on a quite different motivational ground. Unlike Western MNCs' investments in other countries which are basically offensive ones to exploit firm-specific advantages that yield monopolistic rents, the investments by LDCs in the industrialized markets are purely *defensive*. The meaning of "defensive" in the reverse investment context has also to be distinguished from that which is used in the oligopolistic context in Vernon's (1966) or Knickerbocker's (1973) works. The terminology has been used in their works with respect to firms which follow the market leader to maintain the competitive balance, whereas it is used in our case with respect to any firm regardless of its relative competitive position. Whether the firm is a market leader or not, its principal motivation for making foreign direct investment is to *protect its export market* which is closely related to its survival rather than to restore competitive balance. This is what we mean by "defensive." In order to understand the defensive nature of reverse investments more clearly, let's look into the case of foreign investment decision of one leading Korean electronics firm.[11]

It did not take long for Gold Star to seriously consider the possibility of setting up a local production facility in the U.S. Due to the rapidly increasing penetration of the U.S. market by Korean and Taiwanese color TV makers, the U.S. government imposed a quota late in 1978 on imports of color TV's made in Korea and Taiwan in the form of an orderly marketing agreement (OMA). As Table 1

[10] The investment of Sony Corporation of Japan in the U.S. for the production of color TV's in 1972 is a typical example. The company invested in the U.S. far before major trade barriers on Japanese imports set in. See Lyons (1976).

[11] For the detailed background of investment decisions of the two largest electronics firms in Korea, see the chapter 6 of Jun (1985).

Table 1. U.S. Quota vs. Production Capacity of Color Television Sets: The Case of Goldstar Co.

In Number of Sets

U.S. Quota			Annual	Production
Period	Volume		Production	Capacity
Dec. 78 - Jan. 79	36,502	91,013		
Feb. 79 - Oct. 79	54,511		142,000 (1979)	600,000 (1979)
Nov. 79 - June 80	63,175	124,779		
July 80 - Dec. 80	61,604		339,000 (1980)	650,000 (1980)
Jan. 81 - June 81	94,491	206,578		
July 81 - Dec. 81	112,087		936,000* (1981)	840,000 (1981)
Jan. 82 - June 82	— **		969,000 (1982)	1,200,000 (1982)

Source: Company data.

Notes: * Actual production exceeded the capacity due to extended working hours in order to meet newly created domestic market. The Korean gorvernment lifted its ban on domestic sales of color TV in 1981.

** Goldstar had no assigned quota in this period though some other firms were still under the quota.

shows, the quota allocation to Gold Star in the first year was around 91,000 sets, which was just 15 per cent of its total capacity. Compared to the past year's export volume of the U.S. market (167,000 sets), it was a 46 per cent reduction in volume. Furthermore, the OMA was extended another two years after its initial expiration in 1979. At that point, the management of this firm recognized that the trade barrier to the U.S. market would be lasting rather than temporary. The firm started to consider seriously the possibility of local production in the U.S. Here the most dominant motivation was to bypass the *expected* future trade barriers in order to protect the established export market. As the U.S. market had been the largest export market of color TV's as well as of other products for this firm (Table 2), the loss of this market was unthinkable. Even if it might lose in the short-term by investing in local production in the U.S., Gold Star had no other choice but to enter the market. Otherwise, it would be confined to a smaller operation due to expected antidumping charges or continuing voluntary quotas. It was felt that though there was a possibility of diversifying the target market eventually, it would not be accomplished in the short run and the relative sizes of other markets were no match to that of the U.S. Despite some opposition to the idea of local production because of higher labor cost and difficulty in managing foreign laborers, the management finally decided to establish a local U.S. production plant late 1981.

Table 2. Market Portfolio of Gold Star by Region (1983)
In Million Dollars and Percent

	Total Consumer Electronics		Color T.V.	
Region	Amount	Proportion	Amount	Proportion
Domestic	620.3	60.7	163.3	47.3
U.S.A.	135.7	17.8	140.7	40.8
Canada	20.1	2.1	12.0	3.5
Latin America	12.5	1.3	7.8	2.3
Europe	35.3	3.7	3.9	1.7
Asia	20.1	2.1	7.4	2.1
Middle East	13.7	1.4	6.0	1.7
Africa	9.1	0.9	1.7	0.5
Others	0.2	0.0	0.2	0.1
Total	967.0	100.0	345.0	100.0

Source: Compiled from Harvard Business School, *Gold Star Col., Ltd.* Reference # 0-385-264, 1985, p. 21.

From the defensive nature of reverse investments, we may conjecture that reverse investments are basically *premature* strategic moves. They are premature because firms would not have made such investments unless they faced threats to their market security. In other words, they are more or less forced to opt for FDI against their will at an earlier time than economic forces might have led them to do. This can be most clearly demonstrated when we compare the local production cost in a host country with export cost (landed basis) from the home country. If we find that the local production cost of a firm is higher than its pre-trade barrier export cost, we may conclude that the firm was forced to make such an investment for a defensive purpose rather than for an offensive purpose (i.e. to exploit one's monopolistic advantage).

Table 3 shows the comparative production costs of one principal product (color television) of two major Korean electronics firms in the U.S. market. As the information reveals, the local (i.e. U.S.) production cost is higher than the export cost by around 7 per cent, which confirms our argument. If we look into the detailed cost breakdown, the cost data show that the local production in the U.S. is disadvantageous to the production in Korea in material costs, labor costs, and factory overhead. Material costs are higher in the U.S. production even after all the attempts of firms to reduce them, mainly because of higher duties imposed on imported parts than on finished products and inbound transportation costs of parts. The higher labor costs are due to higher wages and lower productivity of U.S. workers in comparison to their Korean counterparts.[12] The reason for the

[12] The main difficulty faced by Korean firms in their U.S. operation is the low productivity of U.S. workers in the assembly process as well as their lack of discipline. Korean firms expect it will take about two years for their U.S. operations to achieve the same level of productivity of their

Table 3. Comparison of Manufacturing Cost of 19″ Color T.V. Sets in Two Locations

	Production in Korea	Production in U.S.A.	Differential
COMPANY A (1983)			
Material	82.1	98.0	15.9
Labor	1.4	4.0	2.6
Factory Overhead	2.2	5.0	2.8
Manufacturing Total	85.7	107.0	21.3
Transportation	7.0	—	−7.0
Damage in Transit	varies	—	?
Duty	7.3	—	−7.3
Total Landed Cost	100.0	107.0	<7.0
COMPANY B (1986)			
Material	82.2	98.8	16.6
Labor	1.1	4.5	3.4
Factory Overhead	3.5	`4.0	0.5
Manufacturing Total	86.8	107.3	20.5
Transportation	6.7	—	−6.7
Damage in Transit	varies	—	?
Duty	6.5	—	−6.4
Total Landed Cost	100.0	107.3	<7.3

Source: Company data.
Note: To disguise the actual figures, every value has been converted into an index by setting the U.S. landed cost of "production in Korea" as 100.

higher overhead is mostly derived from the high depreciation expense on the new equipments of the U.S. plant. However, Table 3 also shows that these disadvantages in material costs, labor costs, and factory overhead are to a certain extent offset by savings in other cost components, such as inbound transportation cost and tariffs on finished products.

We have to note that the overall 7% cost disadvantage is a significant one in view of the low margin of the export business of Korean firms even though the overall cost difference is not big enough to wipe out the whole business.[13] This "defensive argument" leads the author to contend in this article that reverse investment has to be understood in the context of an LDC firm's internationalization process which is basically a "market security seeking" process in which the firm overcomes various market threats along its growth path. Reverse investment is simply a part of the process which distinguishes itself from other preced-

home plants.

[13] Export margins of Korean electronics firms are normally less than 3% of sales.

ing stages such as "export via sales agent" or "local sales through sales subsidiaries" in terms of only the magnitude of commitment of resources. The underlying thrust of the movement is, however, the same defensive "market security seeking" behavior along with enhanced internal capabilities.

Though we argued that the basic motivation for reverse investments is defensive rather than offensive, this does not mean that LDC firms do not have any firm-specific advantage at all. They do have some firm-specific advantages. However, these advantages are *squeezed out* rather than naturally existing. They obtain these advantages through judicious tactical moves. The author believes that LDC firms' main strength lies in their capability to maintain the same advantage they have enjoyed in their export mode (i.e. low cost). They try to retain their low cost advantages even after they change their market entry mode from export to direct investment. We may wonder how they can maintain their home country location-specific advantage (i.e. low labor cost) once they operate their assembly plants in the developed countries. Of course, they cannot completely maintain their low cost advantage as they did in the export mode. However, they try to maintain it to the maximum extent. For example, in the case of Korean firms operating in the U.S. market, they try to save, most of all, both parts and final assembly costs by importing parts in a semi-knocked down (SKD) form, utilizing home labor as much as possible in the SKD kits.[14] In terms of value, they import more than three quarters of their components from Korea, sourcing locally only bulky parts such as cabinets and packing materials. If they have not used these tactics while relying wholly on local supply, the material cost in the Table 3 would have been significantly higher. In short, Korean firms managed to *convert home-country location-specific advantages (e.g. low labor costs) into internationally transferable firm-specific advantages.* By so doing, they could extend a good part of its cost advantage of the pre-trade barrier export mode to the local production mode.

Besides, Korean firms also emphasize the enhancement of productivity to cut the production cost by introducing the most up-to-date assembly equipments as well as by raising employee morale through Korean-style human-relations based management.[15] Some other assets of Korean firms are the commitment and dedication of Korean managers[16] and willingness of the major shareholders to withstand heavy front-end loadings in such risky business as a part of their long-term market strategy. Furthermore, being conglomerates themselves, Korean electronics firms have the capability to subsidize this risky venture (i.e. local production

[14] A SKD kit consists of a picture tube and a printed circuit board or ceramic substrate with components assembled thereon. It needs the final assembly process to become a complete receiver. A SKD kit is different from a CKD (complete knocked-down) one in that it has more preassembled parts.

[15] As for the Korean management style in the U.S. operation. see "Korea's newest export: management style," *Business Week*, January 29, 1987, p. 54.

[16] Korean managers work 70 to 80 hours a week, compared with 60 to 70 hours for Japanese and 50 for Americans. See Kumar, K. and Kim K. (1984), pp. 45-62, for the importance of lower cost and commitment of expatriate staff as a firm-specific advantage of Korean firms.

in industrialized countries) from their "cash surplus" divisions, which may enable the firms to go through the painful "teething" period.

4. CONCLUSION AND SUMMARY

In this paper, we have reviewed major received theories of foreign direct investment for their applicability to reverse investments on the basis of limited experiences of the Korean consumer electronic industry. From this discussion, the following points emerged: (1) The traditional foreign direct investment theories have not provided a clear explanation for the reverse investment phenomenon of Korean firms. This is basically due to the different motivations underlying the traditional theories and the reverse investment phenomenon. Whereas the traditional theories are mostly based on an offensive strategy to exploit monopolistic firm-specific advantages, the reverse direct investment phenomenon is basically an outcome of defensive strategy of LDC firms; (2) The reverse investment is interpreted in this paper as a premature defensive strategic move which was forced upon firms of developing countries in order to protect their export market. We contend that the reverse investment has to be understood in the broader context of the internationalization process of LDC firms which is basically a market security seeking process; and (3) We have noted that Korean firms tried to squeeze as much home country-specific advantages as possible to offset the 'cost of foreignness" of operating in developed countries.

APPENDIX

Appendix Table 1. The Foreign Production of Major Korean Consumer Electronics Firms in Industrialized Countries

Firm	Foreign Location	Product	Production Start	Production Capacity (1987) (sets)
Goldstar	U.S.A.	Color T.V.	1981	1,000,000
		Microwave Oven	1986	300,000
		VTR*	Dec. 1987	N.A.
	W. Germany	Color T.V.*	Sept. 1987	300,000
		VTR*	Sept. 1987	400,000
Samsung	U.S.A.	Color T.V.	1984	1,000,000
	England	Color T.V.*	June 1987	300,000
		Microwave Oven*	June 1987	300,000
		VTR*	June 1987	250,000
	Portugal	Color T.V.	1982	300,000

* The time to begin production and the capacity figures are all projected ones according to company plans.

REFERENCE

Baranson, J., *The Japanese Challenge to U.S. Industry*, Lexington: Lexington Books, 1981.

Buckley, P. J. and Casson, M. C., *The Future of the Multinational Enterprise*, London: Macmillan, 1976.

Caves, R. E., "International Corporations: The Industrial Economics of Foreign Investment," *Economica*, February 1971, 1-27.

Dunning, J. H., "Trade, Location of Economic Activity, and the Multinational Enterprise: A Search for an Eclectic Approach," in B. Ohlin, P. O. Hesselborn, and P. M. Wijkman, eds., *The International Allocation of Economic Activity*, London: Macmillan, 1977.

__________, "Explaining Outward Direct Investment of Developing Countries: In Support of the Eclectic Theory of International Production," in K. Kumar and M. G. McLoed, eds., *Multinationals from Developing Countries*, Lexington: Lexington Books, 1981.

__________, and McQueen, M., "The Eclectic Theory of the Multinational Enterprise and the International Hotel Industry," in A. M Rugman, ed., *New Theories of the Multinational Enterprise*, New York: St. Martin's Press Inc., 1982.

Freeman, C., *The Economics of Industrial Innovation*, Middlesex: Penguin, 1974.

Giddy, I. H. and Young, S., "Conventional Theory and Unconventional Multinationals: Do New Forms of Multinational Enterprise Require New Theories?" *New Theories of the Multinational Enterprise*, in A. M. Rugman, ed., New York: St. Martin's Press Inc., 1982.

Hymer, S. H., *The International Operations of National Firms: A Study of Direct Foreign Investment*, Cambridge: MIT Press, 1976.

Jun, Y. W., 'The Internationalization Process of the Firm: The Case of The Korean Consumer Electronics Industry," Unpublished Ph. D. Dissertation, Sloan School of Management, M. I. T., 1985.

Kindleberger, C. P., *American Business Abroad: Six Lectures on Direct Investment*, New Haven: Yale University Press, 1969.

Knickerbocker, F. T., *Oligopolistic Reaction and Multinational Enterprise*, Boston: Harvard Business School, 1973.

Korea Trade Association, *The International Competitiveness of Korean Products-Views of Foreign Buyers*, Seoul: KTA, 1982-1985 (in Korean).

Kumar, K. and Kim, K., "The Korean Multinationals," *Journal of International Business Studies*, Spring/Summer 1984.

Lall, S., *The New Multinationals: The Spread of Third World Enterprises*, New York: John Wiley & Sons, 1983.

Lyons, N., *The Sony Vision*, New York: Crown Publishers, 1976.

Rugman, A. M., "Internalization as a General Theory of Foreign Direct Investment: A Re-Appraisal of the Literature," *Weltwirtschafliches Archiv*, Vol. 116, 1980, 365-79.

Scott, B. R., "U.S. Competitiveness: Concepts, Performance, and Implications," in B. R. Scott and G. C. Lodge, eds., *U.S. Competitiveness in the World Economy*, Boston: Harvard Business School Press, 1985.

Teece, David J., "A Transaction Cost Theory of the Multinational Enterprise,"

Discussion Papers in International Investment and Business Studies, No. 66, University of Reading, September 1982.

Vernon, R., "International Investment and International Trade in the Product Cycle," *Quarterly Journal of Economics*, May 1966, 190-207.

____________, "The Product Cycle Hypothesis in a New International Environment," *Oxford Bulletin of Economics and Statistics*, Vol. 41, 1979, 255-267.

Wells, L., *Third World Multinationals: The Rise of Foreign Investment from Developing Countries*, Cambridge: MIT Press, 1983.

[21]

OXFORD BULLETIN OF ECONOMICS AND STATISTICS, 50, 4 (1988)

PARENTAGE AND FACTOR PROPORTIONS: A COMPARATIVE STUDY OF THIRD-WORLD MULTINATIONALS IN SRI LANKAN MANUFACTURING*

Premachandra Athukorala and S. K. Jayasuriya

I. INTRODUCTION

A striking development in the scenario of internationalization of economic activity that dates largely from about the late 1960's is the emergence of multinational enterprises[1] from developing countries. As an outcome of rapid industrial development in the post-war era, the more industrialized of the developing countries now provide home to many indigenous firms which have grown in strength to expand production beyond national frontiers, mostly (but not exclusively) to neighbouring developing countries. These 'new' multinationals or Third World multinational enterprises (TWMNEs as they are popularly known), still account for only a minor share of the total stock of direct foreign investment in developing countries,[2] but in a significant number of them the incidence of such investment is already quite substantial (UNCTC, 1983:19). There is evidence that the number of TWMNEs, the sophistication of their activities and their international spread has greatly increased over the years (Lall, 1983).

Beginning with the pioneering works of Diaz-Alejandro (1977), Wells (1977) and Lecraw (1977), a sizeable body of literature, mostly exploratory in nature, has developed on this subject.[3] A basic assertion of this literature is that TWMNEs possess a number of unique characteristics which distinguish them from the 'traditional' (developed-country) multinationals (DCMNEs). One such hypothesized difference relates to the relative appropriateness of their technology to host developing countries. A well known argument in the long-running discussion on labour absorption in the manufacturing sector of

*The authors wish to thank the School of Economics, La Trobe University, for financial support and Ravi Ratnayake for excellent research assistance.

[1] In line with usual practice in this area of study, the multinational enterprise (MNE) is defined here as an enterprise that owns or controls income-generating assets in one or more countries other than the one in which it is based.

[2] By 1980 the share of developing-country investors in the total stock of direct foreign investment in developing countries was between 4 to 8 percent (Jenkins, 1986; 458).

[3] Lall (1984) and Wells (1983) synthesize much of the existing knowledge.

developing countries is that the technology introduced by DCMNEs (which virtually monopolises world trade in technology) is highly capital intensive, and, therefore, tends to reduce the employment potential of industrialization (Sen, 1980; Singer, 1973). This argument is based on the presumption that a given investor's technology reflects peculiarities of the factor market conditions in their home countries. On the basis of the same presumption, the conventional wisdom on TWMNEs holds that the technology of these firms is more appropriate to the relative labour and capital costs in the host (capital-receiving) developing country. This belief has nurtured the hope that TWMNEs might be able to 'make a special kind of contribution to the development of poor countries' (Wells, 1983: 1).

The hypothesis that DCMNE affiliates in developing countries employ relatively more capital intensive techniques than indigenous firms has been subjected to extensive empirical testing in recent years.[4] However, empirical evidence on the relative capital intensity of TWMNE affiliates is sparse. Moreover, even the available evidence comes from studies based on rather sketchy data covering a small number of countries and which employ questionable analytical procedures (see Section II). Much more systematic empirical investigations covering a variety of host country situations are needed before any valid generalization on this issue can be made.

In this paper we present results from an analysis of the differences in capital intensity between TWMNEs, DCMNEs and indigenous private firms in Sri Lankan manufacturing industry. Access to a hitherto unexploited data set has allowed us to avoid some of the major drawbacks of previous studies and to test more rigorously important hypotheses regarding the choice of technique, as well as to explore the dynamic adjustments of MNEs over time to host country market environments.

The paper is organized as follows: Section II surveys the limited empirical evidence available on the subject. In Section III, the trends and patterns of direct foreign investment in the Sri Lankan manufacturing industry are outlined. Section IV sets out the methodology and describes the data base. The results are presented and analysed in Section V. The principal conclusions are contained in Section VI.

II. REVIEW OF PREVIOUS WORK

The hypothesis that TWMNEs are relatively more labour intensive has been apparently supported by the three major studies which have investigated the issue (Wells and Warren, 1979; Busjeet, 1980; Lecraw, 1977).[5] However, these studies had important limitations.

[4] For recent surveys of this literature see Balasubramanyam (1983) and Kirkpatrick *et al.* (1985; 104–116).

[5] Wells and Warren (1979) and Basjeet (1980) support the hypothesis that TWMNEs are relatively more labour intensive than DCMNCs, while Lecraw (1977) demonstrated that they are more labour intensive than either DCMNCs or local (Thai) firms. For a useful summing up of the methodology and findings of these studies see Wells, 1983, Chapter 2.

Wells and Warren's (1979) study of Indonesian manufacturing firms, as well as Busjeet's (1980) study of manufacturing firms operating in the export processing zones of Mauritius and Philippines, compared average factor intensities without controlling for other firm attributes. However, studies which have compared techniques adopted by DCMNEs and local firms have shown that attributes such as firm size, age and scale of operation explain a large proportion of the observed differences in factor proportions (Morley and Smith, 1977; Biersteker, 1978; Chen, 1983; Ahiakpor, 1986; Forsyth and Solomon, 1977). Hence simple comparisons of averages across ownership groups can be quite misleading.

Lecraw's (1977) more carefully designed study of manufacturing firms in Thailand attempted to control for the influence of these factors. However, this study was based on data from the 'old breed' of TWMNEs (set up in the early 1970's) which tended to locate almost exclusively in those sectors employing relatively unsophisticated technologies. There is evidence that in recent years TWMNEs have been rapidly moving into more sophisticated product lines requiring technologies, skills and production scales previously considered to be the exclusive preserve of DCMNEs (Lall, 1984). As the scope for technological adaptation is rather limited in such product lines (Forsyth *et al.*, 1980), it could be argued that differences in labour intensities found in these studies may have reflected conditions prevailing at an early stage of TWMNEs which is now past.

III. DIRECT FOREIGN INVESTMENT IN SRI LANKAN MANUFACTURING

As in many other developing countries, import restriction was the major factor which triggered the entry of DFI into Sri Lankan manufacturing. In response to a deteriorating balance of payments situation, Sri Lanka moved rapidly to a regime of stringent import and exchange restrictions in the 1960's. When their market shares were threatened by import controls, many foreign firms set up affiliates within Sri Lanka to undertake the domestic production and/or assembly of product lines which had previously been supplied from overseas production centres.[6] During the 1960's, facilitated by a favourable government policy stance, MNCs expanded their role in the domestic manufacturing sector. By the end of the decade, there were 51 MNE affiliates in operation, and they accounted for about 28 percent (38 percent if the public sector is excluded) of total manufacturing output (Fernando, 1971, p. 84).

The period from 1970 to 1977 witnessed a marked reduction in the tempo of foreign capital participation in the economy (Table 1). The left-of-centre government in power during this period laid a heavy emphasis on expanding the role of the public sector in the economy and DFI did not receive much encouragement. With the change in Government in 1977 there was a marked

[6] Fernando (1971) provides a detailed and interesting account of this early stage of MNE involvement in Sri Lankan manufacturing.

TABLE 1
Multinational Firms by Parentage in Sri Lankan Manufacturing

Period of establishment	Number of Affiliates DCMNCs	TWMNCs	Total
Prior to 1950	3	0	3
1950–1959	8	0	8
1960–1969	34	6	4
1970–1977	11	9	20
1978–1985[1]	135	87	222
Total	191	102[2]	293

[1] Figures for this period include firms in trial production and under construction.
[2] Country-wise distribution of these firms was as follows: Hong Kong 44, Singapore 21, India 16, South Korea 4, Taiwan 3, Other 14.

Source: Official records of Foreign Investment Advisory Council, Greater Colombo Economic Commission, and the Ministry of Industries and Scientific Affairs (for the period up to 1976).

shfit in the policy towards DFI. The promotion of foreign capital participation in manufacturing, notably in export-oriented industries, was a pivotal element of the development strategy of the new right-of-centre Government (Lal and Rajapatirana, 1986). As demonstrated in Table 1, the new policy orientation certainly proved to be very attractive to foreign investors.[7]

A disaggregation of MNE affiliates operating in the Sri Lankan manufacturing sector by nationality of ownership points to a remarkable improvement in the relative position of TWMNEs over time. Even as recently as 1977, there were only 15 TWMNE affiliates among a total number of 71 MNE affiliates. By the end of 1985 the comparable figures were 102 and 293 respectively (Table 1). Hong Kong, India and Singapore, in that order, were the largest nationality groups of TWMNEs. A nationality-wise disaggregation of foreign equity capital in Sri Lankan manufacturing for 1971 and 1982 shows that the combined share of TWMNEs increased from 2 percent to 34 percent between these two years (Athukorala, 1984).

In Table 2, we present data on the location of TWMNEs by 2-digit SITC industries and their relative output shares in 1982. Clearly, they are strongest in the Textile and Wearing Apparel (32) industry accounting for a third of industry output. Of the 71 TWMNEs in Sri Lanka, 30 were located in this industry. In contrast, the output share of DCMNEs in this industry is considerably smaller, though they, too, have more than a third of their total

[7] Political uncertainty resulting from the worsening of the country's ethnic conflict has greatly reduced the attractiveness for DFI since 1983.

TABLE 2

Output Shares of Public Enterprises, Local-Private Firms and Foreign Firms in the organized Manufacturing Sector[1] in Sri Lanka, 1981.

				Foreign firms[2,3]		
SITC Divisions	*Gross output (Rs. Mn.)*	*Public corporations (%)*	*Local private firms[2] (%)*	*DCMEs (%)*	*TWNEs (%)*	*Total (%)*
31 Food, beverages and tobacco	3,499	40	12	47	2	48
32 Products and footwear	3,233	28	25	13	34	47
				(50)	(30)	(80)
33 Wood and wood products	283	89	10	*a*	0	*a*
				(2)	(0)	(2)
34 Paper and paper products	732	75	25	*a*	1	1
				(3)	(3)	(6)
35 Chemical, rubber and plastic products	2,712	43	19	36	3	39
				(32)	(15)	(47)
36 Non-metallic mineral products	1,367	74	11	15	*a*	15
				(11)	(2)	(13)
37 Basic metal products	527	81	*a*	19	0	19
				(3)	(0)	(3)
38 Fabricated metal products	925	22	36	35	7	42
				(17)	(9)	26
39 Other manufacturing	110	0	82	12	6	18
				(12)	(5)	(17)
Total	13,388	44	19	27	10	37
				(139)	(71)	(210)

[1] Excluding petroleum refining. Estimates are based on data from firms employing 5 or more workers.
[2] '*a*' implies that the share is less than 1 percent. Figures may not add up to 100 because of rounding.
[3] Figures in parentheses are number of firms.

Source: Estimated using unpublished firm-level data from *The Survey on Manufacturing Industries — 1981*, Department of Census and Statistics, Sri Lanka.

number located in this sector. In other industries (31, 35 and 38), where MNEs contribute a large proportion of industry output, DCMNEs are dominant. Overall, TWMNEs contribute 10 percent of total output in the organized manufacturing sector.

When industry location of TWMNEs is examined at the more dis-aggregated 3-digit level, they are seen to be highly concentrated in five 3-digit industries (Textiles (321)), wearing apparel (322), rubber products (355), plastic products (356) and other manufacturing (390). This pattern appears to correspond closely to that predicted by the conventional view of TWMNEs as having their competitive advantage in industries with well defined technologies, low requirements of product differentiation and low intensity of product or process innovations (Wells, 1983; Lecraw, 1977 and 1981).

IV. METHODOLOGY AND DATA

(a) Model

We employ multiple regression analysis to examine the relative capital intensity of TWMNEs in relation to DCMNEs and indigenous (local private) firms while controlling for the effect of other firm attributes expected to affect capital intensity. Depending on the availability of data, four industry characteristics (firm size, export orientation, wage rate and the age of DCMNEs) are taken into account. The impact of product composition is taken into account by performing the regression analysis at individual industry level.

The complete model is as follows:

$$KL = KL(DCMNE, LPF, SZ, WG, XOUT, AG*DCMNE)$$

where

KL = Capital intensity (defined as the beginning-of-the-year book value of machinery and equipment per production worker).
SZ = Firm size (represented by gross output).
DCMNE = A dummy variable set equal to 1 if the firm is a DCMNE affiliate and 0 otherwise.
LPF = A dummy variable set equal to 1 if the firm is a local private firm affiliate and 0 otherwise.
WG = Wage rate (measured as average wage per production worker).
AG = Age of firm.
XOUT = Export orientation of firm (measured by the export- output ratio).

In specifying the nationality-of-ownership (parentage) dummies, we have treated TWMNE ownership as the *base* dummy. Therefore, the estimated coefficients of DCMNE and LPF variables are expected to indicate the difference in capital intensity of affiliates of developed-country multinationals and indigenous private firms respectively in relation to TWMNEs. According to the conventional wisdom on TWMNEs (Section I), the expected sign of the coefficient of DCMNE is positive. In the literature there is no explicit postulate as to the capital intensity difference between indigenous firms and TWMNE affiliates (i.e. as to the sign of the coefficient of the LPF variable in our model). In the only study to test this difference so far (Lecraw, 1977), it was found to be positive (and statistically significant). Unfortunately, Lecraw did not discuss the implications of his result. However, drawing upon the existing literature, such a result can be explained as follows. Local firms usually have to choose their equipment from the currently available range of alternatives in a market dominated by DCMNEs. In contrast TWMNEs which establish affiliates can draw on the technological expertise developed over a long period in their home country. They can either design machinery to suit the relatively low wage situation in the host country drawing upon their own historical experience (Wells, 1982), or can utilize second hand machinery which are now outdated by the factor market situation in the home country but are well suited to the new host country (Wells, 1978). If this were so, we expect the sign of the coefficient of TWMNE to be negative.

A well known neoclassical counter argument to the 'inappropriate technology' allegation against DCMNEs is that, within a given industry, firm size, rather than parentage, is more likely to explain differences in capital intensity between DCMNE affiliates and local firms (Biersteker, 1978). The rationale behind this argument, derived from the theory of firm, is that optimum factor proportions and the scale of operation are intimately linked such that the relative importance of labour declines as the scale of production increases.[8] If this were so the sign of the coefficient of SZ should be positive.

It is generally believed that DCMNEs tend to pay higher wages than indigenous firms (Agarwal, 1976; Leipziger, 1976). The wage rate variable (WG) is included in the model to test if this particular feature of multinational behaviour leads to the choice of capital intensive techniques. Thus the expected sign of WG is positive. However, the direction of causation between these two variables is not entirely unambiguous. For instance, the hypothesis that DCMNEs are more capital intensive implies that wages form a smaller percentage of total cost. If this is the case, wage costs might be a less significant consideration for them in determining the input mix. Further, such firms may employ more skilled labour and higher wages may simply reflect this.

Export-oriented firms are usually set up with the aim of exploiting the comparative advantage of the host country. In contrast, inward-looking (import-substituting) investments are induced mostly by various product and factor market distortions which usually impart a bias towards higher capital intensity. Therefore, we can expect production techniques used by firms engaged in manufacturing for exports to be more labour intensive than those

[8] The assumption here is that the production function of the firm is of the non-homothetic type. This is valid for industries where economies of scale are important.

used by firms which are domestic market oriented (Helleiner, 1978; Chen, 1982:199). Accordingly, the coefficient of XOUT variable is expected to be negative.

There is evidence that affiliates of MNEs do modify and adapt their technology to local factor market conditions (Pack, 1976; Morley and Smith, 1977; Kirkpatrick *et al.*, 1985). Indeed, it is quite possible that affiliates of DCMNEs could have undertaken technological adaptation to the same extent as TWMNEs (Lall, 1984). Such adaptation is essentially time dependent (Watanabe, 1981). We take into account the possibility of such adjustment over time by including the slope dummy variable, AG*DCMNE. The sign of this variable is expected to be negative.

(b) Data

The data for the study comes from the Sri Lankan Survey of Manufacturing in 1981. The identification of MNE affiliates for the purpose of data extraction from unpublished returns was done using the list of firms prepared by Lakshman and Athukorala (1985). The list identifies a firm as 'foreign' if at least 30 percent of the share capital is foreign owned and gives information on the parentage and the date of commencement of operations in Sri Lanka.

Initially, data were obtained for all firms employing more than ten workers for all 4-digit industries each of which contained at least one foreign firm. Whenever returns were incomplete (for at least one variable relevant for the study) or irremediably inconsistent, they were not included in the list. The list at this stage contained 132 firms belonging to sixteen 4-digit industries. However, the number of firms in the three ownership categories was inadequate for statistical analysis in seven 4-digit industries. Hence, 31 firms had to be excluded from the analysis. The remaining firms belonged to four industry groups – textile, wearing apparel, chemicals and metal products. The first two groups were at the 4-digit level while the latter two were combinations of 4-digit industries.[9] The aggregation in the latter two groups was unavoidable given the need for an adequate number of observations in each industry classification.

The survey data contained information on the value of total fixed capital as well as that of plant and machinery in fixed capital. In compiling the data series for the capital intensity variable (KL) we used the latter for the following reasons. Firstly, employment is likely to be more closely related with outlay on plant and machinery than with outlay on land and building. Secondly, the literature suggests that DCMNEs tend to spend relatively more on

[9] The four commodity groups (with relevant ISIC number in parentheses) are:
(i) Textile (3211)
(ii) Wearing apparel (3220)
(iii) Chemicals — paints and varnish (3521), drugs and medicines (3522), soap and cosmetic (3523) and miscellaneous chemicals (3529).
(iv) Metal products — non-electrical machinery (3829) electrical machinery (3829), and hand-tools and general hardware (3811).

buildings compared with TWMNEs (Wells, 1983: 27) and indigenous firms (Agarwal, 1976). Hence, the use of total fixed assets as the measure of capital intensity may lead to misleading results.[10] In Table 3, we present the mean values of the major variables differentiated by parentage.

V. RESULTS

The model specified in the previous section was estimated using ordinary least squares. Both linear and log-linear functional forms were tested. Inspection of the correlation matrix showed high intercorrelation between DCMNE and WG variables in all four industry categories. To test the sensitivity of results to the presence of multicollinearity, for each industry, two equations, one including WG and the other excluding it, were estimated. For the metal product industry, the equations do not contain the XOUT variable because none of the firms in this industry had recorded exports. While broadly similar results were obtained with both functional forms, the linear form generally provided a better fit. Results for the latter form are reported in Table 4.

The regression equations for textile and wearing apparel industries provide statistical support for the hypothesis that DCMNEs are relatively more capital intensive than TWMNEs. The coefficient of DCMNE for these commodities is somewhat sensitive to the inclusion (or exclusion) of the WG variable in the equation but remains significant at least at the 10 percent level in both equations. The coefficient of LPF is, however, not statistically significant in the equations for textiles. It is insignificant in equations for wearing apparel, too, even though in this case both coefficients are positive with *t*-values above unity. Overall, the hypothesis that TWMNEs are relatively less capital intensive than indigenous firms is not supported for these two industries. For wearing apparel, if anything, there is weak support for the alternative hypothesis that TWMNEs are relatively more capital intensive than indigenous firms.

The two equations estimated for the chemical industry do not pass the *F* test for overall significance. This suggests that the variables included in the model are not capable of explaining a significant part of the variation in capital intensity in this industry. This may be because all firms in this group use similar (developed-country) technology without adaptation. A recent study on technology licencing and patent rights in Sri Lankan manufacturing showed that in this sector there was a widespread developed-country management presence through licensing agreements (ESCAP/UNCTC, 1984) which extended to all firms irrespective of ownership. Our division of firms

[10] The use of the book value of fixed assets to construct the KL series is subject to the problem that firms have different accounting practices in their valuation of assets. There is also the well known 'vintage' issue (the difficulties of comparing machines of different ages). In the absence of data on fixed investment by age, it is not possible to overcome these limitations. All previous studies in this area have encountered these problems. For details on various methods of measuring capital intensity and related issues see Bhalla (1975).

TABLE 3

Firm Characteristics by Parentage (Mean Values)

Variable	*Parentage*	*Number of firms*	*Average output (Rs.'000) (SZ)*	*Export output ratio (%) (XOUT)*	*Wage per employee (Rs.) (WG)*	*Machines and equipment per worker (Rs) (KL)*
1. Textile	DCMNE	5	24,375	5.7	8,883	56,059
	TWMNE	6	29,253	35.5	5,285	3,653
	LPRV	11	3,467	8.5	6,329	3,435
2. Wearing apparel	DCMNE	8	24,122	8.0	8,500	11,775
	TWMNE	8	28,324	91.0	7,461	6,488
	LPRV	10	22,500	85.5	6,118	3,850
3. Chemical – products	DCMNE	15	26,861	4.0	18,421	25,264
	TWMNE	6	7,706	2.6	8,422	24,068
	LPRV	16	4,892	9.7	7,466	16,198
4. Metal products	DCMNE	6	39,776	–	14,882	40,236
	TWMNE	5	14,228	–	9,876	13,843
	LPRV	5	1,583	–	6,325	9,456
5. Total sample	DCMNE	34	28,130	28.2	14,059	29,260
	TWMNE	25	20,750	37.4	7,638	11,498
	LPRV	42	8,317	8.7	6,711	9,113

Legend: DCMNE = Developed-Country multinational enterprises
TWMNE = Third-World multinational enterprises
LPRV = Local private firm

Source: Compiled using firm-level data (unpublished) from *The Survey Manufacturing Industry – 1981*, Department of Census and Statistics, Sri Lanka.

TABLE 4
Regression Results

		Variables									Sample size
		Constant	*DCMNE*	*LPF*	*XOUT*	*S̄Z*	*WG*	*AG*DCMNE*	$\bar{R}^2$	*F*	*(N)*
1. Textile	(a)	−7.95	56.63	0.58	−5.66	0.43	2.99	−3.33	0.85	21.61***	22
		(0.61)	(2.27)***	(0.06)	(0.81)	(0.20)	(3.04)***	(1.84)**			
	(b)	19.47	120.13	−7.69	−7.95	−0.25		−8.01	0.78	15.85***	22
		(1.72)	(7.12)***	(0.69)	(0.93)	(0.95)		(6.78)***			
2. Wearing apparel	(a)	7.81	7.81	−1.96	0.06	−0.44	0.04	−0.45	0.50	5.15**	26
		(1.78)	(1.85)*	(1.10)	(0.02)	(1.05)	(0.12)	(0.47)			
	(b)	15.39	10.82	−0.37	5.20	−0.20		1.59	0.45	4.34**	26
		(1.61)	(1.73)*	(0.09)	(0.69)	(2.37)		(0.95)			
3. Chemicals	(a)	26.68	−1.61	−16.04	9.26	0.18	0.11	−0.08	0.02	1.07	37
		(2.13)	(0.09)	(1.17)	(0.52)	(1.09)	(0.12)	(0.18)			
	(b)	27.14	−0.34	−15.75	9.21	0.18		−0.06	0.04	1.32	37
		(2.32)	(0.02)	(1.18)	(0.52)	(1.16)		(0.16)			
4. Metal products	(a)	4.91	−28.85	3.45	1.93		−1.15	0.58	0.53	4.35**	16
		(0.19)	(0.81)	(0.15)	(3.26)***		(0.52)	(0.26)			
	(b)	−4.93	−30.67	8.57	1.78			0.62	0.56	5.77**	16
		(0.30)	(0.89)	(0.44)	(3.51)***			(0.29)			
5. Total sample	(a)	1.92	13.12	0.39	−9.11	0.02	1.65	−0.50	0.24	4.72**	101
		(0.19)	(1.37)	(0.04)	(1.40)	(1.32)	(2.80)**	(1.45)			
	(b)	17.53	15.32	−4.51	−14.20	0.02		−0.14	0.13	3.82**	101
		(1.97)	(1.56)*	(0.51)	(2.20)**	(1.87)**		(0.42)			

Notes: *T*-ratios are given in parenthesis under each coefficient. Level of significance (one-tail test) denoted: *Significant at 10 percent; **Significant at 5 percent; ***Significant at 1 percent.

on the basis of DFI does not capture this element of foreign technology participation.

The equations for the metal product group are significant at 5 percent level. The only statistically significant explanatory variable is firm size which is significant at 1 percent level in both equations. It is interesting to note that the large differences in the mean levels of capital intensity between DCMNEs and the other two groups observed in Table 3 cannot be attributed to parentage; rather, they appear to be related to firm size.

Among the other explanatory variables, the coefficient of XOUT is insignificant and the sign is not consistent when the analysis is conducted at the disaggregated level of industry groups. However, in the two equations for the total sample it has the expected sign and one of these coefficients is significant at 5 percent level. This suggests that the degree of export orientation may be relevant for explaining inter-industry variation of capital intensity of production but not intra-industry variation. The wage rate variable is significant (with the expected sign) only in one industry (textiles). Note that the same is true for the interaction variable of age with DCMNE ownership. In sum, there is no consistency among the four industry groups with regard to the relevance of the four firm-characteristics considered in explaining inter-firm differences in factor intensity.

VI. CONCLUSION

DCMNEs generally exhibit a higher degree of capital intensity compared with TWMNEs and indigenous private firms in terms of average capital per worker. However, such a simple comparison can be misleading as firm attributes other than parentage can affect capital intensity. Our analysis of data from the Sri Lankan manufacturing sector which controlled for the effect of such other factors highlights the fact that *the link between parentage and capital intensity is industry specific.*

There were marked differences in capital intensity between DCMNEs and TWMNEs in the textile and wearing apparel industries. However, no such differences could be observed in the chemical and metal product industries. There were no significant differences beteween TWMNEs and indigenous private firms in any industry.

These results support the view that developing country firms may adopt more appropriate technology only in those industries where the range of technological possibilities is wide enough to enable significantly different techniques of production to be utilized (Lall, 1983). The textile and wearing apparel industries are classic examples of such industries. It is significant that in these industries even the firms with developed-country parentage tended to adopt more labour intensive techniques over time.

Our results also show that the degree of export orientation is more relevant in explaining inter-industry rather than intra-industry differentials in capital intensity. As expected, the labour intensity is relatively higher in those export oriented industries in which labour rich developing countries tend to have greater comparative advantage.

Thus, our results suggest that the inter-industry variations in the degree of technological flexibility are an important determinant of the capacity of developing-country multinational affiliates to adopt more appropriate techniques than developed country multinationals. To the extent that they locate within the more labour intensive industries where such flexibility is generally high, and where most developing countries typically have comparative advantage, they can make a greater contribution to employment and economic growth than developed country multinationals. However, over time these differences tend to diminish.

La Trobe University,
Bundoora, Victoria

Date of Receipt of Final Manuscript: May 1988.

REFERENCES

Agarwal, J. (1977). 'Factor Proportions in Foreign and Domestic Firms in Indian Manufacturing', *Economic Journal*, Vol. 86, pp. 589–94.

Ahiakpor, J. C. W. (1986). 'The Capital Intensity of Foreign, Private, Local and State Owned Firms in a Less Developing Country: Ghana', *Journal of Development Economics*, Vol. 20, No. 2, pp. 145–62.

Athukorala, P. (1984). 'Direct Foreign Investment and Manufactured Exports from Sri Lanka', *Vidyodaya: Journal of the University of Sri Jayawardenepura*, Vol. 12, pp. 21–41.

Balasubramanyam, V. N. (1983). 'Transnational Corporations: Choice of Techniques and Employment in Developing Countries', in B. Weisbrod and H. Hughes (eds.) *Human Resources Employment and Development*, London, Macmillan.

Bhalla, A. S. (1975). 'The Concept and Measurement of Labour Intensity' in A. S. Bhalla (ed.) *Technology and Employment in Industry: A Case Study Approach*, Geneva, ILO, pp. 11–33.

Biersteker, J. J. (1978). *Distortion or Development? Contending Perspectives on the Multinational Corporation*, Cambridge, Mass., MIT Press.

Busjeet, V. (1980). Foreign investors from Less-Developed Countries, Unpublished Doctoral Dissertation, Harvard Business School.

Chen, E. K. Y. (1983). *Multinational Corporations, Technology and Employment*, London, Macmillan.

Diaz-Alejandro, C. F. (1977). 'Foreign Direct Investment by Latin Americans', in T. Agmor and C. P. Kindleberger (eds.) *Multinationals from Small Countries*, Cambridge, Mass.: MIT Press, pp. 167–96.

ESCAP/UNCTC (1984). 'Technology Transfer from Transnational Corporations in Sri Lanka' in ESCAP/UNCTC, *Costs and Conditions of Technology Transfer Through Transnational Corporations*, Bangkok, pp. 151–83.

Fernando, L. E. N. (1971). Some Aspects of Private Foreign Enterprises in Ceylon, Ph.D. Thesis, University of Hull.

Forsyth, D. J. C., McBain, N. and Solomon, R. F. (1980). 'Technical Rigidity and Appropriate Technology in Less-developed Countries', *World Development*, Vol. 10, No. 3, pp. 371–79.

Forsyth, D. J. C. and Solomon, R. F. (1977). 'Choice of Technology and Nationality of Ownership in Manufacturing in a Developing Country', *Oxford Economic Papers*, Vol. 29, No. 2, pp. 259–83.

Helleiner, G. K. (1973). 'Manufacturing for Exports, Multinational Firms and Economic Development', *World Development*, Vol. 1, No. 7, pp. 13–22.

Hill, H. and Lindsay, C. W. (1987). 'Multinationals from Large and Small Countries: A Philippine Case Study', *Banca Nazionale Del Lavoro Quarterley Review*, No. 160, pp. 75–92.

Jenkins, R. (1986). 'Third World Multinationals: Rhetoric or Reality?' *Journal of Development Studies*, Vol. 22, No. 2, pp. 458–63.

Kirkpatrick, C. H., Lee, N. and Nixon, F. I. (1984). *Industrial Structure and Policy in Less Developed Countries*, London, Allen and Unwin.

Lakshman, W. D. and Athukorala, P. (1985). Transnational Trading Corporations and the Structure of Trading Channels in Sri Lankan Foreign Trade, Research Paper, ESCAP/UNCTC Joint Unit on Transnational Corporations, Bangkok (mimeo).

Lal, D. and Rajapatirana, S. (1987). *Impediments to Trade Liberalization in Sri Lanka*, Thames Essay No. 53, London. Trade Policy Research Centre.

Lall, S. (1983). *The New Multinationals: The Spread of Third World Enterprises*, New York, John Wiley.

Lall, S. (1983). 'The Rise of Multinationals from the Third World', *Third World Quarterly*, Vol. 5, No. 3, pp. 618–26.

Lecraw, D. (1981). 'The Internationalization of Firms from LDCs: Evidence from Asian Region' in K. Kumar and M. McLeod (eds.), *Multinationals from Developing Countries*, Lexington, MA: D.C. Heath.

Lecraw, D. (1977). 'Direct Investment by Firms from Less-Developed Countries', *Oxford Economic Papers*, Vol. 29, No. 3, pp. 442–57.

Leipziger, D. M. (1976). 'Production Characteristics in Foreign Enclave and Domestic Firms: The Case of India', *World Development*, Vol. 4, No. 3, pp. 321–25.

Morley, S. A. and Smith, G. W. (1977). 'The Choice of Technology: Multinational Firms in Brazil', *Economic Development and Cultural Change*, Vol. 24, No. 2, pp. 239–64.

O'Brien, P. (1980). 'Third World Industrial Enterprises: Exports of Technology and Capital', *Economic and Political Weekly*, Vol. 25, Nos. 41, 42 and 43, pp. 1831–45.

Pack, H. (1976). 'The Substitution of Labour for Capital in Kenyan Manufacturing', *Economic Journal*, Vol. 86, pp. 45–58.

Sen, A. (1980). 'Labour and Technology' in J. Cody, H. Hughes and D. Wall (eds.). *Policies for Industrial Progress in Developing Countries*, New York, Oxford University Press, pp. 121–58.

Singer, H. W. (1973). 'International Policy and its Effect on Employment' in R. Jolly, *et al.* (eds.), *Third World Employment*, Harmondsworth, Penguin.

United Nations Centre on Transnational Corporations (UNCTC) (1983). *Salient Features and Trends in Foreign Direct Investment*, New York, United Nations.

Watanabe, S. (1981). 'Multinational Enterprises, Employment and Technology Adaptations'. *International Labour Review*, Vol. 120, pp. 693–704.

Wells, L. T. Jr. (1981). *Third World Multinationals: The Rise of Foreign Investment from Developing Countries*, Cambridge, Mass., MIT Press.

Wells, L. T. Jr. (1978). 'Foreign Investment from the Third World: The Experience of Chinese Firms from Hong Kong', *Columbia Journal of World Business*. Vol. 13, No. 1, pp. 39–48.

Wells, L. T. Jr. (1977). 'The Internationalization of Firms from Developing Countries', in T. Agmor and C. P. Kindleberger (1977). *Multinationals from Small Countries*, Cambridge, MIT Press, pp. 69–84.

Wells, L. T. Jr. and Warren, V. (1979). 'Developing Country Investors in Indonesia', *Bulletin of Indonesian Economic Studies*. Vol. 15, No. 1, pp. 69–84.

White, E. (1983). 'Multinational Companies of Developing Countries: The Issues of Correct Policies, in Pavlic, B. *et al.* (eds.), *The Challenges of South-South Co-operation*, Bouler, Colorado, Westview.

[22]

Brazilian Multinationals

Christopher Wells

Brazilian companies, driven by the need to export, are using their advanced management and technical skills to successfully run subsidiaries abroad.

THE TUCANO AIRPLANE, the Labra pencil and the Atlas elevator are hardly household names in the United States or Europe. They are, however, an important part of people's lives in many countries.

- Tucano military training aircraft, designed in Brazil, are a source of jobs for several thousand workers in Belfast, Northern Ireland, who are assembling them for the Royal Air Force;
- Labra pencils, made in Portugal by a Brazilian company, will soon be used by school children throughout Western Europe;
- Every day thousands of people in Buenos Aires, Santiago and Mexico City use Atlas elevators, shipped from Brazil and installed by a Brazilian multinational.

Brazilian multinationals have manufacturing subsidiaries producing a wide range of products in more than a dozen countries. Their arrival on the scene is very recent; a decade ago there were only a handful of Brazilian companies with more than a sales office abroad. The number has grown to at least 33 companies, plus several dozen construction and engineering firms.

The significance of Brazilian multinationals extends beyond the novelty of the phenomenon. Brazilian investment abroad is beginning to play an important role in relations with a variety of countries. These companies have built Paraguay's only steel mill, Chile's first shopping mall and Portugal's leading supermarket chain. Their success abroad is a unique combination of sophisticated technology with management expertise applied to the socioeconomic environment and climatic conditions of developing countries. Given the rapidly expanding trade links between Brazil and the rest of the Third World, these multinationals will certainly affect the course of economic development in Latin America, Africa and even the former mother country, Portugal.

Brazilian multinationals also are surfacing as an important force in the context of the nation's foreign debt, the largest in the developing world. Their investment abroad, now about $1 billion, helps promote exports, the key to any solution of the debt crisis.

Estimates vary as to the exact size of foreign direct investment (FDI) by Brazilian multinationals. Anibal Villela, in his 1982 study of these companies, itemized FDI by firm and arrived at a total of about $1 billion at historical values.[1] My 1986 estimate (detailed in Table I) is roughly comparable at $1.1 billion, although there are conflicting data for some companies. This figure is conservative because it does not include investments in construction projects and sales offices as well as FDI by companies for which no data were available.

The Brazilian Central Bank's figures (Table II) total $1.3 billion. Although this is very close to the two itemized estimates, the Central Bank figure includes investments by banks in branches in the US, Western Europe and the Caribbean, while excluding oil exploration by Petrobras, the national oil corporation, and other capital invested overseas but registered as expense.[2] In essence, therefore, my re-

---

Christopher Wells is editor of the weekly English edition of Gazeta Mercantil, *the major Brazilian business daily. He is based in São Paulo.*

search only covers the tip of a growing iceberg.

RESEARCH BACKGROUND

My research on Brazilian multinationals dates back to 1981, when I spent a year at the University of Sao Paulo. That year I wrote a paper on the subject based on interviews and company articles. After returning to New York, I built files on the companies for several years. I used them for my Master's thesis written in early 1986 while attending the Fundacao Getulio Vargas in Sao Paulo as part of an exchange program with the Graduate School of Business Administration at New York University. I complemented the files with more interviews and submitted the thesis in September 1986.

TRENDS

In conducting a statistical analysis, I used 33 industrial Brazilian multinationals, excluding most construction and engineering firms and Companhia de Pesquisa de Recursos Minerais (CPRM), the federally owned mineral prospection company that operates abroad without subsidiaries. The group of 33 has set up a total of 63 subsidiaries and licensed production operations abroad. At least 12 of these activities had been discontinued as of mid-1988.

Joint ventures account for two-thirds of the subsidiaries, as seen in Table III. Host country legislation is only partly responsible for this tendency. The multinational often needs a joint venture because it is not financially or technologically capable of running the subsidiary alone.

The rate of expansion overseas rapidly accelerated after 1984, when Brazil started accumulating large trade surpluses. Investment in general has grown concurrently with the export drive. Almost half of the multinationals took their first steps abroad between 1984 and 1988.

The pre-1980 investments are characterized by the impossibility of simply exporting the product, such as elevators, supermarkets and oil exploration. The pre-1980 investments generally were not motivated by export priorities but rather by the opportunity to exploit some technological or managerial skill.

Investment overseas in the eighties, propelled by exports, has been linked to the sale of "portable" items such as aircraft, electricity meters, textiles and iron ore.

Two-thirds of the 33 multinationals are leaders in their respective sectors.[8]

TABLE 1

Figures on Investment by Company (where available)

All figures in thousands of US dollars, as of mid-1986

Amount	Company	Note
$767,000	Braspetro (subsidiary of Petrobras)	This represents the total amount invested abroad for oil exploration and setting up service subsidiaries. This figure is not counted in the Central Bank's records probably because Braspetro wrote it off as an expense to be reimbursed by Petrobras. This procedure was discontinued after 1984.
$130,000	Labra	In 1985, Labra acquired a pencil factory in Portugal.
$ 65,000	Interbras (trading company of Petrobras)	As with Braspetro, this represents the total amount disbursed from 1976 to 1985. It is not known whether the same reimbursement procedure was used.
$ 50,100	Cotia	This is a 1980 figure for Cotia's capital in its various Nigerian subsidiaries. Cotia in recent years has been investihg $40 million a year abroad. Cotia writes off all FDI as expense.
$ 38,500	Copersucar	In 1976, Copersucar bought Hills' Brothers Coffee of San Francisco, California.
$ 25,000	Veplan	This represents Veplan's investment in a joint venture to build a shopping center in Chile.
$ 20,000	CVRD	In 1984, CVRD bought 25% of a steel mill in the US.
$ 10,000	Pao de Acucar	This is a 1974 figure for the amount Pao de Acucar lost when the Portuguese government expropriated its supermarket chain.
$ 4,000	Bardella	In 1985, Bardella bought 50% of a capital goods maker in the US.
$ 2,500	Gradiente	In 1979, Gradiente bought the British turntable maker, Garrard.
$ 1,364	Inbrac	This represents the total capital and machinery invested in Inbrac's joint ventures in Paraguay and Ecuador.
$ 500	Securit	In 1979, Securit entered into a joint venture to open a furniture showroom in the US.
$ 500	Cacique	In 1985, Cacique entered into a joint venture to package instant coffee in China. This is the amount to be invested.
$ 400	Inepar	In 1977, Inepar entered into a joint venture to make electrical control equipment in Chile.
$ 300	Nansen	In 1985, Nansen announced it was building a factory to make electrical measurement equipment in Colombia. This is the amount to be invested.

TOTAL OF ITEMIZED FOREIGN DIRECT INVESTMENT: $1,115,164,000

This is a logical result of the economies of scale enjoyed by these companies and in some cases the cramped outlook for expansion at home. The top raw materials producers can guarantee a steady flow of iron ore or coffee to their foreign offshoots by virtue of their world-class volume of output.

About half of the multinationals view their foreign operations as but a small addition to their whole range of activities. (Data were not available for the rest.) Sales by foreign subsidiaries and licensed production abroad make up less than a tenth of total sales for 12 companies, and in many cases the contribution is below 1%.[4] It is important to note that income from subsidiaries is unrelated to export sales. For example, Cacique, the leading instant coffee producer, exports the bulk of its output but plans to commit less than 1% of production to its joint venture in China.[5]

TABLE 2

Distribution of Brazilian Investment Overseas Registered with Central Bank, 1986

(in millions)

Total Investment	US$1,315.8	100.0%
Non-Offshore Destinations		
United States	$608.7	46.3%
Other O.E.C.D.		
United Kingdom	$45.2	3.4%
France	$22.1	1.7%
West Germany	$15.2	1.2%
Spain	$14.8	1.1%
Japan	$10.0	0.8%
Austria	$10.0	0.8%
Subtotal Other O.E.C.D.	$117.3	9.0%
Subtotal O.E.C.D. Including US	$726.0	55.3%
Developing Countries		
Argentina	$74.1	5.6%
Paraguay	$55.7	4.2%
Chile	$52.9	4.0%
Uruguay	$36.1	2.7%
Bolivia	$21.5	1.6%
Venezuela	$15.3	1.2%
Ivory Coast	$11.6	0.9%
Subtotal Developing Countries	$267.2	20.3%
Total Non-Offshore	$993.2	75.6%
Offshore Destinations		
Cayman Islands	$82.0	6.2%
Netherlands Antilles	$78.9	6.0%
Bahamas	$39.1	3.0%
Panama	$23.7	1.8%
Luxembourg	$17.0	1.3%
Bahrain	$13.0	1.0%
Singapore	$11.4	0.9%
Leeward Islands	$11.0	0.8%
Total Offshore	$276.1	21.0%
Other	$46.5	3.4%

Source: **Central Bank of Brazil.** These figures represent all registered capital invested by Brazilian companies outside of Brazil from 1965 to 1985.

MOTIVES FOR INVESTMENT

Import Barriers: Prior Export Experience

This group is composed of companies with several years of export experience in a given market prior to establishing a subsidiary there.[6] These companies are distinguished by their orientation toward exports.

Companies such as Labra (pencils) and Nansen (electricity meters) classically demonstrates the case of building a plant abroad with the express intent of replacing exports from the parent company. Labra, which claims to be the world's second-largest manufacturer of pencils, invested $130 million in a Portuguese factory to beef up exports to the European Economic Community (EEC). Nansen, which exports between 10% and 20% of output to Latin America, opened a plant at Medellin, Colombia, to serve as a springboard for third world country sales.

Embraer's aircraft assembly operations in Cairo and Belfast were necessary because the air forces of Egypt and the U.K. would not have placed orders without local production. A similar obstacle led Bardella, a leading capital manufacturer, to buy a 50% stake in the US offshoot of West Germany's Schuler GmbH. Prior to its Columbus, Ohio acquisition, Bardella lost a contract to supply cranes to San Francisco's port because it did not have a company based in the US. Since the acquisition in late 1985, Schuler Inc. has become the principal supplier of stamping presses to Chrysler Corp. Like Embraer, Bardella needed a local presence to win contracts, in this case to provide a service network.

Import Barriers: Limited Export Experience

Ten companies are distinguished by their lack of export experience to the countries where they invested.[7] In most cases, such as television stations, elevators, supermarkets and soft drinks, it was impossible or impractical to export directly without some infrastructure close to the customer. The motive could not have been to consolidate an export market, therefore, and the answer seems to lie in opportunities rather than necessities.

The opportunity is the exploitation of some technological or managerial skill. This includes tropical technologies related to bottling a soft drink derived from an Amazonian berry or building rugged buses for hot climates. The company's forte can range from low-tech cable-making machinery to sophisticated elevators and escalators. Auto parts manufacturer Eluma went abroad thanks to technology developed jointly with its US partner, Bundy.[8]

Globo, Brazil's dominant television network, bought a Monte Carlo-based television station after it sensed that it could transfer its programming skills to developed countries. The network searched the world for acquisitions and chose Telemontecarlo based on price and expansion prospects.

Few of these companies depend significantly on exports. The absence of an export motive is also reflected in the fact that eight of the ten companies had established some kind of foreign operation in the seventies, before a major export drive took hold.[9]

The best explanation for investment abroad by this group is that each company realized its technology could be applied to other countries and then took advantage of that opportunity. The investments were minimal: "an office with a phone" in the words of an elevator company executive, and previously-used machinery for a stereo equipment manufacturer. The company's managers therefore must have judged the venture worthwhile.

Vertical Integration

Forward vertical integration is a natural reflex of companies that boast a strong raw material advantage and whose volume of production justifies acquisition of the subsequent step as adding value to their commodity. The Brazilian forward vertical integration investments have always had an eye on developed-country markets, principally the US and Japan, a logical consequence of heavy dependence on these markets.

Companhia Vale do Rio Doce (CVRD), the world's top iron ore

TABLE 3

Itemization of Subsidiaries

Parentheses indicate the company no longer has a subsidiary in that country.

Company	Country	Form of Association
BARDELLA (capital goods)	(USA)	(50% stake in joint venture)
BRAHMA (beer)	Argentina	minority stake
CACIQUE (instant coffee)	China	50%
CARAIBA (copper mining)	(Chile)	(joint venture)
CALOI (bicycles)	Bolivia	joint venture
	(Colombia)	(50%)
	Guyana	licensed assembly
	Costa Rica	licensed assembly
CICA (canned foods)	Argentina *	majority *
COPERSUCAR (coffee)	(USA)	(100%)
COTIA (diversified—all in Nigeria)		LIK: minority
		LEMACO: joint venture
		DRINCO: joint venture
		(NRL: 60%)
		(PROJEX: 100%)
CVRD (iron ore mining)	USA	25%
DIMEP (clocks)	Portugal	unknown
ELUMA (auto parts)	Argentina	20%
	Colombia	minority
	(South Africa)	(minority)
	(Venezuela)	(45%)
EMBRAER (aircraft)	Egypt	licensed assembly
	United Kingdom	licensed assembly
GLOBO (TV broadcasting)	Italy	100%
GRADIENTE (home electronics)	(Mexico)	(100%)
	United Kingdom	100%
GRENDENE (plastic footwear)	Argentina	49%
	Colombia	minority
	Mexico	minority
HERING (cotton knitwear)	Argentina	licensed production
	Portugal	joint venture
INCASA (iodine salts)	Chile	joint venture
INEPAR (elec. control equip.)	Chile	40%
LABRA (pencils)	Portugal	97%
MARCOPOLO (buses)	(Ghana)	(licensed assembly)
	(Venezuela)	(licensed assembly)
METAL LEVE (auto pistons)	USA	100%
METALUR (magnesium alloys)	Norway	33%
NANSEN (electricity meters)	Colombia	50%
ODEBRECHT (construction)	Portugal	majority
PAO DE ACUCAR (supermarkets)	Angola	majority
	Poland	minority
	Portugal	majority
	(Spain)	(minority)
	Soviet Union	majority
PARANAPANEMA (tin and gold mining)	Guyana	75%
PETROBRAS (oil exploration)	Algeria	majority
	Angola	minority
	Norway	minority
	USA	joint venture

TABLE 3 (Continued)

Company	Country	Form of Association
SECURIT (office furniture)	(USA)	(75%)
TENENGE (industrial engineering)	Chile	100%
	Paraguay	100%
VACCHI (leather products)	United Kingdom	51%
VEPLAN (shopping malls)	(Chile)	(35%)
VILLARES (elevators)	Argentina	100%
	Colombia	70%
	Chile	100%
	Mexico	87%
	Paraguay	100%
	Uruguay	100%

TOTAL COMPANIES: 33
TOTAL SUBSIDIARIES: 63

Source: I depended primarily on interviews, company documents and newspapers.

* Cica was acquired in 1987 by the Ferruzzi group of Italy. The Argentine subsidiary remained with the original owners of Cica, the Bonfiglioli group of Sao Paulo.

Form of Association		
Joint venture	43	68%
Majority stake	13	21%
50%	4	6%
Minority	19	30%
Unknown	7	11%
Wholly-owned	12	19%
Licensed prod.	7	11%
Unknown	1	2%
TOTAL	63	100%

Legend: figures refer to equity holdings in subsidiaries. When exact figure is not known, the terms minority and majority are used.

Licensed production means the company allowed the foreign partner to manufacture the product in return for royalties.

Licensed assembly is the same as licensed production, except that the product is assembled abroad from kits sent by the Brazilian company.

Joint venture means a partnership with stakes not disclosed.

producer, bought part of a California steel mill in 1984 to cash in on the value added to iron ore at the manufacturing stage.[10] Copersucar, a leading coffee exporter, bought San Francisco-based Hills Brothers Coffee in 1976 to vertically integrate its coffee business and take advantage of a traditional name. (Copersucar sold Hills Brothers in 1983 after failing to make an adequate return on its investment.)

Cacique, the leading exporter of Brazilian instant coffee, entered into a joint venture with a Chinese state farm to bottle coffee starting early in 1987. Cacique cannot afford to export instant coffee bottled in Brazil to the other side of the globe because of the fragile nature of the product. The company's aim is to break out of exporting unpackaged instant coffee and sell most of the bottled coffee to Japan, Australia and other Asian markets.[11]

Securit, Brazil's largest office furniture maker, opened a showroom and assembly point in Houston, Texas, in 1980.[12] The company's strategy was to cut through furniture dealers in Houston and sell directly to the customer, taking advantage of cheap Brazilian wood and labor. Securit aimed at capitalizing on the oil boom in Texas and the large Arab real estate investments in the state. Pressure tactics from local competitors forced Securit to close down the operation.

Domestic Market Slowdown

With the onset of the debt crisis after 1982, GNP growth rates, once among the highest in the world, slid into the negative zone. The recovery beginning around 1984-5 has raised per capita output levels slightly above what they were on the eve of the crisis. Meanwhile, dozens of large local companies (soon to become multinationals) found that their production volumes were exceeding Brazil's absorption capacity.

This glut led to the well-documented export drive that has generated huge trade surpluses. The boost in exports was partly helped by a steady stream of currency devaluations that often outstripped the fast-moving inflation rate. A soft currency helped aspiring multinationals place their product abroad in sufficient numbers to justify FDI.

Growth at home has also been held back by political uncertainty. Since 1985, when a civilian president was restored (though not via direct election), the focus of both politicians and businessmen has been directed at rewriting the constitution, a legacy of the military, and setting a date and procedure for the first direct presidential election in more than a quarter-century. This uncertainty has been reflected by a plunge in fixed asset investment, and has fed a growing pool of capital that is invested on a day-to-day basis in securities. Farsighted businessmen, however, are investing this idle capital abroad.

This FDI can be carried out without creating a drain on international reserves, as the government has invented an innovative scheme using gold. The Central Bank disburses hard currency to the aspiring multinational in return for the equivalent value in gold, acquired by the company from Brazil's booming gold mining industry. This technique was made possible by the almost weekly gold discoveries occuring on the rim of the Amazon Basin.

The domestic glut is particularly apparent in the case of capital goods manufacturers and construction/engineering firms. With a slowdown in government spending on major infrastructure projects, companies such as

Mendes Junior, the leading construction firm, and Bardella, have looked abroad. Today many of these firms depend on foreign contracts as the mainstay of their business. Mendes Junior in the mid-eighties was earning more than a third of its revenue abroad,[13] and in the capital goods industry up to 70% of output was exported in 1984.[14] Many capital goods leaders are forging links with Argentine counterparts, which also suffer from idle capacity, to jointly produce for the Latin American and African markets.

One construction company chose to boost its overseas presence via acquisition. The Odebrecht group, which is already strong in Africa, in 1988 bought a Portuguese construction firm to enhance its grip on the market and break into EEC work.

TABLE 4

Distribution of Foreign Operations

Latin America		
Argentina	6	Brahma, Cica, Eluma, Grendene, Hering, Villares
Chile	6	(Caraiba), Incasa, Inepar, Tenenge, (Veplan), Villares
Colombia	5	(Caloi), Eluma, Grendene, Nansen, Villares
Mexico	3	(Gradiente), Grendene, Villares
Paraguay	3	Inbrac, Tenenge, Villares
Guyana	2	Caloi, Paranapanema
Venezuela	2	(Eluma), (Marcopolo)
Bolivia	1	Caloi
Costa Rica	1	Caloi
Ecuador	1	Inbrac
Uruguay	1	Villares
	31	49% of total foreign operations
Developed Countries		
United States	6	(Bardella), (Copersucar), CVRD, Metal Leve, Petrobras, (Securit)
Portugal	5	Dimep, Hering, Odebrecht, Pao de Acucar, Labra
United Kingdom	3	Embraer, Gradiente, Vacchi
Norway	2	Metalur, Petrobras
Italy	1	Globo
Spain	1	(Pao de Acucar)
	17	29%
Other		
Nigeria	5	Cotia has set up five subsidiaries in Nigeria
Angola	2	Pao de Acucar, Petrobras
Algeria	1	Petrobras
China	1	Cacique
Egypt	1	Embraer
Ghana	1	(Marcopolo)
Poland	1	Pao de Acucar
South Africa	1	(Eluma)
Soviet Union	1	Pao de Acucar
	14	22%

Parentheses indicate the company no longer has a subsidiary in that country.

Government Priorities

Braspetro, the overseas oil exploration arm of Petrobras, was created in 1972 more because of strategic priorities than commercial interest. Brazil, a major importer of petroleum (slightly less than Italy or Spain), felt the need to secure supplies abroad through risk contracts and close relations with OPEC countries. Braspetro's first discovery was the Majnoon field in Iraq, which was later devastated by Iranian forces in the Gulf War. Since its creation, Braspetro has carried out exploration and production in over a dozen countries, including Angola, Algeria, China, India, South Yemen, Libya, Congo and Guatemala.[15] In March 1987 Braspetro won two bids to explore in the Norwegian zone of the North Sea in two consortia with oil majors such as Shell and Exxon.[16]

Braspetro is seeking to expand its share of revenue from oil services as part of a strategy of moving away from being a tool of national policy and toward becoming its own profit center. The subsidiary now sells its expertise in the construction and installation of oil rigs, refineries, storage systems and pipelines.

Petrobras, the parent company, wants to open a subsidiary in London. This new unit, which will probably be named Petrobras Overseas, will fully implement the corporation's strategy to become the oil industry's "eighth sister." Among its objectives are the construction and ownership of refineries overseas, for purely profit motives, and participation in the oil trading market.[17]

COMPETITIVE ADVANTAGES

When investing abroad, Brazilian multinationals must compete against both developed-country multinationals and host (and usually less developed) country firms. Their competitive advantage vis-a-vis major multinationals stems frequently from application of advanced technology or managerial skill in the less developed country (LDC) environment. In cases where the Brazilian company does not possess an advanced technical base, the firm competes on the basis of smaller production runs, raw materials and know-how adapted to tropical climates. At home, Brazilian multinationals can bring to bear skills ranging from supermarket management to oil exploration to gold mining.

Management Skills

The most common competitive advantage of Brazilian multinationals is the management skills they have accumulated over the past decades. These skills can be applied to managing construction projects, cable factories and supermarkets, as well as to marketing canned goods. Possessing the largest and most diversified economy in the Third World, Brazil is in the unique position to offer management of sophisticated technology in the socioeconomic setting of a developing—or even developed—country.

Francisco Sercovich, a consultant to the Inter-American Development Bank, points out that Brazilian engineering firms have gradually accumulated know-how through years of "learning by doing." The technologies for such sophisticated projects as petrochemical complexes, offshore drilling rigs and ferroalloy plants have been successfully absorbed via former licensing arrangements.[18] The management skills associated with these projects have been developed to the point that firms can compete outside Brazil against bidders from developed countries.

Tenenge, an engineering firm with subsidiaries in Chile and Paraguay, can deliver virtually state-of-the-art refineries through a combination of former licensing arrangements and its own technology. The company also completes the projects at a lower cost than developed-country competitors, thanks to the difference in engineers' salaries and perks. In the words of a Tenenge manager, "developed-country firms are pricing themselves out of the market, leaving it to Brazilians, Koreans, Indians and others." [19]

Engevix, a leading consulting engineering firm, is designing part of the Baghdad subway system using expertise gained when it helped plan the São Paulo Metro in the late seventies. The São Paulo project, recalls a senior executive, was "basically handled by Sofrerail, a French company. We absorbed their technology and were able to adapt it to Iraq." [20]

This "learning by doing" approach has also been employed by federally owned CPRM and privately owned Paranapanema, two companies carrying out mineral prospection abroad. Both companies have built up reservoirs of experience within Brazil's vast territorial expanse and are applying that know-how to the rest of the developing world. Gold mining is a particular forte; Paranapanema is developing a gold mine in Guyana, and Andrade Gutierrez, a leading construction company, plans to build the world's third-largest gold mine at Kilo-Moto, in northeastern Zaire.[21]

Petrobras, the oil monopoly, has absorbed the expertise related to oil exploration, in addition to "learning by doing," on its own outside of Brazil. This know-how includes the engineering aspects of drilling for oil plus the managerial skills needed to handle hundreds of workers in the jungle, desert or off the coast of a foreign country. Petrobras has been able to apply this expertise in two ways: 1) via its own exploration and more recently 2) through training programs for foreign cadres or technical support for oil drilling carried out by foreign companies.

The success of Caloi's bicycle manufacturing is partly due to the company's familiarity with small-scale production, a management skill developed since its founding in 1889 to respond to a relatively small home market. As Louis T. Wells puts it, Caloi "remembers how to manufacture bicycles at a scale appropriate for Bolivia because it has not been too long since its home operations were of a similar size."[22] The appropriate scale is also a factor in Inbrac's management of its cable factories in Ecuador and Paraguay.[23]

Villares can compete abroad because it has built a high standard in both manufacturing and servicing elevators in Brazil, enabling it to hold its own against more familiar names such as Otis and Westinghouse. Villares also has developed its management skill by servicing elevators throughout Brazil, including those located hundreds of miles from its plants in São Paulo. Quickly delivering the right part to the right city simulates the challenges faced by a foreign operation.

The management skills of Pao de Acucar, the biggest supermarket chain, and Veplan, a leading shopping mall developer, relate to the construction, logistical and marketing aspects of their stores. The experience was acquired over the past two decades with the emergence of an affluent middle class in the more developed southern region of the country. Pao de Acucar also carefully adapted the supermarket experience in Europe and the US to its home market.

Pao de Acucar's expertise has been exported to Portugal, where the group —already the leader in Brazil—expanded to become the largest chain in the country. Pao de Acucar is also a pioneer in building and managing supermarkets in the Soviet bloc; it runs a store in Warsaw and will build another one in Moscow.[24] The group has supplied technical assistance to stores in Spain and Angola.[25]

Veplan built Chile's first shopping mall, Parque Arauco in Santiago, using know-how developed after completing several such complexes in Sao Paulo and Rio de Janeiro.

Television broadcasting giant Globo has also worked in Italy, where it expanded the reach of the Telemontecarlo station after acquiring it in 1985. The Monte Carlo-based network regained lost ground so quickly that competitors sought legal grounds to shut the company down.[26]

Raw Materials

This group enjoys raw material advantages based on abundance and/ or price in agricultural commodities, iron ore and wood.

For Cacique and Copersucar, two major coffee exporters, the advantage is one of abundance, and not price, as these producers must follow market price fluctuations. Cacique sells to its Chinese instant coffee bottling joint venture at 1% above the international quotation for coffee.[27]

The assurance of a steady supply from the multinational has been a key point in vertical integration investments. Cacique expects to commit less than 1% of its total output to the China venture and Copersucar was able to easily supply its Hills Brothers subsidiary in San Francisco with a large volume of coffee beans for roasting. Metalur, which announced a joint venture to produce high-grade magnesium in Norway, is so advanced in the field that it plans to supply the Norwegian plant with Brazilian equipment.[28]

Other companies enjoy a price advantage. CVRD's low-cost iron ore is an important ingredient for the success of its Fontana steel mill in California. The mining giant secured a foothold in the US by drawing on cheap ore and its own shipping fleet to bring down the cost of Fontana's steel.

Labra's pencil factory in Portugal is an example of a powerful combination of cheap raw materials with advanced technology. The company ships the wood from Brazil and produces the pencils in Portugal for the EEC. It can sell the pencils in the EEC at a competitive price because of its access to forests in Brazil, large-scale production, licensed technology from Europe and cheap labor in both Portugal and at home.

Tropical Technology

"Tropical technology" has become a popular buzzword to describe the success of Brazilian exports to the developing world. The know-how adapted to the tropical environment and technical levels of the Third World, however, seems to limit itself to exports and construction projects. Only a handful of multinationals can compete on this basis.

The value of tropical technology is most clearly exemplified in the work of construction and engineering firms. These companies have paved roads with seashells in Mauritania and built hydroelectric generating plants in the deepest Amazon. They can deliver heavy equipment to remote regions interlaced with unnavigable rivers. This ability is an asset considering that many of today's projects must take place in the harshest climates on earth.

Of the 31 non-construction multinationals surveyed in this article, only two can credit their advantage to the application of technical skills to a tropical environment. Easy dissemination of tropical technology probably robs the multinational of its competitive edge.

Bus bodies made by Marcopolo have large windows, simple interiors and price tags suited to the modest budgets of transportation services in developing countries. The company also shows flexibility by adjusting the bodies to chassis of major non-Brazilian manufacturers. For its Ghanaian operation, a Hino Motors chassis was imported from Japan so that a special body could be adapted for the Accra client.

Cotia's soft drink bottling operation in Nigeria draws on guarana, a berry found in the Amazon region. The drink is extremely popular in Brazil, and Cotia tried it on African tastes. Bottled under the trademark Drinco, guarana reportedly outsells Pepsi Cola in Nigeria and rivals Coca-Cola.[29]

CONCLUSIONS

The dominant competitive advantage of Brazilian multinationals is their strong management skills adapted to LDC environments, but it is not restricted to them. The primary force behind Brazilian FDI is the need to export, derived from both a recession at home and output levels beyond what Brazil can absorb. Brazilian multinationals are looking abroad not just for markets, but also for second bases.

These companies have the capital to acquire foreign firms or to build new ones. The funds are not entirely a sign of wealth but partly of the reluctance to invest in Brazil, given the extremely uncertain outlook on the country's political future (as of mid-1988, when this paper was completed). This atmosphere has caused a catastrophic plunge in industrial investment which, in addition to creating a pool of idle capital, impacts every sector by reducing demand. Even those companies that are investing internally find their orders hanging at break-even levels, and these firms are redoubling their search for customers abroad.

Lackluster demand at home, a product of both the debt crisis and temporary political confusion, is solidifying Brazil's presence abroad, as Brazilian multinationals become an important tool in relations with both LDCs and developed countries. Pao de Acucar runs Angola's only supermarket, which despite damage from the local civil war provides the residents of Luanda, the capital, with one of the few sources of food, virtually all imported from Brazil. In early 1988, Canadian officials visited Brazil to invite Brazilian auto parts manufacturers to set up subsidiaries in Ontario province, just as Metal Leve did in Michigan.

Even the Soviets are interested. Petrobras, the oil monopoly, has been approached about managing a chain of fuel stations in Moscow.[31]

Portugal, the former colonial power and the newest member of the EEC, is being discovered by waves of Brazilian executives eyeing the European market as a whole. Two Portuguese prime ministers visited Brazil in 1987 and 1988 to attract Brazilian capital and technology. Portugal is a valuable stepping-stone for breaking into the EEC market, which buys more than a third of Brazil's exports.

Neighboring Argentina provides a strong partner for development. The two countries, after decades of rivalry in South America, are rapidly moving toward economic integration to gain economies of scale. Already West Germany's Volkswagen and US-owned Ford together have fused their Argentine and Brazilian subsidiaries into one giant holding company, Autolatina.

This trend is finding a parallel among Brazilian multinationals. Aircraft maker Embraer and its Argentine counterpart Fama formally agreed in May 1987 to jointly produce a nineteen-seat turboprop commuter liner, the CBA-123. The total investment is estimated at $300 million, of which two-thirds will be supplied by Embraer. Petrobras, the national oil corporation, and Argentina's federally owned oil monopoly, Yacimientos Petroliferos Fiscales, are studying joint

TABLE 5

Chronology

Year	Company	Country	Activity Initiated
1968	Eluma	Argentina S. Africa	Auto parts joint venture (JV)
1970	Pao de Acucar	Portugal	Supermarket JV
1971	Eluma	Colombia Venezuela	Auto parts JV
	Marcopolo	Venezuela	Assembly of bus bodies
1972	Petrobras	Iraq	First oil exploration contract abroad
1973	Pao de Acucar	Angola	Opened supermarket
1974	Caloi	Bolivia	Bicycle JV
	Gradiente	Mexico	Stereo equipment subsidiary
	Marcopolo	Ghana	Assembly of bus bodies
	Petrobras	Algeria	Oil exploration
1975	Pao de Acucar	Spain	Supermarket franchise
	Tenenge	Paraguay	Engineering subsidiary
1976	Copersucar	USA	Bought Hills' Brothers Coffee
1977	Inepar	Chile	Electrical control equipment JV
	Villares	Chile	Elevator subsidiary
1978	Caloi	Colombia	Bicycle JV
	Cotia	Nigeria	Civil engineering JV
	Inbrac	Paraguay	Cable JV
	Villares	Colombia Uruguay	Elevator subsidiaries
1979	Cica	Argentina	Canned foods subsidiary
	Cotia	Nigeria	Auto parts JV
	CPRM	(Africa)	Began mineral prospection abroad
	Gradiente	UK	Bought Garrard
	Securit	USA	Opened showroom and assembly point in Houston, Texas
1980	Caloi	Guyana	Royalties agreement for bicycles
	Villares	Mexico	Elevator subsidiary
1982	Caraiba	Chile	Aborted JV to mine copper
	Petrobras	South Yemen	Began oil exploration
1983	Embraer	Egypt	$181 million contract to build Tucano military trainers in Helwan, Egypt
	Petrobras	China India	Began oil exploration
1984	Petrobras	Norway	Formed oil services JV
	CPRM	Angola	Gold prospection contract
	CVRD	USA	Bought 25% of steel mill at Fontana, California
	Paranapanema	Guyana	Gold prospection JV
1985	Bardella	USA	Bought 50% of Schuler Inc., a capital goods maker
	Cacique	China	Formed instant coffee JV
	Embraer	UK	$150 million contract to build Tucano trainers in N. Ireland
	Globo	Italy	Bought Telemontecarlo TV station
	Inbrac	Ecuador	Cable JV
	Labra	Portugal	Bought pencil factory for $130 million
	Nansen	Colombia	Formed electricity meter JV
	Petrobras	Angola	$8 million oil services contract
1986	Grendene	Argentina Colombia Mexico	Formed joint ventures with Argentine partner to produce plastic shoes
	Hering	Argentina	Cotton knitwear licensing agreement
	Vacchi	UK	Bought British tannery
1987	Brahma	Argentina	Malt JV at Puan
	Petrobras	USA	Oil exploration JV with Texaco to work in Gulf of Mexico
1988	Hering	Portugal	Plans textile mill
	Incasa	Chile	Plans iodine JV
	Metal Leve	USA	Opened R & D center in Ann Arbor
	Odebrecht	Portugal	Bought construction firm

oil exploration in Argentina and construction of pipelines. Villares, which makes elevators and other heavy equipment, has signed protocol agreements with Argentina's Pescarmona to manufacture together for export to the rest of Latin America.

The global reach of Brazilian multinationals extends into high-technology markets. Embraer has linked up with Aeritalia and Aermacchi of Italy to manufacture the sophisticated AMX fighter-bomber in Brazil and Italy. The AMX, which is marketed out of a London office, is being offered at a flyaway cost of about $13 million, which makes it very affordable to the airforces of Western Europe and developing countries.[32] This places Embraer in direct competition with British Aerospace's Hawk, the similar Alpha Jet built by the Franco-German consortium Dassault/Dornier, and the Soviet Sukhoi-25 "Frogfoot" model.

At the same time, Petrobras is using its deep-sea oil production know-how in the North Sea and Gulf of Mexico, former turfs of only major oil companies.

These are the most colorful examples of the impact of Brazilian multinationals. The more subtle ones, such as school children writing with Labra pencils and executives riding Atlas elevators, have an equally pervasive effect. The switch in the pencil or the fighter-bomber is the fruit of an advanced technological base and strong management skills, combined with a new boldness as Brazilians compete outside their country against major multinationals.

NOTES

1. Sanjaya Lall, *The New Multinationals,* New York: John Wiley & Sons, 1983, p. 242.
2. Information on FDI registered at the Central Bank kindly furnished by Mr. Carlos Eduardo T. Andrade of the Brazilian Central Bank, May 1986. Mr. Mário da Silva Oliveira of Petrobrás also supplied the following information in May 1986:

   Petrobrás had invested $832.2 million abroad as of April 1986. Oil exploration by its subsidiary Braspetro accounted for 83.1% of the total, and equity in Braspetro's own service-based subsidiaries in Angola, Cayman Islands and Norway made up another 9%. All oil exploration had been carried out in developing countries, with 60.4% of Petrobrás FDI concentrated in Iraq, Libya, Angola and Algeria. Non-oil exploration investment accounted for 7.9%, all of which was done via the trading subsidiary Interbrás in its offices in the Cayman Islands, the US, France and Mexico.

   Petrobrás alone accounts for about 75% of my total estimated FDI. Total investment by all Brazilian multinationals in the Third World comes to $845 million, compared with $268 million in developed countries.
3. The following is a list of the multinationals that are the leaders in their respective sectors:
   Brahma (1 of 2 leaders in beer brewing)
   Cacique (leader in instant coffee)
   Caraíba (1 of 2 copper mining companies)
   Caloi (leader in bicycles for leisure)
   Cica (canned foods)
   Copersucar (sugar and coffee)
   Companhia Vale do Rio Doce-CVRD (iron ore mining)
   Eluma (copper products)
   Embraer (aircraft)
   Gradiente (stereo equipment)
   Globo (television networks)
   Grendene (plastic footwear)
   Hering (cotton knitwear, tee-shirts)
   Labra (1 of 2 leaders in pencils)
   Marcopolo (1 of 2 leaders in bus bodies
   Metal Leve (auto engine pistons)
   Pão de Açúcar (supermarkets)
   Petrobrás (oil)
   Paranapanema (tin mining)
   Securit (office furniture)
   Veplan (shopping malls)
   Villares (elevators).
4. Sales from manufacturing or mining activities abroad account for less than a tenth of total sales of the following companies:
   Cacique (instant coffee)
   Caloi (bicycles)
   Cica (canned foods)
   Cotia (a trading company with interests in Nigeria in soft drinks, auto parts, engineering)
   Eluma (copper products, auto parts)
   Globo (television networking)
   Inbrac (cables and wires)
   Inepar (electrical control equipment)
   Paranapanema (gold mining in Guyana)
   Petrobrás (oil exploration and production)
   Tenenge (industrial engineering)
   Villares (elevators). Data for remaining companies unavailable.

5. Interview with Dr. Edmundo Ayres of Cacique, in São Paulo, June 20, 1986.
6. This group includes:
Bardella (crane exports to the US)
Cica (canned goods to Argentina)
Dimep (clocks to Europe)
Embraer (aircraft to many countries)
Labra (pencils to Europe)
Metal Leve (auto engine pistons to the US)
Nansen (electricity meters to Colombia, C. America)
Vacchi (leather products to Europe).
7. This group includes:
Cotia (trading company with interests in Nigeria)
Eluma (auto parts)
Globo (television broadcasting)
Gradiente (stereo equipment)
Inbrac (cables)
Inepar (electrical control equipment)
Marcopolo (bus bodies)
Pão de Açúcar (supermarkets)
Veplan (shopping malls)
Villares (elevators).
8. Eluma, the top copper products maker in Brazil and up until recently a major auto parts manufacturer, set up joint ventures with Bundy of the US in South Africa, Argentina, Venezuela and Colombia, between 1968 and 1971. Eluma had been a partner of Bundy in the Brazilian market since the birth of the auto industry in the 1950s. Information kindly supplied by Eluma director William G. Butler, in interview on September 28, 1981, in São Paulo.
9. The two late ones are Veplan and Globo. Veplan entered into a joint venture to build Chile's first shopping mall in Santiago, and Globo bought the Monte Carlo television station in 1985.
10. In 1984, Companhia Vale do Rio Doce bought 25% of the Fontana steel mill in California from Kaiser Steel Corp. Entrepreneur Michael Wilkinson bought 50% and Kawasaki Steel Corp. of Japan bought the remaining 25%. Together, they formed California Steel Co., of which Wilkinson is president (source: *International Herald Tribune*, August 7, 1984).
11. Interview with Dr. Edmundo Ayres of Cacique.
12. Interview with Mr. Sidney Caser of Securit, in São Paulo, May 6, 1986.
13. *Gazeta Mercantil International Weekly Edition* (English language edition of Brazilian business daily *Gazeta Mercantil*), August 18, 1986. Hereafter referred to as *Gazeta Weekly*.
14. *Ibid.*, June 18, 1984.
15. Petrobrás Annual Report, 1985.
16. *Gazeta Weekly*, March 30, 1987.
17. *Gazeta Weekly*, June 15, 1987.
18. Francisco Sercovich, "Technology Exports from Brazil," *World Development*, Vol. 12, 5/6, p. 582.
19. Interview with Mr. Américo Nogueira de Sá of Tenenge, in São Paulo, May 12, 1986.
20. *South*, July 1985.
21. *Gazeta Weekly*, February 23, 1987.
22. Louis T. Wells, "The Strength of LDC Investors," *Economic Intelligence Unit*, May 1980.
23. Interview with Mr. José Carlos Bazeggio of Inbrac, in São Paulo, May 23, 1986.
24. *Gazeta Weekly*, December 7, 1987 and *Senhor*, December 8, 1987.
25. Pão de Açúcar Annual Report, 1980.
26. *World Screen News*, February 1987 and *Istoé*, April 22, 1987.
27. Interview with Dr. Edmundo Ayres of Cacique.
28. *Brasil Mineral*, August 1986.
29. *Brasil, S.A.*, 1985.
30. The Central Bank disburses hard currency to the aspiring multinational in return for the equivalent value in gold, acquired by the company from Brazil's booming gold mining industry.
31. *Gazeta Weekly*, June 20, 1988.
32. *Gazeta Weekly*, February 29, 1988.

[23]

GeoJournal 22.3 345–354

Sun International: The Making of a South African Tourism Multinational

Rogerson, C. M., Prof. Dr., University of the Witwatersrand, Department of Geography, PO Wits 2050, Johannesburg, South Africa

ABSTRACT: Sun International is a tourism multinational corporation (MNC) based in South Africa. The aim is to examine the formation and geographical spread of activities of this South African MNC engaged in casino-resort development and luxury tourism. Within the geographical literature on MNCs the study of Sun International underlines both the importance of country of origin as a factor in interpreting the heterogeneous character of MNCs and of the distinctiveness of South African MNCs. The spatial scope of Sun International (including its ancestor, Southern Sun) operations was influenced by the enterprise's association with apartheid. Despite several efforts to mask its South African origin through restrictive corporate disclosure and corporate camouflage, planned international expansion was continually frustrated by the stigma of apartheid. Sun International was confined in its international operations to those African states which either were economic or political satellites of South Africa or to the group of 'independent' Bantustans, which were creations of apartheid.

Introduction

Since the beginning of the 1970s the geographies of multinational corporations (MNCs) have been an increasingly popular focus for study by human geographers (Taylor and Thrift 1982; Clarke 1985; Dixon et al. 1986; Taylor and Thrift 1986, 1989; de Smidt and Wever 1990). Initial research centred on the internationalization of production activities and the role of MNCs in constructing a new global industrial order with the extension of manufacturing operations into many parts of the developing world (Clarke 1985; Thrift 1986). Recent work evidences geographers' concern for MNC involvement not only in manufacturing but also in agriculture, banking, property and services (Dixon et al. 1986; Taylor and Thrift 1986; Thrift 1987; Wallace 1990). One important theme highlighted by the geographical writings on MNCs is that such organizations are by no means homogeneous phenomena (Dicken 1982, p. 119). Although several bases for differentiation have been suggested (Taylor and Thrift 1982, 1986), both Dicken (1982) and Watts (1987) draw attention to the different corporate geographies of firms originating in different source nations. Credence to the possible significance of the source nation is seemingly furnished by research on the operations and expansion paths of Japanese-based MNCs (Dicken 1988).

The case of South African-based MNCs offers additional support to the nation state as an axis of cleavage for MNC differentiation. A number or works reveal that, as a result of the stigma attached by apartheid to corporations whose home base is South Africa, the internationalization of South African firms differs in important respects from European or North American-based MNCs on the one hand or developing world MNCs on the other (Kaplan 1983; Innes 1984; Tucker 1985, 1986; Rogerson and Tucker 1985). The objective in this paper is to undertake a micro-study of the making of a South African MNC and of its geographical expansion path. The research focuses on the emergence and spatial growth of Sun International, an enterprise engaged in tourism and leisure operations. Although MNC involvement in tourism activities has been widely recognized (United Nations 1982; Clairmonte and Cavanagh 1984; Ascher 1985) the operations of tourism MNCs have attracted remarkably little attention in the broad geographical literature on tourism (cf. Pearce 1989). One notable exception, however, is a rich series of studies by Britton dealing with MNCs, tourism and underdevelopment in the South Pacific (Britton 1982a, 1982b, 1984).

The examination of Sun International as a South African tourism MNC is divided into two major sections of discussion. First, the origins of this international tourism MNC are traced in the formation and expansion between 1969 and 1983 of the Southern Sun Group's hotel operations and later involvement in casino developments. Against this backcloth, in the second section the birth of Sun International in 1983 as a powerful MNC engaged in luxury resort and casino development is detailed. In addition, an analysis is pursued of the geographical spread of the newly constituted Sun International enterprise in Southern Africa, the Indian Ocean Islands and of the organization's attempts to penetrate Western European markets.

The Expansion of Southern Sun Hotels and Casinos

An understanding of the making of Sun International must begin with an examination of the hotel industry in South Africa during the 1960s and 1970s a period which witnessed the formation and rapid growth of the Southern Sun hotel corporation. Until the late 1960s there was only a limited development of tourist hotel facilities across South Africa. The hotel industry largely comprised a network of commercial hotels, lower quality boarding houses and the limited accommodation facilities offered by a mass of tied 'public houses' linked to South Africa's competing brewing enterprises. During the 1960s the Government sought to encourage the upgrading of South African hotels in order to foster international tourism. This policy prompted the country's leading brewing concern, the South African Breweries Ltd. (SAB) to restructure its involvement in the hotel trade, shedding poorer quality establishments and concentrating attention and investments in the existing larger hotels (Tucker 1985). In 1969 this restructuring precipitated the formation by SAB of two new hotel subsidiaries. The first of these, Transito, took over the bulk of SAB's existent hotel operations catering for the commercial traveller with a spatial grid of hotels in South Africa's major business centres. The second subsidiary, Southern Sun Hotels, was formed as part of a broader diversification programme of SAB away from its core brewing activities (Tucker 1985, 1986). The new enterprise was constituted jointly by SAB together with Safmarine, a large shipping company, and the existing hotel interests of a Durban businessman, producing the Southern Sun Hotel Corporation.

Under the leadership of a flamboyant entrepreneur, Sol Kerzner, the ambitious objective of the Southern Sun Hotel group was to secure a chain of luxury tourist hotel facilities both across South Africa and the surrounding territories. From an initial base in 1969 of six hotels, one in Johannesburg, two adjacent to the Kruger Game Park, and three in Natal coastal areas, the Southern Sun enterprise expanded rapidly. With the financial backing of the large SAB group Southern Sun embarked upon a dual strategy of acquiring and subsequently upgrading existing hotel operations and of building new facilities in South Africa's leading tourist resort areas. For example, during its first three years of business the company acquired existing tourist hotels along the Natal coast region and commenced construction of new developments both in Durban, South Africa's tourist 'mecca' and along the scenic Garden Route at the Southern Cape coastal resort of Plettenberg Bay. The company's geographical range of operations was extended in 1972 to Cape Town and Port Elizabeth by taking-over the operations of a Cape Province-based hotel concern. The acquisition also extended Southern Sun activities into the game lodge market through securing an additional facility in Natal. Further spatial spreading of corporate activities occurred during 1973 with the decision by SAB to merge the Transito chain of nine 'commercial hotels' into the Southern Sun network of tourist facilities.

As a result of these developments in corporate acquisitions, new facilities and the merger with Transito, by 1973 Southern Sun had a network of 24 hotel operations in South Africa covering all the country's major urban centres and most of the leading tourist areas (Fig 1). Throughout the 1970s and early 1980s Southern Sun endeavoured to rationalize, consolidate and extend its hotel interests within South Africa. The most important developments involved the take-over of a hotel situated close to Johannesburg's international airport and the construction of major new luxury hotels in Cape Town, Johannesburg and Durban. Moreover, the enterprise further expanded its operations in the Natal coastal resort areas. By the early 1980s the company enjoyed a dominant position in both the luxury tourist and business hotel trade across South Africa. With limited opportunities for further expansion within South Africa it is not surprising that the company renewed a long-standing interest in overseas expansion.

The geography of Southern Sun's activities in 1973 discloses that the company was already multinational in its operations with a game lodge in northern Botswana and a hotel in Mozambique. These two endeavours represented Southern Sun's first functioning ventures outside of the South African home base. The fledgling attempts made by Southern Sun to go multinational during the early 1970s had a chequered history. Corporate attention initially was directed to the potential of the Indian Ocean islands, a region which it was hoped ultimately would rival the Caribbean, Mediterranean and the Pacific tourist regions (*Rand Daily Mail* 20 March 1972). To facilities overseas expansion Southern Sun Hotels constituted in 1970 an offshore subsidiary, incorporated in Bermuda, to hold the company's investments outside of South Africa (Annual Report (AR) Southern Sun Hotels 1971). The first external investment was to occur in Madagascar where the group planned to acquire an existing facility and construct a five-star luxury hotel at Nossi-Be to tap the country's undeveloped tourist potential. When the initial

GeoJournal 22.3/1990

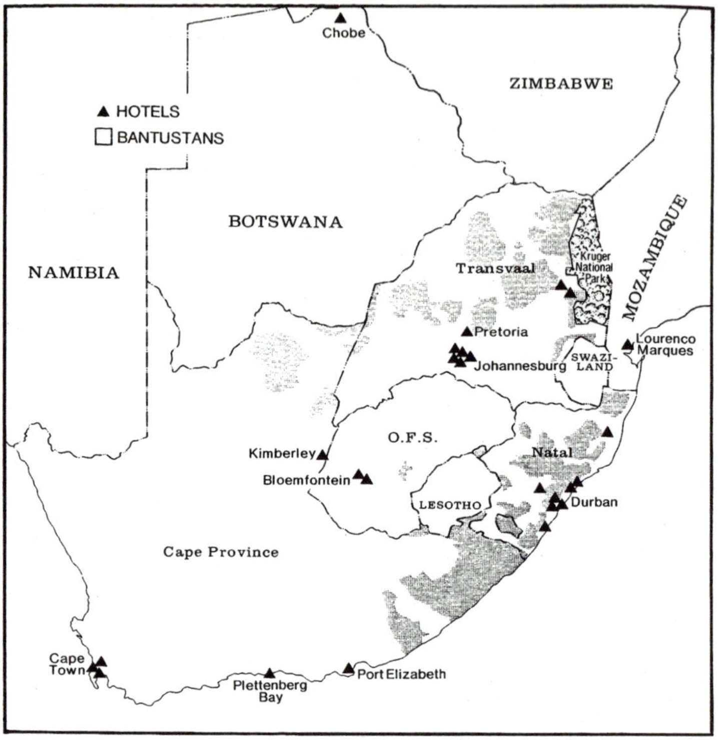

Fig 1
The corporate geography of Southern Sun, 1973
(Source: AR, Southern Sun 1973)

Madagascar project was formulated South Africa was developing close economic ties with the country (Covell, 1987, p. 43). The fall of the Tsiranana regime in Madagascar in May 1972 and the severing of economic and political links with South Africa effectively terminated prospects for a South African corporation to be involved in the island's tourist trade. Equally unsuccessful were plans announced in 1972 by Southern Sun to develop or acquire hotels in Reunion and Seychelles.

The changing political context of Southern Africa during the 1970s greatly influenced the early international operations of Southern Sun. During 1971 Southern Sun entered into a partnership agreement with a Portuguese conglomerate, Companhia Uniao Fabril, to develop a series of hotels along the coast of Mozambique, then still a colony of Portugal *(Sunday Times* 11 July 1971). The first Mozambican development involved a take-over of management and re-furbishing of the famous Polana Hotel in Lourenco Marques (now Maputo). But, the march of decolonization processes in Mozambique and the accession to power in 1975 of the FRELIMO government hostile to South Africa ended any further expansion plans in Mozambique; Southern Sun withdrew from its existing hotel operations in the newly independent country (AR, Southern Sun Hotels 1976). Political developments associated with decolonization struggles in Southern Africa also affected the operations of the Chobe Game Lodge in Botswana. Located on the Botswana-Zambia-Zimbabwe border the game lodge was forced to close in 1977 as a result of the overspill of the independence war surrounding the transition from colonial Rhodesia to independent Zimbabwe (AR, Southern Sun Hotels 1977). In 1983 Southern Sun disinvested from Botswana, selling the game lodge to a group of private investors.

The rapidly changing political complexion of decolonizing Africa and growing opposition to apartheid South Africa circumscribed Southern Sun's ambitious international expansion plans throughout the 1970s. The only step made towards the envisioned chain of Indian Ocean island resorts occurred in Mauritius, where friendly political links were retained with South Africa. The Mauritian development was significant for it marked a breakthrough for Southern Sun into the business of

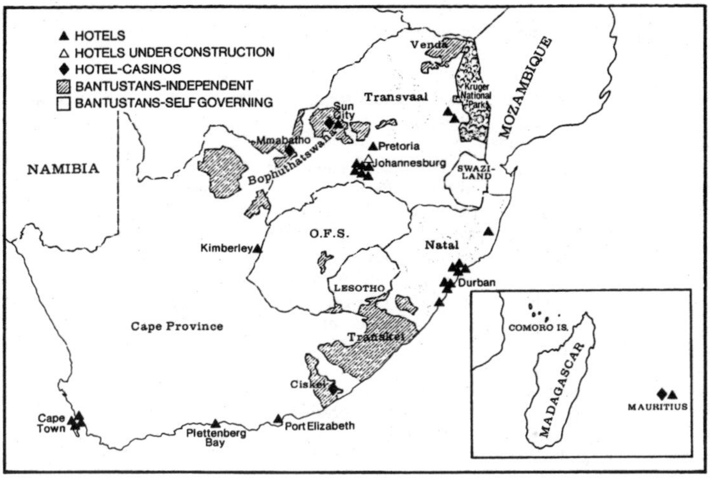

Fig 2
The corporate geography of Southern Sun, 1983
(Source: AR Southern Sun 1983)

casino resort development. The aborted Madagascar project had been linked to a casino development; the Mauritius scheme in 1975 represented the formal entrance of Southern Sun into the gambling industry of Southern Africa. The lucrative gambling trade of the region had been hitherto monopolized by the operations of the Holiday Inn Group of casinos in Lesotho, Swaziland and Botswana which attracted South African gamblers denied such possibilities by legislation banning casinos in South Africa (Crush and Wellings 1983, 1987; Stern 1987). Notwithstanding the election during 1982 of a socialist government in Mauritius the tourist linkages with South Africa remained unaffected. Accordingly, in 1983 Southern Sun deepened its involvement in Mauritius (Fig 2) taking-over a second existing casino resort and an additional tourist hotel on the island (Sunday Express 20 February 1983).

Major new investment prospects opened for Southern Sun with the maturation of apartheid planning and the grant of nominal 'independence' to several of the Bantustan or 'homeland' areas of South Africa (Fig 2). The delegation of independence to such areas as Transkei (1976), Bophuthatswana (1977), Venda (1979) and Ciskei (1981) re-defined the function of these parts of South African space (Crush and Wellings 1983, 1987). New opportunities appeared for Southern Sun to challenge the regional monopoly on gambling held by the Holiday Inn group (Wellings and Crush 1983). By taking advantage of the 'independence' of Bantustans and establishing casino operations there Southern Sun could penetrate the lucrative South African gambling market (Stern 1987). In particular, Southern Sun sought to capture the key market of the Southern Transvaal, the most economically developed and affluent region of South Africa, by securing an agreement with the 'slumlords' of Bophuthatswana for exclusive gambling rights in the territory. After lengthy negotiations Southern Sun agreed to develop the tourist industry in 'independent' Bophuthatswana in return for 10-year exclusive casino licences with five-year options *(Financial Mail* 2 December 1977 Supplement, p. 35). The first hotel/casino complex at Mmabatho, the capital of Bophuthatswana, was constructed and readied for official opening by the time of 'independence' in December 1977. This was followed by construction of an even more ambitious tourism-casino complex, proclaimed "to match Las Vegas" *(Financial Mail Supplement* 2 December 1977, p. 34), situated within the Pilansberg range, a mere two hours drive away from Johannesburg. In undertaking such major developments Southern Sun was in close alliance with the South African state, receiving financial assistance in the form of low interest subsidized loans *(Sunday Express* 11 September 1983). For the South African State this alliance with tourism capital was doubly advantageous; on the one hand "giving considerable weight to its attempts to legitimize Bantustan independence in the international forum", on the other hand allowing the state "to replace a considerable portion of the costs of subsidizing the Bantustan strategy with private capital" (Crush and Wellings 1987, p. 107). Because of its spectacular financial success the massive Sun City complex, inaugurated in December 1979, rapidly became the core of Southern Sun's casino operations. The initial complex was extended by addition of an entertainment complex, a new hotel, golf course and game park. Beyond Bophuthatswana, Southern Sun further obtained the gambling rights for the Ciskei Bantustan, opening in June 1982 a small hotel at the capital, Bisho, and adding a casino during 1983 "to appreciably improve the profitability of the operation" (AR Southern Sun Hotels 1983, p. 9).

The successful casino developments of Southern Sun within the Southern African region encouraged the company to attempt once again to expand operations on an international basis. In planning its investment abroad Southern Sun emphasized the imperative for management control of projects with the company seeking an average 20–25% level of financial participation. In addition, it was stressed that Southern Sun would not scatter its overseas investments around the world rather "cluster them in one or more specific areas" *(Sunday Times* 9 November 1980). As with most South African MNCs, Australia and the USA were the favoured geographical sites for Southern Sun's intended expansion (cf. Kaplan 1983; Innes 1984). But, as in the early 1970s, political factors associated with the corporation's home base being in South Africa thwarted the planned break-out of Southern Sun from Southern Africa. In Australia, Southern Sun sought to participate in an ambitious project to develop a casino on Queensland's Gold Coast tourist area *(The Star* 13 October 1982). However, the hostility of the Australian national government towards apartheid pressured the large Commonwealth Superannuation Fund to threaten its financial withdrawal if a South African corporation were to be associated with the project *(The Star* 19 November 1982).

American investment possibilities were scanned by Southern Sun during the late 1970s but abandoned temporarily due to the corporation's massive commitment of financial resources to the construction of Sun City. In March 1983 it was announced that Southern Sun had concluded an agreement with American Leisure Corporation to establish a US $ 250 million casino/hotel venture in Atlantic City (AR Southern Sun 1983, p. 9). Nonetheless, the 'Camelot Project' attracted considerable opposition from local anti-apartheid groups with Atlantic City councillors introducing an ordinance prohibiting the city government from investing in companies with South African connections. Opposition to Southern Sun's planned involvement in the US gambling industry was even raised in the United Nations General Assembly *(Rand Daily Mail* 17 May 1983). Despite suggestions that Southern Sun might become involved in subsidized local housing construction to temper community opposition toward South African participation, the project was eventually aborted in June 1983 *(Rand Daily Mail* 20 May 1983; *The Star* 16 June 1983). Just after the announced withdrawal of Southern Sun from the scheme, the New Jersey State Senate voted unanimously to ask that the Casino Control Commission deny a licence to the South African firm *(Rand Daily Mail* 20 June 1983).

The failures of Southern Sun to penetrate beyond the Southern African region were mirrored in the overall geography of the corporation in 1983 (Fig 2). Despite several attempts to go multinational Southern Sun operations were confined, apart from South Africa and the 'independent' Bantustans, to its Mauritian projects.

Sun International – Formation and Changing Geography

The partial metamorphosis of Southern Sun into Sun International must be situated in the context of the rationalization of the casino industry of Southern Africa which occurred in 1983. Rationalization of control centred upon a merging of the casino-hotel interests of Southern Sun with those of its rival, the Holiday Inn group, to constitute the new enterprise later christened as Sun International. The corporate merger was orchestrated by Southern Sun's Sol Kerzner who first offered his shareholding in Southern Sun to SAB while simultaneously making a successful bid for control of its casino-hotel operations. The second stage in the birthing of Sun International was acquisition of the casino-hotel interests of the Rennies Group which had operated under the Holiday Inns franchise in Southern Africa (AR Sun Hotels International 1984, p. 9). In a subsequent development a second acquisition took place in 1985 of Holiday Inn's outstanding South African hotel interests by Southern Sun. As a result, the remoulded Southern Sun corporation became the leading force in the hotel industry within South Africa complementing Sun International's dominance of casino-resort development outside South Africa.

The background events which precipitated the formation of Sun International surrounded the heightening competitive struggle set up between the Southern Sun and Holiday Inn casino interests. The struggle was launched by Southern Sun's construction of Bantustan casinos shattering the regional gaming monopoly held for over a decade by Holiday Inn (Crush and Wellings 1983; Wellings and Crush 1983; Stern 1987). In particular, the building of Sun City was a watershed event threatening the existence of Holiday Inn's chain of casinos situated in Botswana, Lesotho and Swaziland. The *raison d'etre* of casino resorts in these independent states was as purveyor of the "forbidden fruit" denied to South Africans by the country's Calvinistic puritanism and anti-gambling codes (Crush and Wellings 1983, p. 683). The Holiday Inn group responded with an imitative corporate strategy which re-oriented its investments 'inward' to South Africa's Bantustans and away from Botswana, Lesotho or Swaziland. During December 1981 Holiday Inn opened a parallel casino resort to Sun City along the Wild Coast of Transkei, close to Durban. The 'casino war' escalated a stage further with an announcement that Holiday Inn had secured monopoly rights on gambling in the economically eviscerate and minuscule territory of KwaNdebele, which in 1982 appeared likely to be the fifth South African Bantustan to accept 'independence'. The significance of the proposed KwaNdebele casino lay in the fact that it severely

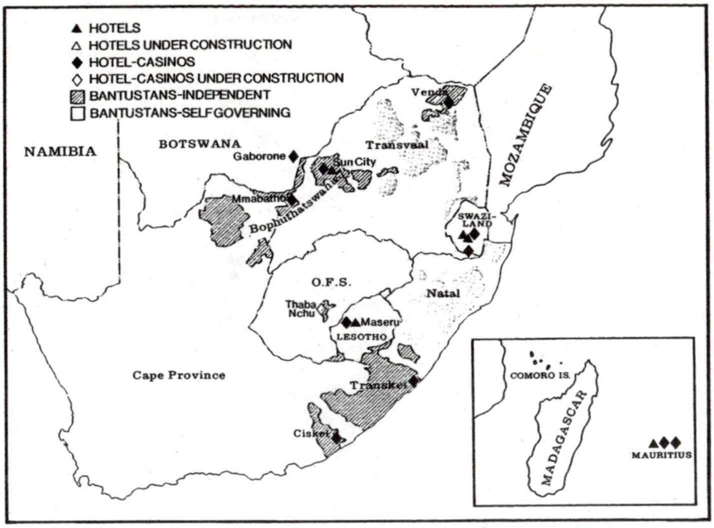

Fig 3
The corporate geography of Sun International, 1984
(Source: AR Sun Hotels International 1984)

threatened to undercut the profitability of Southern Sun's Sun City due to its location less than one hour's drive from Pretoria. This projected casino set in motion the discussions for rationalization of casino operations in Southern Africa which triggered the eventual creation of Sun International.

The newly founded Sun International corporation possessed an extensive geographical spread of operations within Southern Africa. To Southern Sun's existing five casino resorts and two hotels in Mauritius, Bophuthatswana and Ciskei was added a further six casino-hotels and two other hotels in Botswana, Lesotho and Swaziland as well as the two South African 'independent' Bantustans of Transkei and Venda. The new Sun International enterprise now enjoyed control of all casinos in Southern Africa with the single exception of the Hilton Hotel casino situated in Maseru, Lesotho. At the core of the enterprise was the development and management of luxury hotels, resorts and gaming operations, areas in which future investments would be directed (AR Sun Hotels International 1984, p. 11). Within the first year of its establishment Sun International moved to complete its monopoly hold on the gaming industry of Southern Africa by taking-over management and absorbing the Lesotho Hilton casino. With Sun International already in possession of one casino in Maseru, a rationalization of operations was undertaken with the older casino-hotel being downgraded by removing its casino; the closure of one Maseru casino was notable as the first event of its kind in the 20 year unfettered expansionary history of the gambling industry in Southern Africa. Beyond the new Lesotho venture, the lifting of the competitive threat (and subsequent abandonment) of the proposed KwaNdebele casino-resort encouraged Sun International to invest further at the Sun City complex by constructing a spectacular new luxury hotel. Finally, in its first year of operations, Sun International opened a new hotel-casino at Thaba 'Nchu, an enclave of Bophuthatswana favourably located to attract gamblers from urban areas of the Orange Free State.

Accordingly, by 1984 Sun International's multinational spread of activities encompassed a total of 18 hotels, including 12 casinos, situated in four states of Southern Africa in addition to the four nominally 'independent' Bantustans (Fig 3). In the period since 1985 two major themes have shaped the changing corporate geography of Sun International. First, was the enterprise's efforts to expand further its core of casino-resorts within the area of Southern Africa. Second, and more importantly, was the new thrust to extend operations of Sun International beyond the regional sphere of Southern Africa. The geographical direction of Sun International's activities was sealed by a complex financial restructuring in 1985. The enterprise obtained an effective 21% share of the combined Southern Sun-Holiday Inn hotel chain which would be confined geographically to South Africa allowing Sun International to concentrate its endeavours outside the country (*Sunday Times* 14 April 1985).

Between 1985 and 1990 Sun International boosted considerably its regional Southern African operations in casinos and resort development. Five new casino-resorts were opened with a further two being in the planning stages. Spatially, the greatest concentration of invest-

GeoJournal 22.3/1990

Fig 4
The corporate geography of Sun International, 1990
(Source: AR Kersaf Investments 1989 and newspaper reports)

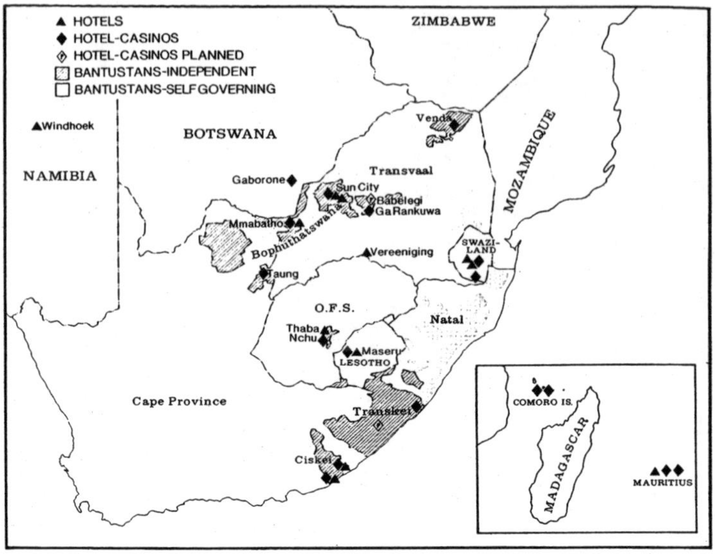

ments was directed 'inwards' to the 'independent' Bantustans (Fig 4). More specifically, a major expansion was undertaken of the existing highly successful casino-resort in Transkei and a new casino-resort and two hotels added in Ciskei. Expansion plans in Transkei for a new casino-hotel at Umtata, the capital, were endangered by a corruption scandal surrounding the payment of bribes to the former prime minister in exchange for his awarding Sun International exclusive gambling rights in the territory. Indeed, the company faced a challenge to its gaming exclusivity in the area which precipitated a suspension in 1989 of further developments in Transkei until the matter was clarified (AR Kersaf Investments 1989, p. 16). In Ciskei, expansion of Sun International proceeded without such controversies. The Ciskei coastal casino-resort and nearby additional hotel completed during 1989, were strategically located between the major South African urban centres of Port Elizabeth and East London. Also Sun International took over and refurbished a small hotel at Mdantsane, East London's satellite city, in Ciskei.

The most significant Bantustan expansions have taken place within Bophuthatswana. Further development has occurred of Sun International's showpiece, the Sun City complex which is projected to become the world's biggest resort of its kind. Among the ambitious large extensions announced in 1990 are proposals for a luxury hotel (tentatively called 'The Palace') set in a spectacular man-made jungle to include a functioning coral reef with tropical fish, scuba diving and a giant wave pool for surfers *(The Mail* 2 March 1990). Alongside further consolidation of the huge Sun City complex, Sun International began the development of a series of smaller casino resorts in the territory, opening the first two such operations at Ga Rankuwa and Taung (AR Kersaf Investments 1989, p. 18). In addition, the existing (1984) casino-hotels at Mmabatho, and Thaba 'Nchu were augmented by hotels at each location. Finally, Sun International began work on a further casino-hotel complex north of Pretoria at Babelegi, a resort which is described will have "a Victorian Mississippi theme" *(The Mail* 2 March 1990).

Outside of the Bantustans, Sun International extended geographically its Southern African sphere of corporate operations with first investments made in the Comoro Islands, Namibia and South Africa itself (Fig 4). As a result of the withdrawal of a British-based hotel group from the management contract regarding a series of new luxury hotels under construction in the Comoros, in 1988 Sun International was afforded the opportunity to broaden its casino-resort operations. Considerable controversy, however, attached to the Comoran projects which drew opposition from local religious leaders who saw the ventures as centres of evils such as gambling and drinking, forbidden activities under Islamic law *(The Star* 19 May 1988). Additional criticism surrounded the reported 'apartheid-style' forcible removal of many villagers to facilitate land for one of the planned hotels *(The Star* 19 May 1988). These problems resulted in the reduction from four to two of the number of Sun International's Comoran ventures. Significantly, despite anti-apartheid sentiment to South

African MNCs investment elsewhere, the Comoros had been evolving close economic and diplomatic ties with South Africa since the mid-1980s. Indeed, Sun International deployed South African government backed loans in refurbishing one of its hotels in Comoros (The *Citizen* 8 February 1989). Eventually the remaining two Comoros hotel resorts opened during 1989 but were almost immediately troubled by political uncertainties surrounding the assassination of the President and the role played by a group of White mercenaries. As a consequence of the political turmoil in Comoros, Sun International closed temporarily its largest casino-hotel in the country (*Business Day* 31 January 1990).

The prospect of changing gambling legislation that might permit new casino developments prompted an interest in Namibia as early as 1987 (*Sunday Times* 15 March 1987). Nonetheless, with the certainty of Namibian independence on the horizon Sun International moved into the territory in 1989 securing a majority shareholding in Windhoek's most luxurious hotel (*Sunday Times* 30 July 1989). This move undoubtedly increased the chances that Sun International would be granted casino rights after Namibian independence in March 1990. An unusual investment by Sun International was its participation in a villa development and time-share resort on the Vaal river at Vereeniging (AR Sun Hotels International 1985, p. 8). The project was unusual both for its location in South Africa and in terms of being a departure from the core business of Sun International. Finally, in terms of regional operations in Southern Africa, in Botswana Sun International invested during 1985 in Chobe Game Lodge, a former Southern Sun venture (*Sunday Times* 3 Feburary 1985). Four years later, however, the company sold out its stake in the game lodge, described as "too different from our central business", in line with corporate strategy to refocus on the core activities of casino-resorts (*Daily Despatch* 21 November 1989). Accordingly, the Gaborone hotel-casino remained in 1990 Sun International's only investment in Botswana (Fig 4).

The final thread in the growth and changing geography of Sun International concerns the enterprise's attempts to spread activities beyond the regional sphere of Southern Africa. In 1985 Sun International announced the objective for the corporation to become "a major force in the international entertainment and leisure industries": noting that the enterprise's activities were "reasonably well spread" the intention was stated to achieve "further geographic diversification . . . outside the Southern African region" (AR Sun Hotels International 1985, p. 9). The ultimate vision was of becoming a geographically expansive MNC "with world-wide operations" (AR Kersaf Investments 1986, p. 3). This goal of going international in scope was clarified, however, with the caveat that the company would "focus on target regions and only expand beyond these should the alternative opportunity be of significant size and offer a higher than usual rate of return" (AR Kersaf Investments 1986, p. 3). Against the backdrop of the prior history of failed attempts by Southern Sun to invest in North America and Australia, it was perhaps not surprising that Western Europe became the selected "target region" for Sun International's drive for overseas expansion.

The beginnings of overseas diversification were signalled in June 1985 with the acquisition by Kersaf, the holding company for Sun International, of a 40% shareholding in a British enterprise, Kunick Leisure group. The diverse interests of Kunick included water theme parks, discotheques, an opera house, zoo, ice skating rinks and the London Dungeon tourist attraction. The acquisition of Kunick was clearly intended as a springboard, "a principal vehicle" for Sun International's further expansion into the United Kingdom and European leisure and entertainment industries (AR Sun Hotels International 1985, p. 9). Nonetheless, while Kunick might engage in small casino-related schemes in the United Kingdom, it was not intended that it become involved in larger casino ventures (*Sunday Times* 19 May 1985). Indeed, the initial investments made by Kunick were to reinforce its role as the entertainment arm of Sun International. In rapid succession the company made three acquisitions variously taking over the leading British popular music impresarios, an amusement machine group and an entertainment management company (*Financial Mail* 7 February 1986). The largest of these acquisitions, Allied Entertainments, was particularly attractive as it held exclusive option on the development of a leisure complex in the London Docklands area (*Financial Mail* 16 August 1985). The South African linkage, however, soon clouded prospects for Kunick fulfilling its designated role of spearheading Sun International's European expansion drive (*Business Day* 6 July 1986). In common with the international boycott of Sun City by leading entertainers, several of the rock artists refused to work with a business having South African connections. With the growing difficulties of Kunick tainted by its South African connections, in May 1987 Sun International disposed of its holding in this venture (*Business Day* 7 May 1987).

A second attempt to penetrate the international leisure market centred on the formation in 1986 of Royale Resorts, a joint partnership with a major UK company, British and Commonwealth Shipping. Although Sun International held 50% of the shares of Royale Resorts and the new company was to be headed by Sol Kerzner, it was claimed that Royale was not a South African company (*Finance Week* 19–25 June 1986). By establishing this offshore subsidiary, based in Bermuda, it was hoped to create a bridgehead for the long-thwarted international ambitions of the managers of Sun International. Through this exercise in corporate camouflage it was planned that Royale Resorts would spearhead the Sun International group into the business of "casino and resort industries" (AR, Kersaf Investments 1986, p. 4). Moreover, to avert possible opposition and unfavourable publicity of its overseas expansion plans, a veil of South African state sanctioned secrecy was to be drawn over Royale Resorts in terms of limited disclosure on its activities (Financial Mail 17 October 1986).

At inception it was stressed that the strategy of Royale Resorts would be to develop on a regional basis concentrating particularly upon Western Europe "rather than trying to operate a string of resorts around the world" *(Business Day* 27 June 1986). Despite restrictions on corporate disclosure (cf. Krumme 1989) it was revealed that projects being examined by Royale included a casino-hotel in Monaco, a resort in Spain and a hotel in Turkey *(Finance Week* 19–25 June 1986). Nonetheless, in a major move during 1987 it was announced that Royale Resorts in alliance with a French company effectively had secured control of approximately half of France's gaming market through a planned take-over of seven of the country's leading ten casinos *(Business Day* 3 August 1987). Once again, the smear of apartheid created problems for this planned expansion into France. Trade union-led protests called on the French government to block the acquisition bid by Royale, urging "Don't let apartheid take over gambling in France" *(The Star* 10 August 1987). It must be acknowledged, however, that trade union opposition was not only fuelled by prospects of South African management of French casinos but also by the impending introduction of slot machines (formerly prohibited in France) which threatened the incomes and jobs of many casino workers *(Business Day* 27 August 1987).

Despite problems Royale did succeed in securing an involvement and operating four casino resorts, three of which were located in France (AR Kersaf Investments 1989, p. 5). Yet the intractable problems of the South African connection forced a reappraisal during 1988–89 of the whole direction of offshore corporate activities. Temporary defeat was admitted during 1989 when it was disclosed that "due to political pressures" and inability to expand into other casino resort operations in France, the decision was taken to divest from the existing French casino and gaming interests (AR Kersaf Investments 1989, p. 5). Moreover, the ambitious goals of major overseas expansion were to be deferred in the wake of "the political and other obstacles" encountered in the overseas expansion drive (AR Kersaf Investments 1989, p. 5).

Concluding Remarks

The making and geographical spread of Sun International as a South African tourism MNC underlines the importance of country of origin as a factor in interpreting the heterogeneous character of MNCs. The spatial extent of Sun International (including its ancestor, Southern Sun) operations was deeply affected by the enterprise's tarring by the brush of apartheid. Despite Sun International's several efforts made to mask its South African origin through restrictive corporate disclosure and corporate camouflage, planned international expansion was continually frustrated by association with the apartheid system. In consequence, this South African MNC was quarantined in its international operations to those African states which either were economic or political satellites of South Africa or, in the case of the 'independent' Bantustans, were creations of apartheid.

The changing South African political environment of the early 1990s appears to offer both new opportunities and potential dangers for Sun International. On the one hand, the possibility of a new South African political order with the re-incorporation of the 'independent' Bantustans places a question mark on the enterprise's gaming rights and lucrative casino-resorts in Bophuthatswana or Transkei. On the other hand, a new political dispensation could remove the core obstacle blocking the internationalization of this vibrant and ambitious South African MNC, namely the stigma of apartheid.

Acknowledgements

Thanks are due to Phil Stickler for preparation of the diagrams. The Financial assistance of the Institute for Research Development of the Human Sciences Research Council towards this research is hereby acknowledged.

References

Annual Reports (AR), Southern Sun Hotels 1971–1983, Sun Hotels International 1984–1985, Kersaf Investments 1986–1989.

Ascher, F.: Tourism: Transnational Corporations and Cultural Identities. UNESCO, Paris 1985.

Britton, S. G.: The political economy of tourism in the Third World. Annals of Tourism Research 9, 331–358 (1982a)

Britton, S. G.: International tourism and multinational corporations in the Pacific: the case of Fiji. In: Taylor, M.; Thrift, N.: The Geography of Multinationals, pp. 252–274. Croom Helm, London 1982b.

Britton, S. G.: Tourism and Underdevelopment in Fiji. Australian National University Press, Canberra 1984.

Business Day (Johannesburg)

The Citizen (Johannesburg)

Clairmonte, F. F.; Cavanagh, J. H.: Transnational Corpoorations and Services: the Final Frontier. University of Sydney Transnational Corporations Research Project Research Monograph No. 19, Sydney 1984.

Clarke, I. M.: The Spatial Organisation of Multinational Corporations. Croom Helm, London 1985.

Covell, M.: Madagascar: Politics, Economics and Society. Frances Pinter, London 1987.

Crush, J.; Wellings, P.: The Southern African pleasure periphery, 1966–83. Journal of Modern African Studies 21, 673–698 (1983)

Crush, J.; Wellings, P.: Forbidden fruit and the export of vice: tourism in Swaziland and Lesotho. In: Britton, S.; Clarke, W. C. (eds.), Ambiguous Alternative: Tourism in Small Developing Countries, pp. 91–112. University of the South Pacific, Suva 1987.

de Smidt, M.; Wever, E. (eds.): The Corporate Firm in a Changing World Economy: Case Studies in the Geography of Enterprise. Routledge, London 1990.

Dicken, P.: Recent trends in international direct investment, with particular reference to the United States and the United Kingdom. In: Robson, B. T.; Rees, J. (eds.): Geographical Agenda for a Changing World, pp. 118–161. Social Sciences Research Council, London 1982.

Dicken, P.: The changing geography of Japanese foreign direct investment in manufacturing industry: a global perspective. Environment and Planning A 20, 633–653 (1988)

Dixon, C. J.; Drakakis-Smith, D.; Watts, H. D. (eds.): Multinational Corporations and the Third World. Croom Helm, London 1986.

Finance Week (Johannesburg)

Financial Mail (Johannesburg)

Kaplan, D. E.: The internationalization of South African capital: South African direct foreign investment in the contemporary period. African Affairs 82, 465–494 (1983)

Krumme, G.: Financial and social disclosures by multinational corporations: geographic segmentation of information and other issues. Paper presented to the IGU Commission on Industrial Change Meeting, Eppenhain, September 1989.

The Mail (Mafikeng)

Pearce, D. (ed.): Geography of tourism and recreation. GeoJournal 19, 250–335 (1989)

Rand Daily Mail (Johannesburg)

Rogerson, C. M.; Tucker, B. A.: Commercialization and corporate capital in the sorghum beer industry of Central Africa. Geoforum 16, 357–368 (1985)

The Star (Johannesburg)

Stern, E.: Competition and location in the gambling industry: the 'casino states' of Southern Africa. Geography 72, 140–150 (1987)

Sunday Express (Johannesburg)

Sunday Times (Johannesburg)

Thrift, N.: The geography of international economic disorder. In: Johnston, R. J.; Taylor, P. J.: A World in Crisis?: Geographical Perspectives, pp. 12–67. Basil Blackwell, Oxford 1986.

Thrift, N.; Taylor, M.: Battleships and cruisers: the new geography of multinational corporations. In: Gregory, D.; Walford, R.: Horizons in Human Geography, pp. 279–297. London, Macmillan 1989.

Tucker, B.: The Growth and Spatial Evolution of a Large Business Enterprise: The South African Breweries Ltd. M.A. Dissertation, University of the Witwatersrand, Johannesburg 1985.

Tucker, B.: The international expansion of an enterprise of the semi-periphery: South African Breweries Limited. In: Taylor, M.; Thrift, N. (eds.), Multinationals and the Restructuring of the World Economy, pp. 86–104. Croom Helm, Beckenham 1986.

United Nations: Transnational Corporations in International Tourism. Centre on Transnational Corporations, New York 1982.

Wallace, I.: The Global Economic System. Unwin Hyman, London 1990.

Watts, H. D.: Industrial Geography. Longman, Harlow 1987.

Wellings, P.; Crush, J. S.: Tourism and dependency in Southern Africa: the prospects and planning of tourism in Lesotho. Applied Geography 3, 205–223 (1983).

Taiwan's Electronic Companies are Targeting Europe

MICHAEL McDERMOTT, *Lecturer, University of Strathclyde International Business Unit*

The market penetrative power of Taiwanese exports is a well-known story. Less is known about Taiwan's strongest export companies, in electronics, which have been targeting Europe in preference to the USA in their marketing strategies since 1986, and have succeeded in making it Taiwan's fastest-growing export market.

Michael McDermott considers the roots of Taiwan's electronics industry, its internationalization, and diversification from consumer to industrial electronics. He then sets out the facts on Taiwan's striking export and investment record in the Single European Market and offers forecasts for the future.

Introduction

In 1990 Taiwan's exports amounted to $67.2bn, making it the world's 12th largest exporting nation. The economic transformation of Taiwan over the past three decades has been due to its successful export-oriented development strategy. Manufactured goods now account for around 95.6 per cent of Taiwan's total exports. Textiles was Taiwan's largest export industry until 1984 when it was superseded by electronics. Electronics remain the largest export sector, and it continues to grow rapidly due to the dynamic information products subsector.

As recently as 1985 the USA still accounted for almost half (i.e. 48.8 per cent) of Taiwan's total exports while Europe absorbed a mere 10 per cent. Europe is now Taiwan's fastest-growing export market and in the first six months of 1991 it accounted for 20.6 per cent of total exports. During the same period, the USA saw its share slip to 28 per cent. This paper thus focuses on a market (i.e. Europe) and sector (electronics) which will be of enormous importance in determining the overall performance of the Taiwan economy during the 1990s.

McDermott (1990) examined the international marketing strategies of South Korean electronics companies. It was seen that the 'big three' (that is, Goldstar, Samsung Electronics and Daewoo Electronics) focused their export efforts on the US market. In 1981 Goldstar became the first South Korean company to establish an overseas production facility, a wholly-owned plant in Alabama, USA. Samsung followed suit in 1984 at Los Angeles and Daewoo did likewise in 1986 in California. Thus by 1986, these three companies had ceased to rely on exports and instead used local production to serve the US market. It should be noted too that Korean electronics production and exports were dominated by just three products: colour television, video cassette recorders and microwave ovens.

Thus during 1986, the Koreans rapidly turned their attention to the EC market. The sudden upsurge in exports led to a series of EC anti-dumping investigations, and indeed the imposition of anti-dumping duties. An examination of Korean electronics plants in the EC reveals that virtually all of these investments coincided with either the investigation process or the implementation of penalties.

In this paper, it will be seen that Taiwan's electronics manufacturers have recently targeted the EC and that 1992 and fears of 'Fortress Europe' will result in a wave of Taiwanese investments in the EC. The location-specific advantages of EC member countries is considered based upon the Taiwanese perspective, and a plant location decision model is provided.

Lastly, the opportunities and threats for and to EC electronics companies and the European industry overall is considered. First of all, it is necessary to trace the development of Taiwan's electronics industry.

The Origins and Growth of Taiwan's Electronics Industry

In 1961, the Taiwan government formally recognized that an outward-oriented economic development strategy was necessary to foster economic growth for its low-labour cost economy which lacked capital and natural resources. It thus passed The Statute for Encouragement of Investment in an effort to attract foreign direct investment (fdi), and boost indigenous

Table 1 Value of electronics production of world's leading producers in 1988 ($bn)

Rank	*Country*	*Value*
1	USA	192
2	Japan	130
3	West Germany	35
4	France	24
5	UK	23
6	South Korea	22
7	Taiwan	16
8	Italy	14
9	Singapore	8
10	Netherlands	7

Source: Electronics. Industrial Development Board. Ministry of Economic Affairs, Taipei, Taiwan, 1990: private discussions with IDB staff

Table 2 Value of Taiwan's electronics exports 1978–88 ($m)

Year	*Value*
1978	1,812.0
1979	2,374.3
1980	2,957.3
1981	3,629.2
1982	3,550.7
1983	4,251.1
1984	5,461.4
1985	5,092.7
1986	7,254.9
1987	11,038.4
1988	13,613.3

Source: see Table 1

Table 3 Distribution of Taiwan's electronic exports by nature of product, 1978–88

	Consumer	*Industrial*	*Parts and components*
1978	51	4	45
1979	50	3	47
1980	47	4	49
1981	47	4	49
1982	42	6	52
1983	36	15	49
1984	33	22	45
1985	27	30	43
1986	27	35	38
1987	26	38	36
1988	21	42	37

Source: see Table 1

investment. The same year Tatung produced the country's first radio.

In 1964, the US MNE, General Instrument, became the first of many foreign investors, establishing a plant to produce radios. The same year saw Tatung diversify its product range when it and indigenous rival, Sampo, commenced production of black and white televisions. Today, these two firms remain Taiwan's leading producers of consumer electronics.

Before the mid-1970s, the growth of Taiwan's electronics industry had been the result of activity by the foreign-owned sector and indigenous manufacturers, acting mainly as subcontractors to US and European MNEs, assembling consumer electronics. In the mid-1970s though, the industry took a new direction when a number of Taiwanese entrepreneurs established information products companies. Today, Acer (founded in 1976) and Mitac (founded in 1974) are Taiwan's leading producers of information products (that is, computers and peripherals).

By 1980, the Taiwanese government had identified information products as a dynamic sector compatible with Taiwan's resource base and development strategy. It thus established Hsinchu Science-based Industrial Park, Taiwan's Silicon Valley, and accorded information products 'priority' status.

By 1988 Taiwan had become the world's seventh largest electronics manufacturer, with output of $16.0bn of which $13.6bn or 85 per cent was exported (see Tables 1 and 2). Consumer electronics accounted for 21.2 per cent of total output, industrial electronics 42 per cent, and parts and components 37 per cent (see Table 3).

The industry consisted of 3,300 factories with 350,000 employees, and it made a disproportionate contribution to the manufacturing sector. It accounted for:

- 4.0 per cent of total manufacturing enterprises;
- 15.6 per cent of total employment;
- 13.8 per cent of the value of total production; and
- 26.0 per cent of total exports.

Even as recently as 1988, the USA accounted for 43 per cent of Taiwan's electronics exports, as against 56.1 per cent in 1978. The section below examines the internationalization strategies of Taiwan's two main consumer electronics companies.

Internationalization of Taiwan's Leading Consumer Electronics Companies

Tatung began exporting in 1954, selling electric fans to the Philippines. Initially it focused its export activities on other Asian markets, finally targeting Japan in 1968. These countries were relatively close to Taiwan culturally and geographically, thus Tatung in its choice of export markets was adhering as far as possible to advice commonly given to exporters:

'An ideal export market is one that is identical to the home market, speaks the same language and is geographically close' (Katz, 1990)

In 1971, Tatung commenced exporting fans to the USA. Despite the fresh challenge involved in exporting to this culturally and geographically remote market, it was immediately successful. A US marketing subsidiary was established in the following year, an indication of greater commitment to the market. In 1974 Tatung opened its and Taiwan's first overseas manufacturing plant, at Los Angeles to produce electric fans. The product line of this facility was extended two years later to include colour televisions. Thus, Tatung was the pioneer in the internationalization of Taiwanese business. Arch-rival Sampo has followed closely behind Tatung.

In 1981 Tatung opened its second plant in the USA, AT Atlanta, to produce colour televisions and home appliances. More significantly though, this year also saw Tatung become the first Taiwanese company with a manufacturing presence in the EC, having established a marketing subsidiary in the UK and Luxembourg in 1980.

Tatung entered the UK market by acquiring the consumer electronic business of Decca Radio and Television Ltd. The following year Samsung became the first Korean company to invest in Europe, establishing a plant in Portugal. During the second half of the 1980s Korea's 'big three' established several plants in the EC, but Tatung remained the sole Taiwanese investor until late 1990. In the meantime though, Tatung had moved in 1985 from its Bridgenorth plant to a 43 acre greenfield site at Telford, England. It has invested circa £20m in the Telford plant which produces daily 1,500 colour televisions and 800 computer monitors. Moreover, 95 per cent of components are produced in-house. Initially the ethnocentric approach to labour relations created tensions between the plant's Taiwanese management and British workforce, but a move towards polycentricism has ameliorated this situation. The unionized Telford plant currently has 900 employees, and a further 100 jobs will be created during 1991 with the expansion of its R&D facility. Again in the context of the European market, Tatung has pioneered Tainwanese expansion, and in terms of Porter's value chain, all primary activities have been transferred to the UK.

During the second half of the 1980s, Tatung and Sampo's internationalization process took a new direction. Rising costs forced them to locate labour-intensive activities in low-cost Asian countries. Tatung has a plant in Malaysia and also one in Thailand. The Thai plant exports all of its output. It has an annual production capacity of 400,000 colour televisions and 350,000 satellite receivers which are destined mainly for the EC, and 1 m printed circuit boards which are exported to Taiwan for final assembly. The Malaysian facilities produce components. Sampo has a joint-venture in Thailand and a plant in China. It is currently considering opening a third facility in Indonesia. Figure 1 summarizes the internationalization process of Tatung, revealing its presence in each region of the Triad (i.e. USA, Europe, Asia). Despite having transferred production overseas, Tatung ranked as Taiwan's second largest exporter in 1989, with exports of $414.5m, behind Nan Ya Plastics Corporation ($508.3m).

In contrast to its larger rival, Sampo is yet to establish a manufacturing presence in the EC. Until recently the USA accounted for 80 per cent of Sampo's total exports from Taiwan, but this share has shrunk to 40 per cent, with the emergence of the EC as a key market. Marketing subsidiaries were established first in Germany (Dusseldorf, 1989) and in the UK (London, 1990). Sampo's main exports to the EC are, in descending order, computer peripherals, telecommunication equipment, and microwave ovens. The company is currently undertaking a review of appropriate locations in the EC for each product. As of September 1990, the preferred locations were as follows:

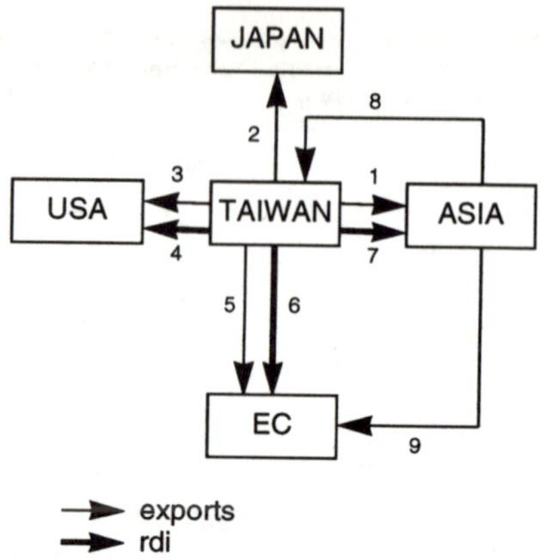

Figure 1 Tatung's Internationalization process

- computer plant — Germany because of infrastructure and market size;
- telecommunications — Spain or North East England. Availability of quality auxiliary suppliers will be the determining factor, given that components account for around 70 per cent of total production costs:
- microwave ovens — North East England where Goldstar and Samsung already make microwave ovens.

Tatung is also likely to open another plant in the EC, most likely in Germany, to produce computers. Thus, clearly both Tatung and Sampo have diversified with success from consumer to industrial electronics. However, the author's view is that those companies which are dedicated to manufacturing information products will provide the bulk of Taiwanese fdi in the EC over the next few years, but especially in 1992.

The Information Industry: Its Achievements and Changing Structure

In 1989 Taiwan's production of information products amounted to $5.5bn, of which exports accounted for $5.2bn or 96 per cent. The industry was responsible for 2.7 per cent of Taiwan's GNP, and information products ranked as the country's third largest export earner. In 1989 there was a total of 5,000 firms engaged in the industry with a total labour force of 80,000.

By 1988 Taiwan was the world's sixth largest manufacturer of information products. Its growth rate was appreciably higher than its nearest rivals (i.e. the

Table 4 Information industry revenues in 1988 of top ten manufacturing countries ($bn)

Rank	*Country*	*Value*	*Growth rate (%)*
1	USA	52.1	9.0
2	Japan	35.7	9.0
3	West Germany	8.8	8.5
4	UK	6.4	8.8
5	France	5.7	8.1
6	Taiwan	5.2	38.7
7	Italy	4.5	6.3
8	Singapore	2.9	26.0
9	Ireland	2.3	12.9
10	South Korea	2.2	45.0

Source: see Table 12

UK and France in fifth and fourth positions) (see Table 4). It is thus very likely that 1990 will confirm Taiwan as the world's number three producer behind the USA and Japan. It is already the leading supplier of monitors, number two in terminals and number three in personal computers. Its worldwide market share for ten major information products is presented in Table 5. This success is largely due to the popularity of Taiwan for offshore production and subcontracting. More recently though, and significantly for the industry's long-term prosperity, indigenous manufacturers (e.g. Acer, Mitac, Tatung etc.) have increased the proportion of own brand sales.

In the first half of the 1980s the growth of the industry was due largely to foreign-owned firms (e.g. Atari,

Table 5 Taiwan's worldwide market share for selected information products (1989)

Product	*Worldwide market share (%)*
Microcomputers	10.5
Colour monitors	34.7
Monochrome monitors	29.4
Mainboard	60.8
Terminals	33.2
Switching power supply	18.3
Keyboards	28.7
Graphic cards	32.9
Control cards	52.0
Disk drive	0.2

Source: Market Intelligence Centre, Institute for Information Industry

Table 6 Breakdown of type of exports of Taiwan's information industry (%)

	OBM	*OEM*	*OSM*
1984	3	40	57
1985	5	37	58
1986	17	39	44
1987	20	41	39
1988	20	44	36
1989	22	43	35

OBM = Own Brand Manufacturing
OEM = Original Equipment Manufacturing
OSM = Offshore Manufacturing

Source: see Table 5

Table 7 Taiwan's top 18 exporters of information products, 1989

Value of 1989 exports	*Rank 1984*	*Rank 1988*	*Rank 1989*	*Company*	*Main export items PCs*	*Terminal*	*Monitor*	*Printer*	*Components*
More than US$300 m	1	2	1	Tatung	X		X		
	16	3	2	Acer	X				
US$200–299 m	—	5	3	Philips			X		
	6	6	4	Atari	X				
US$100–199 m	9	1	5	Wyse	X		X		
	3	7	6	Wang	X		X		
	—	10	7	Mitac	X				
	2	4	8	Digital Equipment	X		X	X	
	—	13	9	DTK Components	X				X
	11	8	10	Captronic			X		
	—	11	11	AST Research	X				
	12	15	12	Sampo		X	X		
US$50–99 m	23	16	13	Copam Electronics	X				
	8	14	14	Zenith		X	X		
	—	19	15	Compal			X		
	15	12	16	ADI		X	X		
	5	18	17	Teco		X			
	—	30	18	TDK					X

Source: *The Way Approaching Miracle: The Digest of Taiwan's Information Industry*, China External Trade Development Council, Industrial Technology Research Institute, Electronic Research and Service Organisation, Institute for Information Industry, Taipei, 1990.

Table 8 Percentage breakdown of production type of selected information products made in Taiwan 1985–88

Year	*OBM*	*OEM*	*OSM*	*Total*
Microcomputers				
1985	9	27	64	100
1986	28	22	50	100
1987	36	23	41	100
1988	39	24	37	100
Diskdrives				
1985	6	29	65	100
1986	—	8	92	100
1987	5	23	72	100
1988	4	21	75	100
Printer				
1985	—	9	91	100
1986	—	2	98	100
1987	3	21	76	100
1988	1	21	78	100
Terminal				
1985	2	35	63	100
1986	7	24	69	100
1987	7	22	71	100
1988	6	25	69	100
Monitor				
1985	4	56	40	100
1986	17	41	42	100
1987	23	37	40	100
1988	23	37	4	100
Other Peripherals Components				
1985	6	32	62	100
1986	5	25	70	100
1987	10	19	71	100
1988	11	19	70	100

Source: see Table 5

Digital, Philips, Wang) which had established a manufacturing presence in Taiwan. Indeed, until 1986 foreign multinationals were responsible for the majority of the industry's exports (see Table 6). In 1984 offshore manufacturing (OSM) accounted for almost three-fifths (i.e. 57 per cent) of the information industry's total exports. In 1984 two US multinationals, Digital and Wang, were the industry's second and third largest exporters (see Table 7).

By 1989 OSM's share of total production had fallen to just 35 per cent. Nevertheless, five of the sector's eight largest exporters, including Wyse (a US company acquired in 1989 by a Taiwanese consortia), were foreign multinationals. In certain products (e.g. disk drives) OSM accounted for the bulk of Taiwan's production (see Table 8).

Despite rising labour costs and labour shortages, not to mention the appreciation of the NT$, it is difficult to imagine a mass exodus of these firms to lower cost locations. Certainly, labour intensive operations with very little value added are likely to be transferred overseas, but OSM will continue to make an important, albeit diminishing, contribution to Taiwan's information sector. However, in 1989 some firms (e.g. Ampex and Commodore) ceased manufacturing in Taiwan.

In the early 1980s Taiwan was still a low-cost location and local manufacturers were awarded large subcontracting contracts from foreign multinationals. Indeed, despite rising costs, original equipment manufacturing (OEM) business has accounted for a steady proportion of the industry's total production during the period 1984–89. Indeed, leading US computer manufacturers (e.g. Apple, Compaq, IBM, Unisys) have all established International Procurement Offices in Taiwan. These and numerous other firms source monitors from Taiwan, so little wonder that it produced one in three of all monitors manufactured worldwide in 1989.

In the long term, OEM business is likely to become less important. Some manufacturers (e.g. Acer and Mitac) are seeking to convert OEM business to own brand manufacturing (OBM). In contrast, other firms — the majority — still rely heavily on OEM business. Hence the loss of subcontracting contracts still represents a serious threat to the information industry in Taiwan.

In 1984 only three per cent of all information products made in Taiwan were sold under a Taiwan company's brand name. Thus, the industry was in a very vulnerable position. Foreign multinationals could decide to close up and move production overseas, or terminate OEM business which is very cost-sensitive. Therefore, by developing OBM, Taiwan's information companies are pursuing stability and simultaneously moving to higher added value products with better profit margins. By 1989, OBM accounted for 22 per cent of the industry's total exports, with particular success recorded in microcomputers and monitors.

Table 9 Value of Taiwan's exports of main information products (US$m)

	1983	1984	1985	1986	1987	1988	1989
Microcomputers	16	152	240	393	761	1,154	1,244
Monitors	130	319	303	500	877	1,081	1,251
Disk drives	15	86	42	71	97	119	115
Printers	12	23	45	41	44	43	39
Terminal	97	207	226	317	414	505	458
Other	104	205	257	299	80	81	102
Sub-total	374	992	1,113	1,601	2,273	2,983	3,209
Parts & components	129	113	112	462	1,428	2,016	2,035
Total	503	1,005	1,225	2,063	3,701	4,999	5,244

Source: see Table 5

Table 10 Analysis of growth in Taiwan's exports of information products to major markets, 1986–87 (US$m)

	Export value			No. of exporters		
	1986	1987	% change	1986	1987	% change
USA	1,175	1,910	63	1,355	1,629	20
Netherlands	140	275	96	283	428	51
West Germany	103	214	108	546	839	54
UK	103	194	88	334	484	45
France	44	108	145	316	497	57
Hong Kong	47	88	87	526	708	35
Italy	30	70	133	262	387	48
Singapore	32	70	119	375	602	61
Total information products exports	2,063[a]	3,701[a]	79	2,788[b]	3,720[b]	33

[a] Including others. [b] Exporters may be duplicated across countries.
Source: *The Way Approaching Miracle: The Digest of Taiwan's Information Industry*, China External Trade Development Council, Industrial Technology Research Institute, Electronic Research and Service Organisation, Institute for Information Industry, Taipei, 1990.

Parts and components account for a significant chunk of Taiwan's exports of information products. In 1989 their export value amounted to $2.03bn or 39 per cent of the sector's total. In 1983 the value of such exports had been a mere £129m, and accounted for just over a quarter of total exports (see Table 9).

Concentrating now on actual equipment, five products (in descending order of importance — monitors, microcomputers, terminals, disk drives, and printers) recorded exports of $3.2bn in 1989. These amounted to 61 per cent of total information product exports or 97 per cent excluding parts and components. Monitors were the single largest export item in every year, except 1988, during the seven-year period from 1983 to 1989. Microcomputer exports have recorded the most impressive growth rate during this period, rising from just $16m in 1983 to $1.24bn in 1989.

Although the USA is the largest export market for Taiwan's information products, exports to other major markets (e.g. France, Germany, Holland and the UK) are increasing at a faster rate (see Table 10). Indeed, Europe is already a much larger market than North

Table 11 Export markets for information products, 1985 (%)

Area	Information products (Including computer components)	Micro computers	Disk drives	Printers	Terminals	Monitors
USA	51.62	33.94	52.92	57.77	70.04	56.70
Canada	1.82	1.62	1.16	0.03	0.13	1.85
North America	53.44	35.56	54.08	57.80	70.17	58.55
Netherlands	7.44	9.44	10.87	21.01	12.29	8.86
West Germany	5.78	6.62	6.67	2.85	1.59	4.91
UK	5.25	7.74	7.07	3.62	4.40	6.20
France	2.93	5.51	2.56	0.24	0.99	2.94
Italy	1.90	3.18	1.15	0.44	1.24	1.71
Switzerland	1.52	3.40	1.05	0.81	0.06	0.64
Belgium	1.04	1.39	4.73	0.14	0.24	1.27
Others	6.16	12.86	1.24	4.60	3.37	4.02
Europe	32.02	50.14	35.34	33.71	24.18	30.55
Hong Kong	2.39	0.36	2.34	1.05	0.73	1.85
Singapore	1.88	1.04	2.66	0.56	1.69	1.41
South Korea	0.51	0.16	0.73	0.07	0.01	0.38
Japan	1.47	0.38	0.80	0.27	0.34	0.69
Australia	2.61	3.32	1.52	3.53	2.08	2.18
Others	1.05	1.07	0.44	1.24	0.19	1.50
Asia & Pacific	9.91	6.33	8.49	6.72	5.04	8.01
Other areas	4.63	7.97	2.09	1.77	0.61	2.89
Total	100.00	100.00	100.00	100.00	100.00	100.00

Source: *The Way Approaching Miracle: The Digest of Taiwan's Information Industry*, China External Trade Development Council, Industrial Technology Research Institute, Electronic Research and Service Organisation, Institute for Information Industry, Taipei, 1990.

Table 12 The World's top 15 markets for microcomputers (000 sets)

	Country	Volume
1	USA	8,715
2	Japan	1,200
3	France	588
4	West Germany	577
5	England (sic)	534
6	Italy	316
7	Holland	215
8	Australia	195
9	Taiwan	165
10	Spain	144
11	Sweden	132
12	South Korea	123
13	Switzerland	115
14	Singapore	48
15	Indonesia	28
16	Malaysia	24
17	Hong Kong	21

Source: see Table 5

America for Taiwan's exports of microcomputers (see Table 11). Within the EC, the Netherlands is the largest market for such exports, reflecting the fact that this country is the major distribution point for the EC market, rather than the one with the biggest domestic export. This fact, plus the relatively high proportion of own brand exports to the EC suggests that a number of Taiwan's microcomputer manufacturers will establish a manufacturing base in the EC prior to 1992. Moreover, the EC accounts for six of the world's ten largest markets for microcomputers (see Table 12).

Despite the entry of the large 'chaebols' (i.e. large conglomerates) into the information industry, the value of South Korea's exports of information products still lags well behind those from Taiwan. In each of the five main products discussed above, plus parts and components, Taiwan leads South Korea. In 1987 South Korea's exports of information products were worth $1.46bn against Taiwan's $3.7bn.

The Internationalization of Taiwan's Information Products Manufacturers

Acer and Mitac began manufacturing computers in 1981 and 1984 respectively. Financial data on both companies is provided in Table 13. Their domestic plant(s) are at Hsinchu and in 1989 they ranked behind Tatung as Taiwan's top, second and third largest exporters of information products.

In 1984 Acer won its first OEM contracts (from the US MNEs, ITT and NCR). The following year, Mitac secured its first large OEM order, also from ITT. In 1986 it gained other business from Memorex (USA), which in 1990 was its largest customer, Commodore (USA) and Philips (the Netherlands). Both companies now derive

Table 13 Selected financial data on Acer and Mitac (US$m)

	Acer		Mitac	
	Sales	Net income	Sales	Net income
1983	28.3	—	50.0	—
1984	51.6	0.4	80.0	—
1985	94.8	5.1	100.0	—
1986	165.3	3.9	130.0	—
1987	331.2	15.3	235.0	—
1988	530.9	26.5	300.0	—
1989	688.9	5.8	380.0	—
1990	949.5	2.4	500.0	—

Source: Acer and Mitac.

a sizeable proportion of their sales from own brand sales, and are investing to boost their brand and corporate image in international markets.

Until 1988 Acer was known as 'Multitech' but the latter name was dropped because it did not possess 'the distinctiveness ... necessary for us to make a real impact on the world market'. In 1990 both companies introduced their new marketing slogan: Acer replaced 'Your Computing Friend Cares Everywhere' with 'Global Partner in Computing', while Mitac abandoned 'Growth Without Chaos' in favour of 'People Committed to Infotech'.

Table 14 shows that Europe is now clearly the largest export market for Acer Inc. and Mitac Inc. This position has been achieved even though Acer has only recently targeted the EC market. In order to enhance own brand sales it adopted a market concentration strategy, beginning with developing countries and gradually moving to more competitive markets once it succeeded (i.e. a top five market position). Its tactics are comparable to those utilized in the Chinese chess game, Go, where the objective is to make territorial gains rather than capture the opponent's pieces. This strategy has worked. Acer is market leader in many less developed countries (LDCs) (Bolivia, Bahrain, Chile, Cyprus, India, Jordan, Mexico, the Philippines and Thailand). It is among the top five best selling brands in countries such as Finland, Singapore, South Africa and the United Arab Emirates.

Table 14 Distribution of sales by market for Acer Inc. and Mitac Inc.

	Acer Inc. (1991, 1–6)	Mitac Inc. (1989)
North America	27	37
Europe	42	27
Rest of World	31	36
Total	100	100

Source: see Table 13.

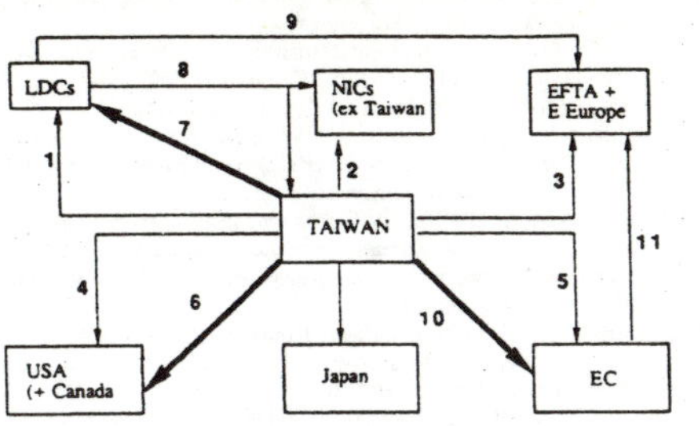

Notes: Numbers indicate (roughly) sequence of internationalisation.

——► equals export (arrows donating origin and destination of products)

▬▬► equals transferral of production (arrows donating origin and destination)

Figure 2 Acer's international markerting development for own brand products — GO tactics

The international marketing development process for Acer's own brand products is shown in Figure 2. Acer reached stage 10 in 1990 when it acquired the Dutch computer company, Kangaroo Computer BV. During 1991, it is expected to select a greenfield site in the Netherlands.

Figure 3 provides a simplified model of the plant location decision-process of Taiwanese manufacturers looking to establish a plant in the EC. This model is appropriate for those Taiwanese manufacturers that intend to develop their own brands. Such firms are also members of Brand International Promotion Association (Bipa), founded in 1989, to promote Taiwanese brands in international markets.

The EC will also attract fdi by Taiwanese subcontractors to the world's major computer companies. In 1990 Delta Electronics, for example, located near Glasgow in Scotland to be near its main customers, IBM and Compaq. As Figure 3 shows, the UK, Ireland and the Netherlands, appear the preferred locations among Taiwanese investors.

In the spring of 1990, Yuen Foong Yu Group, a paper conglomerate and one of Taiwan's largest business groups, purchased a 50-acre site near Cork in Ireland. Its aim is for the site to become a 'Hsinchu in Europe'. A year later, Northern Ireland's Industrial Development Board set aside a 139-acre industrial zone at Ballyhenny, near Antrim, for Taiwanese investors. The project has the support of the Taiwan Electrical Appliance Manufacturers Association (TEAMA) which will encourage its member companies to locate on the zone.

It is the author's view that during the 1990s the contrasting characteristics of Taiwan's and Korea's electronics industry will have important implications for inward investment in the EC. Taiwan may well be the source of a greater number of cases of fdi but in value terms Korea will be much more significant.

Taiwanese electronics companies are also perhaps more likely to establish a manufacturing presence in the EC market through acquisition rather than greenfield investment. In the spring of 1990, Japan's Mitsubishi outbid Acer and Mitac to acquire Apricot Computers for £49m. Both Acer and Mitac have already concluded one large acquisition of a US company. In 1990 Acer paid $94m for Altos Computers and in 1989 Mitac was part of the Taiwanese consortium which paid $270m for Wyse Technology, taking a 12 per cent stake.

Conclusions

The Taiwan electronics industry has successfully diversified from consumer to industrial electronics. The leading consumer electronics companies have moved into information products, but the rapid growth of this subsector is due mainly to the staggering growth of companies which have been founded since the early 1970s and which have focused exclusively on information products. Until recently Taiwan's electronics firms have been heavily dependent on the US market, but they are now being pushed and pulled towards the European market, especially the EC with the prospect of '1992'. Even before the unsuccessful coup in the Soviet Union in August 1991, the Eastern European dimension had little bearing on the plant location decision, with three North Atlantic economies (i.e. Ireland, the Netherlands and the UK) the apparent favourite choices.

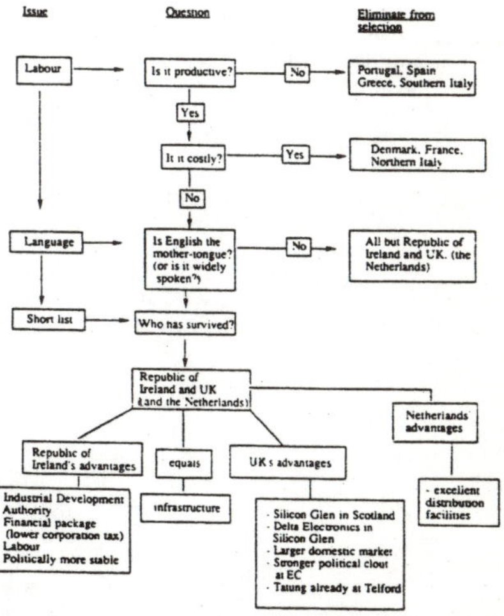

Figure 3 Simplified EC plant-location decision making process of potential Taiwanese manufacturers of information products

The Irish Republic and the Netherlands are likely to attract information product manufacturers, but the UK could well attract Taiwanese investments in consumer electronics and information products. The North East of England and Northern Ireland are likely to prove the preferred location for consumer electronics investments. In June 1991 Wales launched a special initiative to attract information technology companies, especially those from South Korea and Taiwan. Indeed the Welsh Development Agency seems to be focusing increasingly on Taiwan at the very moment its main rivals are finding their powers weakened (i.e. Locate in Scotland — see Hood, 1991) or the agency is being disbanded (e.g. Telford Development Corporation).

Ironically though, this inter- and intra-country competition in the EC to attract Taiwanese investment will accelerate the loss of competitiveness of indigenous European electronics companies and foreign divestment mainly by ailing US computer companies.

Note

This paper is based on primary research conducted by the author during two visits to Taiwan in 1990. To avoid offending through omission, the author would like to express his gratitude to the numerous executives of several leading electronics companies, who kindly agreed to be interviewed and who provided valuable documentation. Officials of Brand International Promotion Association, the Industrial Development Bureau, the Industrial Development and Investment Centre, the Institute for Information Industry, the Taipei Computer Association, and the Taiwan Electrical Appliance Manufacturers Association.

Bibliography

Hamel, G. and Prahalad, C.K. (1989), 'Strategic Intent', *Harvard Business Review* May–June.

Hood, N. (1991), 'Inward Investment and the Scottish Economy: Quo Vadis', *The Royal Bank of Scotland Review*, No. 169, March.

Katz, B. (1987), *Managing Export Marketing*, Gower Business Enterprise Series, Aldershot.

Kotler, P., Fahey, L. and Jatusripitak, S. (1985), *The New Competition: What Theory Z Didn't Tell You About*, Prentice-Hall, Englewood Cliffs, New Jersey.

McDermott, M.C. and Young, S. (1989), *South Korea's Industry: New Directions in World Markets*, Special Report No. 2005, The Economist Intelligence Unit, London.

McDermott, M.C. (1990), *The Development and Internationalisation of the South Korean Electronics Industry*, Sixteenth Annual Conference of the European International Business Association.

McDermott, M.C. (1991), *Taiwan's Industry in World Markets: Target Europe*, Special Report No. 2111, The Economist Intelligence Unit, London.

Porter, M.E. (1986), *Competition in Global Industries*, Harvard Business School Press, Boston, Massachusetts.

Journal of Development Economics 39 (1992) 397–407. North-Holland

Determinants of Taiwan's direct foreign investment

The case of a newly industrializing country

Tain-Jy Chen*

Chung-Hua Institution for Economic Research, Taipei, Taiwan

Received July 1990, final version received April 1991

This paper shows that direct foreign investment (DFI) is motivated by different factors under different macroeconomic conditions. The microeconomic determinants of DFI vary with firm size, although on average, large firms are more inclined to make DFI than small firms. The only common factor that drives both large and small firms to venture abroad is the successful export experience prior to DFI.

1. Introduction

The orthodox theory of direct foreign investment (DFI) emanates from Hymer's (1960) work, which draws primarily on the U.S. experience. Hymer argues that DFI occurs only because firms operating in oligopolistic markets seek to exploit their firm-specific advantages, or intangible assets. By setting up a foreign subsidiary, etc., the firm internalizes or supersedes the market by transferring this advantage abroad at a very low marginal cost. Empirical works attempting to substantiate Hymer's hypothesis have revealed that the firm-specific advantages lie mainly in the areas of technological superiority [Horst (1972), Caves (1974), Wolf (1977), Lall (1980)], greater product differentiation [Caves (1974), Lall (1980)], and larger firm size [Horst (1972), Wolf (1977), Lall (1980)].

A Japanese variant of DFI theory was proposed by Kojima (1973, 1978) and Ozawa (1979). In contrast to Hymer's study, which placed emphasis on the microeconomic characteristics of individual firms, Kojima and Ozawa argue that Japanese firms embarked on a course of DFI because they were in a comparatively disadvantageous position, forged by macroeconomic con-

Correspondence to: Tain-Jy Chen, Research Fellow, Chung-Hua Institution for Economic Research, 75 Chang-Hsing St., Taipeim Taiwan.

*I am indebted to my colleague Hsien-Yang Su, who conducted the difficult survey, Chung H. Lee, C.M. Joseph Yu, and two anonymous referees who provided useful comments.

0304–3878/92/$05.00

ditions. Japanese firms ventured overseas simply to exploit location-specific advantages of the host country (such as low-cost labor) in order to re-establish their international competitiveness. They observed (in the 1960s and 1970s) that Japanese DFI took place mainly in labor-intensive, low-technology industries in which Japan's competitive edge had been eroded by rising wage rates.

The apparent difference between Kojima and Ozawa, and Hymer's hypotheses is only superficial, however. As pointed out by Lee (1984), the fact that the Japanese firms went abroad to continue operating in the traditional industries, in which they had been engaged, instead of switching to new industries, which were favored by the prevailing macroeconomic conditions, suggests possession of certain intangible assets by Japanese firms which are tied to the old industries. Horst (1972) found that the advantages believed to be possessed by U.S. multinational firms are mostly industry specific. Holding industry constant, the only identifiable characteristic that differentiates U.S. multinational firms from other ordinary firms is their relatively large size.

In fact, Kojima and Ozawa, and Hymer probably are looking at the opposite sides of the same coin; macroeconomic conditions and firm-specific advantages are indeed complementary to each other in fermenting firms' decisions to undertake DFI activities. It is possible that, under different macroeconomic conditions, there may exist different sets of firm characteristics that are conducive to DFI. In other words, how an individual firm decides to invest abroad depends on the country's degree of industrialization as well as the underlying international environment that prescribes the company's competitive position. Studies by Lecraw (1977), Lall (1983), and Wells (1983), among others, have shown that multinationals based in developing countries derive their comparative advantage from the following operational characteristics: smallness of scale, labor intensive technology, and flexible product lines. It is also noted that developing-country multinationals are typified by low R&D intensity and advertising outlay, in sharp contrast with Western multinationals. This implies that developing-country multinationals compete through their relatively lower cost of production rather than through superior technology or brand names.

This paper examines the influence of both macroeconomic and microeconomic factors on Taiwan's DFI. The study shows that Taiwan's DFI was motivated by different factors given different macroeconomic conditions. It was also found that the microeconomic determinants of DFI vary with firm size and that growth performance increases the small-scale firms' propensity to invest abroad, while it is an inconsequential factor in the large-scale firms' DFI decisions. On the other hand, dependency on imported raw materials increases the large-scale firms' probability of investing abroad, while the small-scale firms' DFI decisions are not affected by this factor.

2. Taiwan's DFI since 1987

In 1987, firms in Taiwan started to undertake DFI at ever increasing rates; up to that time, DFI by Taiwan enterprises had been rather minimal. In 1987, Taiwan's officially registered amount of outward investment increased by 80.5% (in U.S. dollars). It increased another 112.9% in 1988 and 325.6% in 1989.[1] Statistics compiled by the host countries have further indicated that the actual amount of DFI from Taiwan was several times the figure officially recorded by Taiwan's government [see World Bank (1989)]. The macroeconomic factors that could have conceivably sparked the outburst of DFI are three in number. First, Taiwan's currency appreciated rapidly against the world's major currencies.

Second, wages increased and labor shortages occurred.[2] Third, Taiwan's government dismantled its foreign exchange controls in July 1987, allowing for a virtually free outflow of capital.

Under this new set of circumstances, the author surveyed Taiwan's major businesses on their intention to invest abroad in February 1988, at the onset of the DFI takeoff. The survey covered 2,311 firms whose sales revenue exceeded 100 million NT dollars (Taiwan's currency), or approximately 2.9 million U.S. dollars, in 1986. The data from the questionnaires form the basis of this study. In the questionnaire, we inquired whether the firm planned to invest abroad in the next three years and, if so, why. Our sample consists of 468 valid, returned questionnaires, of which 372 are in the manufacturing sector and 96 are in the service sector. Of the 468 firms, 116 indicated that they planned to invest abroad. Among the DFI-minded firms, 22 are in the electronic and electrical products industry, 12 in the plastics industry, 10 in the textile industry, 7 each in the apparel, chemicals, and transportation equipment industries, 24 in services, and the rest belong to other manufacturing industries. We compared the reasons that the firms in our sample listed with those revealed in another sample of firms that had made overseas investments prior to 1987. The latter data were collected from interviews with 53 firms which had established foreign subsidiaries before 1987. Among those 53 firms, 9 are in the electronic and electrical products industry; 7 in the apparel industry; 3 each in food processing, plastics, non-metal minerals, wood products, and metal products industries, respectively; 16 in services, and the rest in other manufacturing industries. There are four firms which appear in both samples. The comparative results of the two questionnaires are illustrated in table 1 where the relative importance of each DFI

[1]See Investment Commission, Ministry of Economic Affairs, Republic of China, *Statistics on Overseas Chinese & Foreign Investment, Technical Cooperation, Outward Investment, Outward Technical Cooperation* (Dec. 31, 1989).

[2]Taiwan's currency, the NT dollar, appreciated against the U.S. dollar by 41.6% between September 1985 and December 1987. The manufacturing wage measured in terms of the local currency rose 20.7% between 1985 and 1987.

Table 1
Reasons cited for DFI.[a]

Reasons	Before 1987 (%)	After 1987 (%)
(1) Expansion of markets	56.0	25.1
(2) Low-cost labor	3.5	21.3
(3) Raw material supplies	8.2	9.1
(4) Tax incentives	1.6	6.6
(5) Avoidance of trade barriers	6.6	5.5
(6) Collection of market information	6.9	2.1
(7) Others	17.2	30.3
Total	100.0	100.0
Sample size	53	116

[a]The figure shown is the average (weighted) percentage of the respective reason cited by all of the firms interviewed or surveyed.

motivational factor is measured as a percentage and where the sum of all percentages equals one.[3]

Table 1 shows that, before 1987, the predominant reason for firms in Taiwan to engage in DFI was to expand their market base, including the enlargement of existing markets and the exploration and development of new ones. The second most important reason was to secure supplies of raw materials. The rank of the motivational factors changed after 1987, however, Although market expansion remained the top motive behind DFI, its weight of importance was substantially reduced from the overwhelming 56.0% of the pre-1987 era to just 25.1%. The second most important reason, low-cost labor, moved closer to the top of the list with 21.3%. In the catch-all category, 'others', 12.1% of its weight was accounted for by currency appreciation (not shown), which was rarely given as a factor during the interviews with the firms that had undertaken DFI before 1987. Little change of importance is observed in the motive of securing raw material supplies, which stood at 8.2% in the pre-1987 era and increased slightly to 9.1% in the post-1987 survey.

Since the two samples are composed of different industries, there is a possibility that the difference shown in table 1 is a result of the difference in industry composition. However, examining the most important industry in both samples, namely, the electronic and electrical products industry, reveals an even sharper contrast. In the pre-1987 sample, the single, predominant reason for this industry to engage in DFI is expansion of markets, accounting for 75.9%. All the other factors weigh trivially and low-cost labor

[3]The surveyed firms were asked to list and rank the reasons that they considered relevant to their decisions to invest abroad. Each reason is given a percentage value in accordance with its order of importance, with the percentages adding up to one. The percentage for the ith ranked reason is $(n+1-i)n/!$, where n is the number of reasons listed.

was not even mentioned. In the post-1987 sample, expansion of markets accounts for only 26.7%, while the weight of low-cost labor moves up to 25.3%. The shift in DFI motivations within this industry is evident.[4]

To formally test the overall difference between the two periods, in terms of the distribution of the motivational factors behind DFI, Pearson's chi-square statistic may be employed. The null hypothesis that the frequency distribution of the motivational factors are identical yields a χ^2 statistic of 24.2; therefore, our null hypothesis can be rejected at the 1% significance level, given six degrees of freedom. This implies that firms which planned to invest abroad after 1987 were motivated by a different set of considerations, which is distinct from that of the firms which actually invested abroad before 1987.

The change in the motivational factors behind DFI must have had something to do with the change in macroeconomic conditions, although we cannot pinpoint the elements that actually caused the change. From table 1, it appears that rising wage rates and currency appreciation are the probable factors that underlie the change.

3. Microeconomic determinants of DFI

In this section, we will study the microeconomic factors that determine an individual firm's propensity to invest abroad. We will explore the aforementioned survey data to identify the firm characteristics that are conducive to a firm's decision to invest abroad. Since this is a DFI decision made at a point in time, a cross-sectional study can best reveal the kind of firms that are most inclined to invest abroad. Since the international environments for production and investment are conspicuously different for the manufacturing and service sectors, this part of the investigation focuses solely on manufacturing firms.

The firm characteristics included in this study are scale (*SALE*), growth performance (*GR*), dependency on imported raw materials (*RAW*), labor intensity (*LAB*), and export ratio (*EXP*). Scale has been shown to be an important determinant of DFI undertaken by Western multinationals.[5] Large firm-size is usually associated with an oligopolistic market structure, implying some firm-specific advantages. Growth performance is designed to

[4]The service industry also exhibits a similar pattern of change, although the emergence of low-cost labor as a DFI factor in the post-1987 era is less striking. The other industries have too few observations to warrant a meaningful comparison.

[5]R&D intensity and advertising outlay, which have also been shown to be important in determining Western DFI, are omitted from this study because relevant data are unavailable at the firm level. Industry-specific R&D intensity was tried as a surrogate for an individual firm's R&D intensity but turned out to be insignificant.

Table 2
Correlation matrix of explanatory variables; sample size = 266.

	SALE	*GR*	*RAW*	*EXP*	*LAB*
SALE	1.000	−0.004	0.038	−0.162	−0.224
GR		1.000	−0.015	0.086	−0.033
RAW			1.000	−0.188	−0.139
EXP				1.000	0.566
LAB					1.000

reflect the firm's motive behind expanding its markets via DFI. Presumably, a firm with a higher potential growth is more motivated to engage in DFI. This also reflects the Kojima–Ozawa observation that a firm will engage in DFI when its growth is limited by domestic resource availability. The dependency-on-imported-raw-materials and the labor-intensity factor, respectively, reflect the motives of securing raw materials and accessing low-cost labor, which are to be found in the host country. The export ratio factor is designed to detect whether export-oriented firms are in a better position to, or are more heavily pressured to, go abroad. Each variable is measured as follows:

SALE ≡ the scale of operation, measured by sales revenue in 1986 (in billions of NT dollars);

GR ≡ growth performance, measured by the average annual rate of growth in sales in 1984–1986 (in percentages);

RAW ≡ dependency on imported raw materials, an industry dummy variable taking the value of 1 for paper and pulp, and ceramics, 0 otherwise;[6]

LAB ≡ labor intensity, measured by the ratio of employees to value of assets (in man-years/million NT dollars);

EXP ≡ export ratio, measured by the ratio of exports to total sales (in percentages).

The correlation matrix of the explanatory variables is depicted in table 2. It can be seen that, except for the pair of labor intensity (*LAB*) and export ratio (*EXP*), whose correlation coefficient is 0.566, a high degree of correlation is not found between the other variables.

We employ a probit model to estimate the effects of the firms' characteristics on their propensity to invest abroad. The dependent variable, *DFI*, is represented by a binary number, which takes the value of 1 if the sampled

[6]The petrochemical, textile, and steel industries also depend heavily on imported raw materials. However, the firms in the sample obtain their supply from state enterprises which import and process the raw materials. The relevant state enterprises are not included in the sample.

Table 3
Probit model on determinants of DFI: All firms.[a]

Variable	(1)	(2)[b]
Constant	−1.2977 (7.0)	−1.4280 (7.3)
SALE	0.0812 (2.3)	0.7075 (3.3)
GR	0.0012 (1.0)	0.0007 (0.6)
RAW	0.4503 (1.2)	0.3273 (0.8)
EXP	0.0057 (2.0)	0.0055 (1.9)
LAB	0.0539 (0.5)	0.1136 (0.9)
Goodness-of-fit[b]	$\chi^2(5) = 12.2$	$\chi^2(5) = 18.3$
Sample size	266	266

[a]Figures in parentheses following coefficient estimates are asymptotic t-statistics. $\chi^2(n)$ indicates the likelihood ratio statistic on the null hypothesis that the coefficients of all explanatory variables except the constant term are zero, where n is the degree of freedom.

[b]Variable '*SALE*' is replaced by a dummy variable which takes the value of 1 for firms whose sales are above the sample mean and 0 otherwise.

firm indicates an intention to invest abroad and 0 otherwise. The model being estimated takes the following form:

$$DFI = F(SALE, GR, RAW, EXP, LAB).$$

The results are reported in table 3.

From eq. (1) in table 3, we can see that only two variables are statistically significant: *SALE* and *EXP*. It indicates that both the size of the firm and the export ratio are positively related to the propensity to invest abroad. The effect of firm-size seems to suggest that the DFI of Taiwan's firms shares the trait of that of Western multinationals in that larger firms are more inclined to invest abroad. But if we replace the actual sales of a firm by a dummy variable which takes the value of 1 for the firms whose sales are above the sample average and 0 otherwise, the regression equation, (2) in table 3, actually performs better. In terms of the χ^2 statistic, which measures the explanatory power of the independent variables as a whole, the dummy-variable version scores an 18.3, indicating significance at the 0.3% level, while the sales version only scores a 12.2, indicating significance at the 3% level. It seems that large firms as a group have a higher propensity to go multinational than do small firms. But since the sample includes firms from different industries and since the firms from some industries may be larger than others, there is a possibility that the size effect actually reflects the industry effect. To detect this possibility, a series of dummy variables representing two-digit industries (except for those coinciding with the dummy variable *RAW*) were inserted into the regression. None turned out to be

Table 4
Probit model on determinants of DFI: Large and small firms.[a]

	Large firms		Small firms	
Constant	−0.8063 (2.1)	−1.1056 (2.9)	−1.7600 (5.3)	−1.6120 (5.3)
SALE	0.0216 (0.5)	0.0312 (0.7)	0.1679 (0.3)	−0.0439 (0.1)
GR	−0.0024 (0.9)	−0.0023 (0.7)	0.0155 (3.9)	0.0153 (4.0)
RAW	1.1764 (2.0)	1.2761 (2.2)	−2.9244 (0.2)	−3.0393 (0.2)
EXP	0.0123 (1.8)	0.0102 (2.0)	0.0047 (1.3)	0.0064 (2.2)
LAB	−0.3388 (0.7)	–	0.1307 (1.0)	–
Goodness-of-fit	$\chi^2(5)=7.2$	$\chi^2(4)=8.2$	$\chi^2(5)=27.5$	$\chi^2(4)=26.2$
Sample size	63	68	203	208

[a]Figures in parentheses following coefficient estimates are asymptotic *t*-statistics. $\chi^2(n)$ indicates the likelihood ratio statistic on the null hypothesis that the coefficients of all explanatory variables except the constant term are zero, where *n* is the degree of freedom.

significant.[7] We can, therefore, safely pronounce the existence of the size effect. It also suggests that different groups of firms, based on size, may have different inclinations toward DFI. In fact, the null hypothesis that two groups of firms follow the same decision model regarding DFI yields a likelihood ratio statistic of 32.0 (with six degrees of freedom), which indicates that the null hypothesis can be rejected at the 1% significance level.[8]

We therefore separate the sample into two subgroups, using mean sales, 1.029 billion NT dollars (approximately 29 million U.S. dollars in 1986), as the line of demarcation. The above-average sales group is denoted as large firms and the below-average group as small firms. Separate coefficient estimations using the aforementioned probit model are conducted and the results listed in table 4. Differences between the two groups are clearly evident.

First, '*SALE*' ceases to be a significant factor behind DFI in either group. It suggests that firm size, as measured by sales, does not exert a proportio-

[7]The industry distributions of the large firms and small firms are also compared. The null hypothesis that there is no difference in industry distribution between the two groups yields a Pearson's $\chi^2(18)$ statistic of 32.7, which is statistically significant at the 5% level, but insignificant at the 1% level. The major source of the difference is found in the non-metal minerals industry, which is dominated by large firms. When the non-metal minerals industry is excluded from the analysis, the difference in industry distribution is no longer significant even at the 10% level. When the firms in this industry are excluded from the regression, however, the variable *SCALE* in eq. (2) remains highly significant. It indicates that the size of the firm still matters even when the link between firm size and industry is broken. A dummy variable representing the non-metal minerals industry also yields an insignificant coefficient in the regression.

[8]The likelihood ratio statistic is derived by comparing the likelihood function values obtained from the regression that allows the estimated coefficients to be different for large and small firms and from the one that forces the estimated coefficients to be identical. The latter constraint amounts to six linear restrictions. The logarithm of the likelihood ratio multiplied by two is asymptotically chi-square distributed with six degrees of freedom.

nate effect on an individual firm's propensity to engage in DFI, although large firms as a whole do show a stronger inclination toward investing abroad. Second, dependency on imported raw materials tends to lure large firms to look abroad but its impact on the small firms' DFI decision is insignificant. Meanwhile good growth performance in the past years tends to induce small firms to venture overseas, but seems irrelevant in a large firm's DFI decision. Third, the only common factor that affects both large and small firms alike is 'export ratio'. It seems that all export-oriented firms are encouraged or pressured to engage in DFI activities to expand or defend their export markets. Fourth, labor intensity indicates a positive impact on a small firm's decision to go abroad only when its export proportion is excluded from the regression equation (not shown). Thus it may only reflect a spurious effect, stemming from the fact that export ratio and labor intensity are highly correlated. Finally, the negative sign of both constant terms suggest that, without the influence of the firm characteristics specified in the model, the average firm tends not to engage in DFI.

In sum, given the currency appreciation and wage increases that took place prior to 1988, Taiwan's firms, which had thrived on exports, became inclined to engage in production overseas. It seems that the firms that had been performing well in the export markets were in an advantageous position to go multinational, a manifestation of their possession of some firm-specific, intangible assets. This result is also in conformity with Vernon's product-life-cycle hypothesis, in which Vernon argues that foreign investment is often preceded by export and foreign investment made by the exporter is seen as 'a prudent means of forestalling the loss of a market' [Vernon (1966, p. 200)]. This result suggests that both firm-specific advantage and competitive pressure are important factors to firms in their DFI decisions. Firm-specific advantage provides a potent incentive to investing abroad while macro-economic factors act as the catalyst. This argument is re-affirmed by the following observation: In the face of rising wages, more labor-intensive firms presumably were under more pressure to relocate abroad. This study, however, indicates that labor intensity has not had an independent impact on a firm's propensity to invest abroad. This implies that pressure per se will not produce a DFI decision unless it is complemented by some firm-specific advantage – which seems to be associated with export expertise in Taiwan's case.

Growth performance has a positive and significant impact on the small firm's propensity to invest abroad. This further suggests that DFI is undertaken by growing firms as a means of overcoming resource constraints in the source country that tend to limit their expansion. In other words, DFI serves more as a means for healthy firms to exploit their growth potential than as a means for deteriorating firms to salvage their competitive position. It again confirms the notion that competitive pressure alone does not constitute a sufficient condition for DFI. Only the cream of the crop will be induced and empowered to make DFI under such pressure.

On the other hand, large firms' DFI decisions do not seem to be affected by their growth performance. Compared with small firms, the growth rate of large firms is known to be relatively lower and less variable [Jovanovic (1982), Hall (1987), Segal and Spivak (1989)]. While small, efficient firms may be characterized by rapid growth, growth performance may not be a good measure of a large firm's vitality. DFI is thus employed by large firms principally as a means to defend their export markets and secure raw material supplies; this proposition is similar to Lall's (1986) finding in his study of India's multinational firms. Securing raw material supplies via DFI means a vertical integration of production across national borders. While large firms may benefit from such an integration small firms may not: when a firm's needs are small in relation to the market, it is advantageous to buy from the market rather than to own [Williamson (1987, p. 1547)]. This may explain why raw materials dependency does not exert a significant impact on small firms' DFI propensity. Overall, the model performs better in explaining the DFI decision of small firms than it does of large firms, judging by the chi-square statistics.

4. Conclusions

This paper argues that macroeconomic conditions interact with the micro-characteristics of individual firms in fermenting a DFI decision within them. Conventional investigation, aimed at revealing the firm characteristics that are correlated with cumulative overseas investment without referring to the macroeconomic conditions under which DFI is made, may yield misleading conclusions. Drawing on Taiwan's DFI experience, we have shown that different macroeconomic conditions give rise to different motives for DFI.

A study of Taiwan's firms' ex-ante decisions regarding DFI in the aftermath of substantial appreciations in the value of the currency and an increase in wages indicates that small and large firms are depicted by different decision models. The securing of raw material supplies seems to be a major concern of large firms but bears little importance on the DFI decisions of small firms. Small firms with good growth potential are strongly inclined to invest abroad, probably to overcome the resource and market constraints inherent in the source country. The only common factor which is found to affect both large and small firms is their export performance. The firm which draws a higher proportion of its revenue from foreign sales is more inclined to invest abroad. This indicates that the export-oriented firms are either more compelled or better positioned to engage in DFI. The evidence seems to suggest that both the 'pull' and 'push' forces are at work and only the better positioned firms will be induced to make DFI under the right macroeconomic conditions.

The study is obviously limited in scope. One element that is missing in the above analysis is the 'Chinese connection' which greatly affects the direction of Taiwan's DFI and the choice of host-country partners made by the investing firms. Taiwan's post-1987 DFI has largely been directed toward Southeast Asia, notably Thailand and Malaysia, and China due to the vast number of ethnic Chinese businessmen in the region. Large firms in Taiwan may also have better 'Chinese connections', which could make their overseas ventures less formidable.

References

Caves, R., 1974, Causes of direct investment: Foreign firms' shares in Canadian and United Kingdom manufacturing industries, Review of Economics and Statistics 56, 279–293.

Hall, B., 1987, The relationship between firm size and firm growth in the U.S. manufacturing sector, Journal of Industrial Economics 35, 583–606.

Horst, T., 1972, Firms and industry determinants of the decision to invest abroad: An empirical study, Review of Economics and Statistics 54, 258–266.

Hymer, S., 1960, The international operations of national firms: A study of direct foreign investment, Ph.D. Thesis (MIT Press, Cambridge, MA, 1976).

Jovanovic, B., 1982, Selection and the evolution of industry, Econometrica 50, 649–670.

Kojima, K., 1973, A macroeconomic approach to foreign direct investment, Hitotsubashi Journal of Economics 14, 1–21.

Kojima, K., 1978, Direct foreign investment: A Japanese model of multinational business operation (Croom Helm, London).

Lall, S., 1980, Monopolistic advantages and foreign involvement by U.S. manufacturing industry, Oxford Economic Papers 32, 102–122.

Lall, S., 1983, The new multinationals: The spread of third world enterprises (Wiley, New York).

Lall, R., 1986, Third world multinationals: The characteristics of Indian firms investing abroad, Journal of Development Economics 20, 381–398.

Lecraw, D., 1977, Direct investment by firms from less developed countries, Oxford Economic Papers 29, 442–457.

Lee, C., 1984, On Japanese macroeconomic theories of direct foreign investment, Economic Development and Cultural Change 32, 713–723.

Ozawa, T., 1979, International investment and industrial structure: New theoretical implications from the Japanese experience, Oxford Economic Papers 31, 72–92.

Segal, U. and A. Spivak, 1989, Farm size and optimal growth rates, European Economic Review 33, 159–167.

Vernon, R., 1966, International investment and international trade in the product cycle, Quarterly Journal of Economics 80, 190–207.

Wells, L., 1983, Third world multinationals (MIT Press, Cambridge, MA).

Williamson, O., 1987, The modern corporation: Origins, evolution, attributes, Journal of Economic Literature 19, 1537–1568.

Wolf, B., 1977, Industrial diversification and internationalization: Some empirical evidence, Journal of Industrial Economics 26, 177–191.

World Bank, 1989, Industry and Energy Department, Foreign direct investment from the newly industrialized economies, Industry series paper no. 22 (World Bank, Washington, DC).

[26]

Chinese transnational corporations*

Ye Gang**

China's outward investment

Chinese enterprises began to establish affiliates abroad as late as 1979. It has only been since the end of 1985, however, that Chinese foreign direct investment (FDI) abroad began to grow notably. At the end of 1985, the number of non-trade overseas affiliates of Chinese enterprises was 187, while the total value of the investment was equal to $290 million, of which $170 million represented the Chinese equity share. By the end of 1988, the number of overseas affiliates had increased to 526; the value of total investment, to $1.9 billion; and the amount invested by China, to $715 million. The number of foreign affiliates and China's investment abroad increased 1.8 and 3 times, respectively, between 1985 and 1988, while the aggregate value of investment rose 5.5 times. The situation of Shanghai, Beijing and Fujian Provinces largely coincides with the above picture. The number of foreign affiliates of Shanghai-based transnational corporations (TNCs) rose from 16 to 51 between the end of 1985 and June 1989; the Chinese equity contribution rose from $11 million to $27 million during the same period. Similarly, the number of foreign affiliates of Fujian-based TNCs rose from 78 to 190 between the end of 1986 and March 1989.

Outward Chinese investment has become increasingly diversified in terms of destination. At the end of 1985, foreign affiliates were located in 45 countries and territories, but were mostly concentrated in Hong Kong and Macau (54), the United States (21), Thailand (11) and Japan (11). Those countries and territories accounted for 63 per cent of the total number of foreign affiliates. By 1988, foreign affiliates had spread to 79 countries and territories, of which more than 240 were in Asia, more than 80 in Africa, more than 50 in Europe, nearly 40 in Oceania and more than 20 in North America and Latin America. By the first quarter of 1989, foreign affiliates of Shanghai-based and Fujian-based TNCs, formerly concentrated in Hong Kong and Macau, had expanded their activities to a number of countries in Europe, Asia and Africa.

* Investigations were made by both interviews and questionnaires. The reasons for the choice of provinces are that Beijing is the capital of China and the location of most large centrally-owned enterprises; Shanghai is the most highly developed city in China; and Fujian is the province with the greatest number of foreign affiliates.

** Researcher, Shanghai Research Institute of International Economy and Trade, Shanghai, China.

Chinese foreign affiliates have invested in a multitude of industries and continue to diversify the sectoral distribution of their activities abroad. At the end of 1985, there were 45 manufacturing and agricultural projects, accounting for 24 per cent of all projects, 14 extraction projects (8 per cent of the total), 19 construction projects, 15 restaurant and transportation projects and projects combining industrial and trading activities. By the end of 1988, manufacture and agriculture accounted for about 40 per cent of all projects (50 per cent if extraction projects are included). By early 1989, most foreign affiliates from Shanghai and Fujian Provinces were engaged in industrial and services projects.

The number of Chinese TNCs with investments abroad has increased. At the initial stages of opening to the outside world, enterprises which were eligible to have foreign affiliates were limited to the international economic and technological co-operation companies of individual provinces and cities and to the import and export corporations, which were privileged to engage in foreign trade. In 1985, the Ministry of Foreign Economic Relations and Trade decided to allow an increase in the number of parent enterprises with investments abroad. Since then, parent enterprises have not only experienced a gradual increase in their number, but they have also become more diverse. Apart from former foreign trade companies and international economic and technological co-operative companies, enterprises currently engaging in overseas investment are professional enterprises, "group" enterprises and even scientific research units.

The Government at all levels has accumulated valuable experience in administering non-trade overseas investments. At present, the Foreign Economic Relations and Trade Commissions of different provinces and cities have assigned people and institutions to administer overseas investments and find ways of regulating, supporting and servicing foreign affiliates. This early stage of outward FDI from China requires attention and support from all areas in order to make it an integral part of the country's economic development. At present, however, the role of overseas investment in China's economy remains insignificant.

Motives for and benefits from investing abroad

Between the end of 1988 and May 1989, the Institute of World Economy, Fudan University, under the guidance of the International Economic Co-operation Bureau of the Ministry of Foreign Economic Relations and Trade and the International Economic Co-operation Association, carried out a survey through questionnaires and interviews of Chinese enterprises with overseas investment, mostly in industries other than trading, in Shanghai, Beijing and Fujian Provinces. Those provinces were chosen on the basis of their importance as sources of Chinese outward FDI. The Institute interviewed managers of 37 Chinese enterprises—six of which were State-owned—with about 160 overseas affiliates, as well as leading officials of the Foreign Economic Relations and Trade Commissions in the relevant provinces and municipalities. Eighteen enterprises responded to the questionnaire.

The Institute circulated a questionnaire which gave 18 possible reasons behind the motives of Chinese TNCs for operating abroad. They were ranked by the parent enterprises according to their relative significance. The replies showed the degree of importance attached to each of these elements by the parent enterprises. The Institute grouped together some questions and discarded others in order to facilitate the analysis. The relative importance of each motive is shown in table 1.

Motives that were not listed in the questionnaire will be examined next. Centrally-owned, ministry-owned and "comprehensive" enterprises, in particular, have placed great emphasis on the motive of adapting to Chinese economic reforms and on fulfilling the economic needs of local regions and sectors. Several enterprises considered undertaking investment abroad from the viewpoint of their long-term development into "modern international enterprises". Others regarded foreign investment as a method of substituting for domestic investment. Some companies felt that their potential for domestic expansion was limited and that the possibility of investing abroad might solve that problem and enable them to engage in profitable activities. In view of the disadvantages facing foreign enterprises in relation to domestic firms, such as lack of familiarity with the local environment and additional communication costs, the question raised was what the benefits are that Chinese enterprises derive from their overseas investments. Nine items were listed in the questionnaire, and the enterprises were asked to rank their answers according to their relative importance (the degree of importance is classified the same as for motives). The answers from 18 enterprises are presented in table 2.

According to replies to the questionnaire, the advantages advocated by Chinese enterprises fall into the following categories: excellent customer relations and credit, indicating confidence in and recognition of the performance of foreign affiliates; technology of production, indicating that several Chinese products possess a certain comparative advantage, especially in

Table 1. Motives to invest abroad[a]
(Number of enterprises)

Motives	Important (1)	Not important (2)	Not considered (3)	Share in total (%)
Open up new markets	16	–	1	94
Circumvent trade barriers and maintain export markets	10	1	6	59
Promote exports of capital goods, materials and labour	13	–	4	77
Acquire foreign capital technology and managing skills	13	1	3	77
Acquire raw materials	10	3	4	59
Give full play to own advantages abroad	9	1	7	53
Enjoy preferential terms offered by local governments	13	2	2	77
Earn high interest	12	5	-	71
Acquire first-hand information on foreign production and market	16	-	1	94
Create conditions for other business activities of the enterprise	17	-	-	100

[a] Managers of all 37 firms were interviewed, but only 17 questionnaires were received from these firms. The conclusions of most interviews conformed with the results of questionnaires returned.

relation to those goods produced in developing countries; quantity and quality of technical and management personnel; small-scale production, considered to be suitable to the needs of developing countries; cultural links with

Table 2. Main advantages of investing abroad[a]
(Number of enterprises)

Advantages	Very important (1)	Important (2)	Not important (3)	Not considered	Share in total (%)
Technology of production	11	3	0	4	78
Reputable brand names and trade marks	9	0	2	7	50
Excellent customer relations	11	4	2	1	83
Small-size production	9	1	1	7	56
Use of local resources and ability to adapt to local markets	7	2	0	9	50
Quantity and quality of management and technical personnel	12	2	1	3	78
Low costs	5	4	3	6	50
Cultural and ethnic relations with local people (overseas Chinese)	6	4	0	8	56
Excellent credit	15	0	0	3	83

overseas Chinese; use of local resources; and ability to adapt to local markets, low costs and reputable brand names and trade marks.

The advantages of centrally-owned enterprises with investments abroad are more apparent. Those enterprises are large, with an abundance of funds and resources and a long history of operating in an international environment through trade. Management personnel are well-trained and experienced in the conduct of business abroad and knowledgeable about local conditions. In comparison, TNCs from the provinces are small or of medium size, but their advantage is that they are specialized in particular segments of the production process. Their level of technology is lower than that of the centrally-owned enterprises and their operations are more labour-intensive. However, small and medium-size enterprises also possess technical and managerial personnel of quality, which they regard as their most important advantage for investing abroad.

The importance of foreign affiliates for the economy of China

Foreign affiliates of Chinese TNCs have limited experience in the conduct of business abroad, although a number of them have gained a firm foothold. It has been found that, among a diverse range of foreign affiliates, there are some that are well-operated and profitable. By the end of 1989, of 376 TNCs, 208 possessed obvious economic advantages for investing abroad. These efficiently-run affiliates, despite their newness, are increasingly acquiring an important role in the development of China's economy.

Approximately 20 quantitative and qualitative indices regarding the possible economic benefits of overseas affiliates were listed in the questionnaire and parent enterprises were asked to answer them. The response rate was low; enterprises were unwilling to answer such questions in order to protect a sense of secrecy. More significantly, parent enterprises lack the system and habit of regularly issuing balance sheets and annual reports so as to monitor effectively and systematically the activities of their affiliates. Taking into consideration the above, the following conclusions can be reached on the contribution of outward FDI to the Chinese economy.

China faces a slow-down in export growth owing to trading barriers set by its trade partners. The main reason for establishing enterprises to produce abroad is to maintain or increase the existing export market share. Establishing factories abroad in countries where there is no export quota, or using the local quotas, may circumvent trade barriers and help maintain or increase export share. Formerly, most Chinese exports were channelled through Chinese agents and foreign offices abroad. Overseas affiliates can now establish marketing networks to penetrate export markets. Outward investment with advanced capital equipment and technology has promoted

Chinese exports. Raw materials or parts are usually supplied by China. Several TNCs first design and produce samples of goods in their foreign affiliates prior to producing them domestically, in order to be assured that the quality is suitable for sale in overseas markets. All of those factors facilitate the increase of exports and the opening-up of new products and markets.

Outward FDI may play a dual role in introducing or acquiring advanced technology. On the one hand, it can give full play to Chinese-owned technological advantages; on the other, it can help acquire advanced technology locally, that is, a "technology-recycling" type of investment. There have been several ways of acquiring advanced technology through investing abroad:

- By purchasing advanced equipment to start businesses when forming joint ventures from foreign enterprises possessing advanced technology;
- By purchasing shares of foreign enterprises with advanced technology;
- By using semi-advanced equipment in the operation of foreign affiliates;
- By connecting domestically-produced equipment with advanced-technology parts and components from abroad; and
- By acquiring technologically-advanced equipment through foreign affiliates at a lower price than otherwise for fulfilling the needs of China.

There is, however, potential for a more effective utilization of foreign capital. At present, the share of Chinese overseas investment normally accounts for less than 40 per cent of the total investment in joint ventures abroad. In general, when an enterprise sets up a new business abroad, it does not necessarily follow that all capital will come from its own resources. On the contrary, most of it is raised either locally or in the international market. Foreign affiliates are a new form of raising capital, with the difference being that this capital is utilized abroad. Moreover, only part of the investment stems from foreign exchange remitted abroad from China. Some capital stems from technology, equipment, labour and trade marks valued in monetary terms, and a large amount is raised abroad. It should also be noted that foreign investment induces an influx of capital should disinvestments occur. For example, out of $60 million of total outward investment from Fujian Province, $30 million have been repatriated; in that case, loans from abroad exceeded $300 million.

Another possible benefit to the Chinese economy from the operation of foreign affiliates is the acquisition of raw materials. At present, more than 20 overseas investments are in operation in the fields of fisheries, forestry and mining, and they play a favourable role in compensating for the shortages of raw materials in China. The operation of foreign affiliates also encourages the training of managerial personnel. More than 3,000 management and technical personnel are working in Chinese foreign affiliates in an environment where business is conducted according to international standards, thus receiving first-hand training and acquiring invaluable experience. To a certain extent, international competition requires the collection of a diverse range of information, and overseas affiliates play a unique role in that respect. The information obtained is direct, accurate and prompt and its role is not to be ignored in understanding the operations of the international market, in taking advantage of marketing opportunities, in enlarging and opening up the export market and in introducing foreign capital and technology.

Although there is little systematic data concerning the profitability of the operations of affiliates abroad, according to recent reports, several large projects in the primary and manufacturing sectors have shown large profits. A number of small and medium-size enterprises have also shown sizeable profits. There have been, however, some unsuccessful cases. A small number of overseas affiliates registered losses, a few enterprises have wasted precious resources, and a minority have gone bankrupt or have withdrawn their investments. Those unsuccessful enterprises have the following common features:

- Feasibility studies have not been conducted prior to investing abroad;
- In most cases, sales of products have not been ascertained;
- The choice of partners in joint ventures is unsatisfactory;
- The control of the operation is not in Chinese hands, resulting in an unusual phenomenon, namely, that, although the project and operations are sound, the foreign side earns profits while the Chinese side incurs losses;
- Low quality of personnel sent to work in affiliates abroad.

In conclusion, China has achieved a remarkable growth in outward investment during the past few years. It must be affirmed that such investments have opened up new prospects for the Chinese economy. It should also be noted that these investments are only at an initial stage, lagging far behind their full potential, as well as behind those from other countries in the world. There is still ample room for possible changes regarding the number and size of enterprises, industrial and geographical distribution, technical, managerial and organizational standards, structure of company operations, and social benefits. In addition, further changes in the regulatory framework and greater support by the Government are needed in order to strengthen and improve the conditions for outward investment. ■

[27]

The Determinants of Korean Foreign Direct Investment in Manufacturing Industries

By

Yoong-Deok Jeon

I. Introduction

Korean foreign direct investment (FDI) in manufacturing industries has been rapidly growing over the past four years. The total number of overseas investments in manufacturing industries established by Korean firms was 289, and their total volume of direct investment was some $0.5 billion as of December 31, 1989. In particular, 212 out of the 289 occurred from 1987 to 1989. At the same time, a major part of Korean FDI shifted from wholesale trade and natural resources industries to manufacturing ones and from investment in developed countries (DCs) to investment in less developed countries (LDCs), at least in terms of the number of direct investments. The major purpose of this study is to examine Korean firms' foreign direct investment in the manufacturing sector using firm-level data. In addition, we provide evidence that there are quite different motivations of Korean manufacturers' direct investment in manufacturing activities based upon two different regions, DCs and LDCs.

With respect to direct investment in developed countries, the paper introduces and tests two conventional models: the defensive investment hypothesis and the hypothesis that FDI can be viewed as a tariff-jumping technique. Moreover, the paper provides direct evidence that both the size of a Korean firm and the real economic growth of the Korean economy have a positive impact on FDI in the manufacturing sector of DCs. We also find the fact that physical and/or cultural differences among invested countries affect Korean FDI in them.

Remark: I am indebted to the chairman of my dissertation committee, Edward John Ray at the Ohio State University, and an anonymous referee for helpful comments. This research was partially supported by the Asan Foundation.

In terms of Korean FDI in the manufacturing industries of LDCs, there is some evidence that the supply of cheap labor of LDCs has been regarded as one of their comparative advantages in international trade in certain products. It is evident that the labor intensity of each Korean firm is positively related to FDI. The data also suggests that a structural shift has occurred since 1987 perhaps because of the worsening labor-management relationship in Korea. Korean firms investing in labor-intensive industries of LDCs have more incentives to exploit cheap wages in the region than other firms producing non-labor-intensive products do. Additionally, the result shows the fact that the real growth rate of the Korean economy negatively affects FDI in manufacturing industries of LDCs.

The paper has several implications. First, it suggests the implication that the recent rise in non-tariff trade barriers in developed countries has induced Korean foreign direct investment in developed countries' manufacturing industries. Second, it provides evidence that the faster growth of the Korean economy has played a role in promoting Korean foreign direct investment in developed countries. Finally, it provides evidence that, other things being equal, the larger firm is more efficient in exploiting business opportunities in developed countries than smaller firms are.

The structure of the paper will be as follows. Section II will introduce two conventional models and present empirical evidence that Korean foreign direct investment in manufacturing activities of DCs can be viewed as a tariff-jumping technique. In Section III, an idea will be suggested and tested in a systematic manner. The idea is that to exploit cheap labor of LDCs is a main reason why Korean firms invest in those countries. Section IV will contain summary and conclusions.

II. Non-Tariff Trade Barriers and Foreign Direct Investment in Developed Countries [1]

1. The Models

This section introduces two conventional models which predict the pattern of FDI across industries. First, there is the notion that FDI reflects a defensive motive by oligopolistic producers to maintain foreign market shares in an increasingly competitive environment. Hymer [1976], Gruber et al. [1967], and many others argued that the

[1] Developed countries include OECD countries, Hong Kong, and Singapore.

exports of oligopolistic producers might become less competitive over time since technology and/or managerial advantages of oligopolistic producers become weak in local markets. It is presumed that oligopolistic producers establish foreign production facilities to maintain their market positions abroad. As a result, it was hypothesized by the above researchers and accepted for the purpose of this paper that FDI is positively related to market concentration in the production of differentiated consumer goods, and that direct investment and exports could be substitutes for one another.

Alternatively, foreign direct investment can be viewed as an attempt by profit-maximizing firms to minimize their costs of production. Horst [1972b] and many others argued that foreign exporters find it more profitable to establish production facilities inside a country's tariff wall than to write off their investment in the local market or continue to serve it from lower-cost locations abroad through exports. Now, it is expected that trade barriers are positively related to FDI.

The functional relationship we test in this section is basically based upon two models but includes several factors that tend to encourage or discourage FDI. First, licensing or exports are encouraged when the licensor lacks some assets needed for direct investment. These might include a stock of accumulated knowledge and experience with the foreign market, managerial skills, and/or capital. These considerations help to explain why the smaller a firm is, the more likely it is to resort to licensing or exports rather than FDI. There is a minimum level of asset holdings necessary for successful FDI even when a firm has valuable information, patents, technology, and so on. On the cost side, production, administrative and marketing costs would be low when local production facilities and marketing organizations of a licensee are already in place for similar or differentiated goods, whereas direct investment would involve substantial fixed costs. Thus, small firms would favor licensing.[2] The amount of assets owned by a firm is reflected in firm size. It is argued, therefore, that firm size is positively related to foreign direct investment.

Second, the transaction cost approach holds that domestic firms and even international corporations arise in order to overcome the imperfections of arm's-length markets, especially for specific assets.

---

[2] See Buckley and Casson [1976], Casson [1979], Horst [1972b], Mirus [1980], and Vernon [1971] for the argument and empirical evidences regarding the relationship between firm size and the propensity to license versus invest.

Premier among those assets is the knowledge that represents new products, processes, proprietary technology and so on. Specific assets could be transferable via arm's-length trade. However, relatively high policing costs arise because it is not easy to prevent a licensee from pursuing opportunistic behavior. The theory implies that FDI occurs in order to avoid the loss from a licensee's opportunistic behavior.

When is it more costly to a licensor to get rents from a licensee? A firm that owns specific assets is less willing to bear costs in terms of a licensee's opportunistic behavior than the firm with fewer assets. To some degree, specific assets are "public goods." Once a piece of knowledge has been developed and applied at a certain location, it can be put to work elsewhere at little extra cost and without reducing the value of the application at the original site. From society's point of view, the marginal conditions for efficient allocation of resources requires that the price of a specific asset be equal to its marginal cost, which is close to zero. Indeed, specific assets tend to be underprovided and priced inefficiently. Internalization of transactions involving specific assets is a good way to deal with the underprovision and inefficient pricing of them. It is hypothesized that the presence of specific assets in a firm is positively related to direct investment.[3] In general, specific assets are incorporated into product differentiation, and the degree of product differentiation may be highly correlated with the amount of specific assets. In short, we presume that product differentiation is positively related to the amount of FDI.

Third, we include a measure of growth in the domestic country. In part, it is presumed that economic prosperity in the parent company market indirectly helps manufacturing firms to get bigger and accumulate assets for both licensing and FDI. However, a Korean manufacturer may exploit business opportunities in the domestic market, at least in the short run, if the real growth rate of the Korean economy is relatively higher or vice versa. Therefore, the expected sign of a measure of growth in the domestic country is uncertain. To get investment permission from the Korean government, more than a year is needed after the investment decision has been made. Thus, the real growth rate of the Korean economy one year before the permission date is used.

---

[3] Ethier [1986], Grossman and Hart [1986], and Helpman [1984] theoretically focus on specific assets and appropriability of rents. In them, FDI or internalization of transactions involving specific assets is a good way to extract rents that would be difficult to capture licenses.

Fourth, we presume that the value of FDI and the probability of investment in the rest of the world are both positively related to whether or not the subsidiary is producing goods that belong to the same industry as those of the parent firm. That relationship reflects a minimum of diversification between the parent and subsidiary firms.

Finally, we include country dummies based on geographic proximity of the home country to the host country. One country dummy ($CD1$) is 1 if direct investment in Japan, Hong Kong, and Singapore occurs and 0 otherwise. Another country dummy ($CD2$) is 1 if direct investment in the United States and Canada occurs and 0 otherwise.

The estimation equations are of the following forms

$$\mathrm{IV89} = F(FS, KCR3, PD, WPI, GRK1, CD1, CD2)$$

and

$$\mathrm{IV89} = F(FS, PD, WPI, GRK1, CD1, CD2, NTB).$$

The former equation is for the defensive investment hypothesis and the latter is for the hypothesis that trade barriers are positively related to FDI. The definition of variables and their expected signs along with source notes are presented in Table 1.

2. Data and Empirical Results

The empirical analysis was conducted using Korean firm level investment in manufacturing industries of developed countries as of December 31, 1989, obtained primarily from the unpublished sources of the Bank of Korea. The data was supplemented with balance sheets and profit and loss statements of each Korean firm in *Maekyung's Annual Corporation Reports*. It was also supplemented with *Industrial Organization Statistics* [1982] from the Korea Development Institute and the Economic Planning Board, and the *National Accounts 1989* and the *National Accounts* (preliminary) *1990* from the Bank of Korea. The sample includes firms whose ownership is larger than 10% and is limited to those which report complete balance sheets and profit and loss statements to Maekyung's Annual Corporation Reports. The complete sample contains 60, or 67 observations depending upon which countries are included in the estimated equations.[4] The data were analyzed using the Tobit model.

[4] The total number of direct investment in DCs was 97 and their total volume was some $417 million. 30 or 37 observations were deleted due to the reason discussed. In 67 observations, 1 investment is in Australia, 6 in Canada, 4 in Japan, 35 in the United States, and 14 in Western Europe, including both 6 in Hong Kong, and 1 in Singapore.

Table 1 – *The Determinants of Korean Foreign Direct Investment in Developed Countries and Their Expected Signs*

Variable	Definitions and proxies	Expected sign
Common factors		
FS	*TA*87; total asset of Korean firms as of Dec. 1987	+
PD	*AS*87; advertising-sales ratio of Korean firms in 1987	+
WPI	*WPI*; takes on a value of 1.0 if the parent and affiliate firms have the same five-digit SIC code and 0.0 otherwise	+
GRK	*GRK*1; the real growth rate of the Korean economy at the previous year before investment is actually permitted by government	?
*CD*1	*CD*1; includes Hong Kong, Japan, and Singapore	?
*CD*2	*CD*2; includes Canada, and the United States	?
Factor for defensive investment		
*KCR*3	The concentration ratio of three largest firms in 1982 (five-digit SIC)	+
Factor for NTB-jumping		
NTB	Developed countries' non-tariff barriers (five-digit SIC)	+

Source: 1987 data for total asset, advertising and administrative expenses, and total sales volume from Mae-il Kyung Jae Shin Moon Sa, *Maekyung: Annual Corporation Reports*, Seoul 1988. – 1982 data for the concentration ratio from the Korea Development Institute and the Economic Planning Board, *Industrial Organization Statistics (1982)*, 1986. – The real growth rate of the Korean economy from the Bank of Korea, *The National Accounts 1989* and *The National Accounts* (preliminary) *1990*. – 1989 and 1990 data for non-tariff trade barriers from the Korea Trade Association, *Import Restriction Lists of Major Developed Countries*. Seoul, 1989 and 1990.

*TA*87 is employed as a proxy for firm size and is measured as the sum of current assets, properties, plants and equipment, and other assets of each Korean firm in 1987. *KCR*3 is measured as the concentration ratio of the three largest firms at the five-digit industry level in 1982. In order to use *KCR*3 and *NTB* below, we classify the products of a parent company into a five-digit industry. *AS*87 is employed as a proxy for product differentiation and is measured as Korean firms' sales and general administrative expenses divided by total sales of the firm in 1987. *WPI* is measured by a dummy variable that takes on a value of 1 if the parent and affiliate firms have the same five-digit SIC code and 0 otherwise. *GRK*1 is measured as the real growth rate of the Korean economy at the previous year before investment is actually permitted by government. *NTB* is measured by a dummy

Table 2 – *The Determinants of Korean Firms' Foreign Direct Investment in Manufacturing Industries of Developed Countries (Tobit model)*

	(1)	(2)	(3)	(4)
Independent variable				
Constant	−24,802.4***	−32,436.5***	−29,066.6***	−37,052.4***
	(3.35)	(4.00)	(4.27)	(4.95)
*TA*87	0.01412***	0.01497***	0.01357***	0.01459***
	(9.04)	(9.29)	(9.58)	(9.99)
*KCR*3	−3,806.34	−2,740.68	–	–
	(0.69)	(0.46)		
*AS*87	89.3990	78.2119	121.417	110.572
	(0.58)	(0.51)	(0.80)	(0.73)
WPI	7,044.98	7,606.55	6,433.38	6,680.94
	(1.42)	(1.52)	(1.30)	(1.36)
*GRK*1	748.737**	1,242.78***	825.853***	1,379.32***
	(2.22)	(3.05)	(2.44)	(3.37)
*CD*1	8,972.86**	9,737.43*	11,512.4***	12,378.2**
	(2.28)	(1.79)	(2.72)	(2.22)
*CD*2	12,227.8***	13,173.6***	12,792.3***	13,971.6***
	(4.12)	(4.38)	(4.30)	(4.67)
NTB	–	–	3,562.70	4,251.79*
			(1.37)	(1.63)
Statistics				
R^2	0.60	0.63	0.60	0.65
F	12.40	12.72	12.83	13.54
No. of observations	67	60	67	60

Note: Absolute *t*-values in parentheses are asymptotically normal. – The asterisks ***; **; and * indicate significance at the 0.01; 0.05; and 0.10 level.

variable that takes on a value of 1 if the five-digit industry has non-tariff trade restrictions and 0 otherwise.

The results are reported in columns (1) and (2) of Table 2. The regression results in this table are intended to provide evidence on the applicability of 'the defensive investment hypothesis' as an explanation for Korean direct investment in manufacturing industries of DCs. In equation (1), OECD, Hong Kong, and Singapore are included in the estimation. OECD alone is included in equation (2). In both equations, the coefficients of *KCR*3 are not of the expected signs. Consequently, the notion that Korean manufacturers' investment in manufacturing industries of DCs is positively related to market concentration is not supported in any of the equations. The results suggest that the defensive investment motive is not significant in determining the pattern of Korean manufacturers' investment in manufacturing industries of developed countries. The regressions also imply that the proposition that exports and horizontal investment are substitutes across industries is not correct.

The results obtained in columns (3) and (4) of Table 2 address the following question: do protectionist measures induce Korean firms' direct investment in OECD manufacturing industries including or excluding Hong Kong and Singapore? In columns (3) and (4), non-tariff trade barriers are included because the importance of non-tariff trade restrictions as a way to protect the manufacturing industries of DCs has been growing and because tariff data are not available.[5] The coefficients of *NTB* are of the expected signs in both equations. The coefficients of *NTB* is significantly different from zero in column (4), but not in column (3). The reason for the insignificance of the *NTB* variable in column (3) is that Hong Kong and Singapore have no trade restrictions and the inclusion of direct investment in the countries makes the regression less efficient. In effect, column (4) alone fits our purpose very well. The results suggest the fact that the influence of non-tariff trade restrictions on FDI is positive and significant. Such results confirm casual observation that the recent rise in *NTB* protection in DCs has had an inducement effect on direct investment in manufacturing activities of developed countries.

In all columns in Table 2, the coefficient of *TA*87 is of the expected sign and is significantly different from zero at the 0.01 level. The argument that a minimum amount of general assets is required for FDI is supported. Moreover, the coefficient of the *GRK*1 variable is significant and positive at the 0.01 level. The contention that economic prosperity in the parent-company market indirectly helps manufacturing firms get bigger and accumulate assets for both licensing and FDI is well supported. The coefficients of *CD*1 and *CD*2 are significant for discriminating countries based upon physical distances and/or cultural differences. The coefficients of *AS*87 and *WPI* are of the expected sign, but not significant.

[5] See Ray [1981a; 1981b] for the relative importance of non-tariff barriers between tariff and non-tariff trade restrictions in the United States and her major trading partners.

III. Cheap Labor and Foreign Direct Investment in Less Developed Countries

1. The Model

Since 1987, Korean foreign direct investment in manufacturing industries of less developed countries has been rapidly increasing.[6] Casual observation suggests that such an increase is due to rapidly rising wages or high wage rates and less favorable labor-management relations in Korea. In this section, we examine whether relative wage differentials between Korea and other less developed countries may induce Korean FDI in the latter countries.[7]

Korean firms have been losing comparative advantage over time to produce labor-intensive products since nominal wages have been rapidly rising and more frequent labor-management conflicts have been observed. In 1988, for example, when we make the Korean average wage equal to 100, Thailand is 31.6, Malaysia 24.0, Indonesia 13.4, and the Phillipines 34.7 (1986). Many Korean manufacturers still focus on the production of labor-intensive products or assembly of imported parts rather than the production of R&D or capital-intensive products. In fact, such rapidly rising wages or high wage costs make Korean firms lose international competitiveness relative to other less developed countries and profits become smaller. Ceteris paribus, the bigger the wage differences between Korean manufacturers and other less developed countries' are, the more the former invest in the latter.[8]

Establishing production facilities in foreign countries is mostly based on long-term perspectives. However, a firm also considers short-run benefits and costs. The most significant among them is the business outlook in the home country. Given high wage costs, a Korean manufacturer exploits business opportunities in the domestic

---

[6] As of December 31, 1989, the total number of overseas investment in manufacturing industries of LDCs was 192, and their total volume of direct investment was some $186 million. Indeed, $146 or some $108 million were invested in manufacturing industries of LDCs from 1987 to 1989.

[7] Riedel [1975], for example, found that the lower wage costs have been one of the major determinants of the export-oriented FDI in Taiwan.

[8] Nominal wage differences may not induce direct investment if labor productivity is increased at the same rate as wage increase. Firms or industries with high labor productivity may have less incentive to establish a production facility in a foreign country to use cheap labor than those with low labor productivity. Unfortunately, cross-section data about labor productivity is not easily available. In that sense, this study is incomplete.

market if the real growth rate of the Korean economy is higher or vice versa. Thus, it is expected that FDI and the real growth rate of the Korean economy are negatively related. To get investment permission from the Korean government, more than a year is needed after the investment decision has been made. In effect, the real growth rate of the Korean economy one year before the permission date must be used.

The effects of wage increases or high wage rates on a firm or an industry depend upon labor intensity of such a firm or such an industry. For example, rapid wage increases affect a firm which produces labor-intensive goods more badly than the one whose product is less labor-intensive. To be sure, it is expected that FDI is positively related to the labor intensity of each firm in this setting.

To the extent that a high wage rate stimulates Korean FDI in LDCs, it is meaningful to divide up the time series of direct investment. In the case of direct investment in Asian developing countries, three-fourths of total investment in the region were to exploit natural resources until 1986. From 1987 to 1989, in contrast, as major part of Korean FDI in the region was labor-intensive industries such as footwear, textile and clothing, and toys. In addition, three-fourths of total investment in manufacturing industries of Latin America occurred from 1987 to 1989 and almost all of the investment was centered on labor-intensive industries. More than that, many labor-management conflicts have occurred over the past several years. We, therefore, presume that a structural shift has occurred due to both a rapid wage increase and labor-management conflicts. To incorporate a structural shift, we use a year dummy as a way of dividing investment until 1986 and into one since 1987. The year dummy is equal to 1 if investment happened from 1987 to 1989 or 0 otherwise.[9]

Finally, we include an industry dummy because Korean firms go to LDCs to use natural resources even without cheap labor in the region. In fact, high wage rates differently affect industries based upon

---

[9] The increasing rate of Korean average wage was 9.2% in 1985, 8.2% in 1986, 10.1% in 1987, 15.5% in 1988, and 21.1% in 1989, and, therefore, it is likely to see that the increasing rate of average wage was out of trend from 1988. However, the increasing rate of the unit labor cost of Korean manufacturing industries (=labor cost per hour/labor productivity) in terms of dollars was −2.2% in 1986, 12.4% in 1987, 26.0% in 1988, and 43.3% in 1989. Thus, it is correct that the wage rate was out of trend from 1987 rather than 1988. Moreover, the total number of labor-management conflicts was 265 in 1985, 276 in 1986, 3749 in 1987, 1873 in 1988, and 1616 in 1989. Labor union movement has been dispersed in many industries since 1987. Thus, the year of 1987 is a better benchmark.

Table 3 – *The Determinants of Korean Foreign Direct Investment in Developing Countries and Their Expected Signs*

Variable	Definition	Expected sign
*YWE*88	Average year earnings per employee of a firm in 1988	+
*GRK*1	See Table 1	–
*LI*873	Korean firms' total employees divided by total assets in 1987	+
YD	1 if the investment happened from 1987 to 1989 or 0 otherwise	+
ID	1 if subsidiaries produce footwear, textile and clothing, toys, or electrical and electronic goods, or 0 otherwise	+
CD	1 if the host country is one of the Asian developing countries or 0 if it is one of the rest of the developing countries	?

Source: Total payments to employees for 1988, the number of employees for 1987 and 1988, and total assets for 1987 from the Korea Investors Service, Inc., *The Financial Report of Korean Companies*, Seoul 1989. – *YD*, *ID*, and *CD* from the Bank of Korea, unpublished sources.

their labor intensities. The industry dummy is equal to 1, if subsidiaries produce footwear, textile and clothing, toys, or electrical and electronic goods, or 0 otherwise. Similarly, the country dummy is equal to 1 if the host country is one of the Asian countries or 0 if it is one of the rest of LDCs.

The estimation equation is of the following form:

$$\mathrm{IV89} = F(YWE88, GRK1, LI873, YD, ID, CD),$$

where *YWE*88 is average year earnings of each employee of a firm in 1988, *GRK*1 the real growth rate of the Korean economy in a year before investment, *LI*873 labor intensity of the firm in 1987, *YD* the year dummy, *ID* the industry dummy, and *CD* the country dummy. The definition of variables and their expected signs along with source notes are presented in Table 3.

2. Data and Empirical Results

The empirical analysis was conducted using Korean firms' investment in manufacturing industries of LDCs as of December 31, 1989, obtained primarily from the same sources as in Section II. The data was supplemented with balance sheets and profit and loss statements

Table 4 – *The Determinants of Korean Firms' Foreign Direct Investment in Manufacturing Industries of Developing Countries (Tobit model)*

Independent variable						
Constant	*YWE*88	*GRK*1	*LI*873	*YD*	*ID*	*CD*
−11,950.0 (0.11)	0.25875*** (2.92)	−905.216*** (8.41)	10,795.5* (1.81)	2,457.32*** (2.74)	1,189.41** (2.30)	18,835.0 (0.17)

Statistics		
R^2	F	No. of observations
0.51	16.52	101

Note: Absolute *t*-values in parentheses are asymptotically normal. The asterisks ***; **; and * indicate significance at the 0.01; 0.05; and 0.10 level.

of each Korean firm in the *Financial Report of Korea Companies* by Korea Investors Service, Inc. and the *National Accounts 1989* and the *National Accounts* (preliminary) *1990* from the Bank of Korea. We use the same criteria to include observations as in Section II. The complete sample contains 101 observations.[10]

The dependent variable is the amount of Korean foreign direct investment in manufacturing industries of LDCs in terms of dollars. *YWE*88 is measured as a Korean firm's total payments to employees divided by the total number of employees in 1988. *GRK*1 is defined in Section II. *LI*873 is measured as a Korean firm's total employees divided by total assets in 1987. *YD*, *ID*, and *CD* are defined in the first part of this section. The results are reported in Table 4.

The coefficient of *YWE*88 is of the expected sign and is significantly different from zero at the 0.01 level. It would imply that a rapidly rising wage in Korea induces domestic firms to establish their production facilities in cheap labor countries to keep a competitive edge. Additionally, yearly earnings per employee in 1987 were included in the model rather than those in 1988, and an insignificant coefficient was obtained. Such insignificance means that the cumulative effect of a wage increase gives an impetus to transformation of production facility in developing countries. The coefficient of *GRK*1 is of the expected sign and is significantly different from zero at the 0.01 level. Whenever the real growth rate of the Korean economy is

[10] 75 observations are investment in Asian countries, 18 in Latin America, 6 in Middle East, and 2 in Africa.

low given the wage rate, Korean manufacturers have a propensity to move their establishments into relatively cheap wage countries for compensating competitiveness. The coefficient of *LI*873 is of the expected sign and is significantly different from zero at the 0.10 level. It suggests the fact that a rapid wage increase or a high wage rate affects a firm producing labor-intensive goods more badly than the one producing less labor-intensive ones. The more labor-intensive goods firms produce, the more incentive they have to invest in LDCs with relatively cheap labor. The coefficients of *YD* and *ID* are of the expected signs and are significantly different from zero at the 0.01 and 0.05 level, respectively. Foreign direct investment which occurred after 1987 and which is classified into labor-intensive industry is most seriously and directly affected by rapid wage increases and indirectly by less favorable labor-management relations. Such results suggest that a structural shift has occurred over time and across industries. Finally, *CD* is not significantly different from zero. That means that Korean manufacturers seem to be indifferent to less developed countries once the latter countries supply cheap labor to the former or transport costs are no longer a major factor to consider FDI in LDCs. It also suggests that country-specific advantages except labor supply might be insignificant.

IV. Summary and Conclusions

The purpose of this study is to understand the motivations of Korean foreign direct investment in manufacturing industries of both developed and less developed countries in a systematic manner. First, the paper presents empirical regressions based upon two conventional theories of FDI for the examination of Korean FDI in manufacturing industries of DCs. Those results indicate that there is some evidence that Korean firms' direct investments in manufacturing industries of DCs are influenced by DCs' non-tariff trade barriers. They imply that the manufacturer establishes subsidiary production facilities at least to evade DCs' non-tariff trade restrictions which are recently on the rise. However, there is no evidence to support the notion that FDI reflects "a defensive motive" by oligopolistic producers to maintain foreign market shares. These findings should be of interest since they provide some of the quantitative evidence concerning the determinants of Korean foreign direct investment in DCs. In addition, the results shed some light on the determinants of investment and export choices based on firm level data. Interestingly, we find the fact that both firm size and the real growth rate of the Korean economy are significant determinants of Korean FDI in DCs. The macroeconomic environment is important to Korean firms in exploiting business opportunities particularly in DCs.

Second, there is some evidence that Korean FDI in LDCs is consistent with the notion that one of the determinants of this FDI is to exploit the cheap labor of LDCs. The result shows a tendency that wage differentials between Korea and LDCs differently affect Korean FDI in the latter region since 1987 and across industries. It also shows the fact that Korean firms exploit business opportunities of the domestic market in the short run. However, more efforts are required to collect additional data of wage costs of LDCs to directly compare wage gaps between two countries. We suggest further research: there is a possibility that Korean FDI in less developed countries can be used as a way of evading tariff or non-tariff trade barriers of LDCs with the effect of relatively cheap wages.

In sum, Korean foreign direct investment in manufacturing industries is a way to minimize production costs arisen from non-tariff trade barriers of developed countries or to exploit cheap labor of less developed countries.

References

Aliber, Robert Z., "A Theory of Direct Foreign Investment". In: Charles Kindleberger (Ed.), *The International Corporation. A Symposium.* Cambridge, Mass., 1970, pp. 17–34

Baldwin, Robert E., "Determinants of Trade and Foreign Investment: Further Evidence". *The Review of Economics and Statistics,* Vol. 61, 1979, pp. 40–48.

Brock, William, Stephen P. Magee, "The Economics of Special Interest Politics: The Case of Tariff." *The American Economic Review,* Vol. 68, 1978, pp. 246–250.

Buckley, Peter J., Mark C. Casson, *The Future of the Multinational Enterprise.* London 1976.

Casson, Mark C., *Alternatives to the Multinational Enterprise.* London 1979.

Caves, Richard E., "International Corporations: The Industrial Economics of Foreign Investment." *Economica,* Vol. 38, 1971, pp. 1–27.

–, *Multinational Enterprise and Economic Analysis.* Cambridge 1982.

Ethier, Wilfred J., "The Multinational Firm." *The Quarterly Journal of Economics,* Vol. 101, 1986, pp. 805–833.

Grossman, Sanford J., Oliver D. Hart, "The Costs and Benefits of Ownership: A Theory of Vertical and Lateral Integration." *Journal of Political Economy,* Vol. 94, 1986, pp. 691–719.

Grubaugh, Stephen G., "Determinants of Direct Investment." *The Review of Economics and Statistics.* Vol. 69, 1987, pp. 149–152.

Gruber, William, Dileep Mehta, Raymond Vernon, "The R&D Factor in International Trade and International Investment of United States Industries." *Journal of Political Economy,* Vol. 75, 1967, pp. 20–37.

Helpman, Elhanan, "A Simple Theory of International Trade with Multinational Corporations." *Journal of Political Economy,* Vol. 92, 1984, pp. 451–471.

–, **Paul R. Krugman,** *Market Structure and Foreign Trade. Increasing Returns, Imperfect Competition, and the International Economy.* Cambridge, Mass., 1985.

Horst, Thomas O. [1972a], "Firm and Industry Determinants of the Decision to Invest Abroad: An Empirical Study," *The Review of Economics and Statistics,* Vol. 54, 1972, pp. 258–266.

– [1972b], "The Industrial Composition of U.S. Exports and Subsidiary Sales to the Canadian Market." *The American Economic Review,* Vol. 62, 1972, pp. 37–45.

Hymer, Stephen H., *The International Operations of National Firms: A Study of Direct Foreign Investment.* MIT Monographs in Economics, 14. Cambridge, Mass., 1976.

Kravis, Irving B., Robert E. Lipsey, "The Location of Overseas Production and Production for Export by U.S. Multinational Firms." *Journal of International Economics,* Vol. 12, 1982, pp. 201–223.

Kumar, Krishna, Kee Young Kim, "The Korean Manufacturing Multinationals." *Journal of International Business Studies,* Vol. 15, 1984, pp. 45–61.

Lipsey, Robert E., Merle Yahr Weiss, "Foreign Production and Exports in Manufacturing Industries." *The Review of Economics and Statistics,* Vol. 63, 1981, pp. 488–494.

Marvel, Howard P., Edward John Ray, "Intraindustry Trade: Sources and Effects on Protection." *Journal of Political Economy,* Vol. 95, 1987, pp. 1278–1291.

Mirus, M., "A Note on the Choice Between Licensing and Direct Foreign Investment." *Journal of International Business Studies,* Vol. 11, 1980, pp. 86–91.

Ray, Edward John, "Foreign Direct Investment in Manufacturing." *Journal of Political Economy,* Vol. 85, 1977, pp. 283–297.

– [1981a], "Tariff and Nontariff Barriers to Trade in the United States and Abroad." *The Review of Economics and Statistics,* Vol. 63, 1981, pp. 161–168.

– [1981b], "The Determinants of Tariff and Nontariff Trade Restrictions in the United States." *Journal of Political Economy,* Vol. 89, 1981, pp. 105–121.

–, "The Impact of Special Interests on Preferential Tariff Concessions by the United States." *The Review of Economics and Statistics,* Vol. 69, 1987, pp. 187–193.

–, "The Determinants of Foreign Direct Investment in the United States: 1979–85." In: Robert C. Feenstra (Ed.), *Trade Policies for International Competitiveness.* Chicago 1989, pp. 53–77.

Riedel, James, "The Nature and Determinants of Export-Oriented Direct Foreign Investment in a Developing Country: A Case Study of Taiwan." *Weltwirtschaftliches Archiv,* Vol. 111, 1975, pp. 505–528.

Vernon, Raymond, "International Investment and International Trade in the Product Cycle." *The Quarterly Journal of Economics,* Vol. 80, 1966, pp. 190–207.

–, *Sovereignty at Bay: The Multinational Spread of U.S. Enterprises.* New York 1971.

Williamson, Oliver E., *The Economic Institutions of Capitalism: Firms, Markets, Relational Contracting.* New York 1985.

[28]

Internationalization of Turkish Construction Companies: A Lesson for Third World Countries?

This exploratory study examines and evaluates the structure and operations of Turkish construction companies operating in the Middle East and North Africa.[1] The paucity of studies on the performance of Third World international companies, especially regional performance of construction companies, indicates a blind spot in our knowledge of this field.

The initial data for this study was collected in the summer of 1985 in Istanbul and Ankara, where the majority of the Turkish construction company headquarters are located, and in the summer of 1989, from the Turkish Association of Construction Contractors, Istanbul Board of Trade, the State Planning Organization, Construction Industry Special Task Force, and TUSIAD (Turkish Industrial Businessmen Association). The 10 companies in the 1985 study were the 10 largest construction firms in Turkey. They accounted for more than 80% of the total Turkish construction business volume. In 1988, the Turkish construction industry was ranked the eighth largest internationally, just behind Germany, with about 315 contracts involved in over 300 overseas projects worth $17 billion.

Presently, Turkish international construction firms handle contracts in 12 Middle Eastern and African countries and in the USSR. During the last few years, the declining petrol earnings of the Middle Eastern and African countries have caused a fall in these markets. Turkish contractors have had to look further afield with the USSR becoming an important market. To this end, a recent development had been the entry of Turkish contractors into the U.S. market (e.g. Kiska's Brooklyn Bridge shaft contracts). This trend reflects the increasing level of sophistication of Turkish contractors' services overseas.[2]

In our study, the CEOs of the 10 construction companies explained their views on different challenges, opportunities and problems faced by Turkish construction companiesand the industry as a whole. Out of 104 companies involved in 315 international contracts in the construction industry in 1989, the top 10 innovators were the market leaders. They gave role models to the rest of the industry for coping with recurring problems in domestic and international markets. These 10 companies also set an example for the rest of the industry in management, investment and marketing strategies, policies, and even tactics. The marketing and management strategies and policies of these firms are often considered competitive, innovative and effective, thus increasing their international market share and creating additional opportunities for market growth and prosperity.

Erderner Kayank is Professor of Marketing at the School of Business Administration of the Pensylvania State University, Harrisburg. He has served as a business consultant and training advisor to various international organizations, particularly in Turkey, the U.S., Canada, the Netherlands, Peru and Yugoslavia. He has published over 13 books on international marketing.

Tevfik Dalgic is a Head Tutor in Marketing and International Business at the Henley Management College of The Netherlands, Zeist. He has served as a faculty member at the Gazi University in Ankara, Turkey and has conducted a number of training missions through the International Trade Center in Switzerland to the Middle East and Asia.

A History of Turkish Construction Companies

Domestic Construction Companies

During the 1970s, external and uncontrollable forces had a major impact on the operations of Turkish construction companies both regionally and nationally. An expanding consumer and institutional market and an increasing demand for manufactured products in Turkey typified the time period. Turkish construction companies tried desperately to meet the huge demand for private housing as well as for public sector industrial projects. During this period, the country achieved an average of 7% growth rate, one of the highest rates within the OECD countries.[3]

Throughout the 1970s, Turkish universities produced large numbers of civil engineers and architects who mainly entered construction engineering such as dam building, irrigation projects, airports and harbors. According to Sealy[4] many of these bright young civil engineers and architects wanted to set up their own construction firms, yet had very little money to do so. To get around their capital problem, young companies lured investment. Many drew up plans on a lot in a desirable location without buying it. Instead, they would offer the owner payment with several new buildings in the newly-developed lot. The students then would sell the plans for the remaining unbuilt flats for enough cash to finance the work, the cost of the flats due the original owner and, of course, earn some profit. This unique solution created hundreds of contracting firms during the expansion stages of the Turkish economy and, as a result, accumulated a considerable degree of expertise, capital and financial resources in the Turkish construction industry.

In contrast to the rapid growth during the early 70s, the economic environment of the mid-70s posed enormous challenges to the construction industry. In the housing sector, there was a slowdown in both public and private housing demands due to credit facility limitations and government cutbacks. These measures were imposed on Turkey by international credit institutions and the IMF after most Turkish firms failed to pay debts, successive Turkish governments failed to stabilize debt, and foreign exchange earnings continued to shrink.[5] The Turkish government was forced to curb imports of machinery, technical expertise and raw materials. Government spending, especially in construction, was also reduced. As a result, the industry began slowing down in 1975. Turkey's GNP also began declining in real terms during this period. These adverse circumstances created idle labor and capital in the construction industry.

Under this unfavorable economic climate, the Turkish manufacturing industry tried to solve its problems by manufacturing scarce goods the country badly needed, or simply by imitating foreign-origin products. But the same option was not open in the construction sector. The construction industry had at its disposal large machine capacities, easy access to building materials at home, a well-trained work force, and a pool of young engineers and managers who had considerable managerial and technical competence, but had no work. These prevailing macroeconomic forces in Turkey around the mid-1970s motivated construction companies to look for market growth opportunities overseas.

Some of the factors which initially attracted or "pulled" Turkish construction companies to the Middle East and North Africa are: 1) geographic proximity; 2) a common cultural and religious heritage to Turkey; 3) tremendous wealth from the sale of petroleum and natural gas; 4) similar construction needs to that of Turkey; and 5) similar economic development path followed.[6] In each of these markets in North Africa, the Near East, the Gulf States and Non-Arab (Islamic) Africa, there is a single dominant country from which 73% - 98% of the total construction business is obtained. In North Africa, Libya is the dominant country, in the Near East, it is Iraq, and among the Gulf States, Saudi Arabia is placed first. By the end of 1990, out of the total 391 international construction projects completed, some 95% were undertaken in the three countries, namely in Libya, Iraq and Saudi Arabia, thus utilizing a market concentration strategy in international markets (see Table 1).

Turkish Construction Companies Abroad

By the late 1970s, Turkish construction firms began to make headway bidding for some of the world's largest construction projects.[7] Most countries in these regions have five year economic development plans and yearly programs which assist them in the allocating resources and determining socio-economic developmental priorities. The development and improvement of the physical infrastructure and construction sector had utmost importance. This created a need for Turkish construction companies.

The internationalization process of these companies went through four distinct stages. Initially, the companies tried to become low-cost bidders to win projects abroad, and then secondly sought more efficient business opportunities to maintain profitability. In the third stage, the construction companies concentrated heavily on creating economies of scale to improve productivity and efficiency. Finally, they became global companies whose activities are diversified along concentric, horizontal

Table 1

Turkish Construction Contractors Abroad
(As of December 31, 1990)

Sources: Adapted from Business International, *IBS Doing Business in Turkey*, Istanbul: IBS, 1991,
Dunya Newspaper, (in Turkish), Special Issue, June 14, 1991, p. 1.

	Number of Firms	*Number of Employees*	*Number of Construction Contracts*		*Total Value of Contracts Undertaken*		*Work Completed ($Billion)*	*Work Outstanding ($Billion)*
Libya	46	17,100	346	*88.5*	12,535	*58.3*	10,500	3,000
Saudi Arabia	6	8,340	13	*3.4*	4,000	*18.6*	3,900	100
Iraq	6	320	14	*3.5*	3,000	*13.9*	2,450	550
USSR	7	2,220	13	*3.4*	645	*3.0*	150	500
Kuwait	2	20	2	*0.5*	495	*2.3*	200	300
Others	3	100	3	*0.7*	825	*3.9*	720	130
Total	**70**	**28,100**	**391**	*%100.0*	**21,500**	*%100.0*	**17,920**	**3,580**

and conglomerate lines.

From 1978 to 1990, the total contract value undertaken by Turkish contractors abroad increased more than 13 times, reaching $21.5 billion (Table 2). Of the total 391 contracts received, some 83 are carried out in more than one country, and 346 conducted in Libya alone. When one looks at their structure, 81.2% worked as independent contractors, 15.3% worked as a partner to a joint-venture, and the remaining 3.5% had subcontractor status. In later years, because of the economic and financial difficulties Libya faced, a large percentage of the firms (41% of the total 129) moved to Saudi Arabia. Of the total $21.5 billion turnover, some 58.3% ($12.5 billion) was obtained from Libya. Besides Libya, Saudi Arabia, Iraq, Kuwait and Jordan were the major contributors to the income of Turkish construction companies.[8]

In addition to their quantitative achievement during the 1980s, the qualitative performance of Turkish contractors has also been spectacular. Ten years before, Turkish construction companies had to forfeit projects involving the construction of dams, harbors, tunnels, bridges, highways, airports and industrial plants, to foreign multinationals. But in 1988, Turkish companies possessed the requisite highly-organized structure, advanced technology and field experience to undertake projects not only in domestic, but also in foreign markets.

Turkish construction contractors, so far, have undertaken projects in many foreign countries. Among these, Libya is first with 60% of the total amount of the work. This is followed by Saudi Arabia, Iraq, Kuwait, USSR, and others. In Libya by 1988, Turkish companies were responsible for the Al Zahra-Al Jedida and Taruna-Qusabat highways; Tajovra new town construction; housing complexes of 1,000 units or more in Derna, Sebha, Bir Al Ghanam, Fezzan, Tobruq and Tripoli; Tripoli and Sidi Belal harbors; two cement plants in Bengazi; Tajura industrial vehicles plant; sewage network in Missurata and Tobruq. Turkish firms are also interested in Libyan plans to build a $1.5 billion desert city to be named Al-Jufra which will be located 300 miles southeast of Tripoli.[9]

In Saudi Arabia, Turkish companies built dams, irrigation networks and drainage works; tunnels, highways, bridges and airports; turnkey industrial installation; H.T. transmission lines, electrical maintenance, electric power plants, telecommunications installation; construction of houses, hotels, schools and hospitals. In Jordan, Turkish companies are responsible for the Amman and Irbid water and sewage treatment plants; Arab Potash Potassium Refinery; Resadiye Cement plant; 11 water depots in Amman; and 255 villas. And in Iraq, airport and highway construction; surface and underground pipe lines; irrigation and drainage projects; construction of industrial complexes.[10]

A part from the Middle East and North African construction markets in which the Turkish contractors have enjoyed the greatest share of participation in civil engineering and electrochemical erection works, the USSR has opened its construction market to Turkish contractors for such projects as hotels, health centers, hospitals, trade centers, housing and industrial facilities. In the USSR, $675 million worth of 14 projects, namely the health care center in Pitsunda, Georgian USSR with 750 beds, the health care center in Mohachala, Daghestan, foundary works and Petrovski shopping center in Moscow, were already completed.[11]

Officials of the Turkish Ministry of consturction and Housing estimates that Turkish overseas construction firms' revenues from the USSR exceeded the US$1 billion mark in 1991 and that they will reach $2 billion by the end of 1992. Of the total $1 billion worth of construction busiensses generated from the USSR in 1991, the USSR paid for construction services with the products Turkey imported. To this end, $300 million was paid through natural gas purchases and another $400 million worth of

Table 2

Total Value of Contracts Undertaken by Turkish Construction Contractors Abroad
($ Billion)

Sources: Aydin Esen, "Contractors Abroad and Exportation of Construction Materials Symposim," Marmara University, Istanbul, March, 1984.
Preliminary Report of the 6th Five Year Economic Development Plan, Ankara, 1989.
Business International and IBS Doing Business in Turkey, Istanbul, IBS, 1991, p.IV. 7–6.

	1978	*1979*	*1980*	*1981*	*1982*	*1983*	*1984*	*1985*	*1986*	*1987*	*1988*	*1989*	*1990*
Libya	1.182	1.432	2.346	7.100	8.167	8.569	8.657	8.657	9.266	9.266	9.422	9.935	9.935
Saudi Arabia	0.192	0.307	0.684	1.130	3.302	4.125	4.567	4.954	4.959	4.959	4.959	4.964	4.964
Iraq	0.203	0.303	0.403	0.728	0.952	1.031	1.031	1.297	2.098	2.097	2.098	2.230	2.500
Jordan	–	–	0.110	0.043	0.043	0.108	0.108	0.168	0.185	0.185	0.185	0.185	0.185
U.A. Emirates	0.047	0.047	0.035	0.039	0.039	0.039	0.039	0.051	0.051	0.051	0.051	0.051	0.051
Kuwait	0.005	0.005	0.011	0.012	0.016	0.017	0.017	0.017	0.017	0.017	0.017	0.017	0.473
Senegal	–	–	–	–	0.020	0.020	0.020	0.020	0.020	0.020	0.020	0.020	0.020
Algeria	–	–	–	–	0.037	0.037	0.037	0.037	0.037	0.037	0.037	0.037	0.037
Iran	–	–	–	–	–	0.070	0.071	0.071	0.071	0.071	0.071	0.071	0.071
Egypt	–	–	–	–	–	0.016	0.016	0.016	0.016	0.016	0.016	0.016	0.016
Yemen	–	–	–	–	–	–	0.100	0.111	0.111	0.111	0.111	0.111	0.111
Bahrain	–	–	–	–	–	–	–	–	0.001	0.001	0.001	0.001	0.001
Others	–	0.005	0.099	–	–	0.004	0.100	0.100	0.100	0.101	0.288	0.230	0.548
Total	**1.692**	**2.099**	**3.517**	**9.052**	**12.567**	**14.028**	**14.763**	**15.499**	**16.932**	**16.932**	**17.276**	**17.968**	**18.964**

iron and steel, chemical products, coal and arbestos under Turk Eximbank credit. This amount also includes the installment payments of the two Soviet built Iskenderun Iron and Steel and Seydisehir Aluminium Factories. The remaining amount is paid in hard currency provided by the German Government grant. Presently these are also proposals from the Soviet side to engage in construction joint ventures with Turkish construction firms as well as bartering Soviet cotton by Turkish construction services.[12]

During 1990 and 1991, Turkish construction companies have also keenly been interested in the housing projects planned to be built for the Soviet military personnel returning from the former East German territory. This housing project, comprising of 36,000 units in to be completed by a grant worth $5 billion (DM 7.8 billion) provided by the German Government and through international bidding. In the first stage of the project which covers four different cities and 4,000 units, a Turkish-Finnish consortium has won a contract for the construction of 1,056 dwelling units and infrastructure facilities in Shaykovka. During the second stage of the project, more Turkish firms are likely to succeed in the competition.[13]

International Competition

According to a survey conducted by the *Middle East Economic Digest* in 1983, competitors of Turkish companies abroad included the world's largest contractors from the U.S., South Korea, Italy, Japan, the U.K., Germany and France. The South Korean Government provides tax reductions, stand-by letter of credit facility for simultaneous financing, income tax reductions for employees, credit and non-payment risk insurances, facilitation of equipment export and import, satisfactory foreign currency allocation and transfer. Apart from such supports and backing, the construction firms are also provided with the management support when necessary in international markets. Furthermore, a support fund has been established for sectoral development and improvement which South Korean firms use particularly for technological development.

Recent years have also witnessed the influx of mainland Chinese, Pakistani, Indian and Bangladeshi engineering and construction companies, which are moving rapidly into the market with very low labor costs.[14] When compared to Japanese and South Korean companies, Turkish construction firms have suffered the loss due to lack of a well organized contracting sector. During the early 1980s, as Japan and South Korea had a share of 6% and 11% respectively in the international contracting services market, Turkey's share was only 8%. The German contractors share of 6% put them behind Turkish contractors. South Korean firms possessed comprehensive technical and management skills that gave them formidable competitive strength.[15] In addition, tax breaks, export financing from the Korean government make these and other firms in similar situations more competitive than Turkish firms.[16] The diversification and horizontal/vertical integration stratagies employed by Korean and other internationally competitive firms was being imitated by Turkish construction firms by 1980.[17]

Recently, the South Korean authorities have declared construction sector to be a "strategic national industry." As such, a master plan and sectoral coordination plans have been developed to support and enhance the sector. In Turkey, the plans and strategies related to the development and improvement of international contracting services have not been achieved yet. The principles and policies for Turkish construction sector proposed within the 6th Five-Year Economic Development Plan includes only one paragraph regarding the targets, goals, and policies of international construction firms.

Five-yearly economic development plans are prepared by the State Planning Organization. The purpose of these plans are to give direction to the economy of Turkey at a macro level. These economic development plans as well as yearly programs allocate public funds to various sectors of the economy. The plans are inward-oriented and deal mostly with domestic economic issues; and the plans direct the private sector including construction firms in a tangential manner. This situation has created certain problems for those construction firms within the confines of both five-year economic development plans and yearly programs.[18]

In 1981, the total value of Turkish construction market activity in the Middle East and North Africa was $45 billion. It declined to $28 billion in 1984 and to a very low level of $14 billion in 1987. The total dollar amount of the construction projects in this region ran around $12 billion to $15 billion a year in the following period before the Gulf War. In view of the overall market shrinkage in the Middle East and North Africa in

Table 3

Main Turkish Contractors Exposure in Iraq and Kuwait, August 1990
($ thousands)

Source: Business International, IBS Doing Business in Turkey, Istanbul: IBS, 1991, p. IV. 7–7. Turkish Contractor's Union

Note: STFA-Elta figures include STFA's independent exposure.

	Enka Insatt	*Enka Teknik*	*Fuat Soylu*	*STFA-Elta*	*Güris Makina*	*Özgü -Baytur*	*Kiska*	*Tekfen*	*BMB*	**Total**
Guarantee Letters	71,000	1,150	168	3,950	380	13,413	3,500	5,420	107,000	**205,981**
Company Advances	–	–	–	810	–	–	–	–	–	**810**
Equipment	63,000	350	550	160	500	11,000	–	2,320	34,500	**112,380**
Mobilisation Stocks	30,500	783	250	170	–	5,400	–	200	69,300	**106,603**
Wages etc.	10,500	500	44	50	–	438	100	40	2,075	**13,747**
Invoices Outstanding	14,00	–	525	225	626	193	1,000	1,630	10,740	**28,939**
Work in Progress	–	–	–	1,075	–	760	–	–	–	**1,835**
Promissory Notes	50,000	3,610	1,630	2,460	245	2,730	3,500	–	2,000	**66,175**
Other	86,000	940	700	7,170	–	27,350	–	3,330	80,900	**206,390**
Advances Due	19,500	–	–	–	–	–	–	–	–	**19,500**
Total	**344,500**	**7,333**	**3,867**	**16,070**	**1,751**	**61,284**	**8,100**	**12,940**	**306,515**	**762,360**
Labor Force	2,602	12	26	–	48	210	–	–	–	**2,896**

1988 and beyond, a number of large Turkish construction contractors returned to the domestic market. At this time the Turkish government sponsored re-establishing the building of low cost housing Construction Fund. What will happen in the future will depend upon how much countries of the region will suffer from the world-wide economic crisis, the general state of the economies of the area as part of the aftermath of the Gulf War, and the effects of the European Common Market on the area.[19]

Given the magnitude of destruction, the task of rebuilding Kuwait is expected to pose substantial challenges and opportunities through 1995.[20] Turkish construction firms interested in reconstruction business opportunities will closely follow the bidding procedures adopted by the Kuwaiti government in the coming months and assess whether special bidding customs or practices will develop.[21]

Iraq's invasion of Kuwait created a very serious situation for some Turkish contractors. At the end of August 1990, the Turkish Constructors Union estimated that losses by Turkish companies involved could total $800 million, of which some $200 million was bank letters of guarantee. It was stated that virtually none of this was insured with Turk Eximbank. Currently, Turkish Undersecretariat of the Treasury and Foreign Trade is in charge of developing a compensation package. The situation of the 10 major Turkish construction firms is shown in Table 2.

Contribution of Construction Companies Abroad to the Turkish Economy

Since Turkish construction companies have more and more business outside of Turkey, there have been some noticeable effects on the Turkish economy.[22]

Positive Effects on Balance of Payments

Since 1975, balance of payment difficulties have been one of the biggest problems in the Turkish economy. However, inflow of foreign currency into the economy through workers' remittances ($836 million), profit transfers ($660 million), and the exportation of construction materials ($145 million) has helped alleviate this problem. In addition, there have been $750 million in credit commissions and $425 million from construction material exports. For instance, in 1988 some 80% of the wages of the personnel was retained by the employer and directly transferred to Turkey in foreign currency. The remaining 20% was also expected to be repatriated by workers in various ways. Workers' remittances, the greatest item of currency transfers from construction activities abroad, are estimated at $700 million in 1981, $1.2 billion in 1983 and $1.9 billion in 1988. Profit transfers of the construction companies, amounting to 5% of the total contract value for each year, is estimated to be $210 million-$250 million a year for the period 1984-1988 (see Table 3).

Employment Opportunities

Since Turkey's low rate of investment is insufficient to cope with the labor supply growth, construction activities abroad, being a labor-intensive industry, create new opportunities for growth and a possible solution of the unemployment problem in the domestic market. After West European countries halted the immigration of foreign labor, the Middle East and North African construction markets gained even greater importance to Turkey. During the late 1980s, a majority of the Turkish workers emigrating for employment opportunities abroad have been absorbed by the construction sector in the Middle East and North Africa.

Contribution to Exports

During the 1980s, Turkish exports to Middle Eastern countries increased remarkably, reaching approximately 50% of the total volume of exports.[23] Turkish contractors acting in these countries are supposed to have played the most significant role in this reorientation. In fact, Turkish construction companies abroad import cement, construction equipment, wood, marble, ceramics and consumer products from Turkey to be utilized by their personnel, thus complimenting Turkish foreign direct investment (FDI) with these exports. In 1988, the total dollar volume of construction activity taking place abroad was around $4.5 billion. In addition to this, Turkish construction companies made bids totalling $4.6 billion (see Table 4).

Table 4

Turkish Construction Activities Abroad
($ thousands)

Source: State Planning Organization, 6th Five Year Economic Development Plan, Construction Sector Activity Report, Ankara, 1989.

	Continuing Construction Jobs	*Construction Bids of Turkish Firms*
Libya	2,250	4,960
Saudi Arabia	932	504
Iraq	846	818
Other Countries*	473	118
Total	**4,500**	**6,400**

* Other countries include Egypt, Sudan, United Arab Emirates, USSR, Jordan, Iran, Yemen, Senegal, Kuwait, Algeria, and some East European countries.

Contribution to Domestic Economy

Construction sector has an important role in the Turkish economy as its share in the GDP at constant prices is around 6% and together with other sectors supplying imputs, its total role in the overall economy reaches 40%. Furthermore, construction sector has a share of 10% in the employment (agriculture excluded), 50% in expenditures and 24% in taxation. Construction activities of Turkish companies abroad have a carry-over effect on domestic industry and the economy. Major construction companies investing at home produce the construction materials that they need in their construction projects abroad. As a result, there appears to be a rise in capacity, productivity and efficiency at firm and industry levels in Turkey. Turkish industrialists are also forced to improve the quality of their output to meet the higher standards expected in international markets, which also carries over to the Turkish economy.[24] With increased skills and knowledge-base gained overseas, Turkish construction firms are now able to build 2,000 to 3,000 kms long highways and 64 dams at home.

Techonology Transfer

Construction contractors in foreign countries could have the opportunity to follow the most recent technological developments in the sector and also to transfer the most advanced technology in the sector by means of joint ventures and very close international contacts. Turkish contractors and suppliers are now well established in the construction industries of Algeria, Iraq, Kuwait, Libya and Saudi Arabia. Often Turkish construction technologies and their application are more appropriate for the local conditions of the Middle East than those available from the United States and other developed countries.[25] This point clearly illustrates the importance and application of reverse technology in the area of construction, leading to South-South techno-economic cooperation. It is also worth mentioning that other foreign companies with access to higher technological and financial resources could make advantageous deals when they cooperate with strong Turkish companies for jobs in these countries.[26]

As a result, Turkish construction firms have exported their businesses into such countries as Austria, Germany, France, Guatemala, Honduras, Nigeria, Trinidad, Uganda and Zambia.[27]

International Company Characteristics

Managerial Philosophy

General characteristics of the major companies' decision makers show certain similarities. These are related to their performance over the past decade in the same markets under similar socio-economic, legal and technological conditions. The CEOs have used entrepreneurial qualities to improve performance of their companies. This is apparent through:

1 a firm's higher involvement in product/service and technological innovation;

2 a willingness to undertake more risky construction projects;

Chart 1

Evolutionary Internationalization Process of Turkish Construction Companies

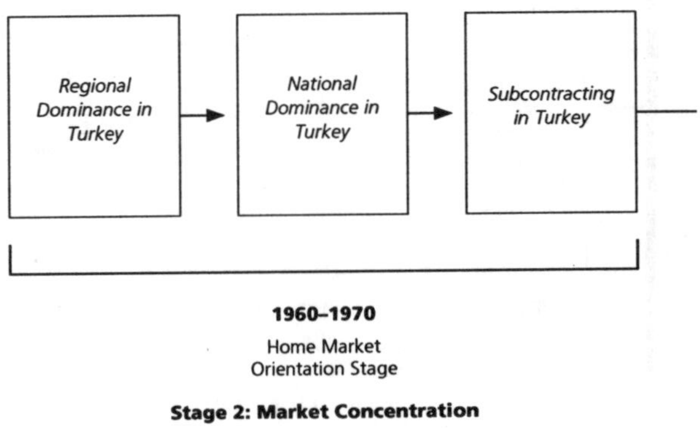

3 initiating rather than imitating the moves of others;

4 a desire to seek market opportunities on a global scale;

5 a highly-fragmented and diversified industry involving construction firms that employ many people to firms (85%) that employ fewer than 10 employees;

6 longer planning horizons than other sectors;

7 a pattern of horizontal and concentric diversification into non-construction areas.

The firms operating in the Turkish construction industry are organically linked to a large number of supplementary industries such as glass, wood, cement, steel and clay. As a result, marketing and organizational strategies adopted may also be influenced by the trends, managerial practices and policies in the supplementary industries.

Social Responsibility of the Firms

Major Turkish construction companies tend to have strong nationalistic feelings. They all contended, essentially to participate in the solutions of the economic ills of the country, to create new options in the foreign currency shortage and the high rate of unemployment. They felt obliged to repay Turkey for educational opportunities and wished to see Turkey raised to international standing and credibility. Managers see the extension of their business outside of Turkey as socially motivated rather than economically.[28]

Policies and Strategies Followed

Among the strategic objectives, "survival" was most important. Diversification strategies have played an important role for a majority of the companies. Under the prevailing economic conditions, companies could not use marketing policies and strategies to increase internal market share, but developed marketing strategies to exploit foreign markets more fully.

By selecting survival as their primary strategic objective, they developed successive levels of internationalization starting from sub-contracting to contracting, then management consultancy and turnkey projects, to joint ventures and, finally, multina-

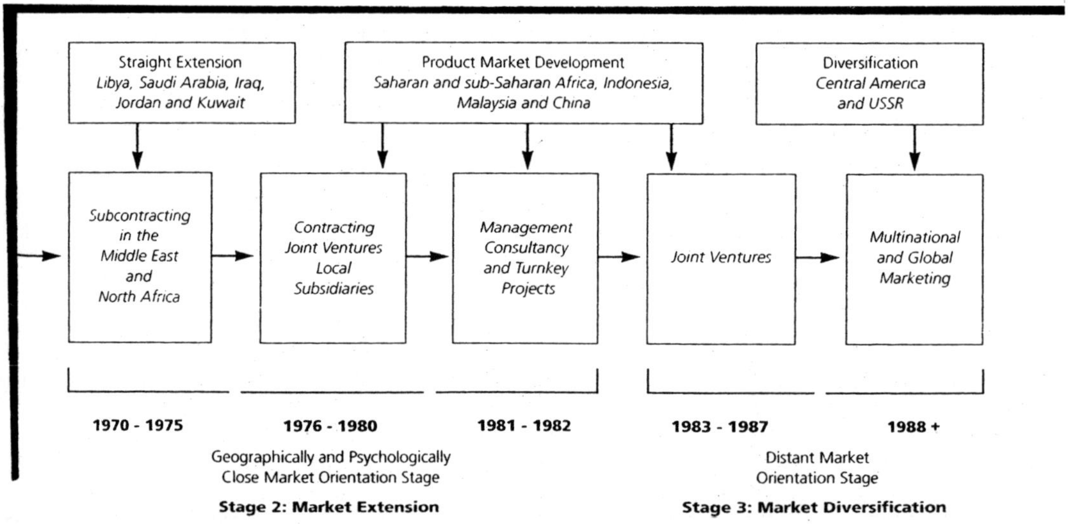

tionality (Chart 1). At the initial foreign market entry stage, sub-contracting was the most viable alternative for them to exploit. Firms' major concern at this stage was to utilize their workforce and capital equipment in the most productive and cost effective way in the field for as long as possible. Only through sub-contracting could these firms employ Turkish labor and integrate it with foreign-made raw materials and equipment by using their technical and managerial power to become competitive in the global building industry. From time to time, these contractors have also used Turkish-made raw materials like cement and tiles. However, West European suppliers were the major purchasers of Turkish raw materials.[29]

The first stage in the internationalization process has been through sub-contracting. At a later stage the firm opens contracting companies overseas (mainly in the Middle East and North Africa) with their own manufacturing plants at home for the procurement of needed construction inputs. During the third stage, the firm, through turnkey projects or joint ventures, coordinates marketing, finance, production and personnel across several countries. Finally, the firm becomes a truly global firm by centralizing production, distribution, marketing, finance and personnel policies and strategies.

Competitive Strategies

Construction firms from developing countries, including Turkey, have managed to build a very successful record abroad. These companies, in addition to low wages, offer additional benefits to the local industries. Their accumulated past experience has taught them how to solve problems that are special to environments similar to those at home. For instance, their competitive strengths in the area of designing small-scale plants, substitution of local materials and design of simple buildings suitable for tropical climates and low income neighborhoods, are some of their competitive advantages.[30]

The accumulated experience also enables Turkish companies, as well as those from other developing countries, to estimate costs more accurately. For instance,

> *the inexperienced firm is likely to build into its bid price a large margin to cover uncertainty. A firm from an advanced country may also bid high to cover the uncertainty of an unknown environment and to cover the high cost of its personnel. The firm from another developing country (like Turkey) with experience on similar projects is likely to offer the lowest bid, since it has fewer uncertainties than other competitors and cheaper resources than the firm from an advanced country.*[31]

Turkish firms tend to bid lower for projects abroad because of the depressed home construction market. Tax incentives and tax rebates offered by the successive Turkish governments pose another motive for these companies to go abroad and be more competitive in their pricing and bidding strategies.

Starting from 1989, Turkish construction firms have been able to increase their sources of financing domestically as well as internationally. In winning large construction contracts in international markets, strong financial position and financial backing is very important. Traditionally, construction contracts in the Middle East and North Africa are in part financed by means of advance payments. These advances usually amount to 20% of the total contract value and in some countries it is as low as 10%. In cases when the advance payment is insufficient to finance the operation, Turkish construction firms look for additional financing, which creates the problem of project risk financing as well as country risk.[32]

The cash flow policies of the companies were mainly based on installment payments by the main contractors, and their early years were the years of cash savings and further investments. One of the keys to the tremendous success of the Turkish contractors was the low-paid Turkish workers, who make only about 60% of their Korean counterpart's pay. As competition in the industry becomes more intense, some companies which are less efficient are being pushed out of the market.[33] Eventually, some of the more than 50 Korean companies working abroad may be forced to merge.[34] These are also some of the emerging trends in the Turkish construction industry.

In order to prevent industrial actions, Turkish workers have been employed on a fuller scale and a number of bilateral agreements have been signed with the Turkish Ministries of Employment and Social Security. The Turkish government acts as a guarantor on behalf of the workers in the enforcement of the signed agreements. In addition to this, several agreements have also been drafted with the host Arab country counterpart organizations. Turkish people

Table 5

Market Opportunity Matrix for Turkish Construction Companies

Products/Services Offered

Markets Served	**Present Product Service**	**New Product Service**
Present Markets	**1 Market Penetration** • Increase sales regionally in Turkey. • Increase sales nationally in Turkey. • Enter into Turkish part of Cyprus. *Dominant market is residential.*	**3 Product Service Development** • Management contracting and turnkey projects. • Joint ventures with Arab companies as well as with West European companies. *Developmental projects are the prime focus of attention which are outlined in five year economic development plans.*
New Markets	**2 Market Development** • Entry into Saudi Arabia, Libya, Iraq, and Jordan as sub-contractors. • Becoming contractors in Libya, Tunisia and Algeria. *Dominant market is public sector buildings.*	**4 Diversification** • Involvement in financing and banking. • Running hotel chains. • Exporting. • Forming trading houses. • Formation of multinational firms. • Manufacturing in non-construction fields, (i.e.; food, vessels, dairy products). *Product/service diversificaton.*

working for subcontractor companies are mainly paid in Turkish currency and their wages are transferred to their families living in Turkey. But the workers themselves are provided with accommodations and given stipends of local currency.

Market Growth Opportunities

When one looks at the market growth strategies of the 10 leading companies since 1975, they have all adopted a similar pattern of development (Table 5). The structural development has shown little difference, but some of the stages have been different. In a study conducted by Sozen and Giritli in 1987 among some 30 Turkish construction contractors, it was found that programming techniques of small firm operations was mostly unsuccessful.[35] Medium-sized firms, on the other hand, cited inadequate staffing levels. The large construction companies, which were the focus of the current study, have shown different characteristics at five stages of organizational development (Chart 2). The successful implementation of any organizational strategy to improve company efficiency depends upon the identification of key problem areas. Exoneration of these problems provides a guideline for developing appropriate operating objectives and procedures.

Among the top 10 construction companies, three of them have been involved with other activities mainly in the areas of banking, newspaper publishing, exporting, carpet and yarn manufacturing.[36] The other three are involved in a variety of contracting businesses, namely building harbors, dams, industrial complexes, bridges, hydro-electric plants, steel construction, cement factories, water storage, pumping treatment, desalination projects, construction of bridges, tunnels, highways, refineries, petrochemical plants, power plants, university campuses, and other construction type of businesses.[37]

What has been the secret behind Turkish construction companies success story in the Middle East and North Africa? Like Taiwan and South Korea, Turkey was assisted by the obvious Saudi policy of pushing work towards countries in need of economic support against communism. Turkey's traditional relationship with U.S. corporations and engineers has played a major role in military construction and construction of other strategic installations. With experience and increased productivity and efficiency, Turkish construction companies are completing projects ahead of time and consistently winning bids, sometimes at the expense of powerful and experienced engineering giants of the West.

Future Directions of Internationalization of Turkish Construction Firms

With such positive contributions to the economy, construction activities abroad have constituted the new prospect for the Turkish economy. Along with freight revenues, overseas Turkish contracting firms create annual revenues of approximately $6 billion. Being aware of this fact, successive Turkish governments have adopted several incentives and facilities for the sector in recent years.

However many Turkish firms feel their potential has not yet been fully exhausted overseas. They are doing work outside Turkey which is well below their technological capacity and, in fact, well below what they have already achieved at home. In the coming years Turkish contractors would undertake greater and more complicated projects in the region as well as elsewhere. As the Gulf strife between Iraq and Kuwait and her Western allies is over, it is expected that many more contracts could become available.

Even before the bombing of Iraq had begun, the government of Kuwait had started to allocate contracts for the rebuilding of its shattered country. There is going to be a construction boom taking place involving $100 billion to rebuild Kuwait's oilfields, highways, prisons, desalination plants and hotels as well as damage

Chart 2

Organizational Development of Companies

Organizational Type Exhibited	*Structural Characteristics*	*Construction Company Type*	*Operational Policy Used*
Simple.	Single Product.	Subcontracting.	Market Concentration
Functional.	Single product and vertical integration.	Contracting.	
Multi-divisional.	Related diversity of product lines and internal growth.	Management consultancy and turnkey project.	Market Expanding
Holding company.	Growth by acquisition.	Joint ventures.	
Multinational. (Global)	Multiple products in multiple countries.	Multinational company.	

Table 6

Turkish Construction Projects in the USSR February 1991

Financed Outside the Natural Gas Protocols

Source: Business International, IBS Doing Business in Turkey, Istanbul: IBS, 1991, p. 4.7 and IV. 7-8.

Note: FX means hard currency
1: Turkish company's share, 2: Completed in 1990

Project	*Location Terms*	*Contractor*	*Foreign*	*Cost Partner*	*Months*	*Currency*
500-Bed Surgical Hospital	Novokuznetsk	Petkontur	ABC, Austria	$70.0m	36	—
320 Luxury Flats etc.	Moscow	Mir	—	$56.0m	36	FX
300-Bed Cardiological Centre	Krasnodar Barter	Mir	Interade and Varnet, Austria	$20.0m[1]	36	—
Cable Factory Renovation[2]	Moscow	Alarko	—	$12.0m	10	FX
250-Bed Clinic	Irkutsk	Tekser	Trachtabel, Belgium	$10.0m[1]	28	FX
Hotel	Sochi	Erna	U.S.-Soviet Joint Venture	$15.0m[1]	na	FX
Polyclinic	Novokuznetsk	Petkontur	—	$10.0m	14	FX
ZAPSIB Infrastructural Works, Bread Plant & Social Buildings	Novokuznetsk	Petkontur	—	$17.0m	12	FX
Jewellery Plant	Krasnoyarsk	Petkontur	—	$35.0m	30	FX
17-Story Housing Building	Krasnoyarsk	Petkontur	—	$12.0m	30	FX
Banknote Factory-Process Water Plant	Leningrad	Alarko	—	$12.0m	30	FX

Financed Under the Natural Gas Protocols

Source: Business International, IBS Doing Business in Turkey, Istanbul: IBS, 1991, p. 4.7 and IV. 7–8.

Note: 1: Originally completed, 2: Originally Koray Baytur, 3: Completed

Name of Project[1]	*Location*	*Contractor*	*Cost*	*Months*	*Workers*
1000-Bed Hospital	Moscow	Enka	$88.0m	35	1,200
Yalta Tourism Complex	Yalta	Tekser	$41.5m	25	—
Pitsunda Rehabilitation Complex	Pitsunda	Baytur[2]	$45.0m	25[3]	600
Makhachkala Rehabilitation Complex	Makhachkala	Baytur[2]	$34.5m	25[3]	400
Renovation of Petrovski Passage	Moscow	Enka	$19.5m	30[3]	600
Yalta Children's Clinic	Yalta	Tekser	$40.5m	36	100
194-Bed Maternity Clinic	Moscow	Baytur	$25.0m	24	350
250-Bed Maternity Clinic	Moscow	Enka			
212-Bed Gynocological Hospital	Moscow	Enka	$100.0m	24	2,000
Bakulev Cardio-Surgical Clinic	Moscow	Enka			

done to hospitals, shopping centers, and amusement parks.[38] Contract preferences have been announced for firms from coalition countries. Although much more slowly and with almost no obvious funding sources, Iraq will join Kuwait and Lebenon as an economy to be reconstructed from devastating damage. Although the Iraqi government might prefer to give its business to the USSR, it is highly likely that there will be greater market opportunities for Turkish construction firms as well.[39]

The natural gas agreement between the USSR and Turkey states that 25% of the value of Turkish natural gas imports from the USSR will be allocated to finance Turkish contracting services in the USSR. Another important development was the signing of a $350 million credit line agreement that Turk Eximbank channels to the USSR, to be used in the turnkey construction of light industrial plants. Table 6 shows Turkish construction projects in the USSR financed under and outside the natural gas protocols in February of 1991.[40]

In particular, the unparalleled growth of Pacific-Rim countries may provide additional opportunities to Turkish companies that face a static period of construction in Turkey and in the Middle East. Parallel to this evolution, interest in joint ventures with Far Eastern and Asian firms is increasing. Joint ventures with Chinese construction companies may prove very successful in the future. Possible areas for Turkish construction in these countries may include energy (construction of power stations and refineries), buildings (residential, industrial and commercial) and services and communications. For instance in China, priority has been on upgrading major domestic, international and Special Economic Zone (SEZ) airports. For the Seventh Five-Year Plan (1986-1990), the largest construction projects are new international airports at Shenzhen and Shanghai.[41] A financial package may need to be developed for future Asian projects, and in order to satisfy the need for a national industrial policy to coordinate domestic and foreign activity, a concerted effort on the part of industry leaders is needed.

Turkish construction firms may find greater competition from these Far Eastern firms. For instance, Chinese firms have a commerical goal to earn foreign exchange. Lower profit margins will be accepted by Chinese firms if they can gain experience. The PRC has some 70 construction firms active overseas, employing over 60,000 engineers and laborers in 100 countries. These firms acquired only 2% of the world's construction business, accounting for $1.7 billion worth of business in 1987.[42]

At present, Turkey is not a member of the Asian Development Bank, nor the African Development Bank. If the country were to be a full member in these two important development organizations, there would be vast construction market opportunities for Turkish contractors in such countries as Pakistan, Bangladesh, Indonesia, Malaysia and the Sudan. Corporate considerations regarding these Pacific-Rim construction projects involve service trade liberalization as well as construction dynamics since such domestic issues as environmentalism, business ethics and collective bargaining are muted abroad.[43] A construction market explosion seems imminent as world wealth and economic impetus gravitate to the Pacific Rim.[44]

One important lesson gained from this study is that contracting is a valid example of technology transfer between Western construction companies and the companies from the developing world.

While not every LDC can rely upon the growth of their domestic construction industry to bolster their GNP and national competitiveness, the Turkish example is worthy. It is a concrete example of a country that has spent years attempting to move firmly into the First World, and the case of their construction industry is actually a move in the desired direction.

The construction companies have achieved several crucial national goals through their growth: the transfer of technology, acquiring business knowledge and increasing international trade. As stated earlier, the growth of the construction sector may not be the answer for every LDC, however, the prosperity and national competitiveness afforded by such growth is a valuable lesson – a lesson as to how a specific industry is able to turn itself around to the greater benefit of an entire nation.

Notes

1 *Middle East Economic Digest*, April 1988, 85-88.

2 Business International, *IBS Doing Business in Turkey*, Istanbul: IBS, 1991, section IV, 7-6.

3 *OECD Economic Report on Turkey*, Paris: OECD, 1985.

4 T. Sealy, "How the Young Entrepreneurs Made Their Way," *Financial Times Survey Turkey: Building and Contracting Industry*, December 17, 1982, VII.

5 State Planning Organization, *The Fifth Five-Year Development Plan (1985-1989)*, Anakara, October 1986, 265-266.

6 Erdener Kaynak, *International Business in the Middle East*, New York: Walter de Gruyter, 1986.

7 "Contracting Operations Abroad," *Economic Dialogue*, September 1983.

8 "Turkish Contractors: It's Time to Take Them Seriously," *International Management*, Volume 40, No. 7, (July 1985): 41-45.

9 "Turkey, Libya to Discuss Libyan Debt to Turkish Contractors," *Turkish Daily News*, August 8, 1989: 3.

10 "Muteahhitlik Isi Ne Oldu?" (in Turkish), *Dunya Newspaper*, June 27, 1989: 2.

11 Turkish Contractors Association, *Turkish Contracting Services Abroad, Ankara*, March 1991: 2.

12 Ibid, 2-3.

13 Telephone interviews held with Turk Eximbank and Turkish Ministry of Construction and Housing Officials on December 11, 1991 in Istanbul, Turkey.

14 Susan Poole, "China Builds Overseas Business," *China Business Review*, Vol. 15, No. 5 (September-October 1988): 20,22.

15 F.D.M. Thomas, "Managing Major Construction Projects" in K.R. Corcoran, ed., *Saudi Arabia: Keys to Business Success*, London: McGraw-Hill Book Co., 1981, 136-7.

16 *Wall Street Journal*, "Korean Construction Aid," Section 2, August 31, 1984: 16E.

17 C. Sweeney, "The End of a Building Boom," *Far Eastern Economic Review*, Vol. 109, No. 31, (July 25, 1980): 38-39.

18 Altinci Bes Yillik Kalkinma Plani 1990-1994 (Sixth Five Year Economic Development Plan) State Planning Organization, Ankara 1990, 281.

19 Turkish Contractors Association, *Review of the Development of Turkish Contracting Services*, Vol. 1, (May 17, 1990).

20 Chetan Shah and Sonal Shah, "Kuwait's Multibillion Dollar Opportunities," *Global Marketing Intelligence*, Portland, Oregon, 1991: 4.

21 Ali M. Radwan and Howard L. Stovall, "Reconstruction of Kuwait: Emerging Legal Issues," *Middle East Executive Reports*, Vol. 14, no. 4, (April 1991): 4.

22 In the preparation of this part the principal authors have received help of Ergin Akyruek of the Istanbul Chambers of Trade.

For more on this, see Ergin Akyurek, "A New Opportunity for Turkish Economy: Contractor Services Abroad," *Journal of the Istanbul Chambers of Commerce*, Volume 4, No. 10, (April-June, 1984): 22-29.

23 "Foreign Contracting Services" (in Turkish), *Daily Dunya*, December 7, 1984: 2.

24 S. Lall, "Exports of Technology by Newly Industrializing Countries," Special Issue of *World Development*, Vol. 12, No. 5/6 (May-June, 1984): 505-533.

25 A. Erdilek, "International Technology Transfer in the Middle East," in Erdener Kaynak, ed., *International Business in the Middle East*, New York: Walter de Gruyter & Co., 1986, 98.

26 Turkish Contractors Association, 43.

27 State Planning Organization, *1991 Yearly Economic Development Program*, Ankara: SPO, 1990: 48.

28 Ergin Akyurek, "A New Opportunity for the Turkish Economy: Contractor Services Abroad,"25.

29 T. Sealy, "How the Young Entrepreneurs Made Their Way," VII.

30 L.T.Wells, *Third World Multinationals*, Cambridge, Massachusetts: The MIT Press, 1983, pp.126-129.

31 U.S.Shim, *Korean Construction in the Middle East*, Seoul: Bub Mun Sa Publishing Company, 1984, 129.

32 Ibid.

33 S.Lall, "Exports of Technology by Newly Industrializing Countries," 505-533.

34 "Korean Construction Aid," *Wall Street Journal*, Section 2, August 31, 1984, 15W.

35 Z. Sozen and H. Giritli, "Factors Affecting Construction Productivity: A Survey," *International Journal of Construction Management and Technology*, Vol. 2, No. 1, (1987): 49-61.

36 B. Lopinto, "Airport Development," *China Business Review*, Vol. 13, No. 4, (July-August 1986):43-48.

37 K. Finneran, "Factory-Built Homes: Beyond the Ticky-Tacky," *High Techonology*, Vol.6, No.1 (November 1986): 53-55.

38 Charles Epstein, "Gulf-War Aftermath: Building Up to a Construction Bonanza," *Multinational Business*, (Spring 1991): 29-34.

39 The Conference Board, *The Gulf War, Global Business White Papers*, No. 1, (May 1991): 4-5.

40 Business International, *IBS Doing Business in Turkey*, 7-8.

41 Lopinto, "Airport Development" 43-48.

42 Turkish Contractors Association, *Turkish Contracting Services*, 44.

43 M.A. Muspratt, "East Asia-Rim Projects," *Project Management Journal*, Vol. 18, No. 1, (March 1987): 63-67.

44 Erdener Kaynak and K.H. Lee, *Global Business: Asia-Pacific Dimentions*, London: Croom-Helm Company, 1989.

[29]

Brazilian Emerging Multinationals: A Conduit for Export of Technology

Raul de Gouvea Neto

Exports of technology by newly industrializing countries are an important development in the global economy. Foreign direct investment is one dimension of these technological trends. Multinational companies from Brazil, South Korea, India, Mexico, and other countries are currently operating in several markets around the globe. In the case of Brazil, exports of technology constitute an important step toward further diversification of exports and gains in global competitiveness. This article shows that Brazilian multinationals have engaged in the exportation of indigenous technology in areas where the level of sophistication is relatively high, encompassing a number of diverse industries, and showing a tendency to invest beyond its regional boundaries.

INTRODUCTION

Since the late 1970s, technological developments have fostered and dramatically influenced trends in international trade (Dunning, 1993; Kenwood and Loughheed, 1993). Exports of technology by newly industrialized countries (NICs) constitute an important phenome-

---

The author wishes to thank Anant Negandhi, Werner Baer, Rachel Davis, Vicki Jones, and anonymous reviewers for their helpful comments and suggestions.

The author is with Anderson Schools of Management, University of New Mexico, Albuquerque, NM 87131.

The International Executive, Vol. 37(6) 583–597 (November/December 1995)
 CCC 0020-6652/95/060583-15

non in the world economy (Lecraw, 1993; Li, 1994b; Porter, 1990; Sim and Theoh, 1994; UNCTAD, 1990).

Foreign direct investment (FDI) by multinationals from NICs challenge the conception that NICs are passive recipients of technology, with few indigenous technological export efforts. Multinationals from NICs are now active members of the estimated 37,000 multinational corporations (MNCs) boosting the world economy. Asia and Latin America are the main source of newcomers.

This article addresses the Brazilian experience. We selected cases from several Brazilian industries that encompass the major categories of technology exports. Our purpose is to illustrate how Brazilian companies are developing their entry strategies in overseas markets. The cases show that indigenous technology, i.e., technology developed in Brazil by Brazilian companies, enabled these companies to develop unique, firm-specific assets that facilitated their expansion overseas. Our cases also show that Brazilian multinationals do not follow the simplified characterization of multinationals from NICs, i.e., being limited to labor-intensive and unsophisticated activities. These cases illustrate the diversification and increasing sophistication of indigenous technologies being exported by Brazilian multinationals.

In the case of Brazil, exports of technology constitute a further step in that country's comprehensive move toward diversification of its exports and gains in global competitiveness (Bell, 1984; Katz, 1987; Lall, 1990). This step toward increased technological sophistication has strong implications for the world and for the Brazilian economy.

EXPORTS OF TECHNOLOGY BY NICs

Previous research on the export of technology tended to focus on the transfer of technology among industrialized countries. NICs were assumed to be buyers rather than creators of technology. Researchers assumed that these countries had an extremely weak technological base. These assumptions, however, began to be challenged in the late 1970s (Copley, 1990; Moore, 1983; Sapir, 1980). Researchers focused on the absorption and suitability of imported technology as well as on the development of indigenous technology. They noted the increasing technological trade among NICs and the appearance of multinationals from NICs on the world trade scene (Ablin, 1985; Aggarwal and Agmon, 1990; Dahlman and Sercovich, 1984; 1985; Li, 1994a; Monkiewicz, 1986). Multinationals from NICs are now conduits for the export of technology from different industries encompassing complex skills and technology. They design and build plants, engage in engineering consulting services, set up foreign direct investment, and engage in licensing indigenous technology to overseas clients (Lall, 1983; Lall and Mohamed, 1983).

Technology exports from NICs fall into seven major categories: infrastructure (construction), consulting, technological services, licensing, industrial projects, capital goods exports, and FDI (Diaz–Alejandro, 1977; Villela, 1983; Wells, 1983; White, 1981).

BRAZILIAN TECHNOLOGICAL EFFORTS

In the early stage of industrialization, Brazil relied heavily on the import of technology (Randall, 1993). The inflows of technology took the form of FDI, disembodied technology (e.g., patents, licenses, technical services, etc.), and capital goods imports. Efforts were made to understand, assimilate, and adapt "alien" technology to meet Brazilian needs (Bastos, 1993; Dahlman and Fonseca, 1987; Randal, 1993; Schmitz and Cassiolato, 1992). Economic growth and export diversification demanded a strong technological base. It was imperative therefore to develop technological capability and indigenous technology. In many cases the state had a decisive role in providing the environment for such developments. Thus, the Brazilian experience is a symbiotic mix of market forces and state intervention (Evans, 1989; Ferreira and Mota, 1987; Franko–Jones, 1992; Vieira, 1991).

There is a considerable degree of heterogeneity in the profile of Brazilian exports of technology. In the late 1970s, the majority of exports of technology were concentrated in licensing, consulting, technical services (LCTS), and industrial projects. In the 1980s and 1990s, however, investments in manufacturing, retailing, banking, and telecommunications increased in importance. This article provides cases to illustrate the breadth of Brazilian indigenous technology exports and also to shed light on the evolution of these exports.

For instance, the integration and development of the Brazilian economy during the last 30 years has been responsible for a massive number of infrastructure projects. Reliance on domestic engineering firms, an infant industry approach sponsored by the Brazilian government, enabled engineering firms and manufacturing firms to complete large scale projects under the most difficult conditions in record time. The building of the Transamazonica and other roads in the Amazon forest, offshore oil exploration, and the large hydroelectric plants, bridges, and highways have resulted in indigenous technological competence and expertise that in the 1990s is being exported to both developed and developing countries (Gomes, 1994; Pedroso, 1992).

BRAZILIAN EMERGING MULTINATIONALS

This section elaborates on the experience of several Brazilian firms and their efforts and strategies to internationalize their operations. Our cases show that Brazilian multinationals do not follow the simplified characterization of multinationals from NICs, i.e., being limited to labor-intensive and unsophisticated technological activities. Rather, these cases show the diversification and increasing sophistication of the indigenous technologies that are being exported by Brazilian multinationals. The cases concentrate on the following industries: oil, construction, aircraft manufacturing, mining, retailing, capital goods, and telecommunications.

Technical Services

Petrobras, the Brazilian state-owned oil company, was established in 1953 through Law No. 2,004 that created the oil monopoly (Dias, 1993). The lack of trained personnel in the area of petroleum geophysics and geology led Petrobras to contract foreign experts. At the same time, the company started an intensive program to train skilled personnel abroad and use them in Brazil to spread their knowledge. Petrobras has improved and developed technologies to meet Brazil's diverse geographic conditions that range from equatorial forests in the Amazon to desert conditions in the northeast (Petrobras, 1993a). In 1972 Petrobras started its operations outside Brazil's borders with its first subsidiary. Braspetro was created mainly to solidify the country's access to oil reserves overseas. Since then, Petrobras has expanded to two international subsidiaries: Braspetro and Brasoil. Braspetro explores oil and sells services abroad, while Brasoil is responsible for drilling operations. Petrobras' engineering department, Segen, has provided technical support in overseas negotiations and bidding (Petrobras, 1993a,b).

As of 1993, by either engaging in joint ventures or operating alone, Braspetro has developed projects in 24 countries on five continents. Braspetro efforts are focused in three main areas: exploration and production, services and technical assistance, and marketing petroleum and other products. In the exploration and production areas, Braspetro discovered two enormous oil fields in Iraq, the Majnoon and Nahr Umr fields. The two oil fields are among the largest in the world in the past two decades, amounting to 10 billion barrels of recoverable oil. In the late 1980s Braspetro also began exploring the Norwegian and British sides of the North Sea, as well as the US gulf of Mexico. In 1993, Braspetro signed an agreement with Yacimientos Petroliferos Fiscales Bolovianos (YPFB) for the supply of 105 billion cubic meters of natural gas. Petrobras will be the company responsible for laying the gas pipeline between the two countries (Petrobras, 1994).

In the service and technical assistance category, Brasoil is also undertaking drilling operations in Africa and Latin America. Braspetro trains engineers from other countries in the fields of geology, geophysics, and petroleum engineering. Braspetro also offers a wide array of technical services, ranging from the processing and interpretation of geophysical data to the optimization of drilling schedules (Petrobras, 1993b).

Petrobras' world recognition for its R&D accomplishments came in May 1992, when the company was awarded the Offshore Technology Conference's (OTC) Distinguished Achievement Award. This award represents the highest international recognition in offshore technology. Because most of Brazil's oil reserves are located offshore, deepwater production technology was given priority after the first oil shock. During the 1980s, the company established indigenous technological programs such as Procap (Petrobras Technological Development Program on Deepwater Production Systems), which have culminated in a number of successful completions and deepwater production records. By 1993, Petrobras had established several world records, such as the deepest oil strike, the deepest pipeline laying, and the deepest producing well (Petrobras, 1993a).

Industrial Projects

In 1975, Brazil launched the National Alcohol Program (Proalcool). This initiative enabled Brazil to substitute alcohol for gasoline in order to reduce its dependence on imported oil (Souza, 1987). The project was feasible because the country had the technology and production capacity. By encouraging the production of alcohol from sugar cane, manioc, and other sources the Proalcool also stimulated the expansion of the equipment industry. As a result of Proalcool's success several countries became interested in developing similar plans. Thus, the sector became an active exporter of alcohol plants, distillery projects, and technology (Ferreira and Motta, 1987).

A good example may be provided by the company Codistil which was established in 1943, and 3 years later, with its own technology, constructed a distillery. Today it produces not only autonomous units connected to sugar mills, but also distilleries producing alcohol from manioc and other sources. Its first activity abroad was in Bolovia in 1964. Since then distilleries have been sold to Paraguay, Venezuela, Argentina, Costa Rica, and Honduras. Codistil supplies equipment, handles construction, accompanies operations, and trains operators.

Infrastructure Projects

Norberto Odebrecht Engineering, the largest private Brazilian multinational, started international operations in Peru in 1979. By 1994, Norberto Odebrecht Engineering was operating in 18 countries. International operations in 1993 accounted for half of the company's US $2 billion gross revenues (Rossi, 1993). By 1994 Norberto Odebrecht was developing operations in Latin America, Africa, Europe, and the United States. In Latin America the company is taking advantage of Mercosul, the South American common market, by expanding its operations to neighboring Argentina. With local partners, the engineering company has built hotels, hydroelectric plants, highways, and airports. The company is now focusing on the American market (Camargo, 1994; Pinto, 1993). Norberto Odebrecht Engineering was attracted to the US $500 billion American market for several reasons. First, the company intends to increase revenues and profits. Second, it desires access to the state of the art managerial and human resources techniques. And third, the company is seeking increased market diversification. In the United States the firm created a joint venture with a American company, resulting in the Odebrecht Chuch & Tower. The joint-venture approach advanced its knowledge of the American market. By 1993 Norberto Odebrecht was developing eight projects in the US market amounting to US $144 million (Rubio, 1993).

Aircraft Manufacturing

In some cases, FDI is being practiced by state-owned enterprises. In spite of the general skepticism regarding the capabilities of public enterprises for effectively manufacturing and exporting high-technology nonstandardized products, the Brazilian government sponsored the creation of Embraer (Vernon, 1981). This company was established in 1969 and specialized in the production of planes with relatively low technological content. The second generation of planes, initiated in the late 1970s, incorporated higher technology. The company began exporting in 1975 (Franko–Jones, 1992; Gouvea, 1991).

By the mid-1990s Embraer had its planes operating on five continents. In addition to its exports, Embraer established subsidiaries in the United States (Embraer Aircraft Corporation) and in France (Embraer Aviation International). These subsidiaries promote foreign sales and after sales services. Recently, the company initiated joint ventures in developed and underdeveloped countries. Embraer developed the T-27 Tucano turboprop, a trainer aircraft, in association with Short Brothers in Ireland. In addition to manufacturing these airplanes in Belfast, both companies have plans to explore activities such as a new generation of commuter aircraft. Another joint venture was established with Egypt in 1983. The Embraer T-27 Tucano is also built in there. Embraer exports structural components to be assembled by the Arab Industrialization Organization. In 1990 Embraer began developing, with the Argentinian state aircraft manufacturer FAMA, the CBA-123, a 19 seat turbofan commuter (Franko–Jones, 1992; Gouvea, 1991).

Mining

Companhia Vale do Rio Doce (CVRD), Brazil's largest state trading company and the world's largest producer and exporter of iron ore, engaged in a massive program of diversification inside and outside the mining field. The company sells ore to over 41 countries around the world. It established subsidiaries in Europe and the United States to serve as marketing arms for the Brazilian parent corporations. These subsidiaries in turn are responsible for keeping stockpiles of iron abroad. In addition, the company undertakes joint ventures with international firms to mine coal in Canada and the Pacific. It has also sold its expertise in mines, ports, and railways to several countries. As part of its verticalization strategy, in 1985 CVRD, in association with the American Wilkinson group and Kawasaki of Japan, acquired Fontana Steel in the United States. The Fontana plant produces steel products for the western American market (CVRD, 1993).

In 1992 CVRD continued its drive toward the diversification, verticalization, and globalization of its activities. This was particularly true in the areas of minerals and forestry resources. CVRD acquired an interest in the Rio Doce Pasha Terminal at the Port of Los Angeles, acquired stock in the French company SEAS, and also acquired interest in the Argentinian company Propulsora Siderurgica (CVRD, 1993).

Retailing

In 1969 the Pao de Acucar retailing chain opened its first foreign supermarket in Europe. The early 1970s saw the company expand its operations to Africa. Pao de Acucar Industria e Comercio, the largest retail company in Latin America, controls 50% of the biggest supermarket chain in Portugal, with 33 stores and 3 shopping centers. The retailer is also the major outlet in Angola. In Spain, Pan de Azucar SA leases the trademark and technical assistance of the Brazilian group. One of the factors behind the success of its operations has been its retail technology. According to the director-superintendent Abilio Diniz:, "In terms of supply, Brazil is now just as up-to-date as any other country. In the areas of supermarkets, shopping centers, department stores and other types of outlets we have just as much know-how as the more developed nations" (Brazil Trade and Industry, 1982). The company has offices in Argentina and the Ivory Coast, and Luxembourg is the headquarters of its international holding company. Pao de Acucar has given priority to Brazilian manufactured products and food items (Loureiro and Santos, 1991).

Telecommunications

Globo TV Network started off in 1965. It is Brazil's largest broadcasting TV network, ranking fourth in the world after ABC, NBC, and CBS in the United States. By 1969 it had become a national network, using the Intelsat satellite for transmissions in Brazil. Today Globo has 94 stations in Latin America and has already set up subsidiaries in both the United States and Europe. The company has successfully marketed its programs abroad. Its main products "telenovelas" (soap operas), miniseries, and movies are being exported to more than 90 countries. In the United States market the company exports dubbed programs for Spanish-language networks. The main factor behind the company's performance abroad is its outstanding production capabilities. In an import substitution strategy, the company considerably reduced its dependence on foreign made programs. Now 78% of its primetime programming is produced in-house. Thus, over time, it has acquired the necessary technology and skills needed to produce its own products (O Globo, 1993).

The company's decision to invest abroad was largely due to two factors: the constraints of the Brazilian market, and a developed and growing market for its programs abroad. Thus, the company followed the steps of an expansionary development growth strategy, paved partially by previous exports. The company established a long-range plan to acquire broadcasting stakes in several European countries. In 1976 Globo TV created an international division; in 1979 it set up an international sales division, based in Rome, to license its programs worldwide, exempting the United States and Latin America. In 1984 Globo TV set up a holding company (Globo International Company Ltd.) based in Nassau, Bahamas. The holding company is composed of four subsidiaries: Globo International London Ltd, Globo TV Distribution SRL–Rome, Globo International New York Ltd, and Sigla Quattro (O Globo, 1993).

In 1985 Globo associated with the Ferruzi Group resulting in Tele-Montecarlo (TMC), giving Globo access to the Italian market. In the same year the company negotiated with the Societe Speciale D'Enterprise (SSE) of Monaco for a controlling position in TMC's broadcasting to the Principality of Monaco and to southern France. Globo's European expansion strategy also included other European countries. In France the company is working in conjunction with Tele-Luxemburg, to develop the operation of a French commercial cable channel (Multi-Ville). In 1992, Globo established the Sociedade Independente de Comunicacao-SIC in Portugal. In the United States Globo TV has established a foothold by purchasing a Los Angeles Spanish-language cable station (O Globo, 1993).

INTERNATIONALIZATION STRATEGIES

Brazilian service and manufacturing multinationals expanded their activities overseas as result of firm- and environment-specific factors and conditions. Table 1 covers some of the main factors related to the expansion of NIC's multinationals to overseas markets.

On the firm-specific side, the Brazilian cases have shown a very

Table 1. Firm- and Environment-Specific Factors Related to Internationalization of NIC's Multinationals

Firm Specific
Indigenous technology breakthroughs (Bell, 1984; Copley, 1990; Dahlman and Cortez, 1984, Dahlman and Sercovich, 1985; Katz, 1987, Lall, 1983; Lall and Mohamed, 1983; Mokiewicz, 1986; Vernon, 1981)
Special asset (Bell, 1984; Dalhman and Sercovich, 1985; Diaz–Alejandro, 1977; Dunning, 1993; Lecraw, 1993; Li, 1994b)
Appropriateness of process and product technologies to overseas markets (Dahlman and Fonseca, 1987; Lall, 1990; Loureiro and Santos, 1991; Schmitz and Cassiolato, 1992; Sim and Teoph, 1994; Villela, 1983)
Natural development of a firm's growth strategy, pecking order stage in the product life cycle of some technologies (Wells, 1983)
Lower operational cost sites (Sim and Teoph, 1994; Li, 1994a)
Economies of scale (Aggarwal and Agmon, 1990; Erramilli and Rao, 1990)
Cultural and ethnic ties (Lecraw, 1993; Li, 1994b; Villela, 1983)
Environment Specific
Size limitation and growth potential of domestic market (Ablin, 1985; Caves, 1982; Papadopoulos, 1993; Root, 1987)
Incentives from international agencies (Li, 1994b; Villela, 1983)
Home government policies inducing export of embodied and disembodied technologies (Villela, 1983)
Regional economic integration (Loureiro and Santos, 1991; Sim and Teoph, 1994)
Exchange rate controls, avoidance of tax burdens, and labor legislation (Aggarwal and Agmon, 1990; Erramilli and Rao, 1990; Lecraw, 1993; Li, 1994; Monkiewicz, 1986)

distinctive and common element: indigenous technology developments. All the examples listed indicate that these companies developed firm-specific assets related to their indigenous technological efforts. For instance, Petrobras has been able to operate internationally largely as a function of its deep-water exploration technology. The aircraft company, Embraer, has developed several product and process technologies allowing the company to export and invest overseas. The possibility of exploiting additional rents from firm-specific advantages was also a factor behind the internationalization of firms like TV Globo and the giant retailer Pao de Acucar.

On the resource side, one single factor is present in all cases: heavy expenditures on R&D and a solid technological base. The mastery of know-how and the development of indigenous technology has contributed to the internalization of these companies.

Appropriate process and product technologies largely explained the penetration of Brazilian engineering companies in overseas markets. The assimilation, adaptation, and innovation steps taken by these engineering companies have allowed them to develop price and nonprice competitive advantages. For instance, Brazilian engineering companies have shown a great deal of flexibility by engaging in labor-intensive and capital-intensive projects. Because they were able to adapt their indigenous technology to meet the needs of different working environments, these companies have become very competitive at the international level. That would also explain their wide market range, from countries in Africa to projects in the American market. These engineering companies have also developed nonprice competitiveness. For instance, they have developed a tradition of working under very difficult environmental conditions on a large scale and have developed the ability to train contingents of nonqualified labor on a large scale.

Several Brazilian multinationals expanded their operations overseas following their growth and development strategies. The aircraft manufacturer Embraer is a good example. The company expanded its operations to follow the global trends of the aircraft industry. Embraer had to be closer to its main markets and competitors to keep abreast of technological innovations in the aircraft industry. In addition, economies of scale were putting pressure on the company's delocalization strategies. Without international markets Embraer would not be able to keep upgrading the technological content of its products. Norberto Odebrecht also moved to the US market to have access to more sophisticated managerial and human resource techniques.

Cultural and ethnic ties were important factors in the internationalization strategies of some Brazilian multinationals international strategies. TV Globo, for instance, started its international involvement in neighboring countries and gradually expanded its operations to Europe and the United States. In Europe priority was given to Latin speaking countries and in the United States the Hispanic community was TV Globo's main target. Another Brazilian multinational, Pao de Acucar, decided to first expand to Portuguese-speaking African countries. Later, the company moved to Portugal and Spain. The cultural and ethnic ties played an important role in the early internationalization process of these companies.

Environment-specific factors have played a meaningful role in the internationalization process of Brazilian multinationals. In all of the cases mentioned, the Brazilian market became too small for these companies to continue expanding their operations. In addition, down swings and slow growth rates in the Brazilian market contributed to the outward-looking strategy of most companies in our sample. Engineering companies, for instance, started their international expansion in the late 1970s. The Brazilian economy was then showing the first signs of what would be called the "lost decade," the 1980s. Heavily dependent on government contracts, Brazilian engineering companies were forced to expand overseas to offset sluggish growth domestically. In all cases, long-term commitment to international markets was achieved when the Brazilian market no longer satisfied the firm's overall growth strategies.

Regional economic integration motivated Brazilian companies to expand their operations to neighboring countries. Mercosul, the South American common market, has induced a number of joint ventures and cross-border investments. Norberto Odebrecht, the engineering company, expanded its operations in Argentina after the creation of Mercosul in 1991 (Camargo, 1994).

The companies in our sample have pursued a wide variety of entry strategies. First, they used exports as an initial approach to international markets. Second, after gaining experience in neighboring countries, most of the companies in our sample moved toward European, American, and African markets. In this second stage, joint ventures were the preferred entry mode. Like European and Japanese multinationals, Brazilian multinationals saw a number of advantages in developing business linkages with partners in these overseas markets. Market knowledge and technology sharing were cited as the major driving forces behind joint ventures. In our sample Embraer, Norberto Odebrecht, and CVRD cited these two factors as driving forces for their joint-venture strategies. Several companies also adopted wholly owned strategies. Pao de Acucar, TV Globo, and CVRD developed 100% ownership strategies by acquiring already established companies instead of building overseas branches.

CONCLUSION

This study shows the importance of indigenous technology to the expansion of Brazilian companies in the global economy. The article argued that the internationalization of Brazilian companies was strongly related to mastery of know-how and indigenous technological efforts. As a common element, all the companies listed have developed firm-specific assets related to their indigenous technological efforts. The existence of competitive process and product technologies facilitated the penetration of these companies in developed and less developed markets.

Other factors related to initial entry can be categorized as firm specific or environment specific. On the firm-specific side, we can mention development of special assets, appropriateness of process and product technology, natural development of a firm's growth, economies of scale, and cultural and ethnic ties. On the environment-specific side, we can mention size limitations and growth potential of the Brazilian market, incentives from international agencies, and regional trading blocks.

The cases indicate that Brazilian companies sought alternative entry strategies. As a rule, exports were their first mode of entry, followed by joint ventures and 100% ownership strategies. Brazilian companies tended to be very flexible in the formulation of their entry strategies.

In conclusion, for the Brazilian economy exports of technology represent a step toward further diversification of its exports embodying a higher technological content and providing a dynamic impact on the comparative advantage of the Brazilian economy.

REFERENCES

Ablin, E. (1985) *Internationalizacion de Empresas y Tecnologia de Origem Argentino,* Buenos Aires: EUDEBA.

Aggarwal R. and Agmon, T. (1990) "The International Success of Developing Country Firms: Role of Government-Directed Comparative Advantage," *Management International Review,* 30, 163–180.

Bastos, M. (1993) "State Policies and Private Interests: The Struggle over Information Technology Policy in Brazil," in H. Schmitz and J. Cassiolato (Eds.), *High-Tech for Industrial Development,* London: Routledge.

Bell, M. (1984) "Learning and the Accumulation of Industrial Technology Capacity in Developing Countries" in M. Fransman and K. King (Eds.), *Technology Capability in the Third World,* London: MacMillan Press.

Camargo, G. (1994) "O Muro da Prata foi Demolido," *Exame,* Vol. 573, 18–25.

Caves, R. (1982) *Multinational Enterprise and Economic Analysis,* Cambridge, UK: Cambridge University Press.

Copley, B. (1990) "Technical Change in Latin America Manufacturing Firms: Review and Synthesis," *World Development,* 18, 1457–1469.

CVRD (1993) *1992 Annual Report,* Rio de Janeiro: Companhia Vale do Rio Doce (CVRD).

Dahlman, C. and Fonseca, F. (1987) "From Technological Dependence to Technological Development: The Case of the Usiminas Steelplant in Brazil," in J. Katz (Ed.), *Technology Generation in Latin American Manufacturing Industries,* Hong Kong: The MacMillan Press.

Dahlman, C. and Sercovich, F. (1984) "Export of Technology from Semi-Industrial Economies and Local Technological Development," *Journal of Development Economics,* 16, 63–111.

Dahlman, C. and Sercovich, F. (1985) "Local Development and Exports of Technology," World Bank Staff Working Papers, No. 667, Washington, DC: World Bank.

Dias, J. (1993) "Petrobras: Organizacao e Subsidiarias," *Revista de Administracao Publica,* 27, 47–68.

Diaz–Alejandro, C. (1977) "Foreign Direct Investment by Latin Americans," in T. Agmon and C. Kindleberger (Eds.), *Multinationals from Small Countries,* Cambridge, MA: MIT Press.

Dunning, J. (1993) *The Globalization of Business,* London: Routledge.

Evans, P. (1989) *High Technology Industry in the Americas,* Stanford, CA: Institute of the Americas.

Ferreira, L. and Motta, R. (1987) "Reavaliacao Economica e Novos Ajustamentos do Proalcool," *Revista Brasileira de Economia,* 41, 117–133.

Franko–Jones, P. (1992) *The Brazilian Defense Industry,* Boulder, CO: Westview Press.

Gomes, M. (1994) "Ser Multi nao e para Qualquer Um," *Exame,* 572, 36–39.

Gouvea, R. (1991) "How Brazil Competes in the Global Defense Industry," *Latin American Research Review,* 26, 83–108.

Katz, J. (1987) "Domestic Technology Generation in LDCs: A Review of Research Findings," in J. Katz (Ed.), *Technology Generation in Latin American Manufacturing Industries,* Hong Kong: MacMillan Press.

Kenwood and Lougheed, A. (1993) *The Growth of the International Economy,* New York: Routledge.

Lall, S. (1983) *The New Multinationals: The Spread of Third World Enterprises,* New York: Wiley.

Lall, S. (1990). *Building Industrial Competitiveness in Developing Countries,* Paris: Organization for Economic Co-Operation and Development (OECD).

Lall, S. and Mohamed, S. (1983) "Technological Effort and Disembodied Technology Exports: An Econometric Analysis of Inter-Industry Variations in India," *World Development,* 11, 527–535.

Lecraw, D. (1993) "Outward Direct Investment by Indonesian Firms: Motivation and Effects," *Journal of International Business Studies,* 24, 589–600.

Li, P. (1994a) "Strategy Profiles of Indigenous MNEs from the NIEs: The Case of South Korea and Taiwan," *The International Executive*, 26, 23–34.

Li, J. (1994b) "Experience Effects and International Expansion: Strategies of Service MNCs in the Asia-Pacific Region," *Management International Review*, 34, 217–234.

Loureiro, F. and Santos, A. (1991) "Internacionalizacao de Empresas Brasileiras," *Revista de Administracao*, 26, 23–34.

Monkiewicz, J. (1986) "Multinational Enterprises of Developing Countries: Some Emerging Characteristics," *Management International Review*, 26, 67–79.

Moore, F. (1983) "Technological Change and Industrial Development," World Bank Staff Working Papers, No. 613, Washington, DC: World Bank.

O Globo (1993) *Organizacoes Globo*, Rio de Janeiro: O Globo.

Pedroso, H. (1992) "Brasileiras Estao Fazendo a America," *Dirigente Contrutor*, XXVIII, 16–18.

Petrobras (1993a) *Petrobras Magazine*, No. 1, Rio de Janeiro: Petrobras.

Petrobras (1993b) *Annual Report 1992*, Rio de Janeiro: Petrobras.

Petrobras (1994) *Annual Report 1993*, Rio de Janeiro: Petrobras.

Pinto, C. (1993) "Expansao da Odebrecht na Europa," *Gazeta Mercantil*, Julho 12, 1.

Porter, M. (1990) *The Competitive Advantage of Nations*, New York: The Free Press.

Randall, L. (1993) *The Political Economy of Brazilian Oil*, London: Praeger.

Root, F. (1987) *Entry Strategies for International Markets*, Lexington, MA: Lexington Books.

Rossi, C. (1993) "Odebrecht Vira uma Gigante Multinacional" *Folha de Sao Paulo*, August 15, 10–11.

Rubio, P. (1993) "Odebrecht vai Fazer Baragem nos EUA," *Gazeta Mercantil*, August 2, 1.

Sapir, A. (1980) "Trade in Non-Factor Services: Past Trends and Current Issues," World Bank Staff Working Paper, No. 410, Washington, DC: World Bank.

Schmitz, H. and Cassiolato, J. (1992) *Hi-Tech for Industrial Development: Lessons from the Brazilian Experience in Electronics and Automation*, London: Routledge.

Sim, A. and Teoph, H. (1994) "Internationalization of Australian Business in the Asia-Pacific Region: Issues and Prospects," *The International Executive*, 36, 435–464.

Souza, M. (1987) Avaliacao Economica do Programa Nacional do Alcool (Pro-Alcool)," *Pesquisa e Planejamento Economico*, 17, 381–410.

UNCTAD (1990) *Transfer and Development of Technology in Developing Countries: A Compedium of Policy Issues*, New York: United Nations.

Vernon, R. (1981) "State-Owned Enterprises in Latin American Exports," in W. Baer and M. Gillis (Eds.), *Export Diversification and the New Protectionism: The Experience of Latin America*, Urbana, IL: National Bureau of Economic and Business Research, University of Illinois at Urbana–Champaign.

Vieira, D. (1991) "Capacitacao Tecnologica na Industria Brasileira," *Revista de Administracao*, 26, 48–57.

Villela, A. (1983) "Multinationals from Brazil," in S. Lall (Ed.), *The New Multinationals: The Spread of Third World Multinationals,* New York: Wiley.

Wells, L. (1983) *Third World Multinationals,* Cambridge, MA: MIT Press.

White, E. (1981) "The International Projection of Firms from Latin American Countries," in Kumar and MacLeod (Eds.), *Múltinationals from Developing Countries,* Lexington, MA: Lexington Books.

[30]

TAIWAN INVESTMENTS IN CHINA AND SOUTHEAST ASIA

"Go West, but Also Go South"

Xiangming Chen

Go West, young man, go West.

—Horace Greeley

The Americans historically went west, the Russians east, the Chinese south.

—S. Gordon Redding, *The Spirit of Chinese Capitalism*

Since the late 1980s, Taiwanese companies have "gone West" by investing heavily in China, primarily through Hong Kong. The early and mid-1990s also saw Taiwanese companies pursue an intensifying "go South" strategy of investing in such Southeast Asian countries as Indonesia, the Philippines, and Vietnam, continuing a trend of investing in Malaysia and Thailand since the late 1950s. The large flows of Taiwanese capital into China and Southeast Asia have begun to reshape the economic and political ties among these countries in the Asia-Pacific, with significant regional and global consequences. While the investment in China has been well documented, there is relatively little in the English literature on recent Taiwanese investment in Southeast Asia. Moreover, much less is known about whether and how the investments in China and Southeast Asia differ in terms of characteristics, determinants, and consequences and, more importantly, about how to explain the observed differences and similarities theoretically. In this article, I employ a systematic comparative approach to examining the charac-

Xiangming Chen is Assistant Professor in the Department of Sociology, University of Illinois at Chicago. An early version of this article was presented at the international conference, Taiwan in Asia, sponsored by the Center for East Asian and Pacific Studies, University of Illinois, Urbana-Champaign, March 31–April 1, 1995. The author is grateful to Hsiao-hung Nancy Chen and Steve J. F. Yan in Taiwan and Kathleen Crittenden, Yi-hsiung Huang and Dan Liou for providing valuable materials; Thomas B. Gold and a referee for comments on earlier drafts; and Yanmei Zhuo for research assistance. This project was supported in part by a grant from the Pacific Cultural Foundation in Taiwan.

teristics and determinants of Taiwanese investments in China and Southeast Asian countries, thus establishing a broad empirical basis and an integrated explanatory framework to guide further comparative research.

I begin by providing a general statistical comparison of Taiwanese investment trends in China and Southeast Asia, and then focus on the salient features of Taiwanese investment in the two areas at the regional, industry, and firm levels; in the next section, I examine how and why Taiwanese companies "go both West and South," thus creating cross-national economic ties between China and Southeast Asia, and assess different arguments about the actual and perceived tradeoffs of Taiwanese companies "going West vs. going South." The next section synthesizes key determinants of Taiwanese investments in China and/or Southeast Asia by suggesting that these investments from the mid-1980s through the mid-1990s have been shaped by a temporal conjuncture of economic comparative and complementary advantages at the national, industry, and firm levels, the internationalization of state-business relations, historical legacy, cultural and ethnic ties, subregional integration, and locational advantages. Finally, I draw brief conclusions and identify primary consequences of Taiwanese investments in China and Southeast Asia for future comparative research.

General Statistical Comparison

Table 1 compares Taiwanese investments in China, five ASEAN countries, and Vietnam during 1959-93. Although trailing some Southeast Asian countries during the late 1980s, China absorbed a much larger volume of Taiwanese capital than all Southeast Asian countries in both 1992 and 1993, during which 66% of Taiwan's total outward investment flowed into China.[1] A dramatic shift of Taiwanese investment from Southeast Asia to China occurred in 1992, when the ratio of investment in China to that in Southeast Asia stood at 2.8:1 compared with 1:2.5 in 1991. Second, Taiwanese investments in all ASEAN countries declined during the early 1990s, when Vietnam received a growing amount of capital from Taiwan. At US$0.92 million per case, Taiwan's cumulative average investment in China was less capital intensive than in all Southeast Asian countries, except the Philippines at US$0.64 million per case. This higher average capital intensity in Southeast Asia reflects two new economic trends in the region: (1) rising production (mainly labor) costs in Malaysia and Thailand and efforts by both countries to stop promoting labor-intensive industries; and (2) growing investment from

1. The referee commented that Taiwan's investment in China involves used equipment that might be spruced up to look new and bring higher valuation, which could benefit the Taiwan investor in determining his equity contribution in a joint venture. There were also contracted investments that were later canceled but went unreported. Both factors might have contributed to an upward bias of the annual statistical series on investment in Table 1.

TABLE 1 *Taiwan's Annual New Investments in China and Southeast Asian Countries, 1959–1993*

	Year							
Country: Indicator	*1959–1986*	*1987*	*1988*	*1989*	*1990*	*1991*	*1992*	*1993*
China[a]								
(1) Capital (US$m)	220.00		420.00	500.00	1,000.00	1,310.00	5,547.00	5,520.00
(2) Case	80		335	547	1,117	1,701	6,430	5,602
(3) 1 ÷ 2 (US$m)	2.75		1.25	.91	.90	.77	.86	.99
Singapore								
(1) Capital (US$m)	61.62	.01	.67	.54	3.16	23.73	.19	—
(2) Case	48	1	3	1	3	4	1	—
(3) 1 ÷ 2 (US$m)	1.28	.01	.22	.54	1.05	5.93	.19	—
Malaysia								
(1) Capital (US$m)	50.89	91.00	313.00	815.00	2,383.00	1,314.00	602.00	346.50
(2) Case	138	37	111	191	270	182	137	86
(3) 1 ÷ 2 (US$m)	.37	2.46	2.82	4.27	8.83	7.22	4.39	4.03
Thailand								
(1) Capital (US$m)	577.45	307.58	859.94	892.20	782.59	593.46	289.92	215.00
(2) Case	157	102	308	214	144	69	44	61
(3) 1 ÷ 2 (US$m)	3.68	3.02	2.79	4.17	5.44	8.60	6.59	3.52
Indonesia								
(1) Capital (US$m)	170.00	8.40	913.00	158.00	618.00	1,056.50	563.30	131.40
(2) Case	3	3	17	50	93	56	23	21
(3) 1 ÷ 2 (US$m)	56.67	2.80	53.71	3.16	6.65	18.87	24.49	6.26
The Philippines								
(1) Capital (US$m)	7.82	9.04	109.87	148.69	140.65	11.61	9.27	5.37
(2) Case	54	43	86	190	158	109	27	21
(3) 1 ÷ 2 (US$m)	.14	.21	1.28	.78	.89	.11	.34	.26
Vietnam								
(1) Capital (US$m)	—	—	—	1.00	104.43	457.66	531.41	436.54
(2) Case	—	—	—	1	18	28	23	47
(3) 1 ÷ 2 (US$m)	—	—	—	1.00	5.80	16.35	23.10	9.29

SOURCES: Taiwan's Ministry of Economic Affairs data on contracted investment approved by the various host governments, adapted from (1) Hsiao-hung Nancy Chen. "An Overview of Taiwan's Investment in Mainland China and Southeast Asia," chap. 5, pp. 188–89 in *Industrial Structural Change and Trends in Interaction Between Mainland China and Taiwan* (in Chinese) (Taipei: Chung-Hua Institution for Economic Research, June 1993), and (2) Steve J. F. Yan, "View the Development of Taiwan's Enterprises from the Westward and Southward Policy" (in Chinese), paper presented at the Conference on Economic Development across the Straits and Economic Cooperation in the Asia-Pacific, Chinese University of Hong Kong, Hong Kong, June 1994.

[a] For China, data for 1959–86 also include 1987 (almost all of the investment during that time period was made from the mid-1980s): the 1993 data are for January through June.

the newly industrialized countries (NICs), primarily Taiwan and South Korea, in more capital-intensive industries such as steel and petrochemicals in Malaysia and cement in Indonesia.[2]

2. Junko Takeuchi, "Trends and Prospect for Foreign Investment in ASEAN Countries in the 1990s," *Rim: Pacific Business and Industries*, 1:27 (1995), pp. 22-41.

TABLE 2 *Taiwan-Invested Factories in China and Southeast Asia, by Employment Size and Type, 1992*

Employment: Size and Type	China		Southeast Asia[a]	
	No. of Firms[b]	*Percentage*[c]	*No. of firms*	*Percentage*
Total employment				
Below 100	20	29.9	9	31.0
101–200	18	26.9	8	27.6
201–300	11	16.4	2	6.9
301–500	10	14.9	2	6.9
501–1,000	7	10.4	7	24.1
1,001–1,500	0	0.0	0	0.0
Over 1,501	1	1.5	1	3.4
Total	67	100.0	29	99.9
Managers				
0	2	3.0	0	0.0
1–10	29	43.3	10	37.0
11–20	18	26.9	8	29.6
21–50	11	16.4	6	22.2
51–100	6	9.0	3	11.1
Over 101	1	1.5	0	0.0
Total	67	100.1	27	99.9
Engineers and technicians				
0	4	7.4	0	0.0
1–10	36	66.7	13	54.2
11–20	8	14.8	4	16.7
21–50	5	9.3	4	16.7
51–100	0	0.0	0	0.0
Over 101	1	1.9	3	12.5
Total	54	100.1	24	100.1

SOURCE: See Table 1, chap. 6, p. 206.
[a] Includes only Malaysia, Thailand, Indonesia, the Philippines, and Vietnam.
[b] Based on an early 1993 survey of 89 and 41 Taiwan-invested factories in China and Southeast Asia, respectively. The discrepancies between the number of factories reported and factories surveyed are accounted for by incomplete responses to the questions.
[c] Some percentages do not add up to 100.0 due to rounding.

Survey data at the firm level confirm the aggregate difference between Taiwanese investments in China and Southeast Asia regarding average capital intensity (see Table 2). Only 11.9% of the surveyed Taiwan-invested factories in China had over 500 employees, compared with 27.5% in the five ASEAN countries. To the extent that firm size is positively associated with capital intensity, a greater share of larger Taiwan-invested factories in Southeast Asia indicates their greater capital intensity. While 26.9% and 11.2% of Taiwan-invested factories in China had over 20 managers and technical staff, respectively, the corresponding figures for Southeast Asia were 33.3% and 29.2%, reflecting a stronger capital and technological orientation than those in China. The tabular data provide a statistical basis for a more focused and detailed comparison of the differences and similarities between Taiwanese investments in China and Southeast Asia.

Go West: Investing in China

The trickle of Taiwanese investment into China through Hong Kong in the early 1980s turned into a torrent late in the decade. The total stock of Taiwanese capital in China, however, remains difficult to estimate, and the figures vary across time periods and information sources. During 1986-91, between 2,500 and 4,000 Taiwanese companies invested approximately US$3 billion in China. By the end of 1992, Taiwan's investment amounted to US$9 billion in 10,245 ventures,[3] making it the second largest foreign investor in China after Hong Kong. According to the data in Table 1, cumulative Taiwanese investment in China reached US$14.5 billion through June 1993 with a total of 15,812 ventures.

By mid-1994, the number of Taiwan-invested factories and establishments in China was estimated to be approximately 15,000, with about US$4 billion in new investment under contract from January to May. The upper end of the total investment was estimated to be close to, or even exceed US$20 billion in some 20,000 ventures, the majority of which are manufacturing facilities. And a more recent report put cumulative contracted Taiwanese investment in China at US$26.3 billion in 29,500 joint ventures by June 1995. In the second half of 1995, the mainland-Taiwan relationship deteriorated, primarily due to Lee Teng-hui's visit to the United States. Investment slowed down considerably, and at the beginning of 1996 China's military threat through missile tests caused a further reduction. The Investment Commission of Taiwan's Ministry of Economic Affairs approved only 36 projects capitalized at US$71 million in January 1996, 27% less than in the same month of 1995.[4] Balancing the above sources leads to a rough estimate that the cumulative stock of Taiwanese investment in China today falls in a range of US$20–25 billion involving between 25,000 and 30,000 ventures.

3. Hsiao-hung Nancy Chen, "An Overview of Taiwan's investments in Mainland China and Southeast Asia," in *Industrial Structural Change and Trends in Interaction Between Mainland China and Taiwan* (in Chinese) (Taipei: Chung-Hua Institution for Economic Research, June 1993), p. 180.

4. Charles H. C. Kao, Chu-Chia Steve Lin, Cher Hsu and Wennie Lin, *The Taiwan Investment Experience in Mainland China: A First-hand Report* (in Chinese) (Taipei: Commonwealth Publishing Co., 1995), p. 43; *Central Daily News* (hereafter *CDN*), intnl. ed., February 11, 1996, p. 1; *Renmin Ribao*, overseas edition, November 1, 1995, p. 5.

Investment in China has generally been labor rather than capital intensive, due to the massive relocation to the mainland of Taiwan's small and medium-sized firms in highly labor-intensive industries. By 1992 plastic and rubber, electrical and electronic products, and food and beverages accounted for 26.3%, 16.5%, and 15.6% of Taiwan's total investment in China, ranking the top three in terms of industry shares. By July 1994 the rankings of the top three industries shifted to electrical and electronics (14%), food and beverages (12.1%), and plastics and rubber (11.7%).[5] More recent Taiwanese investment has shifted from labor-intensive, low value-added, and short-term operations to more capital- and technology-intensive industries with longer investment horizons such as automobiles, computers, machinery, and petrochemicals. During January-August 1994, capitalization of the average approved Taiwan investment project peaked at US$2.1 million. Taiwan's largest PC maker and the world's seventh largest—Acer Computer, Inc.—has invested US$2 million in Suzhou, Jiangsu Province, to manufacture monitors, and half of the capital is valued as technology transfer. Having set up an "electronics street" in Shanghai earlier, some Taiwanese computer and information processing companies have recently planned to create a 2 km^2 science-based industrial park in Shanghai, with a total investment of US$60 million, to promote computer and telecommunications industries. A petrochemical company has committed US$100 million to building a plant in Huizhou, Guangdong Province, to make ABC resin and PVC (polyvinyl chloride). A rubber company and a plastics company have been approved by the Ministry of Economic Affairs to invest US$30 million and US$20 million in China, respectively.

Taiwanese investment in China is generally concentrated in a few geographical areas in Guangdong and Fujian provinces. In 1991 four southeastern coastal cities—Guangzhou and Shenzhen in Guangdong and Xiamen and Fuzhou in Fujian—accounted for 45% of the investment cases and 44% of the contracted capital. Although Taiwanese investment continues to cluster in these cities, it has recently begun to move north and west within China. Shenzhen and Xiamen's shares of Taiwan's total investment dropped from 14.8% and 12.2% in 1991 to 9.6% and 6.9% in 1993, while Shanghai's share rose from 11.5% to 12.1%. During 1991–94 Shanghai accounted for 11.2% and 13% of all Taiwan investment cases and capital in China, leading the top six cities with the most investment (the other five being Shenzhen, Dongguan, Xiamen, Guangzhou, and Fuzhou in that order). By July 1994 Jiangsu Province (excluding Shanghai) took in 13.2% of all Taiwanese investment in China, topping all provincial and municipal shares. The proportion of

5. Ming-ying Chan, "Issues Regarding the Development of Economic and Trade Exchanges across the Strait." (in Chinese) *Tai-Gang-Ao Ji Haiwai Maoyi* (Taiwan-Hong Kong-Macao and Overseas Trade), no. 8 (1995), p. 9.

Taiwanese investment in provinces other than the southeast coastal region (Guangdong, Fujian, Jiangsu, Zhejiang, Shanghai) rose from 22.4% during 1991-93 to 25.4% in 1994.[6]

The spatial diffusion of Taiwanese investment in China has also been fostered by new investment by firms already operating there. One of Taiwan's oldest and largest food processing companies, Wei Chuan, first built factories in Fujian and Guangxi provinces, but in the second half of 1994, it developed new plans to set up a canned food factory in Huangyan, Zhejiang Province, a joint-venture fast food factory in Luohe, Henan Province, and a milk powder factory in Heilongjiang Province. Another giant Taiwanese food company, President Enterprise, has increased its joint-venture or affiliated factories in China from one to 17 since 1992 in all major regions of the country, with cumulative investment of US$180 million, becoming the investor with the widest geographical spread and largest cumulative capital of all Taiwanese companies in China.[7]

Another striking feature of Taiwan-invested factories in China is that they tend to be wholly Taiwan owned. Three separate surveys have shown that about 55% of these factories in the early 1990s involved 100% Taiwanese capital, but varying across industries and localities from a low of 33% for plastics in Shanghai to a medium of 47% for electrical machine tools in Guangdong to a high of 92% for garments in Fujian. Taiwanese investors have preferred wholly owned ventures to joint ventures because of: (1) incompatibility with potential mainland partners in business values, management styles, and company goals and strategies; (2) lack of familiarity with the mainland business environment; and (3) small and medium-sized firms using their own material supplies, production equipment, and export channels.[8] As Taiwanese firms become more familiar with China's business environment, as more large firms begin to invest in China, and as China's domestic market opens up more widely, there should be a gradual shift in Taiwanese investment from wholly owned to joint ventures.

Also Go South: Investing in Southeast Asia

While the Taiwanese government officially initiated the "go South" policy in 1994, companies began investing in Southeast Asia in 1959 when a

6. Ibid., and H. H. Chen, "Overview of Taiwan's Investments," p. 135.

7. *CDN*, intnl. ed., September 7, 1994, p. 8; March 7, 1995, p.6; June 2, 1995, p. 6.

8. H. H. Chen, "Overview," p. 214; Kao et al., *Taiwan Investment Experience*, p. 165; Chang-yung Liu et al., "A Study of the Current Operation of Taiwanese Companies in the Mainland," in *Investing in the Mainland Market: Industry Investment and Cross-Straits Division of Labor* (in Chinese) (Taipei: The R.O.C. Association of Management Science, 1993), pp. 53 and 33; Xiangming Chen, "The New Spatial Division of Labor and Commodity Chains in the Greater South China Economic Region," in Gary Geretti and Miguel Korzeniewicz, eds., *Commodity Chains and Global Capitalism* (Westport, Conn., Greenwood Press, 1994), p. 177.

Taiwanese firm set up a cement factory in Malaysia. In fact, during 1959-80, the bulk of Taiwan's total overseas investment was concentrated in Southeast Asia, especially Malaysia and Thailand. Although declining in the early 1990s (see Table 1), largely due to a diversion of investment to China, cumulative Taiwanese investment in five ASEAN countries and Vietnam during 1959-93 amounted to US$16.1 billion, roughly equal to the estimated total Taiwanese investment in China. By June 1995, contracted cumulative investment in the ASEAN countries and Vietnam reached US$25 billion, US$21.6 billion of which had been committed since 1988, again keeping up with the estimated total investment in China.

By 1993, the ranked order of Southeast Asian countries receiving the volume of Taiwanese capital were Malaysia, Thailand, Indonesia, Vietnam, the Philippines, and Singapore. The order in which Taiwan ranks against other foreign investors in these countries is Vietnam (1), Malaysia (2, behind Japan), Indonesia (3, behind Japan and Hong Kong), Thailand (4, behind Japan, Hong Kong, and the U.S.), the Philippines (5, behind Japan, the U.S., Hong Kong, and the U.K.), and Singapore (13). In the first half of 1995, Taiwan remained the top foreign investor in Vietnam, surpassed Japan to become the largest investor in Malaysia, and moved from the fifth to third largest in the Philippines, while its investment rank in Indonesia dropped from third in 1993 to fifth in 1994 and sixth in the first half of 1995.[9]

During the 1960s and most of the 1970s, Taiwanese investment in Malaysia, Thailand, and Singapore focused on such typical labor-intensive industries as food and beverages, textiles, plastics and rubber, and electrical and electronics assembling. Since the late 1970s, it has involved more capital-intensive industries such as petrochemicals and some advanced electrical and microelectronics manufacturing; it also shifted more to Indonesia and the Philippines in the 1980s and to Vietnam in the early 1990s. Investment in the more capital-intensive industries has grown from the late 1980s; Chi Mei Enterprise, for example, recently planned to commit approximately US$1 billion to making both upstream and downstream petrochemical products in Malaysia and Singapore.[10] And as in China, Taiwanese investment in Southeast Asia is characterized by geographical concentration first and spatial diffusion later. Earlier investment tended to cluster in such major Southeast Asian cities as Kuala Lumpur, Penang, Bangkok, Jakarta, Bandung, and Manila. Since the late 1980s, rapidly growing Taiwanese investment has flowed into several new, smaller locations such as Batam Island and Medan in Indonesia, Subic Bay in the Philippines, and Ho Chi Minh City in Vietnam.

9. Chi Hsueh, "The Go-South Policy and the Asia-Pacific Operational Center," pp. 13–37 in Pai-hsian Peng, ed., *The Go-South Policy and Taiwan's Economic Future* (in Chinese) (Taipei: New Society Foundation, 1995), p. 23; *CDN*, intnl. ed., June 2, 1995; August 28, 1995.

10. *CDN*, intnl. ed., May 31, September 15, 1995.

The primary target of recent Taiwanese investment in Indonesia is Batam Island, 20 kilometers offshore from Singapore. In 1990 Taiwan established a special industrial park on Batam, which attracted a large number of potential Taiwanese investors. But by 1992, with three projects in operation, Taiwan accounted for only 2.1% of the total foreign investment on the island, behind 45.4% from Singapore, 15.7% from the U.S., 11.8% from Japan, 11.3% from Hong Kong, and 4.5% from the Netherlands.[11] More recently, Taiwan's investment has picked up: its machinery industry association has signed a letter of intent to put up a 25-acre assembling and warehousing center, and its ocean shipping giant, Evergreen, plans to build a container dock and shipyard on Batam. Evergreen also bought 10 acres of land in the Taiwan industrial park as a potential site for its Southeast Asian regional headquarters. With a new international airport opened to service in 1995 and a plan to become Asia's third largest duty-free port behind Singapore and Hong Kong, Batam Island is expected to attract more investors from Taiwan and other countries. In May 1995 Taiwan and Indonesia agreed to set up an industrial park primarily for small and medium-size Taiwanese firms in Medan on the eastern coast of Sumatra.

Recent Taiwanese investment in the Philippines has focused on Subic Bay, the former U.S. naval base that has been converted into a special economic and free-port zone of multiple functions, including export processing, financial services, transit shipping, and tourism, administered by the Subic Bay Metropolitan Authority (SBMA). Within Subic Bay's boundaries, 300 acres of land are being developed into a special industrial park for Taiwanese investors by the Taiwanese Subic Bay Development Management Corporation (SBDMC), a joint venture of SBMA and a Taiwanese consortium. With the first phase of land (105 acres) and infrastructure development completed, 47 Taiwanese companies have begun to build factories and facilities, committing to invest US$200–300 million. By the end of 1995, all the available land was occupied. The second phase of land development (70 acres) has also begun and will accommodate 38 small and medium-sized firms. With about 50% of all the approved ventures and 24% of the total contracted overseas investment in Subic, Taiwan is the largest single-country investor. Of the Taiwanese factories already in operation in Subic, a shoe manufacturer employes about 4,000 workers to turn out 180,000 sports shoes a month, and Acer Computer is producing computer motherboards and planning to build complete PCs and set up a global repair center. Acer has projected employment of 19,000 people and annual sales of at least US$1 billion by the year 2000.[12]

11. H. H. Chen, "An Overview," p. 194.

12. Investment activities in Subic Bay assembled from *CDN*, intnl. ed., various; Michael DiCicco, "A Port Prospers in Civvies." *Business Week* (September 25, 1995), pp. 119–20; *Subic Bay Advantage* (official publication of the SBMA), 1:3 (September 1995), p. 4.

Vietnam has recently emerged as probably the most popular country location for southbound Taiwanese companies. By the end of 1995, Taiwanese companies had set up 236 manufacturing projects worth US$3.6 billion, accounting for 18% of total foreign investment in Vietnam. These projects include food processing, shoemaking, textiles, plastics processing, cement production, vehicle parts, and timber processing. Similar to the arrangement on Batam Island and Subic Bay, a Taiwanese development corporation of joint public-private ownership created two export processing zones (EPZs)—Tan Thuan and Linh Trung—in Ho Chi Minh City primarily for Taiwanese investment; by March 1993, 14 of the 20 factories in the Tan Thuan EPZ were set up and running under management of Taiwan firms. The Vietnamese government recently issued a license to the Taiwan Hanoi Industrial Park Development Corporation, which will develop 40 acres of land for manufacturing facilities under a 70-year lease. The largest Taiwanese investor in Vietnam is the Chin Fong Group, which has set up three manufacturing ventures: two vehicle assembly works in Ho Chi Minh City and Hanoi for assembling small motorcycles to compete with Japan in the local market, and a joint venture cement factory in Haiphong, which is capitalized at US$2.8 million, is scheduled to go into production in 1996, and will be capable initially of producing 1.4 million tons of cement per year.[13]

Go West and/or Go South: Ties and Tradeoffs

Instead of seeing them as mutually exclusive, many Taiwanese companies have attempted to create ties among China and Southeast Asian countries by investing in both regions across a number of industries. Taiwan's S.T. Group, which had been an early investor in Singapore's electronics industry, began to invest in China in 1985. From its Singapore-based holding company, S.T. has established and currently controls 17 subsidiary ventures in China, three in Singapore, two in Malaysia, and one in Hong Kong, which are involved in a wide range of businesses such as hotel management, construction materials, plastics processing, petrochemicals, computers, real-estate development, and warehousing and transportation. The rapid expansion of S.T. (Singapore) has followed the move of several large multinational electronics companies such as Motorola and Siemens in establishing facilities in China because it is the world's second largest manufacturer of silicon conductor plastics and a major supplier of these components to those companies. The fifth ministerial economic and trade conference between Taiwan and Singa-

13. *CDN*, intnl. ed., June 2, August 27, 1995, and March 2, 1996; also Yung-ker Lin, "Taiwan Businessmen March with the Southward Policy?" (in Chinese), *China Times Weekly* (January 9-15, 1994) pp. 30–31.

pore in February 1995 emphasized both countries' bilateral links to China and suggested that Singapore may replace Hong Kong after 1997 as the third-party intermediary through which Taiwan would conduct business with China. Located halfway between Hong Kong and Singapore, Subic Bay may also emerge as an alternative to Hong Kong as the gateway to China after 1997. This scenario would help Taiwan in bridging and mediating trade and investment flows between China and Southeast Asia.[14]

Another very large Taiwanese conglomerate, Tundex Group, has also been trying to integrate the westward and southward strategies, but unlike S.T., Tundex went from West to South. In Fuqing in Fujian Province, it set up a garment factory capitalized at US$3 million; then together with the Salim Group headed by Soedono Salim (Liem Sioe Liong), the wealthiest overseas Chinese in Indonesia, Tundex built a huge facility in Xiamen to make PTA (polyterythalic acid), which is used in China and other countries for manufacturing such downstream products as industrial fibers. To increase PTA production, Tundex recently decided to inject US$77 million into its factory in Thailand to double its current annual output of 300 tons in 1996.[15]

In a third case, the Pao Cheng Shoe Co., which earlier set up 17 production lines for making athletic shoes in China, subsequently established 11 similar production lines in Indonesia, and in 1994, committed US$30 million to build a new factory with eight production lines on 20 acres outside Ho Chi Minh City. This expansion from China to Vietnam was intended to meet growing overseas orders from such American companies as Nike and shift them to more competitive production sites. Another Taiwanese shoe company, which has a factory in China, has decided to invest in the Philippines. Although the primary purpose of its southward move is to spread risks, this company also considered that the United States and European Community might impose some restrictions on China's shoe exports.

Although the above Taiwanese companies have "gone West *and* South," there have been debates about the trade offs between investment in China versus Southeast Asia. The arguments for going West are based primarily on comparative economic advantages. Taiwanese companies regard China's cheap and abundant labor, vast land, huge domestic market, and strong engineering and technological capacity in selected industries as complementary to Taiwan's abundant capital, manufacturing experience, management skills, and some research and development (R&D) capacity. This economic integra-

---

14. Hui-hsuan Huang, "Transnational Enterprises Are Flourishing," *China Times Weekly*, September 25-October 1, 1994, pp. 46–49; Dave Savona, "The Road to Hanoi," *International Business*, September 1995, pp. 14–16; Diane Brady, "Subic Bay Seeks to Be Alternative to Hong Kong as China Gateway," *Asian Wall Street Journal*, August 1, 1995, p. 3.

15. Chian-hua Tseng, "Tundex Goes West and South Simultaneously," *China Times Weekly*, May 15–21, 1994, p. 44.

tion, based largely on vertical division of labor, can encourage industries in China to concentrate on low value-added manufacturing while allowing Taiwan to accelerate industrial upgrading. Also, China's traditional orientation toward heavy industries and large state-owned enterprises can be balanced by Taiwan's small and medium-sized firms investing in China; these firms can use their well-established production and marketing networks to help similar firms in China enter the international market. These kinds of economic ventures are generally viewed by government and business in Taiwan as "win-win" or mutually beneficial situations. Taiwanese investors in China also expected to increase the domestic sales of their locally made products from 22% in 1992 to over 30% in 1994, and even more after China joins the World Trade Organization. The secondary arguments favoring going West emphasize cultural and linguistic similarities between China and Taiwan.

The primary argument against going West, as viewed by both the Taiwanese government and business, is that too much trade with, and investment in China is risky due to the latter's potentially unstable domestic policy and tough position on Taiwan's international status. China's missile tests near Taiwan in reaction to President Lee Teng-hui's U.S. visit in June 1995 caused immediate concern among a few Taiwanese investors who have begun to spread risks by increasing investment in Southeast Asia. The Pao Cheng Co., for example, decided to increase its shoe production lines in Indonesia from 11 to 24 in the first half of 1996.[16] Related to the "risky China" argument are the lack of legal protection for investments in China and isolated instances in which Taiwanese businessmen and their factories on the mainland were robbed by local bandits.

Second, trade with, and investment in China may make Taiwan's economy too dependent on China's market. The most commonly used evidence in support of this market dependency argument is that Taiwan's trade with China as a share of its total trade has grown too fast and become too large, from 1.5% in 1986 to 8.4% in 1993; this figure would double to 17% if illegal direct shipment across the Taiwan Strait and other transit trade via places other than Hong Kong were included. Measured more meaningfully in exports, Taiwan depended on the China market for 16.5% of its total exports in 1993. Taipei recently estimated that discontinuing all trade with China could result in an annual loss of US$12 billion (equal to Taiwan's approximate total exports to China through Hong Kong in 1994), and turn Taiwan's overall trade surplus into a deficit.

The third (potential) disadvantage is that heavy manufacturing investment in China may lead to deindustrialization in Taiwan—the so-called "hollowing out." A Taiwan source attributed the loss of close to 20,000 manufactur-

16. *CDN*, intnl. ed. July 24, 1995, p. 3.

ing jobs and US$10 billion in manufacturing output to the shift of production to China through 1993. The "hollowing-out" argument against going West, however, was countered by research showing that: (1) the Taiwanese firms that have relocated most of their manufacturing activities are no longer competitive in Taiwan; (2) the overwhelming majority of the Taiwanese firms with investment in China keep more important functions such as research and development, product design and engineering, finance and accounting, sales and marketing, planning and inventory control, quality control, and after-sales service in Taiwan; and (3) Taiwan's industries have already upgraded to more capital- and technology-intensive production and exports. Government data show that the share of high labor-intensive products in Taiwan's total labor-intensive exports decreased from 47.9% in 1987 to 39.2% in 1992, while the high capital-intensive products' share in Taiwan's total capital-intensive exports rose from 22.4% to 29.3%.[17]

The basic argument favoring going South is similar to the economic rationale behind going West. Besides the complementarity between Taiwanese and Southeast Asian economies, the government sees less political risk in developing close business ties with these countries as they have more compatible ideologies and political systems. Most ASEAN countries also have bilateral government agreements with Taiwan to guarantee its investment. Second, although Southeast Asia is a much smaller market than China, countries such as Indonesia, the Philippines, and Vietnam are potentially large markets because of their sizeable populations and growth momentum. Taiwanese companies are also attracted to Southeast Asia because they have a much longer history of investing in the region and greater familiarity with its business environment. Other conditions favoring going South include recent new incentives introduced by some Southeast Asian countries: both Indonesia and the Philippines in 1994 began to allow foreign companies to have 100% equity ownership, and to attract specific industries, the Philippine government offered Taiwan some of its textile and garment quotas for exports to the United States.

The major economic argument against going South is the increasing cost of investing and manufacturing in Southeast Asia due to high inflation and rapidly rising wages. Another unfavorable factor is the recent policy of Malaysia and Thailand to pull back from labor-intensive industries and withdraw the incentives for foreign investment in them. In addition, physical infrastructure in some Southeast Asian cities remains poor and underdeveloped, such as the lack of handling capacity at Bangkok's port; on the other hand, some investors regard Subic Bay's physical infrastructure as superior to

17. Ibid., July 15, 1994, p. 7, June 11, 1995, p. 3; Shi-chun Hsu, "The Core-Peripheral Firm Relationship Across the Strait," in *Investing in the Mainland Market*, pp. 70, 97; Kao et al., *Taiwan Investment Experience*, p. 18.

many areas in China. One negative reaction toward going South is that the policy tends to benefit Taiwan's large state- or party-owned (KMT) companies, while offering limited opportunity to small and medium-sized private firms. This controversy centers around whether the use of public funds to invest in Southeast Asia is risky and irresponsible. Some cultural, religious, and language barriers may also make it more difficult for Taiwanese companies to invest in Southeast Asia than in China.

Despite these actual and potential trade offs, the policies toward the two regions are regarded as somewhat complementary by most top government officials in Taiwan. Although the government initiated the go South policy to cool down the high "investment fever" in China, some Taiwanese businessmen have suggested that the close cultural, kinship, and language connections with China favor investing there, and small and medium-sized companies may find it difficult to decide which way to go or how to split their limited capital between China and Southeast Asia. A 1994 survey by Taiwan's Ministry of Economic Affairs showed that in the next three years, 48% of the companies surveyed intended to invest in China, compared with 21% planning to invest in Singapore, Malaysia, Thailand, Indonesia, the Philippines, and Vietnam combined, followed by 11% planning to invest in Hong Kong and 9% in the United States.

Synthesizing Key Determinants of "Going West and/or South"

Economic Factors: From Product Cycles to Production Networks

The product cycle model, which predicts a staged shift of production-based investment and trade from the United States to other advanced industrial countries and then to less developed countries, provides a basic useful economic framework for understanding Taiwan's labor-intensive manufacturing investments. The large labor-cost differences make China and Southeast Asia logical locations for labor-intensive manufacturing but the "neat" stages of product cycles do not constitute the sole economic determinant of Taiwanese investments in the two regions. The division of labor between Taiwan and China is not exclusively vertical. Recognizing the engineering and technological capacity and skilled work force in some of China's large state-owned enterprises, Taiwanese companies have begun to ally with them to co-produce some relatively technology- and skill-intensive products such as major computer or vehicle components and parts. In Southeast Asia, especially in Malaysia, Taiwanese companies have also invested in such capital- and technology-intensive industries as computers, steel, and petrochemicals.

The movement of product cycles from Taiwan to China and Southeast Asia varies between and within countries and industries.[18]

The product cycle model, which emphasizes trade and investment between national economies as the basic unit of analysis, limits our understanding of the more varied and complex economic networks between Taiwan and China and Southeast Asia. In some industries, the network rather than the company has become the primary locus of productive and innovative activity. In addition, some of these production networks do not involve the one-way flow of capital from Taiwan to China or Southeast Asia and the return flow of exports from the latter two to the former, as predicted by the product cycle model.[19]

In the automotive industry, for example, some Taiwanese auto companies have become a crucial link between U.S. and Japanese multinational automakers and China. General Motors recently unveiled a long-range plan for including both Taiwan and China in the mutual supply and exchange of components and parts in the Asia-Pacific region; its primary objective is to use its cooperative ties with Taiwan to penetrate the mainland market. In the eventual division of labor, Taiwan and China will be engaged in mutual supply and exchange of components and parts for GM cars and even joint production of whole cars for the United States, Taiwan, China, and other markets. To achieve that long-term goal, GM and its Taiwan partner, Chinese Automobile Co. Ltd., have already established a joint venture in Hong Kong, which has been authorized to sell GM cars to China. After Toyota set up two manufacturing facilities in Shenyang and Hainan Island, and an R&D center in Tianjin, its Taiwan subsidiary followed up with a plan to build a repair facility and another factory to produce Toyota parts in China. This network allows Taiwan to carry out more sophisticated OEM (original equipment manufacturing) production as an experienced subcontractor and supplier of parts for the global auto industry.

Two other economic factors have functioned to induce Taiwanese investments toward China and Southeast Asia. The first was the continued high valuation of the new Taiwan dollar (NTD) from the mid-1980s through the early 1990s. A focused survey of Taiwanese firms in early 1992 showed that 55.4% of the respondents said they could not afford to keep their manufacturing in Taiwan if the exchange rate rose to 25 NTD to US$1, while 19.5% set the bottom line at 26-27.5 NTD to US$1. Of the respondent firms, 30% would move out of Taiwan if the rate hit 25 NTD to US$1; of those, 56%

18. Raymond Vernon, "International Investment and International Trade in the Product Cycle," *Quarterly Journal of Economics*, 41:4 (1966), pp. 190–207.

19. See Mitchell Bernard and John Ravenhill, "Beyond Product Cycles and Flying Geese: Regionalization, Hierarchy, and the Industrialization of East Asia," *World Politics*, no. 47 (January 1995, pp. 171–209.

would likely choose China as their destination and 35% would likely go to Southeast Asia, with only 9% going elsewhere. Thus, the exchange rate staying at around 26 NTD to US$1 through the 1990s has certainly been a "push" behind Taiwan's outward investments to China and Southeast Asia. The second economic factor is the termination of Taiwan's GSP (generalized system of preferences) status by the United States in January 1989. Since 1976, GSP had allowed thousands of Taiwan's small and medium-sized firms to export large quantities of labor-intensive products to the U.S. with no or reduced tariffs. The loss of GSP status has "pulled" the export-oriented Taiwanese firms more toward the ASEAN countries, which have GSP status in the U.S. market, than toward China, which does not.[20]

Political and Policy Factors: The Internationalization of State-Business Relations

The developmental state perspective emphasizes the strong and selective roles of the East Asian governments in Japan, South Korea, and Taiwan in channeling funds for investment, intervening directly in the economy, creating a market system, shaping industrial policy, devising indicative plans, and guiding these economies' incorporation into the capitalist world system. This perspective is useful for understanding the new role of the Taiwanese state in facilitating capital investments in China and Southeast Asia.

Although the state plays a crucial role in shaping Taiwan's economic development, much of its influence is confined to the domestic arena. However, the state has gradually taken on an expanded external role regarding investments in China and Southeast Asia, which may be characterized as the internationalization of state-business relations. While continuing to ban official direct trade, the Taiwanese government has incrementally expanded the list of agricultural and manufactured commodities that can be indirectly imported from China; that list grew, year by year, from 30 items in 1987 to approximately 4,500 at the end of 1994. In 1990 Taipei allowed indirect investment in China, and in 1991 the Ministry of Economic Affairs began to promote a division of labor in which core factories are based in Taiwan ("keeping the roots planted") and peripheral (supporting) factories are set up in China ("letting the branches and leaves grow out"). Between August and October 1994, the government approved hundreds of new products whose manufacturers could invest in China, and most recently it decided to allow trade officials and managers of Taiwan-invested factories in China to visit Taiwan for business purposes.

---

20. Ching-hui Huang, "An Analysis of the Relationship Between Taiwan's Investment on the Mainland and Manufacturing 'Hollowing Out'," in *Winning in the Mainland Market* (in Chinese) (Taipei: The R.O.C. Association of Management Science, 1993).

Taipei has adopted several external policy measures to facilitate investment in Southeast Asia. First, the Executive Yuan enacted the Operational Programs for Economic and Trade Relations with the Southeast Asian Region, whose goals were to: (1) conduct research on economic and trade developments in Southeast Asia through data collection and holding symposiums; (2) strengthen bilateral trade by helping businesses set up marketing channels; (3) promote mutual investment by providing banking and insurance services; and (4) use the government-financed Overseas Economic Cooperation Fund (OECF) to support private businesses indirectly. Second, the government set up special cooperative work groups to focus on promoting trade with, and investment in Singapore, Indonesia, the Philippines, and Vietnam. The work groups on Indonesia and the Philippines, for example, helped develop the industrial parks on Batam Island and in Subic Bay. Under this formal policy structure, Taiwan signed an official agreement with the Philippines to provide a low-interest loan of US$60 million through the OECF to improve the physical infrastructure in Subic Bay; the first installment of US$23 million has already been committed to building the Taiwan industrial park. Initiated by the Economic Affairs Ministry, Taiwan's Overseas Economic Cooperation Council and Central Bank are developing a joint program that, if approved, will allow Taiwanese firms investing in Subic to qualify for 6% low-interest loans. The government also provided US$45 million to help Vietnam improve its business infrastructure.[21]

President Lee Teng-hui's "diplomatic vacation" in the Philippines, Indonesia, and Thailand in the beginning of 1994 gave the highest official blessing to the go South policy. The "inspection" tours by the Minister of Economic Affairs to Batam in November 1993 and Subic in February 1994 provided a strong boost to the investment confidence of Taiwanese companies in these specifically targeted areas. Other lower-ranked government officials have also led private business groups to Southeast Asian countries. These conscious policies reflect the aggressive effort of the Taiwanese state to "seize the chance" to continue advancing Taiwan's position in the capitalist world economy through internationalizing state-business relations, not during a global economic contraction as suggested by world-system theory for peripheral economies, but for a solid semi-peripheral economy during a period of economic expansion in the Asia-Pacific region.

Historical and Sociocultural Factors: Traditional and Ethnic Connections

While product cycles and external state policies are key contemporary determinants of Taiwanese investments in China and Southeast Asia, the impact of

21. *CDN*, intnl. ed., March 3, 1996, p. 6; Chi Hsueh, "The Go-South Policy," pp. 28–30.

these factors is magnified in the favorable sociocultural environment of traditional and ethnic ties among the peoples of the region. As early as the mid-1600s when Taiwan was under Dutch occupation, it served as an intermediary between China, exporting silk, porcelain, and cane sugar to Japan, and Japan sending silver back to China. The same exports from China also went to Southeast Asia via Taiwan. At the turn of the century, after Japan's colonial rule began, investment flowed into China from Taiwan, heavily concentrated in Xiamen, Fuzhou, Shantou, and Guangzhou where it still tends to cluster today.[22] During the 1930s and 1940s, Japan's go South policy of using Taiwan as a base for simple manufacturing activities and Southeast Asia as a source of raw materials also strengthened the existing economic ties between Taiwan and Southeast Asia countries. These traditional ties laid the groundwork for investments in Southeast Asia from the late 1950s and in China from the late 1980s.

Taiwanese investments in China and Southeast Asia are also fostered by the strong, long-standing ethnic ties among overseas Chinese in these countries based on migratory movement, linguistic similarities, family connections, and geographical affiliation by birthplace. This sociocultural environment helps forge four interconnected capital flows across many economic and political entities of Chinese background: Taiwanese and Hong Kong investments in southern China (Taiwan going West), investments from the three NICs of Chinese descent (Hong Kong, Singapore, Taiwan) to Southeast Asia (Taiwan going South), the movement of funds from overseas Chinese enterprises in Southeast Asia to China via Hong Kong and Singapore (Southeast Asia going West), and mainland Chinese investment to Hong Kong and Southeast Asia (China going South).

Other analysts see these investment flows as contained within and channeled through a series of concentric circles embedded in the overarching China Circle.[23] In the Taiwanese-to-mainland China capital flow, Taiwanese businessmen identified similarity in culture and language as one of the three main factors in investing in China, with the other two being cheap and abundant labor and a huge domestic market. Although Taiwanese companies have begun to spread their investments, a disproportionately large share continue to concentrate in Fujian Province, which has particularly close historical and ethnic ties with Taiwan. In the Southeast Asia-to-China flow, Thailand's Chinese-controlled Charoen Pokphand Group, the largest Southeast Asian conglomerate with 200 companies, has been one of the earliest and most active investors in China since the early 1980s. In the capital flow from main-

22. Man-houng Lin, *The Separation and Unification of Taiwan and the Mainland in the Last 400 Years* (in Chinese) (Taipei: Wu Shih Book Publishing, Inc., 1994), pp. 135–58.

23. *Newsletter*, Institute on Global Conflict and Cooperation (IGCC), University of California at San Diego, 11:1 (Spring 1995), pp. 1–2.

land China to Hong Kong and Southeast Asia, it is public knowledge that Chinese red chip companies are listed on the Hang Seng Stock Exchange in Hong Kong but perhaps less known that China National Chemicals Company (CNCC) has set up a soda ash plant in Indonesia and a rubber products project in Malaysia.

Among major locations in Southeast Asia, some Taiwanese companies have expressed a preference for Vietnam over Batam and Subic because Taiwan conducted business in southern Vietnam for many years before the country's unification in 1975. In fact, Taiwan provided logistical assistance to then South Vietnam in setting up its first export processing zones in Saigon (now Ho Chi Minh City) in the 1970s. Today Ho Chi Minh City, whose Cholon district has always been a bastion of ethnic Chinese business, has the heaviest concentration of Taiwanese capital in Vietnam. The shared historical and ethnic ties make it easier for some Taiwanese companies to go West via a southern detour. The crosscutting investment flows among the overseas Chinese economies and companies provide strong support for the sociological perspective on economic transactions being embedded in deep and dense social and personal relations and networks based on trust.[24] The overseas Chinese diaspora in East and Southeast Asia provides the cultural "glue" for sustaining organizationally and spatially integrated economic activities in the region.

Geoeconomic and Geographical Factors: Subregional Integration and Locational Advantages

The China-Hong Kong-Taiwan economic triangle has formed one distinctive subregion of spatially integrated commodity chains. In making garments, bikes, and electrical appliances in China, a Taiwanese firm usually receives overseas orders in Taiwan, brings raw materials from Taiwan or other countries into China through Hong Kong, has the product made partially or completely in a Taiwan-invested Chinese factory, ships the product out via Hong Kong (again) to destined markets, and eventually settles the financial transactions back in Taiwan. The transportation costs incurred in this long and roundabout movement of products will be reduced considerably by the opening of direct shipping between Taiwan and China expected during 1997–99. While Kaohsiung will function as Taiwan's primary port for direct shipping, local governments at Chiayi, Tainan, and Yunlin have begun to campaign for their small ports to compete for freight business to and from Xiamen when direct shipping is established. The Taiwanese government has also approved

24. Mark Granovetter, "Economic Action and Social Structure: The Problem of Embeddedness," *American Journal of Sociology*, no. 91 (November 1985), pp. 481–510; also John Kao, "The Worldwide Web of Chinese Business," *Harvard Business Review* (March-April 1993), pp. 24–36.

direct flights between Taiwan and the mainland via Hong Kong and Macao. This agreement, which began at the beginning of 1996 and is renewable to 2001, allows Taiwan's China Airlines and Evergreen Airlines (EVA), Hong Kong's Cathay Pacific Airways and Dragonair, and Macao Air to fly between Taiwan (Kaohsiung) and China with a stopover in Hong Kong and Macao where flight numbers have to be changed.

As Taiwanese companies search for more investment opportunities in Southeast Asia, the region has seen the emergence of two distinctive cross-national growth zones that cover contiguous or adjacent border economies. The more developed of the two involves a subregional division of labor among Singapore, the Johor state of Malaysia, and the Riau Islands of Indonesia, based on comparative economic advantages, government facilitation, some ethnic ties, and geographical proximity, as well as on their joint effort to attract outside investment.[25] In the meantime, the ASEAN has proposed to create the ASEAN Free Trade Area (AFTA) to gradually formalize free trade among the member countries. Since the AFTA grants favorable tariffs to products with over 40% ASEAN content, it will benefit Taiwanese companies to increase local product content in Southeast Asia by setting up more manufacturing facilities or sending semi-processed materials there for finishing and then exporting to other markets.[26] While the *geoeconomic* factors created by the emergence of the subregional growth zones have become very significant, *geopolitical* conditions remain important in channeling Taiwanese investment to Southeast Asia. After all, the go-South program is a conscious government policy, and some major respondents have been KMT-controlled firms. The recently popular investment sites in Southeast Asia—Batam Island, Medan, and Subic—are also in highly favorable and strategic physical locations.

Conclusion and Future Research

This article has provided a detailed and most updated account of the salient characteristics of Taiwanese investors going West to China and going South to Southeast Asia through the mid-1990s. Taiwanese companies have also been "going East" by investing in California's Silicon Valley and the Los Angeles area since the 1970s, and it is worth noting that the recent military tension in the Taiwan Strait triggered a surging flow of Taiwanese capital into the overseas Chinese-owned banks in southern California. What is more relevant to, but cannot be covered in this article is that Taiwanese companies

25. See Xiangming Chen, "The Evolution of Free Economic Zones and the Recent Development of Cross-National Growth Zones," *International Journal of Urban and Regional Research*, 19:4 (1995), pp. 593–621.

26. Yeh-ping Chen, "AFTA and Taiwan's Go-South Policy" (in Chinese), *National Policy Dynamic Analysis*, no. 81 (March 8, 1994), pp. 10–13.

have already begun to "go Southwest" beyond Vietnam by developing economic ties with, and making initial small investments in Burma, Cambodia, and Laos.

The information presented here has shown that although sharing a similar general orientation, Taiwanese investors in China and Southeast Asia differ by industrial sectors and geographical locations. There has emerged complex investment links and production networks at the industry and firm levels among each of the dyads (Taiwan-China, Taiwan-Southeast Asia, China-Southeast Asia) in a broad regional triangular economic structure. Standing alone, the key determinants of Taiwanese companies going West and/or South—comparative and complementary economic advantages, the internationalization of state-business relations, historical and ethnic ties, or subregional integration and favorable location—offer only partial insights. Together they constitute a causal cluster of interdependent determinants that fully explain the magnitude, features, and spatial distribution of Taiwanese investments in China and/or Southeast Asia.

This article does not attempt to analyze the consequences of Taiwanese investments in China and Southeast Asia for the countries involved and for the regional and global economies. Evidence already points to their strong impact, as investment and trade tend to go together; Taiwan's exports to China in 1994 reached US$12.6 billion, ranking second only to exports to the United States, while Taiwan's exports to the five ASEAN countries and Vietnam amounted to US$11.4 billion, trailing only its exports to the United States and China via Hong Kong.[27] Finally, it is important to point out that the Taiwanese government intends to make investments in China and Southeast Asia dovetail with its official policy of developing Taiwan into the operational center of manufacturing, sea and air transit shipping, financial services, and telecommunications for the Asia-Pacific region. This policy envisions China, and Southeast Asia to a lesser extent, as a large hinterland for Taiwan. But even as the shift to high-tech industries enhances its potential to become a regional manufacturing operational center, Taiwan faces fierce competition from other NICs in several functional areas: South Korea in manufacturing and Hong Kong and Singapore (post-1997) in financial services and transit shipping. More extensive and in-depth comparative analysis based on this explanatory framework will be needed if we want to understand the full impact of Taiwanese investments in China and Southeast Asia at the local, national, regional, and global levels.

27. *CDN*, intnl. ed., June 15, 1995, p. 3; March 2, 1996, p. 3.

The Pacific Review, Vol. 9 No. 4 1996: 531–552

Korean foreign direct investment in Europe: the determining forces

Christopher M. Dent and Claire Randerson

Abstract Korea's more complete integration into the world economy has been stunted by past government policies aimed at preserving comprehensive control over the domestic economy. This situation has recently changed owing to prevailing structural weaknesses in the Korean economy and the dictates of the global competitive environment. Consequently, the level of Korean overseas investment has escalated, particularly in Europe – the Triad region which has traditionally attracted limited inward FDI from Korea's large *chaebol* companies. This paper examines the determining forces that lie behind this trend. It is recognized that early Korean investments in the EU were principally driven by reactionary motives when confronted by actual or anticipated policy threats. While it is argued that the pretext for such investment has not significantly diminished, the imperatives of globalization together with emerging economic conditions in both east and west Europe have provided considerable incentives for more proactive FDI strategies to be adopted. The recent announcements by senior *chaebol* of intended large-scale investments in Europe suggest that this new pattern is becoming increasingly apparent.

Keywords Korea; Europe; investment; *chaebol*; globalization; *segyehwa*.

Introduction

If a defining characteristic of the post-war South Korean[1] economy has been its outward-orientation, this is primarily attributable to fervently pursued export-led growth strategies. However, its relatively low propensity for both inward and outward foreign direct investment (FDI) has until recently limited the degree to which a more comprehensive integration into the world economy has occurred.[2] This was largely owing to past

Christopher M. Dent is a senior lecturer, University of Lincolnshire and Humberside, UK. Claire Randerson is a lecturer, University of Lincolnshire and Humberside, UK.

Addresses: University of Humberside Campus, Cottingham Road, Hull, East Yorkshire, HU6 7RT; University of Lincoln Campus, Brayford Pool, Lincoln, LN6 7TS.

government policies that aimed to preserve extensive control over the domestic economy and finance by attempting to insulate them from certain exogenous influences.

In recent years, though, overseas FDI has become more integral to the wider strategies of Korea's large multi-industrial companies – the *chaebol* – and is being more actively encouraged by the government as part of its recently inaugurated *segyehwa* (globalization) policy. Europe has played an increasingly important role in this process attracting a faster inflow of Korean investment compared to any other global region in the 1990s. At this point it should be disclosed that the FDI levels in question are currently very low relative to those for Japanese investment in Europe.[3] Nevertheless, the dynamics associated with a growing number of Korean firms operating inside Europe extends beyond a simple *prima facie* statistical comparison and warrants serious enquiry into a much neglected area of research.

Thus, the main purpose of this paper is to examine those forces that have determined the escalation of Korean FDI in Europe, as well as both actual and emerging patterns of investment across the region. In the first section, we shall explore Korean outward FDI's general determinants, adopting a 'domestic-push' and 'global-pull' perspective. This will be followed by a statistical analysis at both a global and European level. Finally, our more detailed study of Korean FDI in Europe will show that while the pretext for reactionary investment has not significantly diminished, other conditions have encouraged more proactive FDI strategies to be deployed.

General determining forces behind Korean outward FDI

Domestic-push factors

A multitude of domestic factors are responsible for pushing the *chaebol* into more dynamic overseas investment strategies. These are primarily associated with prevailing structural weaknesses in the Korean economy and recent government policies aiming to address them. In this section, we shall examine these main weaknesses – an under-developed small- and medium-sized enterprise (SME) sector, an excessive technological dependency, uncompetitive cost-structures and widespread debt constraints – and their impact on outward FDI. We shall also discuss how, in endeavouring to provide a solution to these problems, the government's more deregulatory approach to economic policy has diminished the security of the domestic market for the *chaebol*, hence sharpening their focus on opportunities existing in foreign markets. Overseas investments have an important part in exploiting these.

Korea's cost-competitiveness has been steadily eroding since the late 1980s. This stems principally from rising labour costs, an appreciating won, inflated real estate prices and the fluctuating cost of raw material prices. The potential of these inflated costs to hamper export growth is inducing the *chaebol* to embrace outward FDI with a new enthusiasm, in an attempt to maintain their competitive position. In particular, greater trade union power and high wage increases have led to a shift to higher value added, capital-intensive activities by Korean firms, with sectoral production that has experienced declining capital productivity being moved to lower cost East Asian locations (Lee K. 1995). Government policy has attempted to compensate for such disadvantages by favourably influencing certain cost-structures and promoting overseas investment as a means to restore cost-competitiveness.

Although the first permission for overseas investment dates back to 1968, it is only since the 1980s that outward FDI has been more actively supported. The recent *segyehawa* programme, encapsulated in the 7th Five-Year Plan (1993–7), represents the government's recognition of the need for greater integration into the world economy and continues the strong tradition of close collaboration between itself and the *chaebol* (see Amsden 1989; Wade 1990; Westphal 1990; Pilat 1994). *Segyehawa* aims to encourage outward direct investment, introduce economic liberalization and open up the Korean economy to greater foreign competition. As a consequence, the relative attractions of the domestic market have been effectively reduced for the *chaebol*, providing further exigency for overseas investment, to sustain export growth and reduce factor costs.

The investment provisions of *segyehawa* include easing the application process for outward overseas investment and completely removing investment restrictions in all but three real estate related areas. The result has been a remarkable growth in the number of FDI applications and in particular an increase in large-scale FDI projects. Simultaneously, 'prudential guidance' measures for FDI have been implemented in an attempt to prevent reckless overseas investment and minimize potential adverse effects upon the national economy. Hence, the *chaebol* are now required to finance a minimum 20 per cent of a FDI project from domestic sources.

An important strategic objective of *segyehwa*'s promotion of outward FDI has been to acquire an independent technological capability, based on the notion of overseas investment acting 'as a bridge over which necessary, advanced technology can enter the domestic arena' (Korean Ministry of Finance and Economy 1995). Korea's technological dependency remains a significant structural economic weakness, as demonstrated by its persistent reliance on imported technology from Japan and the USA (see Woo 1993; Hobday 1994; Simon and Soh 1994; Ursacki and Vertinsky 1994). This dependence is at least partially attributable to the emphasis the *chaebol* have typically placed on achieving production economies of scale and increasing total sales volume as opposed to profit maximization. Consequently, some *chaebol* have found themselves at a serious disadvantage now that imported technology is increasingly difficult to obtain since Korea has become a serious rival in all major regional markets.[4] Hence, many Korean firms have attempted to redress the imbalance of relationships with their Pacific partners whilst also seeking alternative means of acquiring new technology, such as establishing closer technological links with European counterparts. *Segyehwa*, therefore aims to resolve this significant domestic deficiency and acquire a greater technological capability through merger, acquisition and joint ventures with incumbent firms in Triadic[5] regions.

Despite the crucial role played in Korea's economic development by the *chaebol*, their predominance within the economy has led to other pronounced structural weaknesses (Lee *et al.* 1993), not the least being the relative under development of the SME sector. Recent changes to government policy have attempted to create a more balanced industrial structure through a more proactive policy towards SMEs, consequently depriving the *chaebol* of their accustomed preferential treatment.

For the *chaebol*, the under-developed nature of the SME sector has created specific, long-term problems. For example, it has necessitated the sourcing of industrial components and machinery from countries where the logistical and technological capabilities of local SMEs are superior. This is particularly applicable in the case of Korean automobile manufacturers who require a multi-layered system of suppliers in order to optimize lean production processes. The main benefactor of this technological dependence until recently has been Japan (Simon and Soh 1994). However, the scale of this dependence, in conjunction with the recent strength of the yen, has fuelled Korea's divergent trade deficit with Japan and thus heightened the imperative to find alternative suppliers in Europe and the USA. In theory, increased outward FDI could itself create a virtuous circle in which more favourable financial conditions are generated. Greater direct use of overseas subcontractors by Korean multinationals abroad could relieve this import dependence on Japan and thus assist Korea's capital balance position. This itself would allay financial concerns amongst domestic policymakers which should logically release constraints on outward investment flows.

As part of their efforts to create the more balanced economic structure noted earlier, government policies have attempted to streamline the industrial activities of the *chaebol*, compelling them to adopt a narrower industrial focus set within designated core sectors. From one perspective, this has presented an additional inventive for greater outward FDI, providing these firms with the means to spread and reduce risk by establishing a firmer global position within the industries in question. Nevertheless, it is still unclear as to how closely the *chaebol* are adhering to the government's policy of concentrating on core sectors, given Samsung's recent decision to enter into automobile production and Daewoo's expansion into electronics. It could be argued that they are simply making structural shifts, away from mature technology industries into newer ones.[6]

A final structural weakness relates to the huge debts accumulated by the *chaebol* and has raised concerns over future economic stability. A significant motivation for overseas expansion therefore originates from the need to service their debts, yet these have, under particular circumstances, impinged greater financial constraints on investing overseas. The debt burden, a legacy of Park Chung Hee's early soft loan policies, has not abated given the persistence of the government's 'policy loans' into the 1990s. Cheap credit has played a critical role in the growth and diversification of the *chaebol*. It continues to enable them to expand into new business areas and increase their production capacity, despite the rising tide of government constrictions over recent years. *Chaebol* reliance on domestic sales to enable them to service their debts has left them vulnerable to changes in demand in the home market, a situation causing consternation given the size of debts involved and the deregulation of the domestic economy. Furthermore, the possibility exists that a *chaebol* bankruptcy could threaten the stability of the country's banking system.

To conclude, we have seen how the process of adjustment inherent in the government's liberalization and deregulation programme carries numerous potential hazards for the *chaebol*. Although many undoubtedly welcome their release from the 'burden' of government intervention, their preferential access to soft loans has already become restricted. It is also anticipated that the increased competition they will face in the domestic market could be to the detriment of their profit margins and their ability to service these substantial debts. The establishment of an overseas presence will potentially improve their penetration of strategic markets and reduce their dependence on home market sales. In addition, it offers them the opportunity to acquire relatively low interest rates and capital resources from foreign banks and financial markets, a prospect that has until now been largely denied them.

Global-pull factors

In our analysis of general determining forces, it is also useful to consider the various 'global-pull' factors that have affected the overseas investments of Korean firms. Broadly speaking, these can be understood with reference to the improvement or maintenance of competitiveness in existing markets, or establishing a strategic position where representation is currently weak. In this section, we shall thus examine how securing supply chains for strategic assets, the dictates of global competition, changing relative cost differentials, the exploitation of ownership-specific advantages and responses to foreign government measures, amongst other things, have stimulated Korean outward FDI.

Early overseas Korean investments were permitted in natural resource-based sectors. This was logical given the country's limited indigenous sources and the burgeoning material demands placed upon an economy undergoing rapid economic development (Euh and Min 1986). Such a situation has been compounded by a closed Northern border that effectively negates South Korea's use of overland transportation routes. Natural resource-based investments are still required to secure a key supply chain, although structural changes imply that their relative strategic importance have declined.

The need to procure overseas strategic assets of a different nature originated from rising factoral costs at home. As the 1980s progressed, Korean multinationals were impelled to search for cheap labour in neighbouring low-wage locations. During the 1990s, minimal cost East Asian countries (e.g. China, Vietnam) have increasingly been targeted as Korean producers endeavour to shore up competitive advantages against rivals from others that are closest to developing similar industrial capabilities (e.g. Thailand, Malaysia). This has particularly applied to labour-intensive industries, like electronic and automobile component manufacture, textiles and footwear, in which Korean firms still retain a competitive position albeit less tenable.

Those capital-intensive sectors where Korean firms either currently have, or are endeavouring to develop, a competitive advantage have become particularly globalized, e.g. sectors concerned with automobiles, consumer electronics and semiconductors. To become central players in their respective industries, the *chaebol* have therefore had to compete globally. Moreover, global competition in those sectors where they are prominent is essentially oligopolistic and subsequently a 'follow the leader' pattern has emerged in many of their foreign investments. This is particularly relevant with respect to their Japanese rivals (see Jeon 1992).

Yet, overseas FDI undertaken by Korean firms cannot be distinguished as simply a response to the initiatives of their main competitors. The proclaimed objective of most *chaebol* to become global leaders in their field is consistent with the more recent course of offensive investments. Daewoo's plans to commence automobile production in Uzbekistan, Peru, Iran, India and central and eastern Europe – relatively uncharted commercial territory – best exemplifies such ambition. Moreover, it should be remembered that competition between the *chaebol* themselves is fierce. Overseas FDI can thus provide the means to promote their own domestic status. As we shall later discuss, the recent surge of Korean FDI into Europe also demonstrates a willingness to compete head-on against established Triadic competition.

Given the Korean economy's balance of payments constraints, trade-creating FDI still plays a crucial part in *chaebol* corporate strategy. Although the absolute rise in trade-related FDI over the 1990s reflected lagged or contemporaneous efforts to buttress export positions, its recent flow rate relative to other types has fallen.[7] Persistence in this trend would be indicative of more globally integrative strategies being pursued through both export-substitutory FDI and direct servicing of end-markets. This contrasts with the distributional functions that a significant number of overseas investments have typically performed. In certain sub-sectors this has become increasingly evident. For example, in 1990, Korean exports of colour televisions (CTVs) totalled around $200m, but by 1995 the European-based CTV production of Korean firms had practically reduced this figure to zero. A similar pattern is emerging for market expansion FDI strategies whereby investment activities in host countries act as regional-based export platforms. This has been an integral part of consolidating a strategic position where competition is both intense and conducted at a global level.

In accordance with FDI theory, the global-pull upon Korean firms to invest overseas also derives from the potential benefits of exploiting their own particular set of ownership-specific advantages, or intangible assets. A notable area of commonality lies in their cost advantage held against many of their industrial competitors. Hence, investment is frequent where production conditions safeguard this advantage or where demand conditions are notably price elastic. Furthermore, the multi-industrial portfolios of many *chaebol* can cover a range of interdependent activities that often permit considerable economies of scope to be captured.[8] Under certain circumstances, such advantages have been best realized through outward FDI strategies, especially where a more integrative approach has been pursuable and other associated internalization advantages are feasible. LG Electronics' plans to construct industrial complexes at sites in the UK, within which related electronics production will be clustered, provides an illustrative example.

Acquisitional FDI can enhance a *chaebol*'s portfolio by adding proprietary technology and capital assets once held by other firms to their own. Where this route has not been open, and the ownership-specific advantages of Korean firms have been singularly deficient in realizing corporate objectives, they have sought strategic alliances to develop synergetic and mutually shared advantages. Alliances now characterized by a more equal partnership with Triadic companies carry the potential benefit of attentuating the technological dependence of Korean firms. The abandonment of 'guest' manufacturer roles for those based on producing own brand products[9] signifies the *chaebol*'s growing commercial confidence and technological prowess. Outward FDI has reflected and served as a means to fortify both aspects, as well as establish a firmer market identity for Korean products. Nevertheless, Korea's prevailing technological dependency implies that much of its high-tech overseas investment is still based on procuring sources of strategic technology assets in developed economies as opposed to generating or jointly developing them.

Perceptions of Korean firms as essentially predatory must, though, be tempered by what they themselves have to offer host countries. As Asia's second largest overseas investors in manufacturing, Korean firms have become an important source of standardization industrial technologies, employments, skills and capital formation. Foreign government agencies presently compete to entire inward investment from the *chaebol* by offering a mix of incentive measures. These constitute further location-specific factors for Korean outward FDI, although their influence is more or less confined to regionalized investment decision-making. Moreover, reactive protectionism against competitive Korean exporters is still significant in certain sectors. As a consequence, Korean outward FDI habitually falls into the trade-barrier circumventing category, especially where targeted at traditional producer locations. We later argue, however, that this has become less applicable to European-based investments, and that the more proactive motivations identified in this section have played a greater determining role. Before we do so, let us conduct a general statistical analysis of Korean outward FDI both globally and in Europe itself.

Korean outward FDI: a statistical overview of global and European patterns

Korean overseas investments were still predominantly concentrated in natural resource-based sectors until the mid-1980s.[10] Steady growth was achieved during the early 1980s with total FDI for 1980–5 amounting to $417.9m. Thereafter, accumulated trade surpluses led to a substantial appreciation of the won, which, in combination with rising protectionism against Korean exports and inflated factoral costs at home, gave spur to a considerable increase in outward FDI that amounted to $3.45bn over the 1986–91 period. As Figure 1 indicates overseas investments have continued to accelerate with the total accumulated net invested by 1995 standing at $10.22bn. Manufacturing investment has risen sharply relative to other sectoral FDI categories over the last three years and holds the majority sectoral share with 58.8 per cent of the total net figure (see Table 1). Although SMEs now account for around a quarter of all Korean outward FDI, their investments are largely concentrated in East Asia (Sakong 1993). This contrasts with the global reach of the *chaebol*.

East Asia has re-established its position as the most important host region for Korean FDI with a 44.7 per cent share (see Figure 2). During the late 1970s and most of the 1980s, North America was the preferred global locations, though a large share of this investment was geared to serve the export interests of home production plants. Trade-related FDI remains high in North America at 36.3 per cent compared to only 6.1 per cent for East Asia. It is likely that trade-related FDI in East Asia will rise owing to the intra-regional market dynamics of the region and the export opportunities they afford. A similar argument could also be made, however, for market expansion FDI strategies noted earlier. Meanwhile, manufacturing investment continues to rise in the region and currently holds a 76.6 per cent share of the cumulative sectoral total. As argued earlier, this reflects the appeal of low-cost production that neighbouring East Asian countries hold.

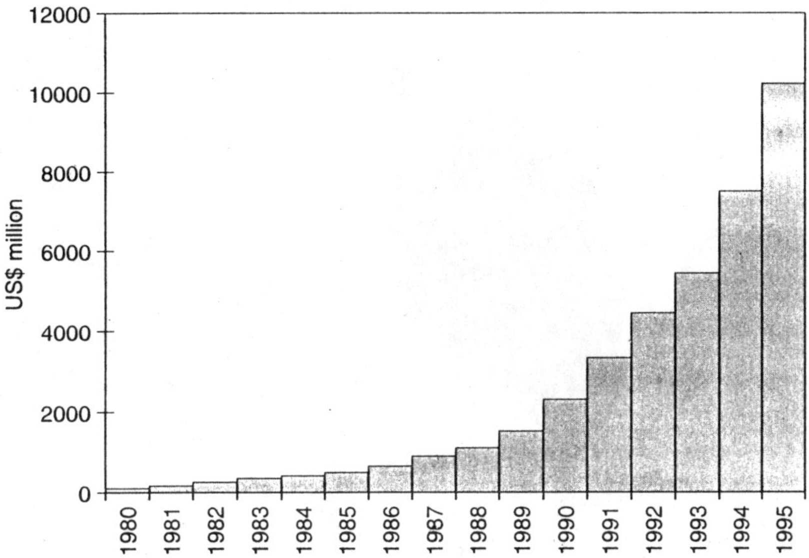

Figure 1 Korean outward FDI: trend for total cumulative net investment 1980-95).

Source: Bank of Korea (1996)

Europe is presently the third favourite overseas location for Korean firms, attracting 15.1 per cent of total FDI by 1995, but more significantly Korean investment in Europe has risen faster than in any other region.[11] Figure 3 suggests that an extrapolation of current trends could soon lead to Europe overtaking North America as the second regional location for Korean FDI. While annual investment flows for the latter have fluctuated considerably during the 1990s, for the former these have consistently risen at significant rates. Indeed, 1995 was the first year that Europe had attracted more Korean FDI than North America. Further examination of the data reveals that both regions possess similar structural profiles with manufacturing and trade-related FDI taking at least three-quarters of the sectoral total. This is in some contrast to Japan's profile where real estate took a 47.2 per cent share,[12] manufacturing 36.4 per cent but trade-related FDI a comparable 40.7 per cent. (While there is evidence of rising Korean investment in Japan, its current level of $227.8m is less than the UK's.)

Europe's traditional hosts for inward FDI – Germany, the UK, France and the Netherlands – all figure highly in attracting Korean multinationals as Figure 4 illustrates. However, in 1995 the CIS became Europe's third most important host, although this position rests on the Bank of Korea's decision

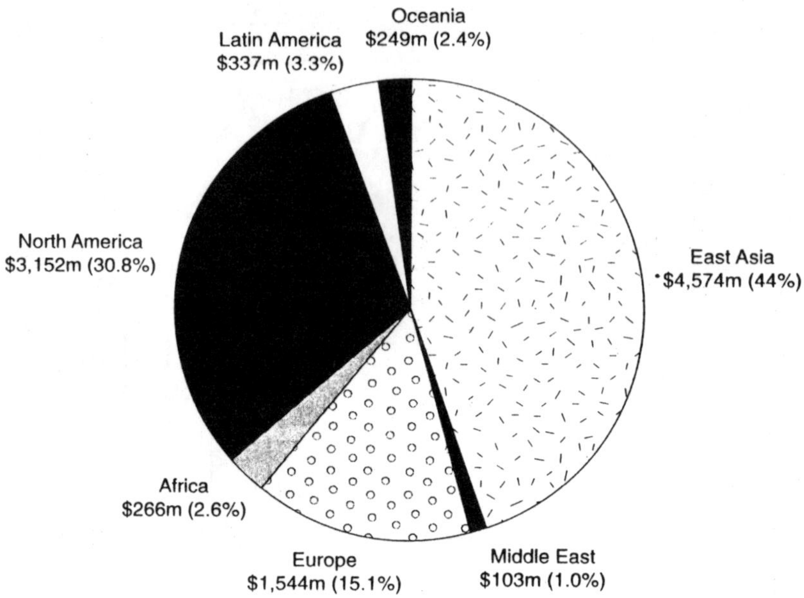

Figure 2 Korean outward FDI: cumulative net investment by region (1968-95)
Source: Bank of Korea (1996)

to include the Central Asian states – where over half the CIS's inward investment from Korea lies[13] – in its European statistical classification. Table 2 would indicate that most Korean FDI in the CIS is driven by production cost-based motivations with 84.4 per cent dedicated to manufacturing but only 2.4 per cent in a trade facilitating role. Amongst the main West European hosts there exists some variance regarding the sectoral distribution of investment, but this follows expected patterns (see Table 2). For example, Germany's high trade-related FDI reflects its position as Korea's largest export market in the region, whilst its low share for manufacturing is indicative of the country's relatively high labour costs. France and the UK's shares for trade-related FDI contrast with a low figure for the Netherlands owing to the smaller market presented to Korean exporters. Indeed, in late 1996 Hyundai announced its intentions to invest £2.4bn ($3.6bn) in a semiconductor plant to be located in Dunfermline, Scotland.

Although trade-related FDI in Germany has enabled it to remain for some time as Europe's leading host country, this is likely to change with senior *chaebol* recently announcing their intentions to conduct large-scale investments in the UK. The most notable of these have been Samsung's $700m investment to be phased in over 1994–2000 and LG's $1.5bn project

Table 1 Korean outward FDI by main host region and sector: cumulative net investment (US$m and percentage, 1968–95)

	Sector							
	Mining	Forestry & Fishing	Manufacturing	Construction	Transportation & Storage	Trade	Other	Total
Europe	14.2	2.8	843.5	5.1	1.5	497.5	179.8	1,544.4
	(0.9%)	(0.2%)	(54.6%)	(0.4%)	(0.1%)	(32.2%)	(11.6%)	
North America	112.9	22.0	1,339.9	82.4	12.4	1,144.0	438.5	3,152.1
	(3.6%)	(0.7%)	(42.5%)	(2.6%)	(0.4%)	(36.3%)	(13.9%)	
East Asia	328.2	46.0	3,502.4	72.3	55.4	277.7	291.7	4,573.7
	(7.1%)	(1.0%)	(76.6%)	(1.6%)	(1.2%)	(6.1%)	(6.4%)	
World	701.0	167.9	6,013.2	211.3	76.7	1,991.9	1,062.7	10,224.7
	(6.9%)	(1.6%)	(58.8%)	(2.1%)	(0.7%)	(19.5%)	(10.4%)	

Source: Bank of Korea (1996).

Table 2 Korean FDI in Europe, main host countries and sector: cumulative net investment (US$m and percentage, 1968–95)

	Sector							
	Mining	Forestry & Fishing	Manufacturing	Construction	Transportation & Storage	Trade	Other	Total
Germany	–	–	60.3	–	1.2	222.3	3.5	287.3
			(21.0%)		(0.4%)	(77.4%)	(1.2%)	
United Kingdom	–	–	104.3	5.0	–	130.5	0.3	240.1
			(43.4%)	(2.1%)		(54.4%)	(0.1%)	
CIS	–	2.6	178.8	–	–	5.2	25.2	211.8
		(1.2%)	(84.4%)			(2.5%)	(11.9%)	
Netherlands	–	–	20.2	–	0.3	6.7	146.9	174.1
			(11.6%)		(0.2%)	(3.8%)	(84.4%)	
France	–	–	97.3	–	–	69.8	2.3	169.4
			(57.4%)			(41.2%)	(1.4%)	

Source: Bank of Korea (1996)

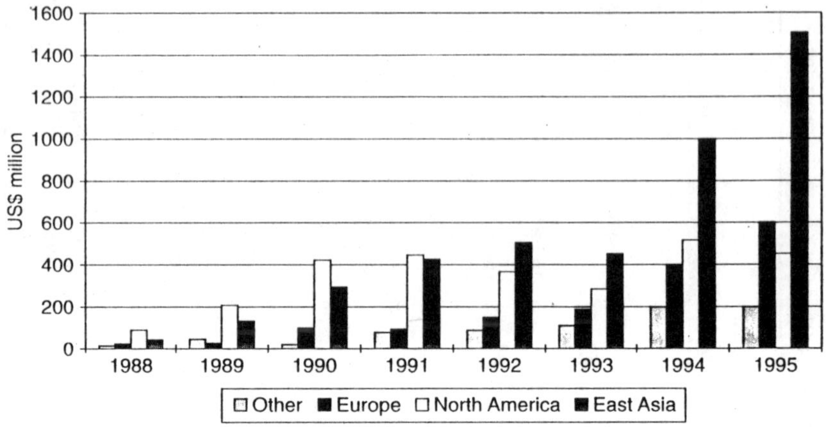

Figure 3 Korean outward FDI: annual net investment by region (1988-95)

Source: Bank of Korea (1996)

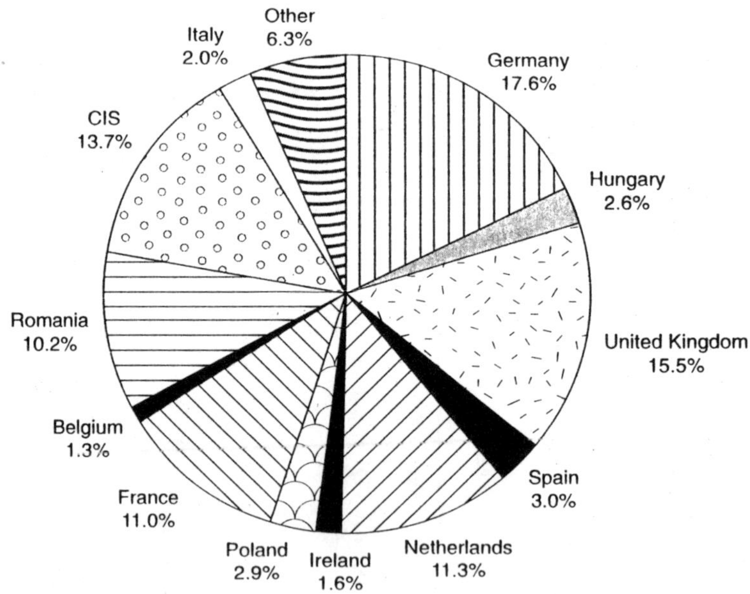

Figure 4 Korean FDI in Europe: host country share of cumulative net investment (1968-95)

Source: Bank of Korea (1996)

Table 3 Main Korean FDI projects in Europe

Samsung
Colour TV factory, Billingham, UK ($15m, 1990)
Semiconductor assembly plant with Texas Instruments, Porto, Portugal ($30m, 1994)
Colour picture tube factory, Berlin, Germany ($120m, 1994–7)
Consumer electronics plant, Wynyard, UK ($700m, 1994–2000)
Hydraulic excavator plant, Harrogate, UK ($16m, 1995)

LG
VCR factory, Worms, Germany ($40m, 1986)
Refrigerator/freezer plant, Naples, Italy ($10m, 1990)
Colour TV and microwave oven factory, Newcastle upon Tyne, UK ($40m, 1994–5)
Semiconductors and consumer electronics, (unannounced location) UK ($1.5bn, 1996–)

Daewoo
VCR plant, Antrim, UK ($42m, 1988)
Microwave oven plant, Longwy, France (£23m, 1988)
Hydraulic excavator plant, Framières, Belgium ($10m, 1990)
Colour TV plant, Fameck, France ($37m, 1993)
Cathode ray tube factory, Lorraine, France ($138m, 1993)
Colour tube factory, Longwy, France ($150m, 1993–5)
Rodae Autos: Car factory, Craiora, Romania ($900m, 1995–2000)
Avia: Commercial vehicles, Czech Republic ($200m, 1995–)
FS Lublin: Car and van factory, Lublin, Poland ($350, 1995–)
FSO: Cars, Poland ($1.1bn, 1996–2001)

Hyundai
Hydraulic excavator factory, Geel, Belgium ($10–15m, 1995)
Automobile dealerships, UK ($240m, 1996–)
Microchip plant, location yet to be determined ($1.3bn)

Source: various journalistic

due to commence later this year (see Table 3). Another significant trend concerns central and eastern Europe (CEE) and its emergence as a favoured location for Korean firms. Until 1993, its share of cumulative Korean FDI in Europe was only 13.5 per cent, but by 1995 this had doubled to over 30.4 per cent. Furthermore, actual and forthcoming investments made particularly by Daewoo and Hyundai in the automotive sector are likely to both increase this share and shift the prevailing bias away from electronics investments for Europe as a whole.

Korean FDI in Europe: a deeper exploration

In this section, we shall make a more considered examination of Korean FDI in Europe with the intention of evaluating those factors that have determined both the level and distribution of investment in the region. Much of the debate will centre on how far the *chaebol* have progressed beyond 'reactive' FDI projects in response to actual or anticipated protectionism. There will also be an emphasis on how emergent economic conditions in Europe could serve to invigorate a more proactive approach from Korean firms.

Examining the pretext for reactionary investment

Induced protectionism and encouraged trade diversion are usually highlighted as the main adverse effects that the SEM potentially poses to 'outsider' firms. In theory, rival EU-based producers will seek protectionist measures to be deployed in compensation for the intensified competitive pressures now faced within the EU as a consequence of market integration. Furthermore, EU policymakers have negotiated for reciprocity gains in exchange for benefits that the SEM affords to non-EU companies.[14] Although *ex ante* studies conducted by Na and Hong (1990) suggested that the trade diverting effects of the SEM on Korean exports would be minimal, such effects have raised fears amongst 'outsider' Korean firms anxious at being excluded from the world's largest unified market place.

Earlier research has indicated that the spectre of protectionism, and anti-dumping duties (ADDs) in particular, were a major stimulant of Korean FDI in Europe during the 1980s (Young *et al.* 1991). Investments made by the *chaebol* enabled them to both avoid such tariffs[15] and potentially capture the economic benefits accruing to 'insider' firms. The peak period of FDI inflows – 1987–8 – coincided with the highest levels of actual or threatened imposition of ADDs on Korean imports.[16] This situation was exacerbated by the EU's decision to suspend Korea's Generalised System of Preferences (GSP)[17] privileges in 1989 after frustrated attempts during negotiations to liberalize the country's import regime. Subsequently, a range of quantitative restrictions were applied on 'sensitive' sector imports from Korean firms.[18]

Recent complexities that have evolved within the EU–Korea relationship have meant that the pretext for reactionary investment is now less definitive. Table 4 shows that the rate at which new ADDs have been introduced against Korean imports has stabilized. This rate may even fall in 1996 depending on the outcome of the current investigations listed. It is nevertheless evident that Korean producers remain sensitive to the ADD issue. For example, Samsung's decision to establish a hydraulic excavator plant in Harrogate, UK, came just a month after Europe's excavator manufacturers formally pressed the European Commission to use ADDs against low-priced rival Korean products. Interestingly, despite receiving similar confirmation that Korean automobile manufacturers were dumping their products in EU markets, ACEA – the European motor manufacturers' association – decided at present not to lobby for equivalent actions that

Table 4 EU Anti-dumping duties on Korean imports

Current ADDs in force (May 1996)

Product	Imposition date	Notes
Video cassette tapes	22.06.89	
Televisions, small screen	27.04.90	
Audio tapes in cassettes	14.05.91	expired: 11.95
Disposable lighters	28.11.91	
Car radios	07.08.92	
Synthetic polyester fibres	19.01.93	
DRAMS	18.03.93	suspended: 09.06.95–08.06.96
Monosodium glutamate	04.09.93	
Electronic weighing scales	22.10.93	
Electronic capacitors	18.06.94	
Microdisks	10.09.94	
Televisions, large screen	01.04.95	
Microwave ovens	01.12.95	

Current investigations initiated (May 1996)

Product	Initiation
Video cassette recorders and key components	25.04.95
Hydraulic excavators (>6 tonnes)	12.05.95
PET video film	14.06.95

Source: Directorate-General I, European Commission

might furnish the *chaebol* with greater incentives to compete directly against European producers from within the SEM.[19]

South Korea's impending graduation from the EU's GSP scheme, as a consequence of its 1995 review, will disadvantage Korean exporters after the country's beneficiary status is phased out in 1998. However, this will be mitigated by three main factors. First, owing to the more advanced industrial state now reached by other dynamic East Asian economies, they too will graduate from the scheme in accordance with a similar schedule. Second, the 'accentuated differentiation' provisions introduced to the scheme in the late 1980s mostly limited the concessions granted to NIC members to mainly 'non-competing' sectors, and hence not those where the European investments of the *chaebol* are mainly targeted.

Third, the recently negotiated EU–Korea Framework Agreement signed in March 1996 could provide more favourable political conditions under which a more liberal trade policy is adopted towards Korean imports. The main economic objectives of the Agreement were: (a) the accordance to each other of MFN status; (b) new concerted efforts to eliminate NTBs and the introduction of more transparency on trade matters; (c) improved mutual market access in both telecommunications and financial service sectors; (d) the encouragement of greater bilateral flows of FDI between both parties. The Agreement, combined with the broader framework of the Asia–Europe Meetings (ASEM), in which both parties participate, could act to further undermine the entrenched 'Fortress Europe' perception of the EU still harboured by many Koreans.

However, a number of potential frictions persist within the EU–Korean relationship that serve to perpetuate the conditions for reactionary investment. For instance, the European Commission retains its objective to match the inroads made by the Korean firms into the SEM with reciprocal access to the Korean market for imports and investment.[20] Furthermore, certain Korean firms have been bewildered by the EU's apparently more political than economic rationale deployed when determining the level of ADDs against Korean imports.[21] There are also some analysts who believe that the Framework Agreement is no more than a 'political gesture' and lacks any real substance to promote economic exchange between both parties.[22]

Exploiting 'opportunity Europe'

We have seen that the pretext for reactionary investment by Korean firms in relation to EU policy regimes has not significantly diminished. Nevertheless, there is increasing evidence that the Koreans are pursuing more long-term, proactive strategies with regards to FDI within both the EU and central and eastern Europe (CEE). The sudden escalation of investment, particularly the establishment of production bases throughout Europe by the *chaebol* must be viewed as an essential part of their ambitious globalization objectives. More specially, it reflects their desire to exploit the locational advantages that Europe has to offer in terms of markets, access to sophisticated technology and key manufacturing facilities.

Although corporations such as Samsung and Hyundai rank fourteenth and eighteenth respectively in the world in terms of size, it has become increasingly apparent that to establish themselves as truly global organizations, they must generate more output outside of Korea.[23] For such companies competing in globalized industries, developing a strategic position in Triadic locations is vital, providing both global balance, risk diversification and vulnerability reduction (Ohmae 1985, 1990). The notable under-representation of Korean multinationals in Europe therefore provides an essential rationale for the current surge of investment into the region.

Increasing competition from Korea's East Asian rivals and market saturation encountered in certain sectors of the American market has encouraged the *chaebol* to widen their search for alternative markets and production plants. Europe is the next logical destination for investment, given its status as a sophisticated, prosperous market and hence a natural alternative to the American market. It is anticipated that, the dynamics of the EU's Single European Market (SEM) together with the promising market and production opportunities emerging in CEE countries, will provide the Korean *chaebol* with potentially their largest market for growth in the short- and medium-term future.

The EU and the CEE region possess fundamentally different location-specific advantages for Korean investors. The EU economy's size and prosperity, enhanced by the microeconomic and macroeconomic opportunities of the SEM, are the most apparent advantages offered. These are being reinforced by recent high-level trade missions and increased political and economic dialogue between national governments, the European Commission and the Korean authorities. The Commission has extolled the locational benefits of the EU economy in their endeavours to welcome this valuable source of investment and have achieved significant success. Despite initial misconceptions about the possible motivations and effects of the SEM programme, the acceleration of investment over the last two years would indicate that the Koreans are now better positioned to take advantage of the EU's production and market opportunities.

Another attraction of establishing an insider position, with respect to the SEM, lies in capturing the wider diffusion of technological exchange within Europe. Acquisitional FDI to enhance technological expertise is a fundamental determinant of Korean investment in Europe. This is clearly illustrated by Samsung's interest in obtaining Fokker, the Dutch aerospace group, and Rollei, the German camera-maker, Daewoo's interest in Lotus and their 65 per cent stake in Steyr-Daimler-Puch. As argued earlier, securing such strategic assets alleviates the *chaebol*'s technological dependency in this area and more specifically helps facilitate their penetration of advanced markets such as Western Europe. Although at present the emphasis is still very much on buying technological assets, there are indications that some *chaebol* are increasingly prepared to create their own capability either alone or through joint ventures.[24] The European Commission's involvement in the development of new technology by European firms in areas such as HDTV (high definition television), is a key attraction for Korean firms. Long-term development programmes such as ESPRIT (European Strategic Programme for Development in Information Technology) provide additional incentives to enter into joint ventures with incumbent firms, as well as acquiring them.

Furthermore, the gradual phasing out of many of the *chaebol*'s 'guest' manufacturer relationships with US and Japanese firms has involved a shift in resources towards building brand loyalty amongst consumers in more established Triadic markets. Europe will not be excluded from this process. It may even transpire that the region will become a prime focus for such a strategy as previously contracting US and Japanese firms attempt to protect their market share against their erstwhile Korean partners turned competitors.[25] The technological and logistical capabilities of the

EU's SMEs, along with their relatively high density, is a significant advantage for the *chaebol* to engage. This is particularly relevant in the case of the Western European automotive component industry which consists of some of the world's most advanced suppliers. Progressive utilization of these networks should serve to improve the *chaebol*'s supply chain functions and hence improve their general competitiveness.

When analyzing the spread of Korean investments throughout the EU, it would seem that no single factor prevails in determining their location. Investments instead result from the successful fusion of a variety of determinants. It is apparent from a number of recent decisions that the UK has the most attractive combination of these factors, even resulting in the intra-EU movement of Korean investments to the UK.[26] The UK successfully combines a reasonably skilled workforce, large domestic market, substantial financial support packages, existing operations – in particular the industrial clustering in regions like the northeast – and a government committed to remaining the primary destination for FDI in Europe. These factors are further compounded by the fact that labour costs in Northern Ireland and parts of northern England are currently reported to be lower than in parts of Korea.

Emerging economic conditions in the CEE region provide contrasting location-specific advantages to those found within western Europe. A vital element of *chaebol* strategy concerns the exploitation of suppressed consumer demand across a range of product markets. Some of these coincide with the existing manufacturing strengths of Korean firms,[27] for example consumer electronics and automobiles where most of the Korean investment in Europe has been concentrated (see Table 3). Investing in both local distribution networks and production facilities serves to satisfy these high growth markets. Buying into companies such as FSO and Rodae has also enabled Daewoo to establish a presence in European car production. This is consistent with its ambition of being one of the top five automobile producers by 2005.

The position of Korean products at the lower end of both the quality and price spectrum provides a specific competitive edge over Japanese equivalents in particular. This derives from an ability to better exploit price-elastic markets within which technical sophistication holds comparatively less importance (Sasseen 1991). Their price advantage has persuaded the *chaebol* investors to enter this region more rapidly than many of their Japanese rivals who are proving uncharacteristically hesitant. Generally, the *chaebol* appear more willing than the Japanese to make high risk, loss-leading, but potentially high return investments, for the sake of acquiring strategic position. From one perspective, future rewards evidently appear to outweigh the relative scarcity of technological expertise and established SME supply networks throughout this region.

As well as the desire to satisfy the immediate demands of the CEE's local markets, other key location-specific advantages regarding Korean investment in CEE lie in the region's geographic proximity to the affluent markets of the European Union and its potential as a low-cost production base. The competitive advantage of this region, in terms of labour costs over Western Europe and preferential access to the European Economic Area, create greater opportunities for the *chaebol* to pursue essential, long-term strategies. Production and service facilities located in these countries will enable the *chaebol* to supply the affluent and more mature markets of Western Europe in the immediate future. The anticipated accession of many of these countries to the EU is an additional motivating factor. Rodae, Daewoo's recent acquisition, have stated that they intend to export about 65 per cent of production, the initial target area being Western Europe as the 'nearest market and furthest from Korea' (*Financial Times* 25 May 1995). The degree of local content in these manufactures will ensure that they are sold almost tariff-free in Western Europe, allowing Daewoo to avoid the anti-dumping duties for which ACEA are considering lobbying the EU. Although some analysts confidently predict that the cars will not be sufficiently sophisticated for the Western European market, this will undoubtedly change over the next decade if companies like Daewoo obtain the high-tech assets they are currently seeking.

A potential problem, however, for the Korean *chaebol* is the possibility they will find it difficult to exploit their existing ownership-specific advantages within Europe, given the mutual lack of experience or understanding in areas such as culture, traditions and psyche. Yet, by exploiting the opportunities that the EU has to offer in terms of high technology, supply networks and prosperous markets – combined with the CEE's provision of low-cost production and high projected growth – the *chaebol* undoubtedly have the potential to develop additional ownership-specific advantages within Europe's industrial fabric.

Conclusion

We have examined how prevailing structural weaknesses in the Korean economy, together with related changes in government economic policy, have created the domestic-based determinants behind the recent surge of Korean outward FDI. Those determining factors that exist beyond Korea's boundaries have also been discussed. More specifically, we have applied this analytical framework to a study of Korean FDI in Europe, in an attempt to explain why this region has the fastest growing share of total Korean outward investment.

It has been recognized that early Korean investments in the EU were primarily driven by reactionary motives with respect to actual or potential policy threats that confronted Korean firms. While the pretext for reactionary investment has not significantly diminished, other factors have provided over-riding incentives for more proactive FDI strategies to be pursued. The globalization of those industrial sectors where the *chaebol* predominate has implied that establishing a direct strategic position in Europe is imperative if they intend to compete effectively against global rivals. In addition, emerging economic conditions throughout both east and west Europe present Korean investors with considerable future opportunities. The recent large-scale FDI projects announced by the senior *chaebol* would indicate their intention to exploit these opportunities and provide Europe with a new source of investment from East Asia.

Notes

1 Hereafter referred to as Korea or Korean unless a contrast is required with North Korea.
2 Korean outward FDI as a percentage of 1995 GDP was only 2.3 per cent.
3 Roughly sixty times greater than Korean levels.
4 Ursacki and Vertinsky (1994) note that recent decisions taken by Japanese companies include up to 200 high tech measures to curb technology transfers firms to Korean counterparts by 1995.
5 Europe–North America–Japan.
6 Although the most senior *chaebol* have announced their intention to reduce the number of their subsidiaries in the short- to medium-term, e.g. Hyundai from 50 to 23, Samsung from 50 to 24 and Daewoo from 21 to 14 (*Economist* 3 June 1995).
7 Trade-related FDI's share of total Korean FDI fell from 23.4 per cent in 1992 to 19.5 per cent by 1995. There was a 55 per cent drop in 1995's absolute level relative to 1994.
8 The progressively higher quotants of electronic componentry found in automobiles has, for example, been partly influential in enticing Samsung into automobile production from 1998 onwards, albeit with the technological assistance of Nissan.
9 Daewoo have produced their own brand automobiles since 1992 after their 14-year joint venture with General Motors ended.
10 Mining investments outstripped manufacturing until 1987.
11 Europe's average annual flow rate over early 1990s increased by a factor of 23 times that of its rate for the late 1980s, well over twice East Asia's own rate and more than six times that of North America.
12 Cumulative 1994 figure.
13 The large Korean communities found in these states may themselves be a significant determining factor.
14 As first exemplified by the 1989 Second Banking Co-ordination Directive.
15 Although under the EU's 1988 'screwdriver plant' legislation (Regulation 2423/88), ADDs were imposed on foreign multinationals deemed guilty of circumventing these duties by establishing low local content production and service facilities within the EU. However, in 1990, a GATT panel upheld a formal complaint by Japan against this legislation on account of its market distorting effects.
16 McDermott (1992) noted that by 1989, 21.3 per cent and 20.3 per cent ADDs had been imposed on Haitai's and Inkel's respective compact disk products. Both firms subsequently embarked on FDI projects in the EU.
17 The GSP scheme affords trade concessions to developing countries.
18 For instance, video cassette recorders, microwave ovens, small-screen televisions, videotapes, polyester film and yarns, oxalic and glutamic acids.

19 Interview with ACEA personnel.
20 A number of deep sectoral imbalances remain in EU–Korean trade. For example, in 1995 European car manufacturers sold only 4,300 units in Korea (*Business Week* 18 March 1996). It should be noted, though, that the EU currently enjoys an overall trade surplus with Korea.
21 Conversation with *chaebol* personnel, May 1996, making a relative judgement when dealing with EU and US trade policy regimes.
22 Conversation with KOTRA official, May 1996.
23 Only around 10 per cent in 1993 for both companies. This is intended to increase to a minimum of 30 per cent by year 2000 (*Lloyd's List* 21 December 1995).
24 Daewoo's establishment of two technical centres in the UK and Germany for automotive development and Ssangyong's joint venture with Mercedes-Benz to develop new four-wheel drive automobiles.
25 This is best illustrated by the 1992 alliance parting agreement between General Motors and Daewoo in which the latter was obliged not to compete against the former's products in Europe before 1995 and in North America before 1997.
26 Samsung recently relocated their European headquarters from Frankfurt to London. Personnel from another senior *chaebol* has, unofficially, indicated the possibility of moving some of their operations from Germany and Italy to the UK.
27 For example, 1995 figures for car ownership per 1,000 population in Romania and Poland were 79 and 175 respectively. This compared to the EU average of 435 (*Financial Times* 25 May 1995).

References

Amsden, A.H. (1989) *Asia's Next Giant: South Korea and Late Industrialisation*, Oxford: Oxford University Press.

Bank of Korea (1996) *Overseas Direct Investment Yearbook, 1996*, Seoul.

Euh, Y. and Min, S.H. (1986) 'Foreign direct investment from developing countries: the case of Korean firms', *The Developing Economies* 24(2): 149–68.

Hobday, M. (1994) 'Export-led technology development', *Development and Change* 25(2): 333–61.

Jeon, Y. (1992) 'The determinants of Korean foreign direct investment in manufacturing industries', *Review of World Economics* 128(3): 527–42.

Korean Ministry of Finance and Economy (1995), *Korea's Outward Direct Investment Liberalisation Policy*, October.

Lee, K. (1995) 'Structural changes in the Korean economy and Korean investment in China and ASEAN' in S. LaCroix, M. Plummer, and K. Lee (eds) *Emerging Patterns of East Asian Investment in China: From Korea, Taiwan and Hong Kong*, London: Eastgate.

Lee, U.O., Lee, J. and Bobe, B. (1993) 'Technological co-operation between European and Korean small firms', *International Journal of Technology Management* 8(6/7/8): 764–81.

McDermott, M. (1992) 'The internationalisation of the South Korean and Taiwanese electronic industries' in S. Young and J. Hamill (eds) *Europe and the Multinationals*, Aldershot: Edward Elgar.

Na, S.L. and Hong, K. (1990) 'The effect of European single market on the Korean–EC trade pattern', *Journal of Economic Development* 15(2): 93–129.

Ohmae, K. (1985) *Triad Power: The Coming Shape of Global Competition*, New York: Free Press.

—— (1990) *Borderless World: Paper and Strategy in the Interlinked Economy*, London: Collins.

Pilat, D. (1994) *The Economics of Rapid Growth: The Experience of Japan and Korea*, Aldershot: Edward Elgar.

Sakong, I. (1993) *Korea in the World Economy*, Washington DC: Institute for International Economics.

Sasseen, J. (1991) 'Japan takes it gently', *International Management* 46(9): 48–51.

Simon, D.F. (1993) 'The international technology market: globalization, regionalisation and the Pacific Rim', *Business and the Contemporary World* 5(2): 50–66.

Simon, D.F. and Soh, S. (1994) 'Korea's technological development', *The Pacific Review* 7(1): 90–103.

Ursacki,T. and Vertinsky, I. (1994) 'Long term changes in Korea's international trade and investment', *Pacific Affairs* 67(3): 385–400.

Wade, R. (1990) *Governing the Market – Economic Theory and the Role of Government in East Asian Industrialisation*, Princeton, NJ: Princeton University Press.

Westphal, L.E. (1990) 'Industrial policy in an export propelled economy: lessons from South Korea's experience', *Journal of Economic Perspectives* 4(3): 41–59.

Woo, M. (1993) 'Export promotion in the new global division of labour', *Sociological Perspectives* 36(4): 335–57.

Young, S., McDermott, M. and Dunlop, S. (1991) 'The challenge of the single market' in B. Burgenmeier and J.L. Mucchielli (eds) *Multinationals and Europe*, London: Routledge.

Journal of Asian Business Volume 12 • Number 2 • 1996

Mainland Chinese Investment in Hong Kong: How Much, Why, and So What?

K.C. FUNG*

We ask *three* questions concerning Mainland Chinese investment in Hong Kong: "How much, why and so what?" From various fragmentary sources, the best guess is that it reached US$25 billion by 1995. More than 90 percent was in non-manufacturing. Using 1992 figures, between 2.65 percent and 4.4 percent was in manufacturing, while between 10 percent and 16.7 percent was in the Hong Kong property market. By 1993, Mainland China was the largest overall cumulative foreign investor in Hong Kong, while it was third among foreign investors in manufacturing. Mainland Chinese investment in Hong Kong is likely to be larger than Hong Kong investment in the Mainland.

There are many reasons why the Mainland Chinese invest in Hong Kong. This includes serving the re-export trade and raising capital through the Hong Kong stock market. Due to moral hazard problems, Chinese state-owned enterprises may likely engage in "excessive" speculation in Hong Kong property and stock markets. The involvement of Mainland Chinese officials and their relatives in the Hong Kong stock market may raise insider trader issues. Lastly, some local Mainland Chinese governments seem to be using the Hong Kong stock market to raise funds to set up more production facilities in China to circumvent the reform process.

In this paper, I focus on *three* aspects concerning Mainland Chinese investment in Hong Kong. First, given that there is little information on this issue, I will assemble fragmented data from different sources and present to the reader an overall picture of such investments. In other words, I want to answer the questions "How much is Mainland Chinese investment in Hong Kong?" and "What are the features of such investments?" Second, I want to examine the different motives of Mainland Chinese investment in Hong Kong. Here I try to answer the question, "Why?" Third, I wish to examine the

* Research Associate Professor, University of California-Santa Cruz and Associate Director, The Hong Kong Centre for Economic Research
The author had productive conversations on this topic with Dan Friedman, Donald Wittman, Mike Dooley and Michael Hutchison. Useful comments from an anonymous referee are much appreciated. Some of the data are supplied by Rob Feenstra and the Institute of Government Affairs at UC-Davis. Funding from UC Pacific Rim Research Grant and the Hong Kong Centre for Economic Research is gratefully acknowledged. The views expressed here reflect the author's thinking only and do not necessarily represent the views of the Centre. All errors are his.

welfare implications of such investments. I will examine the effects on both the economy of Hong Kong and the economy of Mainland China. So the third question to be answered in this paper is, "So what?"

In the next section, I present some historical and institutional background on this topic. In section three, I provide a picture of the size of such investments and in what activities they lie. In section four, I examine the motives of the Mainland Chinese investment in Hong Kong. Section five presents the effects of such investment on Hong Kong as well as on Mainland China. In section six, I conclude.

Historical and Institutional Background

For close to thirty years before 1978, Chinese enterprises in Hong Kong were mostly confined to banking and to services related to the Mainland's commerce, transportation, and tourism. Most of these firms were run directly by the central government in Mainland China. In fact, up until very recently, there were four dominant Chinese investing entities in Hong Kong: Bank of China, China Resources (Holdings) Co. Ltd., China Merchants International and China Travel Services (HK) Ltd. (see Kao 1994). These four government-run companies have built up a significant market share in Hong Kong.

The Bank of China has become the second largest financial institution in Hong Kong. According to the Hong Kong Monetary Authority, the Bank of China operates with 18,000 employees with 350 branches. It has an estimated 25 percent of the total Hong Kong dollar deposits and 10 percent of the total assets of the banking industry. In 1994, the Bank of China was granted the privilege to issue Hong Kong banknotes (see Chan 1994 and Kan 1996).

China Resources, which was set up by the precursor of the Ministry of Foreign Economic Relations and Trade (MOFERT) in 1949 as its trading arm, now has 150 enterprises in Hong Kong. It has its own shipping fleet, port, bank, warehouse, and department stores. China Resources monopolizes the supply of China's fossil oil and foodstuffs to Hong Kong.

The China Merchants International belongs to the Chinese Ministry of Communications. The company's original business was in shipping. In 1992 it had the capacity to ferry one-ninth of Hong Kong's sea-borne trade and one-tenth of total container shipments (see Chan 1994). The company has greatly diversified in recent years, with a total assets of US$2.7 billion in businesses such as manufacturing, trade, construction, finance and tourism.

The last of the historically dominant Chinese companies, China Travel Services (HK) is a subsidiary of the China Travel Services, which monopolizes China's international travel industry. In 1993, it had thirteen branches and more than twenty subsidiary companies, serving more than two million tourists a year. It is listed on the Hong Kong stock exchange.

With economic liberalization since 1979, many provincial and municipal governments and ministries in China set up branch offices in Hong Kong and there has been a great upsurge in the extent of Mainland Chinese investment and presence in Hong Kong. However, information in this area is scarce.

China does not publish data on outward investment (Lardy 1994). Due to Hong Kong's open trade and investment regime, and the absence of statuary reporting requirements, there is also no comprehensive information on inward foreign investment to Hong Kong. According to the General Agreement on Tariffs and Trade (1994), the only restriction on foreign inward direct investment to Hong Kong is in the broadcasting industry. To qualify as a shareholder in a licensed television operator, a person must have resided in Hong Kong for a full seven-year period. However, unqualified shareholders may have a "relevant interest" in up to 10 percent of the voting shares of a TV broadcast company and 49 percent of a satellite broadcaster covering Asian countries from Hong Kong. The latter limit also applies to radio stations.

Companies conducting banking, insurance or securities dealings in Hong Kong, whether they are locally incorporated or not, need a license or authorization. All other companies are required only to register with the Companies Registry of the Registrar General's Department. There are no exchange controls on capital receipts or payments by residents and non-residents. The bottom line is that there are virtually no restrictions on inflow of investment to Hong Kong. At the same time, there are no reporting requirements. Comprehensive and current data on Mainland Chinese investment in Hong Kong are thus difficult to obtain.

Extent and Characteristics of Mainland Chinese Investment in Hong Kong

According to Kao (1994), at the end of 1991, cumulative direct investment from Mainland China to Hong Kong reached US$10 billion, and the number of Chinese-funded enterprises was about 1,000. Sung (1995) reported that assets owned by Chinese enterprises and government agencies totaled US$6 billion by 1984. The magnitude rose to US$10 billion by 1989 (a figure also cited by Chan 1994) and reached US$20 billion by the end of 1992. Chen and Wong (1994) reported that by

1992, China invested about US $15.5 billion overseas, of which US$12 billion (78.2%) was in Hong Kong (table 1). They further pointed out that of the US$12 billion, US$11.54 billion was in the non-manufacturing sector of Hong Kong, while US$0.46 billion was in manufacturing. Within non-manufacturing, it was reported that the Chinese investment in the Hong Kong property market reached US$2 billion in 1992 (Sender 1993). More recently, Kan (1996) estimated that the Mainland Chinese had invested US$25 billion in Hong Kong by 1995. According to a report by the Hong Kong Trade Development Council (1994), by 1993, China passed Japan as the number one overall cumulative foreign investor in Hong Kong. Hong Kong was also the number one destination for Chinese overseas investment.

Table 1
Estimated Cumulative Mainland Chinese investment in Hong Kong

1984	US$6 billion
1989	US$10 billion
1991	US$10-12 billion
1992	US$12-20 billion
1993	US$20 billion
1995	US$25 billion

Source: Sung (1995), Kao (1994), Chen and Wong (1994), Hong Kong Trade Development Council (1994), Chan (1994), Kan (1996).

We can divide investments by Mainland Chinese in Hong Kong into three kinds: banking, listed companies and unlisted companies. Citing statistics from the Hong Kong Monetary Authority, Chan (1994) estimated that investment from the banking group of China came to US$6.4 billion and US$7.4 billion in 1992 and 1993 respectively. The listed companies are estimated to have invested US$7.9 billion by 1993. The unlisted companies are estimated to have cumulative investment of slightly less than that of the Chinese banks. Kao (1994) reported that by 1992, Chinese banks had invested US$5 billion, while the listed companies had invested at least US$1 billion.

Using the 1993 total cumulative figure of US$20 billion, one can provide a good argument that Chinese investment in Hong Kong is in fact greater than Hong Kong investment in China. The amount of cumulative utilized investment from Hong Kong to China for the period of 1979-1992 was US$23 billion. The reported amount of Chinese investment in Hong Kong is likely to be biased downward because some Chinese local authorities and enterprises establish subsidiaries in Hong Kong in order to evade foreign exchange and trade controls. On the other hand, the amount of Hong Kong investment in China is likely to be exaggerated. First, some Hong Kong investment in China is really Chinese capital going back to the Mainland to take advantage of

Mainland Chinese Investment in Hong Kong

the more favorable treatment given to foreign investors.[1] Second, there may be a tendency for the local Chinese officials to overstate the extent of foreign investment in their localities because successful attraction of more foreign investment enhances their job performance evaluations. Lastly, Hong Kong is a entrepot for goods as well as for capital. Some Hong Kong capital going to China is in fact capital from outside Hong Kong that goes through Hong Kong to China.[2]

Table 2
Cumulative Mainland Chinese Investment in Hong Kong, By Major Sectors, 1991 and 1992
(US$ billion)

Year	Total	Manufacturing	Non-Manufacturing	Property
1991	10-12	0.46	11.54	1.3
1992	12-20	0.53	11.47-19.47	2.0

Source: Sung (1995), Kao (1994), Chen and Wong (1994), Hong Kong Trade Development Council (1994), Chan (1994), Sender (1993).
Note: Investment in Hong Kong property is part of the investment in non-manufacturing.

Chronologically, Mainland Chinese investment in Hong Kong can be divided into five stages. 1949-1979 was the gestation period, when Chinese investments were dominated by the four Chinese conglomerates mentioned above. This was followed by an expansion period from 1979 to 1985, when practically all the important ministries of both the central government and the provincial governments came to Hong Kong to invest. 1985 to 1989 was a period of further expansion, but the activities seemed to be guided more by political considerations. 1989 to 1992 was the retrenchment period, with the Chinese government clamping down on hundreds of unscrupulous Mainland firms. As a result, the number of Chinese firms in Hong Kong were reportedly reduced from more than 3,000 to less than 1,000. Following Deng's visit to the South in 1992, we witnessed another period of expansion and proliferation. Presently, there are roughly 1,000 Mainland-funded enterprises in Hong Kong. They are of four types: those that are directly controlled by the central government (e.g. Bank of China Group); those that are directly controlled by provincial governments (e.g. Guangdong Enterprises Holdings); subsidiaries, branches and joint ventures of both the central and provincial governments (e.g. CITIC Pacific); and unauthorized Chinese backed companies (see Lin, Ng, and Tuan 1995, and Kan 1996).

Compared to the past, current Mainland Chinese investment in Hong Kong is relatively diversified. However, the bulk of it is still in non-manufacturing. Table 2 shows that, by the end of 1991, China had invested US$11.54 billion in non-manufacturing and US$0.46 billion in manufacturing. Within non-manufacturing, Chinese investment in the Hong Kong property market reached US$2 billion in 1992.

According to information from the Hong Kong Chinese Enterprise Association, 5.6 percent of the Chinese funded enterprises in 1991 were in manufacturing, 8.28 percent were in construction and real estate, 46.9 percent were in transport business, 4.2 percent were in tourism, 10.15 percent were in transportation and 10.8 percent were in finance and insurance (table 3).

Table 3
Mainland Chinese Investment in Hong Kong by Sectors, 1991
[Number of establishments (percentage)]

Manufacturing	48 (5.6)
Trading	402 (46.91)
Finance and Insurance	93 (10.8)
Transportation	87 (10.15)
Construction and Real Estate	71 (8.28)
Consulting, Advertising, Packaging and Printing	44 (5.13)
Tourism	36 (4.20)
Other	76 (8.87)
Total	857 (100)

Source: Hong Kong Chinese Enterprise Association (1992), Chen and Wong (1994).

Table 4
Cumulative Mainland Chinese Direct Investment in Hong Kong Manufacturing

	Amount (in HK$bill)	Share of All Foreign Investment (percent)
1985	2.40	19.7
1986	2.48	15.9
1988	2.95	11.3
1990	3.28	10.6
1991	3.75	10.9
1992	4.08	11.1

Source: Hong Kong Government Industry Department (1993), Kao (1994), Hong Kong Trade Development Council (1994).

Within *manufacturing*, cumulative Mainland Chinese direct investment in Hong Kong reached HK$4.08 billion by 1992 (table 4). Chinese direct investment constituted 11.1 percent of all foreign investment (with a total of HK$37.3 billion) in Hong Kong. China was the *third* largest foreign investor in manufacturing (number *one* in all sectors), behind Japan and the United States (table 5).

Table 5
Foreign Investment in Hong Kong's Manufacturing Sector, 1992

1. Japan	33.4
2. USA	27.1
3. China	11.1
4. United Kingdom	4.9
5. Netherlands	4.5

Source: General Agreement on Tariffs and Trade (1994).
Note: Figures are percentages of overall foreign manufacturing investment in Hong Kong.

Table 6
Mainland Chinese Investment in Hong Kong by Manufacturing Industry, 1989-1991

	1989	1990	1991
Transport Equipment	939	1,657	2,099
	(29.5)	(50.4)	(56.0)
Electronics	410	255	523
	(12.9)	(7.8)	(14.0)
Textiles and Clothing	295	272	325
	(9.3)	(8.3)	(8.7)
Paper Products	80	NA	221
	(2.5)	---	(5.9)
Non-Electrical Machinery	NA	NA	NA
Metal Products	NA	NA	165
	---	---	(4.4)
Electrical products	NA	93	95
	---	(2.8)	(2.5)
Jade and Jewelry	NA	NA	NA
Chemical products	599	621	81
	(18.8)	(18.9)	(2.2)
Printing and Publishing	NA	NA	NA
Others	48	29	238
	(1.5)	(0.9)	(6.4)
Total	3,178	3,288	3,747
	(100)	(100)	(100)

Source: Hong Kong Government Industry Department (various years), Chen and Wong (1994).
Note: Figures are in HK$million. Figures in parentheses are the percentage share of the total.

As mentioned earlier, Mainland Chinese investment in the manufacturing sector of Hong Kong is rather small. But within manufacturing, most of the 1991 investment was in transport equipment, electronics, and textiles and clothing (table 6).

Looking at the pattern of overall foreign investment in Hong Kong, electronics and textile and clothing were among the top industries, as is the case for Chinese investment. However, unlike the Chinese case, overall foreign investment did not flow much to transport equipment in Hong Kong (table 7).

Table 7
Foreign Investment in Hong Kong's Manufacturing Sector, 1992
(By Industry)

1. Electronics	31.4%
2. Electrical Products	11.1%
3. Textiles and Clothing	11.0%
4. Food and Beverages	6.9%
5. Chemical Products	5.8%

Source: General Agreement on Tariffs and Trade (1994).
Note: Figures are percentages of overall foreign investment in Hong Kong manufacturing sector.

We could further classify Mainland Chinese investment in Hong Kong by their types of ownership. According to table 8, in 1991, 60 percent (28 out of 46) of the firms surveyed were joint ventures with a local interest. This type of organization seemed to concentrate in electronics and textiles and clothing. Joint ventures of Chinese investment can occur at the company, product or project level. For example, Chen and Wong (1994) reported that China Resources, one of the original four dominant Chinese firms in Hong Kong, has 300 joint ventures worldwide in businesses such as toys and furniture manufacturing. It markets the foreign partners' products in China.

Motives of Mainland Chinese Investment

There are several motives for the Mainland Chinese to invest in Hong Kong. Publicly, some Mainland Chinese national enterprises argue that investing in Hong Kong is a way to maintain the social and economic stability of Hong Kong. The Chairman of China International Trust and Investment Corporation (CITIC), an investment arm of the Chinese government's State Council (the highest executive authority in China), had stated this as a reason for investing in Hong Kong. China Resources Enterprises, Ltd. reportedly engages in exporting foodstuffs to Hong Kong as a means of maintaining stable food prices. China Overseas Land and Investment Ltd. is supposed to provide cheap housing to the poor in Hong Kong. However, while there certainly are political-economic reasons for these Chinese entities to invest for the above reasons, it is difficult to judge their significance in particular Chinese investment and operational decisions.

Table 8
Mainland Chinese Investment in Hong Kong
Manufacturing Sector, 1991
(by Forms of Organization)

	Wholly Chinese Owned	Joint Venture without a local interest	Joint Venture with a local interest	Total
Transport Equipment	2 (13.3)	0 (0)	0 (0)	2 (4.3)
Electronics	3 (20.0)	1 (33.3)	8 (28.6)	12 (26.1)
Textile and Clothing	2 (13.3)	0 (0)	6 (21.4)	8 (17.4)
Non-Electrical Machinery	1 (6.7)	0 (0)	1 (3.6)	2 (4.3)
Electrical Products	3 (20.0)	0 (0)	1 (3.6)	4 (8.7)
Others	4 (26.7)	2 (66.7)	12 (42.8)	18 (39.1)
Total	15 (100)	3 (100)	28 (100)	46 (100)

Source: Hong Kong Government Industry Department (1992), Chen and Wong (1994).
Note: The figures are in number of companies. Figures in brackets are the percentage share of the total.

In addition to the above motives, there are other reasons for the Mainland Chinese to invest. First, to China, Hong Kong is still a large and profitable market. So it is natural to invest and set up affiliates in Hong Kong. This is partly reflected in the fact that much of Chinese investment in the manufacturing sector involves a local interest, as the local partner has better information about the domestic Hong Kong market. This reason coincides also with the CITIC announcement that Mainland Chinese investment is in Hong Kong partly to promote Chinese products (Chan 1994).

Second, related to this motive is the desire to provide services to the large amount of trade, traffic and tourist flows between China and Hong Kong. As discussed elsewhere (Fung 1995a, Fung 1995b and

Fung and Lau 1996), trade between Mainland China and Hong Kong involves substantial re-exports between China and the rest of the world via Hong Kong. Servicing the re-export trade can be quite profitable. According to Hong Kong sources, the markup on Hong Kong re-exports of Chinese goods is as high as 25 percent.

A third motive is to bypass restrictions limiting export of advanced technology to China. This reflects China's desire to modernize its economy by acquiring high-technology. The restriction was imposed by the Coordinating Committee for Multilateral Export Controls, which was established by the industrialized countries to regulate the flow of military technology to communist countries. For example, in order to bypass such regulations, it was reported that China set up three electrical products factories in Hong Kong in the 1980s in order to obtain restricted technology (Chan 1994). This motive, however, has weakened somewhat in recent years as the United States relaxed its regulations on high-technology exports with the end of the Cold War.

Fourth, as mentioned earlier, some local Chinese officials set up subsidiaries in Hong Kong to evade Chinese foreign exchange and other controls (Sung 1995). Hong Kong's freedom from capital flow reporting requirements coupled with its higher level of property-rights protection has attracted Chinese capital to Hong Kong, where it can be used and transmitted elsewhere in a much more flexible way.

Fifth, some Chinese enterprises see investing in Hong Kong as a stepping stone to investing abroad. They can test their products, learn about Western management skills and gather more foreign market information in Hong Kong. Hong Kong is the chosen first stop because of proximity, language familiarity and ethnic ties. From Hong Kong, they can next invest in foreign markets such as the United States.

Sixth, some Chinese capital comes to Hong Kong to be designated as foreign capital. It can then in turn be re-invested back to China to take advantage of the favorable tax treatment given to foreign investors. Hsueh and Woo (1991) reported that at least 40 percent of Hong Kong's investment in China is originally from Mainland China.

Lastly, an increasingly important motive for the Chinese presence in Hong Kong is to raise capital. In 1992, China approved the public listing of some state-owned enterprises in the Hong Kong stock exchange. These shares are often called Red Chips and H shares. If we define a Chinese company as one where 35 percent of the shares are controlled by the Mainland Chinese, then there are 39 such firms out of a total of 444 companies listed in the Hong Kong Stock exchange, with about 6 percent of the entire market capitalization. Six of the 39 are state-owned Chinese enterprises listed in the Hong Kong stock exchange (such as Qingdao Brewery and Shanghai Petrochemical

Complex), but they do not engage in any economic activities in Hong Kong (Chang 1994, Chan 1994, Chen and Wong 1994).

Hong Kong has a high savings rate. According to the Asian Development Bank, Hong Kong saved about 31 percent of its Gross Domestic Product (GDP) in 1992. The Hong Kong stock market was the sixth largest stock market in the world at the end of 1993. Chinese enterprises are eager to list in Hong Kong since this could help them raise foreign exchange on a large scale. Some Chinese enterprises also want to be listed in the Hong Kong stock exchange because this is a stepping stone to be listed overseas, such as in the stock markets in New York and London.

This motive of raising capital from Hong Kong also led to some so-called back-door listings. Some Chinese enterprises acquire poorly performed companies listed in the Hong Kong stock exchange, with the sole intention of raising capital through selling stocks of these companies. Over a two year period (1992-1993), a total of nineteen such shell companies have been purchased. These Mainland Chinese shell companies have been able to raise a total of US$1.84 billion from Hong Kong (see Chan 1994, Chen and Wong 1994 and Kan 1996).

Effects of Mainland Investment in Hong Kong

The increase in Mainland Chinese investment in Hong Kong is in general beneficial to both economies. Typically, capital flows from a region of low expected returns to one with high expected returns. Hong Kong benefits from this investment in terms of increased capital formation, growth in output and expansion of employment. Technology transfer tends to be from Hong Kong to China. However, there seems to be some transfer of technology from China to Hong Kong in some selective industries such as cement, chemicals and construction (Chen and Wong 1994). Mainland China also benefits from training, particularly business and managerial training from Hong Kong. However, local Hong Kong staffs trained by Chinese companies can also be useful to Hong Kong if the business is to serve the Mainland market, since this will familiarize the Hong Kong locals with the marketing and institutional aspects of the Chinese market.

Nonetheless, despite the above benefits, there are also some potential concerns. As discussed earlier, a large fraction of the Mainland Chinese investment in Hong Kong is in non-manufacturing. Specifically there is a significant amount of investment in the Hong Kong property market (table 2). The large infusion of Chinese capital in this market has led to a boom. During the two years of 1992-1993, the price of residential property market rose more than 100 percent. Real estate prices in Hong Kong are now higher than those in Tokyo. In fact, even the director of the Hong Kong and Macau Affairs Office criticized the extent of Chinese speculation in the Hong Kong real estate market. These high property prices led to a severe redistribution of income. Although property sellers have benefitted, ordinary Hong Kong residents have witnessed a decline of affordable housing and their standards of living have suffered.

It is also believed that Mainland Chinese capital has led to an expansion of the stock market. In both the real estate and stock market cases, there are some characteristics of Chinese investment that may be of particular concern. One, to the extent that these are investments by state-owned enterprises using Chinese government money, the investors will face the moral hazard problem. The Chinese investor is free to gamble and speculate since if they lose, their losses are covered by the state. But if they win, they can often benefit personally. This leads to property market and stock market speculation that is not consistent with market risks. Excessive volatility is likely to be the result. In addition, the increase in back-door listings by Chinese firms has also led to increased volatility in the stock market. Investors attempt to guess which companies will be the next targets of takeovers and then carry out speculative activities with respect to these stocks. For example, within five months time, the share price of Laws Property tripled while its price/earning ratio increased 25 times after being acquired by Chinese enterprises (see Chang 1994, Chen and Wong 1994, and Chan 1994).

Investments from Chinese state-owned enterprises and other entities using Chinese state funds in Hong Kong have some parallels to the crisis of the American Savings and Loan (S & L) industry in the 1980s and 1990s. S & Ls are, like banks, for-profit financial institutions that borrow money from the public in the form of deposits and then invest it. In the S & L crisis, there were two major problems: one was excessive risky investments that went sour and the second was fraud. The fundamental problem was that deposits in the S & L appeared to be federally protected by the Federal Savings and Loan Insurance Corporation (FSLIC).

While FSLIC served some legitimate functions, its role, (together with lax regulations) encouraged the managers of the S & Ls to invest in very risky projects, including loans on commercial real estate and high-yielding but risky corporate borrowing called "junk bonds". The deposit insurance (and with limited requirements that the owners put their own money at risk) encouraged excessive risk-taking by relieving the S & Ls of the responsibility for poorly performing investments but permitting them to gain if the investments succeeded.

Furthermore, since the deposits were insured, there were less incentives for the lenders (depositors) to monitor and scrutinize which

S & Ls were honest. This allowed some managers and owners of S & Ls to engage in outright fraud. For example, top officers at some S & Ls made loans to themselves, to their other companies, to friends and relatives at reduced interest rates and without adequate collaterals. U.S. government investigation showed that there was fraud in at least 25 percent of the cases of S & Ls.

For the Chinese investments in Hong Kong, the equivalent to the "deposits" are funds from state-owned enterprises, which are implicitly "insured". China's Bankruptcy Law became effective in 1988, but bankruptcy has rarely been used as a way to address the problems of insolvency. Rather, the state budget and the banking system have continued to shoulder a large portion of the losses of the state owned enterprises (World Bank 1993). This soft-budget constraint encourages the Chinese investors to put money in riskier investments, such as real estate and the stock market in Hong Kong. If these Chinese entities raised funds in the Hong Kong stock market, the Hong Kong investors may also feel that their investments are to some extent "insured". In that case, there is much less incentive to monitor the investment activities of these Mainland entities and to ensure that fraud does not take place.

In light of the American S & L experience, what may we expect from some of the Mainland investments in Hong Kong? As we explained earlier, the incentives are such that these Chinese enterprises will engage in risky investments. Some of these speculative investments in the property market and the stock market will eventually sour. When that happens, the state-owned firms will sustain losses, but the losses will be shouldered by the Chinese taxpayers. During good times, the managers/officials involved in the investment can profit personally by siphoning off some of the gains from the risky or fraudulent investments. The Hong Kong shareholders may also be somewhat "insured", depending on exactly what the Chinese government will do to prop up the state-owned firms that engaged in these investments. But unlike the case with the depositors of the S &Ls, the "insurance" to Hong Kong investors is far from certain.

Theoretically, such "moral hazard" problems as discussed above are familiar in the literature of the economics of information (Stiglitz and Weiss 1985, Guesnerie 1989 and Laffont 1990). In a literal sense, moral hazard refers to the negative effects on the insurer due to the provision of insurance. The negative impact may arise because providing insurance can alter the behavior of the insured. As an extreme example, providing fire insurance may induce the policy holder to deliberately burn his house.

Moral hazard issues are often discussed in the context of a principal-agent model. A principal is one who designs a contract to reward the agent, who is supposed to carry out the principal's goal. Due to differences in interests and also due to incomplete information, the principal cannot fully monitor the agent's actions.[3] In our context, the principal is the Mainland Chinese government, which funds the state-owned enterprises through taxes and bank credits. The central government instructs the agent, the local officials and managers of the firms, to maximize profits for the state. In addition, the central government provides "insurance" to the firm since bankruptcy laws are not enforced.

Due to incomplete information, the agent can take certain actions to enrich himself at the expense of the principal, and ultimately the Chinese taxpayers. For example, the agent takes some money out to invest in Hong Kong, ostensibly to get higher returns. Since the money is ultimately "insured," the agent will engage in more risky projects (Milgrom and Roberts 1992). Furthermore, he can write off any bad outcome as a loss from the state-owned enterprises. But for good outcomes, he could make use of the lax regulations in Hong Kong and turn some of the profits into his own returns.

The agent can also raise capital from Hong Kong. He can loan the money to his friends and associates. Hong Kong investors will be less diligent to monitor or to act since they may also feel that they are insured. The agent can also use this raised fund to speculate. Incomplete information and insurance provided by the Mainland Chinese central government can lead to risky investment, and potentially fraud and illegal capital transfers.

In addition to the moral hazard issues, there are two other problems faced by Hong Kong because of the involvement of government and government officials in the Chinese investment. The first problem is that their time horizon may be particularly short-term. Both economically and politically China is a country in transition. As government officials, these investors do not know how much longer they can maintain their privileges, including the privileges of investing the state's money abroad. The incentive here is to speculate fast and get out as soon as sufficient personal profits can be made. This raises the specter that the bubble of Hong Kong's financial sector may burst.[4] Indeed, price increases for property and shares slowed in Hong Kong in the latter part of 1994 and early 1995. Some observers believe that this was due less to the macroeconomic conditions in the United States and China than the fact that as 1997 draws near, Mainland Chinese investors want to move their funds (or funds that belong to the Chinese government) to a place where they cannot be reached by the Chinese central government, say Singapore.[5]

Second, but perhaps more importantly, the involvement of these officials as investors can cause damage to the reputation of the Hong Kong stock market. Some of these investors are directly involved in local decision making in China, and as such, have inside information about potential policy changes. According to Chan (1994) and Chen and Wong (1994), Fujian Enterprises (Holdings) Co. Ltd. is a subsidiary of the provincial government in Fujian. About one-third of its profits, which rose by 40 percent in 1993, came from trading shares of the small and medium companies in Hong Kong. The company's executive director said that the company will continue to have particular interests in trading shares of Hong Kong firms that have businesses in Fujian.

These insiders, being in China, are not subject to the full discipline of the Hong Kong stock market monitoring authorities. Indeed, some of the biggest Chinese investors are descendants of the most important policymakers. For example, Chan (1994) reported that the chairman of Silver Grand International Industries Ltd. and Onfem Holdings Ltd., two companies listed on the Hong Kong stock exchange, is closely related to a powerful leader in China. Potentially, the inside information and the privileges of some of these descendants and relatives of Chinese policymakers can lead to conflicts of interest when they act as investors in the Hong Kong stock market.

The economic involvement of the Mainland Chinese government and officials has caught the public attention. For example, an important Hong Kong businessmen had set up a new Hong Kong company, New China Hong Kong Group, with its shareholders consisting of thirteen Chinese government firms, eleven of which have connections to the national government ministries or bodies. One firm the business arm of the State Council's Hong Kong and Macau Affairs Office (an office that formulates Chinese policy towards Hong Kong and Macau), had to withdraw due to public charges of conflict of interest (Karp 1993). The negative consequence to Hong Kong due to the economic involvement of the Chinese government is that it may damage the reputation of Hong Kong as a modern, competitive, contract-binding, and efficient financial center.

Lastly, Chinese investment in Hong Kong may also have negative consequences for the Chinese reform process. China has been trying gradually to lessen government control over state-owned enterprises. One important part of the recent reform is to allow state-owned firms to set up shareholding companies. The idea is to shift the power of control from the local government to the firm managers, who would then have greater autonomy of decision making. Some local governments responded by acquiring Hong Kong shell companies, raising capital and then setting up factories in China. Thus, the local governments still control production in China, even though on paper the new factories are controlled by a Hong Kong listed company.

Some of the capital raised is also used to strengthen and maintain the monopoly position of locally-controlled firms in China's market. For example, it was reported that Guang Zhou Investment raised HK$1.28 billion from Hong Kong in order to finance acquiring three cement factories in China. When the new factories start to operate, the enterprise will be the largest cement producer in the country, capable of supplying half of the demand of Guangdong (see World Bank 1993, Chan 1994, and Chen and Wong 1994). This may create and strengthen monopolistic practices in China in the future, even as the economy continues to liberalize. The Chinese attempt to weaken ties between local governments and enterprises may be slowed because of the financial connection between China and Hong Kong.

In sum, while financial integration between Mainland China and Hong Kong is in general desirable, it will require much closer monitoring and inspection in order to avoid potentially undesirable outcomes.

Conclusion

There is no comprehensive information concerning Mainland Chinese investment in Hong Kong. This is because Hong Kong does not require reporting on capital flows and China does not keep records on capital outflows. From various fragmentary sources, we gathered data on the extent and characteristics of Chinese investment in Hong Kong. Total cumulative Chinese investments in Hong Kong reached US$25 billion by 1995. It is safe to say that more than 90 percent were in non-manufacturing. Using 1992 figures, between 2.65 percent to 4.4 percent were in manufacturing and between 10 percent to 16.7 percent were in Hong Kong property market. Within manufacturing, the bulk was in transport equipment, electronics and textiles and clothing. The Mainland firms in the manufacturing sector seems to prefer joint ventures with a local partner. By 1993, Mainland China became the largest overall cumulative foreign investor in Hong Kong, while it was third among foreign investors in manufacturing, behind Japan and the United States. Also, by 1993, Chinese investment in Hong Kong was likely larger than Hong Kong's investment in the Mainland.

There are many reasons why the Mainland Chinese invest in Hong Kong. This includes serving the profitable Hong Kong market; serving the re-export trade between China and the rest of the world via Hong Kong; bypassing Western high-technology export control; evading Chinese foreign exchange and other controls; using Hong Kong as a first stop to go further overseas; and raising capital through Hong Kong.

There are clearly some mutually beneficial reasons for such flows of capital, such as capital formation, employment, technology transfer, etc.. However, there are also some concerns. First, the infusion seems to have contributed to the rise of the property market in Hong Kong, which can have negative income distribution effects. Second, as a significant amount of the Mainland Chinese capital comes from government funds, the investors may face moral hazard problems and likely will engage in "excessive" speculation, adding to the volatility of the real estate and stock market. In addition, the involvement of the local Chinese governments as well as the involvement of descendants of important Chinese policymakers in Hong Kong in the Hong Kong stock market means that there are potential conflict-of-interest problems. This may lead to a deterioration of the reputation of the Hong Kong stock exchange as a modern and efficient capital market. Lastly, some Chinese local governments seem to have used the Hong Kong stock market as a way to raise funds to acquire factories in China so that they can continue to control, even though indirectly through a shell company in Hong Kong, establishments in China. This practice is used as a circumvention of the central government's wish to weaken the ties between the local governments and the state-owned enterprises. It has the effect of slowing down the Chinese reform process.

Overall, while Mainland Chinese investment in Hong Kong is generally beneficial, stricter monitoring is required to reduce the likelihood of adverse consequences, either to the Chinese taxpayers, to the Chinese reform process, or to the stability and efficiency of the Hong Kong economy.

Endnotes

1 In recent months, in order to gain entry to the World Trade Organization, Mainland China is preparing to apply the national treatment principle to investment. In other words, formal favorable treatments given to certain foreign investors will soon be eliminated.

2 For a discussion on this point, see Sung (1995), Kao (1994), and Low, Ramsetter and Yeung (1995).

3 For technical discussions of the principal-agent approach, see Tirole 1989: 51 and Mas-Colell, Whinston and Green 1995: ch.14.

4 However, some argue that the size of the Mainland Chinese investment will not be able to cause too much damage to the Hong Kong financial market.

5 I am indebted to Larry Lau for suggesting this possibility to me. But currently, there are some signs that the Hong Kong property market is recovering.

References

Chan Hing-lin, 1994, "The Chinese Investment in Hong Kong: Issues and Problems," BRC Papers on China, Hong Kong Baptist College, Hong Kong.

Chang, C., 1994, "Corporations of the Hong Kong Stock Exchange and Their Subsidiaries in the People's Republic of China, 1993," Institute of Government Affairs, University of California-Davis.

Chen, E. and T. Wong, 1994, "Economic Synergy—A Study of Two-Way Foreign Direct Investment flow Between Hong Kong and Mainland China," mimeo, Centre of Asian Studies, University of Hong Kong, Hong Kong.

Fung, K.C., 1995a, "Accounting for Chinese Trade: Some National and Regional Considerations," paper presented at the NBER Conference on Geography and Ownership as a Basis for Economic Accounting, Washington, D.C.

----------, 1995b, *Trade and Investment Flows: Mainland China, Hong Kong and Taiwan,* Hong Kong Centre for Economic Research Monograph, City University of Hong Kong Press, forthcoming.

---------- and Lawrence J. Lau, 1996, "The China-United States Bilateral Trade Balance: How Big Is It Really?" Occasional Paper, Asia/Pacific Research Center, Institute for International Studies, Stanford University, Stanford, CA.

General Agreement on Tariffs and Trade, 1994, *Trade Policy Review Mechanism: Hong Kong,* Geneva.

Guesnerie, R., 1989, "Hidden Actions, Moral Hazard and Contract Theory," in *Allocation, Information and Markets*, ed. by J. Eatwell, M Milgate, and P. Newman, The Macmillan Press.

Hong Kong Chinese Enterprise Association, 1992, *Directory of Enterprise with PRC Capital in Hong Kong*, Hong Kong.

Hong Kong Government Industry Department, *Survey of Overseas Investment in Hong Kong Manufacturing Sector*, various years, Hong Kong.

Hong Kong Trade Development Council, 1994, "Hong Kong as a Trading Hub in Asia-Pacific," Research department Topical Paper.

Hsueh, Tien-tung and Tun-oy Woo, 1991, "The Changing Pattern of Hong Kong-China Economic Relations since 1979: Issues and Consequences," in E. Chen, M. Nyaw and T. Wong ed. *Industrial and Trade Development in Hong Kong*, University of Hong Kong, Hong Kong.

Mainland Chinese Investment in Hong Kong

Kan, Chak-Yuen, 1996, "Mainland-Funded Enterprises and the Hong Kong Economy," *City Economist*, City University of Hong Kong, Hong Kong.

Kao, C., 1994, "An Investigation of the Relations of the Economic Interactions among Taiwan, Hong Kong and Mainland China," (in Chinese) Chung Hua Institution for Economic Research, Taipei, Taiwan.

Karp, J., 1993, "The New Insiders," *Far East Economic Review*, 27 May 1993: 62-68.

Laffont, J.J., 1990, *The Economics of Uncertainty and Information*, MIT Press, Cambridge, Massachusetts.

Lardy, N., 1994, *China in the World Economy*, Institute for International Economics, Washington, D.C.

Lin, Tzong-Biau, Linda Ng, and Chyau Tuan, 1995, "The South China Growth Triangle: Integration of Economies of South China, Hong Kong and Taiwan," mimeo in possession of author.

Low, L., E. Ramstetter, and H. Yeung, 1995, "Accounting for Outward Direct Investment from Hong Kong and Singapore: Who Controls What?" paper presented to NBER Conference on Geography and Ownership as a Basis for Economic Accounting, Washington, D.C..

Milgrom, P., and J. Roberts, 1992, *Economics, Organization and Management*, Prentice-Hall, New Jersey.

Mas-Colell, A., M.Whinston and J. Green, 1995, *Microeconomic Theory*, Oxford University Press.

Sender, H., 1993, "Cash Dispenser: Fast-moving Money Underpins Economy," *Far East Economic Review*, 144 (42): 26.

Stiglitz, J., and A. Weiss, 1985, "Credit Rationing in Markets with Imperfect Information," *American Economic Review* 71(3), 393-410.

Sung, Yun-Wing, 1995, "Hong Kong and the Economic Integration of the China Circle," mimeo, Chinese University of Hong Kong, Hong Kong.

Tirole, J., 1989, *The Theory of Industrial Organization*, MIT Press.

World Bank, 1993, *China Updating Economic Memorandum: Managing Rapid Growth and Transition*, Washington, D.C.

[33]

GLOBALIZATION AND URBAN CHANGE: TALES FROM VANCOUVER VIA HONG KONG[1]

Kris Olds

Department of Geography
National University of Singapore
10 Kent Ridge Crescent
Singapore 119260
Tel: 65-874-6811
Fax: 65-777-3091
geoko@nus.edu.sg

Abstract: The main aim of this article is to examine some of the sociocultural dimensions of contemporary globalization processes, especially in a "Pacific Rim" context. This broad subject is approached by using the Can$3 billion Pacific Place urban mega-project (UMP) in central Vancouver as a vehicle through which to explore the social processes structuring a trans-Pacific property transaction. I examine the key factors leading the Li Group from Hong Kong to extend their "reach" over space into Vancouver at this particular time in history. Addressing this topic entails attempting to understand (1) the business and personal dynamics of the key actors involved with such global flows of property capital, set within a broader geopolitical and geoeconomic context; (2) the meaning and significance of Vancouver to the actors, especially in the context of immigration flows to the city; and (3) the significance and multiple functions of this type of property development project—the urban mega-project—to the actors. And while this case study is not designed to be representative of the overall nature of the trans-Pacific property development process, it does highlight some important characteristics about Vancouver's changing social and political structure, as well as the need (in theoretical and methodological terms) to produce more modest and provisional accounts about the "global space of flows."

Let me take you on a brief tour through a condominium unit in The Concordia, part of the Pacific Place mega-project on the North Shore of False Creek in Vancouver, Canada. This unit (Fig. 1) and the project it is situated in are elegant markers of the intersection of a burgeoning trans-Pacific residential property market with trans-Pacific migration, and succession plans within one of the world's leading ethnic Chinese corporate groups (the Li Group)—three factors that both constitute and are constitutive of the processes of globalization.

We arrive on the 15th floor and make our way into a unit in the range of 1,100 square feet of "timeless elegance and sophistication" creating "a new standard in home design"—priced at Can$200,000–$300,000 at this floor level.[2] "Finely crafted with care and attention," your home offers views of the water, southern exposure to the sun, and your choice of select materials and equipment to outfit and decorate the unit. The unit and The Concordia express an "ambiance"—a "distinctive residence"—in a "classic estate" on an "exclusive seafront." It is connected with "state of the art fiber optics providing enhanced personal communications," enabling you to carry out a multitude of activities such as: working at home through the exchange of high-speed text, audio, video, and

Urban Geography, 1998, 19, 4, pp. 360–385.

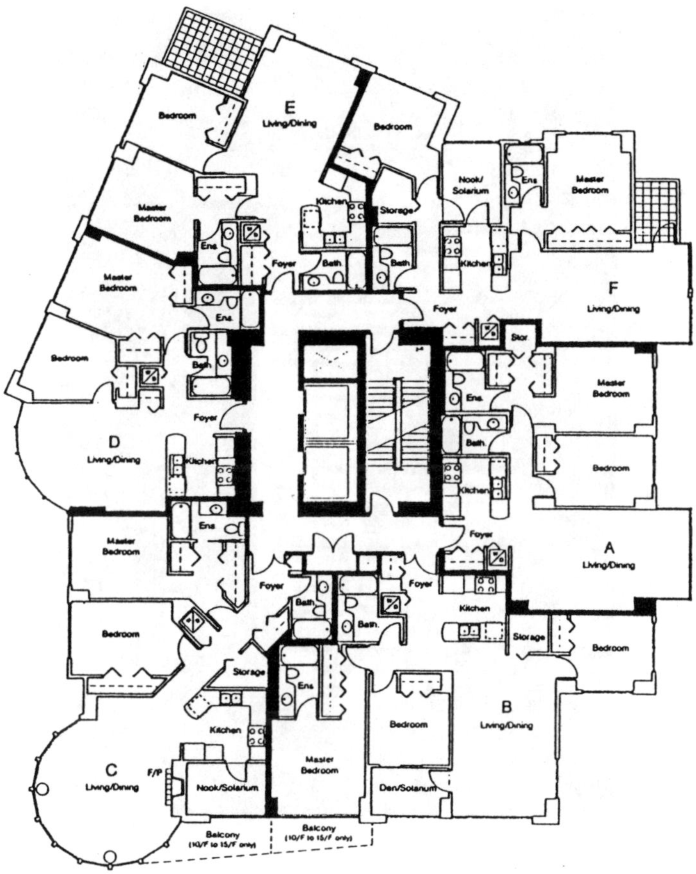

Fig. 1. Floorplan of units in The Concordia, Pacific Place. *Source:* Concord Pacific Developments Ltd.

graphic information with people from around the world; calling home to turn on the oven or adjust room temperature; ordering videos to be "piped in"; and surveillance through the use of high-definition video monitoring equipment to simultaneously view up to four different locations (by splitting your television screen into quadrants) in the private, semi-public, and public spaces in and around The Concordia.

The Concordia itself is situated on a "sheltered Pacific inlet" at the "heart of a great international centre of fashion and finance"—Vancouver—the "Pacific Coast's most dynamic city." In short, you are now a resident of Concord Pacific Place, the "pre-eminent planned community on the Pacific Rim."

This unit did not actually exist in physical reality until mid-1995—two years after the field research that this passage is based on (Fig. 2). We have been inside the display unit

Fig. 2. The Concordia in 1996. *Source:* Author.

of a Can$2 million presentation center where the "pre-sale" process takes place. In the pre-sale process, prospective purchasers of condominium units examine mock suites, graphic images such as Figure 1, models of condominium towers, a model of the entire project site, a large map of the Pacific Rim, and numerous other types of information including mortgage arrangement details with banks in Vancouver and Hong Kong. The atmosphere of a marketplace prevails, with large crowds at certain times of the week. You can mingle with representatives of the development company, fellow buyers, and researchers such as myself. Glass-enclosed meeting rooms permit you to see deals in the making, and each closure is followed by the placing of a red sticker on a graphic of the condo tower announcing "SOLD." Full-page announcements of the sale of new condominium towers are also placed in all of Vancouver's major English- and Chinese-language newspapers. If you prefer a more distanciated mode of viewing the condominium units being built at Pacific Place, log on to the World Wide Web and key in Concord Pacific's internet address (http://www.concordpacific.com/welcome.html). Through the vehicle of communications technology you will be able to examine floor plans, take yacht trips down False Creek, and find out the latest company-sponsored public events planned for the site.

This style of buying property is a relatively recent phenomenon in Vancouver. It became common in the early 1990s when projects such as Pacific Place were being developed and sold in the context of a globalizing residential property market, driven by steadily increasing linkages between Vancouver and Hong Kong. Indeed, the Vancouver Information Centre in Hong Kong acts as a virtual replica of this one, albeit on the 20th floor of the China Tower, Central, Hong Kong. Pre-sale is the most common method of residential property development in the hyperactive temple of money worship—Hong Kong, also known as Mammon's Temple. Pre-sale provides the developer with "capitalism's ultimate fantasy—the world's first perpetual money machine" (Newman, 1993, p. 36), where risk is shifted to the buyer from the seller, where turnover time, gearing levels, and carrying costs are significantly reduced, and where future speculative goals can be more carefully weighed.

Pacific Place is ultimately the product of complex Hong Kong–derived agendas—agendas that have shaped all aspects of the project's development process in Vancouver. As with many cities, especially on the Pacific Rim, the processes underlying the production of new urban spaces are being transformed in our "globalizing era." Urban societies and urban economies are becoming increasingly interdependent, albeit in a highly uneven manner. Networks of a global scale are linking together processes of change within seemingly separate cities, generating new forms of interdependencies, intertwined futures, hybrid social practices, and built forms representative of a plethora of competing and complementary agendas.

While globalization is certainly not a new force, and interdependencies between cities have existed for hundreds of years (cf. Abu-Lughod, 1989), it is clear that the *nature* of contemporary globalization processes is changing (Giddens, 1990; Amin and Thrift, 1994; Bairoch and Kozul-Wright, 1996). As one of the more insightful commentators on globalization writes, "what is new about the modern global system is the stretching of social relations in and through new dimensions of activity—technological, organizational, administrative and legal, among others" (Held, 1996, p. 340). To be more concise, I follow Anthony McGrew's (1992, p. 23) definition of globalization as:

> the multiplicity of linkages and interconnections between states and societies which make up the present world system. It describes the process by which events, decisions, and activities in one part of the world come to have significant consequences for individuals and communities in quite distant parts of the globe. Globalization has two distinct phenomena: *scope* (or stretching) and *intensity* (or deepening). On the one hand, it defines a set of processes which embrace most of the globe or which operate worldwide; the concept therefore has a spatial connotation.... On the other hand it also implies an intensification on the levels of interaction, interconnectedness or interdependence between the states and societies which constitute the world community. Accordingly, alongside the stretching goes a deepening of global processes. (Cited in Dunning, 1994, p. 11, emphasis added)

As McGrew's definition implies, globalization must be seen as a *multi-dimensional* phenomenon, involving "highly intricate interactions between a whole variety of social, political, and economic institutions across a spectrum of geographical scales" (Dicken et al., 1997, p. 159; also see Amin and Thrift, 1994, and Appadurai, 1996, on this point). Globalization is therefore a contingent and ever-shifting mesh of interactive processes that operate at a variety of scales.

It is in such a globalizing context that urban redevelopment processes within Vancouver's central city must be framed. Projects such as Pacific Place are symbols of the increasing interconnectedness of Vancouver and Hong Kong. Global flows of property capital and development models are increasingly binding these two cities together, and in the process transforming the nature of urban life and identity in this Canadian city. And while it is obvious to anyone living in Vancouver that the nature of urbanity is changing, and that "Hong Kong" is playing a key role in this process of change, it is often difficult to make sense of the subtle impacts of these changes and the complex social dynamics that underlie the process of change.

The main aim of this article is to examine some of the sociocultural dimensions of contemporary globalization processes, especially in a "Pacific Rim" context. This broad subject is approached by using the Pacific Place urban mega-project (UMP) in central Vancouver as a vehicle through which to explore the social processes structuring the property development process. In this article, I examine the key factors leading the Li Group to extend their reach over space into Vancouver at this particular time in history. Addressing this topic entails attempting to understand (1) the business and personal dynamics of the key actors involved with such global flows of property capital, set within a broader political-economic context; (2) the meaning and significance of Vancouver to the actors, especially in the context of immigration flows to the city; and (3) the significance and multiple functions of this type of property development project—the UMP—to the actors. By addressing these issues, I hope to clarify how the redevelopment of one-sixth (80 hectares) of Vancouver's central city is intimately related to family/corporate succession plans with the Li Group, plans that required the acquisition of a large portion of the city for use as a property development training tool for the eldest son of Hong Kong tycoon Li Ka-shing. And while this case study is hardly representative of the overall nature of the trans-Pacific property development process, and while Li Ka-shing is only representative of a small elite circle of ethnic Chinese tycoons and their families based in Hong Kong, the case does highlight some important characteristics about Vancouver's changing social and political structure, as well as the need (in more theoretical terms) to conduct culturally sensitive work on the property development industry.

READING GLOBAL FLOWS OF PROPERTY CAPITAL

The implications of the deepening of globalization processes for cities are many, though the concept of social and spatial reordering is a particularly prominent one (e.g., Sassen, 1991, 1994; Hannerz, 1996; Eade, 1997). In a more general sense, Thrift (1996) has characterized such changes in this way:

> What is *place* in this new "in-between" world? The short answer is—compromised: permanently in a state of enunciation, between addresses, always deferred. Places

> are "stages of intensity," traces of movement, speed and circulation. (P. 289, emphasis in original)

Now, I do not mean to imply that this is a homogeneous and uncontested process (cf. Mitchell, 1993; Ley, 1995), or that the forces of globalization have swept through the cities of the Pacific Rim and all that we are left with is an unstable landscape marked by movement and flow, for this is clearly not the case. "Movement and flow" are not overwhelming the "identity of place," as Kevin Robins (1991, p. 13) and Manuel Castells (1989, 1996) have suggested; rather, contemporary flows are reshaping the identity of places that have always been intersected by flows operating at a variety of scales (Massey, 1993; Amin, 1997). This is particularly true in Vancouver—a colonial port city with a long history of contact with "external" forces and diverse cultures.

What has changed though, since the mid-1980s, is that the nature of life in some Canadian cities (in particular Vancouver and Toronto) is increasingly shaped by quite volatile flows that now link Canada to the economically dynamic Asia-Pacific region. The shifting weight of linkages from European nations such as Poland, Sweden, and Scotland (the source nations of my own ethnicity), to Asian nations such as China, Vietnam, and Singapore, underlies a myriad of impacts in the city.

But how might we make sense of urban change in Vancouver (and the property development process in particular) in a manner that incorporates a sensitivity to the complex and subtle nature of flows guided out of Asia and across the Pacific? Fortunately, there is a burgeoning literature to which I can refer because, in the context of expanding global flows, an increasing number of analysts are reimagining the city and emphasizing the need for an ontology of movement and new conceptualizations of the "space of flows" (Thrift, 1996). The urban anthropologist Ulf Hannerz (1992, 1996), for example, wrote of the historical increase in global "cultural flows," the emergence of the global ecumene—"a single field of persistent interaction and exchange between cultures"—and the role of the world city in both symbolizing and enabling such an ecumene to form "open ramifying networks." Sociologists Scott Lash and John Urry (1994) analyzed global "asymmetrical" flows of subjects and objects—the people, ideas, images, technologies, and capital that make up the modern economies of signs and space—which drive "disorganized capitalism." They paid particular attention to the role of the global city as a "switching" center of "information, knowledge, images and symbols" (Lash and Urry, 1994, p. 220) where global flows are mediated by networked institutions employing highly skilled, cosmopolitan, and reflexive professionals. Kevin Robins (1991) summarized several other writers who focus on flows and the city:

> Now... the city has become integrated not only into more complex, international transportation systems, but also into global information and communications networks. We can now talk of a process of globalization or transnationalization in the transformation of urban space and form. Manuel Castells describes the advent of the "informational city," and identifies "the historical emergence of the space of flows, superseding the space of places." Others have described this same process in similar ways. Suggesting that "things are not defined by their physical boundaries any more," the [deconstructionist] architect Bernard Tschumi points to the advent of the "exploded city." Paul Virilio calls it the "overexposed city": "In the place of a dis-

> crete boundary in space, demarcating distinct spaces, one sees spaces co-joined by semi-permeable membranes, exposed to flows of information in particular ways." (Pp. 12–13)

While there is insufficient space to highlight the main arguments within influential texts such as Castells's *The Informational City* or *The Network Society*, it is clear that the argument of Castells (1989, 1996) and many others (e.g., Sassen, 1991, 1994; Lash and Urry, 1994) is fundamentally derived from a series of dualisms:

Future	Past
Flows	Places
Function	Experience
Power	Culture
Global	Local

much like Zukin's (1991) division between "market" and "place," with the left column clearly superseding the right. From Castells's (1989, pp. 169–170) perspective, for example, the networked organizations (such as the Li Group) structuring the global *space* of flows, and the material and nonmaterial *flows* that shift along this spatial architecture, are organizationally placeless and increasingly independent from a place-bound societal logic. In other words, the spatial dimension of the space of flows develops out of the logic of organizations (which are large-scale information processing complexes), which prizes access to the network of flows above all other goals (Castells, 1996).

It could be argued that such conceptualizations of placeless organizational logics, all-powerful organizations restructuring places to facilitate flows, and static places is too firm, too abstract, too focused, and lacking in the dynamism that might be evident in more provisional accounts about globalization (Thrift, 1995; Dicken et al., 1997). As Thrift (1995) argued, the "space of flows" can be

> revealed as a partial and contingent affair, just like all other human enterprises, which are not abstract or abstracted but consists of social networks, often of quite limited size even though they might span the globe. (Pp. 34–35)

More specifically, much discussion about the forces propelling the global space of flows (from Castells, Harvey, and others) falls into three main traps. First, narratives about global flows are fundamentally abstracted, decontextualized, and dehumanized. These narratives are written as if the flows were formulated by homogeneous actors (e.g., developers) who "conceive" of space and formulate objectified representations of space in a Lefebvrian sense (Lefebvre, 1991), and then set associated flows free to accelerate and shift across space and time, pulverizing place in the process of creative destruction (e.g., Zukin, 1991). These are fundamentally disembodied flows, since the subjective views of the formulators, funnelers, and skimmers of the global flows are merely assumed rather than examined. If the subjective perception of the actors is examined, it is rarely situated or problematized, and it is also assumed that agents of flows operate according to a global logic (i.e., "Space is commanded and appropriated by capital and represents the realm of a rootless, fluid reality consisting of flows of capital, commodities, money and information that may take on global dimensions" [Merrifield, 1993, p. 103]). Such analyses (including those on property capital flows) are ultimately reflective of Western perspectives on development processes. For example, the vast majority of neoclassical property market analyses (e.g., Baum and Schofield, 1991; Royal Institution of Chartered Surveyors, 1993) are rooted in the catcheisms of self-equilibrating markets, the workings of "natural" laws, and efficient price-setting markets (Harris, 1994). More critical analysts working under the urban political economy rubric (e.g., Harvey, 1982, 1989a, 1989b; Badcock, 1984; Haila, 1991) perform analyses using different terms, but with many functional similarities, universal causal tenets, and foci (Healey, 1991). The applicability of both approaches to a property development project driven by an Asian Asia-based developer needs to be questioned.

Second, the content of the global flows is homogenized and distanced from the fundamental ordering and signification processes associated with the "authors" of the flows. Commonly associated with the hypermobility of capital thesis, these arguments are "dangerously overgeneralized" and encouraging of many forms of defeatism at the local level (Cox, 1992, 1997). For example, narratives on the flow of money tend to assume that money = money—that is, serves one obvious and clear purpose (capital accumulation via the maximization of returns) in a consistent manner over time—and that the goal of capital accumulation can be satisfied on an isotropic plain.

And third, few analyses provide provisional accounts of the concrete "articulations" that accompany the processes of global flows as "they unfold under geographically and historically specific conditions" (Pred and Watts, 1992, p. xiii; see also Appadurai, 1996). Analyses need to be historically specific because the globalization of Chinese corporate groups is very much a recent phenomenon (Kao, 1993); and they need to be socially and geographically specific in that Chinese business activity is largely associated with the ethnic Chinese diaspora and their geographical concentration in specific Pacific Rim cities such as Vancouver (East Asian Analytical Unit, 1995). It is therefore through provisional accounts that we can better understand the uneven and contingent nature of the global space of flows (Thrift, 1995; Murdoch, 1997; Whatmore and Thorne, 1997).

These gaps are related to, and compounded by, the steady retreat into heavily theoretical work as academics make little effort to access global elites and global networks, or link these actors and networks to transformations at the local level. This article is one small contribution toward deepening and socializing the analysis of the global space of flows, by linking the flows to the actors who formulate them and by interrogating the internal ever-shifting nature of the space of flows. The rationale is to construct a socialized discussion of global property development by examining actors (including groups and institutions within their broader societal context[s]) and their discourses in order to humanize the account of global change. The analysis of intentional acting people within their interwoven "social and historical context" (Ley, 1989, pp. 234–235) in the cause of global change is too rarely examined, since, in "the rush to structure, what Pollner has charmingly dubbed 'the extraordinary organization of the ordinary' [1987, p. xvii] is entirely lost," leading to a "largely lifeless view of human society" (Boden, 1994, p. 5). While such analyses provide important insights, "lost in process is the important intersection of action and structure or, more simply, people and their history" (Boden, 1994, p. 5; see also Whatmore and Thorne, 1997). What is needed, in the opinion of Deidre Boden and others (e.g., Giddens, 1990, 1994; Massey, 1993; Murdoch, 1997) is work that seeks to link details of local action and articulates these "on a scale with the pace of global history in the making" (Boden, 1994, p. 6), realizing of course that these are episodic changes, and with the briefest passing of time, they are unlikely to articulate in the *exact* same manner again even in the same locale.

What I have done in my analysis of the development of the Can$3 billion Pacific Place project is try to look at the globalization of Vancouver in what is hopefully a less economistic (more culturally sensitive) nature via the development of a theoretically informed empirical case study. This article focuses on the global actors (the Li family in particular) associated with the global flows of property capital, images, and property development expertise that are dramatically altering the face of this Canadian west coast city.

In this article, an analytical narrative is constructed through the application of two main sets of literature: Arjun Appadurai's (1990a, 1990b, 1996) concept of the "global cultural economy," and socioeconomic literature that highlights the embeddedness of "economic actors" in networks and institutions which are reflective of the sociocultural and professional systems of which they are a part.

To summarize briefly, Appadurai suggested that we need to focus on the nature and impact of five overlapping and disjunctive "landscapes" through which global flows pass: global "ethnoscapes" associated with increasingly mobile people such as migrants; global "mediascapes" associated with flows of electronic-mediated accounts of human lives and places; global "technoscapes" associated with flows of technological systems and components; global "finanscapes" associated with flows of capital into a myriad of markets; and global "ideoscapes" associated with flows of ideologically derived world views. It is important to recognize that the suffix *scape* indicates "first of all that these are not objectively given relations which look the same from every angle of vision, but rather that they are deeply *perspectival* constructs, inflected very much by the historical, linguistic and political situatedness of different sorts of actors" (down in scale from the nation state to the individual, and including diaspora communities), and that these landscapes are irregularly shaped and fluid (Appadurai, 1990b, p. 296; emphasis added).

Appadurai (1990b) suggested that these landscapes are "navigated" by actors (agents) who "both experience and constitute larger formations, in part by their own sense of what these landscapes offer" (p. 296). This framework, which I conceive of as a decentered version of world-systems theory, implies that it is important to take account of the perspectives and imaginations of the situated actors who formulate, funnel, and skim material and nonmaterial global flows. Given that actors drive flows within and between specific contexts, each related landscape is subject to unique "incentives" and "constraints" that change over time and space, leading them to follow "non-isomorphic" (i.e., they do not have the same form and relations) paths. Following this logic, the more culturally oriented scapes (ideoscape, mediascape) are not *necessarily* subordinate to, or directly associated with, the more economically oriented scapes (technoscape, finanscape) (Holton, 1992, pp. 233–234). This mode of thought is clearly sympathetic to actor-network theory, itself derived from the "bloodline" of poststructuralism where concern rests with "many semiotic systems, many orderings, jostling together to generate the social" (Law, 1994, p. 18, cited in Thrift, 1996, p. 23).

Given my sympathies with Appadurai's approach to globalization, the rationale underlying this analysis is the need to problematize conceptions of global *economic* action (property development action) as if it can be disentangled from the cultural, the social, or the political—one sphere determining the other. Rather, this analysis assumes that economic action by an actor (the Li Group) is socially constructed. Moreover, these actors must also be situated within their historically specific social, cultural, and professional systems, for they work in institutionalized environments that both "constrain and buttress their involvement in economic activity" (Gereffi and Hamilton, 1991, p. 7). In other words, the formulation, funneling, and skimming of global flows is a form of economic action that is socially and culturally embedded and hence impossible to analyze in isolation from issues related to culture and social relations (Granovetter, 1985; Grabher, 1993). In the context of the global space of flows described earlier, however, this account must also address the deterritorialization of cultural flows and associated signs, meanings, and identities in today's thoroughly "complex, overlapping," and "disjunctive order" (Appadurai, 1990b, p. 296; see also Amin and Thrift, 1994; O Tuathail, 1997).

Such a perspective on globalizing cities is further developed through the application of complementary insights from what is broadly termed the "economic sociology" or "socioeconomic" paradigm, along with insights from economic and cultural geographers who are addressing similar issues (though with a firmer understanding of the spatial dimensions of change).[3] This paradigm is related to the "new institutionalism in organizational analysis" approach (e.g., Powell and DiMaggio, 1991) and the "new institutional economics" (e.g., Hodgson, 1994). Writers such as Amin and Thrift (1992, 1994, 1995), Block (1990), Dicken and Thrift (1992), Gereffi and Hamilton (1991), Grabher (1993), Granovetter (1985), Granovetter and Swedberg (1992), Hamilton (1994, 1996), Mitchell (1995), Redding (1990), Yeung (1997), and Zukin and DiMaggio (1990) developed a "socio-organizational" approach to the operation of *capitalisms* in distinct time-space contexts. While there is considerable diversity within these writings, the main propositions (Granovetter and Swedberg, 1992, p. 6) of economic sociology and "socioeconomic geography," as it has been practiced to date, are (1) economic action is a form of social action, (2) economic action is socially situated, and (3) economic institutions are social constructions. The basic idea is that the production of global flows (of property capital in this case) is a form of social action, a social construct that can be more subtly analyzed through provisional accounts focused on specific actors, institutions, relations, and events, albeit set within broader geopolitical and geoeconomic contexts.

These two broad literatures are used to formulate the subsequent narrative I provide on the rationale for why the Li Group "reached" over space into Vancouver (a specific city) in the late 1980s (a particular time in history). As my framework cannot be rigidly applied like a grid forcing data to fit within conceptual boxes, nor displayed in diagrammatic form, relevant insights are used to inform my mind as I construct the narrative, and they underlie all of the subsequent text in this article. I should also add that I have deliberately held back using Appadurai's "scapes" terminology in the remaining part of this essay in the interest of reducing jargon. Moreover, I have used few direct quotes from the many interviews I conducted during the multi-locale research process—instead all formal interviews, informal interviews, secondary sources of data, etc., inform *every* aspect of the subsequent narrative you will read.[4]

Let us now move on to one key event in the actual development of the trans-Pacific property market—the (re)development of 80 hectares of prime land in central Vancouver from 1988 on. While some effort is made to follow a chronological pattern, the need for

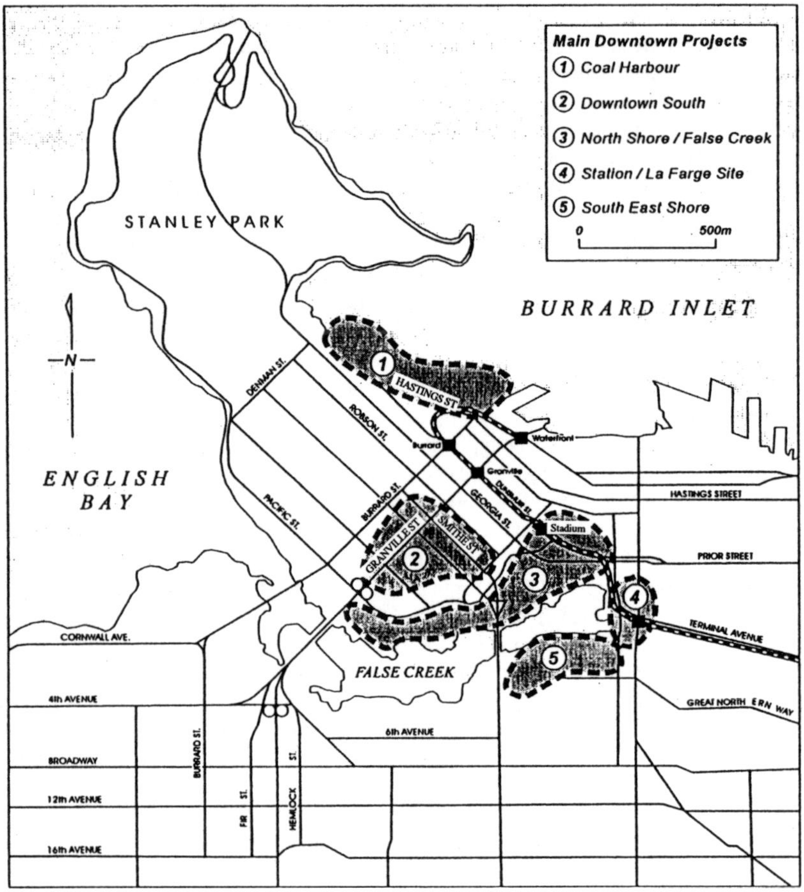

Fig. 3. Pacific Place/North Shore of False Creek. *Source:* City of Vancouver Planning Department, Vancouver, Canada.

brevity precludes much discussion of the actual development process (and in particular the role of City of Vancouver politicians and planners in this process).

LIQUID ASSETS: DEVELOPING "PACIFIC PLACE"

In 1987, the British Columbia Provincial Government decided to sell 204 acres (80 hectares) of land that it owned in downtown Vancouver (Fig. 3). This land (the former Expo '86 site) was put up for sale as part of a newly initiated privatization program. The subsequent acquisition of this land in May 1988 for Can$320 million from the provincial government is the result of the decision of Li Ka-shing, Hong Kong's richest, most powerful and well-connected property tycoon, to deepen his linkages with Vancouver as an individual, as a father, and as patriarch of the Li Group.

Li Ka-shing has two sons—Victor Tzar-kuoi Li (born in 1965) and Richard Tzar Kai Li (born in 1967). Like many of Hong Kong's overseas Chinese business families, the sons were groomed from an early age to take part in their family's firms, and it is impossible to separate "work life" from "home life"—the two are closely intertwined (Chan, 1996).

In 1981, the eldest son (Victor) left Hong Kong to attend Stanford University in the United States, where he enrolled in the civil engineering program. An overseas education at a respected institution is an increasingly common affair in Hong Kong; indeed, there are "strong links between prospective real estate investment and the location of family and friends, and where children and grandchildren were attending university" (Edgington and Goldberg, 1992, p. 7-9). As Goldberg (1985) and Mitchell (1993) also highlighted, the education of children is a critically important factor in most ethnic Chinese cultures, and it reflects the fundamental role of the family in society.

Two years later (1983), when he was 18 years old, Victor became a naturalized Canadian citizen. That Canada was selected as the safe option for Victor's "second home" is related to a number of factors: (1) the variety of property investments Li Ka-shing had accumulated in Canadian cities (including Vancouver) since the late 1960s (Gutstein, 1988, p. 132; Chan, 1996, p. 123); (2) the holiday house where the Li family had vacationed since the early 1970s on a street in Oakridge (a Vancouver neighborhood), where a variety of friends lived; (3) long-term linkages Li Ka-shing had formed with Canadian financial institutions since 1974 (especially the Canadian Imperial Bank of Commerce); (4) the accessible nature of Canada's immigration system; and (5) the social and political climate of the country. All five factors are important in that they gradually encouraged Li Ka-shing to consider Canada a suitable non-Asian country with which to form sustained linkages. As Victor himself stated:

> One of the best things about Canada is the way it treats new people. The cultural diversity makes the investor feel comfortable. There's also political stability. Canada is one of the most comfortable places to do business compared to a lot of Western countries. (Quoted in *An "inside" Asian investor's view of Canada*, 1989, p. 8)

By 1985, Victor had graduated from Stanford with a undergraduate degree in civil engineering and a master's degree in structural engineering. He briefly worked for an architectural firm in Hong Kong before crossing the Pacific once again to set up a base in Vancouver at the age of 21 (Chan, 1996). This move to Canada would have been sanctioned by his father, and it could be seen as a chance for Victor, as one of Li's "boys," to "prove himself" by gaining maturity and new experiences (Kraar, 1992a, p. 108; Kraar, 1992b, p. 62).

As noted above, Vancouver was a chosen as a suitable location for Victor's "second home" (Kraar, 1992b, p. 63). Even though the city (and province) was experiencing an economic recession, steady immigrant flows from Hong Kong (Fig. 4) and other Asian countries had created a diverse ethno-cultural mix in the city (while also creating related market opportunities via the demand for housing units). This steady influx of immigrants

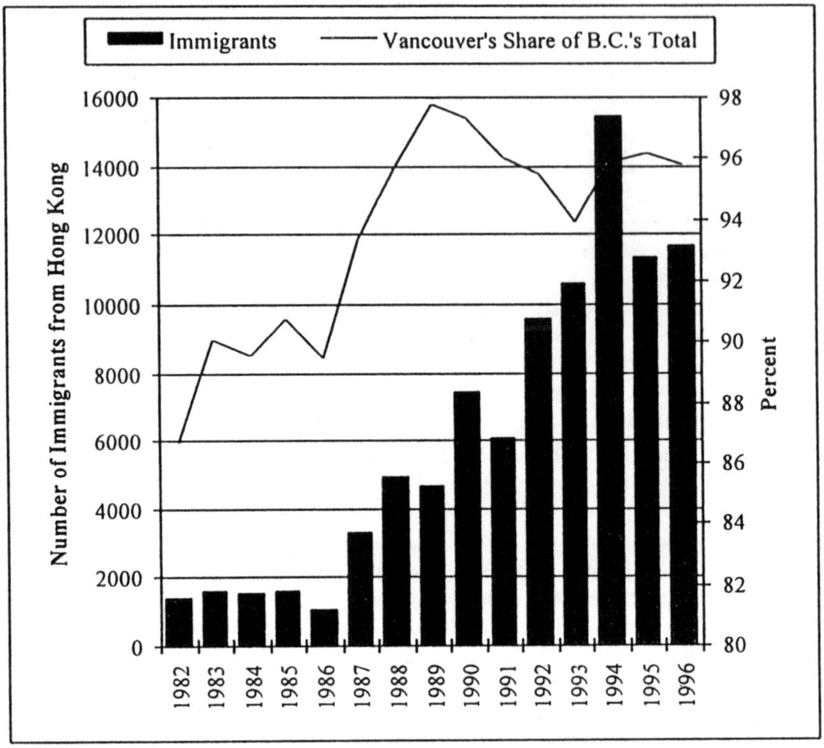

Fig. 4. Immigration to Vancouver, British Columbia (B.C.), fron Hong Kong, 1982–1996. *Source:* Data supplied by Central Statistics Branch, Treasury Board Secretariat, Ministry of Finance and Corporate Relations, Government of British Columbia, Canada.

from Asia (particularly Hong Kong) is transforming Vancouver's social structure. A 422% increase in metropolitan Vancouver's non-European population took place (as opposed to a 28% overall growth rate) between 1971 and 1986, with the vast majority being of Asian ancestry (Ley et al., 1992, pp. 251–252). By 1991, 331,920 people (21%) in the Vancouver Census Metropolitan Area claimed Asian ethnic origin, out of a total metropolitan population of 1,602,502, and it has been estimated that this proportion could rise to 25% by the year 2000. Of this Asian total, 178,820 people (54% of Asians; 11% of the Vancouver total) claimed to be of purely Chinese origin (Asia Pacific Foundation of Canada, 1994, Appendix B). The city of Vancouver itself, with a population of 471,844, had 103,520 people (22%) claiming Chinese origin in the 1991 census (Cleathero and Levens, 1994, p. 68). Clearly, the Chinese population is not homogeneous—it includes people of different genders, ages, religions, source countries (e.g., Hong Kong, Vietnam, Taiwan), linguistic groups, incomes, professions, political beliefs, and lengths of time in Vancouver. Business immigrants are particularly attracted to the city. In 1993, for example, Vancouver attracted 31.9% of all of Canada's business immigrants; by comparison, Montreal and Toronto had 20.9% and 19.3%, respectively (*Pacific Post*, January 27, 1995, p. 17). In short, it is simply impossible to speak of *the* Chinese community. However, the steady increase in the total number and relative proportions of Asians who now live in Vancouver is undeniably altering the nature of what was overwhelmingly a city dominated by people with European (British in particular) backgrounds and linkages. These points were reinforced several years later when Victor suggested to a friend ("Mr. Wong") that Vancouver was a good place to do business:

> Partly because of Canada's immigration policy, the city has experienced profound changes in recent years, becoming more active, international and, in particular, more oriented to the Pacific Rim. A population growth of three per cent annually—more than double Hong Kong's—means increasing demand for various services. And because certain industries are slow in responding to sudden change in demand and taste, there's a great opportunity for those who can fill the vacuum. (Li, 1992, p. 3)

Victor's comments above, and his subsequent involvement in Vancouver, highlight the important role of "destination" sociocultural factors in underlying the ultimate decision-making process of Hong Kong–based ethnic Chinese investors. In this case both the son and the father had to feel comfortable with the sociocultural "atmosphere" in the location where the prospective property investment would be made—a factor highlighted to me by numerous Li Group associates and external advisors. This factor also helps explain why property capital flows tend to be directed to cities such as Singapore, Toronto, Vancouver, and Sydney—all cities where extended social relations are built upon a social formation with a relatively large proportion and number of ethnic Chinese people.

The importance of a supportive sociocultural atmosphere in making ethnic Chinese investors feel comfortable also helps explain why the public and private sector in Vancouver has made such an effort during the 1980s and 1990s to build connections across the Pacific and transform Vancouver into Canada's "gateway" to the Asia-Pacific region. Vancouver's 1997 role as the site for the annual APEC meetings is but the most recent of a long string of programs and projects reshaping the city's identity to that with a more prominent Pacific Rim tenor (Mitchell, 1993, 1995, 1996; Olds, 1996, Chapter 5; see also Dirlik, 1993, on the "Pacific Rim" construct more generally). The elites who fashion public policy, and those who hold sway over private institutions such as the media, understand the critical role of extended social relations in guiding large-scale property capital flows from Hong Kong (cf. Goldberg, 1985). These social relations are best nourished in cosmopolitan locales, where racial tensions are resolved or else repressed from the public sphere (Mitchell, 1993). The aura associated with an emerging Pacific Rim hegemony in Vancouver was also viewed favorably by the Li Group, for it provided an expanding base of support for their activities in the city.

With Terry Hui, a Chinese Canadian friend of Hong Kong origins, Victor Li began developing housing in Vancouver suburbs. Their company (Grand Adex), which initially operated out of a 65 sq. m. office, grew quickly as the partners developed condominiums in Vancouver suburbs, such as Richmond (where large numbers of Hong Kong immigrants were moving) (Kraar, 1992b, p. 63). By the time the company had grown into a mid-sized firm, the pair were responsible for the construction of approximately 1,000 condominium units in metropolitan Vancouver. This modest experience gave the two young men an insight into the planning process associated with residential development projects in Vancouver, the potential market demand of new Hong Kong immigrants, and key design features that would make the residential projects and units more attractive to the immigrants. However, for Victor, the first heir to Hong Kong's largest corporate empire, this type of work was not of sufficient importance and scale to endow him with a local, let alone national or international, reputation.

Victor was 21 years of age when Expo '86 was held. While Expo '86 was underway, there had been some public discussion about the future of the site following the fair's closure. During the course of Expo '86, Premier William Bennett organized a dinner party. One of the attendees was George Magnus, a close associate of Li Ka-shing.[5] Magnus is one of Li Ka-shing's key "interlockers"—a western manager with responsibility for forming the interface between the Chinese and Western management cultures of Li's firms, as well as handling negotiations with Western businesses and governments. After the Bennett dinner ended, Magnus had a brief conversation with the Premier about the future development of the BC Place site following Expo's closure. It was during this time that Magnus first registered his interest (on behalf of Victor Li and Li Ka-shing) in acquiring the site (G. Magnus, interview, April 1994). Victor himself suggested that he "had decided, even before the fair had closed, that he wanted to buy the site" (Matas, 1989, p. A7).

This expression of interest in the land was an early sign of larger plans into which the Expo site and Vancouver as a whole would fit. From the perspective of the eventual developer, the site was much more than a devalued piece of property—a blank "landing strip" for "capital" that was rapidly piling up in Hong Kong with "nowhere else to go" (to use Harvey's [1994] words on another urban megaproject—London Docklands). Rather than thinking of Pacific Place as a "'spatial fix' for capitalism's overaccumulated capital" (Harvey, 1994, p. 427), this large tract of land should be recognized as offering the Li family the perfect opportunity to accomplish a number of interrelated goals during the first five years of the project's development phase. It is also important to note that these goals have changed over time: from 1994 on Pacific Place has been been developed with new agendas and new objectives in mind.

First, the development of the Pacific Place project enabled the 23-year-old (in 1988) Victor to build up his *reputation* in both Vancouver (the city that effectively became the Li Group's North American base) and Hong Kong. The Grand Adex experience was the first level of an incremental climb upward in the management of more-difficult projects, while Pacific Place was widely perceived in Hong Kong to be Victor's "first major business duty" (*South China Morning Post*, January 14, 1994, p. 7; see also Chan, 1996, pp. 117–148). This larger responsibility would have been expected by his father because it permitted Victor to gain business confidence and ensure that his reputation was deserved (in the view of elite overseas Chinese and nonoverseas Chinese Hong Kongers), and not merely related to his family name. This point was hinted at when Victor commented that he sought to "show the world that in Vancouver we can achieve something that we all feel proud of and that will be the cause for envy by the rest of the world" (Hamilton, 1988, p. B2). On this point, it was important that the experience be related to a high-profile, large-scale project. An urban mega-project, on the former Expo '86 site, in Vancouver, Canada (a city and country increasingly connected to Hong Kong), was the ideal type of project and location for "Victor's baby" (as George Magnus, a senior Li Group official termed it in a conversation with me in 1994). Vancouver's social and geographic proximity to Hong Kong enabled information on Victor's achievements to be circulated across the Pacific on a continual basis. However, it is also worth noting that Vancouver was also the perfect place *outside* Hong Kong for this type of learning exercise to take place. In the opinion of Gordon Redding, director of the University of Hong Kong's Business School, Vancouver was probably viewed to be distant enough for any potential problems to be quickly resolved before damaging gossip spread back to key people and institutions in Hong Kong (interview, March 1994).

Second, it was preferable that Victor's reputation and business experience be enhanced through the vehicle of a *large-scale residential* property development project (10,000 units were originally proposed for the site, while 8,500 will eventually be built).[6] Even though they are listed and capitalization levels are in the billions, Li-controlled firms such as Cheung Kong and Hutchison Whampoa are still viewed as "traditional family-run" businesses by associates to the Li Group, as well as the international financial firms that closely monitor their activities (e.g., UBS Global Research, 1994, p. 4). Therefore, Victor, as the eldest son, had to have a sufficient knowledge base and reputation to feasibly take over control of Cheung Kong from his aging father (who was 60 years old in 1988). Cheung Kong is the Li family's "flagship" firm, and it controls three other prominent listed firms within the "Li Group"—Hutchison Whampoa, Cheung Kong Infrastructure, and Hong Kong Electric (together making up approximately 15% of Hong Kong's total stock market capitalization throughout the first half of the 1990s). Cheung Kong is one of Hong Kong's largest property development firms and it has renowned experience and skill in developing mega-projects of a residential nature (Baring Securities, 1995; Ridding and Lucas, 1997). While the transition from one generation to the next is gradual in most ethnic Chinese firms, and stability within Cheung Kong is maintained by a "low turnover of senior staff" (UBS Global Research, 1994, p. 4), the opportunity for Victor to learn through the development of Pacific Place was ideal timing, according to George Magnus (interview, April 1994). The subsequent move of Victor back to Hong Kong to take up an appointment as deputy managing director of Cheung Kong in January 1993, and as deputy chairman for the same firm in January 1994 (a position he shares with George Magnus), clearly highlights the plans that were in place for Victor *before* the Expo site was acquired.

Third, the development of Pacific Place was used by Victor to "build a strong base in Canada...both personally and financially" (Li, 1992). As I noted above, Li Ka-shing has made substantial investments in Canada since the late 1960s, and he has significant connections with Canadian financial institutions (the Canadian Imperial Bank of Commerce) in Hong Kong. Victor also holds a Canadian passport, which guarantees him a safe base should Hong Kong's transition to greater Chinese control ever go awry. In effect, Canada now acts as the Li family's North American base, according to the Li Group officials I interviewed. However, prior to the Pacific Place project, Victor was little known in Vancouver or Toronto, and he had few direct connections to Canadian elites. Pacific Place is a very large urban redevelopment project by Canadian (and even American) standards. The developers knew that acquiring a prominent mega-project site would guarantee them a high profile in business, political, and social circles in both Vancouver and Canada as a whole. A prominent profile (in association with an astute reputation) is important, for the Li family are treated as virtual royalty in Hong Kong, a status that brings with it access to timely and relevant information about the processes that may affect the economic status of the Li Group in the short and long term. The long-term creation of a Vancouver base therefore demanded a suitable method to "insert" Victor (as a representative of the Li Group) into relevant networks, networks that were identified by Vancouver-based contacts and advisors.

Pacific Place, then, was effectively used as a vehicle to "parachute" Victor into the top of Vancouver's social, political, and business hierarchy. He (and his associates) were able to become "players within the mainstream immediately," according to the senior Hong Kong Bank of Canada executive I interviewed in 1994. Indeed, senior officials associated with Concord Pacific are now widely recognized as key actors and spokespersons within Vancouver's business community. Such a maneuver was possible because Vancouver is a relatively small city (in terms of population) by Hong Kong or American standards, and the city's economic influence is dwarfed by Toronto's status as Canada's key financial center. Consequently, Vancouver's power hierarchy is relatively malleable in comparison to established old money, "old boys" network cities such as Toronto or New York—cities where the young, modest, and soft-spoken Victor would have a tougher time fitting in (interview, Hong Kong Bank of Canada executive, April 1994). In short, Vancouver's "very thin layer of Anglo political control" (Seagrave, 1995, p. 259) (or "parochial" nature in the more cynical terms of an anonymous Li Group official I interviewed) contributed to the city's incorporation into a wider web of elite Hong Kong–based influence.

The fourth main rationale for reaching across space into Vancouver is the diversification of the property portfolio of the Li family, along with the portfolios of the two other secondary investors in the site (Hong Kong tycoons Cheng Yu-Tung and Lee Shau Kee). All three tycoons became billionaires by directly and indirectly exploiting the unique development process in Hong Kong as the entrepôt city-state was transformed into one of Asia's key financial centers (see Haggard, 1990, on Hong Kong in comparative perspective). Indeed the "fortunes and prospects" of the various property, energy, and financial firms controlled by Li and Cheng and Lee are "inextricably linked" to Hong Kong's future economic prospects (UBS Global Research, 1994, p. 2; Goldman Sachs, 1996). For example, Cheung Kong, Hutchison Whampoa, and Henderson Land (Lee's firm) generated 98%, 88%, and 95% of their 1993 earnings in Hong Kong, respectively (Alexander, 1994). Overall, 80% of Li's corporate assets were in Hong Kong in 1992 (Kraar, 1992a, p. 107). Investing in Vancouver at a more substantial scale (even if it is personal capital) allowed the tycoons to diversify their portfolio in a geographic sense and "cushion" their holdings in Hong Kong and China (their other main investment location) in the context of geopolitical and geoeconomic uncertainties. And while Canada "does not offer a very high immediate return, it's an essential part of a healthy, balanced portfolio, providing good mid- to long-term asset growth" (Li, 1992, p. 3).[7] In a related sense, Pacific Place also acted as a pilot project for the backers of Concord Pacific (and therefore their Hong Kong firms) in developing additional large-scale (in North American terms) property projects. For example, in 1994, Cheng Yu-Tung became a financial backer of Donald Trump's 56-acre (US$2.5 billion) Riverside South project (also known as "Trump City") on Manhattan's West Side in New York (Hutchinson, 1994). In 1995, Concord Pacific merged with Grand Adex and has since acquired a variety of listed and unlisted property firms with major holdings across key cities in Canada (including Toronto's Railway Lands mega-project). Concord/Grand Adex has now transformed itself into one of Canada's most strategic and well-backed property development firms.

CONCLUSIONS

In this article, I have attempted to examine some of the sociocultural dimensions of contemporary globalization processes, especially in a "Pacific Rim" context. Vancouver's Pacific Place urban mega-project was used as a lens through which to explore the social processes structuring the development of the city's largest-ever redevelopment project. This trans-Pacific property transaction has spurred on the restructuring of Vancouver's central city, facilitating an influx of middle- and high-income residents from Vancouver, other parts of Canada, and Asia to a former industrial area bordering the central business district and the lower-income Downtown Eastside (the area discussed by Jeff Sommers in this special issue of *Urban Geography*).

In a standard economic sense, Pacific Place is the product of investment capital from a corporate group in Hong Kong—a transaction that could be tabulated as foreign direct investment, given that a significant proportion of development capital is flowing across national boundaries. Many urban (and especially property) analysts would conceive of this development process as being reflective of a search by the Li Group (i.e., multinational capitalists) for profit (capital accumulation), in response to perceived opportunity (a rent gap) in conjunction with sufficient demand (from consumers). Together, the ongoing interaction of such multinational firms with consumers forms a trans-Pacific property market, subject of course to state regulations at a variety of levels. Given the increasingly "global reach" of such developers, the choice of cities in which to invest is becoming enlarged. Choice is also magnified because of the adoption of neoliberal policies that spur on new forms of entrepreneurial governance at the local level (Harvey, 1989b), leading to interurban competition and direct city marketing to property developers. Intra- and inter-firm networks are formed, flows are activated, and the global space of flows emerges, ready to pummel and dismember "the local" should the flows' "functional logic" (Castells, 1989) suggest so.

However, my narrative (guided by Appadurai and a variety of "socioeconomic" literature in association with multi-locale field work in Hong Kong and Vancouver) suggests that the rationale for investing in an urban mega-project in central Vancouver during the late 1980s was a more complex affair. Indeed, this perspective would probably not be adopted if I had viewed the transaction through a standard neoclassical or political economy framework. This is *not* to deny the importance of material goals or suggest that the Li Group (or any other Chinese corporate group) is not seeking to maximize profit as a general rule. However, it is important to be aware that property yields are significantly higher in Asian cities such as Hong Kong, Beijing, or Shanghai, three cities in which the Li Group has invested billions (Hiller Parker, 1995; Colliers Jardine, 1997). Given this relative state of affairs, why invest in central Vancouver, where returns are limited and the development time scale is extended (given the nature of the regulatory process)?

Quite simply, the Pacific Place project primarily represented a timely opportunity to further a variety of familial and corporate goals related to succession plans within the Hong Kong–based Li Group. Pacific Place was effectively used as an educational tool to enhance the skills, reputation, and confidence of Li Ka-shing's eldest son in the large-scale property development industry. The acquisition of such a large and high-profile site in Vancouver enabled Victor Li to be "groomed" in a strategic non–Hong Kong locale for his eventual (1993) appointment as a Cheung Kong (Holdings) Ltd. executive.

The purchase of 80 hectares of Vancouver's central city also enabled the Li Group to use Pacific Place as a vehicle to establish a "bolt hole" in North America: Vancouver now acts as a base for development activities in cities across Canada (including Vancouver) and the United States. And finally, simple material goals also inspired the Li Group to extend their reach over space: the Pacific Place project enabled Li and a small circle of Hong Kong–based property tycoons to diversify their property portfolio while enjoying steady (if unspectacular by Asian standards) returns.

Contextual factors played a fundamental role in shaping all aspects of the investment process. For the Hong Kong–based Li Group, Vancouver increasingly was becoming an "in" city. Flows of immigrants and capital linking both sides of the Pacific are transforming Vancouver's social structure, turning it into a relatively welcoming and "open" Western city for elite Asian investors. An open social structure is important, for it enabled ethnic Chinese developers who are used to being treated as elites in Hong Kong to become respected players within Vancouver's business mainstream immediately. The basic point here is that global cultures, such as the elite ethnic Chinese, thrive in cosmopolitan settings, cities open to global flows.

In Appadurai's (1990a, 1990b, 1996) terms, the "ethnoscapes" played a critical role in underlying the "finanscapes" associated with the urban restructuring process in this particular case. Flows of mobile people to Vancouver created the demand for services, which these highly educated and well-connected property developers knew how to supply. Moreover, migration to Canada enabled Li Ka-shing's sons (Victor Li and his younger brother Richard) to establish some form of semi-permanent links to Canada. These links, in the context of a *perceived* policy of multiculturalism and a reframing of Vancouver's development discourse in "Pacific Rim" terms, enhanced the actors' commitment to investing short- and long-term resources in Vancouver.

What these findings highlight is the need to work with theoretical frameworks that address the subject of globalization and urban change in a more flexible manner, one that can take into account the fundamental role of actors, their relations, their diverse and ever-shifting objectives, and their knowledge systems in formulating, funneling, and skimming global flows. Such an approach to the global space of flows suggests a higher level of provisionality in analysis, one that rejects representations of globalization as monolithic, absolute, and homogeneous in nature (Thrift, 1995). As Whatmore and Thorne (1997, p. 290) put it, "global reach" is a "laboured, uncertain, and above all, contested process of 'acting at a distance'." In affinity with actor-network theory, this approach to analysis is at odds with the "peculiarly modernist geographical imagination that casts globalisation as a colonisation of surfaces which, like a spreading ink stain, progressively colours every spot on the map" (p. 287). Indeed:

> Rather than conceptualising the spatial orderings of economic activity in territorial terms—a globalisation of surfaces—this approach implies a conception of the spatial ordering of economic activity in mobile terms—a globalisation of flows. It shifts concern from a predictable unfolding of social structures in space to the means whereby networks of actors construct space by using certain forms of ordering which mobilise particular rationalities, technological and representational devices, living beings (including people), and physical properties. More than this, unlike the filled in surfaces of globalisation, this approach opens up space-time to

the coexistence of multiple cross-cutting networks of varied length and durability.... (P. 302)

In short, the global space of flows does not float in ethereal space, guided by a transcendental logic of its own, dropping from place to place in a "footloose" and unexpected manner. The global *flows* of the material and nonmaterial are processes designed by and incorporating humans. The majority of these flows are formulated, activated, and legitimized by powerful human beings who are unevenly spread across the world in (primarily) global cities (Sassen, 1991; Hamnett, 1995). These actors, within their broader relational systems, draw themselves and others into the same "social space" and the same "historical time" in order to implement their goals (the transformation of urban space in this case). This cosmopolitan network of humans (Hannerz, 1992, 1996) is a continually evolving social space constructed by dynamic "networks of social relationships stretched across the globe" (Allen, 1995, p. 135; see also Amin and Thrift, 1994; Thrift, 1996), peopled with the resources (material and otherwise) to maintain and enhance such social spaces. The concept of "extended social relations" enables us to "reevaluate" the concepts of "global" and "local" and recognize that they offer "points of view on networks that are by their very nature neither global nor local, but more or less long and more or less connected" (Latour 1993, p. 122; see also Amin and Thrift, 1994).

The main methodological implications of such an approach is the need for an increased focus on elites within their broader relational systems. Practically, this will require multi-locale empirical field work in long-term research projects. Unless the researcher becomes entangled within these networks, "stretched out" social relations—the nexus of the "global" and the "local"—will remain out of reach from academic discourses on the global, and we shall degenerate further into the "global babble" that Janet Abu-Lughod (1991) rightly worried about.

NOTES

[1]This paper is primarily derived from my doctoral dissertation (Department of Geography, University of Bristol, Bristol, UK, 1996). The dissertation is currently being revised into a book titled *Globalization and Urban Change: Capital, Culture and Pacific Rim Mega Projects* (Oxford University Press, in press). Funding or other significant assistance for the dissertation research was kindly provided by institutions including the Association of Commonwealth Universities, the Social Sciences and Humanities Research Council of Canada (SSHRC), the University of Bristol, UK, the University of British Columbia, Canada, and the Chinese University of Hong Kong (Hong Kong Institute of Asia-Pacific Studies). Follow-up work was funded by the Government of Canada through a SSHRC Postdoctoral Fellowship, and the Vancouver Centre for the Study of Immigration and the Metropolis. Thanks also go to Keith Bassett, Don DeVoretz, David Ley, Nigel Thrift, and four anonymous referees for comments on all or portions of this text, and Concord Pacific Developments Ltd. for various forms of data. Of course, none of the above institutions or individuals should be in any way held responsible for the opinions expressed in this paper.

[2]All of the above quotations are taken from one promotional brochure titled "The Concordia at David Lam Park," which was published in February 1994 and distributed at Concord Pacific's presentation center on the Pacific Place project site. The themes are in keeping with other materials published by Concord Pacific Developments Ltd. and with the concepts expressed by the firm's representatives in both formal interviews and casual discussions with me.

[3]Economic sociology, as it is defined now, is derived out of the classic writings of Marx, Weber, Schumpeter, Veblen, and Polanyi (a disparate group, which explains variations in the analyses pro-

duced under this "banner"). Still, all recognized the importance of starting analyses at the central "institutional order that comprises a society's cultural and economic infrastructures" (Zukin and DiMaggio, 1990, p. 2; see Smelser and Swedberg, 1994, for a detailed overview of the intellectual tradition of economic sociology).

[4]The analysis in this article draws from three main stages of research: (1) relevant pre-Ph.D. experience in Vancouver from 1984 to 1992 when I was both a student and an urban planner for the City of Vancouver; (2) during the three years (1992 to 1995) I was registered at the University of Bristol as a doctoral candidate; and (3) during the last two years while working at universities in Vancouver, Bristol, and Singapore. The three stages are interdependent, and knowledge gained during all periods informs the construction of this article. The earliest phase in particular was key, for it enabled me to form trusted social networks with Vancouver-based actors—networks that I subsequently drew upon during the second and third phases of research.

With regard to specific methodology, the vast majority of the data for this article was collected during *multi-locale* field work in Hong Kong and Vancouver during extended periods of time from 1993 to 1997. Research methods consisted of literature searches, company searches, formal open-ended interviews, informal interviews, and casual "conversations."' I also drew upon periods of participant observation in Vancouver from 1988 to 1992. Formal open-ended interviews with over 50 people were conducted in both cities from 1993 on, while I interacted with a much larger number of relevant people on an informal basis during this same time period. The vast majority of the interviews were conducted in person, and the interviewees included senior representatives of the Li Group in both Vancouver and Hong Kong; senior, mid-level, and junior government officials in Vancouver; municipal politicians in Vancouver; and an assortment of lawyers, bankers, journalists, academics, chartered surveyors, and community representatives.

The key factor underlying the acquisition of insightful data was the ability to identify and then insert myself into disparate, constantly evolving social networks, using what "social capital" and "cultural capital" I possess or could accrue during the course of the research process. Unless the researcher becomes entangled within these networks, critical social relations—the nexus of the global-local dialectic—will remain out of reach from academic discourses on the global. However, even with a complex research strategy, a broad informational base, and a focus on *the global*, the analysis presented in this article is partial, and it represents one decentered perspective on the nature of globalization processes and urban change today. For too long, geographers have claimed to "see all"—a claim bound up with, in Gillian Rose's (1993, pp. 70–71) view, the assumption of a "vantage point far removed from the embodied social world, and this transcendent, distanced gaze reinforces the dominant Western masculine subjectivity in all its fear of embodied attachment and in all its universal pretensions." As Gregory (1994, p. 9) pointed out, it is impossible to claim a stable vantage point, since perspectives are formed in a world "in which the observers and the observed are in ceaseless, fluid and interactive motion." Instead, this article is my construction of a deeply perspectival analysis of the global space of flows as they relate to the production of new urban spaces such as Pacific Place. However, by conducting multi-locale field work and by using a myriad of techniques to insert myself into the stretched out and tangled social relations that guide global flows across space, I believe that this partial perspective cuts into the core issues. And provided the reader is aware of the author's subject position, these partial perspectives, these incisions into our continually evolving world-system, can shed some light on why our cities are developing the way they are.

[5]George Magnus's titles include Deputy Chairman of Cheung Kong (Holdings) Ltd., Chairman of Hong Kong Electric Hldgs. and CEF Holdings Ltd., and Executive Director of Hutchison Whampoa Ltd. and Green Island Cement (Hldgs.). Magnus is British.

[6]What we have here is a case of the confluence of the goals of the Li Group (which wanted a high-density residential project for Victor's experience, as well as enhanced financial returns) and the goals of the City of Vancouver (which wanted higher densities than those on South Shore of False Creek, as the development was taking place in the context of a growing jobs-housing imbalance at the metropolitan scale, and the push for more ecologically friendly, higher-density housing).

[7]The gradual diversification of Li's corporate assets continues to the present day. Moreover, in June 1995, Li raised considerable speculation about Hong Kong's future by placing his 34.95% controlling interest in Cheung Kong in a Cayman Islands trust. While his rationale was that he

sought to avoid inheritance tax (for his sons' sake), the action was seen as embarrassing for Li, given his excellent connections in Beijing (Holberton, 1993, 1995).

LITERATURE CITED

Abu-Lughod, J., 1989, *Before European Hegemony: The World System A.D. 1250–1350.* Oxford, UK: Oxford University Press.

Abu-Lughod, J., 1991, Going beyond global babble. In A. King, editor, *Culture, Globalization and the World System.* London, UK: Macmillan, 131–138.

Alexander, J., 1994, HK top 10 urged to expand their horizons. *Eastern Express,* April 5, p. 21.

Allen, J., 1995, Global worlds. In J. Allen and D. Massey, editors, *Geographical Worlds.* Oxford, UK: Open University and Oxford University Press, 105–142.

Amin, A., 1997, *Placing Globalization.* Paper presented at the RGS-IBG Annual Conference, Exeter, UK, January 9.

Amin, A. and Thrift, N., 1992, Neo-Marshallian nodes in global networks. *International Journal of Urban and Regional Research,* Vol. 16, 571–587.

Amin, A. and Thrift, N., editors, 1994, *Globalization, Institutions, and Regional Development in Europe.* Oxford, UK: Oxford University Press.

Amin, A. and Thrift, N., 1995, Institutional issues for European regions: From markets and plans to socioeconomics and powers of association. *Economy and Society,* Vol. 24, 41–66.

An "inside" Asian investor's view of Canada, 1989. *Invest Canada,* November, pp. 8–9.

Appadurai, A., 1990a, Disjuncture and difference in the global cultural economy. *Public Culture,* Vol. 2, 1–24.

Appadurai, A., 1990b, Disjuncture and difference in the global cultural economy. *Theory, Culture and Society,* Vol. 7, 295–310.

Appadurai, A., 1996, *Modernity at Large: Cultural Dimensions of Globalization.* London, UK: University of Minnesota Press.

Asia Pacific Foundation of Canada, 1994, *Canada's "Hidden Advantage": Asian Canadians.* Summary of Roundtable Discussions, November. Available from Asia Pacific Foundation of Canada, 666–999 Canada Place, Vancouver, BC V6C 3E1, Canada.

Badcock, B., 1984, *Unfairly Structured Cities.* Oxford, UK: Basil Blackwell.

Bairoch, P. and Kozul-Wright, R., 1996, *Globalization Myths: Some Historical Reflections on Integration, Industrialization and Growth in the World Economy.* Geneva, Switzerland: United Nations Conference on Trade and Development, Discussion Paper No. 113, March.

Baring Securities, 1995, *Stock Market Review: Interest Rates: The Spark.* Hong Kong: Author.

Baum, A. and Schofield, A., 1991, *Property as a Global Asset.* Working Papers in European Property, Centre for European Property Research, University of Reading, Reading, UK, March.

Block, F., 1990, *Postindustrial Possibilities: A Critique of Economic Discourse.* Berkeley, CA: University of California Press.

Boden, D., 1994, *The Business of Talk: Organizations in Action.* Cambridge, MA: Polity.

Castells, M., 1989, *The Informational City.* Oxford, UK: Blackwell.

Castells, M., 1996, *The Rise of Network Society: Economy, Society and Culture, Volume I*. Oxford, UK: Blackwell.

Chan, A., 1996, *Li Ka-shing: Hong Kong's Elusive Billionaire*. Toronto, ON, Canada: Macmillan.

Cleathero, J. and Levens, B., 1994, *Environmental Scan of the Lower Mainland: A Compilation of Socio-Economic Trends. Part Two: Socio-Economic Trends*. Burnaby, BC, Canada: United Way.

Colliers Jardine, 1997, *Asia Pacific Property Trends: Conditions and Forecasts*, January. Hong Kong: McGraw Hill.

Cox, K., 1992, The politics of globalization: A sceptic's view. *Political Geography*, Vol. 11, 427–429.

Cox, K., 1997, *Spaces of Globalization: Reasserting the Power of the Local*. London, UK: Guilford.

Dicken, P., Peck, J., and Tickell, A., 1997, Unpacking the global. In R. Lee and J. Wills, editors, *Geographies of Economies*. London, UK: Edward Arnold, 158–166.

Dicken, P. and Thrift, N., 1992, The organization of production and the production of organization: Why business enterprises matter in the study of geographical industrialization. *Transactions of the Institute of British Geographers*, Vol. 17, 279–291.

Dirlik, A., editor, 1993, *What is in a Rim?: Critical Perspectives on the Pacific Region Idea*. Boulder, CO: Westview Press.

Dunning, J., 1994, *Globalization, Economic Restructuring and Development*. The Sixth Raúl Prebisch Lecture, United Nations Conference on Trade and Development, Geneva, Switzerland, April 29.

Eade, J., 1997, *Living the Global City: Globalization as Local Process*. London, UK: Routledge.

East Asia Analytical Unit, 1995, *Overseas Chinese Business Networks in Asia*. Parkes, Australia: Department of Foreign Affairs and Trade.

Edgington, D. and Goldberg, M., 1992, Vancouver: Canada's gateway to the Rim. In E. Blakely and R. Stimson, editors, *New Cities of the Pacific Rim*. Monograph 43, Institute of Urban and Regional Development, University of California at Berkeley, Berkeley, CA, pp. 7-1 to 7-29.

Gereffi, G. and Hamilton, G., 1991, *Modes of Incorporation in an Industrial World: The Social Economy of Global Capitalism*. Working Paper No. 34, Program in East Asian Business and Development, Institute of Governmental Affairs, University of California at Davis, Davis, CA.

Giddens, A., 1990, *The Consequences of Modernity*. Stanford, CA: Stanford University Press.

Giddens, A., 1994, Living in a post-traditional society. In U. Beck, A. Giddens, and S. Lash, editors, *Reflexive Modernization: Politics, Tradition and Aesthetics in the Modern Social Order*. Cambridge, MA: Polity, 56–109.

Goldberg, M., 1985, *The Chinese Connection: Getting Plugged In To Pacific Rim Real Estate, Trade and Capital Markets*. Vancouver, BC, Canada: University of British Columbia Press.

Goldman Sachs, 1996, Cheung Kong Infrastructure. *Hong Kong Research*, September 3.

Grabher, G., editor, 1993, *The Embedded Firm: On the Socioeconomics of Industrial Networks*. London, UK: Routledge.

Granovetter, M., 1985, Economic action and social structure: The problem of embeddedness. *American Journal of Sociology*, Vol. 91, 481–510.

Granovetter, M. and Swedberg, R., editors, 1992, *The Sociology of Economic Life*. Boulder, CO: Westview Press.

Gregory, D., 1994, *Geographical Imaginations*. Oxford, UK: Blackwell.

Gutstein, D., 1990, *The New Landlords: Asian Investment in Canadian Real Estate*. Victoria, BC, Canada: Press Porcépic Limited.

Haggard, S., 1990, *Pathways from the Periphery: The Politics of Growth in the Newly Industrializing Countries*. Ithaca, NY: Cornell University Press.

Haila, A., 1991, Four types of investment in land and property. *International Journal of Urban and Regional Research*, Vol. 15, 343–365.

Hamilton, G., 1988, Questions raised over Li legacy. *The Vancouver Sun*, December 17, pp. B1, B2.

Hamilton, G., 1994, Civilizations and the organization of economics. In N. J. Smelser and R. Swedberg, editors, *The Handbook of Economic Sociology*. Princeton, NJ, and New York, NY: Princeton University Press and Russell Sage Foundation, 183–205.

Hamilton, G., 1996, Overseas Chinese capitalism. In W. M. Tu, editor, *Confucian Traditions in East Asian Modernity: Moral and Economic Culture in Japan and the Four Mini-Dragons*. Cambridge, MA: Harvard University Press, 328–342.

Hamnett, C., 1995, Controlling space: Global cities. In J. Allen and C. Hamnett, editors, *A Shrinking World? Global Unevenness and Inequality*. Oxford, UK: Oxford University Press and the Open University, 103–142.

Hannerz, U., 1992, *Cultural Complexity: Studies in the Social Organization of Meaning*. New York, NY: Columbia University Press.

Hannerz, U., 1996, *Transnational Connections: Culture, People, Places*. London, UK: Routledge.

Harris, R., 1994, *Office Property Development and the Role of Marketing Research*. Unpublished paper, Stanhope Properties, London, UK.

Harvey, D., 1982, *The Limits to Capital*. Oxford, UK: Blackwell.

Harvey, D., 1989a, *The Condition of Postmodernity*. Oxford, UK: Blackwell.

Harvey, D., 1989b, From managerialism to entrepreneurialism: The transformation of urban governance in late capitalism. *Geografiska Annaler*, Vol. 71, 3–17.

Harvey, D., 1994, The invisible political economy of architectural production. In O. Bouman and R. van Toorn, editors, *The Invisible in Architecture*. London, UK: Academy Editions, 420–427.

Healey, P., 1991, Models of the land development process: A review. *Journal of Property Research*, Vol. 8, 219–238.

Held, D., 1996, *Models of Democracy*. Cambridge, MA: Polity.

Hillier Parker, 1995, *International Property Bulletin*. London, UK: Author.

Hodgson, G. M., editor, 1994, *The Economics of Institutions*. Aldershot, UK: Edward Elgar.

Holberton, S., 1993, HK's superman finds warmer winds from China. *Financial Times*, June 23, p. 30.

Holberton, S., 1995, Mr. Li sets Hong Kong a puzzle. *Financial Times*, June 6, p. 26.

Holton, R., 1992, *Economy and Society*. London, UK: Routledge.

Hutchinson, M., 1994, Donald Trump. *A. D.: Architectural Design*, Vol. 64, VIII–XI.

Kao, J., 1993, The worldwide web of Chinese business. *Harvard Business Review*, March–April, pp. 24–36.

Kraar, L., 1992a, A billionaire's global strategy. *Fortune*, July 13, 106–109.

Kraar, L., 1992b, The legend of Li Ka Shing. *Asiaweek*, July 17, 56–67.

Lash, S. and Urry, J., 1994, *Economies of Signs and Space*. London, UK: Sage.

Latour, B., 1993, *We Have Never Been Modern*. London, UK: Harvester Wheatsheaf.

Law, J., 1994, *Organizing Modernity*. Oxford, UK: Blackwell.

Lefebvre, H., 1991, *The Production of Space*. Oxford, UK: Blackwell.

Ley, D., 1989, Fragmentation, coherence, and the limits to theory in human geography. In A. Kobayashi and S. Mackenzie, editors, *Remaking Human Geography*. Boston, MA: Unwin Hyman, 227–244.

Ley, D., 1995, Between Europe and Asia: The case of the missing Sequoias. *Ecumene*, Vol. 2, 185–210.

Ley, D., Hiebert, D., and Pratt, G., 1992, Time to grow up? From urban village to world city 1966–91. In G. Wynn and T. Oke, editors, *Vancouver and Its Region*. Vancouver, BC, Canada: University of British Columbia Press, 234–266.

Li, V. T. K., 1992, Why we invest in Canada. *Dialogue* [Asia Pacific Foundation of Canada], Vol. 6, February, pp. 3, 8.

Massey, D., 1993, Power-geometry and a progressive sense of place. In J. Bird, B. Curtis, T. Putnam, G. Robertson, and L. Tickner, editors, *Mapping the Futures: Local Cultures, Global Change*. London, UK: Routledge, 59–69.

Matas, R., 1989, Mystery, unanswered questions remain about B.C.'s land deal of the century. *The Globe and Mail*, June 17, pp. A1, A7.

McGrew, A., 1992, Conceptualizing global politics. In A. McGrew and P. Lewis, editors, *Global Politics: Globalization and the Nation State*. Cambridge, UK: Polity, 1–30.

Merrifield, A., 1993, The struggle over place: Redeveloping American Can in Southeast Baltimore. *Transactions of the Institute of British Geographers*, Vol. 18, 102–121.

Mitchell, K., 1993, Multi-culturalism, or the united colors of capitalism. *Antipode*, Vol. 25, 263–294.

Mitchell, K., 1995, Flexible circulation in the Pacific Rim: Capitalisms in cultural context. *Economic Geography*, Vol. 71, 364–382.

Mitchell, K., 1996, Visions of Vancouver: Ideology, democracy, and the future of urban development. *Urban Geography*, Vol. 17, 478–501.

Murdoch, J., 1997, Towards a geography of heterogeneous associations. *Progress in Human Geography*, Vol. 21, 321–337.

Newman, P., 1993, The master builder. *Vancouver Magazine*, September, pp. 34–42.

Olds, K., 1996, *Pacific Rim Mega-Projects and the Global Cultural Economy: Tales from Vancouver and Shanghai*. Unpublished doctoral dissertation, Department of Geography, University of Bristol, Bristol, UK.

O Tuathail, G., 1997, At the end of geopolitics? Reflections on a plural problematic at the century's end. *Alternatives*, Vol. 22, 35–55.

Pollner, M., 1987, *Mundane Reason*. Cambridge, UK: Cambridge University Press.

Powell, W. and DiMaggio, P., editors, 1991, *The New Institutionalism in Organizational Analysis*. London, UK: University of Chicago Press.

Pred, A. and Watts, M., 1992, *Reworking Modernity: Capitalisms and Symbolic Discontent*. New Brunswick, NJ: Rutgers University Press.

Redding, G., 1990, *The Spirit of Chinese Capitalism.* Berlin, Germany: Walter de Gruyter.

Ridding, J. and Lucas, L., 1997, Li to revamp Hong Kong business empire. *Financial Times*, January 7, pp. 15, 20.

Robins, K., 1991, Prisoners of the city: Whatever could a postmodern city be? *New Formations*, Vol. 15, 1–22.

Rose, G., 1993, Some notes on thinking about the spaces of the future. In J. Bird, B. Curtis, T. Putnam, G. Robertson, and L. Tickner, editors, *Mapping the Futures: Local Cultures, Global Change*. London, UK: Routledge, 70–86.

Royal Institution of Chartered Surveyors, 1993, *Understanding the Property Cycle*. Working Paper Two, The Royal Institution of Chartered Surveyors, London, UK, March.

Sassen, S., 1991, *The Global City.* Princeton, NJ: Princeton University Press.

Sassen, S., 1994, *Cities in a World Economy.* Thousand Oaks, CA: Pine Forge Press.

Seagrave, S., 1995, *Lords of the Rim: The Invisible Empire of the Overseas Chinese*. London, UK: Bantam Press.

Smelser, N. J. and Swedberg, R., 1994, The sociological perspective on the economy. In N. J. Smelser and R. Swedberg, editors, *The Handbook of Economic Sociology.* Princeton, NJ, and New York, NY: Princeton University Press and Russell Sage Foundation, 3–'26.

Thrift, N., 1995, A hyperactive world. In R. Johnston, P. Taylor, and M. Watts, editors, *Geographies of Global Change: Remapping the World in the Late Twentieth Century.* Oxford, UK: Blackwell, 18–35.

Thrift, N., 1996, *Spatial Formations.* London, UK: Sage.

UBS Global Research, 1994, Cheung Kong (Holdings) Ltd.—a big gun loaded with firepower. *Hong Kong Equities*, April, entire issue.

Whatmore, S. and Thorne, L., 1997, Nourishing networks: Alternative geographies of food. In D. Goodman and M. Watts, editors, *Globalising Food: Agrarian Questions and Global Restructuring.* London, UK: Routledge, 287–304.

Yeung, H. W. C., 1997, Business networks and transnational corporations: A study of Hong Kong firms in the ASEAN region. *Economic Geography*, Vol. 72, 1–45.

Zukin, S., 1991, *Landscapes of Power: From Detroit to Disney World.* Berkeley, CA: University of California Press.

Zukin, S. and DiMaggio, P., 1990, *Structures of Capital: The Social Organization of the Economy.* Cambridge, UK: Cambridge University Press.

Name Index